International Information

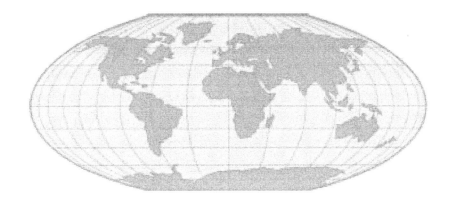

International Information

Documents, Publications, and Electronic Information
of International Organizations

Volume 2

Second Edition

Peter I. Hajnal, Editor

2001
Libraries Unlimited, Inc.
Englewood, Colorado

*To the memory of Bob Schaaf—
friend, mentor, inspiration*

Copyright © 2001 Libraries Unlimited, Inc.
All Rights Reserved
Printed in the United States of America

No part of this publication may be reproduced, stored in a retrieval system, or transmitted, in any form or by any means, electronic, mechanical, photocopying, recording, or otherwise, without the prior written permission of the publisher.

Libraries Unlimited, Inc.
P.O. Box 6633
Englewood, CO 80155-6633
1-800-237-6124
www.lu.com

Library of Congress Cataloging-in-Publication Data

Library of Congress has catalogued previous volume.

International information : documents, publications, and electronic
   information of international governmental organizations / Peter
   I. Hajnal, editor. -- 2nd ed.
      xxxvi, 528 p. 17x28 cm.
      Includes bibliographical references and index.
      ISBN 1-56308-147-4
      1. International agencies--Information services. 2. International
agencies--Computer network resources.   I. Hajnal, Peter I., 1936-   .
JZ4850.I58   1997
021.6'4--dc21   97-23470
                                                                       CIP

Volume 2 : International Information: Documents, Publications,
   and Electronic Information of International Organizations
   ISBN 1-56308-808-8

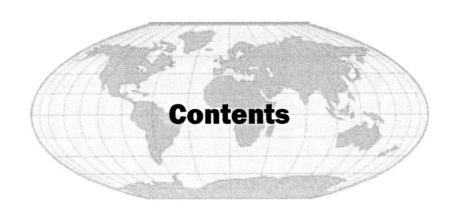

Contents

Illustrations xiii
Preface xv
Preface to Volume 1 xvii
Acknowledgments xix
Contributors xxi
Abbreviations and Acronyms xxv

Part I
INSTITUTIONS

1—INTERGOVERNMENTAL ORGANIZATIONS AS PUBLISHERS 3

(A) Intergovernmental Organizations As Publishers 3
J. J. Cherns

IGOs and Publishing 4
Frameworks of Publishing Activity 6
Organization of IGO Publishing 10
Dimensions of the Specific Publications Activity 14
Some External Aspects and Suggestions 18

(B) An Intergovernmental Organization As Publisher: The Case of the World Bank 23
H. Dirk Koehler

Introduction 23
What Is a World Bank Publication? 25
   The Registry of Print Publications 26
   Documents 26
   Electronic Publications 27
The Governance and Development of Publications 28
   Publishing and the Office of the Publisher until 1996/97 28
   The Cost-Effectiveness Review of 1997 29
   The Office of the Publisher Today 30

1—INTERGOVERNMENTAL ORGANIZATIONS AS PUBLISHERS (*continued*)

Policies of the Office of the Publisher 33
    Revenue Sharing Policy 34
    Cost Sharing Policy 35
    Pricing Policy. 35
    Internal Pricing Policy 37
    Free Dissemination Policy 38
    Copublishing and Licensing Policy 38
    Results of the New Policies 39
Special Initiatives of the Office of the Publisher 40
    African Publishing Initiative 40
    Staff Exchange Programs. 41
Notes and References. 42

2—THE INTERNATIONAL MONETARY FUND:
Operational and Research Documentation 44
    Donald F. Ross

Introduction. 44
Brief History 45
The Fund's Operational Process and Derived Documentation 47
Mission Travel, Reporting, and Review 47
SAF, ESAF, and Now PRGF 50
Poverty Reduction and Growth Facility and the PRSP. 52
Recent Economic Developments 52
Data and Research Compilation 53
Research Documentation 55
Translation of IMF Publications 58
The Executive Board 59
    Minutes of Meetings of the Executive Board 59
    Documents of the Executive Board 60
The Board of Governors 62
The International Monetary and Financial Committee
        (previously Interim Committee) and the
        Development Committee. 62
Finding IMF Publications and Documents 64
Opening of the IMF's Archives. 65
Notes and References. 66

3—THE GENERAL AGREEMENT ON TARIFFS AND TRADE AND THE WORLD TRADE ORGANIZATION. 72

**(A) Historical Overview, Present Structure, and
        Functions of the WTO** 72
    Susan Hainsworth

Introduction 72

The WTO: Historical Overview 73
The ITO Charter and the Origins of the GATT............ 73
The Proposed Structure of the ITO 74
The GATT (1947–1994) 75
    Membership 75
    Governance.............................. 76
    Decision-Making........................... 77
    Secretariat 77
    Functions............................... 78
The WTO (1995–) 80
    Membership 80
    Governance.............................. 80
    Decision-Making........................... 83
    Secretariat 84
    Functions............................... 84

(B) Documentation and Publications of the GATT and WTO. 91
Charles Eckman
Major Publication Series and Areas 91
    Annual Reports............................ 91
    Current Awareness.......................... 91
    Basic Instruments and Selected Documents (BISD)........ 92
    Analytical Index 93
    Trade Rounds and Associated Legal Texts............. 93
    Uruguay Round............................ 94
    Panel Reports............................. 95
    Trade Policy Reviews 95
    Statistics 95
    Reference Material.......................... 96
Documentation 96
    GATT 1947, Tokyo Round, and
                Uruguay Round Documentation 97
    WTO Documentation......................... 98
Bibliographic Control........................... 99
    Publications of GATT and WTO................... 99
    GATT Documentation 99
    Uruguay Round Documentation 99
    WTO Documentation......................... 99
Availability and Dissemination 101
    Sales Program............................. 101
    Depository Library Program 101
    Restriction of Document Distribution................ 101
    Documentation Distribution (Print)................. 102
    Documentation Distribution (Microform) 102
    Documentation Distribution (Internet) 103

3—THE GENERAL AGREEMENT ON TARIFFS AND TRADE AND THE WORLD TRADE ORGANIZATION (*continued*)
Future of the WTO as an Information Provider 103
    WTO Website 103
    Copublishing 104
    Derestriction 104
Notes and References 104

4—LA FRANCOPHONIE: An Emerging International Governmental Organization 108
    Juris Dilevko

Introduction 108
The Early History of OIF 112
Modernizing OIF Through the Summit Structure 118
General Information about the OIF 124
Structure and Documentation of OIF Component Parts 126
    Summits 126
    Secretariat and Secretary General 126
    Conférence Ministérielle de la Francophonie (CMF) 127
    Other Permanent and Sectoral Ministerial Conferences 127
    Conseil Permanent de la Francophonie (CPF) 128
    Agence Intergouvernementale de la Francophonie (AIF) 128
    Agence Universitaire de la Francophonie (AUF) 129
    TV5 130
    Université Senghor in Alexandria 130
    Association Internationale des Maires Francophones (AIMF) . . 131
    Assemblée Parlementaire de la Francophonie (APF) 131
    Forum Francophone des Affaires (FFA) 132
    Organisations Internationales Non Gouvernementales (OING) . 132
Conclusion 133
Notes and References 135

5—INTERNATIONAL NONGOVERNMENTAL ORGANIZATIONS AND CIVIL SOCIETY 138
    Peter I. Hajnal

(A) Nongovernmental Organizations and Civil Society 138
Introduction 138
Definitions 139
NGO Relations with the UN System and Other IGOs 140
The Growing Influence of Civil Society: Some Recent Examples . . 142
    Landmines 142
    The International Criminal Court 144
    The Multilateral Agreement on Investment 145
    The "Battle of Seattle" and the New Power of Civil Society . . . 146
Internet Sources of Information about Civil Society Organizations . 147

(B) Nongovernmental Organizations: Three Case Studies 148
OXFAM International 148
   Introduction 148
   Mandate, Governance, and Structure 150
   Activities 152
   Financing 153
   Information and Publishing 153
   Library and Archival Resources 155
   Concluding Remarks 155
IUCN—The World Conservation Union 156
   Introduction 156
   Mandate, Governance, and Structure 157
   Activities 158
   Financing 161
   Information and Publishing 161
   Library and Archival Resources 164
   Concluding Remarks 164
Médecins Sans Frontières (Doctors Without Borders) 165
   Origins, History, and Worldwide Presence 165
   Mandate, Governance, and Structure 168
   Activities 169
   Financing 171
   Information and Publishing 171
   Library and Archival Resources 174
   Concluding Remarks 174
Notes and References 174

Part II
RESOURCES

6—ICAO PROMOTES SAFETY AND UNIFORMITY IN AERONAUTICAL CHARTING WORLDWIDE 183
   David Lewtas
Introduction 183
The International Civil Aviation Organization (ICAO) 185
Aeronautical Charts—ICAO 186
Technological Change and Safety Aspects Affecting Charting 188
   Other ICAO Products Related to Aeronautical Charting 191
Notes and References 193

7—ARCHIVES 194
   Markku Järvinen
Introduction 194
Records of Intergovernmental Organizations 197
Finding Aids 203

7—ARCHIVES (*continued*)
Access Policy and Services 212
Use of the Archives 216
Conclusion 217
Notes and References 217
    General Note 217

8—MICROFORM 222
(A) Documentation in Microform 222
Robert W. Schaaf

Introduction 222
Microform and the Newer Technologies 222
Silver Versus Other Films for Libraries and Archives 224
Secondary Services Making IGO Microform Available 225
Survey of International Documentation in Microform 226
    United Nations 227
    Unesco 231
    Food and Agriculture Organization of the
            United Nations (FAO) 234
    General Agreement on Tariffs and Trade (GATT) 234
    International Telecommunication Union (ITU) 236
    International Labor Organization (ILO) 236
    International Atomic Energy Agency (IAEA) 237
    Organization of American States (OAS) 238
    European Communities [EC, now European Union] 239
    Organization for Economic Cooperation and
            Development (OECD) 241
    Andean Pact (Junta del Acuerdo de Cartagena) 242
    Conclusion 242

(B) Documentation in Microform and Alternative
       Formats: An Update 243
Michael McCaffrey-Noviss and Andrea Sevetson

Microform Technology 243
    Historical Coverage 244
    Access Technology and Alternative Formats 245
Notes and References 247

9—ELECTRONIC INFORMATION RESOURCES OF
THE UNITED NATIONS HIGH COMMISSIONER
FOR REFUGEES 249
Elisa Mason

Introduction 249
The Organization 249
    Background 249

Establishment of UNHCR 250
 The High Commissioner 250
 UNHCR's Mandate and Activities 250
 Governing Bodies 254
 Staff and Budget 255
The Information and Publication Context 255
Electronic Resources 257
REFWORLD CD-ROM 258
 Background 258
 Sources 258
 Platform and Structure 259
UNHCR Website (<www.unhcr.ch>) 260
 Background 260
 Sources 260
 REFWORLD 263
Conclusion 263
Notes and References 263
Annex: Comparison of Contents on REFWORLD CD-ROM
 and REFWORLD on Web 265

Part III
PROCESSES

10—UNITED NATIONS INFORMATION-GATHERING FOR PEACE AND SECURITY 275
 A. Walter Dorn

Introduction: The Information Cycle 275
Information Sources and Methods 276
 Governments 277
 The Media 282
 Field Operations 284
 UN Information Centres, Field Offices, and Agencies 288
 NGOs and Individuals 290
Conclusion 292
Notes and References 293
Appendix: Memoirs of UN Officials and Peacekeepers 296
 UN Secretariat Staff (Including Secretaries-General) 296
 Peacekeepers and Individuals on Secondment 296

11—TRENDS IN REFERENCE SERVICE FOR UNITED NATIONS SYSTEM MATERIALS 298
 Mary Fetzer

Accessibility of Information: A Time to Reassess 299
The UN: Moving Forward 301
The Dag Hammarskjöld Library: Leading the Way 302

xii / Contents

11—TRENDS IN REFERENCE SERVICE FOR UNITED NATIONS SYSTEM MATERIALS (*continued*)

Indexes and Catalogs of United Nations Materials 304
Bundling and Blurring: Collection and Service Implications 305
Statistics in Electronic Formats: Enhancing the Options 306
FAQs, AAL Services and Listservs: Their Influence on
      the Reference Process 307
Changing Patterns in Model UN Research: Chat Rooms
      and Remote Access 309
Independent Learning 311
Preserving the IGO Legacy: A Final Note 312
Conclusion. 313
Notes and References 313

12—CITATION FORMS 315
Diane L. Garner

Introduction 315
    Print Formats 316
    Electronic Formats 317
Standards 317
    ISO Standard 690-1975 318
    ISO Standard 690-2 319
    ANSI Standard for Bibliographic References Z39.29-1977 . . . 319
Manuals 320
Bibliography Formatting Software 325
The Citation 325
    Sources of Information 325
    Authorship 326
    Title 326
    Edition. 328
    Imprint 328
    Series Statement. 329
    Notes 329
    Citing Nontraditional Media 330
    Translation and Romanization 331
Sample Citations. 331
Appendix—Manuals Consulted 350
Notes and References 351

Bibliography 353
Compiled by Peter I. Hajnal and Gillian R. Clinton

Index 387

Illustrations

Figures

1.1	Mission Statement of the World Bank's Office of the Publisher	31
1.2	Organizational Chart of the World Bank's Office of the Publisher	32
3.1	Structure of the WTO	81
3.2	The WTO Dispute Settlement Process	88
4.1	Organisation internationale de la Francophonie	113
6.1	Format—*Instrument Approach Chart—ICAO*	187
6.2	Sample *Instrument Approach Chart—ICAO*	189
7.1	Cover Page of Unesco's *List of Documents Issued by the Archives Service, 1947–1994*	205
10.1	The UN Information Cycle	277
12.1	UN Masthead Document	332
12.2	UN Official Record	334
12.3	UN Sales Publication	336
12.4	IGO Item Copublished with Another Press	338
12.5	Multiple Authors	340
12.6	Annual Report without Imprint. Necessary to Consult Text for Imprint Data	342
12.7	Journal Article	343
12.8	Microformat, Multiple Series	345
12.9	IGO Material Online Source: Website	346
12.10	IGO Material in Tangible Electronic Medium	348

Tables

1.1	Results of New Policies of the Office of the Publisher, World Bank	40
3.1	Key GATT Document Series	97
3.2	Tokyo Round Documents	97
3.3	Uruguay Round Documents	98
3.4	WTO Document Series	98
3.5	Lists and/or Indexes to GATT Documentation	100
4.1	Member Countries of the Organisation internationale de la Francophonie and Commonwealth	109
7.1	Finding Aids of Unesco Archives (Selective List)	206
7.2	Guides and Other References to Archives of International Organizations (Selective List)	208
9.1	UNHCR's Predecessor Organizations	251
9.2	UN High Commissioners for Refugees	252
9.3	Persons of Concern to UNHCR	253
9.4	UNHCR Document Symbols	255

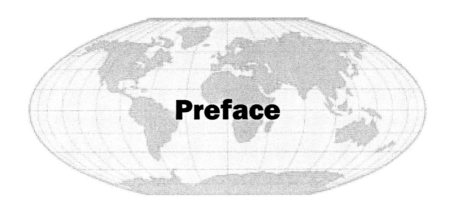

Preface

This second volume follows the publication of the first by some three years—a short time that has seen major changes in international governmental organizations (IGOs) and their information, documentation, and publication patterns. The most striking changes have been greater transparency and therefore greater access to the information generated by these organizations; and an explosive growth of information technology, leading to increased ease of communication as well as to constant challenges to the way information is disseminated, processed, organized, and used.

Chapter 1 reflects those changes clearly. International organizations and, especially, IGOs, have come under closer scrutiny by governments and civil society alike. A new political and economic climate has made institutional reform not only possible but inevitable, and these reforms, along with technological changes, have affected IGO publishing significantly. J. J. Cherns's earlier analysis of IGO publishing philosophy and habits remains largely valid. Dirk Koehler's up-to-date essay, focusing on one major IGO, the World Bank, offers an interesting contrast in its discussion of current IGO publishing.

In Chapter 2, Donald Ross presents a thorough historical survey and guide to information policies and practices as well as documentation and publishing patterns of one of the most prominent IGOs of our day, the International Monetary Fund. Chapter 3 deals with the World Trade Organization, a new IGO, and its less powerful predecessor, the General Agreement on Tariffs and Trade. In the first part of the chapter, Susan Hainsworth traces the evolution and role of this organization from the point of view of international trade law; and Charles Eckman discusses these organizations as information providers.

Juris Dilevko, in Chapter 4, presents the politics and information output of an organization that is not as well known in the English-speaking world as it deserves to be: la Francophonie, which brings together wholly or partially French-speaking countries from several continents. The author highlights the evolution of this IGO and provides a comprehensive guide to its documents and publications. In Chapter 5—the closing chapter of Part I, dealing with institutions—Peter Hajnal discusses nongovernmental organizations (NGOs) and the broader civil society (an increasingly significant and fast-growing phenomenon), focusing on the role of information in these organizations and movements, and providing detailed case studies of three major NGOs.

Part II centers on resources. It opens with Chapter 6, in which David Lewtas discusses a special cartographic resource: aeronautical charting carried out by the International Civil Aviation Organization. This is followed by Markku Järvinen's description and analysis of archives of international organizations (a rich but often-neglected gold mine of source material for research) in a historical context, focusing on Unesco. Another type of resource, microform material—a well-established medium that has survived the challenge of information technology to continue as a valuable complement to other formats—is explored in Chapter 8 in an older but still valuable contribution by Robert W. Schaaf, and is updated by Andrea Sevetson and Michael McCaffrey-Noviss. Finally, in Chapter 9, Elisa Mason discusses electronic information resources of the United Nations High Commissioner for Refugees, an important and highly regarded international agency of humanitarian assistance.

Part III concentrates on processes. In Chapter 10, Walter Dorn describes and analyzes information input—contrasted with information output, which is the subject of most writings on international organization information—concentrating on information-gathering to support the peace and security activities of the United Nations, and on the path that the information takes as it progresses to and through the UN. In Chapter 11, Mary Fetzer looks at the impact of new information technologies and other recent trends in reference service involving materials produced by the United Nations system and other IGOs. Finally, in Chapter 12, Diane Garner presents an updated version of her guide to citation forms relevant to documents, publications, and electronic information from IGOs.

This companion to the 1997 first volume bridges the divide between traditional and new media of information emanating from international governmental and nongovernmental organizations. The book should help researchers, academics, government officials, media personnel, librarians, and the general public in understanding and using crucial information from international organizations.

Peter I. Hajnal
Toronto, July 2000

Preface to Volume 1

The momentous changes that have taken place in the world since the first edition of this book was published in 1988 have affected international governmental organizations (IGOs) fundamentally. The end of the Cold War, the technological revolution, the spreading of democracy, and globalization have all contributed to transform the role, functioning, participants, and programs of international institutions. These changes have occurred in the areas of information, documentation, and publishing no less than in the political and economic realm. A clear need exists, therefore, to survey the present status, characteristics, and trends of IGO information—hence this thoroughly revised and expanded edition.

Part 1, comprising seven chapters, examines a number of international institutions and their documents, publications, and electronic information. Chapter 1 sets the organizational stage necessary to understand the relationship between international institutions and the source material they produce; it reviews characteristics of international organizations, including problems of definition and classification. Chapter 2 discusses the United Nations (UN); sources of information about it; patterns of its documentation and publishing, including publication policies and practices, information dissemination, and documentary implications of recent efforts for organizational reform.

In contrast to the UN—the foremost global international organization—the European Union (EU) is an extraordinarily complex grouping that has acquired many supranational characteristics. The EU is the subject of Chapter 3—a detailed discussion of its treaties and institutions; publishing and information organizations, activities and networks; legislative process; documentation, bibliographic guides and electronic information. Chapter 4 deals with the Organisation for Economic Co-operation and Development (OECD)—a major multiregional institution—and with OECD's information policies, services, and products.

The rest of Part 1 presents three institutions, each of which is special in its own way. Chapter 5 discusses the historical predecessor of the UN, the League of Nations, and its complicated but important documentation. Chapter 6 describes the International Development Research Centre (IDRC) which, although a Canadian federal crown corporation, is internationally oriented. IDRC provides extensive and creative ways to disseminate knowledge and build research support and scientific capacity in developing countries; it is in the forefront of technology in a variety of fields, including the environment, sustainable development, and information and communications. Chapter 7 analyzes the increasingly influential but still little-understood Group of Seven Industrialized Countries (G7), an institution with no secretariat and therefore elusive documentation.

Part 2 concentrates on resources and processes. Chapter 8 discusses the fast-changing and ever-expanding electronic information sources in the UN system of organizations. Chapter 9 is a survey of the document resources of the Dag Hammarskjöld Library—the UN headquarters library. Chapter 10 describes the United Nations Scholars' Workstation at Yale University, an imaginative website devoted to UN studies, research and documentation, with links to many other major internet resources.

Chapter 11 looks at the role of academic and commercial publishers, and other entities that are not part of IGOs, in the distribution, indexing, copublishing, and promoting of access to IGO information. Chapter 12 includes interview information from sixteen academics, media personnel, government officials, businesspeople, and other regular users of IGO information. It discusses how they gain access to the information, the difficulties they encounter, the value they perceive in those sources, and the manner in which they integrate IGO information into their research, writing, and other works.

The final two chapters comprise Part 3 and concern library processes. Chapter 13 deals with establishing, developing, and maintaining collections of IGO source material, including access to the internet and other electronic resources. Chapter 14 discusses the multiple aspects of reference and information work with IGO material, with special emphasis on UN resolutions, statistics, and electronic and printed sources that have recently become available.

Work is proceeding on a second volume to this book to augment and further update the information in this volume. It is planned that Volume 2 will discuss additional resources and processes. This should include the role of IGOs as publishers; microform documentation; maps and other cartographic material; IGO archives; UN information-gathering in the area of peace and security; cataloging and classification of IGO source material; and forms of citation of IGO documents, publications, and electronic information.

Scholars, government officials, researchers, media personnel, librarians, and other information professionals should find this book informative and useful. It should benefit everyone concerned with information produced by and pertaining to international governmental organizations.

Peter I. Hajnal
Toronto, July 1997

Acknowledgments

Space does not allow mentioning here all those who have encouraged and helped me in preparing this second volume of *International Information*. I would, however, like to offer my thanks to the Munk Centre for International Studies, University of Toronto, for granting me office space and many other forms of support, and express particular gratitude to my colleagues Dr. Sylvia Ostry and Professors Louis Pauly and John Kirton.

I am grateful to the contributors for sharing their insight and experience. My special thanks go to my wife Edna and my son Mark for their understanding and valuable editorial assistance, and to my research assistant Gillian Clinton, who provided excellent bibliographic and editorial help, and worked against deadlines with dedication, initiative, perseverance, and a high degree of competence.

Finally, I thank Carmel Huestis and her colleagues at Libraries Unlimited for meticulous editing and for helping in many other ways to develop the manuscript for publication.

I am indebted to them all for their role in making this a better book. Any omissions or inaccuracies are my sole responsibility.

Peter I. Hajnal
Toronto, July 2000

Contributors

J. J. Cherns is a former senior official of Her Majesty's Stationery Office (HMSO), United Kingdom, responsible for its publishing activities. He has also examined at first hand the information and publishing organizations of many other governments and the major IGOs. In retirement he has done academic research on official information and publishing as a component of the political system.

Juris Dilevko teaches at the Faculty of Information Studies, University of Toronto.

A. Walter Dorn is a Senior Research Fellow at Cornell University (Center for International Studies) and on Faculty at the Pearson Peacekeeping Centre in Canada. He is also the UN representative of Science for Peace, a Canadian civil society organization working for a just and sustainable world. He holds a Ph.D. in physical chemistry from the University of Toronto but now devotes almost all his time to issues of global peace and security. His latest book is *World Order for a New Millennium: Political, Cultural and Spiritual Approaches to Building Peace* (St. Martin's Press, 1999). He can be reached at wdorn@chem.utoronto.ca.

Charles Eckman is Principal Government Documents Librarian at Stanford University's Green Library. He has written and lectured on a variety of topics in international documents librarianship. He currently manages a project undertaken by the Stanford Libraries in cooperation with the WTO to digitally preserve and provide access to historic GATT archival and documentary resources.

Mary K. Fetzer is Government Resources Librarian at Rutgers University's Alexander Library, Chair of the New Brunswick Libraries Faculty, and Acting Political Science Librarian. She has been a frequent contributor to the literature of and speaker on international documents and their use.

Diane L. Garner is Librarian for the Social Sciences at Harvard College Library. She is the co-author, with Diane Smith, of *The Complete Guide to Citing Government Information Resources*, revised edition, 1993. She has served as chairperson of the American Library Association's Government Documents Round Table and on the Depository Library Council to the (U.S.) Public Printer.

Susan Hainsworth is currently a Legal Affairs Officer in the Rules Division of the World Trade Organization, Geneva. She has S.J.D. and LL.B degrees from Osgoode Hall Law School, York University, Canada, an M.A.E.S. from the College of Europe, Bruges, Belgium, and a B.A. in International Relations from Trinity College, University of Toronto, Canada.

Peter I. Hajnal is Research Associate, Munk Centre for International Studies, and Adjunct Professor, Faculty of Information Studies, University of Toronto. He has been a member of the G7/G8 Research Group of the University since 1988 and has attended the summits in 1989–1992, 1994–1998, and 2000. He retired from the University's Library in December 1997 as International Organizations and Government Information Specialist. Earlier he had worked for the United Nations. He has written and lectured extensively about international organizations and their documentation; his latest book is *The G7/G8 System: Evolution, Role and Documentation* (Ashgate, 1999). He received the American Library Association's 1997 James Bennett Childs Award for a significant, lifetime contribution to documents librarianship.

Markku Järvinen received his M.A. from Helsinki University in 1961. He was archivist at the National Archives of Finland, Helsinki, from 1961 to 1974, then archivist at Unesco, Paris, from 1974 to 1994 when he retired as Chief of the Unesco Archives.

Hans Dirk Koehler has been Publisher of the World Bank in Washington, D.C. since September 1996. He was a member of the STM Executive Board from 1992 to 1998. From 1981 to 1996 (the last seven years as CEO) he was with VCH Publishing Group, a scientific publisher that was acquired in 1996 by John Wiley & Sons and is based in Weinheim, Germany. Prior to that, he worked for Walter de Gruyter & Co. in Berlin, Germany. He has an M.A. in industrial engineering from Technical University, Berlin.

David Lewtas is the Chief of the Cartographic Unit of the Aeronautical Information and Charts Section in the Headquarters of the International Civil Aviation Organization, Montreal. His background includes a university degree with specialization in physical geography and over twenty years of experience in surveying or cartographic production. He also enjoys navigating as a glider pilot and sailor.

Elisa Mason spent six years with the United Nations High Commissioner for Refugees. From 1994–1998, she served as an information officer in the Centre for Documentation and Research in Geneva. Prior to that, she worked in the Washington, D.C. branch office of UNHCR. Now based in London, she currently conducts research in the field of refugee and forced migration studies, and has published a number of articles on information resources in this area.

Michael McCaffrey-Noviss currently teaches government documents at the University of Toronto's Faculty of Information Studies. Formerly, he was head of the Government Publications and Maps Department at Northwestern University.

Donald F. Ross was International Organizations Librarian at the British Library of Political and Economic Science at the London School of Economics and Political Science from 1979–1987 and Librarian of the Marshall Library of Economics in the Faculty of Economics at Cambridge University from 1988–1992. Since 1992 he has been with the Joint Library of the World Bank and the International Monetary Fund in Washington, D.C. where he is now Senior Librarian, Research Services Team.

Robert W. Schaaf (1926–1997) had an M.A. degree from Johns Hopkins University's School of Advanced International Studies and spent his entire career at the Library of Congress; he retired in 1993 as Senior Specialist in United Nations and International Documents. He published a number of articles and book chapters, and lectured widely, on international documentation. He received the American Library Association's 1987 James Bennett Childs Award for a significant, lifetime contribution to documents librarianship.

Andrea Sevetson has been employed at the University of California/Berkeley Libraries since 1989, and has been Head, Government Information since 1996.

Abbreviations and Acronyms

AACR 2	Anglo-American Cataloguing Rules II
AAL	Ask-a-Librarian
ACCT	Agence de coopération culturelle et technique
AFELSH	Association des facultés et établissements de lettres et sciences humaines
AI	Amnesty International
AIF	Agence intergouvernementale de la Francophonie
AIMF	Association internationale des maires et responsables des capitales et métropoles partiellement ou entièrement francophones
AIP	Aeronautical Information Publication
AIPLF	Assemblée internationale des parlementaires de langue française
AIS	Aeronautical Information Services
ALA	American Library Association
ANSI	American National Standards Institute
APA	American Psychological Association
APF	Assemblée parlementaire de la Francophonie (Assembly of Francophone Parliamentarians)
AUF	Agence universitaire francophone
AUPELF	Association des universités partiellement ou entièrement de langue française
AUPELF-UREF	Association des universités partiellement ou entièrement de langue française—Université des réseaux d'expression française
BBC	British Broadcasting Corporation
BCIS	Biodiversity Conservation Information System (IUCN)

BIFFA	Bureau international du FFA
BIGA	Banque d'Information des Gens d'Affaires
BIS	Bank for International Settlements
BISD	*Basic Instruments and Selected Documents* (GATT and WTO)
BPCD	Biodiversity Policy Coordination Division (IUCN)
CAB	Executive Office of the Director-General (Unesco)
CAFTIC	Centre africain de formation aux technologies de l'information et de la communication
CAR	Computer-assisted retrieval
CAS	Country Assistance Strategy (World Bank)
CIA	Central Intelligence Agency (US)
CIS	Congressional Information Service
CD-ROM	Compact disk/read-only memory
CDR	Centre for Documentation and Research (formerly Centre for Documentation on Refugees) (UNHCR)
CEC	Commission on Education & Communication (IUCN)
CEESP	Commission on Environmental, Economic and Social Policy (IUCN)
CEL	Commission on Environmental Law (IUCN)
CEM	Commission on Ecosystem Management (IUCN)
CER	*Cost Effectiveness Review*
CERN	European Organization for Nuclear Research
CFIT	Controlled Flight into Terrain
CG	Conférence Générale (AIF)
CG-18	Consultative Group of Eighteen (GATT)
CHP	Checkpoint
CIDMEF	Conférence internationale des doyens des facultés de médecine d'expression française
CIECC	Consejo Interamericano para la Educación, la Ciencia y la Cultura (Inter-American Council for Education, Science and Culture)
CIFDI	Centre international francophone de documentation et d'information
CIP	Cataloging-in-Publication
CIP	Comité international de préparation du Sommet (Francophonie)
CIS	Comité du Suivi (Francophonie)
CITRA	International Conference of the Round Table on Archives

CMEF	Conférence des ministres de l'Économie et des Finances
CMF	Conférence ministérielle de la Francophonie
CNN	Cable News Network
CNTS	*Cross-National Time-Series*
COCOM	Co-ordinating Committee for Multilateral Export Controls
COM	Computer-output microform
COM documents	Commission documents (EU)
COMECON	Council for Mutual Economic Assistance
CONFEJES	Conférence des ministres de la jeunesse et des sports des pays francophones (Conference of Youth and Sports Ministers)
CONFEMEN	Conférence des ministres de l'éducation nationale des pays francophones (Conference of Education Ministers of French-speaking Countries)
CONFEMER	Conférence des ministres francophones de l'enseignement supérieur et de la recherche
CONGO	Conference of Non-Governmental Organizations in Consultative Relationship with the United Nations
CPF	Conseil Permanent de la Francophonie
CRMS	Co-ordinated records management system
DCI	Division of Communication and Information (UNHCR)
DDF	Document Dissemination Facility (WTO)
DEP	Depository Library (EU)
DEPOLIB	Depository Libraries (UN)
DHL	Dag Hammarskjöld Library (UN)
DM	*Departmental Memorandum* (IMF)
DPA	Department of Political Affairs (UN)
DPI	Department of Public Information (UN)
DPKO	Department of Peace-keeping Operations (UN)
DSB	Dispute Settlement Body (WTO)
DSBB	Dissemination Standards Bulletin Board (IMF)
DSU	*Understanding on Rules and Procedures Governing the Settlement of Disputes*
EBAM	Executive Board Administrative Matters (IMF)
EBAP	Executive Board Administrative Papers (IMF)
EBD	Executive Board Document (IMF)
EBS	Executive Board Specials (IMF)

EC	European Communities
ECE	Economic Commission for Europe (UN)
ECOSOC	Economic and Social Council (UN)
EDC	European Documentation Centres (EU)
EIS	Electronic Information System (IMF)
ERIC	Educational Resources Information Center
ESAF	Enhanced Structural Adjustment Facility (IMF)
ESU	Economics Service Unit (IUCN)
EU	European Union
EXCOM	Executive Committee (UNHCR)
EXR	External Relations Department (IMF)
EXTAC	Acquisitions and Client Relations Unit (World Bank)
EXTIN	InfoShop (World Bank)
EXTMT	Marketing Unit (World Bank)
EXTOP	Office of the Publisher (World Bank)
EXTPO	Production Services Unit (World Bank)
EXTRF	Rights, Contracts and Free Publications Unit (World Bank)
FAD	Fiscal Affairs Department (IMF)
FAO	Food and Agriculture Organization of the United Nations
FAQ	Frequently asked questions
FBIS	Foreign Broadcast Information Service
FC	Force Commander
FF	French franc(s)
FFA	Forum francophone des affaires (Francophone Business Forum)
FFI	Fonds francophone des Inforoutes
FICU	Fonds international de coopération universitaire
FMS	Flight Management System
G8	Group of Eight industrialized countries
GA	General Assembly (UN)
GATS	*General Agreement on Trade in Services*
GATT	General Agreement on Tariffs and Trade
GB	Great Britain
GDDS	General Data Dissemination System (IMF)
GEF	Global Environment Facility
GFS	*Government Finance Statistics* (IMF)

GIMCU	Groupe d'intervention médical et chirurgical d'urgence
GIS	Geographic Information System(s)
GODORT	Government Documents Round Table (ALA)
GPO	U.S. Government Printing Office
Habitat	United Nations Centre for Human Settlements
HIPC	Heavily Indebted Poor Countries (IMF)
HMSO	Her Majesty's Stationery Office (United Kingdom)
HRW	Human Rights Watch
IAEA	International Atomic Energy Agency
IASC	Inter-Agency Standing Committee
IBRD	International Bank for Reconstruction and Development
ICA	International Council on Archives
ICAO	International Civil Aviation Organization
ICBL	International Campaign to Ban Landmines
ICC	International Criminal Court
ICITO	Interim Commission for the International Trade Organization
ICJ	International Court of Justice (UN)
ICRC	International Committee of the Red Cross
IDRC	International Development Research Centre
IEPF	Institut de l'énergie des pays ayant en commun l'usage du français
IFLA	International Federation of Library Associations and Institutions
IFOR/SFOR	NATO forces sent to Bosnia
IFR	Instrument Flight Rules
IFS	*International Financial Statistics* (IMF)
IGC	Institute for Global Communications
IGO	International governmental organization; Intergovernmental organization
IHO	International Hydrographic Association
IICI	International Institute for Intellectual Co-operation
IIS	*Index to International Statistics*
IISH	International Institute of Social History
ILC	International Law Commission (UN)
ILO	International Labour Organisation; International Labour Office
ILOSTAT	International Labour Organisation's statistical database

IMF	International Monetary Fund	
IMG	Information Management Group (IUCN)	
IMO	International Maritime Organization	
INCREP	Incident report	
INFOCIECC	CIECC Information System (OAS)	
INIS	International Nuclear Information System (IAEA)	
Inter-Action	American Council for Voluntary International Action	
ISAD	International Standard for Archival Description	
ISBN	International Standard Book Number	
ISCC	Information Systems Coordination Committee (UN)	
ISO	International Organization for Standardization	
ISSN	International Standard Serial Number	
ITO	International Trade Organization (proposed)	
ITU	International Telecommunication Union	
IUPN	International Union for the Protection of Nature; World Conservation Union	
JOLIS	Web-based catalog used for access to World Bank and IMF documents and publications	
JUNINDEX	Computer-assisted bibliographic tool (Andean Pact)	
KAL	Korean Air Lines	
KFOR	NATO forces sent to Kosovo	
KIMS	Knowledge and Information Management System (UNHCR)	
LABORDOC	Database of the International Labour Organisation	
LC	Library of Congress	
LID	Labour Information Database (ILO)	
LLMC	Law Library Microform Consortium	
MAE	Money and Exchange Arrangements Department (IMF)	
MAI	Multilateral Agreement on Investment (proposed)	
MERCOSUR	Mercado Común del Sur (The Southern Common Market)	
MIB	Military Information Branch	
MLA	Modern Language Association	
MSF	Médecins Sans Frontières	
MUNDA	Model United Nations Discussion Area	
NAFTA	North American Free Trade Agreement	
NATO	North Atlantic Treaty Organization	

NGLS	Non-Governmental Liaison Service (UN)
NGO	Nongovernmental organization
NTIS	National Technical Information Service
OAMCE	Organisation africaine et malgache de coopération économique
OAS	Organization of American States
OAU	Organization of African Unity
OCAM	Organisation commune africaine et malgache
OCHA	Office for the Coordination of Humanitarian Affairs (UN)
ODS	Official Documents Search; formerly Optical Disk System (UN)
OECD	Organisation for Economic Co-operation and Development
OEEC	Organisation for European Economic Co-operation
OI	Oxfam International
OIF	Organisation internationale de la Francophonie (La Francophonie)
OING	Conférence francophone des Organisations internationales non gouvernementales
OLF	Office de la langue française (Office of the French Language)
ONUC	UN Operation in the Congo
ONUCA	United Nations Observer Group in Central America
OP	Observation post
OPCW	Organization for the Prohibition of Chemical Weapons
ORCI	Office for Research and the Collection of Information (UN)
OTC	Organization for Trade Cooperation
OXFAM	Oxford Committee for Famine Relief
PDF	Portable document format
PDR	Policy Development and Review Department (PDR)
PERSUMS	Periodic summaries
PFP	Policy Framework Paper (IMF)
PI	Public Information Section (UNHCR)
PIC	Public Information Center (World Bank)
PIFS	*Papers on International Financial Statistics* (IMF)
PIN	Policy Information Notice (IMF)
PKO	Peace-keeping operations
PRGF	Poverty Reduction and Growth Facility (IMF)
PRSP	Poverty Reduction Strategy Paper (IMF)

RAMP	Records and Archives Management Programme (Unesco)
RED	*Recent Economic Developments* (IMF)
REFER	Réseau électronique francophone d'information
RSQ	*Refugee Survey Quarterly*
RWF	Reporters without Frontiers
SAF	Structural Adjustment Facility (IMF)
SARPS	Standards and Recommended Practices (ICAO)
SC	Standing Committee
SCAF	Sub-Committee on Administrative and Financial Matters (UNHCR)
SCIP	Sub-Committee of the Whole on International Protection (UNHCR)
SDDS	Special Data Dissemination Standard (IMF)
SDR	Special Drawing Rights (IMF)
SG	Secretary-General
SIO	Section of Archivists of International Organizations (ICA)
SITCEN	Situation Centre
SITREP	Situation report
SM	Staff Memoranda (IMF)
SMF	Secours médical français
SSC	Species Programme & Species Survival Commission (IUCN)
SUPINFOREPS	Supplementary information reports
SUR	Surveillance Documents (IMF)
SYFED	Systèmes francophones d'édition et de diffusion
TPRB	Trade Policy Review Body (WTO)
TPRM	Trade Policy Review Mechanism
TRAFIX	*Trade Facilitation Information Exchange*
TRIPs	*Agreement on Trade Related Aspects of Intellectual Property*
TV5	International French Television Network
UAM	Union africaine et malgache
UAMCE	Union africaine et malgache de coopération économique
UAP	Universal Availability of Publications
UBC	Universal Bibliographic Control
UDC	Universal Decimal Classification
UK	United Kingdom of Great Britain and Northern Ireland

ULDP	*Unesco List of Documents and Publications*
UN	United Nations
UNA-USA	United Nations Association of the United States of America
UNBIS	United Nations Bibliographic Information System
UNCTAD	United Nations Conference on Trade and Development
UNDEX	*United Nations Documents Index*
UNDOC	*United Nations Documents Current Index*
UNDOF	United Nations Disengagement Observer Force
UNDP	United Nations Development Programme
UNEF	United Nations Emergency Force
UNEP	United Nations Environment Programme
UNESBIB	Unesco Bibliographic Data Base
Unesco	United Nations Educational, Scientific and Cultural Organization
UNESDOC	Unesco Electronic Document Management Data Base
UNHCR	United Nations High Commissioner for Refugees
UNIC	United Nations Information Centre
UNICEF	United Nations International Children's Fund
UNIDO	United Nations Industrial Development Organization
UNIFIL	United Nations Interim Force in Lebanon
UN-I-QUE	United Nations Info Quest
UNISAT	Université audiovisuelle
UNISIST	Intergovernmental Programme for Co-operation in the Field of Scientific and Technological Information (Unesco)
UNITA	União Nacional para a Independencia Total de Angola
UNOPS	United Nations Office for Project Services
UNOSOM	UN Operations Somalia
UNPROFOR	United Nations Protection Force
UNREF	United Nations Refugee Fund
UNSCOM	United Nations Special Commission (of the Security Council)
UNTAC	United Nations Transitional Authority in Cambodia
UREF	Université des réseaux d'expression française
URL	Uniform Resource Locator
US	United States
USAID	U.S. Agency for International Development
USG	Under-Secretary-General (UN)

USSR	Union of Soviet Socialist Republics
UVF	Université virtuelle francophone
WCPA	World Commission on Protected Areas (IUCN)
WEO	*World Economic Outlook* (IMF)
WEP	World Employment Program (ILO)
WGS-84	World Geodetic System-1984
WHO	World Health Organization
WHOSIS	World Health Organization's Statistical Information System
WIPO	World Intellectual Property Organization
WISTAT	*Women's Indicators and Statistics Database, Version 3*
WMO	World Meteorological Organization
WTO	World Trade Organization
WWF	World Wide Fund for Nature, formerly World Wildlife Fund

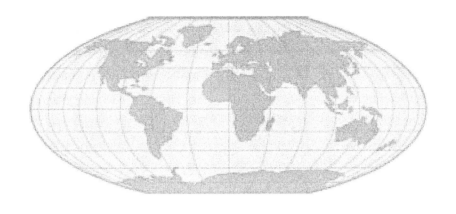

Part I

INSTITUTIONS

CHAPTER 1
Intergovernmental Organizations As Publishers

Editor's note: The two sections of this chapter provide an interesting contrast. Section A, written some twenty years ago, is a thoughtful analysis of the philosophy of publishing in general and IGO publishing in particular. That analysis, and the description of organizational habits and mindset that underlie IGO publishing practices, have stood the test of time. Section B is an up-to-date case study of a major IGO that not only discusses the salient features of World Bank publishing but shows also the tremendous changes brought about in recent years by rapidly expanding information technology, with wide-ranging implications for all aspects of publishing as well as disseminating, organizing, and using the information, documentation, and publication output of IGOs.

(A) INTERGOVERNMENTAL ORGANIZATIONS AS PUBLISHERS

J. J. Cherns*

International governmental organization (IGO) is a term covering upward of three hundred organizations whose scale of operation and functions are very varied. They have in common their intergovernmental constitutions; their interests may have as little in common as those of the Administrative Centre of Social Security for Rhine Boatmen and the Inter-American Music Council. Many are worldwide in scope, such as the World Bank and the International

---

*Chapter 1 (A), republished essentially as it appeared in the first (1988) edition of this work, is substantially based on a paper submitted to the Second World Symposium on International Documentation, Brussels, 1980, and included in the proceedings of the Symposium, *International Documents for the 80's: Their Role and Use*, edited by Theodore D. Dimitrov and Luciana Marulli-Koenig (Pleasantville, NY: UNIFO Publishers, 1982). Used by permission of UNIFO.

Civil Aviation Organization. The largest and most complex groupings, such as the United Nations family and its offshoots, and the European Communities [now European Union—ed.], produce the bulk of IGO recorded outputs, and the problems which go with them.

In toto, the IGOs produce very large amounts of recorded information. Its volume is generally conceded to be overwhelming, indeed stultifying. Its general or specific value is often questioned; **information** is an unselective term. But much of it finds its way into established information bases, and its peculiarities of origin and output have long been a matter of international concern to the library world in particular, which is said to absorb some 90 percent of what is published.[1]

IGOs and Publishing

To what extent these outputs constitute publishing—in the broadest sense, making information available on a limited or general scale outside its originating base—is a matter of definition and discussion. They are certainly a special type of publishing. But consideration of IGOs as publishers is complicated from the outset by the distinction which IGOs make, not itself altogether clear in practice, between the **documents** produced to inform and support their work and the **publications** specifically intended to further their objectives and programs outside their organizational framework. The distinction is blurred in operation, and the professional contributions to both volumes of this work deal with both the definitions and the confusions in more detail.

However, when IGOs refer to **publications**, they are referring to the outputs produced, marketed, or distributed usually under the aegis of their specific publishing organizations and authorities. These are a very small proportion of their total outputs; Luciana Marulli-Koenig has estimated that within the UN family, the largest IGO publishing group, some 180,000 documents produced annually outnumber the 7,500 publications by almost twenty-five to one.[2] More terminological confusion arises from an IGO habit of considering **publications** descriptively rather than conceptually, in terms of "books" or "pamphlets," studies or works of reference, whether priced, and so on. In plain language the essence of a publication is whether it achieves a public circulation, irrespective of its internal classification or the form in which it is produced.

The distinction between documents and publications is paralleled by publishing on two different levels. On the documentary level, IGOs are publishers by virtue of regular and systematic distribution to a wide spread of recipients, including depository libraries accessible to the public, and to the press. This is publication of the material for all practical purposes, however it may be described, though it is passive in form. The material is not initially designed for or targeted to specific external readerships; the recipients, especially libraries, must make it available if it is to have further circulation. On the publications level, the material is produced ostensibly for specific readerships or general public interest and is distributed, if priced, through commercial means and channels, including mail order, and bookshops run by the IGOs themselves, and by the bookselling trade, many of which are designated as agents for particular IGOs. Unpriced publications cannot be commercially distributed; they are distributed through standing lists. Many documents are reissued as publications. Some publications are commercially distributed or produced through arrangements with commercial publishers. The specific "publications" activities of IGOs will be the main, though not the sole, concern of Section A of this chapter.

It was inevitable that the first preoccupations of IGOs were the purposes for which they were established, and that the importance of their documentation and other recorded information outputs as a publishing activity, with research and wider public dimensions, was not always adequately appreciated. Some IGOs have very long histories, some as organs of the pre-1945 League of Nations (e.g., the International Labour Organisation, ILO), with established or inherited habits of documentation and publishing. Even among the many organs of the UN and its offshoots there is no uniformity of organization or of output classification. These are understandably related to the character and tasks of the specific organization. IGOs not infrequently make the valid point that they do not exist to provide material for researchers. Nevertheless, if they produce and distribute recorded outputs on a massive scale, these are bound to become the subject of wide interest and research. By virtue of the very nature of IGOs these are, in effect, internationally public documents.

It was equally inevitable that concerns about form and manageability of these rapidly accumulating outputs should take time to manifest and organize themselves on an international basis. Since the early 1970s those concerns have been expressed in international forums, which have been landmarks in knowledge and treatment of the subject. The International Symposium of 1972, the 1980 Second World Symposium on International Documentation, and the 1982 International Congress on Universal Availability of Publications, following previous meetings about and interest in Universal Bibliographic Control (UBC), have placed on record in their proceedings and reports a wide body of international experience and opinion as well as information; they have identified problems; and they have suggested positive courses of action. Correspondingly, the body of organized knowledge about the documentary and publishing activities of IGOs has been increasing. Theodore Dimitrov lists an impressive corpus of bibliographic and organizational published work about them.[3] They are professionally discussed in journals and at meetings. They have been the subject of comprehensive works such as Peter Hajnal's books on the UN and Unesco.[4]

Discussion has not, however, been matched by action. Rapporteurs of the 1980 Symposium voiced a feeling that not much progress had been made in dealing with problems discussed at the 1972 Symposium. It may be that some of the problems are simply not soluble from the point of view of IGOs rather than of the users. It may be that the sheer complexity of the context frustrates any approach on a broad front and that different strategies might produce better results. There seems no reason to assume that some problems cannot be at least alleviated, if not eliminated.

Many IGOs have primarily a political dimension which is their main interest to the world at large. The special importance to the library world of IGO published outputs is that these reflect very accurately the proceedings and work of their parent organizations and are found whole, or reasonably whole, nowhere else outside these IGOs. Dealing with the collection and organization of IGO material is a limited professional task, but it has wider dimensions. It calls attention not only to the sheer volume of the outputs, but to the question of value which Dimitrov mentions.

These questions are linked through the documentary and publications organizations of the IGOs and the policies behind them. This author took some detailed note of these in connection with a wider survey of official publishing some ten years ago, but the fundamentals have not changed.[5] They underlie the outputs and their characteristics, and an appreciation of them is necessary for understanding the problems. To look at IGOs as publishers one needs to understand how they see themselves in that role and thus how they organize themselves (or should organize themselves) to fulfill it. This in turn necessitates some wider view of publishing as an activity.

Frameworks of Publishing Activity

Publisher and **publishing**, like **IGO**, are terms covering a variety of activities and objectives. The form and organization of publishing are related to the objectives of the publisher. In looking at the broad forms of publishing, one can begin with the commercial publisher; he sets the most widespread and commonly understood framework and objectives for the activity. This provides a basis of comparison for the activities of other types of publishers.

The commercial publisher carries on an entrepreneurial process within a financial framework. His activities are essentially consumer-oriented, governed by the capacity of specific consumers (the market) to pay a price for a recorded information product and by his ability to choose the product and to organize its production and distribution in order to satisfy the market within costs which will leave him a surplus (profit). His market orientation requires a degree of editorial control, which may range from light to dominant, and which must be exercised at a very early stage, in the choice of the product itself. Increasingly, commercial publishers tend to identify markets and seek or commission works to meet their special needs and interests (such as microform editions of back runs or out-of-print material). There is much publishing specialization. But the commercial motivation extends throughout the acceptance/commissioning and production processes, with distribution supported by promotion, in order to present a product attractive to the market in form and substance. This does not necessarily mean glossy covers and illustrations; it extends to format (size), medium (e.g., microfiche), make-up (e.g., loose-leaf editions), and after-sales service for continuing works. In short, the commercial publisher is a merchandiser, aiming to maximize his return from ventures of his choice, and under no obligation to satisfy marginal demand regardless of cost.

Distribution is vital to marketing. One can look at modern commercial publishing as an activity concerned as much with distribution as with commissioning, editing, and production supported by adequate cataloging and descriptive material to meet the needs of booksellers or direct customers for identification of their requirements. Financial discipline imposes a common framework for evaluative judgments. It exerts pressure to confine free distribution to legal deposit requirements, to the few copies given to authors, and to review and other promotional purposes. To give away copies which would be bought is commercial anathema. To give away copies which cannot be sold devalues the product and undermines the market. Publishers sometimes bury their dead in the "remainder" market, but on conditions and after a lapse of time controlled within the book trade.

Other forms of publishing maintain the commercial framework while modifying the commercial objectives. Many academic works would never see publication through entrepreneurial publishers. They find outlets through university presses whose primary aim is distribution, if necessary by subsidization from noncommercial sources or from remunerative items. Private (sometimes known as **vanity**) publishing has always been an outlet for authors more convinced than publishers of the merit of their works and prepared to underwrite them. **Prestige** publishing by large organizations is a promotional expense, though it may sometimes develop into commercially viable ventures (examples from the United Kingdom are the *"Shell" Guides* and the *Guinness Book of Records*).

In commercially based forms of publishing there is no doubt about the fact of publication. Outputs bear a publisher's imprint and recognized publishing identification (e.g., ISBN), have a price printed on them or cataloged, and have defined sources and channels of availability. Commercial publishers do not produce material which they do not intend to sell. The mechanisms of the publishing and bookselling business do not provide channels for free distribution, and publishers now rely less than formerly on the network of the bookselling trade. Mail order, subscription (e.g., book clubs), and other promotional means which identify specific markets and cut out the retail distributor's margins are in common use. Moreover, the highly diffuse retail booksellers' network cannot cope satisfactorily with the increasing range and variety and new media (e.g., microform) of published products. It has been forced to adopt a more merchandising approach, in which it is reluctant to handle complex types of publication which involve unremunerative orders and reference work, or items of very limited demand and turnover, or titles difficult to obtain from publishers.

With official publishing (which for immediate purposes can be considered as publishing emanating from governments and IGOs), one enters a world whose publishing is essentially distributive rather than commercial, in pursuit of objectives to which commercial criteria may be irrelevant even if commercial forms are used. The objective tends to be stated in terms of "dissemination" rather than "distribution," with an implicit sense of mission which sometimes seems to inhibit other judgments.

Governments have characteristics and responsibilities of territoriality and authority in relation to specific populations with whom they must communicate. Their published outputs have diverse and diffused bureaucratic and political origins. They begin with compliance outputs; laws must be known and textually available if they are to be obeyed and enforced. Defined government accountabilities may require regularly published information outputs. Bureaucratic and other guidance and information are made available. The published outputs of parliamentary institutions are important sources of public record and reference. These forms of political communication are by no means all a matter of choice. Many of them are mandated by law or custom. Free distribution, sale, or amplification through the media are used as necessary for dissemination objectives. The bookselling trade may be used; but diffuse demand for these products in the public market and the variety and bibliographic difficulty of the outputs make extensive direct-mail order a feature of developed government publishing.

Diffuse departmental sources and lack of coherent control give rise to "grey" areas of bibliographically ill-defined material across the range of government departments and functions. There is no high degree of co-ordination even in the better-organized government publishing operations. But government publishing, aimed at a defined population, has specific roles in the governmental process to which its "value" can be related. It has a "market," but for penetration rather than financial exploitation. Moreover, governments maintain a clear and deliberate distinction between internal and administrative documentation and published information, and usually buttress it by legal sanctions, subject to any formal access legislation.

IGOs have some similarities to governments, but without the territorial authority which governments exercise. They function through their member governments by consent rather than by authority. They are departmentalized bureaucracies, complex and hierarchical, whose accountabilities to member governments tend to be remote. They administer themselves, producing internal documentation. They produce very extensive "parliamentary" documentation from the plenary sessions, ad hoc meetings, standing committees, and consultative bodies which are the framework for their operations, backed by extensive preparatory papers and studies. They give effect in further documentation to the resolutions and decisions of these meetings, for record or for action.

When, by consent or mandate, IGOs direct themselves to populations rather than governments, through programmatic rather than procedural activities, through "publications" rather than "documents," their "markets" are often uncertain and ill-defined. The Cocoa Producers' Alliance has a limited membership defined by its purpose; it is unlikely to originate highly varied or extensive outputs (though it is easy to imagine how these might be developed in agricultural, economic, and political directions). The World Health Organization (WHO) has a very much wider, but still definable subject range. The UN and Unesco can and do interest themselves in almost everything under the sun. The original territorial limitations of the European Communities have been progressively widened by territorial association and a consequent extension of interest range. Though IGOs are in many ways comparable with governments in their publishing activities, it is difficult to set for these the limits which governments naturally find for themselves in the exercise of a territorial authority. "Since its inception the United Nations has attempted to provide information to the world."[6] How far can such an ideal go?

The larger the IGO, the more extensive and extended is its bureaucracy. Bureaucracy as a phenomenon has a well-established place in the theory of government, but it requires little knowledge of bureaucratic theory to appreciate the rigidities and inertia which can develop within internationally composed bureaucracies. These have been characterized as hierarchical and authoritarian, with corresponding habits of thought which affect the style of their documents.[7] The international membership, at its most extensive in the UN family, comprises states with very different levels of development and varied political organization and orientation which make demands on the services and outputs of the organizations, in distribution and in language editions, for example. All these influences bear on the origination and control of outputs, on what is produced, what (or whose) purpose it serves, its publishable quality, and its volume and style of production—questions which vitally concern a publisher before and during production.

As with governments, published outputs of IGOs originate in the various departments according to the responsibilities of each department. Publishing control is thus decentralized, without the overriding controls which naturally establish themselves, even if somewhat loosely, in relation to government publishing. In the first place, government publications originate for the most part in some specific administrative, political, or public requirement. Secondly, in the specific processes of governing, the governmental machine has many forms and points of contact with the public to which it is catering, including feedback. This is the essence of the political system and its response to its environment. The overt demonstration of waste of money and resources in publication of unwanted and irrelevant material issued for ideological considerations for which there is no public interest can cost votes or support; thus, there is some inhibition on it. In short, while there are inefficiencies and imperfections in any government, there is at source usually some knowledgeable consideration of value and utility. This is one reason why governments do not attempt to centralize control of their publishing, except in provision of technical assistance, printing, and distribution.

IGOs are much further removed from the ultimate users of their published outputs, outside the circle of the organization and its official governmental membership, than are governments from their populations. The immediate "public"—apart from member governments—for IGO outputs of documents and many publications is overwhelmingly concerned professionally with the organization of the collection and of its accessibility to others, and not with the content; with volume and classification, not with value. The four groups of libraries—international, national, parliamentary, and research—which are reckoned to absorb 90 percent of the IGO outputs may be remote even in their own countries from any general public. This emphasizes the specialized and limited use made of them. This is not in itself surprising, but it does pose problems for the occasional member of the public interested in these outputs. The material is difficult for the nonspecialist to identify, locate, and use. Indeed, the wider public interest hardly seems to find adequate expression among the papers of international symposia on availability and use. The problems aired are predominantly from the library world, in terms of handling rather than usage or utility. A survey report, *The Availability and Use of Official Publications in Libraries*, touched only incidentally on publications of IGOs but disclosed a general lack of organized information in libraries themselves about the use of collections, while comments and complaints centered almost entirely on mechanical aspects of collections and supply.[8]

Organization of IGO Publishing

For the smaller IGOs—the majority—publishing in all senses is an uncomplicated activity, requiring no elaborate organization. Its function is to produce and distribute meeting records or summaries, and specialized papers, reports, and statistics. Circulation is to member states and to standard lists of recipients, including depository and parliamentary libraries, various other international agencies, and the press. Some IGOs have sales agents for priced publications. Such relatively limited outputs are not usually segregated by libraries in an "IGO" category, but are shelved by subject or organization. Most demand comes from users who know the field and where to look in it, and how to obtain the material if they want to acquire it. Casual users may experience difficulties of access or acquisition. These may be bibliographic or practical, such as tracing needs, finding out where to obtain the material, whether it is free or priced, and how to pay to distant addresses, especially if transactions take place between developing countries with administrative and monetary complications at both ends. It would not seem too difficult for, say, African and Malagasy or South American or other groups of common area or interest to organize some bibliographic and order-processing center in order to ease irritations. But the specialized nature of the smaller IGOs limits both their outputs and associated problems.

The vast mass of documentation and publishing, with the familiar problems which go with it arises, of course, from the major IGOs of the UN family and the large intercontinental and regional IGOs such as OECD and the European Communities. The outstanding characteristics of their outputs are their huge volume, complex diversity, different and sometimes uncertain "publics," and the formidable bibliographic problems which they present for libraries. Eighty-five percent of the material is said to be unread; it is not necessarily unused. Most of it is documentary record and reference material, and the "read" and "unread" components are not constant (if they were, there would be questions about the very need to collect).

The excessive production of documentation, its deficiencies of drafting and style, its complexities of classification and distribution have long concerned IGOs themselves. The enormous volume is constantly deplored and is accepted within the UN itself as an impediment to proper use,[9] but attempts made from time to time to stem the tide have met with no dramatic or lasting success. It may be that they can only marginally reduce the rate of acceleration. Statistics of page-print outputs have reached the point of meaninglessness. They could be reduced if delegations would say less, keep to the point, demand fewer linguistic versions, require less information, presented their material more tersely, were served by bureaucracies capable of exercising these disciplines, had fewer meetings and committees, set up fewer studies, and, paradoxically, rebelled against being smothered by their own outputs. But behind each delegation is a government; a great deal of activity has political motivation in which it is considered important to speak at length and for the record, and to seek to make political points and capital in setting up and debating inquiry. Only the IGOs themselves can deal with these problems, and it may be that only arbitrary disciplines financially expressed can hope to have any effect on them. There is a Parkinson's law at work that activities and documentation will expand to the extent of the funds available for them.

In any case, publication by distribution is a secondary consideration. IGOs are unlikely to give high priority to the problems recipient libraries have in dealing with the complexities of the material, compounded by successive stages of issue in mimeograph and full documentary form, incomplete (though improving) bibliography, lengthy delays in supply, difficulties in obtaining missing items which have gone quickly out of print, and so on. Almost every library has its own system of indexing the material in order to facilitate use, and all but habitual users are likely to need the services of an expert librarian to guide them. The main preoccupations of the library world are, rightly, to improve acquisition, control and bibliography, and to select the appropriate forms of this material.

The publication output of IGOs emerges not as a quasi-administrative by-product, but as a deliberate function of public information. There are, however, considerable limits. Publications programs usually have a substantial content of originally documentary material converted into publications because of a presumed public interest to be satisfied by something more positive than "passive" documentary distribution. There are also, as will be seen, organizational links.

One can hardly do better initially in considering IGOs as publishers than to examine the views of IGOs themselves in that role, and to see how they behave in it. This can be done from some recent accounts of the publishing activities of the UN and its family. This is, of course, not completely comprehensive for IGOs, but it relates to the bulk of IGO publishing, and is applicable in greater or lesser measure to major IGOs outside the UN family. The chief of the Sales Section of the UN in New York, albeit expressing his own views, has recently written specifically on "The United Nations as a Publisher" in *Government Publications Review*.[10] There is also an up-to-date (1984) inspection report on *Publications Policy and Practice in the United Nations System*.[11] This system comprises the UN headquarters and fourteen major UN organs, and ten main organizations of the UN family, including the Food and Agriculture Organization of the United Nations (FAO), WHO, ILO, and Unesco, the main publishers. This thirty-two-page report, incidentally, is a document, not a publication, and is incomplete for examination without three other documents: the twenty-three-page *Comments of the Secretary-General*,[12] a one-page *Corrigendum*,[13] and the twenty-page *Comments of the Administrative Committee on Co-ordination*.[14] (This is a total of seventy-six pages marked for "general" distribution, the widest distribution category of the UN, all arising in the normal course as documents of the thirty-ninth session of the General Assembly. In English alone, on the appropriate distribution scale,[15] this would make a six-figure contribution to the page-prints which stream out of the system.)

In the following discussion these UN documents are referred to as *Insp*, *Sec-Gen* and *Admin Cttee*, with appropriate paragraph numbers. Text references to the *Government Publications Review* article will be to *Hinds*, with page numbers.

Despite the distinction which IGOs make, imprecise language and concept surround the term **publications**. Of the four hundred new titles issued under that description by the UN each year, "many, if not most of the books issued are not intended as books at all. . . . They are the material that goes into, or comes out of the many meetings and international conferences, the development projects, and the programmes and ruminations of offices, departments, and deliberative and legislative bodies of a highly diverse organization" (Hinds, 298). A good deal of this will already have been distributed in mimeographed or other documentary form, in various documentary classifications. That writer seems to have in mind a distinction between "publications" proper and what are in fact fully published documents.

Similar imprecisions are evident in the UN documents. It is suggested that of ten categories of publications issued in English in 1981 by twelve IGOs, three categories ("Official," "Conventions, Codes and Treaty Texts," and "Conference Proceedings, Meeting Reports and Abstracts") would not generally qualify as "books," and should therefore be considered as "documents," unless they have an identifiable saleability (Insp, para. 16) (here, too, many will have already been issued as documents). Among the criteria by which documents may be considered for issue as publications is "substantial sales potential," a surprisingly low figure of 500 copies or more (Sec-Gen, paras. 21-25). Documents which cannot pass even this nominal threshold could be issued as "non-sale publications," that is, not documents, but not sold or offered to the general public. Responsibility for getting these to the target users then rests primarily with the author department (Sec-Gen, para. 25). This comes as part of the response to a recommendation that "publications in respect of which sales are not a viable proposition should be issued in the form of documents rather than books which demand print runs in the thousands" (Insp, para. 112). This confusion of purpose and published form is corrected with the incidental note that print runs of documents are usually considerably higher than those of publications (Sec-Gen, paras. 21-23). The suggestion that the possibility of free distribution—characteristic of documents—rather than the test of publishability—aimed at commercial sale—may be an influence on decisions about publications, in guarded bureaucratic language "merely to serve as proof that an activity has taken place," is presumably based on some observation of practice (Insp, paras. 111-112).

Nominally, the distinction between publications and documents in IGOs is clear. They serve different purposes. But the Inspectors' report and the comments of the UN organization on it suggest more than marginal ambiguities. Considerations of publication are associated with questions of production form and saleability rather than with purpose. **Books**, a term internationally defined in relation to number of pages (Insp, para. 10), is repeatedly used instead of **publications**.

This ambiguity is rooted within the major IGOs in both organization and control, perhaps most markedly within the UN itself. The UN attempts "to provide information to the world," but its Publishing Division is a branch of the Department of Conference Services, and "the role of the publishing activity is to execute the printing programs of the United Nations Secretariat and other United Nations bodies and special conferences. Thus the United Nations does not act as a publisher in the generally accepted sense" (Hinds, 297-98). The printing programs are concerned overwhelmingly with the production of documents: the staff and finances involved in production of documents and publications are often not readily distinguishable; most publication units "have little control over the choice of subject, the quality and style of the manuscript, or the publishability and 'marketability' of the text" (Insp, para. 32).

Organizations may have impressively constituted publication boards and committees. But it is clear that these can function only in budgetary and programmatic terms. They are "organs of co-ordination and general supervision advising the Executive Head. They satisfy themselves that programmes conform to the mandates given to the organizations . . . but they do not enter into the details of individual publications" (Insp, para. 31). Other control is equally general. The UN Publications Board "determines for the UN Secretariat and ensures the implementation of policies governing the preparation, production, distribution, and sale of United Nations documentation and publications" and "co-ordinates . . . and supervises the execution of the publishing programme" (Hinds, 300). Publications of the more specialized organs of the UN family tend to be more closely geared to their work programs than do those of the UN itself, and probably receive more editorial influence from supervising bodies. Some agencies have arrangements for independent reading and peer evaluation of manuscripts. Unesco, whose work is expressed largely in its publishing program, has made an organizational separation between responsibilities for documents and for publications by establishing the Unesco Press as the publications authority, though this does not free it from much small-edition publishing derived from departmental programs, without coherent editorial policy (Admin Cttee, para. 18).

Outside the UN family, OECD (which defines its publications by virtue of a price on the cover) has a large output more closely aligned to the organization's purposes than is the case in most IGOs. The European Communities have a more diffused organization and publishing output, but have improved their publishing control in recent years. In almost all cases, the major IGOs embrace documents and publications within the same broad control, and they present a similar general picture of diffused origination for which central supervising bodies can lay down general principles, but cannot exercise editorial control. In the UN, the Publications Division has no say over origination at all. First, it is organizationally outgunned in a hierarchical bureaucracy. Directors of Publications do not have the authority to make publishing decisions "which might run counter to the will of more senior technical or administrative personnel" (Insp, para. 114). Secondly, it is not competent in the subject-matter. It "may have an opportunity to comment on proposals for publications but it can exercise little pressure to change their basic concept or content." Perhaps most crucial, in the initial departmental request to embark on a publication project, it "has no say in this process" (Insp, para. 47).

What are the implications for the fundamental publishing functions of control of quality and production? The organizational hiatus need not in itself be crucial to quality, and the major IGOs all voice impeccably sound views about quality of writing and alignment to specific readerships. Nevertheless, within the UN, the general quality of manuscripts is openly acknowledged to be poor, "a matter of serious concern" (Insp, para. 56). Many of these begin life as documents, drafted by staff working indiscriminately on both documents and publications, and recruited for some expertise "along with factors such as geographical distribution and other elements of recruitment policy." The function of editorial units "consists primarily of measures to achieve stylistic uniformity and to ensure adherence to the regulations set forth in the *Editorial Manual* as well as checking the accuracy of references" (Sec-Gen, para. 37). (The "chilly professional jargon" which is said to infect UN publications is clearly environmental.)

Production is largely in-house, and the documents cited are clear that publications take second place to the urgencies of documentary production geared (sometimes frenetically) to work and meeting programs. The *Yearbook of the United Nations* itself appears up to four years late, and Unesco, perhaps the most publishing-conscious IGO, calculates some twenty-five months—three or four times longer than need be according to ILO—for a manuscript to achieve publication in the first language-version (Insp, para 53). That is to say, many publications are out-of-date or have forfeited timely impact by the time they appear.

Dimensions of the Specific Publications Activity

The dimensions of the UN family's publication operations are very large indeed. The system produced in 1981 over 14 million copies of some 3,747 publications, fairly evenly split between books and periodicals; and these figures are incomplete, lacking Unesco's external production—that is, by commercial printers—and some organizations' internal production (Insp, Table I). Nobody knows how much this costs. The Inspectors had to make an "educated guess" of about U.S. $150 million on direct costs alone, including some extra-budgetary finance (Insp, para. 4). The Secretary-General refutes this figure as far too high, but ventures no others for internal costs or for the total (para. 66). This is symptomatic of a lack of financial grasp on publication activities; internal production costs do not differentiate between documents and publications. The careful bureaucratic phrasing is dismissive: "Above all, the financial statistics relating to publications left much to be desired" (Insp, para 4).

What is the result of all this work and expenditure? It is, to begin with, very specialized for outputs aimed at the public, even accepting the specialized nature of some IGOs. Of 572 English-language and multilingual titles issued in 1981 by twelve IGOs in the UN family, 310 (54 percent) were monographs, studies, handbooks, and training materials (Insp, Table II). The remaining 262 included 144 (25 percent) reckoned to be essentially documentary material. Statistical works and yearbooks numbered 63 (11 percent), of which 39 came from the UN and 10 from FAO. The remaining 10 percent consisted mainly of 41 repertories, directories, and bibliographies (7 percent) with only 3 percent for general studies and public-information material. The number of items would be substantially increased by language editions, and the figures do not cover periodicals or IGO items issued by commercial publishers. But the general composition is of reference and specialized material (with no wide public appeal), a good deal of which has a documentary rather than publications origin. Much of it has, no doubt, established itself in reference collections—for example, statistical works and yearbooks. Such collections sometimes take works of this kind merely because they are published. Source material, the quality of manuscripts and editing, and timely publication all have a bearing on the value of a given item. Some doubt has been cast on the reliability and pertinence of some statistical sources; nevertheless, statistical publications of IGOs are considered to have specific value.[16]

The mainly specialized character of publications can be seen against a 1952 comment on publications in the UN system: "Most of the publications involved would constitutionally require to be published if there were no purchasers for them at all while, on the other hand, they are not written to appeal to the so-called general reading public" (Insp, para. 19). The position does not seem to have changed significantly: "The option of whether or not to publish normally arises only in the case of studies and reports" (Sec-Gen, para. 3). Hinds refers to "the educated general reader" (298). Clearly, most IGO publishing is not conceived for the purpose of reaching mass audiences with mass messages.

Sales are a measure of publishing effectiveness, both in quality of material and its distribution. In 1981 sales income totaled U.S. $14 million in the UN family (Insp, Table IV). It is impossible to relate this to direct production costs, on which there seem to be no accurate or even agreed-upon figures; but, even if one reduces the Inspectors' "educated guess" of U.S. $150 million by half, it is clear that sales are a marginal factor in distribution. They sometimes lean heavily on a few items—for example, Unesco's sales of around U.S. $2.8 million are "in large measure" from sales of *The Unesco Courier*. They are made overwhelmingly in developed countries—from 70 percent to 90 percent, depending on the IGO. No less than 60 percent of Unesco's sales were made in four countries, of which its own territorial base (France) is foremost (Insp, paras. 78, 82; Admin Cttee, 42). No doubt the IGOs have some idea of the type of customer, but the figures indicate no breakdown. Hinds states specifically for the UN, however, that "most of those sold are bought by libraries" (298). As publications are aimed specifically at the public and are distributed and sometimes published through commercial networks and mechanisms, it seems reasonable to assume that a greater proportion of the publications sold than of the documents distributed finds its way to a wider public, particularly in case of public-information material. The likelihood is that some, especially handbooks and training manuals, find their way into institutional hands, and more may percolate further down library systems to school, public, institutional, and nondepository university libraries.

Some technical publications have substantial "sales; they have little competition to face" (Insp, para. 89), and statistical and reference works which have established themselves may average sales of from 5,000 copies (*Yearbook of the United Nations*) to over 18,000 copies (Unesco's *Study Abroad*) per year. But sale editions are on the whole surprisingly small—in the general range of

1,500–3,000 copies, even for Unesco (Insp, Table I). And these are bodies which operate on a world scale!

The financial aim of the sales is generally to recoup some production costs and to feed revolving funds for reprints. The profit motive is fairly loftily eschewed—though this is somewhat academic; in no sense could these be considered commercially profitable operations, despite their commercial forms. For example, for the UN, "gross sales of publications, in 1983 at $5.5 million, cover the costs of contractual printing, but not much more" (Hinds, 302). Gross sales are presumably not net revenue, nor would contractual printing cover internal production, the greater element. Sales income is tempered by the costs of maintaining sales organizations, including bookshops, mail-order organizations, visits to agents, promotion, and so on. It is not possible to arrive at any coherent commercial assessment for these publishing programs, or, since they include continuing sales of past issues and reprints, to evaluate the position for any one year's publishing.

The publishing programs do not, however, account by any means for total distribution of the material, because the declared aim of the IGOs is above all dissemination. In pursuit of that aim, partly in conformity with obligations to and requests from member states, and particularly in developing countries which find it difficult to pay for them, publications, like documents, achieve very liberal free distribution. Again, comprehensive figures are not available; figures for the same principal UN publishing bodies in 1981 indicate a preponderance of free issue. For example, Unesco gave away 450,000 books and sold 160,000 (though most of its periodicals are sold). FAO, ILO, and WHO gave away rather more than half their publications, even though they are more conscious that sales are some assurance of use. The more specialized the agency, the more, proportionally, it tends to sell—for example, the World Intellectual Property Organization (WIPO) sold 6,000 books and gave away 1,000 (Insp, Table III). The UN is recorded as having an output of 2,238,000 copies of publications in 1981, of which 740,000 were sold, leaving about 1.5 million copies mostly for free distribution (Insp, para. 75). (However, the organization is said to have distributed free over 7.5 million copies in 1981, including possibly some documents; it is difficult indeed to separate documentary and publications figures.)

It is a telling comment that when a publication is given to an external publisher, "the number of free copies which the external publisher will furnish is often extremely limited" (Sec-Gen, para. 51). It is no surprise to find "substantial stocks of unsaleable [sic] publications" (Insp, para. 102) inadequately controlled and weeded, and it seems clear that many copies of publications achieve only recycling as waste paper (the appointment of a consultant by the UN to advise how overstocks can be turned into waste-paper revenue [Sec-Gen, para. 70] is an intriguing example of a revolving fund).

Extensive free distribution of sales publications has aspects other than undermining sales possibilities. Sale is a means of distribution which, on the whole, gets the product to its genuine market, and some agencies explicitly recognize this advantage, for example, FAO. To print two or three times as many copies as are likely to be sold undermines also the basis of pricing on a formula related to production cost per copy, a formula which most of the IGOs use. More fundamentally, it undermines the publishing judgment at source.

Matching both price and distribution to the market is a job more accurately done by commercial and academic publishers, who are in the business of publishing. In the process they achieve a dissemination which reflects the real value of the material to users. If information is really worth disseminating, there is a market for it with which commercial publishers are in closer touch than an IGO can ever be. (This, however, should not obscure the fact that a great deal of IGO information should reach a public regardless of ability to pay for it, especially in developing countries. Properly managed, this need not undermine commercial arrangements.) Varieties of arrangements with commercial publishers have financial as well as dissemination advantages to IGOs, and are used by Unesco and others. But IGOs in the UN family are criticized for not using them enough (Insp, para. 61). They could cut down some of the more wasteful aspects of their own publishing activities while achieving probably greater impact for the material. The European Communities, which make extensive use of commercial publishers, have long accepted their advantages.[17]

The Inspectors' report and the associated documents on the publishing policies and practices of the UN family repay careful reading for connoisseurs of the language and rituals of bureaucracy. They cover also questions of duplication of material, overlapping of coverage, and lack of co-operation and co-ordination among IGOs. The arrangements for sale of publications are particularly uncoordinated. So far as it can be identified from the figures given, income from agents' sales amounted to U.S. $6.6 million out of the total of U.S. $14.3 million in 1981 (Insp, Table IV). U.S. $2.6 million of this was accounted for by sales agents of Unesco, and U.S. $3.1 million by sales agents of the UN and WHO. To achieve these results, IGOs in the UN family maintain extensive and uncoordinated agency networks throughout the world. In 1979, Unesco had no fewer than 275 sales agents in 112 countries; other IGOs had considerably fewer. Bernan/ UNIPUB in the United States is a major, though incomplete, general agency. There are some general agencies in the hands of governments, for example, Her Majesty's Stationery Office (HMSO) in the United Kingdom. Regional centers and information offices help to provide tracing information.

The association of agency spread with sales figures indicating heavy sales concentration in very limited geographical areas suggests that effort and visiting must be going into agencies which do very little business (much of it with libraries?). In developing countries, the potential of these agencies is likely to be undercut by liberal free distribution through governments. Many such agencies must be little more than ordering points with scant knowledge or experience of a complex body of publishing output. Unesco has the largest number of sales agents, with a marked geographical concentration of sales, and varied output; a handful of items produce the bulk of the revenue, and the major revenue item (*The Unesco Courier*) is a subscription periodical. OECD and the European Communities operate agencies on a much more modest scale, and OECD makes a deliberate effort to sell direct by standing order to eliminate distribution delays. It is difficult to pass final judgment without some breakdown of agency sales and knowledge of whether figures represent actual net cash income or invoiced sales and are on a uniform basis.

Indeed, the lack of comprehensive and authoritative figures for operations in which IGOs are among the world's major publishers of nonfiction must strike others besides the Inspectors, who complain of insufficient management information for intelligent planning (para. 133.3). The words are well chosen; there would be little point in castigating the financial outcome itself for the kind of publishing in which financial objectives are clearly unimportant. The real role of the financial framework is to provide the basis which the Inspectors find deficient. If it is known that a publication will produce an estimated loss of, say, U.S. $1,000, that is the cost of attempting to achieve a designated objective—in effect, a subsidy to it. If objectives cannot be assessed in absolute terms, there would at least be a common comparative basis on which to assess priorities and consider other possibilities.

The arbitrary 25 percent cut in the volume of publications which the Joint Inspection Unit considered a possibility was watered down in a recommendation that a ceiling should be placed on publications budgets until governing bodies are more satisfied with the results (Insp, paras. 119-20). In the *Comments of the Administrative Committee on Co-ordination*, the Committee expresses the considered reactions of UN agencies to the Inspectors' report, but does not suggest any drastic action. Some minor improvements may be made, committees will be set up, investigations may be started; but most of the criticism will blandly fade into the records, leaving some deposit behind. One agency comes as near as bureaucratic prose will allow to telling the Inspectors to mind their own business (Admin Cttee, para. 7); governments are obliquely (and no doubt correctly) blamed for failure of attempts to reduce free distribution (Admin Cttee, para. 10). Some comments are not illuminating: "One measure that deserves further attention is the adaptation of the print run of each publication to the likely demand, which would presumably effect economies"; Unesco is relieved to find itself in good company with its publishing problems, but finds it distressing that they "are inherent in the workings of an international organization" (Admin Cttee, para. 6).

Some External Aspects and Suggestions

Some of the basic organizational problems, such as the separation of editorial and other publishing responsibilities common to all IGOs in varying degrees, cannot really be solved from the outside. The publishing performance of IGOs is varied; some agencies are more able than others to steer their publications toward target audiences.

Sales are, in effect, a commercial framework for the distribution of the lesser proportion of publications, concentrated in relatively few developed countries. Many of these will be periodicals on subscription; many others, sales to nondepository libraries and institutions. Hinds states that most UN publications sold are bought by libraries which need bibliographic information rather than sales promotion (296). Many sales in developing countries will also be made to institutions. The extensive networks are unlikely to satisfy much casual demand in remote regions. Outside developed areas the sales operations probably function at heavy cost in relation to net revenue.

Given the volume of IGO-published outputs, the ultimate question is how such information can be distributed, stored, and accessed conveniently, economically, and quickly. Significantly, distribution has been singled out as "the weakest link in the chain between author and reader."[18] IGO distributions to libraries are predominantly by surface mail. Consignments are slow to arrive, often do not arrive sequentially, and losses in transit are not infrequent. Even by the time these arrive, libraries may not yet have the bibliographic information necessary to check them against what has been published or distributed. Agents have the same problem. The process of getting the material from the publisher to the user could benefit from more practical co-operation among major IGOs. Though every depository library does not have the same collecting range, many collect from more than one IGO. Air-freight (and sea-freight) costs can be reduced by the co-operative use of cargo containers. Air-freight for IGO consignments to regions distant from their production centers would revolutionize speed of supply. Commercial publishers co-operate these days to form container loads going to distant markets. Some IGOs do hold stocks at distant points; but co-operation among them in relation to supply seems hardly considered. No doubt, difficulties as well as advantages can be identified, but some kind of pilot study seems called for.

The heavy concentration of "public" distribution in libraries makes it difficult to measure the effectiveness of publications in relation to the IGOs' objectives, though sporadic sampling efforts are made. But it is a problem to identify users when there is little direct contact with them. Government publishing also is characterized by the absence of unified publishing control, and, as with IGOs, much of it is "parliamentary" output not susceptible to normal publishing criteria. For the rest, government publications circulate widely in the community. Library collections are a back-up and more permanent reference repository, rather than a first line of usage. The published outputs of IGOs, however, are funnelled into very much narrower channels, mainly into "élite" libraries and documentation centers. The estimated 90 percent which goes into international, national, parliamentary, and research libraries by deposit is probably supplemented by institutional, university, and public libraries. The last command scant funds, are generally poorly served for publications of their own governments, and in any case collect IGO material very selectively; many hold little more than standard reference works.

Given a suitable research framework, useful information about usage and users of both documents and publications could probably be gathered from libraries. Most libraries specializing in IGO collections find them being used by very limited numbers of academic researchers, professionals such as lawyers, and government officials. (One of the points which emerged from the study, *The Availability and Use of Official Publications in Libraries*, is that, because governments themselves do not hold official collections, but simply archive copies, officials are often dependent on library collections for their own official needs.)

Research into usage must prompt other directions of inquiry. Libraries may rightly emphasize that their function is to maintain collections and provide expert guidance to them. But cost cannot be disregarded in relation to use. Storage of these constantly growing acquisitions is expensive; Peter Hajnal gives a figure of an 18–20 linear feet accretion of shelf-space per annum for a full deposit of UN documents and publications alone.[19] Costing is not yet a highly developed feature of either libraries or IGOs. Much of the total cost is made up of heavy production and distribution expenses in IGOs, for material which is held at growing and continuing expense by the main collecting libraries, for an apparently very low rate of specialist usage. Regardless of where all these costs fall, they comprise the costs of the system as a whole. The cost of serving each library-use must be large, and probably remarkable in relation to the total costs involved. One doubts whether there is a large untapped pool of potential users unaware of this material.

Identification of assembly, packing, transportation, and holding costs would be relevant also to other possibilities, much discussed intermittently, of supplying microform instead of hard copy. Depository libraries have not generally received microform from IGOs except on payment, for which most of them do not have the financial resources. But there are savings to IGOs themselves in that medium of supply. Advantages and disadvantages of microform have been exhaustively reviewed (for a detailed discussion of IGO material in microform, see Chapter 8), and newer technologies are now available. The 1982 International Congress on Universal Availability of Publications concluded that microform and electronic text are not at present likely to supersede the printed page.[20] Some situations, however, may be more suitable for the use of modern technology; for example, where there is a vast amount of material and relatively few users, some of whom are already accustomed to microform or computerized information systems. Publications are sold mainly in developed countries where electronic transfers of information and texts, for example, are now commonplace, and serious users even of public libraries are accustomed to using microform catalogs and indexes. "Mixed" publications in print, but with bulky background material annexed in microform (the published proceedings of the 1980 World Symposium on International Documentation, *International Documents for the 80's: Their Role and Use*, is a good example) are increasingly common. IGOs could use more of this with advantage.

The computerized information, indexing, and retrieval systems already existing or in prospect within major IGOs have a part to play there. It is generally conceded that they are underutilized, a form of specialized publishing restricted to those in the various networks. In 1972, in reviewing briefly historical attempts to organize international documentation, J. W. Haden drew attention to the accepted need for a co-ordinated interagency system, especially of indexing, and to the factual existence of several unharmonized systems which offered little help to outside users.[21] Progress has been made since then, in the development of such systems as UNBIS and its associated outputs within the UN, including the highly important construction of computerized terminologies on an interlingual basis. Such information systems, which are a key to the mass of IGO information, are another factor in reducing the need to hold expensive physical stocks, and eventually will have an influence on the concept of library collection.

Moreover, only the most populous developed countries are likely to cover in one way or another the whole range of IGO output, and "publications" are not normally collected separately from "documents." Smaller countries are likely to have more selective and incomplete depository and other IGO collections, in their national libraries, institutions, and universities. Major IGOs may be older than the country itself, though there will often be an inheritance within the collections from previous political and territorial arrangements. Survey experience shows that whatever the range of official publication collections, a high proportion (37 percent) had significant gaps in subject or period coverage—even in highly developed countries—for all sorts of local and historical reasons.[22] Interlending cannot completely bridge such gaps. Procurement through commercial agencies can be a protracted and expensive business. Such agencies change hands from time to time, mark-ups are often high, and supply may take months. The researcher in smaller countries will often have to try to visit other collections on travels abroad or use contacts abroad to send material in microform or original form.

Rationalization of collections is a matter of national policy, in which the 1982 International Congress on Universal Availability of Publications stressed the critical role of information professionals and governments.[23] Established patterns of collection are difficult to change; all sorts of vested interests are involved. But whatever improvements may be made in national patterns of collection, there are many countries in which IGO material will never be easily or totally accessible within local facilities. The clearing-house idea seems a natural line of development for IGOs. It is mentioned in discussion and symposia; it is mentioned, though not pursued, in the context of the International Congress on Universal Availability of Publications[24]; it becomes more feasible for IGOs as their massive outputs are increasingly produced in microform. Unesco is already engaged in a pilot project in Latin American countries within the UNISIST framework in document-delivery services. The co-operation of IGOs generally, or of groups of IGOs, in clearing-house facilities could ease many problems of access which cannot otherwise be satisfactorily resolved.

These are not new ideas, but they have not been approached in any planned sequence involving publisher, library, and user. Current outputs are taken more or less for granted, and present evidence suggests that IGOs are not capable of taking in hand a determined attempt to reduce their published outputs. There is an uneasy circularity linking collection, free issue, and publication. A publication is distributed and collected because it has been published; it is published because it will be distributed and collected. These processes are indiscriminate in relation to the intrinsic value of the material. Publications may become potential material for research demand simply because they are published. Even sales, the most direct indication of value, often contain a substantial weighting of library and other institutional sales derived from collection policies and the fact of publication, rather than from any assessment of the value of the contents.

The whole question of IGOs as publishers requires more thought. The problem is how to evaluate works drafted by corporate or sometimes unprofessional authors, somewhat mechanistically edited, at times of dubious quality, and overseen into production and publishing by corporate supervising bodies which may be unable to concern themselves effectively with content, for users whose interest may be rooted in the existence rather than the value of the material. The volume of IGO material, deplored by many as an obstacle to absorption, may also be seen as an impediment to consideration of the problem itself.

This is the sort of problem which large bureaucratic organizations like governments and IGOs are characteristically slow and reluctant to take in hand whole, until forced into action through exposure of instances of absurdity, abuse, and waste. Perhaps the most potentially effective strategy to restrain unnecessary output would be to establish a systematic program of post-mortems, to follow individual publications and documents through the whole process—origination, approval, drafting, production, distribution and marketing, and actual use—taking costs into consideration. It would be surprising if this did not result in some re-evaluation of programs, as well as items, which could not withstand a complete and ruthless dissection, independent of sectoral and hierarchical approvals and certifications. Perhaps, the next time around, the Joint Inspection Unit might try its hand at this approach or perhaps a panel of publishers or librarians (who know what there is in the field) could take a regular sample. Some leverage could be generated around this fulcrum—working outward instead of trying to push inward.

This review has not pursued many subsidiary issues, and it would not claim a place in the very extensive and expert pool of professional knowledge concerned internationally with the activities of IGOs as publishers. It is impossible for the outsider not to be impressed with the expertise, inside and outside IGOs, evident in the published papers of international meetings. It is not difficult from experience in government to appreciate the problems which arise in hierarchical bureaucracies. It is at the same time permissible to wonder whether the specific publishing activities of the major IGOs particularly, with their very broad mandates, are sufficiently aligned in subject-matter and public penetration with their own wide objectives or with the requirements of the Universal Availability of Publications (UAP) which they sponsor. The International Congress on Universal Availability of Publications, significantly, identified weaknesses in publishers' knowledge of users and the lopsidedness between developing and developed countries in both utility and availability of published material. These general features of publishing are apparent in many major IGOs.

Internal publishing problems of IGOs may be more those of management than of professional expertise. Some can clearly be alleviated in technical matters of quality, timeliness, and distribution. Others are probably insoluble, given the nature and organization of IGOs; they are unlikely to be resolved by the importation of commercial publishing expertise, to which the organization, constraints, and criteria of IGOs are alien. Perhaps, as the internal reports suggest, movement might be more effective in the other direction, toward more intensive use of commercial publishers, whose disciplines are tighter and sensitivity to possible users closer and more acute. IGO objectives not susceptible to these disciplines might be achieved by subsidization (as with some academic publishing), which would at least pinpoint the cost as an index of priorities. A number of variations on the theme are already in use by IGOs, particularly Unesco, but there is a good deal more to be done. This might also help to free the publications programs of what seem to be excessive dependence on documentation. Otherwise, effort expended on distribution activities for IGO publications might be better applied to improvements in co-operative physical arrangements than in promotion of material which for the most part has low potential.

Publications on their own are hardly an acute problem for libraries, though there are bibliographical complications in identifying a greater volume of commercial titles emanating from IGOs indirectly. Library problems are primarily those of documentation. As the main nongovernment consumers, libraries must be prepared to question some of their own practices and assumptions in rationalization or concentration of collections, and they should consider increased use of modern technology which might improve access, as well as co-operation in efforts to achieve a clearer and more detailed picture of usage.

It is hardly possible to close without suggesting that IGOs could make a general contribution to dealing with their outputs by dropping the confusing nomenclature of "documents" and "publications," at least for external purposes. They are in fact publishers of priced and unpriced publications of both varieties, whose essential distinction is that they receive different internal treatment and different scales and methods of publishing distribution.

(B) AN INTERGOVERNMENTAL ORGANIZATION AS PUBLISHER: THE CASE OF THE WORLD BANK

*H. Dirk Koehler**

Introduction

The previous section (A) of this chapter is an excellent description of the paradigms, problems, and dilemmas of IGO publishing in general. This section (B) describes the specific publishing approach of the World Bank, with quite a different mission and culture compared to the UN—which forms the core of Cherns's considerations—and in a publishing environment that has changed enormously through technological development since Cherns's article was written, almost twenty years ago.

---

*The author is the Publisher of the World Bank. The views expressed here are his own and should not be attributed to the World Bank, its board of Executive Directors, or the countries they represent. The author wishes to thank Connie Eysenck, Publications Officer in the Office of the Publisher of the World Bank, for editing this article and many of the internal documents on which it is based.

This section necessarily reflects the perspective of the author—that is, an internal perspective. Rather than describing the World Bank's publishing program, this article aims to lay open the anatomy and mechanisms of the publishing efforts at the World Bank. Compared to the UN, the World Bank's publishing scope is narrower, focused on development issues, particularly economic growth and poverty alleviation, and for the most part the World Bank is not required to issue transcripts and proceedings of official meetings.

Under the leadership of its current president, James D. Wolfensohn, the World Bank has undertaken a major process of institutional renewal in recent years and many of the changes have had an impact on its publishing efforts:

- The World Bank strives to become a "knowledge bank" (in addition to being a lending institution), carefully managing and sharing knowledge, both internally and externally. For that purpose, a knowledge management infrastructure has been developed. The importance of *Knowledge for Development* has been recognized and assessed in the 1998/1999 *World Development Report*.[25]

- As a new matrix organization, the World Bank has established networks that are accountable for technical quality and compliance with institutional safeguard and fiduciary policies (in addition to their responsibilities for sector strategy formulation, strategic staffing, and knowledge management). The External Affairs Vice Presidency (which includes the Office of the Publisher), although officially not a network, now operates like one.

- The World Bank endeavors to work in partnership with nongovernmental organizations (NGOs) and the private sector. Consequently, cooperation with commercial publishing houses is sought after and external sponsorships for and advertising in World Bank publications are currently being explored in pilot projects.

- Tight budgets have enforced greater cost-effectiveness—and a more commercial approach to publishing. In 1997 a *Cost-Effectiveness Review*[26] was undertaken, which included an analysis of publishing activities and requested an action plan that has guided a reform of publishing activities since then.

Technological developments have revolutionized publishing in general and at the World Bank in particular:

- Desktop publishing and inexpensive printers enable almost everyone to generate print documents, making professional typesetting less necessary, allowing a decentralization of publishing efforts, and potentially weakening an already fragile coordination of publishing efforts across the institution.

- Intranets permit more and more internal (but in the case of the World Bank nevertheless global) communication to be paperless, making it more environmentally friendly and less expensive. Full-text publications on the intranet should make the internal dissemination of paper copies of these publications superfluous.

- Externally, the internet and e-commerce—together with broad-bandwidth long-distance communication and inexpensive remote printing and binding capabilities for short print-runs (on-demand printing)—allow electronic delivery of content and a reversion of the print-dissemination into a dissemination-print chain.

- CD-ROM and the internet permit new types of publications, utilizing the advantages of the electronic medium, such as nonlinearity, audio and video, and interactivity.

- Electronic communication and electronic publishing have increased the speed of publishing. While Cherns still reports that Unesco calculated some twenty-five months for a manuscript to achieve publication in the first-language version (see p. 14 above), four months is now considered standard at the World Bank—with a much shorter turnaround for small or urgent publications.

What Is a World Bank Publication?

The definition of *publication* is important at the World Bank:

- For *external* reasons, because publications are included in the complete catalog of publications, allowing the public to search and eventually access them;

- For *internal* reasons, because publications have to meet established quality standards and approval criteria—content should be in line with the communication and knowledge-sharing goals and policies of the World Bank; production and dissemination should follow the rules and procedures set up for World Bank publications.

The World Bank recently, for the first time, defined a print publication in the *Registry of Print Publications* (an internal database). The question of which *Board Documents* are to be made accessible to the public is regulated by the *Disclosure of Information Policy*. A definition of an electronic publication does not yet officially exist in the World Bank.

The Registry of Print Publications

The *Cost-Effectiveness Review* requested the Office of the Publisher to create a central registry to:

- provide bibliographic information for all print publications produced by anyone within the World Bank, in order to make them easier to find and disseminate, and to refer queries to the originating unit or author;
- allow the Bank to keep track of how much it spends on print publications, and hence improve transparency and accountability.

The Registry was implemented as of October 1, 1999. The Office of the Publisher will report annually to senior World Bank management on the number of publications, their production cost and other data, and will recommend actions or changes of policies.

For purposes of the Registry a print publication is defined as:

- a book, booklet, or brochure thirty-two or more printed pages long, or a serial (annual, journal, newsletter) irrespective of its length;
- written for an external audience, or written mainly for an internal audience (that is, a *document* other than a Board Document), but with more than five hundred copies disseminated externally.

Originating departments are required to register publications, but can voluntarily also register printed material that does not meet these criteria. The limits of five hundred copies and thirty-two pages are, of course, arbitrary. The consideration was that small brochures of less than thirty-two pages are in most cases short-lived promotional or public relations materials that do not need to be cataloged. And a small external circulation of an internal document should not change it to a publication. The Registry does not deal with *Board Documents*, especially not with *Operational Documents*, because these are regulated by the *Disclosure of Information Policy* and registered separately.

Documents

Publications are distinguished from documents; the latter are defined as mainly written for an internal audience. The goal to make the institution more transparent has led to a *Disclosure of Information Policy* that makes an ever-increasing number of documents, particularly *Operational Documents* (that is, documents on World Bank projects) and other *Board Documents*, accessible to the public. The need to actively alert the public to these documents has resulted in similar marketing activities for documents as for publications (e.g., on the web) and, consequently, has made the distinction between the two less conspicuous for the public; as Cherns remarks "the distinction is blurred in operation"(see p. 4 above). However, discussions with librarians have shown that a majority of them and of library users understand, appreciate, and do not want to give up this distinction. In addition, modern search capabilities have made the issue less important; visitors to the World Bank's website can search at their discretion in the combined catalog of publications and documents, or in one category only. Disclosed documents are available in full text on the internet. Paper copies are printed in small quantities and on demand only.

Electronic Publications

The first electronic publications—in the form of diskettes—could easily be identified as publications. They were "books on plastic." CD-ROMs were not principally different. However, the internet has made it much more difficult—some may say impossible—to distinguish between communication and publishing. In fact, Cherns's statement, "In plain language the essence of a publication is whether it achieves a public circulation, irrespective of its internal classification or the form in which it is produced"(see p. 4 above), seems to declare everything on the internet a publication.

A recent attempt to define a publication starts from the following requirements:

- It must be fixed (i.e., it must be durably recorded on some medium).
- It should, in principle, be publicly available (not necessarily free of charge).
- It should be persistent (i.e., it should remain in the same form and at the same location, so that it is reliably accessible and retrievable over time).[27]

In addition, the same source requires the following for a *formal publication*:

- Authenticity must be guaranteed (i.e., versions should be certified as authentic and protected from change after publication).
- Assignment and persistence of a Web address/location that identifies the work unambiguously.
- A bibliographic record (metadata) that describes the work and its various versions, and which must be public and freely accessible for any given address location.
- A commitment to public access and retrievability through archiving and long-term preservation.[28]

Most content on the World Bank's website(s) does not meet these requirements; it is changed and moved around often and, hence, is better characterized as information sharing or exchange.

For practical purposes, at the World Bank, because of governance issues, the Office of the Publisher has suggested defining electronic publications as:

- all priced electronic material (CD-ROMs and other offline products, web products);
- electronic versions of print publications (because of the interface between print and electronic dissemination and sales) and add-ons to print publications (e.g., electronic updates or background material).

In effect, electronic publications are thus defined as publications channeled through the Office of the Publisher. This internally motivated definition is certainly not satisfactory from the users' viewpoint. It seems likely that a registry of electronic publications, very similar to the registry of print publications and also administered by the Office of the Publisher, will be a next step, but internal discussion has just started and the technical infrastructure for e-commerce at the World Bank is still in its infancy. The Office of the Publisher would ensure that the above requirements for formal publications are met by all electronic publications included in the registry.

The Governance and Development of Publications

Publishing and the Office of the Publisher until 1996/97

In the 1980s and early 1990s publishing at the World Bank resembled the situation at the UN as described above by Cherns. Publishing was fragmented; in addition to the official publications issued by the Office of the Publisher and carrying an ISBN, many more free publications without an ISBN were produced by departments at the headquarters in Washington, D.C. and in overseas World Bank offices. There was no Bank-wide definition of a publication, so that an institutional overview of the publishing activities and their cost was impossible. (All numbers for other than official publications from that period are therefore estimates only.)

The Office of the Publisher was considered more an editorial, typesetting, and printing service than a publisher. In fact, editing was in most cases limited to copyediting and consisted "primarily of measures to achieve stylistic uniformity and to ensure adherence to the regulations set forth in the *Editorial Manual* as well as checking the accuracy of references" (cited by Cherns on p. 14 above).[29] Moreover, most publications were required to arrive at the Office of the Publisher in camera-ready copy and were published as facsimiles. Only a few, more prestigious publications underwent a formal peer review process under the supervision of the Editorial Committee and, consequently, a thorough developmental or substantial editing. This does not imply that the unofficial publications and the facsimiles were not reviewed and edited, but this was undertaken, or not, at the discretion of the originating departments. In general, the Office of the Publisher was more reactive to incoming publishing (i.e., mostly printing and dissemination) requests than proactive in pursuing, influencing, or initiating publishing projects.

While the Office of the Publisher has always had a monopoly for selling priced publications and for collecting the revenues, these revenues were deposited in a central World Bank account and, hence, neither the originating departments nor the Office of the Publisher had an incentive to increase their number. Free copies of priced publications were disseminated generously, both internally and externally. Prices of publications were therefore more a nominal fee, with most publications priced at less than U.S. $10.00.

The Cost-Effectiveness Review of 1997

The report on the *Cost-Effectiveness Review* from October 1997 (*CER*), already mentioned above, came to the conclusion (with regard to publications) that

- the Bank is a paper-dominated organization;
- the Bank's output for external audiences is often supply-driven, rather than demand-driven, and is not subject to a rigorous institutional review process for its relevance to the Bank's knowledge management and communication goals and
- a more strategic and focused publication effort would better support the Bank's knowledge dissemination obligations.[30]

The *CER* stated as guiding principles "to enhance accountability and ensure that the publications meet key knowledge management objectives and their commercial potential is fully exploited"[31] and requested a major reform of the World Bank's publishing efforts, to be implemented within the following two years, by:[32]

- Establishing a central registry to capture information about the source, content, and cost of all World Bank publications. The *CER* did not, however, define the term *publication*. But from the context it was clear that electronic publications were not included.
- Eliminating independent publication efforts by individual units unless channeled through the Office of the Publisher.
- Distinguishing sharply between institutional publications and individually authored output.
- Developing and reviewing a three-year rolling plan for institutional publications.

- Fully exploiting the commercial potential of the publications by pricing and marketing them appropriately.
- Sharply restricting free distribution.
- Fully utilizing electronic media.

As many of these recommendations were based on suggestions made by the Office of the Publisher, this was a welcome and strong but challenging mandate. The *CER* expected savings of about U.S. $5 million and an increase in revenues of U.S. $2 to U.S. $3 million per year from the reform.

The Office of the Publisher Today

The Office of the Publisher, in order to rise to the challenges of the *CER*, had to be reoriented and restructured. For this purpose, a mission statement was drafted. (See Figure 1.1.) The Editorial and Production unit was broken up into an *Acquisitions and Client Relations* unit (EXTAC) and a *Production Services* unit (EXTPO); and a new *Rights, Contracts, and Free Publications* unit (EXTRF) was created; *Controlling* and *Web Coordination* have been established as staff functions. The current organizational chart of the Office of the Publisher is shown in Figure 1.2, page 32.

Given the long tradition of "babies-on-the-doorstep publishing" in the World Bank, the Acquisitions and Client Relations unit (EXTAC) is the most important unit to implement the changes required by the *CER* and has the most challenging task. Success in the long term will depend not so much on a strong mandate, because policing is rarely successful even in a bureaucracy, but on EXTAC's performance and on policies that convince the clients (the internal authors) that the new way of cooperating with the Office of the Publisher is advantageous to them. EXTAC is the equivalent of an acquisitions unit in a commercial publishing house, but is limited to internal authors. Beginning as early in the evolution of the idea or planning stage of a publishing project as possible, EXTAC staff are in contact with the (potential) authors to consult about ideas; advise about the appropriate publishing medium, about targeting, packaging, and presentation; and marketing the material or messages. EXTAC supervises the review and approval process, is instrumental in the creation of departmental and serial editorial boards, and cooperates with the Bank-wide Editorial Committee. It coordinates publishing projects and plans between departments across the World Bank and develops a three-year publishing plan in order to strengthen the strategic orientation of the publishing program.

The second new unit is the Rights, Contracts, and Free Publications unit (EXTRF). The unit has a strong commercial and legal mandate to draft, oversee, and execute copublishing and licensing agreements and permissions, cooperating with the legal department of the World Bank in legal matters. EXTRF is instrumental in further developing and implementing the ambitious new copublishing and licensing policy (see below). For free publications EXTRF plays the same role and faces the same challenges as EXTAC does for priced

Figure 1.1. Mission Statement of the World Bank's Office of the Publisher.

Office of the Publisher (EXTOP) Mission Statement

EXTOP works to advance the Bank's knowledge management objectives and the communication goals of External Affairs (EXT) by initiating, developing, producing, promoting, and disseminating World Bank publications, to:
- disseminate knowledge, research results, and data gathered by the Bank or on behalf of the Bank;
- generate support -- in industrial countries -- for the Bank's work on development issues; and
- enhance understanding in developing countries about the Bank's work program, mission, and operations.

It is EXTOP's mandate to ensure, in close cooperation with originating departments and other institutional bodies:
- the quality, coherence, and impact of the Bank's publishing program and its compliance with Bank policies;
- the cost-effectiveness of the Bank's publishing activities, including full exploitation of its commercial potential (where appropriate).

To fulfill its mandate, EXTOP must:
- Develop, implement, and enforce publishing policies and procedures for the Bank as a whole.
- Provide guidance to originating departments on how to develop their ideas into publications, and on how to structure, package, target, disseminate, and (where appropriate) commercially exploit the content for maximum impact.
- Exploit additional dissemination and cost-saving potential by granting reprint permissions.
- Negotiate and enter into license and copublishing contracts with (commercial) publishing houses and other partners (especially for translations). This is to maximize the accessibility of our material by cooperating with local publishing partners to work within their distribution networks and produce material in local languages.
- Manage the production process to meet time, cost, and quality objectives.
- Promote, sell, give access to, and disseminate publications worldwide, directly and via local partners.
- Develop electronic dissemination systems via the intranet (e-commerce and on-line availability of publication summaries, full text, and embargoed information).
- Maintain a highly visible outreach facility (the InfoShop), where customers can easily and quickly access the Bank's publications, as well as books from other publishers on development issues and the operational documents that are for public access (in compliance with the Bank's Disclosure of Information policy).

World Bank publications comprise printed material (books, booklets, periodicals, etc.) and, increasingly, electronic products (CD-Rom, web publication). Publications are disseminated for free or priced for sale.

Figure 1.2. Organizational Chart of the World Bank's Office of the Publisher.

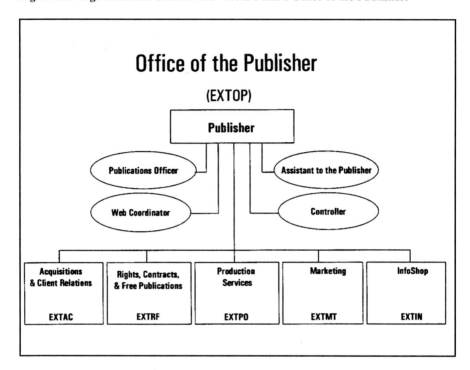

publications. The combination of both functions in one unit was due to staff resources and other specific circumstances; it is not necessarily an optimal long-term solution. However, the combination has been proven useful in dealing with free books funded by space advertising and published for the World Bank by a commercial partner. Obviously, the acceptance or nonacceptance of advertisers and advertisements is a delicate commercial, ethical, and legal issue for an IGO.

The changes in the production function mirror what has happened over the previous years in the publishing industry in general. Staff of the EXTPO unit manage the production process (balancing quality, cost, and time considerations), advise on production issues, and provide cost and schedule estimates. Other traditional production functions—substantive and copyediting, typesetting, and design—are, for reasons of lower cost and better utilization of capacity and specialization, outsourced to freelancers and other vendors.

The Marketing unit (EXTMT) has been strengthened. The former Distribution unit, which handled order fulfillment and distribution, was abolished, and these functions are now fulfilled by a contractor who is supervised by EXTMT. EXTMT maintains the marketing-oriented web pages, including a catalog and full-text and summary online publications. It produces and disseminates an annual *Publications Catalog*, a quarterly *Publications Update* brochure, and other promotional material as needed. An experiment to rely exclusively on the catalog on the web faced strong resistance from librarians and booksellers. EXTMT also places advertisements and represents World Bank publications at book fairs and professional and library meetings worldwide. Staff maintain a network of more than eighty distributors and authorized booksellers, as well as a network of approximately 250 depository libraries. The role of the distributors is further discussed below in the paragraph on *Pricing Policy*; the World Bank's library program is dealt with in the paragraph on *Free Dissemination Policy*.

The InfoShop (EXTIN) is a development bookstore in downtown Washington. It is also a reference center providing quick access to documents, databases, and information about operational policies and procedures, as well as other information and World Bank material. The latter function was originally hosted in a separate *Public Information Center*. The merger of bookstore and Public Information Center was guided by the idea of providing the public with a one-stop information and shopping source, not distinguishing between publications, documents, and other information. The recent expansion of also carrying publications by other publishers (IGOs, NGOs, and commercial) and souvenirs has made the InfoShop a true full-service development bookstore, and public response has been overwhelmingly positive. The World Bank also maintains small Public Information Centers in some of its overseas offices, and the InfoShop has an advisory role to aid these centers. The most recent development is the creation of a Development Center in Hanoi, Vietnam, to be opened in 2000, that will on a small scale replicate and expand the idea of the InfoShop. It will combine a bookstore, a library, an information center with internet access for the public, and a distance learning center—and will be maintained by the World Bank in partnership with other IGOs, bilateral aid agencies, and NGOs. This could become a model for many developing countries.

Policies of the Office of the Publisher

As mentioned above, the previous policies and procedures for publishing at the World Bank did not provide incentives to be cost-effective. Enforcement of new rules without providing incentives for compliance would seem to have had little chance of success. Therefore, the Office of the Publisher, guided and supported by the Vice President of External Affairs and based on a *Publications Task Force Report* (the *"Choksi Report,"* an internal document issued in July 1995), and later on the *Cost-Effectiveness Review* (issued in October 1997 and described above), developed and implemented a coherent set of policies to:

- foster fewer, more marketable publications;
- channel more departmental publications *at an earlier stage* through the Office of the Publisher;
- encourage electronic publication;
- decrease publication costs across the World Bank;

- promote a more targeted, cost-effective dissemination effort; and
- increase revenues.

Revenue Sharing Policy

The Revenue Sharing Policy is probably the most significant new policy introduced. It was implemented in 1996 (and slightly revised in 1999). The objective is to reward the originating departments/authors and the Office of the Publisher for market success by sharing the revenues from the sales of publications. To avoid internal negotiating and contracting for each publication, a uniform sharing of the revenues—60 percent for the originating department, 40 percent for the Office of the Publisher—has been implemented. It is not intended that these shares reflect the cost incurred by the originating department and the Office of the Publisher, respectively. However, the assumption is that the additional funds will be reinvested by the originating departments into new publications or reprints and used by the Office of the Publisher to increase its marketing and distribution efforts.

The motivational impact of the policy was initially severely hampered by its so-called "budget-neutral" implementation. Budget-neutral meant that revenues were transferred to the departments only after the retroactively computed revenues of the previous fiscal year had been deducted from their budget; in other words, only the variances compared to last year's revenues had an impact on the departmental budgets. Especially for departments with decreasing revenues this was not attractive. Another issue (in the original version of the policy) was that the originating department for the purpose of the revenue transfer was defined as "Vice Presidency." But many Vice Presidencies did not forward the received revenues to the lower-level units that had paid for the production of the revenue-producing publication, so that the intended incentive could not work. A major communications task has been to explain the technical details of the policy to staff. The figures reported by the Office of the Publisher for each publication are sales figures (based on net invoice values), but the actual cash received naturally differs in time and amount from sales. For this reason the sales are allocated to departments and the percentages of sales are proportionately applied to the cash received in the same time period (which is not completely correct, particularly with distributors who have payment terms of up to six months).

Despite these initial problems and occasional discussions about the fairness of the share percentage, after three years of practice the policy has been extremely successful. Most departments now have an interest in revenue-creating publications, and act accordingly to improve the content of their publications, to target them better, and work more closely with staff at the Office of the Publisher. In addition, approximately one-third of the budget of the Office of the Publisher is now funded by revenues from publications.

Cost Sharing Policy

Historically, while the production costs of some series and titles were borne by the Office of the Publisher, production costs of other series were the responsibility of the originating departments. Depending on specific budget situations, exceptions (in both directions) were common, and in many cases there was no rationale why one or the other had to pay.

The new Cost Sharing Policy (a slight euphemism), implemented in 1997, requires that the out-of pocket production costs (editing, typesetting, printing, and binding) for all publications are borne by the originating departments. The overhead (the costs of the Office of the Publisher for managing the production process, and for marketing and distribution) is free for priced publications, but is charged to the originating departments for free publications. The additional charging of overheads for free publications increases the awareness of the true cost of publishing. While the new policy increases the accountability of the originating departments, it also has its downside:

- It empowers the originating departments in relation to the Office of the Publisher ("The one who pays has the say"). This can increase an already existing imbalance in power.

- The strengthened position of the originating departments can make quality control, coordination with institutional goals, and *in extremis* rejection of a publication by the Office of the Publisher very difficult.

- The originating departments bear the financial risk of the publications almost alone. There is no incentive for the Office of the Publisher to reduce production costs.

The policy is also a departure from the model of the commercial publisher who has to invest into a publication. But this principally preferred commercial model would have required a shift of publication budgets from all originating departments to the Office of the Publisher. This would have been an unrealistic proposal at the time of implementation of the policy.

Pricing Policy

To fully exploit the commercial potential of World Bank publications, a new Pricing Policy was implemented. The new policy aims at setting U.S. dollar list prices in line with those of other (commercial) publishers in the U.S. market. There is no reason for the World Bank to subsidize wealthy customers in industrialized countries by underpricing publications. The new prices no longer follow a predetermined scheme of pricing by number of pages, but are set for each title in a "planning meeting" of staff from the Office of the Publisher, following a common procedure of commercial publishing houses. The proposed prices are then discussed with the originating departments and revised if necessary.

Part of the new policy was the implementation of a minimum list price of U.S. $20.00 in July 1997 (increased in March 1999 to U.S. $22.00). Before the new pricing policy took effect, more than 80 percent of titles were priced at under U.S. $20.00. In 1998 only 3 percent of the titles published in that year were priced below U.S. $20.00, 64 percent were priced at U.S. $20.00, and 33 percent were priced higher. The rationale behind the minimum price is that most of the publications are ordered as single copies, and that the transaction costs for billing and collecting are fixed per order and are so high that it is not worth selling single copies at a lower price. Also, the book trade (in industrial countries) does not like to handle specialized publications with low prices, and consequently low margins for the retailer, irrespective of how large the trade discount is as a percentage. Effectively, the policy enforced publishing booklets as free publications—with all the disadvantages associated with free publications. As most publications by the World Bank are, for good reasons, in fact booklets with fewer than one hundred pages, this minimum price policy can be problematic and is, therefore, currently being reviewed. An alternative under consideration is a lower minimum price (say, U.S. $10.00) that is acceptable for slim publications, in combination with charging the originating department for the losses incurred.

While market-oriented prices for World Bank publications are adequate in industrial countries, these prices would make the publications unaffordable in developing countries. In light of the World Bank's mission to alleviate poverty and disseminate knowledge in developing countries, this would be unacceptable. Therefore, a system of geographic price discrimination, using local commercial distributors, was implemented. The distributors are granted high discounts (up to 90 percent of the U.S. $ list price) and are contractually obliged to set the prices in local currencies so that their margin is percentage-wise the same as for distributors in industrial countries. In addition, the World Bank pays for the shipment of publications to the distributor, so that this business in most cases generates losses for the World Bank but is profitable for the distributor. The hope is, of course, that this motivates the distributor to promote World Bank publications while providing an effective service to the public.

Although geographic price discrimination seems to be an obvious tool to reach developing country markets, not many IGOs, or even NGOs, are using it. A representative of Oxfam argued that Oxfam publications are targeted at "the North in the South" and that this market can afford to buy the publications at the full price. Although this is also true for some World Bank publications, others aim at the "real" South, too. Another argument is that even a price equivalent to U.S. $4.40 (which could be the result of a 90 percent discount on a U.S. $22.00 publication) is still too high for someone with an annual income of U.S. $1,000.00 (or U.S. $3.00 a day) or less. And finally, an obvious weakness of the system is that it relies on local distributors who sometimes are not available, particularly in very poor countries, and who do not always comply with the contract and mark up the local prices.

Modern technology offers an ideal solution for the future—publications could be ordered via the internet in local currencies at local prices and delivered via a local print-on-demand capability (of the customer, a commercial contractor, or the World Bank office overseas). Although the technology is for the most part available, unfortunately many developing countries have currently neither the internet connectivity and bandwidth, nor the local printing and binding capacity for single copies (for example, Docutech machines).

Internal Pricing Policy

In the past all World Bank publications were free for World Bank staff (to use them internally or give them away for free; resale was not allowed). This sometimes had unwanted consequences (the typical problems of "free goods"):

- Staff ordered large quantities of books "to have them available when needed." Some offices were quasi-converted into mini-warehouses and secretariats converted into mini-mailing houses. If then the need for the books did not arise in the assumed quantities, the remaining stock was sometimes returned to the Office of the Publisher—often after some years, when the publications were outdated and no longer saleable or useful.

- Groups or individuals in the World Bank, other than the originating department, ordered large quantities of a publication, and when the originating department needed copies there was not enough inventory left to satisfy their own needs—and no budget available to reprint the publication.

To avoid these problems an internal price for all priced publications was implemented. The Office of the Publisher informs the originating department of the unit cost (technical cost only) of a publication and suggests an internal price, which is confirmed by the originating department. Internal orders are fulfilled via the Office of the Publisher which serves as a clearinghouse, charging the budgets of the ordering departments and crediting the originating departments on a monthly basis.

Besides allowing the originating department to reinvest revenues from internal sales (into a reprint or a new project), the internal pricing also increases transparency and accountability. It allocates the cost of outreach via print publications to the department that may determine a strategy of giving them away. Although the concept seems to be logical and fair, implementation was difficult because the departments, and particularly the offices overseas, had no budget for this new kind of expense and, furthermore, the implementation took place at a time of shrinking budgets. Also, knowledge sharing was propagated in the World Bank at the same time, and staff felt that internal pricing contradicted this goal and deprived them of a knowledge source. However, internal pricing has become increasingly popular with most originating departments. Even some overseas offices now agree with the argument that an internal pricing policy supports a demand-driven publishing program and decentralized decision-making: Internal orders, in the same way as external orders, signal value attributed to the publication; lack of orders will lead to changes in the publication program and eventually stop further publications of this kind.

Free Dissemination Policy

In 1996 about 80 percent of all copies of priced publications were given away free. This percentage has been reduced to approximately 50 percent in 1999. The remaining free dissemination consists mainly of the *institutional free dissemination* to:

- senior World Bank management, the Executive Directors, overseas offices, and internal libraries of the World Bank;
- Depository and Regional Libraries; and
- media contacts and academic journals for reviews and other media purposes.

Depending on the category of the publication, between approximately seven hundred and twelve hundred copies of a publication are disseminated free to these recipients. It seems almost impossible, and not desirable, to reduce this free dissemination further. On the contrary, the Depository Library program, for example, has recently been expanded.

The Depository Library program follows the model of the national libraries in industrial countries. A *World Bank Depository Library* receives one copy of all World Bank publications for free, and is expected to preserve these publications as a separate collection. For some libraries in developing countries this is a burden more than a help; they have limited shelf space and no interest in specialized publications on subjects of little interest to them; for example, a library in sub-Saharan Africa would probably not be interested in a publication on transition in postcommunist countries in Europe. For this reason, a new type of depository library has been created: the *World Bank Regional Library*. A Regional Library receives one or more copies of publications that are selected according to the library's profile. The opportunity to get more than one copy of the often-used publications seems to be especially valuable for public and university libraries.

For flagship publications (World Bank annuals and titles in the Policy Research Report Series) a greater number of publications are given free of charge to overseas World Bank offices for distribution in their countries. The cost of this outreach is borne by the originating departments as part of the total production cost. Often they also pay for the shipping costs. This is a regrettable legacy of the old system, blurring accountability and transparency, but a transfer of budgets to the overseas offices has not been enforceable.

Copublishing and Licensing Policy

Unlike the UN, the World Bank has no official languages. Major World Bank publications are traditionally translated into certain languages, but most publications are published in English only. Whether or not a translation should be published is usually dependent on the originating department's intention and budgetary capacity. The Office of the Publisher does not have the marketing ability to sell a publication in any other language than English in enough copies for sales to fund a translation.

The obvious way to save money for the World Bank and to increase market penetration is cooperation with a local commercial publisher who undertakes the translation and production at its own risk and cost. Concerns about the quality of the translation sometimes lead to a translation done or supervised by the World Bank. This also can be seen as a subsidy to the local publisher. Buying back copies for free dissemination by the World Bank or for sale through its InfoShop is another way of indirect subsidizing.

The considerations leading to cooperation with "local" publishers are also valid for market segments that the Office of the Publisher has difficulty reaching. In these cases cooperation with a specialized publisher is sought. For the academic market, such arrangements have for a long time existed with Oxford University Press and the Johns Hopkins University Press.

A good example of what can be achieved by copublishing with commercial publishers is the *World Development Report*, probably the World Bank's most prestigious publication, which has traditionally been published in English together with Oxford University Press and in French, Spanish, Japanese, German, Russian, Chinese, Arabic, and Portuguese by the World Bank alone. As part of the increased copublishing efforts, the Arabic, Chinese, French, German, Russian, and Spanish editions of the *World Development Report 1998/99* were published by commercial publishers, resulting in a total savings of approximately U.S. $185,000 for the World Bank and—presumably—much better market penetration. In developing countries such copublishing arrangements can also have a capacity-building and supportive effect for the indigenous publishing industry, which is so important for democratic development in these countries.

The licensing activities have reached a considerable level. In the World Bank's fiscal year 1999 there were eighty-seven license agreements signed, and fifty-five licensed titles (World Bank content published by a commercial publisher) in fifteen languages have been published. Overall royalties contributed almost U.S. $400,000 to the income of the World Bank.

Results of the New Policies

The numeric results of the new policies seem to demonstrate that they are working in the desired directions. Table 1.1, page 40, illustrates these results for fiscal years 1997, 1998, and 1999.

Table 1.1
Results of New Policies of the Office of the Publisher, World Bank

	1997	1998	1999
Priced print publications	237	200	178
Free publications	42	47	46
Net sales (million U.S. $)	2.8	3.6	4.2
Number of copies sold externally*	190,000	133,000	147,000
Royalties received (U.S. $)	220,000	250,000	387,000
Production cost (million U.S. $)**	4.5	3.4	3.2

* These numbers do not include the dissemination of the editions licensed to other publishers.
** For publications managed by the Office of the Publisher.

Special Initiatives of the Office of the Publisher

African Publishing Initiative

Cooperation with distributors in Africa and participation at the Zimbabwe International Book Fair led to the idea of founding an *African Publishing Initiative* by the Office of the Publisher. The objectives of the initiative are:

- to develop long-term partnerships with African publishers;
- to help build the African publishing capacity by having books written, designed, and printed locally;
- to encourage a reading culture;
- to create awareness of critical development issues;
- to increase access to World Bank material by publishing in local languages;
- to more effectively and widely develop and disseminate this material to children and parents through local publishers; and
- to improve the understanding of the World Bank's work in these countries.

With only a tiny budget for this purpose, the specific way to work toward these goals consists mainly of close cooperation with African publishers to support them in kind and granting them free licenses of World Bank material. In addition, cooperating with the Africa Regional Vice Presidency of the World Bank, it was possible to initiate the publication of two bilingual (in English and Kiswahili) children's books on themes of interest to the World Bank (girls' education and environment) by a Tanzanian publishing house. Publication is expected soon and this program will be continued in other African regions.

At first glance it might seem surprising that a unit with the mandate to publish the World Bank's intellectual output is involved in a "real" development activity, but there are not many publishing specialists even in such a big organization as the World Bank. The close understanding among publishers—anywhere in the world—facilitates such projects enormously.

Staff Exchange Programs

In the same spirit as and partly resulting from the experience with the African Publishing Initiative, the Office of the Publisher has launched two staff exchange programs, one with African publishers, a second with publishing departments of other IGOs. This is in cooperation with an institution-wide initiative (the World Bank's Staff Exchange Program), which aims to:

- Develop closer partnerships and long-lasting relationships with other organizations operating in the global development arena.

- Enhance the professional and technical skills and expertise of participants (both World Bank staff and those of partner organizations) through a variety of learning and skills development opportunities.

- Foster cultural change, exchange, diversity, and a sharing of people and talent with global development partners.

Specifically, the Office of the Publisher's program for African Publishers also supports the goals of the African Publishing Initiative. The program with other IGOs recognizes that publishing units in IGOs face similar problems, which are different from those in commercial publishing houses. Communication between the publishing professionals in these organizations through articles such as this one and at conferences is useful, but does not suffice to create a full understanding of the various approaches and solutions in other organizations. For that purpose, a much longer immersion into another organization is necessary. This knowledge would allow a more effective evaluation and assessment of the structures, processes, and policies, as well as developing a collaborative network to strengthen collective operations and work together. This in turn should lead to "best practices in publishing for IGOs."

Notes and References

1. Theodore D. Dimitrov, *Documents of International Organizations: A Bibliographic Handbook* (London/Chicago: International University Publications/American Library Association, 1973), x.

2. Luciana Marulli-Koenig, "Documentation of the United Nations System: Bibliographic Control and Coordination," in *International Documents for the 80's: Their Role and Use*, ed. Theodore D. Dimitrov and Luciana Marulli-Koenig (Pleasantville, NY: UNIFO Publishers, 1982), 422.

3. Dimitrov, *Documents of International Organisations*, chap. 4. See also Theodore D. Dimitrov, *World Bibliography of International Documentation* (Pleasantville, NY: UNIFO Publishers, 1981).

4. Peter I. Hajnal, *Guide to United Nations Organization, Documentation and Publishing for Students, Researchers, Librarians* (Dobbs Ferry, NY: Oceana, 1978); and Peter I. Hajnal, *Guide to Unesco* (London/Rome/New York: Oceana, 1983).

5. J. J. Cherns, *Official Publishing: An Overview; An International Survey and Review of the Role, Organisation and Principles of Official Publishing* (Oxford, England: Pergamon, 1979), chap. 24.

6. Thomas S. Hinds, "The United Nations as a Publisher," *Government Publications Review* 12 (July/August 1985): 297.

7. Bernard Charlesworth, "The Need for Modernization in Production, Editing and Distribution of IGO Documentation," in *Sources, Organization, Utilization of International Documentation; Proceedings of the International Symposium on the Documentation of the United Nations and Other Intergovernmental Organizations, Geneva, 1972* (The Hague: International Federation for Documentation, 1974), 264. FID Publication No. 506.

8. Unesco, General Information Programme and UNISIST, *Availability and Use of Official Publications in Libraries*, prepared by J. J. Cherns (Paris: Unesco, 1983). PGI-83/WS/30.

9. Joint Inspection Unit [of the United Nations System of Organizations], *Report on United Nations Documentation and on the Organisation of the Proceedings of the General Assembly and Its Main Bodies* (Geneva: JIU, 1971). JIU/REP/71/4. Transmitted in United Nations, General Assembly, 26th sess., *Pattern of Conferences* (New York: UN, 1971). 2 June 1971; A/8319.

10. Hinds, "United Nations as a Publisher," 297–303.

11. Joint Inspection Unit [of the United Nations System of Organizations], *Publications Policy and Practice in the United Nations System* (Geneva: JIU, 1984). JIU/REP/84/5. Transmitted in United Nations, General Assembly, 39th sess., *Questions Relating to Information* (New York: UN, 1984). 14 May 1984; A/39/239.

12. United Nations, General Assembly, 39th sess., *Publications Policy and Practice in the United Nations System; Comments of the Secretary-General* (New York: UN, 1984). 7 August 1984; A/39/239/Add.1.

13. United Nations, General Assembly, 39th sess., *Publications Policy and Practice in the United Nations System; Comments of the Secretary-General; Corrigendum* (New York: UN, 1984). 10 October 1984; A/39/239/Add.1/Corr.1.

14. United Nations, General Assembly, 39th sess., *Publications Policy and Practice in the United Nations System; Comments of the Administrative Committee on Co-ordination* (New York: UN, 1984). 2 October 1984; A/39/239/Add.2.

15. R. Furstenberg, "Distribution and Acquisition of UN Documents," in *International Documents for the 80's: Their Role and Use*, ed. Theodore D. Dimitrov and Luciana Marulli-Koenig (Pleasantville, NY: UNIFO Publishers, 1982), 66.

16. J. Fletcher, "International Comparative Statistics Produced by International Organizations," in *International Documents for the 80's: Their Role and Use*, ed. Theodore D. Dimitrov and Luciana Marulli-Koenig (Pleasantville, NY: UNIFO Publishers, 1982), 32-47.

17. John Jeffries, *A Guide to the Official Publications of the European Communities*, 2d ed. (London: Mansell, 1981), 10.

18. International Congress on Universal Availability of Publications, Paris, 1982, *Main Working Document* (Paris: Unesco, 1982), para 104. 22 March 1982; PGI-82/UAP/2; PGI-82/CONF.401/COL.2.

19. Hajnal, *Guide to United Nations Organization*, 204.

20. International Congress, *Main Working Document*, para. 78. See also para. 219.

21. J. W. Haden, "Some Previous Attempts at Organizing International Documentation," in *Sources, Organization, Utilization of International Documentation; Proceedings of the International Symposium on the Documentation of the United Nations and Other Intergovernmental Organizations, Geneva, 1972* (The Hague: International Federation for Documentation, 1974), 271-74. FID Publication no. 506.

22. Unesco, *Availability and Use of Official Publications*, 7.

23. International Congress, *Main Working Document*, para. 260.

24. Ibid., para. 12.

25. World Bank, *World Development Report 1998/99: Knowledge for Development* (New York: Oxford University Press for the World Bank, 1999).

26. International Bank for Reconstruction and Development, *Report on the Cost-Effectiveness Review* (IBRD Board Document R97-231; Washington, DC: IBRD, Oct. 30, 1997), 30ff.

27. *Defining and Certifying Electronic Publication in Science: A Proposal to the International Association of STM Publishers* (Frankfurt: AAAS/ICSU Press Working Group, 1999), 3.

28. Ibid.

29. The World Bank's editorial manual is titled *The World Bank Publications Style Guide* (Washington, DC: World Bank, 1997); the earlier edition was entitled *The World Bank Publications Style Manual* (Washington, DC: World Bank, 1991). Both editions are internal documents.

30. *Report on the Cost-Effectiveness Review*, 30.

31. Ibid.

32. Ibid., 31.

CHAPTER 2

The International Monetary Fund: Operational and Research Documentation

*Donald F. Ross**

Introduction

Asked by a friend, "What is the IMF?", I replied unconsciously, buying time to compose an answer to this notoriously difficult question: "The International Monetary Fund." "I know that," she answered, "but what does it do?" This is a question many people ask. It is a handicap the IMF itself suffers, challenged as it so frequently is, to make its purpose clear. It is in fact the same difficulty that any technocratic organization faces, though made still more difficult for the IMF, by having its technocracy embedded in the "dismal science."

A continuously updated pamphlet entitled *What Is the International Monetary Fund?*[1] has tried to make apparent the purposes of the IMF. It is a good starting point for anyone wanting to get a quick overview of the organization. A number of other pamphlets produced by the IMF describe more specific aspects of what the Fund does.[2]

This chapter is not intended to quell unrequited questions about what the Fund does, but is rather an attempt to reveal the process by which the IMF does its work and the documentary output that results. The hope is that this will address some unanswered questions of process in the public mind.

---

*Donald F. Ross has been with the Joint Library of the World Bank and the International Monetary Fund in Washington, DC since 1992. The author is greatly indebted to the following IMF staff: Ken Friedman, Craig Sevy, Susan Yeager, Michelle Dolbec, David Hawley, David Cheney, and Ramana Ramaswamy, all of whom provided invaluable assistance to him in writing this chapter. All remaining faults, factual or otherwise, are, needless to say, entirely the author's.

For most of its more than fifty years' existence, the International Monetary Fund, the brain child of Harry Dexter White and John Maynard Keynes,[3] has remained an aloof body, avoiding publicity and revealing very little of what it does. This aloofness has earned it an unhelpful reputation for uncommunicativeness. As with so many technocratic organizations, it has assumed that there is little public interest in the detail of its work, and that the detail in which some may show interest is not suitable for public consumption. Now with the series of recent major international economic crises, the calls for a new global economic architecture and the availability of web technology, the IMF is beginning to introduce an open information policy that renders the institution almost unrecognizable from its former, guarded self. I hope below to reveal this new openness.

I must first, however, pay full respect (and record my thanks) to a remarkable study by Richard Harper[4] whose ethnographic approach to the IMF and the generation of its documentation provides an extraordinarily clear insight into what it is that the organization does, by describing, in some detail, how the staff of the organization approach their work. For anyone contemplating, or being offered, employment by the IMF, this is a "must read," as it is for those of us already employed there. For anyone else wanting an insight into the organization, it will prove a revealing and humanizing source on an organization renowned for its public reserve.

Brief History

The history of the IMF typically divides the past fifty years into four periods. Each period has been introduced by some large-scale event or change in international circumstance that has occasioned a change in the role and function of the organization.

When originally created at the end of World War II, the IMF was intended as part of a tripartite, permanent management system for the global economy. The World Bank (or International Bank for Reconstruction and Development, IBRD as it was then referred to) was designed to promote economic development, the International Trade Organization was to manage international trade, and the IMF was to manage national currencies and their exchange, as a means of maintaining a stable international monetary system. Due to lack of ratification by the U.S. Congress, the International Trade Organization was stillborn. The IBRD came into being in 1946, providing, as its first act, development loans to France to rebuild after the devastation suffered in World War II. The IMF commenced operations in May 1946 with a relatively simple mandate, to ensure adherence, by its then thirty-nine member states, to a system of fixed but adjustable exchange rates, with parities fixed in relation to the price of gold. A member country could adjust its exchange rate if the Fund certified the need. To establish any such need, the Fund had the role of monitoring the member countries' economic policies. In addition, member countries would have to pay a membership fee on joining the Fund. These fees would provide a pool of funds from which a member country, finding itself in deficit, could then apply to borrow. Before such borrowing happened, or in conjunction with it, a country would be expected to adjust its economic policies as part of its recovery from a deficit condition. It was to control this adjustment that the IMF was instituted, to ensure that any adjustment was undertaken within an internationally coordinated regime. This arrangement worked well enough until gold ceased to be a workable basis for the valuing of currencies.

A second phase in the IMF's history was then entered in 1966 with the introduction of the SDR or Special Drawing Rights, introduced by the IMF to make good the imbalance between member countries' dollar holdings and the available quantities of gold. The SDR became an alternative currency that member countries could hold. In 1970 the United States, faced with a run on the dollar, ceased its convertibility into gold and the erstwhile system of dollar convertibility collapsed.

In 1972 the Committee of Twenty[5] was established to investigate an alternative regime. The Committee recommended, in 1974, leaving the international exchange system free-floating to allow the system to find its own equilibrium. This raised a large question about the role of the IMF. The combination of the loss of dollar convertibility and the arrival of the first oil crisis exposed a number of IMF members, who needed to turn somewhere for help. The IMF's role as a lender of currency to support countries through these crisis times began to emerge very rapidly in this phase, a role now very recognizable as the Fund's prime purpose. The borrowing system with the Fund has always been related to the member country's quota, or their membership deposit. But further borrowing mechanisms have been introduced as other and greater international crises have erupted.

During the third phase of the IMF's history, the second oil crisis and the international debt crisis (between 1978 and 1985) led to the Fund providing massive assistance to allow countries to meet their obligations to commercial lenders, who had loaned heavily to Third World countries, but who in turn, could not meet these obligations, as interest rates and oil prices rose and the world economy fell into a slump. When Mexico defaulted on its debt repayments in 1982, closing its foreign exchange market, the entire system came very near to collapse. Out of the ashes rose the Baker Plan, which provided IMF loans to the worst-indebted countries, requiring these countries to make structural adjustments in their economies, whilst meeting their debt payments to their commercial lenders.

The fourth phase in the IMF's history began in 1985, with the Soviet Union under Gorbachev warming to membership in the Bretton Woods institutions, followed by the collapse of the Soviet system in 1989. This brought not only fifteen new members (in the form of the individual former Soviet republics) plus Switzerland, who decided to join at this same moment, but also all the problems and demands of converting centrally planned economies into market economies. A huge increase in Fund resources was agreed (150 billion SDRs) as well as a massive increase in the size of the staff of the organization. This latter increase was not only to manage the increased level of economic surveillance these new economies called for, but also to provide the other form of IMF support, technical assistance. This is the role the Fund plays in instilling into countries with relatively weak infrastructure the necessary methods and training, to allow countries to manage their economies and run them along lines that conform to the methods of the Western capitalist economies.

Arising out of these series of events are the various interventionist tools the organization has developed over the years, tools that have changed the organization's role considerably from that with which it first commenced over fifty years ago, and that have kept it centrally located in the economic management of the global economy.

The Fund's Operational Process and Derived Documentation

To perform its varied roles, the IMF has developed a division of labor, which can be simplified as surveillance, review, research, and decision. The *Articles of Agreement*,[6] in Article VIII Section 5a, lay down the information that each member country is required to report to the IMF. Section 5b takes account of the member's ability to report and Section 5c stipulates that the Fund shall collect further data with the country's agreement, and provide studies to assist members in developing policies that "further the purposes of the Fund."[7]

From this Article arises most of what the Fund does. Section 5c establishes the right of the Fund to investigate in detail the economic policies of the member country, the principal basis of surveillance, of which detailed review is a major exercise. Section 5a is the basis of the research work and data compilation the Fund carries out, a large part of which finds its way into published output from the Fund. The final decision-making body of the IMF is the Executive Board, where the decision process is formalized and enacted. Each of these four areas of activity generates documentation, from which ultimately are derived the Fund's decisions. Decisions by the IMF are arrived at, for the most part, by consensus, reached within a set of rules and established policies, which determine the outcome of most negotiations between member countries and the organization. Let us look a little more closely at each of these four activities and set them within the working context of the IMF, identifying the documentation to which each gives rise.

Mission Travel, Reporting, and Review

The principal activity of the IMF is surveillance, which it conducts mainly through sending mission teams of three or four economists to each member country, to gather and analyze economic data from government ministry and central bank officials. These missions are of two types, those conducting regular surveillance under Article IV of the Fund's *Articles of Agreement* and those conducted in response to a request from a member country for IMF resources, that is, a request to borrow. In both cases a very intense process of information gathering and analysis is undertaken to provide an immediate analysis of the state of the country's economy, against which the second stage of the mission can be conducted, namely to propose a new direction or adjustment to meet the demands of the new economic situation in the country. The Fund is constantly engaged upon conducting these missions, and it is only by regarding the IMF as a body in constant review of all its now 182 members' economies, reviewing them by visiting the countries themselves, that the real work of the organization can be understood. The reviews are carried out by the economists from the area departments, departments of the IMF that are charged with maintaining a constant vigilance over the economies of all the countries under that area department's purview. There are presently six of these departments: Asia and Pacific, Africa, Middle East, Western Hemisphere, European I and European II, Eastern and Western Europe being divided between two departments. (Unlike the World Bank, the IMF keeps the economies of all its members under review, not just those in a state of development.) Within each of these departments there is a country desk responsible for the surveillance of one or more countries. Under the guidance of a Division Chief, who holds ultimate responsibility for the Fund's knowledge of the countries within that Division, each country desk will maintain a watching brief on a country. It is the country desk economist who will be responsible for putting together a briefing paper on a country that is to be visited by a mission and the country desk economist will be a member of every mission that visits the country. Each mission will be lead initially by a Deputy Division Chief, who will enter the country with the mission team, followed typically some time later by the Division Chief. This allows the team to commence gathering the initial data from the country officials. At the point at which the data gathering process has been largely completed, the Division Chief will arrive to review the information gathered and to direct the economic approach that the team deems it prudent for the country to take. The role of the Division Chief is also very much as orator and presenter of the findings of the mission, a political role, that has the responsibility of ensuring that the country officials and government representatives accept the mission's findings and agree to the proposals of the team. It is a diplomatic role in cajoling or exhorting country officials and politicians to provide information if this has not been forthcoming and to discern when the country is not being entirely honest with itself or the team. The Desk Economist is responsible for ensuring that all the data gathered by the team is compiled into a reliable form and is useable by the team in reaching its conclusions.

Once returned to Washington, after, typically, a two- or three-week mission in the country, the mission team commences the process of writing the mission report. These reports are required, under the present rules, to reach the Executive Board within six weeks of the mission having set off for the country in question, which means that the mission has, at most, four weeks after its return to complete the report.

The writing of a mission report is as intense an exercise as the mission. It is also the part of the process that involves the review function. Besides the six area departments, the Fund also has three departments that are the policy monitoring agents for the organization. Principal among these is the Policy Development and Review Department, to which all mission reports, once drafted, are submitted for review. The review process is not concerned with checking the accuracy of the content of the report. It is the concern of the mission team, and ultimately the Division Chief, as leader of the mission, to get that right, the real burden for probity of factual data in a report falling on the Desk Economist of the mission team. The Policy Development and Review Department (PDR) is concerned with ensuring that the proposals made in the mission report are consistent with Fund policy. There is also a considerable amount of notation that a mission report receives from PDR, which is exclusively concerned with the language used in the report. A good deal of semantic rectitude is employed in the writing of a report, all of it concerned with maintaining a consistent approach across the different member countries, not leaving open to interpretation some policy approach that may suggest a departure from the established policies of the Fund. The other two reviewing departments, the Fiscal Affairs Department and the Monetary and Exchange Affairs Department, bring to bear their own areas of specialist expertise, ensuring that those specialist aspects of a mission report are consistent with Fund policy.

Once the report has been written and reviewed, it is submitted as a final report to the Managing Director and Deputy Managing Directors (of which there are now three). It is the Managing Director, through the services of the Secretary's Department, who distributes the report to the Executive Board of the IMF, the body of twenty-four Executive Directors, who are the appointees and representatives of the 182 member countries. They in turn send copies of the report to their member countries. (Given the numerical disparity between the number of Executive Directors and the number of member countries, all but eight Executive Directors[8] represent more than one country on the Executive Board.)

The documentary result of each mission undertaken by the IMF is the report to the Executive Board. In the case of Article IV missions, the regular surveillance missions, these reports have, since 1999, begun to be released on a pilot basis, by those countries agreeing to have their surveillance reports made public, on the IMF website.[9] An Article IV staff report (each report is stated to contain the views of the IMF staff and not necessarily those of the Executive Board) consists of a background overview of the country's economy in the previous year; reports on the discussions held between the mission staff and the government officials on fiscal, monetary, external, and structural policies; provides a medium-term economic outlook for the country and the staff appraisal of the country as a result of their investigation on mission. Attached to the report are various statistical tables, the content of which will have been derived largely from the discussions with the authorities during the mission. It is worthwhile, even important, to point out that the statistical data used by IMF staff in writing mission reports on a country are not derived from the large database of economic data held centrally by the IMF. That data is invariably too old to be of use to the mission team that is looking to get very current data and, therefore, asks the government officials to provide the latest data they have. Where data is missing, the mission team will make assumptions, based upon their best judgment and other information they have gathered from their discussions with government and central bank officials. By the same token, the data presented in the Article IV reports is itself not proven data as would be found published in an annual statistical report. It is data established beyond reasonable doubt and often stated to be an estimate. The footnotes to the data tables will seldom refer to a published source of data, as this usually does not exist at the time of publication of the report. These staff reports should be understood, therefore, to be well informed analyses of the current economic situation in a country, derived from the expertise and methodology employed by the IMF in conducting these reviews of a country's economic health. It should also be remembered that they have been put together within a six-week period.

A further product of the Article IV consultation work is the release, since April 1997, of what are termed *Public Information Notices* (*PINs*).[10] These are released following the completion of each Article IV consultation, usually five to ten days after the Board has discussed the report. A PIN is a brief report and consists of two sections:

- background factual information on the economy of a member country; and
- the Fund assessment of the member's prospects and policies. This latter section will correspond closely to the Executive Board Chairman's summing up.

It is assumed that the member country will consent to the release of the PIN, prior to the issuance of the Chairman's summing up, as a Fund document.

SAF, ESAF, and Now PRGF

Besides Article IV missions there are also "use of Fund resources" missions; these are missions conducted in member countries, where the country has asked for financial assistance. The process here is similar to an Article IV mission and report, except that different and often more stringent conditions may be recommended by the IMF team. There will also have to be conformity to other rules, which will be derived from the various funding instruments the IMF has developed over the years. The documentary output is similar, however, except that in preparation for receiving assistance, the country in question must itself prepare its own economic review paper.

Until 1999 these papers were entitled *Policy Framework Papers* or *PFPs*.[11] A PFP was a requirement of any member government seeking financial help under the Enhanced Structural Adjustment Facility (ESAF).[12] This was a concessionary lending instrument introduced by the IMF in December 1987, a year following the introduction of the less concessionary Structural Adjustment Facility (SAF). Under SAF a country could borrow up to 70 percent of its quota on a three-year term. Under the ESAF, up to 250 percent of quota could be borrowed over a three-year period, with provision for 350 percent to be borrowed in exceptional circumstances. Repayment terms and conditions were the same for both instruments: an interest rate of 0.5 percent, with the principal repayable over five and a half to ten years, with a grace period of five years. *PFP* was the major documentary product associated with the ESAF (and to a lesser extent the SAF, for which it was strongly recommended, though not required). The PFP described the government's medium-term policy framework and identified a set of core policy reforms. It was intended to help forge an internal consensus on the country's reform effort through substantial involvement of the national, economic institutions, with ultimate release of the PFP report to the public, if agreed to by the government.

The PFP and ESAF requests were submitted simultaneously to the World Bank and the IMF Boards, though in the Bank the PFP was circulated to the Executive Directors for information only. The current PFP was also circulated for information in the Bank when a World Bank Country Assistance Strategy (CAS) was submitted to its Board. The PFP accordingly played an important role in assisting co-ordination between the World Bank and the IMF. It was also intended to provide donors (commercial lenders) with a consistent policy framework, against which they could consider providing their assistance. The Bank staff contributed expertise on sector policies to a PFP, whilst the IMF provided input on macroeconomic stabilization and exchange rate policies and balance of payments issues. To ensure ownership of the PFP, a country's authorities were encouraged to initiate the drafting of the PFP, or at least to provide input on selected issues. PFPs were a forward-looking analysis of current economic and structural problems and prospects, providing a focus on key policy objectives over a three-year period to address major problems, and a focus on the priorities of the policy strategy. Further PFPs were ideally drawn up in the second and third years of the three-year period, to update the original policy framework identified in the first year's PFP. Each PFP was required to provide a minimum of four tables:

- a policy matrix on specific measures and timing;
- a table of selected economic and financial indicators;
- a table of selected social indicators; and
- a table on external financing requirements.

A fifth table on external debt indicators was expected for Heavily Indebted Poor Countries (HIPCs).[13]

Bank and Fund staff encouraged governments to involve a broad segment of their administration, and all relevant parties, in the drawing up of a PFP. Both Bank and Fund staff tried to persuade country authorities to release PFPs to their publics themselves, though the Bank and the Fund stood ready to do so if a country itself could not. A government had to say, in the covering letter conveying the PFP to the Bank and the Fund, whether it agreed to the release of its PFP or not. In 1996 new guidelines were issued by the Bank and the Fund on the drafting of PFPs; the guidelines stated quite unambiguously that the PFPs were the documents of the member governments and not of the Bretton Woods institutions. They were, however, prepared in close consultation with the staffs of the Bank and the IMF, and formed part of the deliberative process of each institution, particularly the IMF. If the government wished, the Bank and Fund would distribute the document for the government. After 1994 all publicly available PFPs were placed in the Bank's Public Information Centers (PICs) and, from 1998 made available on the IMF website.[14]

Poverty Reduction and Growth Facility and the PRSP

On November 22, 1999, the Enhanced Structural Adjustment Facility was transformed into the **Poverty Reduction and Growth Facility (PRGF)**,[15] and its purposes were redefined. It is intended that PRGF-supported programs will be based on country-owned, poverty reduction strategies, adopted in a participatory process involving civil society and development partners, and articulated in a **poverty reduction strategy paper (PRSP)**.[16] This is intended to ensure that each PRGF-supported program is consistent with a comprehensive framework for macroeconomic, structural, and social policies to foster growth and reduce poverty. Once completed and broadly endorsed by the Executive Boards of the IMF and the World Bank, the PRSP will provide the policy framework for future reviews under this PRGF arrangement. PRGF loans carry an interest rate of 0.5 percent a year, and are repayable over ten years with a five-and-a-half-year grace period on principal payments.

Under the new framework, the country-led strategy is presented in the Poverty Reduction Strategy Paper (PRSP) which is expected to become a key instrument for a country's relations with the donor community. In the context of lending operations and assistance strategies, the Boards of the Bank and the Fund will be asked to endorse the PRSP insofar as it relates to policies and programs supported by each institution in its area of responsibility. This will provide a basis for Bank and Fund concessional lending to support the country as well as debt relief under the HIPC Initiative.

Recent Economic Developments

In 1994 a further document series was released to the public, the *REDs* or *Recent Economic Developments* and *Country Statistical Appendices*. These are prepared as background reports on a country's economic condition for members of the Executive Board, as a form of briefing for the Executive Directors prior to discussion of a staff report on a particular country. *REDs* are prepared by the mission staff of the IMF. The information they convey is essentially factual and already within the public domain in the country concerned. Some editing of the content of the Executive Board briefing paper is done, prior to its publication, to remove sensitive policy discussion matter, such as policy advice, balance of payments projections and medium-term scenarios. It is assumed that each *RED* will be released without objection, though there is provision for a member country to prevent publication. This provision is aimed at preserving the relationship under which information is provided to the Fund by member countries in confidence.

REDs are not released to the public until after the Executive Board has discussed the particular country for which the RED has served as background. REDs are issued as paper documents, but are also accessible in pdf format via the IMF's web page.[17]

As a source of insight into the work performed by the IMF, an interesting publication was issued by the Research Department in 1995, *A Manual for Country Economists*.[18] This *Manual*, by Marcello Caiola, was addressed mainly to new staff members in the area and functional departments of the IMF. It presents different ways to tackle specific problems that desk economists encounter in analyzing country data, but it is not intended to be a unique, comprehensive volume. It is a guide to analyzing financial developments in a country and to evaluating the quality of data at the disposal of the IMF's staff. As such it provides a useful insight into the work of economists at the IMF.

Data and Research Compilation

Thus far we have considered only documentation that arises from the IMF's surveillance and lending functions. There is another form of IMF documentation, quite distinct in both its origins and nature from the operational documentation, produced by the country and review departments. This documentation has two principal forms: compiled information or data and research output. This involves primarily—though by no means exclusively—in the case of the former, the Statistics Department and, in the case of the latter, the Research Department.

Article VIII Section 5C[19] of the *Articles of Agreement* calls for the collection and exchange of information on monetary and financial problems from member countries, "designed to assist member states develop policies, which further the purposes of the Fund" through the production of studies revealing:

- holdings of foreign exchange;
- total values of exports and imports;
- international balance of payments;
- the international investment position;
- national income;
- price indices and inflation rates; and
- exchange controls if any.

This data is then used to produce policy analyses, in the production, for example, of the Research Department's *World Economic Outlook* and in various statistical compendia and manuals, of which the prime example is the *International Financial Statistics (IFS)*.

The **IMF Statistics Department** consists of about 160 staff of whom about 100 are economists. This Department is concerned with the routine collection, collation, and publication of statistical data. The economists in the Department are divided up according to particular statistical topics: balance of payments, financial institutions, government finance and country economic data. The information collected is derived from two sources: information collected on missions or information submitted directly to the Department by members under their IMF obligations. This latter information is usually in response to questionnaires sent out monthly or quarterly by the Department. The data is returned in a variety of ways and is raw data, not in the form that it is needed. The data is entered into the EIS (Electronic Information System) database, from which are produced nearly all the Statistical Department's publications, of which the *IFS* is the flagship title.

The Department's other concern is with defining and establishing methodologies—work it carries out principally through working parties, such as the Working Party on the Measurement of International Capital Flows and the International Working Group on External Debt Statistics. The methodology as applied by the Statistics Department to national accounts has rendered these figures comparable across countries. In other statistical compilations (e.g., in *Government Finance Statistics, GFS* and with the calculation of monetary and other financial statistics) this consistency is missing. The Department also produces manuals such as the *Balance of Payments Manual*,[20] the *Government Finance Statistics Manual*[21] and the *System of National Accounts*.[22]

A third area of activity of the Statistics Department is the provision of technical assistance to member countries—primarily missions to countries needing training in the application of statistical methodologies. Many poor countries are dependent upon the IMF for statistical expertise. The Statistics Department sends out its own missions, as well as joining Article IV missions, which incorporate technical assistance. Statistical mission travel has increased recently, particularly with the arrival of the fifteen former Soviet Union states as member countries, each in its own right. The Statistics Department, in conjunction with the **IMF Institute**,[23] has provided a considerable amount of technical assistance in helping these countries to convert from centrally planned to market economy methodologies.

A fourth area the Statistics Department has contributed to is policy formulation, in which technical assistance missions or Article IV missions, having technical assistance components, will assist reporting by member countries. This has been particularly the case in the former Soviet Union countries and Latin America.

The Statistics Department itself only uses *ex-post facto* data. It does not use or even accept member countries' estimates or forecast data (the way Country Desk missions are forced to). It is because of the resulting omissions that Country Desk officers and Chiefs of Missions retain their own data sets for the reports they submit to the Executive Board. It is possible to formulate policies upon approximation, but published statistical tables cannot depend upon such vagaries.

The Statistics Department has also helped lead the way in disseminating its information much more widely over the web. Through the IMF website, it publishes the International Monetary Fund **Dissemination Standards Bulletin Board (DSBB)**, which provides information to guide countries that have, or that might seek, access to international capital markets, in the dissemination of economic and financial data to the public via the **Special Data Dissemination Standard (SDDS)** established in 1996 and the **General Data Dissemination System (GDDS)**, established in 1997, this latter to guide countries in the provision to the public of comprehensive, timely, accessible, and reliable economic, financial, and sociodemographic data.[24]

The Statistics Department has also partnered with the World Bank, the Bank for International Settlements, the European Union and the OECD, to put up on the web an extensive database system on external indebtedness of Third World countries, the **Joint BIS-IMF-OECD-World Bank Statistics on External Debt**.[25]

The IMF publishes paper versions of the Statistics Department's *International Financial Statistics*,[26] *Balance of Payments Yearbook*,[27] *Government Finance Statistics*,[28] and *Direction of Trade Statistics*.[29] There are also CD versions of each of these titles, the *International Financial Statistics* also being available on CD in a Windows version. All sales of IMF statistical publications, in whatever format, are handled by the IMF Publications Services Section, part of the External Relations Department.[30]

Research Documentation

The IMF Research Department has been the principal—though not the unique—source of research documentation in the organization. Other departments also create research documentation. The Policy Development and Review Department, the Money and Exchange Arrangements (MAE) Department and the Fiscal Affairs (FAD) Department are particular sources of research documentation.

Most of what has appeared in print during the IMF's history has been the published output of this research. The prime source of research documentation in the first years of the IMF was the *Departmental Memorandum (DM) series*. This was established on May 12, 1953. It remained an internal series of research papers until November 1965, when the Research Department proposed that these papers be attributed to the staff members responsible and distributed to selected outside institutions or persons for comment. From 1966 these documents appeared, with a disclaimer on the masthead that they were not formal statements of the Fund's position, and bearing the name of the author.

The papers in the *DM series* were by authors from different Fund departments and occasionally written in collaboration with authors from outside the Fund. Authors were free to distribute copies outside of the Fund, unless the papers (unusually) contained sensitive material. *DM papers* could also be submitted for publication outside the Fund, though the IMF retained the right of first publication.

As from September 1, 1986, the *DM series* was modified and renamed the *IMF Working Papers* and incorporating another series, the *PIFS—Papers on International Financial Statistics*. All papers issued were now produced as Fund publications under the N Rules.[31] The disclaimer concerning authorship was retained, though modified, but removed from the masthead was the statement: "IMF Document not for public use." The External Relations Department (EXR) of the Fund continued to provide the Fund's management (The Managing Director and then single Deputy Managing Director and their advisers) with abstracts of all working papers prior to their publication, as they had done previously for papers issued in the *DM series.*

A select group of research institutions and international organizations was drawn up, with whom the IMF wished to maintain a regular exchange of research work "in the interest of the Fund." A set of these new *Research Working Papers* was deposited with each institution, as well as being deposited in the Joint Library (of the World Bank and the IMF), which entered details of each paper in the JOLIS database.[32] Beyond this, despite these papers being considered publications under the IMF's rules, there was no other distribution. Any requests that were received for such papers were handled individually by EXR. The authors themselves continued to be free to distribute copies of their own papers to interested individuals. Those papers in the *DM series*, which had contained sensitive material, were then issued in a new series of *DMX papers* and thereby removed from the new "public" *Research Working Paper series.*

This erstwhile *Research Working Paper series* is now generically referred to as the *Working Papers series*, and titles are mailed out on requests received from any interested person or organization. However, the advent of the web has provided an opportunity for the IMF's External Relations Department to publish, from 1996 onward, to a wide and undefined audience, much, if not most, of the research output of the organization. Besides the *Working Papers* and *Policy Discussion Papers series*, an increasing number of additional research documents and operational documents are now also accessible, in full-text, via the IMF's web page. The principal research report out of the Research Department is the *World Economic Outlook,* the twice-yearly review and forecast by the Research Department. This report, issued in both paper and web form, is a comprehensive analysis of prospects for the world economy, individual countries and regions and an examination of various economic issues of concern. It begins life as an internal report, drafted by the staff of the WEO Studies Division of the Research Department, in collaboration with other Fund Departments, and which is first presented by the Economic Counselor (the Director of the Research Department) to the Executive Board for discussion, prior to its publication in May and October of each year, with an occasional third issue, depending on need. Its final (glossy) publication form is always preceded by a press release from the IMF that takes the form of a partial version of the full (glossy) report.[33] The full report is not printed at the time of the presentation of the report to the Executive Board and its immediate subsequent issue in partial form as a press release and on the web. It is only released in full published form some weeks later, typically in June and November. In its partial form, it is announced on the IMF web page, where each chapter of this partial form is provided as a separate pdf file. With the May 1999 report, the IMF web page has been further enhanced with the provision of the **WEO Database**.[34] The database provides statistics on Selected World Aggregates, Real Gross Domestic Product, Gross Domestic Product, Inflation and Net Capital Flows for all member countries and from 1970 to date, with forecast figures into the following year in some instances. Besides the WEO Report itself and now the WEO Database, there are also a number of accompanying reports, the *Supporting Studies for the World Economic Outlook*,[35] which comprise supporting material for the analysis and scenarios in the *World Economic Outlook* and provide a more detailed examination of the theory and evidence on some major issues affecting the global economy, commodity prices, and individual countries. These are not currently available via the web, but exist only in hard copy in the *World Economic and Financial Surveys Series*. This series is also the home to the *World Economic Outlook* and the *International Capital Markets Report*, the latter issued as an annual publication since 1984.[36]

Another title worthy of note here is the *Annual Report on Exchange Arrangements and Exchange Restrictions*, published every year since 1950, under the provisions of Article XIV, Section 3 of the *Articles of Agreement*.[37] This report relates to one of the key activities for which the IMF was created. The report is much in demand when it is published each year, usually in August, as it is then most up-to-date. It provides detailed reporting on the state of each member country's foreign exhange regime, covering the existing exchange arrangements in each country, its arrangements for payments and receipts, for resident and non-resident accounts, and for payments for invisibles and capital transactions. It is compiled under the direction of the Monetary and Exchange Affairs Department with assistance from the six area and other departments. It is not available over the web, but needs to be acquired as a paper document. The 1999 edition runs to some 970 pages in length.

All other IMF research documentation that reaches publication is issued under a number of series or as individual monographs. Included among these are the periodical publications issued by the IMF. The major source of research disseminated via periodical is the *IMF Staff Papers*, published four times a year in March, June, September, and December. The purpose of this periodical is to publish high-quality research produced by IMF staff and invited contributors, addressed to a wide audience of academics and member-country policy makers. It has been published since 1951, and with the March 1998 issue, is available in full-text (via pdf) from the IMF web page. As of October 2000, the latest issue published is the September/December 1999 issue, Vol. 46, No. 3. Links to working paper versions of accepted papers for subsequent issues are provided on the web page, but it should be noted that these are preliminary versions of the papers submitted to the journal, and may be amended or revised significantly before final acceptance for publication.

Another periodical title from the IMF with a wide readership is the quarterly, *Finance and Development* which, from its first issue in 1964 until the March 1998 issue, was jointly published by the World Bank and IMF External Relations Departments. In 1998, the World Bank External Affairs Department decided to withdraw from joint publication for budgetary reasons. The content of this title is geared to providing short, incisive views of economic development questions, contributed by experts in the field or staff of the IMF or the World Bank on issues of current interest and topicality. The journal is edited by the editorial staff of the IMF's External Relations Department. From the March 1996 issue, it has also been published on the web.[38]

The third periodical title of note from the IMF is the *IMF Survey*, which provides topical coverage of IMF activities, policies, and research in global economics and financial developments, with reproduction of IMF statements and reportage of international meetings and seminars organized by the IMF. As with the previous titles, this biweekly publication is also accessible via the web.[39]

A fourth periodical title, added in May 1998 to the IMF's output, is entitled *Economic Reviews*. Intended to make available on a more timely basis the Executive Board Reviews of member economies previously released in the *Annual Report*, it compiles and publishes *IMF Public Information Notices* (not to be confused with the *Public Information Notices* (*PINs*) released following the completion of Article IV consultations; these are discussed later). Only two issues have been published to date, No. 1 in May 1998 and No. 2 May–August 1999, published in September 1999. This title is currently only available in hard copy.

The monographic research output of the IMF is delivered through publications issued in a number of series, the principal titles of which are the above mentioned *World Economic and Financial Surveys, IMF Occasional Papers, IMF Pamphlet Series, IMF Working Papers, IMF Policy Discussion Papers* and a more recent series, *Economic Issues*, this lattermost series being devoted to presenting to a broad, nonspecialist readership economic issues faced by the IMF. The IMF also publishes books and *some* seminar reports on topics of "Fundwide importance." Seminar reports not published in hard copy are issued exclusively on the IMF website.

All published titles are listed in the *International Monetary Fund Publications Catalog*, produced annually by the publishers of IMF titles, the External Relations Department. The *Catalog*, besides being issued and distributed as a paper publication, is accessible via the IMF's web page in a constantly updated form, where all the latest titles issued, as well as those previously published, are now mostly available as full-text documents.

Translation of IMF Publications

Some periodical and series titles are translated into other languages, including French, Spanish, Russian, Chinese, and Arabic, after their initial publication in English, the official language of the Fund. Not every publication is translated and not all the languages, used for translations, are employed with every publication. Decisions on language versions are made per title. The translation work is carried out by the Bureau of Language Services, the Department that publishes the *IMF Glossary* [40] and the terminology bulletins.[41]

The research output of the IMF is not large as a proportion of the amount of actual research work conducted, but with the arrival of web technology, the External Relations Department of the IMF has exposed to immediate access a far greater degree of the research work released for public view than had ever been achieved in the past. Though it may still not be possible to track the organization's research thinking as it develops, it is certainly possible now to have a very good idea of the nature of the IMF's thinking, both in research terms and operationally. The Executive Board must be paid its due for having agreed to the proposals of the IMF management to make transparency more of a reality than just a good intention. The External Relations Department must, likewise, be acknowledged for having taken advantage of the available technology to deliver a vastly expanded amount of the organization's documentation in a very easily accessible and timely fashion. This has been a sea change in the organization's attitude to the outside world's right of, and reason for, access to its inner workings.

The Executive Board

There are a number of issues, other than policy issues affecting member countries, on which the Board takes decisions—administrative policies being prime among these—that form the framework within which the staff operate. To undertake its work in 1997, the Executive Board[42] met on 166 occasions, holding 132 formal discussions, 6 informal meetings, 22 private meetings, and 6 seminars.[43] In that same year 58 percent of the Board's time was spent in considering country matters (Article IV consultation reports, reviews, and loan arrangements). Thirty-six percent of its time was devoted to policy issues: the *World Economic Outlook*, developments in international capital markets, the IMF's financial resources, data issues, the debt situation and issues related to IMF loan facilities and programs. In the *Articles of Agreement*, Article XII Section 3 (g) states that the Executive Board "functions in continuous session" (a sensation Board members and the staff must feel to be all too literal at times).

It is worth detailing some of the document series that have been derived over the past fifty years, as the IMF has, in strong contrast to its previous attitude to public disclosure, now opened much of its archives to public access (about which details are given below).

Minutes of Meetings of the Executive Board

The minuting of meetings of the Executive Board of the IMF has a somewhat quaint history. On May 6, 1946, at the inaugural meeting of the IMF's Executive Directors (they were not referred to collectively as the "Executive Board" until April 1, 1978 with the adoption of the Second Amendment of the Fund's *Articles of Agreement*), they agreed that the Secretary would read aloud and in full the draft minutes of meetings before their approval, a practice that was later abandoned. After a brief period of this oratorical practice, Harry Dexter White, a principal author, with John Maynard Keynes, of the IMF's creation, and the first United States Executive Director, called for a *verbatim transcript* of all meetings of the Executive Board. This led to a series of discussions on this topic, giving rise to an opposing view that proposed the Secretary of the IMF alone have access to such records for reference purposes only. Wide dissemination of such records, it was argued, would inhibit discussion and hinder the effectiveness of open exchange at the Executive Board. A compromise was reached, whereby *verbatim records* of the Board's proceedings were permitted to assist the Secretary in preparing *summary records*, with the requirement (subsequently incorporated in 1978 into Rule C-15[44]), that the *verbatim records* then be destroyed!

The early *summary records* were soon felt to be too brief and a more detailed record of discussion was agreed on. By 1966, however, Executive Directors were complaining of the delay of several months in the production of the minutes. This was resolved by the hiring of additional staff in the Secretary's Department to prepare these summary minutes in a more timely manner, the principal cause of the delay having been the increase in the number of Board meetings.

Meetings of the Executive Directors, as shown above, take a number of forms besides the regularly scheduled Board meetings, including informal sessions, seminars, meetings of various committees and meetings of the Committee of the Whole. Each of these separate meetings has a separate document series. The purpose of these "other" meetings is, among other things, to move a policy debate forward between Executive Directors, in the hope of shortening the debate at the regular meetings of the Board. Final minutes of Board meetings are now distributed to Executive Directors and their Alternates and Advisors, to the Managing Director and three Deputy Managing Directors, the Directors of the Departments and selected other members of the IMF staff.

Documents of the Executive Board

As with the minutes, the documents around which discussion has taken place have also had a varied career. At the outset there was only one document series, the prosaically named **EBD (Executive Board Document)** series, which contained all Executive Board documents. EBD1[45] provides the *Articles of Agreement*, as issued in 1944. EBD2 is a copy of the documents of the inaugural meeting of the Executive Directors on May 6, 1946. EBDs include, *inter alia*:

- reports and agenda for the Annual Meetings of the Board of Governors;
- memberships of the Executive Board committees;
- Executive Board decisions and results of Executive Board by-elections;[46]
- exchange market developments;
- monetary policy measures notified by member countries;
- amendments to the Rules and Regulations of the IMF;
- general reviews of members' consent to quota reviews; and
- requests for, and evaluations of, reports on technical assistance.

Monthly reports on foreign currency, gold prices and international reserves data used to be included in this document series, but are no longer. Confidential reports on the above topics caused a new series to be introduced, the **Executive**

Board Specials (EBS) series. Such was the concern for privacy by the organization that it was not until 1992 that the EBS series distribution was extended downward to include Division Chiefs, distribution prior to that date being confined to Executive Directors and Department Directors.

In 1948 the **EBAPs** or **Executive Board Administrative Papers** were introduced. These contained documents on a variety of subjects, including, besides the *restricted discussion minutes* mentioned above, the Annual Audit, the Fund's Accounts, the Administrative Budget, papers of the Joint Committee on Executive Directors' Remuneration, on office space, staff official travel, personnel and recruitment policies, and staff salaries and benefits. From 1992, the EBAP series excluded the Executive Directors administrative business, and the distribution of the series was opened up to all IMF staff, the Executive Directors' business being issued in a new series, **EBAMs (Executive Board Administrative Matters)**.

A curiously named series, **BUFFs**, so called because of the color of their cover sheets, convey statements by IMF staff and the Managing Director to the Executive Board. Prior to 1992, BUFFs included statements to the Board by Executive Directors and the distribution of the series was very limited. From that year another series, the yet more tantalizingly named **BUFF EDs**, were introduced to cater for these statements by the EDs, thereby allowing the distribution of the BUFFs to be open to all IMF staff. Likewise in 1992 the **SUR (Surveillance** document) series was also opened to all IMF staff.

The staff reports (**SMs** or **Staff Memoranda**) series was introduced on December 11, 1946 at the request of the Executive Directors, who wanted these reports separated from the EBM series. The **SM** series consists of reports prepared by the IMF staff and includes policy papers, research papers and studies on underlying Fund policies and their formulation, staff mission reports, and economic surveys.

More recently, as has been detailed earlier, there has been the dramatic release of a growing number of SMs, such as Article IV staff reports and REDs or Recent Economic Developments, to the public at large via the IMF's web page. Where the SM series conveys operational reports, the erstwhile DM (*Departmental Memoranda*) series, now entitled the *Working Paper series* (detailed above) is where research reports first emerge. As this series has grown from being an entirely internal document collection to a now publicly web-accessible document collection, there is little of it that is not now fully revealed to public view.

A collection of Executive Board documents that has long been made available to the public, in printed form, is the *Selected Decisions and Selected Documents of the International Monetary Fund*.[47] The latest issue of this title is the twenty-fourth, published on June 30, 1999. The volume, like its predecessors, reproduces selected decisions and documents of the Executive Board and of the Board of Governors. Decisions of the Executive Board are laid out in order of the *Articles of Agreement*, whereas the decisions of the Board of Governors are presented in chronological order. These decisions and documents (which include documents drawn from the various series mentioned above—EBDs, EBMs and SMs) are an historical record in one volume of the principal documents of the organization, and as such form a kind of working constitution. These are documents to which frequent reference is made by the Fund in the conduct of its activities, and they include other Fund documents that relate to the relationship between the Fund and other international organizations. As a publication in excess of eight hundred pages, it is blessed with a fairly detailed index at the end.

The Board of Governors

The IMF's Executive Board is charged with managing the day-today business of the IMF, but it does so under the jurisdiction of a higher body, the **Board of Governors**. This Board, made up typically of Finance Ministers and Governors of central banks, meets once a year in the autumn. It is a large gathering, as the bringing together of these representatives from the 182 member countries would imply. The purpose of the meeting is to review the policies of the IMF (*and* the World Bank, over both of which organizations this single, but separate[48] Board of Governors presides), and to set any new broad policy directions, to be carried out by the IMF's Executive Board. It is also the opportunity for the Fund's Managing Director (and the Bank's President) to address the "shareholders" of the two organizations and to report on the previous year's work. To facilitate this reporting, both the IMF and the World Bank each present their annual reports. Prior to its printing and presentation to the Board of Governors, the IMF's *Annual Report of the Executive Directors* is approved by the IMF Executive Board at one of its regular meetings. The *Annual Report* is a valuable source of information on much of the detailed work of the organization in the previous year, providing policy statements and decisions of the Board, overviews of the economic issues faced by the organization, descriptions of loans made, and technical assistance given, to member countries, as well as details of the organization's financial standing and operations. Among the appendices are reproductions of the principal policy decisions of the Executive Board, a listing of the Executive Directors with their voting power and changes in the membership of the Board during the year. There are, too, a number of statistical tables, boxes, and figures. As a single, authoritative source upon the principal developments of the organization, it is a unique document and worth close study by anyone wishing to become familiar with the details of Fund programs and policies.

The International Monetary and Financial Committee (previously Interim Committee) and the Development Committee

The *Annual Report* also contains (among its appendices) the press communiqués issued by the (erstwhile Interim Committee now renamed) International Monetary and Financial Committee and the Development Committee. These two committees were set up as committees of the Board of Governors in October 1974. Each committee meets twice a year, once at the Annual Meeting of the

Board of Governors and again in April each year. The purpose of the **Interim Committee** was to advise the Board of Governors of the IMF on supervising the management and adaptation of the international monetary system, as well as dealing with disturbances that might threaten the system. In the wake of the Asian financial crisis in 1997/1998, this Committee was renamed on September 30, 1999, the **International Monetary and Financial Committee of the Board of Governors**, and its purpose defined as:

- supervising the management and adaptation of the international monetary and financial system, including the continuing operation of the adjustment process, and in this connection reviewing developments in global liquidity and the transfer of real resources to developing countries;
- considering proposals by the Executive Board to amend the *Articles of Agreement*; and
- dealing with sudden disturbances that might threaten the system.[49]

The principal difference in the Committee's role is the making overt of its concern with international financial questions, which resulted from the eruption of the Asian financial crisis. Its membership is similar in size and make-up to that of the Executive Board, each country or group of countries being entitled to one representative on the Committee. The Chairman is appointed by the Board of Governors.

The **Development Committee**, whose full title is the dreadful mouthful, **Joint Ministerial Committee of the Boards of Governors of the Bank and the Fund on the Transfer of Real Resources to Developing Countries,** was also established in October 1974, its purpose being to advise and report "to the Boards of Governors of the Bank and the IMF on all aspects of the broad question of the transfer of real resources to developing countries."[50]

Much of the documentation of these two committees is not made public, apart from those documents issued in the *Selected Documents and Selected Decisions of the International Monetary Fund* (mentioned above) or in the *Summary Proceedings of the Annual Meeting of the Board of Governors* (to be discussed next). A number of papers are generated for the meetings by the staffs of the IMF and the World Bank, of which only the press communiqué issued by each Committee is made available at the conclusion of their sessions.[51]

Each annual meeting of the Board of Governors of the Bank and the Fund is publicly documented in the *Summary Proceedings of the ... Annual Meeting of the Board of Governors*.[52] In contradiction of the title's suggestion, this report contains the full-text of the speeches made at the Annual Meeting, which includes the opening and closing addresses of the Chairman of the Meeting, the speeches of both the Managing Director of the Fund and the President of the Bank, plus all the speeches of all the Governors of the member countries who address the meeting. It also includes various documents and resolutions of the Board of Governors, including the agenda of the meeting, and major documents of the International Monetary and Financial Committee and the Development

Committee. If you wish to know, for example, the salary and allowances of Executive Directors of the IMF, this is published as Resolution No. 53-3 of the Board of Governors, adopted at their Fifty-Third Annual Meeting in 1998.[53]

Finding IMF Publications and Documents

The IMF, as has been stated, has done a great deal to make its publications and publicly released documents available to the public via its web page (<www.imf.org>). Through the search facility or the site index, it is possible to find and identify quite easily the published output of the organization for recent years, mostly since 1997. There is, however, another search engine well worth using to identify IMF publications and documents issued publicly. That engine is the JOLIS Library Catalog mentioned above. The JOLIS Catalog is a web-based catalog, accessible at <http://jolis.worldbankimflib.org> the public website of the Library Network of the IMF and the World Bank, a network formed by a common database—the JOLIS Catalog—of some twelve libraries across the institutions. The Catalog is available to anyone having access to the web, and is a very effective tool for identifying not only individual publications and public documents of the IMF and the World Bank, but also for identifying individual articles published in IMF and World Bank periodicals. With the advent of the web, the Library Catalog has taken full advantage of this great enhancement to computer connectivity, and has links from each record in the database to any document described therein, where there is a full-text version of the document on the web. In the case of the IMF, any document or publication available to the public via the web is cataloged in the Library Catalog and the record linked to the IMF website, thus making finding the document and retrieving it all of a piece. The same applies to World Bank documents, as it does to many other items cataloged in the database, which have freely available, full-text versions on the web. For those IMF and World Bank titles not available on the web, the Library Catalog is an effective means of identifying them, as it is a useful way of establishing what each organization has published on a particular subject. Searching the database, using the full name of either organization (i.e., International Monetary Fund or World Bank) will reveal all the monographic items published on that subject by the organizations from the inception of the Bretton Woods institutions up to the day of the search. Journal articles published in IMF and World Bank periodicals, along with articles from about eight hundred other journals have been entered in the JOLIS Catalog since 1982.[54] Besides IMF and World Bank publications, the Catalog is a valuable tool as a source of bibliographic reference on a wide variety of subjects in the field of economic development and financial management.

Opening of the IMF's Archives

Public access to IMF documentation has been still further enhanced by the opening of the IMF's archives to *bona fide* researchers. From the Executive Board document series identified above, selected series are now accessible by the public in what has become, very recently, a remarkably open archive, having only a five-year restriction on access. The first step toward opening the Fund's archives came with **Executive Board Decision 11192-(96/2)**, adopted by the Board on January 17, 1996, which opened to access by outside persons, upon request, the documentary materials maintained in the Fund's archives that were over thirty years old. A prime condition applied, which provided that those documents, originally classified as "secret" or "strictly confidential," would only be accessible upon the Managing Director's consent to their declassification. It was understood that this consent would be forthcoming, except for those documents, which, despite the passage of time, remained highly confidential or sensitive. **Decision No. 11915-(99/23)**, however, taken by Executive Board at its meeting on March 8, 1999, reduced the thirty-year rule for access to Executive Board documents to five years, and for access to other Fund records in the Archives to twenty years, with the same proviso regarding archival records originally classified "secret" or "strictly confidential."[55]

Under both decisions, there are certain classes of these archival records that have not been released to the public. These include legal documents and records maintained by the Legal Department, which are protected by attorney-client privilege; documents furnished to the Fund by external parties, such as member countries, which bear confidentiality markings, unless these parties consent to their declassification; personnel files and records pertaining to individuals; and the documents of the IMF Grievance Committee.[56]

The facilities available for archival research consist of a reading room in the Archives office with seating for several researchers at a time. Access to the IMF's archives may be made by telephone, facsimile, electronic mail, or post.[57] In all cases, requests should be directed to the Archivist of the IMF at least ten working days in advance of an anticipated visit. In preparing a request, researchers are encouraged to be as specific as possible in describing their topic of interest. A clear description will assist the Archivist in identifying potentially useful material and ensuring its availability.[58] The Research Room is open, by advance appointment, from 9.30 A.M. to 5.00 P.M. Monday to Friday, except on public holidays.

It should be apparent from the above that the IMF has made great strides to respond to the mounting demands upon it, to open up its treasure trove of information derived from the member governments and the assiduous hard work of its economists and supporting staff. This is a difficult demand to meet, given that the organization is entrusted with data and information by member countries, its shareholders, on the basis of confidentiality. There are many instances to which the organization can point, where it has been more than willing to share information it has compiled or derived, but where the member country concerned has disallowed such disclosure. The underlying policy behind the PFP and now the

PRSP of moving governments to disclose to the public the details of their economic health is a clear instance of the efforts of the organization to move governments to a greater openness, in the spirit of a more democratic relationship between the governments and the people they serve. Undoubtedly, the IMF has been the victim of its past, in which the sense of its own propriety, in its formative years, took precedence over any sense of duty to inform the wider public. That has now largely gone, and the organization is taking its place among the great open international, governmental institutions—one of the great public inheritances of the twenty-first from the twentieth century.

Notes and References

1. David D. Driscoll, *What Is the International Monetary Fund?* (Washington, DC: IMF, 1998).

2. For a listing of the available **IMF Pamphlet series**, see the IMF Publications web page at: <www.imf.org/external/pubind.htm>. Select Pamphlet Series from the "Series" menu and click search. For a complete listing of the IMF Pamphlet Series, search the JOLIS Catalog of the Joint Bank-Fund Library at: <http://jolis.worldbankimflib.org> entering the search term: "Pamphlet Series International Monetary Fund" as a "Series/Source" search.

3. Harry Dexter White and John Maynard Keynes led, respectively, the United States and British delegations to the Bretton Woods Conference, held at the Bretton Woods Hotel in New Hampshire in 1944, at which the two "Bretton Woods" institutions were created by international conference. Both White and Keynes had variant plans for the institutions. White's plan eventually predominated, which led Keynes to comment that there had now been created a Bank that was a fund, and a Fund that was, in fact, a bank.

4. Richard H. R. Harper, *Inside the IMF: An Ethnography of Documents, Technology and Organisational Action* (London: Academic Press, 1998).

5. The Committee of the Board of Governors on Reform of the International Monetary System and Related Issues (The Committee of Twenty) was convened in September 1972 and met over the following two years. It completed its work in June 1974. In October 1974 the Annual Meeting of the Boards of Governors of the Fund and the World Bank adopted a composite resolution, formally ending the work of the Committee of Twenty. Full documentation and detail of the Committee's history is given in: Margaret Garritsen de Vries, *The International Monetary Fund 1972–1978: Cooperation on Trial* (Washington, DC: IMF, 1985).

6. International Monetary Fund. *Articles of Agreement, 1946—As Amended.* Accessible via the IMF web page at: <www.imf.org/external/pubs/ft/aa/>.

7. International Monetary Fund. *Articles of Agreement, 1946—As Amended.* **Article 8: General Obligations of Members. Section 5: Furnishing of Information.** Accessible via the IMF web page at: <www.imf.org/external/pubs/ft/aa/aa08.htm#5>.

8. The eight individual country representatives are Saudi Arabia, Germany, the United States, the Russian Federation, the United Kingdom, Japan, China, and France, these being the largest shareholders in the IMF. The other 15 Executive Directors represent the remaining 174 member countries.

9. The **Article IV Reports** of those countries, which have joined the pilot publication project, are available in full-text at: <www.imf.org/external/np/a4pilot/doc.htm>, where it is stated: "The policy for publication of Article IV staff reports under the pilot project allows for the deletion of market sensitive information. Additional documentation prepared by Fund staff for the Article IV consultation may be posted on this website separately as part of **Staff Country**

Report series, and subsequently [sic] to the posting of the Article IV staff report. The Fund will review the experience with the publication of Article IV staff reports under the pilot project after a year. Comments on the reports and the project are invited."

10. As stated on the IMF's website <www.imf.org/cgi-shl/create_x.pl?pn+1999>: **Public Information Notices** (**PINs**) are issued, (i) at the request of a member country, following the conclusion of the Article IV consultation for countries seeking to make known the views of the IMF to the public. This action is intended to strengthen IMF surveillance over the economic policies of member countries by increasing the transparency of the IMF's assessment of these policies; and (ii) following policy discussions in the Executive Board at the decision of the Board.

11. For a list of all available **PFPs**, select **Policy Framework Papers** from the IMF web page "site index" at: <www.imf.org/external/indexlst.htm#P>.

12. For a fuller description of the ESAF, see **IMF Concessional Financing through ESAF** on the IMF web page under **About the IMF** at: <www.imf.org/external/np/exr/facts/esaf.htm#pfp>.

13. **HIPC (Heavily Indebted Poor Countries)** is a framework, designed by the IMF and the World Bank to provide special assistance for the most severely indebted poor countries looking for IMF and World Bank adjustment and reform programs, and for whom traditional debt relief mechanisms are insufficient. The HIPC Initiative involves the international financial community, including multilateral institutions, in reducing, to sustainable levels, the external debt burden of these countries. The HIPC Initiative, and progress in its implementation, through to the end of August 1999, is accessible via the IMF web page at: <www.imf.org/external/np/hipc/hipc.htm>.

14. Reports produced *by the countries themselves* (such as **Policy Framework Papers**) and released for publication by the member country concerned can be retrieved from the IMF's Publications web page by clicking on "**Member Country Publications**" at <www.imf.org/external/pubind.htm>.

15. For a detailed description of the **Poverty Reduction and Growth Facility (PRGF)** see the IMF web page under About the IMF at: <www.imf.org/external/np/pdr/prsp/poverty2.htm>. The transformation of the ESAF to the PRGF is also well detailed under **Overview: Transforming the Enhanced Structural Adjustment Facility (ESAF) and the Debt Initiative for the Heavily Indebted Poor Countries (HIPCs)** on the IMF web page under About the IMF at: <www.imf.org/external/np/esafhipc/1999/#sub3>.

16. For a description of the **Poverty Reduction Strategy Paper** see the IMF web page under About the IMF at: <www.imf.org/external/np/pdr/prsp/poverty1.htm>.

17. **REDs** (or **Recent Economic Development papers**) are accessible from the IMF web page <www.imf.org/external/pubind.htm> under the Series heading "**IMF Staff Country Reports**." Doing a search by selecting this series on the IMF Publications web page will provide a list, in alphabetical order of country, of all IMF reports on member countries, published on the Web, including all and any RED reports.

18. Marcello Caiola, *A Manual for Country Economists* (Washington, DC: International Monetary Fund, 1995). See IMF Publications web page at: <www.imf.org/EXTERNAL/PUBS/CAT/longres.cfm?sk&sk=567.0>.

19. As in note 7 above.

20. "The *Balance of Payments Manual* presents concepts, definitions, classifications, and conventions for compilation of balance of payments and international investment position statistics. As the international standard, the manual serves as a guide for IMF member countries that regularly report balance of payments data to the IMF. The Fourth edition in English was

reprinted in 1987." [IMF web page at: <www.imf.org/EXTERNAL/PUBS/CAT/longres. cfm?sk&sk=575.0>.] The *Balance of Payments Manual* itself is not available on the web.

21. "The *Government Finance Statistics Manual* deals with concepts, definitions, and procedures for the compilation of statistics on government finance. It is intended as a reference tool for those who are called upon to prepare or evaluate such statistics. Focusing on financial transactions such as taxing, borrowing, spending, and lending, the Manual emphasizes the summarization and organization of statistics appropriate for analysis, planning, and policy determination. . . . English version reprinted in 1995. The 1986 edition is being revised."[IMF web page]. Draft chapters are available at: <www.imf.org/external/pubs/ft/gfs/manual/index.htm>.

22. "The new version of the **System of National Accounts** is a comprehensive, consistent and flexible set of macroeconomic accounts to meet the needs of government and private-sector analysts, policy makers and decision takers. It is designed for use in all countries, whatever their economic, social or institutional arrangements and stage of economic development. The new SNA updates and clarifies the 1968 SNA and harmonizes the SNA with other sets of international standards in statistics, particularly balance of payments, government and other financial statistics and employment statistics. It deals more fully with the integration of balance sheets, lays the groundwork for dealing with interaction between the economy and the natural resources of the environment, and elaborates an analytical approach to the assessment of poverty through social accounting matrices. Prepared under the auspices of the Inter-Secretariat Working Group on National Accounts of: the Commission of the European Communities—Eurostat; International Monetary Fund; Organization for Economic Co-operation and Development; the Statistical Division, Department for Economic and Social Information and Policy Analysis, and regional commissions of the United Nations; and the World Bank." [IMF web page at: <www.imf.org/EXTERNAL/PUBS/CAT/longres.cfm?sk&sk=575.0>.] This title is not, however, available via the web.

23. The IMF Institute is a training institute, created by the IMF, to provide training in technical aspects of economic management to government employees of member countries. Only officials of economic ministries or agencies, with formal sponsorship by a responsible official of their parent ministry or agency, can apply for these courses. Fund training at the Joint Vienna Institute is only for officials from economies in transition of Central and Eastern Europe, the Baltic States, Russia, and other republics of the former Soviet Union, plus Asian countries in transition: Cambodia, China, Laos, Mongolia, Myanmar, and Vietnam. IMF courses are by application only. All IMF seminars are filled by invitation only. See the IMF Institute web page at: <www.imf.org/external/np/ins/index.htm>, which is presented in English, French, and Spanish.

24. See the IMF web page at: <http://dsbb.imf.org>.

25. This **Joint BIS-IMF-OECD-World Bank Statistics on External Debt** database can be accessed via the web pages of **each** of the co-operating agencies, which link to the database itself on the OECD web page at <www.oecd.org/dac/debt>.

26. "This [*International Financial Statistics*] monthly publication is a standard source of international statistics on all aspects of international and domestic finance. It reports, for most countries of the world, current data needed in the analysis of problems of international payments and of inflation and deflation, i.e., data on exchange rates, international liquidity, international banking, money and banking, interest rates, prices, production, international transactions, government accounts, and national accounts. Information is presented in country tables and in tables of area and world aggregates." IMF web page at: <www.imf.org/EXTERNAL/PUBS/CAT/longres.cfm?sk&sk=397.0>. This data can be purchased electronically on a CD from IMF Publications.

27. "This publication [The *Balance of Payments Statistics Yearbook*] consists of a two-part yearbook (usually published in December) containing balance of payments statistics for most of the world, compiled in accordance with the IMF's Balance of Payments Manual. Part 1 includes aggregate as well as detailed information in the form of analytical and standard component presentation for countries. Part 2 provides tables of data, featuring area and world totals of balance of payments components and aggregates." [IMF web page at: <www.imf.org/EXTERNAL/PUBS/CAT/longres.cfm?sk&sk=7.0>.] At present there is no electronic version of this data available for sale.

28. "This annual publication [*Government Finance Statistics Yearbook*] provides detailed data on revenue, grants, expenditure, lending minus repayments, financing and debt of central governments, and indicates the amounts represented by social security funds and extra-budgetary operations. Also provided are data for state and local governments and information on institutional units of [national] governments." [*IMF Publications Catalog* 1998]. At present there is no electronic version of this data available for sale.

29. "**Quarterly issues** of this publication [the *Direction of Trade Statistics*] provide, for about 150 countries, tables with current data (or estimates) on the value of imports from and exports to their most important trading partners. In addition, similar summary tables for the world, industrial countries, and developing countries are included. The *Direction of Trade Statistics Yearbook* provides, for the most recent seven years, detailed trade data by country for approximately 184 countries, the world and major areas." [*IMF Publications Catalog* 1998]. At present there is no electronic version of this data available for sale.

30. All inquiries and orders about **IMF publications** should be addressed to: IMF, Attention: Publication Services, 700 19th Street NW, Washington, DC 20431, USA. telephone 202-623-7430; fax: 202-623-7201; e-mail: publications@imf.org.

31. See International Monetary Fund. **By-Laws Rules and Regulations. Part II. Rules and Regulations of the International Monetary Fund, Section N Staff Regulations. [Rule] N5**. This rule controls the right of staff to publish outside of the organization. Accessible on the IMF Publications web page at: <www.imf.org/external/pubs/ft/bl/rr14.htm>.

32. **JOLIS** was the name given to the first computerized catalog of the Joint Library. The present JOLIS, a SIRSI system catalog, continues as a web accessible database at <http://jolis.worldbankimflib.org> and is an invaluable source for the identification of publicly available IMF and World Bank documents and publications.

33. The partial version of the **World Economic Outlook (WEO) Report** is available in full-text at: <www.imf.org/external/pubs/ft/weo/1999/02/index.htm>. The distinction, between the full, glossy (hard copy only) edition of the report, and this pre-publication, partial version, accessible on the web, is one ignored by, or not made apparent to, journalists, who quote from the latter, as though it were available as a final, glossy published document. This is often a cause of confusion for librarians being asked to provide the report, extensively referred to in the press. The web availability of the partial version has meliorated this situation, but it should be remembered that the web version is not available in hard copy, nor is it the complete report.

34. The **WEO Database** is presented in the form of a series of Excel spreadsheets, accessible on the IMF Publications web page at: <www.imf.org/external/pubs/ft/weo/1999/01/data/index.htm>.

35. For details of the **Supporting Studies for the World Economic Outlook** currently available, search under the Series selection "**World Economic and Financial Surveys**" on the IMF Publications web page at: <www.imf.org/external/pubind.htm>.

36. For earlier developments in international capital markets, see *IMF Occasional Papers* Nos. 1, 7, 14, 23, and 31; since then *International Capital Markets: Developments, Prospects, and Policy Issues* has been issued annually under the "**World Economic and Financial Surveys**"

series. From the September 1998 issue, this title is available in full-text on the IMF Publications web page at: <www.imf.org/external/pubs/ft/icm/icm98/index.htm>.

37. **Section 3 of Article XIV of the Articles of Agreement** concerns the Fund's duty to make annual reports on the exchange restrictions in force in member countries, which the countries may introduce under Section 2 of Article XIV. See **Articles of Agreement** of the International Monetary Fund, Article XIV, accessible at: <www.imf.org/external/pubs/ft/aa/aa14.htm#3>.

38. The full-text of the latest and back issues of *Finance and Development* is available on the IMF Publications web page at: <www.imf.org/external/pubs/ft/fandd/1999/12/index.htm>.

39. The full-text of the *IMF Survey* is accessible at: <www.imf.org/external/pubs/ft/survey/surveyx.htm>.

40. The *IMF Glossary*, 5th edition, 1997, compiled by the IMF's Bureau of Language Services, presents English, French, and Spanish words, phrases, and names of institutions most commonly encountered in IMF documents. There is a 1998 English, French, and Spanish edition available as a CD-ROM. The English, French, and Arabic edition (1996) and the English, French, and Russian edition (1998) are available in paper only. No edition (at the time of writing) is accessible on the web.

41. Various terminological bulletins have been published over the years by the IMF Bureau of Language Services. The latest of these bulletins are *Organizational Structure of the IMF* (1999), *IMF Staff Titles* (1998), and *A Terminology Bulletin on Statistical Terms* by the BLS Arabic Section (198?). These titles are entered in the JOLIS database, but are not listed as publications on the IMF web page.

42. The representation of countries by Executive Directors in the IMF and their voting power is detailed in the IMF's *Annual Report*, Appendices 7 & 8, published each year prior to the Annual Meeting of the Boards of Governors of the World Bank and the IMF, held at the beginning of October. The full-text of the *Annual Report* is available via the web in pdf format from 1996 to date. From 1997 the Report is available on the web in English, French, German, and Spanish <www.imf.org/external/pubs/ft/ar/index.htm>.

43. IMF *Annual Report* 1998. Chapter XII, Organization, staffing and budget. p. 97. This statistical information on Board activities has not been updated in subsequent annual reports.

44. See International Monetary Fund. **By-Laws Rules and Regulations. Part II. Rules and Regulations of the International Monetary Fund, Section C, Minutes**, accessible on the IMF Publications web page at: <www.imf.org/external/pubs/ft/bl/rr03.htm#p5>.

45. Prior to 1946, the symbol "BED" was used for this then-unique series. Use of EBD was applied retrospectively.

46. These are elections of Executive Directors where unexpected vacancies occur. See International Monetary Fund. **By-Laws Rules and Regulations. Part I. By-Laws of the International Monetary Fund, Section 17, Vacant Directorships**, accessible on the IMF Publications web page at: <www.imf.org/external/pubs/ft/bl/bl17.htm>.

47. International Monetary Fund. *Selected Decisions and Selected Documents of the International Monetary Fund*, First Issue (1962) to Twenty-Fourth Issue (1999), irregular, with Supplements (1976 and 1983) and Annexes (1989 and 1995). Washington, DC, The Fund, 1962– . From the 23rd Issue this title is accessible on the web at: <www.imf.org/external/pubs/ft/seldec/index.htm>.

48. Though each organization shares the same Board of Governors, legally each organization is deemed to hold a separate meeting with the Board at the same time and place.

49. See **IMF Press Release** No. 99/47 September 30, 1999 accessible on the web at: <www.imf.org/external/np/sec/pr/1999/pr9947.htm>.

50. See the IMF website at: <www.imf.org/external/np/exr/facts/groups.htm#DC>, where an extremely useful set of descriptions of most of the international Groups (Group of 7, Group of 24, Group of 77, etc.) as well as these two Committees is given.

51. Besides their printed form, the **Communiqués** of these two Committees and other Groups related to the IMF are accessible via the IMF web page at: <www.imf.org/cgi-shl/create_x.pl?cm+1999>.

52. International Monetary Fund. *Summary Proceedings of the Annual Meeting of the Board of Governors*, First (1946) to Fifty-Third (1998). Annual. Washington, DC, The Fund, 1946- . From the Fiftieth Meeting report, this title is accessible in full-text on the web at: <www.imf.org/external/pubs/ft/summary/sum50.htm>.

53. Ibid., Fifty-Third (1998) p.285.

54. The **JOLIS Library Catalog** contains records for all **monographic items** still held by the Libraries going back to their inception in 1947. The entries for **journal articles** and **working papers** date back to 1982. There is presently under way, however, a program, adding records to the database for newspaper and journal articles *published before 1982*, and held in the **Bretton Woods collection**, a cuttings collection devoted to coverage of the Bretton Woods institutions, that is maintained to this day.

55. See *Annual Report 1999 of the International Monetary Fund*, **Appendix lll K** p.174.

56. These details are specified in the **Information for Researchers**, a guidance note provided to researchers when applying to access the archives. There is also a **Researcher Registration Form**, which the Archivist requires each researcher to complete upon arrival. On the obverse of this form, the **Research Room Rules** are laid out. Full details are given on the Archives entry on the IMF web page at: <www.imf.org/external/np/exr/facts/archive.htm>.

57. The contact details for the IMF Archives are: telephone: 202-623-8625; fax: 202-623-7175; e-mail: archives@imf.org. Postal address: International Monetary Fund, Archives Division, Technology and General Services Department, 700 19th St., NW, Washington, DC 20431.

58. See the IMF Archives website for a detailed description of the files and document series available, at: <www.imf.org/external/np/exr/facts/archive.htm>.

CHAPTER 3
The General Agreement on Tariffs and Trade and the World Trade Organization

(A) Historical Overview, Present Structure, and Functions of the WTO

Susan Hainsworth*

Introduction

For most of the post-World War II period, the international trade regime reflected a broader conflict over principles and mechanisms that would guarantee stable, fair, and equitable trade policies. The Bretton Woods accords anticipated the emergence of an "International Trade Organization" (ITO) to work in conjunction with the World Bank, International Monetary Fund, and several associated treaty agreements to guarantee international economic stability. However, the attempt to create an ITO failed in the late 1940s. The General Agreement on Tariffs and Trade (GATT), an interim multilateral commercial agreement established in 1947 to work within the organizational framework of the proposed ITO, emerged as the *de facto* primary legal instrument for international trade regulation. During the post-Soviet period, the international context within which trade is conducted changed fundamentally. In 1995, the World Trade Organization (WTO) came into existence, embodying many elements of the proposed ITO.

---

*Copyright © Susan Hainsworth. Susan Hainsworth is a Legal Affairs Officer in the Rules Division at the World Trade Organization. The views expressed here in Section A are the author's own and should not be attributed to the World Trade Organization.

The first part of this chapter presents an evolutionary history of the GATT and WTO. This includes sections exploring the principal functions, governance structures, and policy-making environments of the GATT (1947–1994) and WTO (1995–). The second part commences with a review of the major "publication" and "documentation" series of the GATT and WTO. The subsequent section covers bibliographic control and intellectual access to the information products of GATT and WTO. The final section covers availability and dissemination of GATT and WTO information products. A brief conclusion considers the future of WTO as an information provider.

The WTO: Historical Overview

The *Agreement Establishing the World Trade Organization*[1] (the *WTO Agreement*) was concluded by 125 states on 15 April 1994, the result of the eight-year Uruguay Round of Multilateral Trade Negotiations. Its entry into force on 1 January 1995 created the World Trade Organization (WTO), heralding a striking reform of the postwar international trading system. The WTO grew out of the General Agreement on Tariffs and Trade, an international treaty that was signed in 1947 (referred to as the GATT 1947). The GATT 1947 was originally intended as an interim international trade agreement pending the creation of the International Trade Organization (ITO). However, after the attempt to create the ITO in 1948 failed, the GATT 1947 emerged as the primary international legal arrangement governing international trade until the establishment of the WTO in 1995.

The ITO Charter and the Origins of the GATT

The origins of the GATT are inextricably interwoven with the unsuccessful attempt to create the ITO in the early postwar period. Postwar commercial discussions between the United States and the United Kingdom led to the publication in November 1945 of the "Proposals for Consideration by an International Conference on Trade and Employment,"[2] which included "Proposals Concerning an International Trade Organization." They listed suggested areas which could be covered by a future charter for an international trade organization, including trade barriers and restrictions imposed by governments; trade restrictions caused by private cartels; market disorder in primary commodities caused by intergovernmental agreements; and disruptions in domestic production and employment. The Proposals also called for separate negotiations for tariff reduction. The original intent was to create the ITO to complement the work of the International Monetary Fund and the World Bank.

At its first meeting in February 1946, the United Nation's Economic and Social Council (ECOSOC) convened the United Nations Conference on Trade and Employment (Havana Conference). The Havana Conference was charged with drafting a Charter for an ITO and pursuing tariff reduction negotiations.

Early in the preparations, the United States published a "Suggested Charter for an International Trade Organization of the United Nations,"[3] which furnished the foundation for the negotiations. It contained seven chapters, including Chapter IV on commercial policy. The latter evoked the basic commercial principles of most-favored nation (MFN) treatment to the trade of other members, subject to established preferences; negotiations for the reduction of tariffs and the elimination of preferences; and limitation of quotas.

There were four preparatory sessions held from 1946–1948—in London,[4] New York (drafting committee only),[5] Geneva[6] and Havana—in order to negotiate and draft the Havana Charter. In a parallel process, negotiation and drafting of the GATT 1947 occurred at the sessions in 1946–1947 among countries that desired to negotiate to reduce and bind customs tariffs promptly. The GATT 1947, with its schedules indicating the tariff commitments of the contracting parties, was signed by twenty-three countries in Geneva on 30 October 1947. The GATT 1947 was an international commercial agreement and did not create an organization. Because the GATT 1947 was intended only as an interim arrangement pending the entry into force of the Havana Charter and was to be folded into the broader institutional and administrative context of the ITO,[7] contracting parties applied the GATT 1947 only provisionally, through the Protocol of Provisional Application.[8]

The fifty-six-country Havana Conference opened on 21 November 1947. The Final Act, including the text of the Havana Charter, was signed on 24 March 1948.[9] Simultaneous with the signing of the Final Act, the Conference adopted a resolution establishing the Interim Commission for the International Trade Organization (ICITO), on the theory that "pending the establishment of the Organization certain interim functions should be performed."[10] The ICITO had the task of preparing the administrative foundations for the entrance into force of the ITO and clearing up several matters left unresolved at Havana.

The Proposed Structure of the ITO

The Havana Charter would have created the ITO, a full-fledged international trade organization with legal personality and an organizational infrastructure to administer, apply, develop, and enforce the detailed and extensive substantive obligations contained in the Havana Charter. These substantive obligations related to employment; economic development and reconstruction; commercial policy; restrictive business practices; investment and intergovernmental commodity agreements.

The Havana Charter contained provisions concerning governance, decision-making, and dispute settlement. It provided for decision-making by the plenary Conference and the eighteen-member Executive Board by simple majority vote in most situations, although certain decisions (such as amendments to the Charter) required a qualified majority vote. The Havana Charter envisaged a relatively elaborate dispute settlement mechanism for settling state-to-state disputes. Initially, a complaint would be referred to the political organs of the organization for investigation. While the ITO retained the final word on economic and financial questions, a remarkable degree of legalism was apparent in the possibility of requesting an advisory opinion from the International Court of Justice (ICJ) on pure questions of law. The ITO itself retained the responsibility for enforcement, through the authorization of sanctions on a limited and compensatory basis.

After the Havana Charter had been agreed upon at the Havana Conference, factors emerged in the domestic political orders of both of its chief proponents—the United States and Britain—that led to its nonratification in their national legislatures. While the idea of establishing the ITO had floundered, the negotiating and preparatory process for the Havana Conference had borne some fruit. The GATT 1947, and the negotiations proceeding under its aegis, had demonstrated that international trade cooperation was feasible, if in a more limited domain and under a less rigid legal regime. Notwithstanding the ITO's failure, the signatories of the GATT's Protocol of Provisional Application were still bound by the Geneva tariff concessions, as well as major commercial obligations parallel to those that had been contained in the Havana Charter concerning trade and tariff barriers, preferences, and quotas.

The GATT (1947–1994)

The story of the legal and institutional development of the international trade system thus begins with the failed attempt to establish the ITO in 1948–1949. The GATT 1947 had been negotiated as an interim multilateral commercial agreement—devoid of any institutional or organizational elements—to be integrated into the legal and institutional framework of the ITO when the Havana Charter entered into effect.[11] Despite its "provisional" application, it then emerged as the primary legal instrument for international trade regulation. It did not have its own organizational or administrative infrastructure, and borrowed the services of the Secretariat for ICITO (the entity that had been established to make arrangements for the ITO before it became evident that the Havana Charter would not be ratified).

The GATT 1947 evolved from its peculiar origins as a provisional international treaty to a *de facto* international organization. Its informal institutional growth has been cited as an important precedent in international law for the formation of necessary institutional attributes without express legal foundation.[12]

Membership

The GATT 1947 had twenty-three founding contracting parties (because the GATT 1947 was technically an international agreement, rather than an international organization, signatories were referred to as "contracting parties" rather than "members"). By the time of the Tokyo Round negotiations in 1973–1979, there were 102 contracting parties. Just prior to the entry into force of the *WTO Agreement* on 1 January 1995, there were 128 contracting parties.

Governance

The GATT contracting parties,[13] acting jointly, were the only quasi-institutional entity acknowledged in the GATT 1947. The contracting parties based their actions and their exercise of legislative authority on the broad mandate provided to them by Article XXV:1 of the GATT 1947 to further the objectives and facilitate the operation of the Agreement. The GATT contracting parties held regular annual sessions. In 1951, they created an Ad Hoc Committee on Agenda and Intersessional Business to administer matters between sessions.

During the early years of the GATT, the contracting parties acknowledged the need for a more robust institutional structure to support its operation. At the review session in 1954–1955,[14] they made a modest attempt to create an organization (the Organization for Trade Cooperation or "OTC") to administer the GATT 1947. It would have integrated arrangements that had evolved under the GATT 1947 to that time, while leaving the substantive rules of the GATT 1947 intact. The OTC Agreement was a separate legal instrument that consisted exclusively of institutional and procedural provisions. The OTC was to have international legal personality and to establish cooperative arrangements with other intergovernmental organizations. The OTC Agreement made explicit provision for an organizational structure with executive and administrative organs, including a secretariat. Decision-making by a seventeen-member Executive Committee elected by the plenary Assembly would have required a two-thirds qualified majority vote, although the OTC would have had no authority to amend the GATT 1947 nor to take any decision or other action that would have had the effect of imposing a new obligation on a Member that it had not specifically consented to undertake. The OTC Agreement contained no specific provision for an institutionalized legal procedure for the settlement of disputes. Despite the limited nature of this proposed international organization to administer the GATT 1947, the OTC Agreement also met with defeat.

In 1960, the contracting parties created the Council of Representatives. It became the GATT's chief institutional organ.[15] Composed of "representatives of all contracting parties willing to accept the responsibilities of membership," the Council was charged with: considering and making recommendations concerning matters arising between the sessions of the contracting parties requiring urgent attention; considering any other work delegated to it by the contracting parties and "such other matters with which the CONTRACTING PARTIES may deal at their sessions"; supervising committees, working parties, and other subsidiary bodies and making recommendations on their reports; and preparing for sessions of the contracting parties. After 1968, the Council dealt with almost all decision-making and other matters, except for final decision on waivers. It took on most functions relating to dispute settlement under GATT 1947 Article XXIII:2, including the appointment of panel members, the establishment of panel terms of reference and the adoption of panel reports.[16]

In addition to the Council, other organizational entities and subentities were established. For example, the Council or the contracting parties struck standing or *ad hoc* committees to conduct in-depth examinations of certain matters. They also established working parties and panels to conduct dispute settlement functions.

The Council established the Consultative Group of Eighteen (CG-18) in 1975.[17] It was made permanent in 1979.[18] The CG-18 was intended to facilitate the execution by the contracting parties of their responsibilities. The CG-18 was chaired by the Director-General and its membership was broadly representative of GATT composition. It was motivated by the belief "that the GATT should have at its disposal a small but representative group which would permit existing and emerging trade policy issues to be discussed in confidence among responsible officials from capitals and thus facilitate a concentration of policies in the trade field."[19] While it had the potential to act as a nonplenary executive steering group, it never realized this potential. It initially met about three to four times per year, but did not meet in 1988 and was not reconvened for the remainder of the Uruguay Round.

It should be recalled that the Tokyo Round (1973–1979) resulted in a number of side agreements,[20] most of which contained specific institutional arrangements, including an administering Committee to administer the particular agreement. The GATT Secretariat also serviced these Committees.

Decision-Making

Under the GATT 1947, each contracting party technically had one vote. Most decisions of the contracting parties, and of the Council, were technically to be taken by a simple majority vote.[21] Certain decisions—including waivers, accession decisions, and some amendments—had special two-thirds qualified majority voting requirements. Some amendments required unanimous approval. Despite these explicit voting requirements, the practice of consensus prevailed in decision-making. The Chairperson of the body concerned would declare a decision adopted if no delegation formally objected to it. The Committees established under the Tokyo Round agreements also followed this practice.

Secretariat

The GATT was serviced by a small Secretariat headed by a Director-General, who was assisted by a number of deputy directors-general. The Secretariat was divided into divisions, each headed by a director. Each division came under one of the deputy directors-general or directly under the director-general. After the Tokyo Round (1973–1979), the Secretariat also serviced the Committees set up to administer the Tokyo Round Agreements. Certain of the divisions served specific committees or bodies or had other specific duties. The Secretariat also provided technical and legal support to dispute settlement panels. The Statistics Division was responsible for the provision of quantitative information relating to economic and trade policy issues and the publication of annual trade statistics. The Economic Research and Analysis Division provided economic analysis and research in support of the GATT's operational activities, including monitoring and reporting on economic trends developments. The Secretariat produced publications, including the GATT *Annual Report* and the *GATT Focus* newsletter.

Functions

Reduction of Trade Barriers

As stated in the preamble to the GATT 1947, a primary purpose of the Agreement was to enter into "reciprocal and mutually advantageous arrangements directed to the substantial reduction of tariffs and other barriers to trade and to the elimination of discriminatory treatment in international commerce."

A pre-eminent function of the GATT was to act as a forum for negotiations to reduce trade barriers among the contracting parties. Such negotiations occurred at the eight successive rounds of multilateral trade.[22] The first round of tariff negotiations under the GATT resulted in forty-five thousand tariff concessions affecting approximately one-fifth of the total value of global trade. As a result of this and successive rounds, industrial countries' tariff rates on industrial goods had declined steadily to about 6.3 percent.[23]

Along with tariffs, the contracting parties also turned their attention to non-tariff barriers to trade in the Tokyo Round (1973–1979). Because of the procedural and substantive difficulties in amending the GATT 1947 and in the absence of a consensus concerning the scope and content of newly negotiated substantive rights and obligations among all of the contracting parties, the results of the Tokyo Round were limited to a series of side agreements. Most of these agreements contained specific institutional arrangements, including a Committee to administer the operation of the agreement and specific dispute settlement procedures. There was no legal obligation for GATT 1947 contracting parties to adhere to these side agreements, and signatories varied from agreement to agreement.

Dispute Settlement

The GATT 1947 contained dispute settlement procedures in Articles XXII and XXIII to deal with disagreements that arose between contracting parties over the application of the Agreement. These Articles were relatively sparse. They set out the broad parameters for consultation and dispute settlement, but did not contain details concerning the precise procedures to be followed. Practice developed under these Articles, and they were supplemented by successive negotiated texts. The major secondary legal instruments supplementing these basic dispute settlement provisions were: the 1979 *Understanding Regarding Notification, Consultation, Dispute Settlement and Surveillance*[24] (1979 Understanding) negotiated during the Tokyo Round; and the 1989 Decision on *Improvements to the GATT Dispute Settlement Rules and Procedures*[25] (1989 Decision) resulting from the Mid-Term Review of the Uruguay Round. Minor changes to the procedures were introduced in 1958,[26] 1982,[27] and 1984.[28] Procedures concerning disputes with developing countries under Article XXIII were recorded in the Decision of 5 April 1966.[29]

Article XXII of the GATT 1947 set out consultation procedures. Article XXIII furnished the basic principles of dispute settlement, and supplied the foundation for action by the contracting parties. Article XXIII:1 provided that a contracting party could have recourse to dispute settlement when it deemed that any benefit accruing to it was being nullified or impaired or that the attainment of any objective was being impeded as a result of: (a) an alleged violation of the rules by another contracting party; (b) the application by another contracting party of any measure, whether or not it involved a violation; or (c) the existence of any other situation.

Article XXIII:2 provided the broad parameters for dispute settlement procedures. It stated that, if consultations failed to result in a satisfactory adjustment, the matter could be referred to the contracting parties. It further stated: "The CONTRACTING PARTIES shall promptly investigate any matter referred to them and shall make appropriate recommendations to the contracting parties which they consider concerned, or give a ruling on the matter, as appropriate." The contracting parties could authorize a contracting party or parties to suspend concessions or obligations under the Agreement.

Beyond these general guidelines, the GATT 1947 did not elaborate any more precise dispute settlement procedures. It did not indicate the modalities of investigation and review by the contracting parties. In particular, it made no mention of panels or other mechanisms for third party adjudication. Nevertheless, on the basis of this provision, GATT 1947 dispute settlement practice gradually developed. The primary means of resolving disputes were consultations aimed at finding a mutually satisfactory solution. However, where consultations proved fruitless, more formal dispute resolution procedures gradually became available. The procedures evolved pragmatically to accommodate the requirements of particular cases. Early complaints that could not be resolved by negotiations between the parties were dealt with by a "ruling" by the Chairperson of the session of the contracting parties, or by reference to a working party.

Subsequently, the practice evolved of referring unresolved complaints to a panel. The panel was composed of three to five individuals, usually government officials who were not citizens of parties to the dispute. The panel would "assist the CONTRACTING PARTIES" by investigating and making a ruling or recommendation on the matter referred to it, pursuant to its terms of reference. Panels established their own working procedures. The practice was to receive written and oral submissions and to hold two or three informal meetings with the parties. In its report, a panel could recommend the withdrawal of a measure if it was found to be inconsistent with obligations under the Agreement. Where a panel found nonviolation nullification and impairment, it could direct the party concerned to consider ways to make a satisfactory adjustment, without requiring withdrawal of the measure. The panel report would then come before the GATT Council, acting on behalf of the contracting parties, for consideration. Technically, decisions of the Council were to be taken by simple majority vote. However, in practice, decisions were taken by consensus. If there was a consensus among the contracting parties concerning the rulings and recommendations in the report, the report would be adopted.

Adoption of the panel report by the contracting parties gave it binding legal force with respect to the parties to the dispute. It was generally accepted that unadopted reports had no legal value. Counterbalancing the quasijudicial nature of panel examination, the adoption procedure offered a pragmatic safety valve to avoid the imposition of a binding legal obligation on an unwilling contracting party. The practice of seeking consensus on adoption meant that a losing party could block the adoption of a report.

In practice under the GATT 1947, panel reports were not made public unless and until they were adopted. Panel reports consisted of two distinct sections. The first section contained a description of the parties' arguments. As submissions to the panel were confidential, and panel meetings were closed, the descriptive part was the only indication an "outsider" would have of the parties' positions. The second part of the panel report contained the "findings and recommendations" of the panel.

It should be recalled that these dispute settlement procedures developed under the GATT 1947, and so did not automatically apply to disputes arising under the other legal instruments in the GATT system, namely the Tokyo Round Codes. Some of the codes contained their own procedures for the settlement of disputes, which applied only to signatories.

In general, GATT 1947 dispute settlement procedures were effective, and were perceived as such.[30] From 1948 to 1994, 196 complaints were brought under Article XXIII of the GATT. Panels were established in 104 of these cases. Reports were circulated in ninety cases, and eighty-one of these reports were adopted. Thus, resort to dispute settlement was relatively frequent, numerous panels were established, and the majority of panel reports were adopted. Practice under the Tokyo Round Agreements did not reflect quite the same pattern. For example, fewer than half of the ten reports released by panels under the *Tokyo Round Antidumping Code* were adopted.

The WTO (1995–)

Membership

The WTO is a truly global trade organization. As of 17 April 2000, it had 136 Members and over 35 observer governments, including Russia and China. All but five of the observers have applied to accede to the Organization.

Governance

The tasks of the WTO are carried out by the WTO members in an array of councils, committees and subsidiary bodies, assisted by the Secretariat. Figure 3.1 shows the structure of the Organization. The chief decision-making bodies of the WTO, each composed of the entire WTO membership, are the Ministerial Conference and the General Council. A range of subsidiary bodies assists the

Ministerial Conference and the General Council in executing their functions. The subsidiary bodies are also open to the whole WTO membership. In practice, the individuals that actually attend the meetings of these bodies vary depending upon the level of seniority and expertise which may be required to fulfill the functions of a particular body.

Figure 3.1. Structure of the WTO.

```
WTO structure
All WTO members may participate in all councils, committees, etc, except Appellate Body, Dispute Settlement panels
Textiles Monitoring Body, and plurilateral committees

                          ┌─────────────────────────┐
                          │  Ministerial Conference │
                          └───────────┬─────────────┘
                                      │
    General Council meeting as    ┌───┴───────────┐   General Council meeting as
          Trade Policy            │ General Council│       Dispute Settlement
          Review Body             └───┬───────────┘              Body
                                      │
                                                                 Appellate Body
                                                             Dispute Settlement panels

Committees on           Council for          Council for             Council for
 Trade and Environment  Trade in Goods    Trade-Related Aspects    Trade in Services
 Trade and Development                    of Intellectual
 Sub-committee on Least-                    Property Rights
  Developed Countries    Committees on                              Committees on
 Regional Trade           Market Access                              Trade in Financial Services
  Agreements              Agriculture                                Specific Commitments
 Balance-of-Payments      Sanitary & Phytosanitary Measures         Working parties on      Plurilaterals
  Restrictions            Technical Barriers to Trade                Professional Services   Committee on Trade in
 Budget, Finance and      Subsidies & Countervailing Measures        GATS rules                Civil Aircraft
  Administration          Anti-Dumping Practices                                              Committee on Government
Working parties on        Customs Valuation                                                     Procurement
 Accession                Rules of Origin
                          Import Licensing
Working groups on         Trade-Related Investment Measures
 the Relationship between Safeguards
  Trade and Investment
 the Interaction between  Textiles Monitoring Body
  Trade and Competition
  Policy                  Working parties on                  Key
 Transparency in           State-Trading Enterprises           ▬▬▬ Reporting to General Council (or a subsidiary)
  Government Procurement   Preshipment Inspection              ▬ ▬ Reporting to Dispute Settlement Body
                                                               ■ ■ ■ Plurilateral committees inform the General Council of their activities
                                                                     although these agreements are not signed by all WTO members
                                                               The General Council also meets as the Trade Policy Review Body and
                                                               Dispute Settlement Body
September 1997
```

Ministerial Conference

The Ministerial Conference is at the apex of the WTO structure. It meets at least once every two years. The first Ministerial Conference took place in Singapore in December 1996; the second convened in Geneva in May 1998, and the third took place in Seattle in late November and early December 1999. The Ministerial Conference injects high-level political impetus into the WTO system. It is responsible for executing the functions of the WTO. It has authority to take decisions on all matters under any of the Multilateral Trade Agreements, if so requested by a member.

General Council

The General Council assumes the powers and responsibilities, and carries on the functions, of the Ministerial Conference when the latter is not in session. It meets "as appropriate" in the intervals between the meetings of the Ministerial Conference. In practice, the General Council meets approximately once every two months. It conducts the day-to-day operations of the WTO. For example, the General Council considers requests for waivers of obligations under the *WTO Agreement* and considers accessions to the WTO. It also has the authority to adopt interpretations of the *WTO Agreement*. It grants observer status to requesting countries; establishes committees and subsidiary bodies as appropriate; provides a forum where members can voice their views on matters of concern to them; and sets general policy guidelines for the Organization, such as the derestriction of WTO documents adopted in July 1996. These procedures serve to make the operation of the WTO more transparent and are discussed below.

The General Council bears the responsibility for making appropriate arrangements with nongovernmental organizations and with other intergovernmental organizations having mandates relating to that of the WTO. With respect to arrangements for effective cooperation with other intergovernmental organizations, the General Council approved agreements between the International Monetary Fund and the WTO and the World Bank in late 1996.[31] The General Council adopted guidelines on observer status for international intergovernmental organizations, which enable international organizations with competence and a direct interest in trade policy matters, or with responsibilities related to those of the WTO, to follow WTO discussions on matters of direct interest to them. Except where a formal arrangement for cooperation has been made,[32] requests for observer status are considered on a case-by-case basis by each WTO body to which such a request is made. The General Council has also adopted guidelines for arrangements concerning relations with nongovernmental organizations,[33] which direct that the Secretariat should play an active role in its direct contact with NGOs, and develop interaction with NGOs through symposia and arrangements for the exchange of information.

The General Council convenes as appropriate to discharge its duties as the Dispute Settlement Body (DSB) and the Trade Policy Review Body (TPRB). This arrangement promotes consistency in the three functions. The body nevertheless has a different chairperson and particular rules of procedure for each of the three functions. In practice, the DSB meets approximately once a month, or more often if necessary, to carry out its dispute settlement tasks, including the establishment of panels, the adoption of panel and appellate body reports, and the surveillance of implementation of DSB recommendations and rulings resulting from adopted panel and appellate body reports. The TPRB convenes as often as necessary to carry out periodic reviews of individual members' trade policies.

Subsidiary Bodies

To aid the Ministerial Conference and the General Council in executing their functions, there are three Councils. These are: the Council for Trade in

Goods, the Council for Trade in Services and the Council for Trade-Related Aspects of Intellectual Property. Each of these three Councils, which again consist of all WTO members, bears the responsibility for overseeing the substantive multilateral trade agreements under its authority.

Numerous subsidiary bodies report to the Council for Trade in Goods and the Council for Trade in Services. For example, reporting to the Council for Trade in Goods are eleven committees dealing with separate subjects (market access; agriculture; sanitary and phytosanitary measures; technical barriers to trade; subsidies and countervailing measures; anti-dumping; safeguards; rules of origin; customs valuation; import licensing; and investment measures); as well as the Textiles Monitoring Body, and three working parties (notifications; state trading; and preshipment inspection). The bodies reporting to the Council for Trade in Services deal with professional services, General Agreement on Trade and Services (GATS) rules and specific commitments.

There are also several committees that report directly to the General Council. Again, these committees are composed of all WTO members. They concern trade and the environment; trade and development; regional trade agreements; balance-of-payments restrictions; and administrative issues. The Singapore Ministerial Conference in December 1996 struck three working groups on the relationship between trade and investment; the interaction between trade and competition policy; and transparency in government procurement.

The bodies responsible for the two remaining Plurilateral Trade Agreements, dealing with government procurement and trade in civil aircraft, also report directly to the General Council.

Decision-Making

The *WTO Agreement* contains several provisions on decision-making. The general rule is that decisions are taken by consensus. In most cases, consensus is a practice that is a first alternative to voting: where consensus cannot be achieved, the matter is generally put to a simple majority vote. In other cases, consensus is a requirement with no alternative. There are four specific situations in which special voting rules are contemplated: an interpretation of any of the multilateral trade agreements or a waiver of a member's obligation under any of the multilateral trade agreements may be adopted if three-quarters of the members vote in favor. Decisions to amend the multilateral trade agreements can be approved either unanimously or by a two-thirds majority of members depending upon the nature of the amendment concerned. Finally, a decision on the accession of a new member can be taken by a two-thirds majority.

As in the GATT 1947, consensus decision-making is an integral feature of the WTO. It allows every WTO member to ensure that its interests are taken into account. The emphasis on consensus is evident, *inter alia*, in the rules of procedure of the subsidiary bodies: in the event that a decision cannot be reached within a particular council or committee, the matter at issue is to be referred to the General Council for a decision.

Secretariat

With approximately five hundred staff members, the WTO Secretariat is small in comparison with other major international organizations. The Secretariat is headed by the Director-General, currently Mike Moore of New Zealand, who is assisted by four deputy directors-general. Each of the twenty-three divisions, headed by a director, comes under one of the deputy directors-general or directly under the director-general. Some of the divisions serve specific committees or bodies or undertake other duties. For example, the Rules Division services the Committees on Anti-Dumping, Subsidies and Countervailing Measures, Safeguards and Trade in Civil Aircraft, the Working Party on State Trading, and co-services the Working Party on Trade and Competition. The Agriculture Division services the Committees on Agriculture and Sanitary and Phytosanitary Measures. The Secretariat also provides technical and legal support to dispute settlement panels. The Appellate Body has its own small, institutionally distinct secretariat. The Trade Policies Review Division undertakes economic research and analysis of individual members' trade policies and practices in the context of the Trade Policy Review Mechanism. The Statistics Division is responsible for the provision of quantitative information relating to economic and trade policy issues to WTO members and the Secretariat, and the publication of the annual WTO *International Trade Statistics*. The Economic Research and Analysis Division provides economic analysis and research in support of the WTO's operational activities, including monitoring and reporting on current economic developments, and produces publications, including sections of the WTO *Annual Report*. The Information and Media Relations Division publishes, *inter alia*, the *WTO Focus* newsletter. There are approximately thirty in-house translators to facilitate work in the three working languages of the organization (English, French, and Spanish).

Functions

The WTO has five main functions:[34] to facilitate the implementation, administration and operation, and to further the objectives of, the *WTO Agreement* (the essential objective being trade liberalization through the reduction of tariff and non-tariff barriers to trade); to provide a forum for trade negotiations; to settle international trade disputes; to monitor national trade policies; and to cooperate with the IMF and the World Bank. Each of these will be examined briefly.

Implementation of the *WTO Agreement*: Reduction of Trade Barriers

The *WTO Agreement* creates an integrated legal order and establishes the WTO to furnish a unified institutional framework for the conduct of international trade among WTO members. The primary objective of the *WTO Agreement* is trade liberalization through the reduction and elimination of tariff and non-tariff barriers to trade in goods, services, and intellectual property.

The *WTO Agreement* itself is a brief document consisting of a preamble and sixteen Articles. It establishes the WTO and outlines its functions, institutional structure and procedures. The text of the Agreement does not contain any substantive obligations. Rather, the substantive obligations, as well as certain further institutional obligations, are contained in the four annexes to the Agreement. Article II:1 provides that "The WTO shall provide the common institutional framework for the conduct of trade relations among its Members in matters related to the agreements and associated legal instruments included in the Annexes to this Agreement."

Annex I contains the principal substantive agreements. These are the Multilateral Agreements on Trade in Goods, including the GATT 1994[35] (Annex 1A); the *General Agreement on Trade in Services (GATS)* (Annex 1B) and the *Agreement on Trade Related Aspects of Intellectual Property (TRIPs Agreement)* (Annex 1C).

Institutional and procedural agreements for surveillance and enforcement of the obligations set out in Annex 1 follow in Annexes 2 and 3. Annex 2 contains the *Understanding on Rules and Procedures Governing the Settlement of Disputes* (DSU), the dispute settlement rules governing disputes arising between WTO Members under any of the "covered agreements." Annex 3 contains the Trade Policy Review Mechanism (TPRM), providing for the periodic multilateral review of members' trade policies in order to enhance transparency and promote rule-adherence.

Annex 4 contains two Plurilateral Trade Agreements: the *Agreement on Trade in Civil Aircraft*, and the *Agreement on Government Procurement*. These are binding only upon those members that have accepted them. Two additional agreements—the *International Dairy Agreement* and the *International Bovine Meat Agreement*—were originally included in Annex 4. However, in latter years the activities under these agreements were limited to information gathering and the publication of annual reports. Their signatories deemed that these two agreements were no longer serving a useful purpose, and thus decided to dissolve them, with effect from 31 December 1997.

It is the substantive Multilateral Trade Agreements in Annex 1 to the *WTO Agreement*—the GATT 1994 and related goods agreements, the *GATS* and the *TRIPS Agreement*—that spell out the principles of trade liberalization.

Under the GATT 1994, members are subject to the cardinal principle of nondiscrimination in trade in goods, which has two aspects: "most-favored-nation" treatment and "national treatment." The former means that each member must treat all other members equally; the latter means that a member must treat products of other members the same as its own products. In the *Marrakesh Protocol to the GATT 1994*, members have listed their individual tariff and nontariff commitments and concessions on specific categories of goods that were agreed during the Uruguay Round. These include commitments to reduce and "bind" their customs duty rates on imports of goods. In some cases, tariffs were reduced to zero and bound. Once a tariff is "bound" it is difficult to raise (a member would have to negotiate with the countries most concerned and might have to compensate them for loss of trade).[36]

Tariff bindings and nondiscriminatory treatment are essential for securing the smooth and predictable flow of goods. Some of the WTO goods agreements provide for certain derogations in limited circumstances: measures to counteract dumping (selling at an unfairly low price) are governed by the *Agreement on Implementation of Article VI of the GATT 1994 (Anti-Dumping Agreement)*; subsidies and countervailing duties to offset subsidies are governed by the *Agreement on Subsidies and Countervailing Measures*; and emergency safeguard measures are governed by the *Agreement on Safeguards*. In addition, a number of the goods agreements deal with technical, administrative, or legal elements that could constitute barriers to trade: technical regulations and standards; sanitary and phytosanitary measures; import licensing; customs valuation; preshipment inspection; rules of origin and trade-related investment measures.

The GATS is the first set of international legal norms covering international trade in services. It covers all internationally traded services, that is, services supplied from one country to another; consumers or firms using a service in another country; foreign companies setting up branches to provide services in another country; and individuals traveling to supply services in another country. The GATS provides for most-favored-nation treatment, with certain special temporary exceptions. It also provides for national treatment, but only where a member has made a specific commitment in its GATS Schedules, which list a member's commitments to open its markets in specific services sectors. Like tariff commitments under the GATT 1994, commitments under the GATS are "bound" and can only be modified with difficulty, that is, after negotiations with affected countries, which might lead to compensation.

The *TRIPs Agreement* deals with the protection and enforcement of intellectual property rights, that is, rights relating to inventions, designs and creations, such as copyrights, patents, and trademarks. As under the GATT 1994 and GATS, the key to the protection of intellectual property rights under the *TRIPs Agreement* is nondiscrimination (most-favored nation treatment and national treatment). The *TRIPS Agreement* also contains norms to ensure that adequate standards of protection exist in the domestic legal systems of all members relating to: copyright; trademarks; geographical indications; industrial designs; patents; layout designs (topographies) of integrated circuits; and trade secrets.

Forum for Trade Negotiations

The WTO provides the forum for negotiations among members concerning their multilateral trade relations in matters dealt with in the *WTO Agreement*. Many of these agreements explicitly call for further work to be done (the so-called "in-built agenda"). Some of this work has already been accomplished (such as the negotiations held under the auspices of the GATS on financial services and basic telecommunications in 1997–1998), but much of it remains to be done.

The WTO also provides a forum concerning members' multilateral trade relations in other matters as decided by the Ministerial Conference. Thus, members retain the option to pursue negotiations outside the aegis of the WTO concerning trade-related matters not currently within the scope of the *WTO Agreement*.

Dispute Settlement

The WTO dispute settlement system is governed by the DSU, as well as certain special or additional rules and procedures. The DSU introduced significant improvements to the dispute settlement system that had evolved under the GATT 1947. These improvements include: an integrated dispute settlement system administered by the DSB that covers all disputes arising under the *WTO Agreement*; a more structured and timely process; the addition of the Appellate Body to foster consistency in the development of WTO law; automaticity[37] in the establishment of panels, the adoption of panel and Appellate Body reports; and more precise procedures concerning implementation.

The dispute settlement process is becoming more transparent. Panel and Appellate Body reports are now available to the public on the date of their circulation to WTO members, without the necessity of awaiting their adoption by the DSB. As under the GATT 1947, panel reports (and Appellate Body reports) consist of two sections. The first section contains a description of the parties' arguments, while the second contains the panel's findings and conclusions. As submissions to the panel have traditionally been confidential, and panel and Appellate Body meetings have been closed, the descriptive part is the only indication that anyone outside the process would have of the parties' arguments. However, there are indications that certain members may be willing to have their submissions annexed in full to the panel report. If this is the case, general practice may evolve in this direction.

Figure 3.2, page 88, depicts the WTO dispute settlement process. Briefly, the dispute settlement process under the DSU begins when a WTO member launches a complaint by requesting consultations with the member concerned. If consultations fail to result in a mutually agreed solution within sixty days, the complaining party may request the establishment of a panel. At the latest meeting following that at which a first request for a panel is made, the DSB will establish the panel (unless it decides not to do so by consensus). Other members with a substantial interest in the matter may opt to become third parties and enjoy certain rights throughout the panel and appellate process. The panel's terms of reference and composition are then established.

The panel examines the matter referred to it and (within six to nine months) releases its report. The report may either be adopted by the DSB (unless there is a consensus against adoption), or it may be appealed to the Appellate Body. If the report is appealed, the Appellate Body examines the appeal and (within sixty to ninety days) issues its report. The Appellate Body report, and the panel report as modified by the Appellate Body report, are then adopted by the DSB (unless there is a consensus against adoption). If the member concerned is found to be acting inconsistently with its WTO obligations, the DSB will recommend that the member bring its measure into conformity. The member concerned must implement this recommendation within a reasonable period of time.

Figure 3.2. The WTO Dispute Settlement Process.

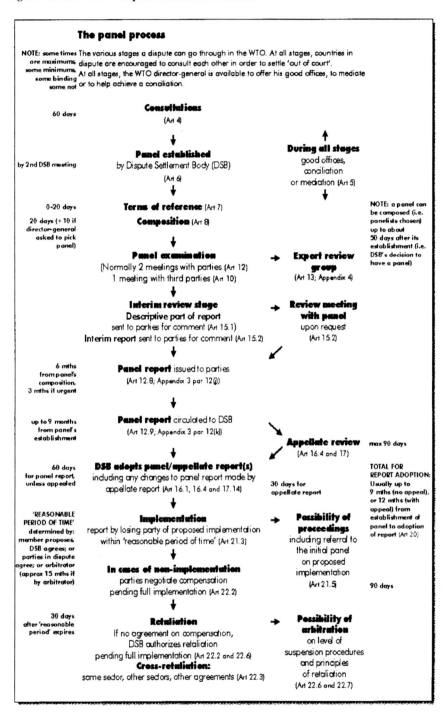

The DSB keeps the implementation of the recommendations and rulings under surveillance. If there is no compliance within a reasonable period of time, the member concerned may negotiate temporary compensation. If the negotiations fail to reach an agreement on mutually acceptable compensation, the complaining party may request that the DSB authorize retaliation through the suspension of concessions or other obligations. Arbitration is available in the event that there is disagreement about the level or type of retaliation.

Binding arbitration is also available as an alternative means of dispute resolution. The DSU also contemplates procedures for good offices, mediation, and conciliation.

WTO dispute settlement has largely been successful. Since the *WTO Agreement* came into effect in January 1995, the number of dispute settlement cases has increased significantly as compared to experience under the GATT 1947. In the almost fifty-year history of the GATT 1947, approximately two hundred complaints were filed. As of 14 March 2000, 190 requests for consultations have been filed since 1 January 1995, concerning approximately 149 distinct matters. The disputes to date have covered a broad range of issues, including many of the issues that were newly integrated into the WTO, such as trade-related aspects of intellectual property, services and trade-related investment measures.

Monitoring Members' Trade Policies

Transparency concerning the trade policies and practices of WTO members is essential to the smooth functioning of the international trading system. It is achieved in two ways. First, WTO members must inform the WTO membership of specific measures, laws, and policies through regular notifications. Second, the WTO conducts regular reviews of individual members' trade policies in the TPRM.

The TPRM trade policy reviews are conducted by the Trade Policy Review Body (TPRB). These "peer reviews" are a multilateral assessment of the individual members' trade policies and practices and of their impact on the world trading system. They aim essentially to improve adherence by all members to the rules in the *WTO Agreement* and to increase transparency and understanding of trade policies. Trade policy reviews are not intended to serve as a basis for the enforcement of specific obligations or for dispute settlement procedures.

While the function of the review is to examine the impact of a member's trade policies and practices on the world trading system, the review takes place against the background of the wider economic and development needs, policies, and objectives of the member concerned. Each trade policy review is conducted on the basis of two documents: a policy statement by the government of the member under review and an economic assessment by the WTO Secretariat. These two reports, together with the proceedings of the Trade Policy Review Body's meetings, are published shortly after the review meeting occurs.

The frequency with which a member's policies come under review depends upon the impact of that member on the functioning of the world trading system, defined in terms of its share of world trade. The Quad countries (Canada, the

European Union, Japan, and the United States) are reviewed once every two years. The next sixteen countries are reviewed every four years. Other members come under review every six years, although a longer period may be set for least-developed countries.

The TPRM was one of the early results of the Uruguay Round, agreed to at the December 1988 Montreal Mid-Term Review, and subsequently adopted in April 1989.[38] While the Uruguay Round's single undertaking approach raised the threat that the TPRM might be eliminated if the rest of the Uruguay Round did not succeed, a GATT Council Decision of 19 July 1989 formally brought the TPRM into effect on a provisional basis, reducing this threat.[39] The entry into force of the *WTO Agreement* in 1995 made the TPRM a basic and permanent function of the WTO and broadened its mandate to cover trade in services and intellectual property.

Cooperation with the IMF and the World Bank

The *WTO Agreement* formally confirmed the status of the WTO as an international organization with a distinct international legal personality. The WTO was established outside the United Nations system and without any formal link to the United Nations. One of the tasks expressly assigned to the WTO is to cooperate with the IMF and the World Bank in order to achieve greater coherence in global economic policy-making. On the basis of this mandate, elaborated in the Uruguay Round *Declaration on the Contribution of the World Trade Organization to Achieving Greater Coherence in Global Economic Policy-making*,[40] the Director-General negotiated agreements with the IMF and the World Bank on behalf of WTO members. These Agreements were approved by the WTO General Council[41] and signed by the Director-General on behalf of the WTO in December 1996 and April 1997, respectively. The Agreements provide for participation of, and cooperation between, the secretariat staffs of the organizations. They deal principally with improving the exchange of information between the organizations to ensure that each organization is cognizant of the rights and obligations of members. They also provide for observer status in certain of each other's decision-making bodies.

The WTO has formalized a relationship with one additional international organization. In December 1995, the WTO concluded an agreement with the World Intellectual Property Organization (WIPO) providing for cooperation between the WTO Secretariat and the international bureau of WIPO concerning technical assistance to developing countries, and the notification and compilation of intellectual property laws of WTO members. This agreement entered into force on 1 January 1996.

(B) DOCUMENTATION AND PUBLICATIONS OF THE GATT AND WTO

Charles Eckman

Major Publication Series and Areas

Throughout GATT's existence, its publishing focused on legal materials related to the trade rounds, studies on the topic of tariff reduction, and gathered and published statistics related to international trade. The WTO has greatly expanded the organization's scope of publishing to include a broad range of trade-related topics, including significant publications in the areas of trade and its impact on environmental degradation and economic development. Some representative recent WTO studies on topics of broad interest include: *Regionalism and the World Trading System* (1995); *Electronic Commerce and the Role of the WTO* (1998); *World Trade and the Environment* (1999); and *Opening Markets in Financial Services and the Role of the GATS* (1997).

Annual Reports

Between 1959 and 1995 the GATT produced an annual overview of trade policy issues and other work before the GATT contracting parties and secretariat entitled *GATT Activities in . . .* (the 1994 and 1995 editions were combined in a single issue). Prior to 1959, an equivalent review appeared in an annual statistical publication entitled *International Trade* described under statistics below. Beginning in 1989 an *Annual Report of the Director General* was issued (the 1993 edition bore the title *Review of Developments in International Trade and the Trading System*).

In 1996 the WTO began issuing a two-volume *Annual Report*. The first volume gives an overview of major events and trends in world trade and the second volume provides statistics, tables and charts. The *Annual Report* is available in both paper and CD-ROM editions.

Current Awareness

Between 1981 and 1995 the newsletter *GATT Focus* was published six times per year. It contained updates on current GATT activities, including extensive reports on Ministerial, Council and various committee meetings. Fifteen issues of a newsletter entitled *GATT WTO News: From GATT to the World Trade Organization* were published between June 1994 and January 1995 documenting the transformation of the organization. In January 1995 the first issue of the *WTO Focus* newsletter was issued, including extensive coverage of activities in the General Council and Ministerial meetings, sections on dispute settlement and trade policy review, and excerpts from substantive reports. In addition to the newsletter, the *WTO Press Release* series reproduces official statements and announcements of activities, publications and other matters of interest to the public. The *Trade and the Environment* press release series (PRESS/TE) beginning in 1995 provides current information on the topic of environmental aspects of trade barrier reductions.

The WTO website [www.wto.org] serves as the most extensive single current awareness service for WTO activities. It includes full-text of all *WTO Focus* issues published since August 1996, a list of meetings, statements and biography of the Director-General, list of new publications, "frequently asked questions" (FAQ) regarding the organization, list of vacancies, and several publications describing the functions and activities of the organization. A more extensive discussion of the website appears below.

Basic Instruments and Selected Documents (BISD)

Between 1952–1969 the GATT published a four-volume set of basic documentation titled *Basic Instruments and Selected Documents (BISD)*. Volume I issued in 1952 reproduced the text of the *General Agreement*. Volume II produced the same year included a set of decisions, declarations, resolutions, and reports. Volume I was subsequently revised in 1955. Volume III incorporating subsequent changes to the original treaty was produced in 1958, and Volume IV reflecting further changes to the treaty was issued in 1969.

Beginning in 1953 a set of annual *Supplements* to the *BISD* have been issued reproducing key protocols, decisions, declarations, understandings, recommendations, and reports. A cumulative subject index is included in each supplement. A searchable CD-ROM version of the comprehensive set—the base set and supplements number 1(1953)–42(1995)—was published in 1998 under the joint imprint of the WTO and Bernan Press.

The WTO in association with Bernan Press plans to resume the series as a WTO publication in both paper and CD-ROM formats. At this writing (May 2000), two to three volumes per year are anticipated in the new *WTO Basic Instruments and Selected Documents* series.

It should be noted that the *BISD* is the most widely distributed compendium of official GATT and WTO documentation. The series was distributed both through sales, and free of charge to all GATT depository libraries from the inception of the organization. Documents published in *BISD* are considered to possess the same legal status as the originals. Citations to the *BISD* are made in the following format:

- *BISD* 27S/131—the cited document is located in the 27th annual supplement to the *BISD*, starting at page 131.

- 1 *BISD* 86—the cited document is located in volume 1 of the four-volume base edition, starting at page 86.

Analytical Index

The *Analytical Index* [symbol ST/LEG/2] is a guide to the interpretation and application of the GATT and a repertoire of GATT practice and drafting history. Six editions have been published since 1952: 1952 (1st); 1966 (2d); 1970 (3d); 1984 (4th); 1989 (5th); and 1994 (6th). The most recent edition—entitled *Analytical Index: Guide to GATT Law and Practice*—is current as of March 1994 and published in both paper and CD-ROM editions under the joint imprint of WTO and Bernan Press. Each chapter covers an article of the *General Agreement*. Included within each chapter are: (1) text of the article and interpretive notes; (2) excerpts from documents concerning the interpretation of the GATT and Havana Charter as well as the practice of the Contracting Parties in the area covered by the article; (3) general account of the relevant preparatory work of the GATT and Havana charter; and (4) a list of relevant documents from the preparatory meetings and early years of GATT through 1954–55. A new edition is in preparation.

Trade Rounds and Associated Legal Texts

Seven of the eight trade rounds conducted between 1947 and 1994 resulted in final acts and associated sets of country tariff schedules negotiated during the rounds. In addition, the Tokyo Round resulted in a number of framework agreements and the Uruguay Round produced the schedules of specific commitments on services, the tariff schedules for trade in goods, and the so-called Plurilateral Agreements. The following list reflects the publication history of the trade rounds in terms of final acts and tariff schedules:

- Geneva 1947. *General Agreement on Tariffs and Trade, with Annexes and Schedules of Tariff Concessions*. Published in four volumes. 30 October 1947.

- Annecy 1949. *Annecy Protocol of Terms of Accession*. 10 October 1949.

- Torquay 1951. *Torquay Protocol*. 21 April 1951.

- Geneva 1956. No final act.

- Geneva 1960–61 (Kennedy Round). *Protocol Embodying the Results of the 1960–61 Tariff Conference*. 16 July 1962.

- Geneva 1973–79 (Tokyo Round). *Geneva 1979 Protocol*. 30 June 1979. Published in four volumes.

- Geneva 1986–1994 (Uruguay Round). *Final Act Embodying the Results of the Uruguay Round of Multilateral Trade Negotiations*. 15 April 1994.

Supplementary to the trade rounds, protocols of modification and rectification to the schedules are issued, along with protocols modifying treaty texts, accession instruments, and supplementary protocols. These are published after the final act and can be identified within a legal instruments series registered by the Legal Affairs Division: *certified legal instruments.* The certified legal instruments series gathers together all GATT and WTO legal instruments and numbers them sequentially.

A numerical and subject index to the certified legal instruments series is found in the loose-leaf publication *GATT: Status of Legal Instruments* [symbol ST/LEG/1]. Entries in this loose-leaf title include reference to sources of the legal text, either as an official numbered GATT publication, citation to the *BISD*, or the *United Nations Treaty Series.* As of 1998, the number of certified legal instruments recorded in the *GATT: Status of Legal Instruments* was 209. A new edition of this loose-leaf title was published in 1997, *World Trade Organization: Status of Legal Instruments* [symbol ST/Leg/1]. As of May 2000, fifteen WTO legal instruments have been certified.

Uruguay Round

The seven-year Uruguay Round was the longest trade round in GATT negotiating history, and it resulted in a larger publishing output than any of its predecessors. A complete publication including all the country schedules of commitments in services, the tariff schedules for trade in goods was published in 1994 in a thirty-four-volume set under the title *Legal Instruments Embodying the Results of the Uruguay Round:*

Volume 1:	*The Results of the Uruguay Round of Multilateral Trade Negotiations: The Legal Texts.* A six-hundred-page compilation of the basic legal texts.
Volumes 2–26:	*Tariff Schedules for Trade in Goods.*
Volume 27:	*Legal Texts* (those not included in Volume 1).
Volumes 28–30:	*Schedules of Specific Commitments for Trade in Services.*
Volume 31:	*Plurilateral Agreements.*
Volumes 32–34:	*Schedules on Services and Goods* submitted after 15 April 1994

A CD-ROM version of the complete thirty-four-volume set was published in February 1996.

Panel Reports

As indicated earlier in this chapter, publication of final panel reports under GATT 1947 depended upon their adoption. Those reports that were not adopted were not made public. Those that were adopted were published in the *BISD* series.

Under the rules of the WTO, panel and Appellate Body reports are made available to the public on the date of their circulation to WTO members, without the necessity of their adoption by the Dispute Settlement Body. They are made immediately available on the WTO website under the document series symbol WT/DS. A collective annotated set of full-text panel reports has been published by Bernan Press since 1996. The series—*World Trade Organization Dispute Settlement Decisions: Bernan's Annotated Reporter*—includes the final report, procedural history, conclusions, annotations, a table of references, index by countries party to disputes, and a subject index.

Trade Policy Reviews

As described earlier, the Trade Policy Review Mechanism was established as a function of the GATT in 1989 during the Uruguay Round. The evaluation is conducted by the GATT Council on the basis of two reports: one presented by the government of the country concerned; and the other presented by the GATT Secretariat including a background report generated by the Secretariat, concluding remarks by the Chairman of the Trade Policy Review Board, and minutes of the Board meeting at which the country and Secretariat reports were reviewed. Reviews are conducted once every two years for the world's four top trading countries, every four years for the next sixteen top trading countries, and every six years for other countries. Since 1989 more than one hundred reports have been issued in paper format. A cumulative CD-ROM covering all reports issued 1995–1998 was published in 1999. These reports are rich sources of country information, frequently including within the Secretariat reports original trade data organized by the Statistics Division on the basis of its internal statistical database.

Statistics

The Statistics Division of the WTO is responsible for statistical support functions, including both internal and external dissemination of statistics. With regard to published materials, the Division plays a key role in gathering data for the background reports that are published in the Trade Policy Review series described earlier. In addition, the Division produces data for an annual publication covering statistics of international trade beginning in 1952 entitled *International Trade* (1952–1990/91), *International Trade: Statistics* (1991/92–1993) and *International Trade: Trends and Statistics* (1994–1995). Issues for 1988–1991/92 were produced in two volumes, the first volume entitled *Review of Developments in International Trade and the Trading System* and the second volume containing charts and tables. Since the establishment of the WTO, the statistical annual appears as volume two of the WTO *Annual Report* and is available in both print and CD-ROM versions.

The Statistics Division has also been responsible for providing data necessary to the conduct of the various trade negotiating rounds. Most of this data is never made available outside of the organization. One significant exception was the GATT Tariff Study prepared for the Kennedy and Tokyo Rounds. A CD-ROM version of the Statistics Division internal database for tracking tariff rates—the *Integrated Database*—has been published and made available for internal use by WTO members.

Reference Material

Both GATT and the WTO have published useful reference materials, including directories, bibliographies, thesauri, and organizational primers. A few examples follow.

The *GATT Bibliography* (1947–1971) listed books, pamphlets, journal articles, newspaper reports, and editorials that refer to the General Agreement on Tariffs and Trade. The *GATT Bibliography* was divided into a chronological listing of references, grouped in alphabetical order month by month. The first edition appeared in March 1954 and covered the time period 1947–1953. Annual supplements were published between 1954 and 1971.

The *Trilingual Glossary* (1998) is a thorough glossary—in English, French, and Spanish—of WTO and international-trade related words, phrases and acronyms, with definitions and references to original sources. It includes terminology developed during the Uruguay Round and incorporated within the legal instruments in the Final Act.

Trading into the Future: Introduction to the World Trade Organization (1st ed. 1995, 2d ed. 1998) serves as an excellent introduction to the history, organization, functions, and policy-making process within the WTO. A case study is used to depict the dispute settlement process.

Documentation

GATT and WTO documentation refers to the internal information products of the two organizations. As distinct from publications, intended for a general audience, documents are produced primarily for internal circulation within the Secretariat and among member governments. The documents of the two organizations include meeting minutes, meeting summaries, agendas, lists of participants, reports and working papers, and other sources of interest to anyone tracing the history of a particular policy decision of the organizations.

The single best introduction to the extensive and complex documentation series produced by GATT and WTO is the *World Trade Organization Guide to Documentation* (WTO Document Systems Section, Translation and Documentation Division, 2d ed., August 1998). In general, the document symbol numbers for the two organizations use common standard abbreviations. **INF** for Information note, **LET** for Letter, **M** for Minutes, **N** for Notification, **R** for Report, **SPEC** for Special Series, **SR** for Meeting Summary, **W** for Working Paper.

GATT 1947, Tokyo Round, and Uruguay Round Documentation

Documents of the GATT were issued under a symbol number system based on the issuing body. Basic reports and other documents not related to a particular division or body were assigned a number in the general document series "L/" (limited distribution) or the information series "INF/". Table 3.1 shows examples of other key document series issued by GATT. Tokyo Round documents were issued under a variety of symbols including those shown in Table 3.2. Uruguay Round documents were generally issued under the "MTN" symbol subdivided by the specific negotiating or working group, including examples shown in Table 3.3, page 98.

Table 3.1
Key GATT Document Series

Committee on Balance-of-Payments Restrictions	BOP/, BOP/R/, BOP/W/
Council	C/, C/COM, C/M/, C/W
Committee on Trade and Development	COM.TD/
Textiles Committee	COM/TEX/, COM/TEX/W
Dispute Settlement	DSNUMBER/
Contracting Parties meeting records	SR.NUMBER/
Committee on Tariff Concessions	TAR/
Working Documents relating CP sessions	W.NUMBER/

Table 3.2
Tokyo Round Documents

Committee on Anti-Dumping Practices	ADP/, ADP/M
Committee on Trade in Civil Aviation	AIR/, AIR/M/, AIR/W/
International Dairy Products Council	DPC/, DPC/W/
International Meat Council	IMC/, IMC/W/
Committee on Subsidies and Countervailing Measures	SCM/, SCM/M, SCM/Spec/

Table 3.3
Uruguay Round Documents

Group of Negotiations on Goods	MTN.GNG
Negotiating Group on Market Access	MTN.GNG/MA/
Negotiating Group on Tariff Measures	MTN.GNG/NG1
Negotiating Group on Non-Tariff Measures	MTN.GNG/NG2/
Negotiating Group on Agriculture	MTN.GNG/NG5
Negotiating Group on Trade-Related Aspects of Intellectual Property Rights . . .	MTN.GNG/TRIPS/
Group on Negotiations on Services	MTN.GNS/
Trade Negotiations Committee	MTN.TNC/, MTN/TNC/W

In 1997, a compilation of over ten-thousand Uruguay Round, GATT 1947 and Tokyo Round documents entitled *GATT and Uruguay Round Documents September 1986–December 1996* was issued on CD-ROM for internal use of the WTO membership.

WTO Documentation

The WTO has applied a new series of symbols to its basic documentation. The basic scheme is twofold. The first element of the symbol describes a "common legal framework." Within the legal framework, a second element describes a "series" concept. Table 3.4 provides selected examples.

Table 3.4
WTO Document Series

World Trade Overseeing Bodies	General Council (WT/GC/) Balance of Payments (WT/BOP/) Dispute Settlement (WT/DS/)
Trade in Goods	Council (G/C) Anti-Dumpting (G/ADP/) Safeguards (G/SG/)
Trade in Services	Council (S/C/) Trade in Financial Services (S/FIN/)
Intellectual Property	Council (IP/C/) Notifications (IP/N/)

Bibliographic Control

Publications of GATT and WTO

Intellectual access to publications of the GATT and WTO is gained through the standard indexes to international organization publications. In terms of historical GATT material, these indexes include the *United Nations Documents Index* that between 1950–1962 indexed the publications of the specialized agencies, IAEA and GATT, and the quarterly *International Bibliography, Information, Documentation* published 1973–1991. The annual publications catalogs of the GATT and WTO in continuous print since 1964 provide lists of sales publications available at the time the catalog was printed. Statistical publications are indexed since 1983 in the *Index to International Statistics* (IIS), published since 1999 as a component within the *Statistical Universe* web service.

GATT Documentation

There is no single cumulative index to the entire internal documentation of the GATT. The latest annual supplement to the *BISD* series provides a good index to a selection of the public documentation of the GATT. But for a thorough search, the researcher must rely upon a series of "lists" and "indexes." Between 1953 and 1980 a numerical list and/or index of documents issued was published on an annual basis. During this time, the *List of Documents Issued* was published separately from a parallel *Documents Index*. In 1981 these publications were merged to form a *List and Index of Documents Issued*. Annual editions of this index were produced through 1997. In addition, cumulative editions covering the periods 1984–1988 and 1989–1992 were produced. The *List and Index* includes indexes by subject, product, country, and articles of the main legal texts. Table 3.5, page 100, identifies the existence of individual Lists and/or Indexes to GATT documentation for the time period 1953-1980 including their specific INF/symbol number.

Uruguay Round Documentation

A separate paper index to the documentation of the Uruguay Round was printed in 1994. The *List and Index of Uruguay Round Documents Issued Between 1986–1994* includes a detailed listing of all Uruguay Round documents, both restricted and derestricted.

WTO Documentation

WTO documentation that has been made public is searchable on the WTO website. The *List & Index of Documents Issued* is also available on the site. Visitors to the site can browse all documents released in the past thirty days, or search by document symbol number, title word, or full-text.

Table 3.5
Lists and/or Indexes to GATT Documentation

	List	Index
November 1953–31 March 1955 + 23/Add.1	INF/23	
1 April–December 1955	INF/35	
1 January 1954–31 March 1955		INF/3/Rev.2
1956	INF/42	INF/44
1957	INF/55	INF/54
1958	INF/68	INF/67
1959	INF/81	INF/79
1960	INF/86	INF/87
1961	INF/95	INF/98
1962	INF/99	INF/100
1963	INF/105	INF/106
1964	INF/110	INF/111
1965	INF/118	INF/117
1966	INF/123	INF/124
1967	INF/129	INF/130
1968	INF/134	INF/135
1969	INF/138	INF/139
1970	INF/141	INF/142
1971	INF/148	INF/149
1972	INF/151	INF/153
1973	INF/155	INF/157
1974	INF/159	INF/161
1975	INF/165	INF/167
1976	INF/169	INF/171
1977	INF/173	INF/177
1978	INF/179	INF/180
1979	INF/189	INF/191
1980	INF/198	INF/196

Availability and Dissemination

Sales Program

Both GATT and the WTO have maintained extensive sales programs and promoted them through issuance of annual publication lists continuously since 1964. The WTO has developed an increasing array of electronic resources and relies more and more on copublication as a vehicle for broader distribution of its sales publications. The current contact for WTO publications is the Information and Media Relations Division, Centre William Rappard, Rue de Lausanne 154, CH-1211 Geneva 21, Switzerland. The latest publications list contains an updated list of distributors worldwide.

Depository Library Program

The GATT supported a wide network of depository libraries that were automatically sent a range of sales publications. According to the latest official list there were more than three hundred GATT depository libraries worldwide in May 1994 [*GATT Depository Libraries*, INT(94)16]. All depository libraries were entitled to receive free of charge a range of monographs and legal texts as well as all publications in the following series:

- *Basic Instruments and Selected Documents*
- *International Trade*
- *Activities of GATT*
- *GATT Studies in International Trade*
- *Trade Policy Review*

The latest official list of titles deposited can be found in *GATT Depository Libraries, List of the Publications Deposited in Each Library*, INT(94)15 May 1994.

The WTO continues to supply a broad range of its monographic publications—as well as titles in the current incarnation of the GATT series listed above—to former GATT depositories.

Restriction of Document Distribution

The vast majority of WTO documentation (as was GATT documentation) is produced specifically for the use of member governments to inform them during negotiations. There is an increasing awareness within both the WTO membership and Secretariat that the citizenry of member and nonmember countries is interested in access to this information. Under the GATT, almost all documentation was automatically designated "restricted." Derestriction of this material was a cumbersome process requiring the approval of GATT contracting parties. The Secretariat could propose documents for derestriction, but contracting parties retained the final right to approve derestriction. As a result, as of May 2000, roughly 40 percent of GATT documentation remains restricted and inaccessible to public scrutiny, as does nearly all the documentation of the Tokyo and Uruguay Rounds.

On July 18, 1996, the WTO's General Council agreed to make more information about WTO activities available directly to the public, and decided that public information, including deresticted internal documentation, would be made available freely over the internet. This decision was codified in *Procedures for the Circulation and Derestriction of WTO Documents* (WT/L/160/Rev.1) issued 26 July 1996. According to the new procedures, "documents circulated after the date of entry into force of the Marrakesh Agreement Establishing the World Trade Organization shall be circulated as unrestricted with the exception of documents specified in the attached Appendix . . ." (WT/L/160/Rev.1/ page 1). In fact, the list of exceptions was extensive. However, under the new guidelines, any member can propose documents for derestriction. A semiannual list is distributed and failing objection by any member any document proposed for derestriction is automatically made public. Documents remaining restricted due to a member's objection are automatically resubmitted for derestriction after one year has elapsed. The streamlining of document derestriction practices in the organization and the design of a freely accessible online documentation system for WTO documents, the Documents Dissemination Facility (DDF), have greatly enhanced access to information on the WTO's internal policy-making environment.

Documentation Distribution (Print)

Print documentation of the GATT and WTO has been strictly limited to internal use, including Secretariat staff, GATT contracting parties, and WTO members. Some documentation is not made available to Secretariat staff.

Documentation Distribution (Microform)

In the 1970s the GATT established a microfiche publication service. The Microfiche Service produced two standing order plans: a *Microfiche Collection for Governments* and a *Microfiche Collection for Libraries*. Both plans involved the distribution of an annual set of microfiche. The collection for governments was available only to GATT contracting parties and WTO members and included all documents, both restricted and derestricted, issued since 1948. The collection for libraries was made available generally to libraries and excluded all restricted documentation. The WTO eliminated its microfiche services after the 1997 sets were published and distributed.

Documentation Distribution (Internet)

Since 1996 all WTO documents with certain exceptions are published on the WTO web server. Documents excluded at present include the following series: Administrative Memo; G/TMB/Spec; G/TMB/W/; IDA/W/; IMA/; IMA/INV/; IMA/SPEC/; IMA/W/; INT( ); Office Circular; OFFICE (except external vacancy announcements); and Vacancy Notice (internal). The public has access to all derestricted documents through the DDF available directly on the public WTO website (<www.wto.org/english/docs_e/ddf_e/ddf_e.htm>). The web service allows searching by document symbol number, title words, and full-text. Documents are stored in word-processed format. Over two hundred thousand documents in the three official languages of the WTO (English, French, and Spanish) were available in early 2000.

Future of the WTO as an Information Provider

Dramatic technological change continues to dominate the global information and publishing environments. It is therefore very difficult to make informed predictions regarding any organization's information practices in the near or long term. However, it does appear that the following three current trends are driven by internal and external factors and conditions that are likely to persist for the next several years:

- increased reliance on and vitality of the WTO website;
- copublishing with the commercial sector; and
- pressure to derestrict more quickly a broader range of internal and administrative documentation.

WTO Website

The WTO website has grown at a phenomenal rate. At present it provides one of the richest sources of freely available information maintained within the community of international governmental organizations. A large amount of public information pertaining to the history, functions, and structure of the organization is available. In addition to press releases, vacancy announcements and other "current awareness" material, the site is being used to distribute panel reports, all derestricted internal documents and selected statistics. The WTO is even considering the possibility for using the website to facilitate communication with individuals and nongovernmental bodies interested in international trade and related issues. International public interest in the activities of the WTO has grown quickly since the founding of the organization, and it is likely that this avenue of access to information about itself will be its most effective means of responding to the international community's need for information.

Copublishing

The WTO has established an apparently broad working relationship with the commercial publisher Bernan Press in the area of sales publications. This relationship includes several major print and electronic publications, constituting a wide range of core organizational information products. The extensive nature of the relationship suggests that the partnership is likely to be a long-term one. However, this could change. Other international governmental organizations are finding "external printing" less cost-effective as a result of technological changes within their organizations (see the recent provisional report by the Secretary-General to the Advisory Committee on Administrative and Budgetary Questions, "Internal and External Printing Practices at the Organization: Note by the Secretary-General," UN Document A/C.5/54/18, 15 October 1999).

Derestriction

As noted earlier, the WTO has made tremendous strides in providing public access to information about the organization's policy-making process. This is evidenced both by the WTO's commitment to a streamlined process for derestriction of its documentation and by its continued commitment to free public distribution of documentation over the internet. Given the heightened interest of citizens throughout the world in the activities of the WTO, as evidenced most dramatically at the Seattle Ministerial in late 1999, it is unlikely that these access-friendly policies will be overturned. Unfortunately, legal responsibility for derestricting GATT documentation remains ambiguous. And it is not clear when, if ever, the public will gain access to a large amount of historic restricted GATT policy documentation, the original grounds for whose classification as restricted or confidential have long since disappeared.

Notes and References

1. Done at Marrakesh, 15 April 1994. GATT, *The Results of the Uruguay Round of Multilateral Trade Negotiations: The Legal Texts* (Geneva: GATT, 1994).

2. United States, Department of State, *Proposals for Expansion of World Trade and Employment* (Washington, DC: Department of State, November 1945). Commercial Policy Series No. 79; Department of State Publication No. 2411.

3. United States, Department of State, *United States Suggested Charter* (Washington, DC: Department of State, 1946). Commercial Policy Series No. 92; Department of State Publication No. 2598.

4. See *Report of the First Session of the Preparatory Committee of the United Nations Conference on Trade and Employment*, United Nations Document E/PC/T/33 (London: UN, October 1946) ("London Report").

5. See *Report of the Drafting Committee of the Preparatory Committee of the United Nations Conference on Trade and Employment 20 January–25 February 1947*, United Nations Document E/PC/T/34 (New York: UN, 1947) ("New York Report"). The Drafting Committee produced the first full draft of the GATT 1947.

6. See *Report of the Second Session of the Preparatory Committee of the United Nations Conference on Trade and Employment*, United Nations Document E/PC/T/186, 10 September 1947 (Geneva: UN, 1947) ("Geneva Report").

7. See GATT 1947, Article XXIX. See also Drafting Committee of the Preparatory Committee of the United Nations Conference on Trade and Development, *Report of the Technical Sub-Committee (covering Articles 15–23 and 37)*, United Nations Document E/PC/T/C.6/55/Rev. 1 ([Geneva?]: UN, 1947).

8. *Final Act Adopted at the Conclusion of the Second Session of the Preparatory Committee of the United Nations Conference on Trade and Employment* 55 UNTS at 187 and 194. See United Nations Document E/PC/T/C.6/55 (1947) and London Report, p. 22–25; New York Report, p. 45.

9. *Final Act and Related Documents*, United Nations Conference on Trade and Employment, Havana, Cuba, November 21, 1947 to March 24, 1948, United Nations Document ICITO/1/4 (1948). The text of the Charter is also published in: E/Conf.2/78 (March 24, 1949), reprinted as United Nations Document ICITO/1/4/ (1948) and in U.S. Department of State Publication No. 3206, Commercial Policy Series No. 114 (1948).

10. "Resolution establishing an Interim Commission for an International Trade Organization Adopted upon Signing of the Havana Conference Final Act," 24 March 1948 in *Final Act and Related Documents*, E/CONF.2/78 or ICITO/1/4. The ICITO was to cease to exist upon the appointment of the ITO Director-General.

11. See GATT 1947, Article XXIX. See also United Nations Document E/PC/T/C.6/55 (1947).

12. John Jackson, *World Trade and the Law of GATT* (New York: Bobbs-Merrill, 1969), p. 153.

13. The CONTRACTING PARTIES, in capital letters, refer to the contracting parties acting jointly and collectively.

14. General Agreement on Tariffs and Trade, "Agreement on the Organization for Trade Co-operation." *Basic Instruments and Selected Documents (BISD)*. Volume I (revised). 75–84 (Geneva: GATT, 1955). See also the *Report on Organizational and Functional Questions* (L/327), adopted 28 February, 5 and 7 March, 1955, *BISD* 3S/231.

15. The Ad Hoc Committee on Agenda and Intersessional Business was made permanent by the CONTRACTING PARTIES in 1955 and renamed the "Intersessional Committee" (*BISD* 3S/9, 246). By the Decision of 4 June 1960, the CONTRACTING PARTIES terminated the Intersessional Committee and delegated its functions to the Council of Representatives (*BISD* 9S/7).

16. The Decision taken at the Twenty-Fifth session, 25 November 1968, SR.25/9, December 1968, p. 176, gave the Council an expanded role to allow the contracting parties to concentrate on major issues at their sessions.

17. Council Decision of 11 July 1975, *BISD* 22S/15.

18. *BISD* 26S/289.

19. L/4869, *BISD* 26S/284, p. 285.

20. *Agreement on Technical Barriers to Trade*, BISD 26S/8; *Agreement on Implementation of Article VII of the GATT—Protocol to the Agreement on Implementation of Article VII of the GATT*, BISD 26S/116, 151; *Agreement on Implementation of Article VI of the GATT* (the "*Tokyo Round Anti-Dumping Code*"), BISD 26S/171; *Agreement on Interpretation and Application of Articles VI, XVI and XXIII of the General Agreement on Tariffs and Trade* (the "*Tokyo Round SCM Code*"), BISD 26S/56; *Agreement on Import Licensing Procedures*, BISD

26S/154; *Agreement on Government Procurement*, BISD 26S/33; and *Agreement on Trade in Civil Aircraft*, BISD 26S/162.

21. The 1960 Decision establishing the Council clarified that Council decisions were technically to be taken by a majority of the contracting parties, including those who were nonmembers of the Council and those who were absent (*BISD* 9S/7-80).

22. The eight Rounds of Multilateral Trade Negotiations were: Geneva (1947); Annecy (1949); Torquay (1951); Geneva (1956); Dillon Round (1960–1961); Kennedy Round (1964–1967); Tokyo Round (1973–1979); Uruguay Round (1986–1993).

23. See World Trade Organization. Information and Media Relations Division. *Trading into the Future: WTO, the World Trade Organization*, 2d ed. (Geneva: WTO, 1998), paras. 1.8 and 1.4. This is also available on the WTO website, <www.wto.org>.

24. Adopted 28 November 1979, *BISD* 26S/210.

25. Decision of 12 April 1989, *BISD* 36S/61.

26. Procedures Under Article XXII on Questions Affecting the Interests of a Number of Contracting Parties, adopted 10 November 1958, *BISD* 7S/24.

27. The 1982 Ministerial Declaration on Dispute Settlement, *BISD* 29S/9, pp. 13–16.

28. Decision of 30 November 1984: Dispute Settlement Procedures, *BISD* 31S/9.

29. *BISD* 14S/18.

30. See Robert Hudec, *Enforcing International Trade Law: The Evolution of the GATT Legal System* (Salem, NH: Butterworths, 1993).

31. WT/L/195, 18 November 1996. See Minutes of the General Council Meeting on 7, 8 and 13 November 1996, WT/GC/M/16, 6 December 1996. Both are internal WTO documents.

32. International organization observers to the General Council include: United Nations (UN), United Nations Conference on Trade and Development (UNCTAD), International Monetary Fund (IMF), World Bank, Food and Agricultural Organization (FAO), World Intellectual Property Organization (WIPO), Organisation for Economic Co-operation and Development (OECD). Observers in other councils and committees may differ.

33. WT/L/162, 23 July 1996, adopted 18 July 1996; WT/GC/M/13, 28 August 1996. Internal WTO documents.

34. These functions are listed in Article III of the *WTO Agreement*.

35. The GATT 1994 is basically an updated version of the GATT 1947. All references to "contracting parties" have been replaced by "Members." All references to the "CONTRACTING PARTIES acting jointly" have been replaced by either "the WTO" or "the Ministerial Conference."

36. See WTO, *Trading into the Future* (WTO: Geneva, 1997), para. 2.3. This is also available on the WTO website, www.wto.org. Developed countries' tariff cuts were largely to be phased in over a five-year period from 1 January 1995. The resulting cut in tariffs on industrialized products will be 40%, falling from an average of 6.3% to 3.8%. The value of industrial product imports that receive duty free treatment in developed countries will increase from 20% to 44%. In addition, fewer products are subject to a high duty of 15% or more: for developed country imports from all sources, the proportion has declined from 7% to 5%; for developed country imports from developing countries, the proportion has gone from 9% to 5%. Moreover, Members increased the number of products subject to tariff bindings: for developed countries, the number of bindings went from 78% of product lines to 99%; for developing countries, the increase was from 21% to 73% and for economies in transition, the increase was from 73% to 98%. In addition, tariffs on agricultural products are now bound.

37. "Automaticity" means that the decision is taken by the DSB unless there is a consensus *against* taking it.

38. "Functioning of the GATT System," adopted 12 April 1989, *BISD* 36S/403 (1990).

39. "Trade Policy Review Mechanism—1989 & 1990," 19 July 1989, *BISD* 36S/406 (1990).

40. This declaration is among the Ministerial Decisions and Declarations adopted by the Trade Negotiations Committee on 15 December 1993. It is reproduced in GATT, *The Results of the Uruguay Round of Multilateral Trade Negotiations: The Legal Texts* (Geneva: GATT, 1994), p. 442.

41. WT/L/195, 18 November 1996. See Minutes of the General Council Meeting on 7, 8 and 13 November 1996, WT/GC/M/16, 6 December 1996.

CHAPTER 4

La Francophonie: An Emerging International Governmental Organization

Juris Dilevko

Introduction

La Francophonie, officially called the Organisation internationale de la Francophonie (OIF) since 1998, may best be characterized as a little-known international organization that in the late 1990s made a number of structural changes in an attempt to become a significant international institution and an indispensable participant in world political and economic affairs. As its name suggests, OIF is the official voice of the world community of French-speaking countries and regions, or the collective unit formed by French-speaking people. Although France is the nominal leader of the OIF, it is by no means its dominant power. Of the approximately 150 million francophones worldwide (some 105 million speak French on a daily basis, while another 50 million know French either as a second or third language), about 60 percent live outside France in more than fifty countries on five continents. OIF thus consists of forty-four member states, three regional subnational governments (called "participating governments"), and three observer nations (see Table 4.1).

It is approximately the same size as the Commonwealth organization of nations, which has fifty-three member states, seven of which overlap with OIF.

In one sense, OIF sees itself as a French-oriented counterweight to the growing hegemony of English-speaking countries, especially the United States, and, more particularly, to the all-encompassing, ubiquitous reach of English language and culture. And because it is neither a continent-centered political and economic organization like the European Union (EU) nor a continent-based economic and trading bloc such as NAFTA (North American Free Trade Agreement)

Table 4.1
Member Countries of the Organisation internationale de la Francophonie and Commonwealth

Francophonie (OIF)	Commonwealth
Benin	Antigua and Barbuda
Bulgaria	Australia
Burkina Faso	Bahamas
Burundi	Bangladesh
Cambodia	Barbados
Cameroon	Belize
Canada	Botswana
Cape Verde	Britain
Central African Republic	Brunei
Chad	**Cameroon**
Comoros	**Canada**
Congo-Brazzaville	Cyprus
Congo-Kinshasa	**Dominica**
Djibouti	The Gambia
Dominica	Ghana
Egypt	Grenada
Equatorial Guinea	Guyana
France	India
Gabon	Jamaica
Guinea	Kenya
Guinea-Bissau	Kiribati
Haiti	Lesotho
Ivory Coast	Malawi
Laos	Malaysia
Lebanon	Maldives
Luxembourg	Malta
Madagascar	**Mauritius**
Mali	Mozambique
Mauritania	Namibia
Mauritius	Nauru
Moldova	New Zealand
Monaco	Nigeria
Morocco	Pakistan
Niger	Papua New Guinea
Romania	St. Kitts and Nevis
Rwanda	**St. Lucia**
St. Lucia	St. Vincent and the Grenadines
Senegal	**Seychelles**
Seychelles	Sierra Leone
Switzerland	Singapore
Togo	Solomon Islands
Tunisia	South Africa
Vanuatu	Sri Lanka
Vietnam	Swaziland
	Tanzania
New Brunswick (participating government)	Tonga
Quebec (participating government)	Trinidad and Tobago
Wallonia-Brussels (participating government)	Tuvalu
	Uganda
Albania (observer)	**Vanuatu**
Macedonia (observer)	Western Samoa
Poland (observer)	Zambia
	Zimbabwe

or MERCOSUR (Mercado Comun del Sur: The Southern Common Market consisting of Argentina, Brazil, Paraguay, Uruguay, Bolivia, and Chile), it also views itself as being able to transcend regional and parochial interests in order to speak with an authoritative global voice about social and cultural principles that it feels are being neglected.

However, OIF is a newcomer on the international stage, and, up to the end of 1999, it has had relatively little influence on world affairs—a consequence, in part, of its tangled history, somewhat fluid organizational structure, and membership requirements. Moreover, because its members include very rich and very poor nations—on one end of the spectrum, there are, for example, Canada, Belgium, and France; on the other end, there are, among others, Chad, Haiti, and Laos—OIF policy decisions and declarations have, for the most part, adopted a nuanced, ultimately pragmatic, perspective that may be described as incrementalist insofar as the needs of both developed and developing nations must be taken into account. This incrementalism—or, according to others, pusillanimity tinged with powerlessness—is in large part a direct function of the large number of member nations, mostly African, whose governments are headed, from the viewpoint of Western nations, by dictators or one-party state leaders. Internal tensions generated by such considerations have meant that the voice of the OIF has been less forceful and influential than it might have been. Still, there are a growing number of indications that a newfound political spirit among OIF members determined to assume a more prominent role in international affairs has, at the beginning of the twenty-first century, begun to assert itself. Concerted attention is being paid to the question of human rights among member nations as well the growing inequality between rich and poor nations, and taken together with an emphasis on the principle of cultural diversity and plurilingualism, the OIF is thus serving notice that it is symbolically equating the dangers inherent in sociocultural uniformization, the hegemony of market-oriented economic policies, and arbitrary and nonaccountable political rule.

Yet, despite the myriad of problems besetting it, some 20 percent of the world's nations are OIF members, drawn together not by political or economic interests, but by linguistic and cultural commonalties. Indeed, one of the salient features of OIF is the circumstance that countries with very small percentages of French speakers and with no inherent relationship to the former French empire may petition to join OIF. Some see this as an advantage, pointing to the need to establish organizations on a basis other than artificial boundaries. Others, however, point out the negative aspects of tenuous membership requirements: marginal participation in and weak commitment to institutional life and principles.[1] Nevertheless, the decisions and compromises reached by the OIF may therefore serve as a needed corrective and alternative voice to decisions taken by more influential institutions such as the Group of 8 (G8), which consists exclusively of wealthy or politically important countries, or the OECD (Organization for Economic Co-operation and Development), whose policies and pronouncements are typically filtered solely through an economic prism. In addition, the OIF has the potential to be an influential actor at the international level in an era marked by the rise of communities formed not because of political borders, but by extrapolitical issues of unifying interest. As globalization continues apace, as continual massive immigration renders superfluous the concept of a national identity, as the internet and web bring together geographically removed and heretofore isolated communities, the OIF may be seen as a new type of hybrid international organization. On the one hand, it most certainly is a governmental organization, since it engages the elected and duly constituted administrative and political apparatus of its approximately fifty member countries. In fact, at the end of the twentieth century, OIF has delineated an organizational structure such that it now has a permanent Secretary General and a Secretariat devoted specifically to intergovernmental political matters as well as to political relationships with other world bodies and non-OIF nations. On the other hand, and perhaps more importantly, it is a nongovernmental organization by virtue of the fact that it makes a nonpolitical characteristic—in this case, language and culture—the catalyst for concerted action in the world arena through the auspices of a wide array of single-interest associations and citizen groups. Issues of importance touching specific interest groups are brought forward and discussed at meetings and conferences at the nongovernmental level. The results of these debates are then filtered upward to the governmental level by a number of coordinating agencies. Similarly, these coordinating agencies (called *opérateurs* in French) attempt to translate the political decisions of the governmental level into concrete actions, often using the organizational reach of the nongovernmental sector.

Broadly speaking, the OIF therefore has an hourglass organizational structure, with ideas, proposals, and plans flowing in both directions. Figure 4.1 shows some of the relationships between and among OIF units. At the top, some fifty governments meet every two years at summits to formulate general principles of action in a variety of spheres. Between summits, organizational and decision-making power rests with the Secretary General, a Permanent Council, and a Ministerial Conference. This triumvirate in turn relies on the five coordinating agencies to carry out specific mandates. These two levels, mingling both political and administrative aspects, may be understood as the narrow part of the hourglass. At the bottom of the hourglass are approximately ninety nongovernmental associations; for example, the International Association of French Women and the International Federation of French Teachers. These particular organizations, through a liaison committee to the principal coordinating agency and through their own formally constituted Conférence francophone des Organisations internationales non gouvernementales (OING), work toward achieving their broadly based priorities, which include advocating for increased educational opportunities and implementing programs designed to improve the living conditions of women and children through the elimination of poverty, corruption, and violence. Finally, two quasi-independent bodies—the Assembly of Francophonie Parliamentarians (Assemblée parlementaire de la Francophonie [APF]) and the Francophone Business Forum (Forum francophone des affaires [FFA])—function as observers which, while possessing political and economic agendas of their own, also advise the OIF, generate ideas, lobby, and act, in the case of the FFA, as intermediaries to the for-profit sector. There are thus three main centers of decision-making, corresponding to the political, administrative, and grassroots organization levels of OIF. And although the OIF increasingly sees itself as a political forum that speaks out about and takes concerted action on vital policy questions such as justice, democracy, and human rights, much of its most effective work consists of "mobilizing resources for cooperative activities"[2] among French-speaking peoples in such diverse fields as agricultural development, environmental projects, culture, information technology, communication networks, scientific information, and education and training initiatives. The sharing of ideas and experiences is paramount.

The Early History of OIF

The philosophical antecedents of OIF can be traced back to a time when French was one of the most widely used languages in the world and the language of international diplomacy. As Latin gradually began to be replaced by local dialects after the Middle Ages, French assumed linguistic supremacy in a large swath of Europe extending from Belgium to the Aosta Valley in Italy, to modern-day Luxembourg and Monaco, and to the western cantons of Switzerland. Two waves of colonization further expanded French reach into diverse parts of the world. By the late sixteenth century, France had well-established colonies in what are today the Canadian provinces of Québec and New Brunswick, Louisiana in the United States, as well as such Caribbean countries as Guyana-Cayenne, Haiti, Martinique, and Guadeloupe. The Pacific island of Mauritius and the Indian enclave of Pondicherry were also under French control by 1720. Rivalry with England led to the collapse of the first French empire, and with the rise to power of Napoleon I, France had been reduced to almost no overseas possessions. The second French empire centered on Western Africa and Southeast Asia. Starting with a military expedition to Algeria in 1830, France extended colonial control to such modern-day countries as Algeria, Senegal, Ivory Coast, Niger, Togo, Mauritania, Gabon, and Mali in Western and Central Africa; Cambodia, Laos, and Vietnam in Southeast Asia; and Tahiti, New Caledonia, Seychelles, Comoros Islands, and Madagascar in the Pacific and Indian Oceans. Following World War II, an inexorable wave of decolonization inaugurated a new type of relationship between France and its possessions. In 1946, a new French constitution declared the birth of what came to be called the French Union, wherein each former colony would develop its own political and socio-economic institutions with the help of France. While local executive bodies and legislative assemblies were established in many Western and Central African areas, full sovereignty was not granted, since France maintained control of such matters as defense, currency, and foreign relations. In 1958, France went further, offering all its overseas territories three options: the status quo, an autonomous state within the framework of a larger French community, or outright independence. All former French territories opted for the latter two choices, and between 1959 and 1963, France signed about two hundred separate agreements with its former colonies, inaugurating a patchwork quilt of political arrangements and a complex division of responsibilities with respect to military presence, cultural cooperation, and developmental aid.

Figure 4.1. Organisation internationale de la Francophonie.

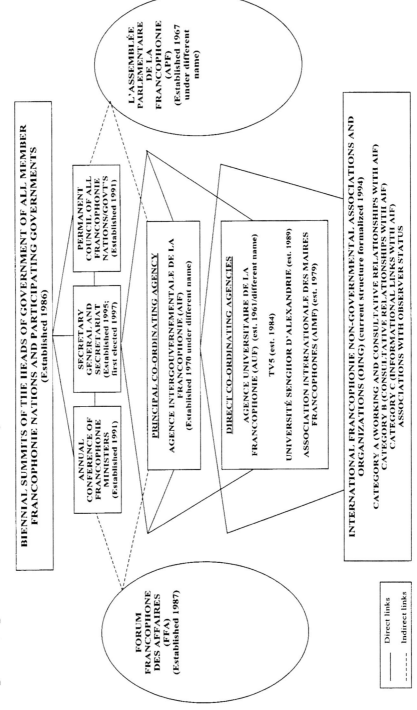

As the French empire expanded, the geographer Onésime Reclus coined the term *francophonie* in his book *France, Algérie, et colonies* (1880) to denote the sum total of countries and populations using the French language. Reclus's word did not gain general popularity, and the concept behind his word was not resurrected until 1962 by President Léopold Senghor of Senegal. Concerned about the wrenching changes experienced in the difficult postcolonial transition years and wanting to ensure that these changes were managed in such a way as to avoid "the Balkanisation of the African continent," Senghor believed that what he called *francité*—defined, according to the *Grand Larousse*, as the set of characteristics unique to French civilization—could serve as an extraordinary tool to forge cross-cultural connections between the black and white races.[3] Senghor viewed the French language as more than a mere linguistic tool; it was, rather, "a way of thinking and of action: a certain way of asking the question and of finding solutions" based on a rich heritage of centuries.[4] Almost concurrently with Senghor's coinage, the magazine *Esprit* devoted a large portion of its November 1962 issue to an extended consideration of Reclus's *francophonie*. As a metaphor for the power relations still existing between France and its former colonies, *francophonie*, instead of *francité*, became the preferred term to describe the confluence of four overlapping senses of "Frenchness." Following the classification established by Xavier Deniau in 1995, *francophonie* includes a linguistic aspect (defined as the totality of French speakers worldwide), a geographical aspect (defined as all the places in the world where French is either the maternal, official, administrative, or popular language), a spiritual or mystical aspect (defined as a set of shared values that give rise to a sense and sentiment of belonging to a community), and an institutional aspect (defined as all the public and private organizations active in *l'espace francophone*).[5]

As decolonization progressed apace in the late 1950s and early 1960s, leaders of many newly independent French-speaking countries were interested in creating "new mechanisms of consultation, co-operation, and, whenever deemed appropriate, policy coordination at the political level ... as a way to expand their access to sources of development assistance [and to establish] a mini-North-South dialogue."[6] The first expression of this desire was the birth in 1960 of CONFEMEN (Conférence des ministres de l'éducation nationale des pays francophones), an organization devoted to improving educational standards in member countries.[7] Almost at the same time, the Association des universités partiellement ou entièrement de langue française (AUPELF) was created in 1961, in Montréal, Québec. Here again the primary interest was educational, linguistic, and cultural, but, while CONFEMEN was a governmental entity, AUPELF was, at the beginning, a loose network of like-minded universities concerned with ensuring their own survival and continued growth. In these two early organizations, the rough outline of the OIF can be seen in embryonic form. Official government political and administrative units mobilized concurrently with private individuals and institutions to achieve similar goals through two separate organizations. From the period 1961–1998, evolving patterns of cooperation between Francophonie nations provide a formal superstructure to integrate and link the aspirations of such diverse social actors.

The first attempt at forging an international umbrella organization was the L'union africaine et malgache (UAM) in 1961. Comprising former French African colonies on the mainland as well as Madagascar, the UAM was primarily concerned with initiating cooperation and resolving differences among members in order to achieve coherence and cohesion in their foreign policy approaches. UAM produced such offshoots as the L'Organisation africaine et malgache de coopération économique (OAMCE), which had a specific mandate to bring about closer economic ties and integration among members. The UAM is significant in large part because, in 1963, the former Belgian colony of Rwanda joined it. UAM was no longer thus solely a group of former French colonies; it had taken the first step to becoming an amalgam of nations sharing linguistic and cultural traits. UAM was dissolved and reincarnated in 1964 as the L'Union africaine et malgache de coopération économique (UAMCE), and it was further rebaptized as the L'Organisation commune africaine et malgache (OCAM) in 1966. The former Belgian colony of Congo (later Zaire, now Congo-Kinshasa) joined OCAM, thus giving credence to "the premise" of a true *francophonie* in Africa.[8]

OCAM was partly the result of a suggestion by the President of Tunisia, Habib Bourguiba, that the linguistic and cultural aspects of *francité* (or *francophonie*) referred to by Senghor be expanded to include regular multilateral meetings among all governments of French-speaking countries. His call for the establishment of a "French Commonwealth" was echoed by the President of Niger, Hamani Diori, who also urged the creation of a formal international francophone organization. Indeed, Diori was instrumental in the development and submission of the first detailed plan of the organizational structure for the nascent international Francophonie. He envisioned three levels of membership, progressing outward in concentric circles. At the first level, what he called *Francophonie* A (consisting of France, Madagascar, and all former French colonies in Western and Central Africa), economic and political ties would predominate and linkages between various national administrative entities would be the most intense. At the level of *Francophonie* B (consisting of Tunisia, Algeria, Morocco, Lebanon, Cambodia, Laos, and Vietnam), the ties would be looser and mostly consultative in nature. At the level of *Francophonie* C (consisting of such countries as Canada, Luxembourg, and Switzerland), the ties would be looser still, essentially restricted to cultural matters.[9] Although Diori's plan did not come to fruition, it had the virtue of reconstituting and solidifying, on paper at least, an international network of relationships that had the potential to become completely frayed in the wake of decolonization. And by proposing three levels of adherence, it focused attention on the multidimensionality of the French-language experience, accepting the reality that not all member countries would have the same commitment to maintaining and preserving the conditions for the growth and success of francophone institutions.

The years 1967–1970 were marked by a large-scale debate and controversy about the status of the Canadian province of Québec. For OIF, the controversy meant an expansion of membership requirements. No longer were internationally recognized countries the only entities eligible for membership: subregions of countries that had cultural and linguistic links to the French language and hence participated in the spiritual and mystical sense of the term *francophonie* were also welcome. In broad terms, French President Charles de Gaulle considered Québec to be in a neocolonial situation within the Canadian federation. During a trip to Montréal in 1967, he pronounced the famous phrase "Vive le Québec libre!" from the balcony of Montréal city hall, causing both national and international consternation. Politicians in Québec understood de Gaulle's speech as support and sanction for their efforts to wrest more powers from the federal government in Ottawa, achieve independence, and be recognized on the international scene. De Gaulle's speech was one of the high points in Québec's "Quiet Revolution" because it legitimized the attempt of the people of Québec to assert their cultural and linguistic rights within the English-speaking sea of Canada. Québec also took comfort from the fact that the international climate was favorable to countries and regions seeking control over their own institutions and fighting for economic equality. The speech put Québec on the world map, whetting its appetite to participate at international venues as its own representative, and not as part of a heterogeneous Canadian delegation.

As one of the few Francophonie institutions existing in 1967, CONFEMEN took the big step of directly inviting Québec to participate in its 1968 meeting in Gabon. According to the Canadian constitutional division of powers, education was a provincial responsibility, and Québec thought that it was within its rights to attend an international education conference in its own name. The federal government in Ottawa, however, believed otherwise, viewing the invitation as a challenge to its sovereignty. Nonetheless, a delegation from Québec traveled to Gabon in 1968 without the authorization of Ottawa, setting off a series of disputes that continue to this day about the extent of Québec's participation at various international fora. In 1969, when Congo-Kinshasa hosted CONFEMEN, the invitation to Québec was repeated. This time, federal-provincial negotiations between Canada, Québec, and New Brunswick—another Canadian province with a significant French-speaking population—led to a situation whereby the official Canadian delegation came under the codirectorship of provincial representatives from the above-named provinces. Nametags of delegates specified that they were not from Canada, but from Canada–Québec or Canada–New Brunswick.

In 1969 and 1970, during a series of two conferences in Niamey, Niger, the principle that subregions of countries could be admitted as "participating governments" to *Francophonie* institutions was formally accepted, with the provision that the nation to whose territory the subregion pertained and upon whose territory the subregion exercised some form of governmental authority, agreed and had worked out some arrangement with the subregion. Known as the Jurgenson compromise, this clause was enshrined in the founding document of L'Agence de coopération culturelle et technique (ACCT), together with a clause that differentiated full-member states from associated states. Although it is possible to see the outlines of Diori's 1966 tiered A-B-C plan in the threefold demarcation among member states, participating governments, and associated states, the Niamey agreement ratified a worldview in which linguistic and cultural affinities trumped, at least in principle, the artificial limits imposed by national boundaries. To be sure, the politics and rhetoric of neocolonialism played a large role in this development, yet the fact remains that the founding of the

ACCT formally recognized and codified, at the international diplomatic level, that generally accepted national boundaries were not the only means of expressing affiliation and belonging. There was, indeed, a greater community beyond that of the nation-state.

ACCT, which in 1996 changed its name to L'Agence intergouvernementale de la Francophonie, was the key intergovernmental agency of the Francophonie until the establishment of the biennial Summit system in 1986. From its inception, ACCT was in a precarious position. Its financing depended, for the most part, on the largesse of France, Belgium, and Canada, but because these countries now contributed to a multilateral organization, they felt that they could reduce bilateral aid arrangements with many of the developing ACCT member nations. Accordingly, many African nations saw no clear benefit from ACCT. In the middle 1970s, ACCT expanded its field of operations from purely cultural matters to encompass economic and educational questions. Emphasis was put on rural development, and its program structure was reorganized into four streams: economic and social development; cultural, technical, and educational cooperation; training institutes; and the promotion of indigenous national languages and cultures.[10] Leadership difficulties, a haphazard funding structure, political corruption and interference, however, meant that ACCT, throughout the 1970s, was not as efficacious as it could have been. Numerous projects were never completed (some commentators mention a figure of 50 percent), and there were calls for its dissolution.

In 1975, Senghor, the Senegalese President, made a written proposition to France urging the establishment of a Francophonie summit of heads of state at regular intervals. The proposition received mixed reviews; indeed, many African nations felt that such a summit would be prejudicial to the existing annual French–African summit. Canada was opposed for a different reason. While it was willing to grant Québec and New Brunswick "participant government" status at the ACCT and CONFEMEN ministerial level, it did not want to enshrine such status at higher political echelons. France took exception to Canada's position, and issued an official statement in 1977 through its Minister of Foreign Affairs that it "could not participate in any Francophone meeting or summit of heads of government to which Québec could not be invited."[11] The situation was not resolved until 1986, at which time the first Francophonie summit was held in Paris. As some analysts have pointed out, the period between 1970 and 1986 was, to a great degree, a time of intense competition between France and Canada for institutional control of Francophonie.[12] Trying to raise its international profile at the same time as it was faced with the growing threat of Québec separation, harboring a grudging admiration for Québec's cultural and linguistic survival, Canada finally agreed to French demands for the extension of "participant government" status to all levels of Francophonie deliberations. Although it recognized that Québec could use the Summits to discuss issues of cultural and language relevant to its own situation, Canada also realized that Summits could have an important political and macroeconomic dimension that would serve its own purposes.[13] However, participant government status within the OIF has become such a well-entrenched concept that, in the early part of 2000, Canadian Prime Minister Jean Chrétien stated that he had no objection to extending it to the province of Ontario and its well over three hundred thousand French-speaking population.[14]

Modernizing OIF Through the Summit Structure[15]

The summits inaugurated a series of far-reaching organizational and policy changes that have, concurrently, expanded the spheres of action of the OIF and streamlined it by giving each of its constituent parts a clear set of responsibilities and tasks. In addition, they helped in bringing about a change in the mindset of Francophonie by helping it grow beyond its traditional function as a promoter of French language and culture. Because the summits bring together about forty or fifty world leaders on a biennial basis, they became forums to promote discussion about and cooperation in major international political and economic matters. First held in Paris in 1986, then in Québec City in 1987, and thereafter every two years, the summits changed the very face and landscape of Francophonie cooperation. Tracing the often serpentine paths taken by OIF in its institutional life gives a sense not only of the progress made over the years in endowing OIF with a transparent organizational basis, but also gives provides insight into the inherent difficulty in coordinating multiple political and cultural agendas.

The tone was set at the very first meeting. In addition to discussions centering on the indebtedness of many African nations and the economic disparity between developed and developing countries, the Paris Summit, with forty-one national and regional participants, established three main areas for future work: development, broadly defined as training, technology transfer, agriculture, and energy; communications, broadly defined as the creation of information and telecommunications networks, as well as databases about the French-speaking world; and culture, with particular emphasis on the diffusion of print publications. Not wishing to entrust its work to the discredited ACCT, the Summit created a temporary Comité du Suivi (CIS), a follow-up committee, to see that its decisions were carried out in the interval between Summits. In hindsight, this was the most significant accomplishment of the Paris Summit. Originally composed of nine members, later expanded to twelve, CIS was given the responsibility of reforming the ACCT and determining which tasks could be entrusted to it. In fact, it had the overall task of deciding which organism within Francophonie would be best suited to carrying out the wishes of Summit participants. CIS thus became an early guarantor of the continuity and decision-making power of the Summit structure, charged to oversee and report back on twenty-eight Summit-approved projects.[16] As well, the Paris Summit saw the creation of l'Université d'expression française (UREF), described as the first multilateral university with a presence in some forty countries. UREF would later combine with AUPELF, eventually becoming l'Agence universitaire francophone (AUF) in 1998.

On the political level, the Québec City Summit (1987) was marked by Canada's announcement that it would cancel some $325 million of debt owed by such countries as Senegal, Zaire, Madagascar, Gabon, and Cameroon. On the structural level, CIS announced that it had formed five coordinating committees or oversight bodies to report on progress in different areas of responsibility: agriculture; communications and communications networks; energy; scientific information and developmental technology; and cultural industries. Its membership increased to twelve members, CIS also made clear that it alone, and not the ACCT, was the chief coordinating agency of work to be done between summits. Two new institutions were also formed. Member nations decided to create L'Institut de l'énergie des pays ayant en commun l'usage du français (IEPF) and the Comité international de préparation du Sommet (CIP) to work on plans for future Summits.

While France made headlines by completely expunging the public-aid debt of thirty-five countries at a cost of some $4.5 billion, the Dakar Summit (1989) also saw the gradual rehabilitation of ACCT and the handing over to it of some CIS responsibilities. The Summit agreed that all multilateral programs should henceforward be under the aegis of ACCT, and that it should integrate within its organizational umbrella the five sectoral committees established in 1987 by CIS. ACCT also saw itself given responsibility for following up on the ministerial-level decisions taken by such entities as CONFEMEN and CONFEJES, the Conférence des ministres de la jeunesse et des sports des pays francophones, created in 1969 to deal specifically with matters pertaining to youth and sports. Nevertheless, there was a certain amount of confusion because the Summit did not explicitly demarcate the responsibilities of ACCT and CIS. In a very real sense, organizational confusion and opacity was a hallmark of the early Francophonie institutional network. Member nations, according to some commentators, were enamored with "institutional pluralism," and by their inaction about organizational matters did nothing to discourage infighting among such existing coordinating agencies (*opérateurs*) as the International French Television Network (TV5), created in 1984, AUPELF-UREF, and the new Université Senghor in Alexandria, Egypt, created in 1989.[17]

Originally scheduled to be held in Zaire (Congo-Kinshasa), the Fourth Summit (1991) was instead held in the Chaillot Palace in France in order to protest the antidemocratic nature of the Zairian government. Moreover, the official government of Haiti was not allowed to participate, and the Summit welcomed the duly elected, but exiled Haitian leader Jean-Bertrand Aristide. Chaillot thus saw the clearest expression to date of a commitment by Francophonie members to denounce human rights violations. And while Bulgaria, Cambodia, and Romania were admitted as member nations, the Summit is best remembered for the creation of a Permanent Council—Conseil Permanent de la Francophonie (CPF)—and a ministerial-level committee—Conférence ministérielle de la Francophonie (CMF). For the first time, a formal politically based buffer layer was created between the Summit and the various administrative entities of Francophonie.

CMF came about as a result of a dispute between France and Canada over the role of ACCT. Wanting to clarify the relationship between the Summit and ACCT, the heads of state decided to create a compromise intermediary body—CMF—made up of the Foreign Ministers of all member nations. In large measure, CMF replaced CIS, since it was given the dual task of ensuring that

Summit resolutions and projects were carried forward by Francophonie *opérateurs* and of sitting as the Board of Directors of ACCT. CMF also instituted a yearly ministerial conference to discuss pending issues. On the other hand, CPF, consisting of only fifteen member nations (later expanded to eighteen), functioned as a Board of Directors of the Francophonie summits, ensuring the preparation of the following Summit as well as serving in an oversight role of previous Summit decisions. To a certain extent, CPF also had attributed to it some of the former functions of CIS, since it was responsible for offering analyses of ACCT actions to the governing council of ACCT. Finally, it was told to establish rules with respect to the approximately six hundred nongovernmental associations wishing to contribute to the Francophonie political process. Various categories of associations were to be defined, and procedures for accreditation and the creation of a parallel NGO forum at each Summit were to be formulated. ACCT itself was accorded a significantly enlarged and exclusively nonpolitical role, and the entire structure of the *opérateurs* was clarified. ACCT became the *opérateur principal* of Francophonie—the central administrative entity charged with coordinating many of the numerous projects given form by Summit political decisions. Its administrative purview extended to the spheres of culture and communication, education, youth, sports, development issues, and environmental matters. In addition, it was given the heavy task of serving as the political Secretariat for the Summit, CMF, and CPF. Subsidiary *opérateur* status was formally given to AUPELF-UREF in the relatively narrow sphere of universities and research, while TV5 was allowed to maintain its independence as a French-language broadcaster.

If the Chaillot Summit was referred to as "the summit of maturity," the Summit in Mauritius (1993) could be called the "summit of consolidation." The principles of North-South solidarity were confirmed, and relative to previous summits, few far-reaching organizational changes were made. Nevertheless, a few important developments took place. First, l'Association internationale des maires et responsables des capitales et métropoles partiallement ou entièrement francophones (AIMF), originally established in 1979, was given associate *opérateur* status (changed to official *opérateur* status in 1995) in order to coordinate activities and share ideas between developed urban centers and less-developed cities and towns, especially in Africa. As well, l'Assemblée internationale des parlementaires de langue française (AIPLF) was accorded a formal consultative role within Francophonie. Finally, because of disappointment with the work of CPF in its function as overseer of ACCT and in its function as the international face of Francophonie, an ad-hoc committee was created to explore ways to strengthen its role.

The Cotonou Summit in Benin (1995) took the last step toward organizational and structural transparency by initiating a process leading to the creation of a Secretary General position and a Secretariat by 1997. On an external political level, the Francophonie nations believed that a well-known person in the Secretary General position would raise their international profile, allowing them to speak with increased authority and prestige on important world issues through a dynamic and active spokesperson. Clearly, the CPF was not filling this role adequately, and the Secretary General position was conceived of as a way to put a single public face on an OIF that was, still, diffuse, structurally unwieldy, and philosophically ambiguous. On an internal level, the Secretary General position would go a long way toward resolving the seemingly never-ending series of nightmares involving the accountability of ACCT. As a result, the Secretary General was given the onerous task of directly overseeing ACCT through the appointment of an Administrator-General with reporting responsibility to the Secretary General and Secretariat. The Secretary General also was given the responsibility of presiding over the CPF in a nonvoting executive capacity. Elected every four years by member nations, the Secretary General was placed under the authority of the CMF, CPF, and the Summit of Nations.

In 1996, the ministerial conference held at Marrakesh adopted a formal Charter consisting of twenty-one articles and seven annexes delineating the functions and responsibilities of each of its constituent parts. As if to completely turn over a new leaf, the perpetually troublesome ACCT was renamed l'Agence intergouvernementale de la Francophonie (AIF). At the 1997 Summit in Hanoi, Boutros Boutros-Ghali, the former Secretary-General of the United Nations (1992–1996) and former Egyptian diplomat, was elected Secretary General of the Francophonie, which at the ministerial conference in Bucharest in 1998 officially changed its name to Organisation internationale de la Francophonie. From one perspective, Boutros-Ghali's election to the head of OIF was symbolic insofar as the United States made it clear in 1996 that it would not support his re-election bid at the United Nations. Boutros-Ghali thus assumed the mantle of an alternative voice to American cultural and economic hegemony, and his election to the head of OIF substantiated its vision of itself as an organization dedicated to cultural diversity and an international bulwark against the looming presence of English-language monolithism and cultural uniformity.

By the end of the twentieth century, Boutros-Ghali had already made progress in affirming a place for OIF on the world stage.[18] In 1998, OIF was granted observer status at the United Nations (UN) and opened two diplomatic liaison offices at UN headquarters in Geneva and New York. It also established diplomatic relations with the EU, and signed cooperation agreements with the Commonwealth, the Organization of African Unity (OAU), and the Arab League. OIF organized joint missions with the Arab League to observe elections in Djibouti, and with the OAU, in Togo. In 1999, it sent election observation teams to Burkina Faso, São Tomé and Príncipe, and Gabon, among others. As evidence of its willingness to serve as international mediator, Boutros-Ghali appointed special envoys to resolve political conflict in Togo and Congo-Kinshasa. OIF also forged close ties with the Commonwealth. In addition to forming a joint team to monitor elections in the Seychelles Islands in 1998, OIF and the Commonwealth jointly organized a colloquium on "Democracy in Pluralistic Societies" in Cameroon in early 2000. As another example of his attempt to make the OIF a multidimensional organization, Boutros-Ghali, understanding the growing importance of transnational economic matters and cross-border capital flows in the twenty-first century, was instrumental in the OIF's decision to hold the first annual conference of Economic and Finance Ministers. This conference, held in Monaco in 1999, enshrined OIF as an economic actor on the world stage, since the ministers debated and took official positions concerning World Trade

Organization (WTO) developments as well as the renegotiations of the trade-centered Lomé Convention, which defines financial and trade arrangements between the European Union and less developed countries, mostly former colonies in Africa and the Caribbean.[19] In sum, the first Secretary General of OIF, through his vast personal network and knowledge of other world organizations, has played a significant role in the maturation and internationalization of OIF, completing its transformation from an entity primarily concerned about language and culture to an organization with strong interests across a wide spectrum of political, economic, and social issues.

Despite the optimism generated by the wholesale restructuring of OIF in the 1990s, significant problems remain. Many of these problems were on display at the Moncton (New Brunswick, Canada) Summit in 1999. Although much of the French-language press in Canada stressed the significance of the event for the French-speaking Acadian population of New Brunswick and concentrated on the Summit theme dealing with issues of importance to youth, the English-language press focused on the presence of many leaders of countries accused by Amnesty International (AI) of major human rights violations. The leaders of Burkina Faso, Burundi, Congo-Kinshasa, Rwanda, and Togo were the particular focus of ire, although AI reported that, of the fifty-two countries participating at Moncton, as many as thirty-two were guilty of practicing executions, arbitrary arrests, and torture. Similarly, Reporters without Frontiers (RWF) provided evidence that 120 journalists had been imprisoned by twenty OIF nations.[20] A leading Canadian newspaper neatly summed up world reaction to OIF. Despite its changes, opined *The Globe and Mail*, OIF "remains the Seymour Milquetoast of international organizations: little known, and even less respected" in part because of its "dubious membership" roster. Moreover, an editorial cartoon showed "a uniformed African dictator seated on a pile of skulls [as] a nattily dressed Frenchman ... sips champagne and says, 'Still, his accent is flawless.' "[21]

The obvious point was that, despite wholesale structural and political reorientation, OIF still retained its early reputation as an organization primarily devoted to the protection and perpetuation of the French language. To be sure, while the expressed views contained more than a little of the long-standing French and English cultural antagonism at the very core of the Canadian mosaic, they also contain more than a kernel of truth. Just how much was revealed by the unexpected intervention of a young woman named Anne-Marie Kabongo, a twenty-five-year old law student from the University of Kinshasa, at a closed Summit session in Moncton. Directly addressing a roomful of African leaders, Ms. Kabongo harshly criticized their lack of respect for human rights and basic democratic principles as well as their constant reliance on wars and power struggles to further their personal aspirations at the cost of untold lost young lives.[22]

But, despite OIF's "dubious membership" list, there were some encouraging signs at Moncton. First, much of the official Summit agenda brought up questions put forward by union groups and human rights organizations participating in the parallel nongovernmental Summit. Thus, there is now clear precedent that internationally based NGOs not part of the extensive OIF family of associations have an important role to play at OIF meetings. Second, the Summit, as part of its final communiqué, adopted a rigorous statement averring that

OIF could in no way "accommodate itself" to situations where human rights and democratic principles were scorned. Realizing that such words may seem empty given past experiences, it directed the AIF to establish a "democracy observatory" and to hold a major international symposium in 2000 about the state of democracy in the French-speaking countries (it was held in Bamako [Mali], 1–3 November). Third, the Summit promised to support international law concerning genocide, urging all its members to adhere to the Rome Treaty of 1998.

There are other indications that African OIF member nations are becoming increasingly aware of the importance of democracy and human rights. Voters in Niger, Guinea-Bissau, and Senegal have, at the end of 1999 and at the beginning of 2000, chosen new presidents in monitored elections that included runoffs. The president of Mali, promising not to change the Constitution to allow him to run for a third term, has pledged to retire in 2002.[23] Perhaps the most encouraging development, however, is the trial in Senegal of the former leader of Chad, Hissène Habré, on charges of political killings and torture. Inspired by the case against former Chilean leader General Augusto Pinochet, the Habré trial is sending a message to other African leaders accused of human rights violations that "nothing will be the same any longer [and] that Africa can also play a role in the fight for human rights and can fight on its own soil."[24]

When all is said and done, the OIF has a difficult task before it as it attempts to outgrow its reputation as the "Seymour Milquetoast of international organizations." For instance, there are persistent reports that at least three OIF members aided Angolan rebels (UNITA) in their protracted conflict with government forces—a conflict financed in large part by the selling of Angolan diamonds by rebel forces on the world market. The United Nations brought forward evidence in early 2000 that Togo and Rwanda served as transshipment points and refueling stops for flights delivering Bulgarian arms to UNITA; that Burkina Faso and Gabon sent the rebels planeloads of diesel fuel; and that Rwanda, despite an international moratorium on purchases of diamonds from UNITA, provided facilities so that Belgian diamond buyers could meet with diamond-selling Angolan rebels.[25] Taken together, these actions by four OIF members have had the effect of prolonging the Angolan conflict at the cost of thousands of lives—the very point so poignantly brought to the attention of OIF members by Anne-Marie Kabongo.

The issues raised by the Moncton Summit are thus very much alive at the start of the twenty-first century, and the degree to which OIF becomes a respected leader of the world community largely depends on the type of concrete actions it takes to convince its members that respecting human rights is the best guarantor of cultural diversity and economic equality.[26] Certainly, a great deal of progress has been made since the early 1960s in terms of solidifying, clarifying, and extending the reach and influence of the OIF. Structurally, the organization is unrecognizable from its early days. Its philosophical stance with regard to cultural and linguistic diversity, on the one hand, and its firm grounding in the politics of North-South economic relationships, on the other hand, puts it at the forefront of world debates about the impact of economic and social globalization. Accordingly, it has the potential to bring to the debating table a counterforce and a counterargument to a world increasingly dominated by an often myopic financially based free-trade focus, best evidenced by the decision-making framework used by the World Trade Organization to resolve disputes. Of course, the lack of respect for human rights is an issue that is not unique to OIF, but because it has come to be so closely identified with the organization, OIF will likely not have as much influence on the world stage as it could have as long as it does not forcefully deal with this issue. Having resolved the human rights question once and for all, OIF will be well placed to take its rightful place among major international governmental institutions.

General Information about the OIF

General information about OIF can be best derived from two electronic and two print sources. First, the official OIF website (in French, English, Spanish, Portuguese, and Arabic), located at <www.francophonie.org/oif.cfm>, contains a complete organizational overview of the main constituent parts of the OIF, with links to the five *opérateurs* as well as a description, and links, to many documents and publications produced on a regular basis by OIF. It also contains a brief history of OIF, as well as a copy of the 1996 Charter. More detailed documentation can be found through the web presence of the Centre international francophone de documentation et d'information (CIFDI), located at <http://cifdi.francophonie.org>. The CIFDI site has full-text collections of the official texts of all OIF Summits, ministerial conferences, sectoral ministerial conferences, the deliberations of the CPF, as well as deliberations of the *opérateur principal*, originally ACCT, later changed to AIF. CIFDI acts as the main publishing arm of AIF, collecting, storing, and disseminating a wide variety of OIF documentation. In addition to the primary documents mentioned above, it has searchable bibliographic databases for any book or report ever published by AIF, and for the over seven hundred periodicals received by AIF.

Although these two websites are probably the most easily accessible way to collect information about OIF, print sources should not be overlooked, since they give unparalleled information about each member of the OIF as well as a complete summary of yearly OIF events. *L'année francophone internationale* (1991-) is an annual compendium published, under the auspices of AIF and l'Association des facultés et établissements de lettres et sciences humaines (AFELSH), itself a member of AUF, by the Faculté des Lettres at Laval University in Québec. In addition to information about OIF institutional activity and country-by-country events of significance for a given year, there are obituaries of well-known recently deceased francophone personalities as well as subject-based essays touching upon such topics as Créole culture, French cinema and music, and the condition of women in various French-speaking regions. *L'année francophone internationale* typically contains more than four hundred pages of up-to-date and diverse facts about OIF. It does have a web presence at <http://francophone.net/AFI>, but the site only contains a table of contents of the print version. Of course, this may change in the near future.

The second indispensable print publication for understanding OIF is *État de la Francophonie dans le monde*, a biennial book of about six hundred to seven hundred pages published by Haut Conseil de la Francophonie, an entity under the auspices of the Office of the French President. In addition to primary source documents from OIF Summits, ministerial meetings, and ad-hoc conferences, *État de la Francophonie dans le monde* contains exhaustive statistics and accounts of activities in all member nations in the following areas: education; language; culture; communication and media; science; economics; and social factors. As well, there are lengthy topical essays about such contemporary issues as migration of peoples within OIF nations and the prospects for bilingual education.

Irreplaceable as reference works about OIF, these two publications appear with a significant time lag from the events they cover. Thus, one way to get the most current information about francophone issues and OIF is through a subscription to the Montréal-based newspaper *Le Devoir*. One of the few noncorporate owned newspapers remaining in Canada, *Le Devoir* frequently publishes special sections in its Saturday editions dealing with cultural and linguistic issues of interest to French speakers. For example, in early March of each year, in conjunction with *Semaine internationale de la francophonie* (Francophonie week), *Le Devoir* prints a retrospective section that look backs at key OIF events of the past year and contains interviews with important OIF figures. Moreover, a week before each biennial Summit, there is a lengthy section taking stock of achievements since the previous Summit and a look ahead at the agenda, debates, controversies, plans, and aspirations swirling around the upcoming Summit. *Le Devoir* also gives special coverage to the many cultural, educational, and technology symposia sponsored annually by OIF. And, since Québec belongs to OIF as a "participating government," many OIF administrative institutions and associations are either based there or have significant branch offices. As these entities carry out their projects and mandates, intervening both internationally and locally, they generate a great deal of news that is covered extensively by *Le Devoir*. Because the Québec government is a strong proponent of and key actor in OIF, it produces numerous policy announcements and position papers on francophone issues on a regular basis, and these too make the news. From a more general perspective, the position of Québec within Canada is symbolically equivalent to the position of francophones worldwide and the position of the OIF vis-à-vis more well-established international governmental bodies: there is a constant struggle to have one's voice heard, one's political viewpoints and cultural contributions respected, and one's problems taken seriously. For those who read it on a daily basis, Québec-based *Le Devoir* provides rare insight both into the psychological, spiritual, and mystical aspects of *francophonie* as well as the more concrete accomplishments and work of OIF.

Structure and Documentation of OIF Component Parts

Summits

The Summit is the chief decision-making body of OIF. Bringing together the heads of state from some fifty countries, the Summit meets every two years to discuss both specific politically charged issues of immediate concern and broader, more thematic issues with general social relevancy. The Secretary General reports to the Summit on work undertaken in the international political arena and in the arena of multilateral cooperation among OIF members. Complete texts of the final communiqués of all OIF summits are available at the website for the 1999 Moncton Summit at <http://sommet99.org>. This site also contains specific information about the Moncton Summit, including the official program and overviews of Summit themes with supporting documentation from past ministerial conferences. Future Summits will undoubtedly also have a web presence.

Secretariat and Secretary General

The post of Secretary General was established in 1995 at the Cotonou Summit. Elected for a renewable term of four years by the heads of state and government, the Secretary General acts under the authority of the Summit, the Ministerial Conference and the Permanent Council. In addition to chairing the Council, the Secretary General is the international political spokesperson and official representative of OIF. The Secretary General is also the titular head of the AIF, but delegates day-to-day power to an Administrator-General. The incumbent is specifically given signing power over all international agreements, but this power is delegated to the Administrator-General for cooperative agreements directly related to the mission of the AIF. Based on decisions taken by the Summit, the Secretary General assigns and coordinates multilateral projects among the five *opérateurs*, has a direct say in the allocation of budgets among the five *opérateurs*, and chairs a coordinating committee of the five *opérateurs*.

Since the Secretariat only began functioning in 1997, documentation is still thin, although it is quickly growing. All press releases from the Secretariat, all speeches made by the Secretary General, and all articles from the French press written about the Secretary General are collected at <www.francophonie.org/frm/secretaire/frm.html>. Press releases are arranged in chronological order, while speeches are searchable by date and subject matter. In addition, the Secretariat publishes the biennial report of the Secretary General about OIF activities from Summit to Summit. The first such report, entitled *Rapport du Secrétaire général de la Francophonie: de Hanoi à Moncton*, is available for downloading at <www.francophonie.org/frm/publications/frm.html. The same site also has downloadable reports from OIF election monitoring teams. Finally, under the link labeled "Events," there are full-text reports that may have been produced by any official OIF conference or meeting.

Conférence Ministérielle
de la Francophonie (CMF)

Normally held once a year, this conference brings together all members of OIF either at the Foreign Minister level or at the level of ministers responsible for the Francophonie. The Foreign Minister of the government hosting the Summit is in charge of CMF during a two-year period immediately before and after the Summit. Some of the functions of CMF are: preparing the agenda of summits; seeing that decisions taken at summits are carried out; and recommending new members and observers. In addition, it handles the financial reports and examines the budget estimates of AIF and other *opérateurs*, and appoints the Administrator-General of AIF upon the Secretary General's recommendation. In other words, it provides continuity between summits, and keeps an eye on the progress of various initiatives decided upon by the Summit as these initiatives make their way through the OIF administrative layer.

Other Permanent and
Sectoral Ministerial Conferences

In addition to the CMF, OIF has two permanent "information and cooperation structures" at the ministerial level: CONFEMEN and CONFEJES. Inaugurated in 1960, the Conference of Education Ministers of French-speaking Countries (CONFEMEN) is the oldest official institution of OIF and has its permanent secretariat in Dakar. It has numerous missions, including financing the building of schools in developing countries, improving the management, planning, and evaluation capacities of already established schools, encouraging schooling for girls and women, preparing educational material, and giving support to teachers. Its website is available at <http://confemen.org>. Established in 1969, the Conference of Youth and Sports Ministers (CONFEJES) concentrates on initiatives for young people. CONFEJES is responsible for the Francophone Games (Jeux de la Francophonie), typically held every four years. More information is available at <http://confejes.org>.

Sectoral ministerial conferences are convened periodically on an ad-hoc basis at the instigation of summits in order to develop policies and programs in specific narrowly defined areas. For example, the Conférence des ministres de l'Économie et des Finances (CMEF) met in Monaco in April, 1999, to discuss trade and investment. CMEF intends to promote sophisticated financial management practices and battle against corruption so as to create a healthy economic environment conducive to foreign investment. It also has committed itself to supporting the growth of small business startups, as well as the creation of a judicial and regulatory framework necessary for business confidence. As another example, OIF ministers responsible for communications networks and information technology met in Montréal in 1997. Ministerial conferences devoted to scientific research were held in 1984 and again in 1995, while a conference about children's issues took place in 1993 in Dakar. Conferences devoted to women's issues have also occurred.

Conseil Permanent de la Francophonie (CPF)

Under the authority of the Ministerial Conference, CFP plans Summits and meets at least twice a year. Consisting of the personal representatives of all OIF heads of states and participating governments, CFP is chaired by the Secretary General. Its specific missions include ensuring that the decisions made by CMF are carried out and overseeing the budgets of administrative entities. It also presides over three broadly based commissions dealing with policy, economic, and cooperation questions. CPF is committed to a consensus style of governance, and it is therefore interesting to note that decisions require majority support of 90 percent of those present and voting.

Agence Intergouvernementale de la Francophonie (AIF)

The central administrative agency of OIF, AIF is responsible for coordinating many of the cooperative cultural, scientific, technical, economic, and legal programs that have been established by the OIF Summit, and for helping member states to better understand principles of democratic governance. Formerly called l'Agence de coopération culturelle et technique (ACCT), it also facilitates links among member states and governments, multilateral and regional cooperation organizations set up under the auspices of the OIF, francophone associations, and international nongovernmental organizations. As well, it promotes distance education and the use of communication technologies among member nations. To this end, AIF signed, early in 2000, an agreement with the WorldSpace Foundation, trustees of the Afristar satellite, to permit the broadcast of an educational radio station, called Canal EF, to Africa and the Middle East.[27]

Headed by an Administrator-General appointed for a renewable four-year term by the Ministerial Conference upon the recommendation of the Secretary General, AIF has two oversight bodies: the Conférence Générale (CG), acting as a Board of Directors, and CPF, acting in an executive capacity. Three of its offices are under the authority of the Secretary General. The other three offices, under the authority of the agency itself, are in West Africa, Central Africa, and the Asia-Pacific region, and their presence in Togo, Gabon, and Vietnam is evidence of its engagement with local problems and its commitment to develop local solutions. Having undergone a substantial reorganization from top to bottom in 1998, AIF intends to take a more community-based and multisectoral approach than previously and to concentrate its efforts on projects in less-developed countries that will give tangible results because all stakeholders participate. This is an approach that will more closely involve francophone nongovernmental associations and international NGOs.[28]

AIF is also involved in administering the Fonds francophone des Inforoutes (FFI), created in 1998 to aid in developing and using internet and web information technologies by businesses, universities, the press, and isolated villages. Financed by thirteen governments, including Canada, France, Monaco, Senegal,

Benin, Cameroon, and the Ivory Coast, FFI is supporting such projects as the web-based networking of African universities and other educational institutions as well the implementation of diverse portal sites on such topics as intellectual property, international legislation, business management practices, and ethnology. FFI is also working to implement regional-specific electronic libraries in the Asia-Pacific and Indian Ocean areas, the creation of an online francophone cultural journal, and a megasite that links the works of all francophone writers and artists.[29]

Through the FFI, AIF has been involved in establishing the Centre africain de formation aux technologies de l'information et de la communication (CAFTIC)—an indication of its realization that heavy emphasis should be put on updating the technological infrastructure of developing African countries. The younger generation is another special focus, and the Belgian association Ynternet.org is in the process of establishing ten training centers where young people will learn about the capabilities of information technology by setting up and managing their own websites. In addition, a site entitled *Leaweb* aims to present a series of integrated reading and writing activities for the benefit of teachers and students, while the e-journal *Interre-actif* is meant to be an entirely student-run enterprise.

AIF produces a bimonthly publication (downloadable full-text) entitled *Le Journal de l'Agence Intergouvernementale de la Francophonie*, formerly called *Lettre de la Francophonie*, which provides an overview of its numerous activities. It also publishes *Echoweb*, which deals with OIF documentation, and *Liaison Francophone*, which deals with many aspects of information technology communications networks as they pertain to OIF. The main website of AIF is available at <http://agence.francophonie.org>.

Agence Universitaire de la Francophonie (AUF)

Formerly known by the unwieldy name and acronym of Association des universités partiellement ou entièrement de langue française–Université des réseaux d'expression française (AUPELF-UREF), AUF is responsible for developing a strong French-language university network. With headquarters in Montréal and status as an *opérateur direct* of OIF, it has relationships with more than four hundred postsecondary institutions, and works particularly on the task of linking researchers from developing countries with facilities and personnel in more developed nations. A special interest has been to develop and expand electronic communications network among French university researchers. An early example of this was UREF, a "virtual" networked university linking resources and academics worldwide. The work of UREF has been supplemented and extended through the Réseau électronique francophone d'information (REFER), essentially a communications network, which has been established in twenty-six countries at SYFED centers (Systèmes francophones d'édition et de diffusion). SYFEDs are physical locations that provide electronic, print, and audiovisual resources for university-level teaching and research. In 1998, AUF was mandated to create l'Université virtuelle francophone (UVF) in order to offer the possibility of formal distance-learning opportunities at the university level. Making use of the latest in information technology infrastructure and web/internet content for the delivery of university courses and research collaboration, UVF aims to play the same role as a traditional university. Piggybacking on the SYFED and REFER networks, the first "virtual" campus had been established in Cameroon by the end of the twentieth century, and plans were under way for campuses in Madagascar, Senegal, Haiti, Hungary, and Vietnam.[30]

In the late 1990s, AUF also created three institutes of information technology and management studies in Cambodia, Vietnam, and Bulgaria. It also administers the Secretariat of the Higher Education and Research Ministers' Conference (Conférence des ministres francophones de l'enseignement supérieur et de la recherche (CONFEMER), which meets every two years, and the Conférence internationale des doyens des facultés de médecine d'expression française (CIDMEF). It also administers the Université audiovisuelle (UNISAT), which produces distance education courseware for undergraduate and graduate studies as well as programs for the general public. AUF is also a project-sponsoring body through the Fonds international de coopération universitaire (FICU). AUF publishes an online magazine called *Universités*—a comprehensive overview of all AUF activities and initiatives. AUF also publishes three monograph series: *Cahiers Agricultures, Cahiers Santé*, and *Cahiers Sécheresse*. The main website of AUF is located at <http://aupelf-uref.org>. UVF is located at http://aupelf-uref.org/uvf/accueil.htm.

TV5

Another *opérateur direct* on the OIF organization chart, TV5 is the international Francophonie television network. The partners involved are Canada, Quebec, France, Switzerland, the French community in Belgium, along with a number of African countries, including Cameroon, Ivory Coast, and Senegal. Considered one of the greatest accomplishments of OIF, TV5 is managed by the Montréal-based Consortium de télévision Canada-Québec as an amalgam of independent broadcasters; for instance, in Europe the founding members were TF1, Antenne 2, FR3, RTBF, and SSR. From its European beginning in 1984, it has expanded to include TV5 Québec-Canada in 1988, and TV5 Afrique in 1992. By 1996, TV5 was beaming its programming into Southeast Asia and the Pacific Rim, and in 1988 it had created special programming for TV5 Orient. In 1998, it began to offer a pay-TV subscription service in the United States. TV5 maintains an impressive web presence at <www.tv5.org>.

Université Senghor in Alexandria

Founded in 1989 following the Dakar Summit and accorded status as an *opérateur direct*, Université Senghor is a private postgraduate institution whose mission is to train the future leaders of African Francophonie. Initially, the university had two departments—Health and Nutrition, and Management and

Administration—but in the middle 1990s the Departments of Cultural Heritage Management and Environmental Management were added. In 1998, the René-Jean Dupuy Center for the Study of International Law was established at the university. From the North American perspective, Université Senghor dispenses short- and medium-term continuing education courses to professionals already holding at least a four-year degree and with at least three years of experience in their respective fields. It sponsors conferences, workshops, and seminars, and has an extensive publishing program that includes the proceedings of conferences, the ongoing reference series *Patrimoine francophone*, and its quarterly journal *La Lettre d'Alexandrie*. Detailed information about its activities is available at <www.refer.org>.

Association Internationale des Maires Francophones (AIMF)

AIMF is the *opérateur* for urban development, and includes mayors and other officials from more than ninety cities in over forty countries. Social intervention is a key aspect of the work of AIMF, and to this end it has financed the construction of community youth centers, medical and health clinics, and playgrounds in numerous African cities. It has also undertaken projects on a larger scale: water supplies, roadways, protection of aquifers, waste disposal, and urban landscaping. In 1989, it launched an initiative to modernize city management practices in developing countries through the use of information technology tools. AIMF publishes a surprisingly eclectic range of books: poetry collections from Western Africa, Central Africa, and the Maghreb region (Tunisia, Morocco, Algeria, Mauritania), and the Histoire de l'Afrique. Its website is available at <www.aimf.asso.fr>.

Assemblée Parlementaire de la Francophonie (APF)

The Parliamentary Assembly, established at Luxembourg in 1967, acts in a consultative capacity to the Summit, the Ministerial Conference, and the Permanent Council on specific issues. It meets yearly, and, at the end of the twentieth century, it included representatives from almost sixty legislative bodies. Its work is divided into six components, all designed to entrench a fair electoral process in member nations: organizing conferences on important political issues of the day; monitoring elections; holding seminars about parliamentary practices and procedures; giving advice about the organization of parliamentary libraries; helping parliamentary transcription services in developing countries to raise standards; and offering internships for African parliamentary administrative personnel so that they can observe the functioning of long-standing Western parliaments. APF has also taken a leading role in denouncing human rights violations. At its 1998 meeting it suspended the memberships of Rwanda and Congo-Brazzaville, and in 1999 it added the Comoros Islands and Niger to the suspension list.[31] Its website is available at <www.francophonie.org/aiplf>. APF publishes *Parlements et Francophonie*, a bimonthly newsletter *La Lettre de L'Assemblée Parlementaire de la Francophonie* (downloadable full-text), and *Parlons Doc*, a newsletter for parliamentary librarians (downloadable full-text).

Forum Francophone des Affaires (FFA)

Founded in 1987, FFA is primarily focused on economic development in "emerging nations." While not an *opérateur* as such, it performs many of the functions of a coordinating agency, since it works with the AIF and international development agencies to initiate, develop, and complete projects. Financed by the AIF, Canada, and Québec, FFA consists of about fifty national committees, with headquarters in Montréal (Bureau international du FFA [BIFFA]). There is a large emphasis on the benefits of information technology for business, and to this end, FFA had opened, by the end of 2000, two Centres du FFA (Ceffanet) in Senegal and Mali.[32] Established because of the prohibitive expense of private internet connections in isolated regions, Ceffanets are, essentially, offices where business people and entrepreneurs can search the web to locate new export sources, establish partnerships, and trade goods. FFA is the publisher of three journals and newsletters: *Liaison*, which discusses currents projects and other FFA-sponsored events; *Économies francophones*, a general interest publication with feature articles about economic developments in French-speaking nations; and *Bourse d'affaires*, a business and information technology magazine. Its website is located at <www.ffa-i.org>, and is designed specifically for small- and medium-sized businesses and organizations in the nonprofit sector. It contains a searchable database called BIGA—Banque d'Information des Gens d'Affaires.

Organisations Internationales Non Gouvernementales (OING)

OING comprises about forty accredited associations that meet every two years. It brings together nongovernmental actors to discuss vital issues, makes recommendations for cooperative action and projects to the AIF, contributes to the accomplishment of AIF-initiated projects, and functions as a sounding board for innovative ideas. Its voice is heard at the AIF level through a five-member Liaison Committee elected for a two-year period. At its 1999 conference it adopted a set of principles emphasizing, among other things, full employment, the importance of volunteer organizations as a means of self-actuation, proactive steps for including women and young people in the changing world economy, and linkages with the private sector for the purpose of increasing training and work-study opportunities. OING has a website at <http://oing.francophonie.org>. Some noteworthy participants are:

- Association francophone internationale des directeurs d'établissements scolaires (International Francophone Association of Directors of Educational Institutions) <www.afides.qc.ca>

- Association internationale francophone des aînés (International Francophone Association of the Elderly) <www.francophone.net/aifa>
- Centre internationale d'études pédagogiques (International Center for the Study of Education and Teaching) <http://ciep.fr>
- Comité international des femmes africaines pour le développement (International Committee of African Women for Development)
- Conseil francophone de la chanson (Francophone Song Council) <www.chanson.ca>
- Conseil pour le développement du français en Louisiane (Council for the Development of French in Louisiana) <www.codofil.org.indexfr.html>
- Fédération internationale des professeurs de français (International Federation of French Teachers) <www.fipf.com>
- Forum internationale des jeunes pour la Francophonie (International Francophone Youth Forum) <http://jeunefra.citeweb.net>
- Groupe d'études et de recherche sur la démocratie et le développement économique et social en Afrique (Study and Research Group on Democracy, Economic and Social Development in Africa) <www.gerddes.org>
- Institut de l'énergie et de l'environment de la Francophonie (Energy and Environment Institute) <www.iepf.org>
- L'office de la langue française (Office of the French Language) <www.olf.gouv.qc.ca>
- Union internationale des journalistes et de la presse de langue française (International Union of Francophone Journalists) <www.francophonie.org/uijplf>

Conclusion

The extent to which OIF moved away, in the late 1990s, from being an organization primarily concerned with the promotion of French language and culture toward a predominantly political institution can be symbolized by the juxtaposition of two minor, yet telling, controversies involving the relationship of French speakers to the English language and the United States. These incidents must, however, be understood against the background of the establishment, in 1961, of L'Office de la langue française (Office of the French Language) (OLF) in the Canadian province of Québec. OLF was founded as an integral part of Québec's self-assertion and desire to function in French despite being surrounded by an English-speaking North American ocean. To be sure, highly contentious language laws regulating, for example, the use of English in advertising, schools, hospitals, and the workplace facilitated the spread of French in the 1970s, 1980s, and 1990s. But, from one perspective, it was the OLF, with its mandate to create and disseminate French terminology as replacements for

English lexical items in common use, that made it possible for citizens of Québec to live and work entirely in French. Its *Banque de Terminologie* contains thousands of French equivalents for English terms in hundreds of specialized fields and industries. Indeed, OLF is striving to keep up with the burgeoning information technology sector (e.g., *courriel* in place of e-mail, *logiciel* instead of software, and *baladeur* in place of Walkman).

Because it was contemporaneous with many of the political developments outlined in previous sections, the founding of OLF was seen by some as a key moment in the birth of OIF, especially in light of an agreement signed in 1965 between France and Québec in which both parties jointly accepted responsibility for the international promotion and diffusion of the French language.[33] Thus, in early 2000, when Air France ordered its pilots to speak English to air-traffic controllers at Charles de Gaulle airport in Paris, Québec expressed grave discontent. The company had been under increasing pressure from international pilots to adopt universal standards for reasons of air safety. Relying on the fact that the use of French in Québec airspace since 1979 and at the Ottawa International Airport since 1990 had never caused an accident, Louise Beaudoin, Québec's Minister for Intergovernmental Affairs interpreted the decision as a "scandalous" attack on cultural diversity: "The imperialism of the English language has to have a limit somewhere." If France cedes ground to English so readily, Beaudoin wondered, "well, just imagine us. I often tell them that what happens there in fifty years is foreshadowed by what is going on here. Our resistance must be echoed somewhere, it must have some resonance."[34]

What did she mean? On one level, she was pointing out the irony of the situation. In essence, Québec was telling France that it was not French enough. On a second level, she was referring to the legal, social, and cultural struggles Québec had experienced, and continues to experience daily, in order to be able to work and live in French. These struggles, she was trying to tell the French, were not to be taken lightly; they were not now to be viewed as in vain. With a little will and backbone, French can be an international working language; after all, it is spoken on five continents by over 100 million people. The struggles of Québec to assert its identity, to resist drowning in an English-language ocean, must have resonance. If Québec is to be viewed as a microcosm of the French-language situation worldwide, then the lesson to be drawn is that only by fighting indefatigably can one hope to maintain an identity, maintain a presence, and gain respect.

Some ten days later, during a visit to France by the Premier of Québec, Air France announced that it was withdrawing its decision.[35] Whether the withdrawal is temporary or permanent, numerous commentators have pointed out the ever-expanding degree to which the English language is present in the everyday life of the French, especially in Paris. The French, it seems, blithely go about their business, talking about "start-ups" instead of *jeunes pousses d'entreprises* as they walk past restaurants offering menus exclusively in English.[36] Beaudoin's point is simply this. If Québec had done nothing about its linguistic situation, it would have, sooner or later, succumbed to English-language predominance. If France does nothing, it will, inevitably and incrementally, succumb. Thus, it should, as a key player in OIF and in the larger mystical and spiritual senses of *francophonie*, do something. For Beaudoin, linguistic infiltration is a Trojan horse for cultural and political hegemony. While English-speaking North Americans, in late 1999 and early 2000, were passionately following the game show *Who Wants to Be a Millionaire?*, French-speaking residents of Québec were avid listeners to and participants in *Des mots et des maux*, a quiz show about French grammar that tested knowledge of definitions, spelling, complex plurals, etymology, and finding errors in paragraphs.[37]

France, though, has chosen another path, to judge by such books as *Non merci, Oncle Sam!* by Noël Mamère and Olivier Warin.[38] Mamère, a member of the French Parliament, has written a scathing indictment of American society, from its fascination with the death penalty, to its health care system that turns away the poor, to its worship of wealth and profit, to what he calls its globalizing and totalitarian tendencies in economic and foreign policy. His voice is not alone: there are other titles such as *The World Is Not Merchandise* and *Who Is Killing France? The American Strategy* that bespeak a profound malaise with American influence, mores, and social phenomena. It can therefore be argued that France has forcefully chosen to show its resistance to American hegemony on the political and philosophical level, not on the linguistic level. To a greater or lesser extent, it is accepting the universal presence of the English language, but it is taking a stand on important political and economic issues. In this respect, its stance is parallel to that of OIF, which has moved away from an emphasis on culture and language to embrace questions of economic equity and political power. Yet, as the Québec experience informs us, language and culture are powerful agents of political resistance. And while Québec has steadfastly embraced its linguistic difference, it has just as steadfastly embraced and welcomed such economic arrangements as the NAFTA. The task of OIF in the coming century will be to find the right balance among cultural concerns, economic issues, and political interests so as to become a significant voice on the world stage for its member states.

Notes and References

1. For example, only five OIF countries or regions have a true French-speaking population of 50 percent or more: France, Québec, Wallonia-Brussels, Luxembourg, and Monaco. Some twenty countries have less than 10 percent real French-language speakers, including Mali, Niger, Senegal, Burkina-Faso, Bulgaria, Vietnam, and Cambodia. See Dennis Ager, *Francophonie in the 1990s: Problems and Opportunities* (Clevedon, UK: Multilingual Matters, 1996), p. 45.

2. Canada, Department of Foreign Affairs and International Trade, *Overview: Canada and la Francophonie* (Ottawa: DFAIT, 1998), p. 2.

3. Jacques Barrat, *Géopolitique de la Francophonie* (Paris: Presses Universitaires de France, 1997), pp. 51–52.

4. Janice Hamilton, in *Canada in Action: The Commonwealth, La Francophonie*, edited by Rupert J. Taylor (Waterloo, ON: R/L Publishing Consultants, 1994), p. 21.

5. Barrat, *Géopolitique de la Francophonie*, pp. 13–14.

6. Canada, *Overview: Canada and La Francophonie*, p. 2.

7. A sister organization, also on the ministerial level and called La Conférence des ministres de la jeunesse et des sports des pays francophones (CONFEJES), was created in 1969. It deals specifically with matters pertaining to youth and sports.

8. François-Pierre Le Scouarnec, *La Francophonie* (Montréal: Boréal, 1997), p. 45.

9. Ibid., p. 51.

10. Ibid., p. 65; see also Barrat, *Géopolitique de la Francophonie*, pp. 26–27.

11. Quoted in Dennis Ager, *Francophonie in the 1990s: Problems and Opportunities*, p. 118.

12. Ibid, p. 118. Ager quotes J. P. Thérien, "Cooperation and Conflict in la Francophonie," *International Journal* 48(3), 492–526.

13. Canada, *Overview: Canada and La Francophonie*, pp. 3–4.

14. Michel Venne, "L'Ontario dans la Francophonie? Pourquoi pas!" *Le Devoir*, 28 August 1999, p. E6.

15. My overall account of the accomplishments of the various Francophonie summits relies on François-Pierre Le Scouarnec, *La Francophonie*, pp. 71–91, Dennis Ager, *Francophonie in the 1990s: Problems and Opportunities*, pp. 119–128, and *L'année francophone internationale* (1997, 1998, 1999, 2000).

16. Le Scouarnec, *La Francophonie*, pp. 74–75.

17. Ibid., pp. 81–82.

18. Michel Venne, "Boutros Boutros-Ghali: La Francophonie, médiatrice pour la paix et la democratie," *Le Devoir*, 28 August 1999, p. E3.

19. Pierre Vallée, "Déclaration de Monaco: Un espace francophone élargi," *Le Devoir*, 28 August 1999, p. E3.

20. Michel Venne, "Les droits de la personne, invité surprise de la Francophonie," *Le Devoir*, 3 September 1999, pp. A1, A10.

21. James Brooke, "A Meeting of Francophones, with Insults in Plain English," *New York Times*, 4 September 1999, p. A6 [National].

22. Michel Venne, "Anne-Marie contre les dictateurs," *Le Devoir*, 7 September 1999, pp. A1, A8.

23. Norimitsu Onishi, "With Africa Watching, Senegal Casts Votes That Count," *New York Times*, 27 February 2000, p. A3 [National].

24. Norimitsu Onishi, "African Dictator Faces Trial Where He Once Took Refuge," *New York Times*, 1 March 2000, pp. A1, A3 [National].

25. Blaine Harden, "United Nations Sees Violation of a Diamond Ban by Angola Rebels," *New York Times*, 11 March 2000, pp. A1, A4.

26. For example, Michel Venne, "Le ton se durcit face aux dictateurs," *Le Devoir*, 4 September 1999, pp. A1, A12.

27. Michel Venne, "L'après-Moncton: Une série de réalisations à portée limitée," *Le Devoir*, 11 March 2000, p. E3.

28. Christian Rioux, "Une nouvelle agence au service de 160 millions de personnes: Le Sud ne fera plus les frais de la politique de 'dumping' du Nord," *Le Devoir*, 28 August 1999, p. E9.

29. Claude LaFleur, "Brancher le Sud et joindre le Nord sur Internet: Art, culture, éducation ou législation lancés sur une inforoute francophone," *Le Devoir*, 28 August 1999, p. E11.

30. Claire Harvey, "Une université populaire: L'Université virtuelle francophone manque déjà de fonds," *Le Devoir*, 28 August 1999, p. E10.

31. Michel Venne, "Les parlementaires font la leçon aux chefs d'État: L'APF a exclu des ses rangs quatre pays coupables de violations des droits humains," *Le Devoir*, 1 September 1999, p. A5.

32. Pierre Vallée, "Le Forum Francophone des affaires est l'acteur privilégié de la Francophonie économique," *Le Devoir*, 28 August 1999, p. E10.

33. William Bostock, *Francophonie: Organisation, Co-ordination, Evaluation* (Melbourne, Australia: River Seine, 1986), p. 15.

34. Michel Hébert, "Air France scandalise Louise Beaudoin," *Le Devoir*, 29 March 2000, p. A2; Rhéal Séguin, "France not French enough, PQ says," *The Globe and Mail*, 29 March 2000, pp. A1, A9.

35. Christian Rioux, "Québec fait reculer Air France," *Le Devoir*, 7 April 2000, pp. A1, A10.

36. See, for example, Alan Freeman, "The English Patience of France," *The Globe and Mail*, 1 April 2000, p. A13.

37. Russell Smith, "A Quiz Show About Grammar…," *The Globe and Mail*, 1 April 2000, p. R7.

38. Suzanne Daley, "More and More, Europeans Find Fault with U.S.," *New York Times*, 9 April 2000, pp. A1, A8 [National].

CHAPTER 5
International Nongovernmental Organizations and Civil Society

*Peter I. Hajnal**

Copyright © Peter I. Hajnal

(A) NONGOVERNMENTAL ORGANIZATIONS AND CIVIL SOCIETY

Introduction

Nongovernmental organizations (NGOs) such as local voluntary mutual-help groups for farmers or fishermen have existed in some form or another for many centuries. After World War II, and especially since the end of the cold war, NGOs have proliferated. The 1999/2000 edition of the *Yearbook of International Organizations*—the most authoritative directory of international organizations—counts 5,825 "conventional" international NGOs and 26,881 international NGOs of all types.[1] Such organizations and, more broadly, civil society, appear with increasing frequency in media coverage as well as in the consciousness of governments, international governmental organizations (IGOs), and the public.

NGOs have extended their concerns and activities into every area of human interaction ranging from development, human rights, humanitarian action and the environment to peace and security, scientific and technical cooperation, and

---

*I am grateful to Dr. Sylvia Ostry and Professors Louis Pauly and John Kirton, all of the Munk Centre for International Studies, University of Toronto, for their encouragement and insights shared. I also wish to thank Gabor Lipcsey for assistance in research for this chapter.

ethical and moral life. Their diversity, role and influence have enjoyed a corresponding increase. Thanks to their efficient use of information technology and of the news media, civil society movements and NGOs are now widely known; yet, they are incompletely understood. Part A of this chapter examines NGOs and civil society in a brief but systematic fashion, focusing on the role of information in their functioning and output. Part B examines three major international NGOs in more detailed case studies.

Definitions

Despite significant growth in the scholarly literature about NGOs and civil society, there is no widely agreed single definition of these entities. The *Yearbook of International Organizations* relies on the definition of NGOs first formulated by the United Nations (UN) Economic and Social Council in 1950, updated in 1968. Council resolution 288 (X) of 27 February 1950 states that "[a]ny international organization which is not established by intergovernmental agreement shall be considered as a non-governmental organization."[2] In resolution 1296 (XLIV) of 25 June 1968 the Council adds that NGOs "includ[e] organizations which accept members designated by government authorities, provided that such membership does not interfere with the free expression of views of the organizations."[3] This is a rather technical and legalistic definition. Anthony Judge of the Union of International Associations (the publisher of the *Yearbook of International Organizations*) notes that "[a] clear and unambiguous theoretically acceptable definition of international NGOs remains to be formulated."[4]

The following definition (or rather, description) gives a flavor of the variety of NGOs and civil society organizations. These organizations

> include officials, independent sector, volunteer sector, civic society, grassroots organisations, private voluntary organisations, transnational social movement organisations, grassroots social change organisations and non-state actors. . . . [T]hese organisations consist of durable, bounded, voluntary relationships among individuals to produce a particular product, using specific techniques.[5]

The Commission on Global Governance offers an explanation for the increasing importance of civil society in general and NGOs in particular. These groups "can offer knowledge, skills, enthusiasm, a non-bureaucratic approach, and grassroots perspectives. . . . Many . . . also raise significant sums for development and humanitarian work, in which their dedication, administrative efficiency, and flexibility are valuable additional assets."[6]

The Commission notes that "civil society" is a broader concept than "NGOs" and adds that "[t]he core of civil society includes those citizen-based associations devoted to advancing any of a wide range of civic, cultural, humanitarian, technical, educational or social purposes, whether at a local, national, regional or global level. These groups are the embodiment of citizen activism, from which they draw their vitality and their legitimacy."[7] Another term found in the literature on civil society is "transnational social movements."[8]

NGO Relations with the UN System and Other IGOs

The UN has had a long-standing, structured relationship with NGOs. This relationship has taken various forms and has had several points of contact within the organization; foremost among these is the Economic and Social Council (ECOSOC) which has set up consultative relations with NGOs under Article 71 of the UN Charter; these relations were more recently revised by ECOSOC Resolution 1996/31, adopted on 25 July 1996.[9] By 2000, the number of NGOs in consultative relations with ECOSOC reached 2,012. A small number are in the "general" consultative category—large, well-established NGOs that are "concerned with most of the activities of the ECOSOC and its subsidiary bodies" according to Resolution 1996/31; others are termed "special"—these are generally smaller NGOs interested only in certain ECOSOC activities; and the largest number—more highly specialized, technical NGOs—are on ECOSOC's "roster."[10] Representatives of these NGOs, especially in the "general" and "special" categories, participate at certain UN meetings and are able to have input into the agenda or to act as expert consultants; they also report periodically on their activities to ECOSOC. These NGOs have formed their own association, the Conference of Non-Governmental Organizations in Consultative Relationship with the United Nations (CONGO; website: <www.conferenceofngos.org>). On its part, ECOSOC has a Committee on NGOs to review applications for consultative status, and an NGO Section to administer the consultative relationship.

The UN Department of Public Information (DPI) has had its own long-standing arrangements with a host of NGOs; these are expected to assist DPI and the UN in general in disseminating UN-related information. These NGOs (1,641 of them in early 2000) are thus an extension of the information arm of the UN. DPI has its own NGO Section to administer the relationship. In addition, DPI has organized annual conferences for its associated NGOs; the 53d such conference took place 28–30 August 2000.

In addition to ECOSOC and DPI, the UN has a number of focal points throughout the Secretariat for contact with NGOs relevant to their work. Most specialized agencies, programs and bodies of the UN system have formal or less formal association with NGOs. A UN system interagency institution established to assist and advise the myriad associated NGOs is the United Nations Non-Governmental Liaison Service (NGLS; website: <http://ngls.tad.ch>).

NGOs have been important participants at a number of major conferences convened by the UN over the years, especially in the 1990s: the 1990 World Summit for Children, the 1992 Rio de Janeiro UN Conference on Environment and Development (also known as the Earth Summit, where civil society really came into its own), the 1993 Vienna World Conference on Human Rights, the 1994 Cairo International Conference on Population and Development, the 1995 Copenhagen World Summit for Social Development, the 1995 Beijing Fourth

World Conference on Women, the 1996 Istanbul Second UN Conference on Human Settlements, the 1996 Rome World Food Summit, and the 1997 "Earth Summit + 5" (the five-year review of the Rio Summit), the 1998 Rome UN Conference on the Establishment of an International Criminal Court. An informative work on NGO-UN relations, including NGO role in UN conferences, is Thomas Weiss and Leon Gordenker's *NGOs, the UN, and Global Governance*; an excellent brief analysis can be found in Chadwick F. Alger's 1999 paper, "The United Nations System and Civil Society."[11]

UN Secretary-General Kofi Annan has on many recent occasions emphasized the importance—indeed, the necessity—of UN-civil society partnership[12] but on a practical working level the relationship is not always easy, even though cooperation between the UN and NGOs has often been mutually beneficial. Access to UN premises, officials, and meetings has been problematic for some NGOs and their members. There has been a certain resistance to NGOs on the part of some UN officials and institutions. In fairness, however, the UN, with its strained resources, could not possibly cope with the potentially huge numbers of organizations and people involved, and with the sometimes unreasonable demands and occasionally reprehensible behavior of certain individuals associated with the more irresponsible sort of NGO. It is also important to realize that while physical access to the Secretariat building is in the purview of the UN administration, permission for NGOs to attend meetings—let alone speak at those meetings—is the prerogative of governments of UN member states.

Looking beyond ECOSOC, DPI and the above-mentioned Secretariat focal points, the desirability of greater UN openness toward civil society has been raised with increasing urgency. In its 1995 report, *Our Global Neighbourhood*, the Commission on Global Governance noted the essential contribution of civil society to global governance and the need for the UN to provide appropriate space for civil society participation. One of the Commission's proposals was to convene an annual forum of civil society that would consist of representatives of civil society organizations accredited to the General Assembly.[13]

Five years after the Commission's report, world civil society convened a Millennium Forum at the UN from 22 to 26 May 2000. The Forum brought together some 1,350 representatives of more than 1,000 NGOs and other civil society organizations from 106 countries. The main themes for discussion were: peace, security and disarmament; poverty eradication, including debt cancellation and social development; human rights; sustainable development and the environment; facing the challenges of globalization; and strengthening and democratizing the UN and other international organizations. In his keynote address to the participants of the Forum, Secretary-General Annan praised "the pioneering role of NGOs on a range of vital issues, from human rights to the environment, from development to disarmament [and stated:] We in the United Nations know that during the cycle of world conferences of the last decade, it was you who set the pace on many issues. You did that through advocacy and through action; by pressuring governments and by working with governments as partners and implementers." He added: "We know that the NGO revolution was made possible by something you also understood before governments did: how to use to your advantage the tools of the information revolution. Communications technology has enabled you to connect and interact across almost all frontiers."[14] The main document, issued at the conclusion of the Forum with the title *We the Peoples: Millennium Forum Declaration and Agenda for Action*, sets forth a series of proposals, grouped around the six themes, for governments, for the UN, and for civil society itself.[15] The Declaration, along with six thematic reports, was subsequently issued as a General Assembling document (A/54/959 of 8 August 2000), and submitted to the UN's own Millennium Assembly in the fall of 2000.[16]

If regular civil society/General Assembly links are difficult politically, links between civil society and the Security Council are an even more challenging and sensitive idea. Nevertheless, in a 1999 addendum to *Our Global Neighbourhood*, the Commission on Global Governance notes that "members of the [Security] Council now hold regular sessions with a group of selected NGOs to discuss questions of common interest" and states that the Council "should take further steps towards regularising procedures for gaining the substantive and timely input of NGOs and other civil society groups with expertise on the issues on its agenda."[17]

This brief section has concentrated on NGO/UN relations. Space does not allow detailed discussion of civil society relations with other IGOs but it should be noted that many IGOs, within and outside of the UN system, have had regular and more or less formalized contact with civil society, and have created web pages reflecting these relations. Some of these sites are quite rich in content; others are less informative. Here are some examples:

- Council of Europe: <www.coe.fr/ong/ngo.htm>
- Organisation internationale de la Francophonie: <www.oing.francophonie.org>
- Organization of American States (OAS): <www.civil-society.oas.org>
- United Nations: <www.un.org/partners/civil_society/home.htm>
- Unesco: <www.unesco.org/general/eng/partners/ong/index.html>
- World Bank: <http://wbln0018.worldbank.org/essd/essd.nsf/NGOs/home>
- World Trade Organization: <www.wto.org/wto/ngo/ngo.htm.>

The Growing Influence of Civil Society: Some Recent Examples

Landmines

One of the major recent successes of civil society was the adoption in 1997 of the treaty banning antipersonnel landmines. In October 1992, six NGOs—Handicap International, Human Rights Watch, Medico International, Mines Advisory Group, Physicians for Human Rights, and Vietnam Veterans of America Foundation—formed the International Campaign to Ban Landmines

(ICBL). At the time of this writing, ICBL has grown to a coalition of more than "1,100 human rights, demining, humanitarian, children's, veterans', medical, development, arms control, religious, environmental, and women's groups in over 60 countries, who work locally, nationally, regionally, and internationally to ban antipersonnel landmines."[18]

ICBL worked hard on getting wide public support for its aims. It participated in a number of conferences, conducted "a public relations campaign to disseminate a clear and consistent humanitarian message" and "enlisted international personalities such as Princess Diana, Archbishop Desmond Tutu, and General Norman Schwarzkopf to champion the issue and provide media salience."[19] Since Princess Diana's death, Queen Noor of Jordan has remained an enthusiastic and articulate supporter of the campaign. Using the internet and the news media skillfully and lobbying various governments energetically, ICBL was able to catalyze what became known as the "Ottawa Process." First the French, then the Canadian government became actively involved politically; with the 3–5 October 1996 Ottawa strategy conference—hosted by Canadian foreign minister Lloyd Axworthy—the diplomatic process took hold, leading to the adoption of the Treaty at the 1–19 September 1997 conference held in Oslo, Norway. Having been ratified by September 1998 by forty countries, the treaty came into force on 1 March 1999—exceptionally speedy progress in international treaty-making. As of 11 September 2000, 139 states signed or acceded to the treaty (formally called Convention on the Prohibition of the Use, Stockpiling, Production and Transfer of Anti-Personnel Mines and on their Destruction) and 94 states have ratified it or deposited instruments of accession or approval.

Most significantly, some governments—notably the Canadian government—recognized the importance of partnership with civil society during the official negotiating process, so that members of the ICBL coalition had direct access and opportunity for direct input. This cooperation has become known as the "new diplomacy."

In 1997, ICBL and its coordinator, Jody Williams, were awarded the Nobel Peace Prize for their role in achieving this treaty. The Norwegian Nobel Committee stated on the occasion of the award that "[t]he ICBL and Jody Williams started a process which in the space of a few years changed a ban on antipersonnel mines from a vision to a feasible reality. The Convention . . . is to a considerable extent a result of their important work."[20] ICBL does not rest on its laurels; its current strategy is to campaign for universalization and implementation of the treaty—including the targeting of nonsignatory states such as countries of the former Soviet Union, the Middle East, North Africa, and the United States—demining action, mine victim assistance, and legal and ethical issues. ICBL's website (<www.icbl.org>) is an excellent source of information on the continuing campaign, on legal texts and other related information. One of the important information resources available on this site and reflecting a core activity of ICBL, is the "Landmine Monitor," a civil society-initiated network that monitors and documents country compliance with the provisions of the treaty. This complements an official, government-based reporting system required by the treaty. "The main elements of the Landmine Monitor system are a global reporting network, a central data base, and an annual report. *Landmine Monitor Report 1999: Toward a Mine-Free World* is the first such annual report."[21]

ICBL's website links to some hundred and forty governmental, academic, NGO, media, UN, private, and other sites relevant to landmines. A good example is the Canadian government's website called "Safe-Lane" (<www.mines.gc.ca>).

The International Criminal Court

The adoption of the Statute of the International Criminal Court in the summer of 1998 (popularly known as the Rome Statute) was a milestone of post-World War II international law. This achievement was a long time in coming. An international congress that met in Paris in October 1946 on the heels of the Nuremberg judgment, called for an international criminal code outlawing crimes against humanity and the establishment of an international criminal court (ICC). By 1949, the UN's International Law Commission (ILC) started drafting a statute for an ICC but it was not until 1989, with the end of the cold war, that the UN General Assembly mandated the ILC to prepare a draft statute for the ICC. The draft was submitted to the Assembly in 1994 and, after a great deal of work by a UN preparatory committee and much lobbying by civil society as well as support by several governments, the UN Diplomatic Conference of Plenipotentiaries on the Establishment of an International Criminal Court met in Rome, Italy, from 15 June to 17 July 1998. One hundred and sixty countries participated, and the Rome Statute was adopted on 17 July by an overwhelming majority.[22]

Although one hundred and fifteen countries have signed the treaty, the ratification process has been slow; sixty countries must ratify the treaty in order for it to come into force. As of 24 October 2000, only twenty-two countries have done so (notably excluding the U.S. and China, which have not yet signed, let alone ratified, the treaty; Russia has signed but has not yet ratified; and the United Kingdom, a signatory, has ratification legislation pending). Nevertheless, this new instrument of international law is on the books, ready to serve as legal basis for a permanent court for trying individuals accused of committing genocide, war crimes, and crimes against humanity. Civil society played a major role in this achievement. "The gathering momentum that led to Rome was only created ... because public opinion led by civil society pressured United Nations Security Council members to establish ad hoc tribunals" on Rwanda and the former Yugoslavia.[23]

In yet another example of "the new diplomacy," the NGO Coalition for an International Criminal Court has been closely involved not only in lobbying and public consciousness-raising about the Court but in working with governments and with the UN during the negotiating process. Under the Coalition's umbrella, 136 NGOs (led by Amnesty International, Human Rights Watch, the Lawyers Committee for Human Rights, the International Committee of the Red Cross, and other major NGOs) gained accreditation to the Rome conference as observers. Civil society representatives in Rome included experts from academia and former government officials, so that their input was knowledgeable and authoritative. A number of official conference delegations, as well as the news media, actually relied for information on newspapers issued and briefings conducted by the Coalition—a proof of the highly effective and sophisticated civil society strategy.[24] The Coalition remains an active provider of information: its website (<www.iccnow.org>) is a comprehensive source on the continuing campaign, including a regularly updated country-by-country ratification status report, and links to documents. In fact, one of the main activities of the Coalition is the development and maintenance of this website. The Coalition conducts electronic conferences and administers a listserv "to facilitate the exchange of NGO and expert documentation and information concerning the ICC negotiations and the ad hoc Tribunals and to foster discussion and debate about substantive issues arising from the process of establishing a permanent International Criminal Court."[25] It also publishes a newspaper, *The International Criminal Court Monitor*, available in print as well as on the website. Another important internet source of information is the UN's web page on the ICC (<www.un.org/law/icc/>).

The Multilateral Agreement on Investment

If the landmines treaty and the International Criminal Court are examples of success achieved by civil society when able to use the "new diplomacy" and to participate in political processes, the defeat of the Multilateral Agreement on Investment (MAI) shows another NGO role in circumstances where civil society is excluded from participation. Although the civil society community often cites its victory in bringing about this defeat, there were multiple factors at play.

It was the proliferation of bilateral investment rules that led to the desire on the part of a number of countries to negotiate a multilateral agreement that would provide a single set of rules governing cross-border investments on a global basis. The Organisation for Economic Co-operation and Development (OECD) was the venue of preference for the start of the negotiating process, with further plans to expand the agreement through the World Trade Organization (WTO). This, from the outset, was part of the problem: OECD was too small as a negotiating forum, excluding most developing countries. Some of the major industrial countries lost the interest or the capacity to continue the process. The U.S. Congress refused to grant the administration fast-track negotiating authority; and France began to demand suspension of the talks and broadening the negotiations.[26] At any rate, "[t]hree years of negotiations to conclude the . . . MAI . . . at the . . . OECD came to an ignominious end on 20 October 1998."[27]

Although civil society was only one of several factors in the demise of the MAI, its role was an important one. And information technology was crucial: it empowered NGOs to form a coalition, raise public awareness of the issues, and communicate its concerns and goals through the effective use of internet and the news media; for example, when it disseminated the text of the leaked draft agreement on the internet. Among the many civil society organizations actively opposing the MAI were the Third World Network centered in Malaysia (website, with its server in Singapore, is at <www.twnside.org.sg>), and various environmental and development NGOs. In a study presented at the 2000 annual meeting of the International Studies Association, Peter Smith and Elizabeth Smythe analyze the role of civil society and technology in defeating the MAI. They have found that practically all concerned NGOs

> used a website, e-mail and a listserv as part of their anti-MAI activities.... [The] main function [of the websites] was to provide a means of gathering, and sharing information and mobilizing those concerned about the agreement.... E-mail, especially automated mailing lists, were used by all groups to maintain links with other activists and concerned citizens ... [linking] local, national and international organizations in the campaign to share strategy and intelligence and coordinate activities with allied groups.... [T]he key advantages of using the internet were its speed, the capacity to move large amounts of information easily, and the over all lower costs for NGOs in comparison to traditional methods [of communication].[28]

Although the anti-MAI campaign is over and the Canadian creator of the original "MAI-NOT website died in late 1999, a related site is still available at <http://mai.flora.org>. It is maintained as "the central information exchange for many people opposed to these types of 'trade' agreements."[29] It includes an "Information and Resource Kit" and a "Library" of full-text documents and articles on globalization and trade issues.

The "Battle of Seattle" and the New Power of Civil Society

The ministerial meeting of the WTO, held 30 November–3 December 1999, attracted an unprecedented number of civil society protesters and demonstrators. In what became known as the "Battle of Seattle," tens of thousands marched in the streets. Some were trade union groups, marching with a permit; others were various NGOs unhappy with globalization and peaceful but not always well informed about the content of the proposed trade liberalization talks or even about the WTO itself; still others were anarchists apparently more interested in breaking windows and wreaking havoc than in influencing the talks within. And there was the small number of NGOs co-opted by and working with the WTO on technical or legal aspects of international trade. As before but with even more technological sophistication, many NGOs involved used the internet and the media to good advantage. In addition to legitimate civil-society use of technology, this time an unnamed group launched a fake WTO website that is still active.

Some civil society organizations consider Seattle a success but this is not convincing. For example, the Seattle protest showed once again the North/South split in civil society. Most of the protesters were from the North, and their goals could be seen as contrary to the interests of developing countries' greater access to the benefits of world trade. So, it is not clear who the "winners" were at Seattle. The losers may have been the developing countries, other governments and, according to *The Economist*, especially intergovernmental organizations themselves.[30]

As was the case with the defeat of the MAI, the failure of the WTO to launch the millennium round of multilateral trade negotiations had several causes. Protesters could not have prevented these talks without the disarray within the WTO. The ministerial conference revealed lack of adequate preparation; problems caused by the long, contentious process of choosing a new Director-General; conflict between governments of advanced countries and developing countries on issues such as labor standards and the environment; and disagreements between the U.S. and Europe over agricultural trade. This partial list indicates the range of problems that did not augur well for the Seattle conference. Also, as in the MAI debacle, civil society largely found itself outside—this was not "new diplomacy" but rather the old one.

Seattle was a watershed: it is hard to imagine any large gathering of IGOs without a strong civil society presence bringing together the same variety of organizations ranging from the serious and respectable groups that seek to influence and improve the outcome to those whose main interest is to disrupt the proceedings. This was clearly the case at several high-level meetings in the year 2000: the IMF and World Bank spring meeting in April in Washington, DC, the OAS General Assembly session in June in Windsor, Canada, and the annual meeting of the OECD Council at ministerial level held in Paris, also in June.

Civil society has without a doubt become a power that IGOs and governments can no longer disregard. They will influence international decisions, programs and treaties, and they will use information technology with increasing efficiency. At best, they will work in partnership with IGOs and governments for the benefit of the greatest number of people.

Internet Sources of Information about Civil Society Organizations

Because information is the bread-and-butter of NGOs and other civil society organizations, movements and coalitions, most (except for groups such as some local grassroots organizations in developing countries) have achieved an internet presence. Websites vary greatly in sophistication, content, structure, state of maintenance, ease of access, search capability, and other characteristics. Here is a sampler of general sites (as distinct from sites of a single NGO) and sites that serve as gateways to and sources of information about a number of organizations:

- Association for Progressive Communications: <www.apc.org>
- The Global Policy Forum's NGO page: <www.globalpolicy.org/ngos/index.htm>
- Institute for Global Communications (IGC): <www.igc.org/igc/gateway/members/index.html>

- The International Studies Association's Directory of Internet Resources: <http://csf.colorado.edu/isa/netsources.html#O>
- NGO Café (a "virtual library on nongovernmental organizations"): <www.soc.titech.ac.jp/ngo/index.html> (includes a bibliography: <www.soc.titech.ac.jp/ngo/ngo-refer.html>)
- NGO Global Network (for NGOs associated with the UN): <www.ngo.org>
- NGONet (NGOs active in Central and Eastern Europe): <www.ngonet.org>
- The North-South Institute's "VOICES: The Rise of Nongovernmental Voices in Multilateral Organizations": <www.nsi-ins.ca/ensi/research/voices/index.htm>
- Third World Network: <www.twnside.org.sg>
- The Union of International Association's "International Organizations and NGOs" page: <www.uia.org/homeorg.htm>

(B) NONGOVERNMENTAL ORGANIZATIONS: THREE CASE STUDIES

OXFAM International*

Introduction

Oxfam International (OI) was established in 1995 and was formally registered in 1996 as Stichting [charitable foundation] Oxfam International, in the Netherlands. It groups together the following eleven autonomous affiliates, located in ten countries:

- Oxfam Great Britain (Oxfam GB), established in 1942 (274 Banbury Road, Oxford, OX2 7DZ United Kingdom; tel.: 44 1865 311 311; fax: 44 1865 312 600; website: <www.oxfam.org.uk>; e-mail: oxfam@oxfam.org.uk)
- Oxfam in Belgium, established in 1963 (39 rue du Conseil, 1050 Brussels, Belgium; tel.: 32 2 512 99; fax: 32 2 514 2813; website: <www.oxfamsol.be>; e-mail: oxfamsol@oxfamsol.be)

---

*I acknowledge with thanks the information and insight kindly shared by Ernst Ligteringen, Executive Director, and Katy Fletcher, Information Officer, Oxfam International; Sarah Totterdell, Publications Team Leader, and Rosalind Buck, Librarian, Oxfam Great Britain; and Françoise Hébert, former Acting Executive Director of Oxfam Canada.

- Oxfam Canada, established in 1963 (Suite 300, 294 Albert Street, Ottawa, Ontario KlP 6E6, Canada; tel.: 613-237-5236; fax: 613-237-0524; website: www.oxfam.ca>; e-mail: enquire@oxfam.ca)

- Oxfam America, established in 1970 (26 West Street, Boston, MA 02111-1206, USA; tel.: 617-482-1211; fax: 617-728-2594; website: <www.oxfamamerica.org>; e-mail: info@oxfamamerica.org)

- Community Aid Abroad (CAA), established in 1970 (156 George Street, Fitzroy, Melbourne, Victoria, Australia 3065; tel.: 61 3 9289 9444; fax: 61 3 9419 5318; website: <www.caa.org.au>; e-mail: enquire@caa.org.au)

- Oxfam Quebec, established in 1973 (2330 rue Notre-Dame ouest, Bureau 200, Montreal, Quebec, Canada, H3J 2Y2; tel.: 514-937-1614; fax: 514-937-9452; website: <www.oxfam.qc.ca>; e-mail: info@oxfam.qc.ca)

- Oxfam Hong Kong, established in 1986 (Head Office, 9th Floor Breakthrough Centre, 191 Woosung Street, Jordan, Kowloon, Hong Kong; tel.: 852 2520 2525; fax: 852 2527 6307; website: <www.oxfam.org.hk>; e-mail: info@oxfam.org.hk)

- Oxfam New Zealand, established in 1991 (1st Floor La Gonda House, 203 Karangahape Road, Auckland, New Zealand; tel.: 64 9 358 1480; fax: 64 9 358 1481; website: <www.caa.org.au/oxfam/nz/index.html>; e-mail: oxfam@oxfam.org.nz)

- Nederlandse Organisatie voor Internationale Ontwikkelingssamenwerking (Novib), established in 1995 (Mauritskade 9, 2514 HD The Hague, The Netherlands; tel.: 31 70 342 1621; fax: 31 70 361 4461; website: <www.novib.nl>; e-mail: admin@novib.nl)

- Intermón, established in 1997 (Roger de Lluria 15, 08010 Barcelona, Spain; tel.: 34 93 482 0708/0; fax: 34 93 482 0707; website: <www.intermon.org>; e-mail: intermon@intermon.org)

- Oxfam Ireland, established in 1998 (9 Burgh Quay, Dublin 2, Ireland; tel.: 353 1 672 7662; fax: 353 1 672 7680; website: <www.oxfamireland.org>; e-mail: oxireland@oxfam.ie)

Oxfam America and Oxfam GB have special consultative status with the Economic and Social Council of the United Nations (UN). OI also has consultative status with the United Nations Conference on Trade and Development (UNCTAD), and OI and Oxfam America are associated with the UN Department of Public Information. Of other IGOs, OI also has links with the Organization of African Unity, the World Bank, and the International Monetary Fund.[31]

As the list above shows, Oxfam GB was the first of the Oxfams. It was created in 1942 as the Oxford Committee for Famine Relief (hence the abbreviated name Oxfam) with the aim of helping to get food, clothing, medicine, and other needed items to the people of war-torn Europe. It has had gift shops and engaged in many fundraising and educational campaigns from its early years. Later, it gradually expanded its scope geographically (with projects in the Middle East,

India, Korea, Hong Kong, Bangladesh, Africa, and elsewhere), cooperatively (working with more and more international, national, and local charitable and community organizations, governments, and intergovernmental organizations), and in range of activities (the most important change was a shift of emphasis to development issues, although disaster relief has remained an important concern). Oxfam GB still is the largest member of the Oxfam family, producing 37 percent of the income of all Oxfams as of 1999.[32] Maggie Black's *A Cause for Our Times: Oxfam, the First 50 Years* is a very readable and informative history of Oxfam GB.[33]

The independent Oxfams are guided by a common philosophy and operate in largely similar ways but all participate in collective action, addressing inequality, injustice, hunger, poverty, armed conflict, and natural disasters wherever these occur. The Oxfams, collectively, have projects in more than one hundred countries, working mostly through local operational organizations. The relationship among the autonomous Oxfams is generally cordial but there have been strains; for example, Oxfam Canada not only showed its independence from Oxfam GB, but its radical activists were "influenced . . . by . . . their dislike of Oxford's paternalistic attitude towards its colonial offspring" and in their political stance "made a much stronger showing than their counterparts in Oxford."[34]

The recognition that globalization of trade, economy, communications, conflicts, social trends, and policies has had a major impact on the well-being of people was a contributing factor to Oxfam's decision to internationalize. OI came into being in order to strengthen cooperation and share resources among the independent Oxfams. An example of sharing is OI's reliance on Oxfam GB staff, resources, and facilities, since both OI and Oxfam GB are headquartered in Oxford. Similarly, OI's Washington Advocacy Office has benefited from the presence in Washington, DC, of an Oxfam America office. An even better, and more recent, example of sharing is the program harmonization project, described later in more detail.

OI considers that the total is greater than the sum of its parts; that is, OI can have a larger impact in its work against poverty and injustice by working together with all member organizations. Citing the example of Oxfam's response to the November 1998 disaster in the wake of Hurricane Mitch in Central America, OI's 1998 *Annual Report* comments on the way "Oxfam affiliates and partners were able to join together—not only in delivering immediate assistance to those in most need but also to call for longer-term policy changes on the debt issue. . . . Now we are all communicating about the same issues with the same message."[35]

Mandate, Governance, and Structure

OI's constitution is an internal document but its mission statement is public; it states that

> Poverty and powerlessness are avoidable and can be eliminated by human action and political will.

> Basic human needs and rights can be met. These include the right to a sustainable livelihood, and the rights and capacities to participate in societies and to make positive changes to people's lives.
>
> Inequalities can be significantly reduced both between rich and poor nations and within nations.
>
> Peace and substantial arms reduction are essential conditions for development.[36]

Through its programs, OI aims to

> [a]ddress the structural causes of poverty and related injustice; [w]ork primarily through local accountable organizations, seeking to strengthen their empowerment; [h]elp people directly where local capacity is insufficient or inappropriate for Oxfam's purposes; [and a]ssist the development of structures which directly benefit people facing the realities of poverty and injustice and which are accountable to them.[37]

The main policymaking body of OI is the *Oxfam International Board*. It consists of the Chair and the Executive Director of each affiliated Oxfam. It meets every October to approve OI's plan and budget. The *Council of Executive Directors* meets after the Board meeting and again in May, to prepare the OI plan and budget.

At the next level of OI governance are four *committees*: Program Directors' Committee, Information Systems Coordinating Committee, Marketing Coordinating Committee, and Advocacy Coordinating Committee. The OI *Secretariat* has a small staff of eleven; plays a coordinating and supporting role in the areas of cooperation and communication among the eleven member organizations; and promotes and monitors the implementation of OI's constitution and plans. The Secretariat is assisted by a number of *working groups*; for example, the [African] Great Lakes Working Group, the OI Campaign Consultative Group and the Middle East Harmonisation Group. The Secretariat, headed by Ernst Ligteringen, Executive Director (executive directors are appointed by the Board), is located at Prama House, 2nd Floor, 267 Banbury Road, Oxford, OX2 7HT, United Kingdom (tel.: 44 1865 31 39 39; fax: 44 1865 31 39 35; websites (identical): <www.oxfam.org> and <www.oxfaminternational.org>; e-mail: administration@oxfaminternational.org). There is also an *Advocacy Office* in Washington, DC, whose primary goal is lobbying the International Monetary Fund, the World Bank, and the United Nations. Its address is 733 15th Street, NW, Suite 340, Washington DC 20005, USA (tel.: 202-783-3331; fax: 1-202-783-5547; website: <www.oxfaminternational.org>; e-mail: advocacy@oxfaminternational.org).

Activities

OI is both an operational (although OI itself favors the term "program" to "operational") and advocacy organization. Its policy—based on its experience and its research—is to link these two types of activities. Its programs (or, rather, the programs of the Oxfams) include emergency response as well as development projects. An example of emergency response during the Kosovo crisis of 1999 is the following set of activities: a water supply survey prepared for the Office of the United Nations High Commissioner for Refugees (UNHCR); a laboratory for water testing set up in an Oxfam field office; a team to assist people with disabilities by distributing orthopaedic and other equipment; organizing summer camps for 150,000 children and youth; setting up counseling programs for women and girls.[38] Other recent programs have included aid in Rwanda, in Central America in the aftermath of Hurricane Mitch, and help to El Salvador after the civil war. These projects all involve Oxfam collaboration with other organizations active in the field.

A current example of development work is Oxfam's fair trade initiative in Australia, Great Britain, Belgium, and Spain. The chief aim of this campaign is "to create awareness of the injustices in world trade . . . [and] to influence consumers, traders, and governments to alter trade conditions to benefit poor producers."[39]

An example of advocacy activity is "Education Now," the first global campaign of OI, launched in 1999. The campaign aims at major policy changes to achieve education for all: removing the debt burden of developing countries; increasing aid for education, reforming IMF programs of structural adjustment, and establishing a global action plan for basic education. The campaign has targeted policymakers, the media, and the public. All eleven Oxfams have collaborated in this campaign, with consensus-building being an important part of the process.[40]

An important concern for OI is its program harmonization project, which brings together program staff of the Oxfams, especially in Southern Africa, Central America, the Mekong region and the Caribbean, to improve coordination and integration of program activities, leading eventually to "a single Oxfam International program framework" and the sharing of resource costs.[41] The harmonization project also covers information, communications and financial systems. A specific example of how harmonization works is Oxfam's response to the East Timor emergency of late 1999. "Under the umbrella of Oxfam International, . . . Oxfam in Australia, CAA, is coordinating the Oxfams['] emergency response ... to provide protection and relief to the people of East and West Timor. With improved security, the Oxfam International response program has now been implemented in East Timor, where . . . [the] specialised team [is] working to provide water and sanitation, as well as shelter."[42] More detail and updates are available on OI's website at <www.oxfam.org/programs/timor.htm>.

Financing

It is not easy to get a detailed picture of OI's finances. The 1998 *Annual Report* gives a statement of the financial activities of "Stichting Oxfam International," presenting the core budget only. This shows the total incoming resources for 1998 at U.S.$812,371, made up of: subscriptions from affiliates (that is, the independent Oxfams), $549,788; donations received, $188,000; and other income, $74,583. Against this, resources expended during 1998 totaled $992,259, of which $336,998 was spent on development fund projects; $348,061 on employment costs; and $307,200 went for office and other expenditure. Funds on 31 December 1998 stood at $276,350. Another chart shows program expenditures of a much higher amount, reflecting expenditures of all Oxfams, U.S.$233,058,025, of which $92,546,520 was spent in Africa, $67,311,081 in Eurasia, $171,360 in the Pacific, $66,470,512 in South America, and $6,558,552 consisted of "international expenditure/home country."[43]

OI is well aware of the inadequacy of publicly available financial data about itself. It plans to expand the 1999 report so as to reflect financial data more completely.

Information and Publishing

OI's draft information strategy (an internal document that is still evolving) includes an agreement to develop the internet as the organization's major vehicle of communication to the public; it also serves OI's goal of transparency. The website (<www.oxfam.org>) went "live" in September 1998 and was re-launched in March 1999 with OI's new logo. The site has good basic information (though not enough for more detailed study) about OI, its mandate, structure, and programs. OI's first *Annual Report*, covering 1997, was on the website and has subsequently been replaced on the web by the 1998 report. The expanded 1999 report will, in turn, appear there. The site, as is usual on the web, has the latest news and other announcements. As of October 2000, the site has no search engine—a shortcoming that should be remedied as soon as possible.

In addition to giving an overview of what OI does and believes in, the website also serves as a gateway to the various Oxfams and provides other useful links. To facilitate the goal of getting more people involved, the site provides information on volunteering or making a donation to the Oxfams or to OI itself; it also allows the public to send e-mail messages to the Oxfams.

A particularly useful feature of the website is the full-text version of OI policy papers. These are produced by the Washington Advocacy Office, but the underlying research is a collaborative effort. The full list of papers is given on OI's website as well as at <www.caa.org.au/oxfam/advocacy/index.html>, a web page of Community Aid Abroad, the Australian Oxfam affiliate. The papers are carefully researched and presented documents. They cover the following main subject areas: debt, trade and investment, conflict and emergencies.

One of the pages of the OI website is devoted to the education campaign, described earlier. It can be found at <www.oxfam.org/educationnow/default.htm>.

For a full-text of the resulting report as well as of the related press releases, one must visit the above-cited Australian site, at <www.caa.org.au/oxfam/advocacy/education/report/index.html>.

Besides the public website, OI has created an intranet for internal communication within OI and among the Oxfams. Striving to ensure compatibility among the Oxfams, OI has set up a strong distribution system, with a contact person in each Oxfam office. Among the internal documents on the intranet are meeting documents. Oxfam working groups and the webmasters of the Oxfams use e-mail as well, quite extensively.

Although OI's main information product is electronic, there is a small amount issued in paper form. Examples are the *Annual Report* and the report *Education Now: Break the Cycle of Poverty*. The latter is in document form; it was published as a book by Oxfam GB in October 2000 with the title *The Oxfam Education Report*.[44] This is not atypical; given OI's small staff and scarce resources, it is natural for it to use the facilities of Oxfam GB, located within a city block or so from OI's headquarters in Oxford. Even in electronic dissemination of information, Oxfam GB can act on behalf of OI; for example, it is on Oxfam GB's website—rather than on OI's—that a press release responding to the 1999 East Timor crisis appeared.[45]

While the subject of this study is OI rather than one of the independent Oxfams, it is worth mentioning that Oxfam GB is a major publisher; it releases twenty to twenty-five books per year, plus two journals. Its publications team has twelve members. The aims of its publishing program are education (rather than fundraising), capacity building in developing countries and promoting good practices. Since 1985, Oxfam GB's mandate has included a provision "to educate the public concerning the nature, causes, and effects of poverty, distress and suffering ..., to conduct and procure research concerning these and to publish or otherwise make the results thereof available to the public."[46]

Publications can serve Oxfam's advocacy function as well. Through its publications, Oxfam communicates its accumulated experience, reflects its successes, but also provides self-criticism.

There are three major categories of Oxfam GB publications (most issued in series, with the occasional "free-standing" monograph):

- publications aimed at development professionals; for example: *The Oxfam Handbook of Development and Relief* by Deborah Eade and Suzanne Williams; *The Oxfam Poverty Report*, by Kevin Watkins; *The Oxfam Gender Training Manual*, by Suzanne Williams, Janet Seed, and Adelina Mwau (Oxfam is planning to prepare a second volume). The principal journal, published in five issues a year (two combined to deal with a special topic each year), is *Development in Practice*, published by Carfax Publishing on behalf of Oxfam GB;

- more popular titles such as cookbooks and children's books—usually published for Oxfam GB by an outside publisher;

- development education—publications in this category are intended for educators or for children and tend to be produced by Oxfam itself rather than jointly with other publishers.

It was not possible for this study to inspect OI's information strategy which, as mentioned earlier, is an internal document. Oxfam GB's International Division, however, has an available publications strategy. Its aims are: to develop and maintain a publishing program that reflects and supports the work of the division; to maintain consistently high standards of writing, editing, and design; to encourage reading, writing, and thinking throughout Oxfam and to contribute to Oxfam's institutional learning; and to support the effective sales, promotion, marketing, and distribution of Oxfam books.[47]

Library and Archival Resources

Lacking its own, OI shares the library of Oxfam GB. Located at Mayfield House, 274 Banbury Road, Oxford OX2 7DZ, United Kingdom, the library's first task is to serve the information needs of Oxfam's staff; it is, however, open to the public by appointment. It specializes in material (whether Oxfam-produced or external) on development issues. Its resources include books, journals, newspapers, CD-ROMs, videos, and a database, as well as access to the internet. It provides, among other services, routine and in-depth reference service, a current-awareness service, and a book token scheme which allows Oxfam project partners to obtain needed resource materials.

Oxfam GB's archives document the organization's work since its inception. They include the project files of Oxfam GB's Overseas Division. OI does not plan to use the Oxfam GB archives but intends instead to move toward increased use of electronic filing and archiving.

Concluding Remarks

How well does OI's information output reflect the organization's mandate, programs, and aims? OI communicates to the public basic information about its programs, both in the operational and advocacy areas, in order to arouse interest and help mobilize public support. The questions remain: How much concrete public support (financial support as well as getting involved as a volunteer) for OI is due to the information disseminated in print and via the internet? What contribution has the information made to policy or program changes by target governments and organizations?

How could OI information be improved? Although enough basic information is made available, it would be useful to add richer content for those who wish to explore OI in more depth. Specifically, more information on the history, constitution, and structure (to the level of working groups) would be helpful. More detail on OI's finances would be useful, too, and change is in the works; OI is committed to transparency and is planning to have its 1999 *Annual Report* reflect such details—a welcome development. Technical improvements to the OI website should include installation of a search engine and provision (for faster access) of a nongraphic (text only) option. One must, of course, bear in mind that OI must weigh carefully how to balance its programs and advocacy work and information activities—notwithstanding the role of information in both programs and advocacy—given its limited resources.

Information supporting OI's advocacy work is more comprehensive than information on programs. This is illustrated by the full-text of policy studies produced by the Advocacy Office in Washington and available on OI's website. These are thoroughly researched, well-prepared, and carefully targeted papers. It is difficult to gauge the effect of these advocacy studies (or, indeed, of Oxfam's advocacy work itself) in changing the behavior of policymakers in governments and international governmental organizations, especially the IMF and the World Bank. OI, on its part, feels that "[i]nternational institutions have come to accept [it] as a partner—a partner with a critical voice."[48] Oxfam states that "[t]he Oxfam International network has had significant success promoting debt relief for poor countries, most notably Mozambique, to allow more money to be spent on education and health services in the country."[49]

IUCN—The World Conservation Union*

Introduction

The World Conservation Union was established in Fontainebleau, France, in 1948 as the International Union for the Protection of Nature (IUPN). Its name was changed in 1956 to International Union for the Conservation of Nature and Natural Resources (IUCN), and in 1991 the "short descriptive title" World Conservation Union was adopted.[50] The acronym IUCN continues to be used by the organization.

IUCN is more of an operational and facilitating organization than an advocacy one, bringing together many different kinds of stakeholders. It characterizes itself as "a union of governments, government agencies, and non-governmental organisations working at the field and policy levels, together with scientists and experts, to protect nature."[51] It is, thus, a hybrid organization rather than a "pure" NGO. It is an umbrella organization that has 955 members, including 76 governments, 111 government agencies from various countries (for example, in the case of France, the ministries of foreign affairs, environment, and cooperation have three separate memberships), 732—mostly environmental—NGOs and 36 nonvoting affiliates.[52] Although IUCN has only institutional members (except for a very few honorary members), individuals can also participate as members

---

*I acknowledge with thanks the information kindly provided by Cécile Thiéry, IUCN Librarian, and Jean Thie, Head of the IUCN Information Management Group.

of expert commissions or as volunteers. As of late 1999, there were more than 9,000 such individuals.[53] The address of IUCN's headquarters is 28, rue Mauverney, CH-1196, Gland, Switzerland (tel.: 41 22 999 0001; fax: 41 22 999 0002; website: <www.iucn.org>; e-mail: mail@hq.iucn.org).

IUCN has special consultative status with the Economic and Social Council of the UN and is also associated with the UN Department of Public Information, UNCTAD, the United Nations Development Programme (UNDP), the United Nations Environment Programme (UNEP), the World Bank, Unesco, the Food and Agriculture Organization of the United Nations (FAO), the World Health Organization (WHO), and the World Meteorological Organization (WMO). Outside the UN system, it maintains links with the Council of Europe and the Organization of American States as well as with multilateral development banks. It has been in partnership with many civil society organizations, notably with the World Wide Fund For Nature (WWF, formerly World Wildlife Fund) which has served as a major source of IUCN's financing.[54]

Mandate, Governance, and Structure

IUCN's *Statutes and Regulations* are the charter of the organization.[55] Its "[m]ission is to influence, encourage and assist societies throughout the world to conserve the integrity and diversity of nature and to ensure that any use of natural resources is equitable and ecologically sustainable."[56]

The World Conservation Congress (prior to 1996 it was called General Assembly), IUCN's highest body, convenes every three years. It sets policy, approves the triennial program, and elects the President and Council members. These congresses and meetings have provided a valuable forum for wide-ranging discussions of environmental issues, and have produced a large number of recommendations.

In earlier years, technical meetings were held simultaneously with some General Assembly meetings. With the change from General Assembly to World Conservation Congress, a somewhat similar structure was re-established. In 1996 a series of workshops devoted to specific technical themes were organized to coincide with the Congress; in addition to members' representatives, outside participants were invited to these workshops. IUCN has planned similar events during the second World Conservation Congress, held in October 2000.[57]

The Council consists of the President, the Treasurer, twenty-four regional councillors, the chairs of the six commissions (see below), and up to five appointed councillors selected on the basis of regional representation and their experience. The Council provides continuity, meeting twice a year and guiding the Secretariat in its work.[58]

The Secretariat serves IUCN's membership by implementing policies and programs set by the Congress. Only about one hundred of its staff of around 1,000 works at headquarters; the rest are employed in forty-two other countries in regional and country offices, and specialized centers. Staff members' work includes conservation in the field, and analysis and communication of information resulting from IUCN activities.[59]

IUCN is aided in its work by the following six global commissions, each of which is an international network of volunteer experts: Species Survival Commission, World Commission on Protected Areas, Commission on Education and Communication, Commission on Environmental Law, Commission on Ecosystem Management, and Commission on Environmental, Economic and Social Policy. The experts making up the six commissions number more than eighty-five hundred; they represent technical, scientific, and policy areas, and include leaders in conservation, environmental education, and sustainable use of renewable natural resources. Chairs of the commissions, elected by the World Conservation Congress, serve on the Council.[60]

National and regional committees, formed by IUCN's governmental and nongovernmental members, have an increasing role in setting its priorities, coordinating membership, and implementing programs. These committees must ask for recognition by the Council.[61]

Thus, IUCN's "constitutional structure . . . makes the Secretariat accountable to the Council and the Council and Commissions to the General Assembly of all the members. The latter [that is, the General Assembly] determine the broad policies—and adopt the resolutions and recommendations that express aspects of that policy."[62]

Activities

In addition to advising and assisting governmental and other organizations as well as local communities worldwide in developing conservation strategies and in implementing those strategies, IUCN shares widely its accumulated knowledge and expertise (publication and information activities are described below in more detail). "IUCN's activities include helping save endangered animal and plant species; working with communities to achieve sustainable development, the creation of national parks and other kinds of protected areas; and assessing the status of ecosystems."[63] Some examples of IUCN activities are:

- preparation and publication of the "Red Lists" of threatened species
- restoring a wetland ecosystem in Cameroon
- coastal zone management and debt-reduction in Guinea-Bissau
- working with communities to protect a national park in Uganda
- helping to manage a mangrove ecosystem in Costa Rica
- collaborating with the World Bank and the Global Environment Facility (GEF)
- serving in the capacity of technical advisors to the Biodiversity Convention
- managing a database of global environmental legislation; and
- integrating gender and social issues within IUCN itself.[64]

IUCN's website lists the following "themes" covering the whole range of programs:

- Antarctica Advisory Committee
- Biodiversity Policy Coordination Division (BPCD)
- Commission on Ecosystem Management (CEM)
- Commission on Education & Communication (CEC)
- Commission on Environmental Law (CEL)
- Commission on Environmental, Economic and Social Policy (CEESP)
- Economics Service Unit (ESU)
- Economics of Biodiversity
- Environmental Education & Communication
- Environmental Law Programme
- Forest Conservation Programme
- Global Policy & Partnerships Unit
- Indigenous Peoples and Conservation
- Information Management Group
- International Coral Reef Initiative
- Marine & Coastal Programme
- Monitoring and Evaluation Initiative
- Protected Areas Programme
- Social Policy Programme
- Species Programme & Species Survival Commission (SSC)
- Strategies for Sustainability
- Sustainable Use Initiative
- TRAFFIC (joint wildlife trade monitoring program of the WWF and IUCN)
- Wetlands Convention—Ramsar
- Wetlands Programme
- World Commission on Dams
- World Commission on Protected Areas (WCPA)
- World Conservation Monitoring Centre.[65]

How successful has IUCN been? Former Director-General Martin Holdgate acknowledges some failures of the international conservation movement:

> The ozone-depleting substances continue to erode our protective screen even though further emissions are being curbed. There is still too much pollution in the world and it threatens to be a scourge of newly-industrializing countries unless they are helped to install the latest technology. Biodiversity is in decline, and further losses are inevitable as forests are cut or burned, coral reefs destroyed, intensive agriculture expands, and species are transported around the world, leaping ancient biogeographical barriers. . . . But . . . [h]ow much worse would all this have been had there been no global conservation movement? . . . [M]y guess is much, much worse.[66]

Perhaps the most important achievement of IUCN in the course of its history is the World Conservation Strategy, completed in 1980 after many years of planning, preparation, and consultation (not always smooth sailing) with Unesco, UNEP, FAO, the WWF, and other partner organizations as well as individual scientists. An interesting description of the preparatory process and salient features of the strategy may be found in Holdgate's *The Green Web: A Union for World Conservation.*[67] The text of the strategy was published by IUCN under the title *World Conservation Strategy: Living Resource Conservation for Sustainable Development.*[68] The main goals of the strategy are "the maintenance of essential ecological processes and life-support systems, the preservation of genetic diversity, and the sustainable utilization of species and ecosystems."[69] It is interesting that the strategy had used the term "sustainable development"earlier than the Brundtland Commission did in its widely known report, *Our Common Future.*[70] In 1991, a revised and updated strategy was published jointly by IUCN, UNEP and the WWF with the title *Caring for the Earth: A Strategy for Sustainable Living.*[71] Much broader in scope than the 1980 strategy, *Caring for the Earth* postulated the following principles for sustainable development:

- Respect and care for the community of life;
- Improve the quality of human life;
- Conserve the Earth's vitality and diversity;
- Minimize the depletion of non-renewable resources;
- Keep within the Earth's carrying capacity;
- Change personal attitudes and practices;
- Enable communities to care for their own environments;
- Provide a national framework for integrating development and conservation; and
- Create a global alliance.[72]

Caring for the Earth was less influential than the 1980 strategy, partly because it was overshadowed by the Rio Earth Summit which met some six months later. Nonetheless, *Caring for the Earth* conveys some of the same message as the Earth Summit and its Agenda 21.[73] Another important related item, completed and published in 1992 under the title *Global Biodiversity Strategy: Guidelines for Action to Save, Study, and Use Earth's Biotic Wealth Sustainably and Equitably*, discusses the causes of losses of biodiversity, and outlines a strategy for biodiversity conservation including the creation of the appropriate international policy environment and national policy frameworks.[74]

Financing

As is the case with many other NGOs, it is not easy to find detailed information on the finances of IUCN. The organization derives its income from individual governments (in 1998 more than 70 percent came from government grants), bilateral aid agencies, foundations, IGOs, NGOs (notably the WWF), corporations, and membership dues. Funding is often provided for particular projects; for example, the Zambezi River Basin Conservation Project in southern Africa has been able to draw on funds from the International Development Research Centre (IDRC). *Global Greens*, a recently published work that is rather hostile to the international environmental movement, provides a few figures on NGO funding, including, for IUCN, a 1996 Ford Foundation grant of U.S.$208,000 and a two-year grant of $360,000 plus $225,000 from the Charles Stewart Mott Foundation. The same book also mentions a two-year U.S.$360,000 foundation grant awarded for 1996–1997 to IUCN's Washington office for the Green Accounting Initiative. This information is too fragmentary and selective to be particularly useful.[75]

About one half of IUCN resources is spent on projects. For 1998, IUCN reported total expenditures of 84,571,000 Swiss francs, of which 15 percent was spent on wetlands and water resources, 14 percent on "representation and management," 11 percent on institutional development, 10 percent on forests, 9 percent on biodiversity, 6 percent on protected areas and natural heritage, 5 percent on communications and environmental education, 4 percent on conservation strategies, 4 percent on environmental law, 4 percent on networking, 4 percent on social policy, 4 percent on the species program, 3 percent on marine and coastal programs, 3 percent on the Sustainable Use Initiative, 2 percent on environmental assessment, 1 percent on the Economics Service, and 1 percent on natural heritage (shown as a separate item from "protected areas and natural heritage").[76]

Information and Publishing

IUCN has no written publications policy but it is considering one. In the wider area of information, however, IUCN's Information Management Group (IMG) has been actively providing direction for the development of coordinated data and information systems and services. Here are two examples of IMG's achievements:

- a major role in the establishment of the Biodiversity Conservation Information System (BCIS; website: <www.biodiversity.org>), which is run as a consortium of nine IUCN programs and partners; and

- responsibility for the electronic virtual World Conservation Bookstore (at <www.iucn.org/bookstore/index.html>), which was designed jointly by IMG and the Publications Services Unit. The Bookstore—in which the IUCN Library plays an important role—is the major component of the overall "Union-Link"—IUCN's term for its program of using electronic communications technology to manage and disseminate information within the organization's constituency worldwide, including the Secretariat, the Commissions, and IUCN members.[77]

IUCN publications are issued in the following major subject categories: biodiversity (including economic aspects); conservation and protected areas; development; forest, marine, wetlands and other ecosystems; environmental education; environmental management; information resources; environmental law; national conservation strategies; species; world conservation strategy; and reference materials about IUCN. In addition to doing its own publishing, IUCN often uses external publishing and joint publishing with other organizations. The following paragraphs highlight some major publications and information sources.

The Green Web: A Union for World Conservation is a thorough history of IUCN and its predecessors.[78] Other good sources of information are *A Pocket Guide to IUCN, the World Conservation Union*; the IUCN *Annual Report*; the journal *World Conservation* (former title: *IUCN Bulletin*); and the *IUCN Membership Directory*.[79] Beginning with the April/June 1999 issue, *World Conservation* is available online at <iucn.org/bookstore/bulletin/wc3/contents/index.html>.

The "Red Lists" of threatened species are authoritative, comprehensive compilations and evaluations; the most recent ones are the *1997 IUCN Red List of Threatened Plants* and the *1996 IUCN Red List of Threatened Animals*. The predecessors of the "Red Lists" were the even more detailed "Red Books." The categories of threatened species used in the "Red Books" and the "Red Lists" are listed in the *IUCN Red List Categories* prepared by IUCN's Species Survival Commission.[80] The three major reports on IUCN's world conservation strategy, *World Conservation Strategy: Living Resource Conservation for Sustainable Development* and its updated, revised version, *Caring for the Earth: A Strategy for Sustainable Living*, and *Global Biodiversity Strategy: Guidelines for Action to Save, Study, and Use Earth's Biotic Wealth Sustainably and Equitably* are described earlier in more detail.[81]

The latest (1996) *World Directory of Environmental Organizations: A Handbook of National and International Organizations and Programs* describes more than twenty-six hundred organizations—governmental and nongovernmental—active in environmental and natural-resource issues. It was published for IUCN by the California Institute of Public Affairs and Earthscan Publications.[82]

The latest edition (1997, published 1998) of the *United Nations List of Protected Areas*, prepared under a UN mandate by the IUCN World Commission on Protected Areas and World Conservation Monitoring Centre, lists more than thirty thousand protected areas designated by government authorities worldwide.[83] The "World Conservation Atlas," a long-term, web-based project, is in preparation.

Proceedings, resolutions and recommendations of the World Conservation Congress (and its predecessor, the General Assembly) are issued as publications for sale. Due to insufficient resources, documents of the World Conservation Congress are not always issued. Press releases, announcing new developments, programs, conferences and publications, are available on IUCN's website.[84]

IUCN Publications 1948–1998: A Catalogue of Publications Produced by IUCN—the World Conservation Union or in Collaboration with Other Organizations or Publishers is a comprehensive bibliographic guide to publications issued over the first fifty years of the IUCN. It lists more than sixteen hundred in-print as well as out-of-print titles. There is a shorter version, *The World Conservation Bookstore, 1948–1998* which lists recent in-print titles.[85] The online version of the larger catalog, accessible at <www.iucn.org/bookstore/catalogues.html>, is updated regularly and is fully searchable. In addition to publications of IUCN proper, both versions of the catalog also list publications of the Convention on International Trade in Endangered Species (CITES); the Ramsar Convention on Wetlands (this convention was signed in Ramsar, Iran, in 1971), TRAFFIC; and the World Conservation Monitoring Centre (WCMC). *IUCN Reports, 1960–1995, Including an Appendix on IUCN Periodicals* lists reports and documentation resulting from field visits, meetings, and projects, and other grey literature, as well as periodicals, issued by the IUCN, and its commissions and collaborating organizations.[86]

Publications may be ordered direct from IUCN Publications Services Unit, 219c Huntingdon Road, Cambridge, CB3 ODL, United Kingdom (tel.: 44 1223 277894; fax: 44 1223 277175; e-mail: info@books.iucn.org). Customers in the U.S. and Canada can also order English-language publications from Island Press, Box 7, Covelo, CA 95428, USA (tel.: 800-828-1302 or 707-983-6432; fax: 707-983-6414; e-mail: ipwest@igc.apc.org; website: <www.islandpress.org>).

Certain IUCN publications are distributed by IUCN's regional and country offices. An online catalog of these titles is *IUCN Publications Available from Regional and Country Offices* (<www.iucn.org/bookstore/cat_rco.pdf>). These publications are also covered in *IUCN Publications 1948–1998*.

In addition to its publications, internet resources and other electronic information, IUCN has set up and is still developing a network of depository libraries in order to reach an even broader constituency. The objective of the IUCN depository library system is to supplement "traditional distribution mechanisms [that] can not reach all who want access to IUCNs information..., particularly... in developing countries where difficulties in obtaining foreign exchange, high communication costs and unreliable postal services make it difficult to obtain needed information." These depository libraries "may receive a copy of each IUCN publication and a fully searchable database to help speed access to specific publications." In exchange, the depository libraries are responsible for "making this information available to the local/regional community, . . . responding to specific requests referred to it by other network libraries or IUCN regional or country offices, . . . identification and acquisition of publications produced in the country/region for the IUCN . . . [and providing] an annual report on the status and use of IUCN publications."[87] As of 1999, there are depository libraries in Australia, Colombia, Costa Rica, El Salvador, France, India, Jamaica, Mexico, Samoa, Saudi Arabia, and Vietnam. IUCN maintains publication exchange agreements with libraries in the United Kingdom and the USA but these are not in the depository program.

Library and Archival Resources

The IUCN headquarters library and archives in Gland, Switzerland—administratively part of the IMG—serves as the authoritative repository of monographic and periodical publications, documents, and scientific and technical reports issued by all offices, including regional and country offices, commissions, and partners of the IUCN from the beginning of the organization. As a result of IUCN's collaboration in the preparation of the *World Directory of Country Environmental Studies*, the library has a nearly comprehensive collection of reports listed in the *Directory*.[88] Among other resources available in the library are the Van Tienhoven collection, dating back to 1928; the video collection; the Forest Conservation Programme collection; and the International Environmental and Natural Resources Assessment Information Service (INTERAISE).

IUCN's Environmental Law Centre Library has a comprehensive collection of books, periodicals, and unpublished reports in its field. Its holdings are listed in the Environmental Law and Policy Literature Database which contains more than fifty-five thousand records. The address of the Environmental Law Centre is Godesberger Allee 108-112, 53175 Bonn, Germany (tel.: 49 228 2692 231; fax: 49 228 2692 250; e-mail: secretariat@elc.iucn.org).

Concluding Remarks

Its broad constituency, embracing both governmental and nongovernmental members and associates, has made IUCN particularly influential. Its program extends to a wide array of environmental and related issues. Unlike many of its fellow NGOs in the environmental field, it has been cautious and scientific in its approach, and has concentrated on operational activity and facilitation of nature protection and conservation rather than engaging in advocacy; consequently, it has not been in the news very much. Being a knowledge-based organization, it has quietly achieved good results and has assisted the work and policies of some other organizations as well as governments in its spheres of interest.

IUCN has a very active and productive information and publishing program. Over the years it has produced a number of authoritative titles, some of which have become indispensable reference works in the area of conservation and sustainable development of natural resources. It has developed an informative, rich, user-friendly internet website as well as a depository library network. Still better transparency would, however, be desirable: more detailed information of its finances would add to better public understanding of the organization's workings. Within its financial means, IUCN has done a great deal to reach out and increase worldwide awareness of major environmental issues.

Médecins Sans Frontières (Doctors Without Borders)*

Origins, History, and Worldwide Presence

Médecins Sans Frontières (MSF) was founded by two groups of French doctors as an NGO specializing in emergency medical assistance. The first group had been active with the French Red Cross in Biafra from 1968 to 1970; and the second group of volunteers had treated victims of a tidal wave in what was then east Pakistan (now Bangladesh) in 1970. Both groups "discovered . . . the shortcomings of international aid: it offered too little medical assistance and was too deferential to international law to be effective in crisis situations. . . . [They were determined to] provid[e] more medical assistance more rapidly and . . . [to be] less deterred by national borders at times of crisis."[89]

In 1970 the Biafra group established the Groupe d'intervention médical et chirurgical d'urgence (GIMCU); and the Bangladesh group set up Secours médical français (SMF). GIMCU and SMF merged on 20 December 1971 into the new MSF. MSF's two main objectives are to "provid[e] medical aid wherever it is needed, regardless of race, religion, politics or sex and [to] rais[e] awareness of the plight of the people [it] help[s]."[90]

In the first few years, MSF's operations were limited. Its volunteer doctors (it was then entirely a volunteer organization) tended to work with development aid agencies rather than independently, and they had a small budget and little experience in the field. After 1978, as a consequence of worldwide proliferation of conflicts, many refugee camps were set up (often by the UNHCR) and MSF stepped in to fill the need for qualified medical personnel in these camps. The resulting expansion of MSF led to a more professional operation by 1979. This was accompanied by the emergence in MSF's ranks of pragmatists who recognized the importance of not only providing assistance but also informing the public about their work through the media. This led to a split with the purists in MSF who did not wish to discuss their experiences.[91]

Thereafter, MSF established an administrative structure with paid staff to supplement the volunteers, and to conduct successful public fundraising campaigns. Parallel with this, MSF devised standardized recruitment practices and

---

*I acknowledge with thanks the helpful comments and information kindly provided by Dr. James Orbinski, President, MSF International Council, Iseult O'Brien, Communications Office, MSF International Office, and MaryBeth McKenzie, Communications Officer, MSF Canada.

expanded its logistics networks. The latter, in addition to communications and transportation, included the preparation of kits of medical and other supplies ready to be sent out and used in any emergency.[92]

The new generation of doctors that joined MSF after 1986 needed increased technical resources to support their work. To fulfill this need, MSF prepared around forty medical guidelines, including guidelines for specialists. Administratively, the organization set up specialist departments; for example, for vaccination, nutrition, and sanitation. During this period MSF also distinguished itself from the Red Cross by its "aggressive humanitarianism" by "violat[ing] the two intangible principles imposed on ICRC [International Committee of the Red Cross] workers: respect for national sovereignty and the duty to remain silent. . . . MSF . . . [spoke] out (in Cambodia, Afghanistan, and Ethiopia) and . . . conduct[ed] clandestine missions (in Afghanistan, Kurdistan, El Salvador, and Eritrea)." In Ethiopia, MSF denounced the diversion of aid and forced transfers of population; as a result, MSF was expelled by the Mengistu regime.[93]

MSF's International Office was set up in the early 1990s. Its address is 39, rue de la Tourelle, B-1040 Brussels, Belgium; tel.: 32 2 280 18 81; fax: 32 2 280 01 73; e-mail:office-intnl@brussels.msf.org; website: <www.msf.org>. In addition, there are the eighteen autonomous sections in the following countries and territories:

- Australia: MSF-Australia, Suite C, Level 1, 263 Broadway, Glebe NSW 2037, Australia; postal address: GPO Box 5141, Sydney NSW 2001, Australia; tel.: 61 (0) 2/95.52.49.33; fax: 61(0) 2/95.52.65.39; e-mail: office-syd@brussels.msf.org

- Austria: Ärzte ohne Grenzen, Josefstädter Strasse 19, Postfach 53, A-1082 Vienna, Austria; tel.: 43 1 409 72 76; fax: 43 1 409 72 76 40; e-mail: msf-wien@eunet.at; website: <www.aerzteohnegrenzen.at>

- Belgium: Médecins Sans Frontières / Artsen Zoonder Grenzen, rue Dupré 94, B-1090 Brussels-Jette, Belgium; tel.: 32-2-474.74.74; fax: 32-2-474.75.75; e-mail:zoom@brussels.msf.org; website: <www.msf.be>

- Canada: Médecins Sans Frontières/Doctors Without Borders, 720 Spadina Avenue, Suite 402, Toronto, ON M5S 2T9, Canada; tel.: 1-800-982-7903 and 416-964-0619; fax: 416-963-8707; e-mail: msfcan@passport.ca; website: <www.msf.ca>

- Denmark: Læger uden Grænser, Bernstorffsvej 20, DK-2900 Hellerup, Denmark; tel.: 45 39 626301; fax: 45 39 626104 e-mail: e-mail: msf-copenhagen@msf.org; website: <www.malaria.dk/msf/index.html>

- France: Médecins Sans Frontières, 8, rue Saint-Sabin, F-75544 Paris Cedex 11, France; tel.: 33 1 40.21.29.29; fax: 33 1 48.06.68.68; e-mail: office@paris.msf.org; website: <www.paris.msf.org>

- Germany: Ärzte ohne Grenzen e. V., Lievelingsweg 102, D-53119 Bonn, Germany; tel.: 49 228 / 55 95 00; fax: 49 228 / 55 95 0 - 11; e-mail: office@bonn.msf.org; website: <www.aerzteohnegrenzen.de>

- Greece: Giatri horis Synora, 57, Stournari Street, 10432 Athens, Greece; tel.: 30 1 520.05.00; fax: 30 1 520.05.03; e-mail: office-ath@brussels.msf.org

- Hong Kong: Médecins Sans Frontières, GPO Box 5803, Hongkong; tel.: 852 2 338 82 77; fax: 852 2 304 60 81; e-mail: office-hgk@msf.org; website: <www.enmpc.org.hk/msf>

- Italy: Medici senza Frontiere, Via Ostiense 6/E, I-00154 Roma, Italy; tel.: 39 6-57300900/901; fax: 39 6-57300902; e-mail: office-roma@msf.org; website: <www.msf.it>

- Japan: Médecins Sans Frontières, Takadanobaba 3-28-1, Shinjuku-ku, Tokyo 169-0075, Japan; tel.: 81 3 3366-8571/72; fax: 81 3 3366-8573; e-mail: msf-tokyo@msf.org; website: <www.japan.msf.org>

- Luxembourg: Médecins Sans Frontières, 70, route du Luxembourg, 70, L-7420 Béreldange, Luxembourg; tel.: 352.33.25.15; fax: 352.33.51.33 e-mail: office-lux@luxembourg.msf.org; website: <www.gms.lu/~msf>

- The Netherlands: Artsen zonder Grenzen, Max Euweplein 40, P.O. Box 10014, 1001 EA Amsterdam, The Netherlands; tel.: 31 20 52 08 700; fax: 31 20 62 05 170; e-mail: hq@amsterdam.msf.org

- Norway: Leger Uten Grenser, Rådhusgate, 30 A, N-0151 Oslo, Norway; tel.: 47 22 33 45 55; fax: 47 22 33 45 51; e-mail: office-osl@oslo.msf.org; website: <www.leger-uten-grenser.no>

- Spain: Médicos sin Fronteras, Nou de la Rambla, 26, E-08001 Barcelona, Spain; tel.: 34 93 304.61.00; fax.: 34 93 304.61.02; e-mail: oficina@barcelona.msf.org; website: <www.barcelona.msf.org>

- Sweden: Läkare utan Gränser, Atlasgatan, 14, S113 20 Stockholm, Sweden; tel.: 46 8 31.02.17; fax: 46 8 31.42.90; e-mail: office-sto@msf.org; website: <www.stockholm.msf.org>

- Switzerland: Médecins Sans Frontières, rue du Lac 12, Case postale 6090, CH-1211 Genève, Switzerland; tel.: 41 22 849 84 84; fax: 41 22 849 84 88; e-mail: office-gva@geneva.msf.org; website: <www.msf.ch>

- United Kingdom: Médecins Sans Frontières, 124-132 Clerkenwell Road, London, EC1R 5DL, United Kingdom; tel.: 44 171 713 56 00; fax: 44 171 713 50 04; e-mail: office-ldn@msf.org

- USA: Doctors Without Borders USA, Inc, 6 East 39th Street, 8th Floor, New York, NY 10016; tel.: 212-679-6800; fax: 212-679-7016; e-mail: dwb@newyork.msf.org; website: <www.dwb.org>

Of these, five (in France, Belgium, Netherlands, Switzerland, and Spain) are operational sections. Each section is slightly different but they all share MSF's philosophy and charter objectives. The French MSF is especially active in advocacy and publishing.

MSF has consultative status with the Economic and Social Council of the United Nations (UN) and is also associated with the UN Department of Public Information. On an operational basis, MSF maintains daily contact with various UN agencies and has liaison offices with the UN in New York and Geneva. It also connects with the WHO and the European Union.

Mandate, Governance, and Structure

MSF's charter states that all of its members are committed to honor these principles:

> Médecins Sans Frontières offers assistance to populations in distress, to victims of natural and man-made disasters and to victims of armed conflict without discrimination and irrespective of race, religion, creed or political affiliation.
>
> Médecins Sans Frontières observes neutrality and impartiality in the name of universal medical ethics and the right to humanitarian assistance and demands full and unhindered freedom in the exercise of its functions.
>
> Médecins Sans Frontières' volunteers undertake to respect their professional code of ethics and to maintain complete independence from all political, economic and religious powers.
>
> As volunteers, members are aware of the risks and dangers of the missions they undertake, and have no right to compensation for themselves or their beneficiaries other than that which Médecins Sans Frontières is able to afford them.[94]

Each of the eighteen MSF sections has its own board headed by a president. The eighteen presidents make up the International Council. As mentioned earlier, five of these are operational centers; among them they provide training and other services to all sections. There are international committees on medical issues, communications, human rights, and logistics.

The International Secretariat has a small staff of eight or nine people. The MSF core personnel includes around 170 doctors, journalists, lawyers, and others, but globally, in all sections, the staff numbers around five hundred and is supplemented by some two thousand volunteers. Around 20 percent are physicians and 30 percent are other health-care workers; the rest work in communications, fundraising, advocacy, and lobbying.

Activities

MSF maintains a careful balance between field action and advocacy. It has some four hundred projects in eighty-four countries. The vast majority of operations take place in Africa, but no continent or country is exempt. MSF is concerned not only with medical assistance in natural and man-made disasters and emergencies but with preventive public health as well. The following examples from the July 1998/June 1999 *Activity Report* illustrate the broad gamut and geographic range of these operations:

- Afghanistan—mother and child health care (in both Taliban-controlled and Alliance-controlled areas)
- Albania—massive refugee aid program
- Bolivia—assistance to the Yuracare, Yuqui, and Quechua indigenous groups
- Bosnia—treating psychological scars of war
- Burkina Faso—bringing aid to Ouagadougou's street children
- Côte d'Ivoire—bringing aid to prisoners
- Guinea—support for national TB program
- Honduras—emergency program in the wake of hurricane
- Iran—aid to Afghan and Iraqi refugees
- Italy—assistance in Roma (Gypsy) camps
- Kenya—AIDS program in Nairobi slums
- Peru—safe sex program for youth
- Romania—helping the homeless
- Tajikistan—rehabilitation of mental hospitals
- Uganda—relief for victims of sleeping sickness
- Yemen—assistance to isolated communities[95]

The primary goal of MSF's advocacy work is to witness and share with as many people as possible the basic reality of genuine human suffering of civilians and others, whether in consequence of war or social instability beyond the reach of formal state structures. MSF lobbies governments to ensure that they take their responsibilities seriously and that they respect, support, and promote the intention and the form of international humanitarian law as well as the basic ethos of humanitarian principles in practice.

Witnessing (*témoignage* in French) is therefore an important part of what MSF does. For example, in Rwanda in 1994, witnessing became a priority.

There, many Hutu refugees were involved in the genocide, and their leaders subsequently manipulated aid provided in the Goma refugee camps in Zaire by international agencies. MSF called for a separation of the leaders from the ordinary refugees. It finally pulled out of Zaire in spring 1996—after what turned out to be a frustrating and disappointing experience—abiding by the Hippocratic maxim "Do no harm."

MSF cooperates with governments and with other groups and organizations, but is not afraid to expose governments, international organizations and other groups that cause or exacerbate emergencies and humanitarian crises or that impede assistance. North Korea, for example, has a noncooperative government. The Sudan conflict, too, has made it difficult to get aid to the victims of war, famine, and disease; not only has the government used the flight ban to prevent aid from reaching those in need, but the rebel SPLA (Sudan People's Liberation Army) has also been guilty of food diversion, and even UNICEF's "Operation Lifeline" has, according to MSF, been somewhat culpable. In Kosovo in 1999, NATO became a party to the conflict, raising questions about the effectiveness of it also engaging in humanitarian action. In Rwanda, MSF has been critical of a number of actors, including the governments of France and the USA as well as the United Nations.[96] And in the Democratic Republic of the Congo, following a conflict not only between government and rebel forces but between ethnic groups, and apparent manipulation of MSF's neutrality toward the local population, MSF withdrew its team from the district in question.[97]

MSF received the highest tribute when on October 15, 1999, the Norwegian Nobel Committee announced its decision to award it the Nobel Peace Prize for 1999 "in recognition of the organization's pioneering humanitarian work on several continents." In its tribute, the Committee added that MSF, throughout its history,

> has adhered to the fundamental principle that all disaster victims, whether the disaster is natural or human in origin, have a right to professional assistance, given as quickly and efficiently as possible. National boundaries and political circumstances or sympathies must have no influence on who is to receive humanitarian help. By maintaining a high degree of independence, the organization has succeeded in living up to these ideals.
>
> By intervening so rapidly, [MSF] calls public attention to humanitarian catastrophes, and by pointing to the causes of such catastrophes, the organization helps to form bodies of public opinion opposed to violations and abuses of power.
>
> In critical situations, marked by violence and brutality, the humanitarian work of [MSF] enables the organization to create openings for contacts between the opposed parties. At the same time, each fearless and self-sacrificing helper shows each victim a human face, stands for respect for that person's dignity, and is a source of hope for peace and reconciliation.[98]

In another appreciation of MSF following the Nobel Peace Prize award, *The New Republic* notes in an article that over the period of its existence "MSF has literally redefined humanitarian action." It goes on to state that "[f]rom Afghanistan to Kosovo, the results of MSF's work have been extraordinary, not only in terms of lives saved and victims succoured, but also in harsh truths told." And in *Maclean's: Canada's Weekly Newsmagazine*, James Paupst states that "MSF has become an examplar of humanitarian aid because of the strength of its advocacy for victims who are unable to speak out against crushing bureaucracy and political systems that rule by terror and fear."[99]

Dr. James Orbinski, President of the MSF International Council, in his acceptance speech, stated that MSF's "action is to help people in situations in crisis. . . . [In addition to] offering material assistance . . . [and] bringing direct medical aid to people in need . . . [, MSF's larger aim is] to enable individuals to regain their rights and dignity as human beings. . . . [Moreover, MSF workers tell] the world of the injustice that they have seen . . . in the hope that the cycles of violence and destruction will not continue endlessly."[100]

Financing

MSF makes financial information available in its *Activity Report*. In 1997 the organization's total income was U.S.$231,000,000. Fifty-four percent came from private contributions and 46 percent were grants from governmental and IGO sources: the governments of Norway (2.61 percent), Belgium (2.19 percent), the USA (2.09 percent) and Luxembourg (1.76 percent), the European Union (23.51 percent) and UNHCR (4.63 percent). The total 1997 expenditure of U.S.$228,000,000 was distributed as follows: Africa, 62 percent; Asia, 18 percent; Eastern Europe, 9 percent; Latin America, 8 percent; Western Europe, 2 percent; and the Middle East, 1 percent. Of all expenditures, 81.18 percent went for operations, 8.72 percent for fundraising, 6.91 percent for administrative costs, and 3.19 percent for advocacy and public awareness campaigns.[101]

The ratio between institutional and private funding has been constantly shifting from earlier years when institutional funds predominated; by mid-1999 (the income for the 1998/1999 fiscal year was around U.S.$280,000,000) 64 percent of revenue came from private funds and only 36 percent from institutional sources.[102] This progression indicates an active policy to remain independent of governments and, at the same time, implies a lessening of dependence on the largesse of governmental institutions.

Information and Publishing

The annual *Activity Report* describes MSF's work in the field and includes some feature articles as well.[103] It has a general and a medical introduction, reports on MSF action in a number of countries, and gives information (including financial data and historical highlights) about MSF. The report covering July 1997–June 1998 features special articles on street children, drug-resistant infectious diseases, and MSF's work to combat the East African cholera epidemic. At the time of writing (February 2000), the report for July 1998–June 1999 is on MSF's website. "The Médecins Sans Frontières Experience," a chapter in *A Framework for Survival*, is a brief history of MSF from its creation in 1971 to 1991, written by Rony Brauman, a former president of the organization.[104] MSF is now preparing an updated history. One of the pages on the website gives a brief history and identifies milestones in the twenty-eight years of MSF.[105] Another overview of the organization is *Lettres Sans Frontières*, issued by a commercial publisher under the aegis of MSF Belgium.[106] Three personal accounts—not published by MSF—deserve mention here: in the first, *Touched by Fire: Doctors Without Borders in a Third World Crisis*, Elliott Leyton describes and Greg Locke photographs their impressions of MSF's work in the midst of the Rwanda genocide and its aftermath; the second, by Leanne Olson, a Canadian nurse who has worked for MSF in Bosnia, Burundi, and Zaire, was published in late 1999 with the title *A Cruel Paradise: Journals of an International Relief Worker*; and in the third, two physicians, Paul B. Spiegel and Peter Salama, give an "epidemiological testimony" of the 1998–99 Kosovo crisis in the medical journal *The Lancet*.[107]

Country reports are another type of publication; for example: *Living in a Minefield: An MSF Report on the Mine Problem in Afghanistan*. This report is available on the MSF website at <www.msf.org/intweb99/library/2pub1197.htm>. Another example is an MSF report on Kosovo.

Several years ago MSF instituted an "MSF Day—International Day for Populations in Danger." One result was a 1995 book entitled *Populations in Danger*.[108] This work, a sequel to a 1992 publication with the same title, highlights five crises: Burundi, Rwanda, Zaire, Haiti, and Bosnia. In addition to a summary of these crises, it includes several opinion pieces and an informative "humanitarian atlas." A similar publication is planned with education as its theme.

Some other studies, published for MSF by commercial publishers, are:

- *Refugee Health: An Approach to Emergency Situations*. Basingstoke, Hampshire, England: Macmillan, 1997.

- *World in Crisis: The Politics of Survival at the End of the 20th Century*, edited by Médecins sans Frontières; MSF project coordinator: Julia Groenewold; associate editor: Eve Porter. London; New York: Routledge, 1996.

Some medical reports lead to advocacy campaigns targeting the international community. For example, an article published in the 27 January 1999 issue of the *Journal of the American Medical Association* reports on MSF's "Access to Essential Medicines" program which aims to encourage research in tropical medicine and to promote access to essential medicines in developing countries.[109] In these countries "life-saving essential medicines are either too expensive, are not available because they are not seen as financially viable, or because there is virtually no new research and development for . . . tropical diseases."[110]

Manuals, guides, and handbooks for field operations, referred to earlier, constitute a distinct category of MSF publications. Based on MSF's own experience as well as on input from major medical institutions, these are intended mostly for physicians and other health professionals. Examples are:

- *Clinical Guidelines: Diagnostic and Treatment Manual.* 3rd ed. 1993.
- *Essential Drugs: Practical Guidelines.* 1st ed. 1993.
- *Minor Surgical Procedures in Remote Areas.* 1st ed. 1989.
- *Public Health Engineering in Emergency Situations.* 1st ed. 1994.
- *Nutrition Guidelines.* 1st ed. 1995.
- *Obstétrique en situation d'isolement.* 1st ed. 1992.[111]

Doctors' diaries, published on the MSF website, convey a powerful message about disasters and the involvement of MSF personnel and volunteers. An example is the diary of Dr. Raymond Vanholder who arrived in Turkey with the MSF team within twenty-four hours following the major earthquake that occurred on August 17th, 1999.[112]

MSF's International Office regularly issues press releases. They are available on its website under subjects or countries covered. For example, the award of the 1999 Nobel Peace Prize to MSF was announced at <www.msf.org/events/1999/nobel/statement.htm>; and several press releases are included, along with a number of MSF reports, on the "Timor" page of the site, at <www.msf.org/projects/e_timor/>. National sections also produce press releases, in consultation with other sections.

From the beginning, MSF has been aware of the role of the media in bringing the plight of victims of war, famine, and disaster to the attention of the general public.[113] Press releases, campaign literature, and other publications testify to that awareness and adroit use of the media by MSF. The internet plays a major role on disseminating information not just to the media but to the broader international community as well. Although there is not the same internet culture in Europe and elsewhere as in North America, this is changing rapidly, so that the internet promises to become an even more important vehicle of communication. On average, around seven hundred people visit the MSF website daily, but on the day when the award of the Nobel Peace Prize was announced (15 October 1999), the site had more than fifteen thousand visitors.[114]

There is a good deal of internal communication within and among the MSF sections. Daily situation reports are shared by e-mail. Relations among sections are not always smooth, but MSF considers debate to be very important; for example, there were ethical differences on how to respond to the 1994 genocide in Rwanda.

Library and Archival Resources

MSF International has no resource center of its own. It relies instead on MSF Belgium, which has a documentation center in Brussels. The operational sections and some (but not all) other national sections have resource centers of various kinds.

Concluding Remarks

MSF is a productive and relatively nonbureaucratic aid organization, with highly motivated, committed staff. It has achieved very impressive results both in its operational and advocacy work. It has courageously exposed governments, international organizations, and other groups when these caused or exacerbated emergencies and humanitarian crises or impeded assistance. MSF was highly acclaimed when it received the 1999 Nobel Peace Prize in recognition of its humanitarian work.

Information and publishing are important aspects of the program. The publishing output ranges from country reports, special studies, and medical reports to practical field guides and handbooks, and general informational material including press releases. The MSF website is rich in content and has many useful links, but, at the time of writing, does not yet have a working search engine. The output, both printed and electronic, not only reflects the work of this multifaceted NGO but serves as an important information resource in the organization's subject areas. Moreover, MSF not just preaches but also practices transparency; it is more open than many other NGOs in presenting detailed accounts of its activities as well as its finances.

Notes and References

1. *Yearbook of International Organizations*, 36th ed., 1999/2000 (Brussels: Union of International Associations), Appendix 3, Table 1.

2. United Nations, Economic and Social Council, Resolution 288 (X), 27 February 1950.

3. United Nations, Economic and Social Council, Resolution 1296 (XLIV), 25 June 1968.

4. Anthony Judge, "Types of International Organization", Section 2.2. Union of International Associations website (www.uia.org/uiadocs/orgtypec.htm, accessed 4 May 2000).

5. Leon Gordenker and Thomas G. Weiss, "Pluralizing Global Governance: Analytical Approaches and Dimensions," in *NGOs, the UN, and Global Governance*, edited by Thomas G. Weiss and Leon Gordenker (Boulder, CO: Lynne Rienner Publishers, 1996), p. 18.

6. Commission on Global Governance, *Our Global Neighbourhood: The Report of the Commission on Global Governance* (Oxford: Oxford University Press, 1995), p. 33.

7. Commission on Global Governance, *The Millennium Year and the Reform Process: A Contribution from the Commission on Global Governance* (London: Commission on Global Governance, 1999): 22–23.

8. See, for example, *Transnational Social Movements and Global Politics: Solidarity Beyond the State*, edited by Jackie Smith, Charles Chatfield, and Ron Pagnucco (Syracuse, NY: Syracuse University Press, 1997).

9. United Nations, Economic and Social Council, "Consultative Relationship Between the United Nations and Non-governmental Organizations," Resolution 1996/31, 25 July 1996.

10. United Nations, Economic and Social Council, "NGOs in Consultative Status, by Category" (<www.un.org/esa/coordination/ngo/table.htm>, accessed May 16, 2000).

11. Thomas G. Weiss and Leon Gordenker. *NGOs, the UN, and Global Governance* (Boulder, CO: Lynne Rienner Publishers, 1996); Chadwick F. Alger, "The United Nations System and Civil Society," paper presented at the International Studies Association Convention, Washington, DC, February 1999.

12. See, for example, the Secretary-General's address at the World Civil Society Conference, Montreal, 8 December 1999. United Nations, Department of Public Information, *Secretary-General Says 'Global People-power' Best Thing for United Nations in Long Time, Needing Response in Partnership With Civil Society*; Press Release SG/SM/7249/Rev.1 (New York: UN, 7 December 1999).

13. Commission on Global Governance, *Our Global Neighbourhood*, p. 258.

14. United Nations, Department of Public Information, *Secretary-General, Addressing Participants at Millennium Forum, Calls For Intensified 'NGO Revolution'*. Press Release SG/SM/7411; GA/9710 (New York: UN, 22 May 2000): 1.

15. Millennium Forum, New York, 22–26 May 2000, *We the Peoples: Millennium Forum Declaration and Agenda for Action* (New York, 26 May 2000).

16. See the Millennium Forum's website at <www.millenniumforum.org>.

17. Commission on Global Governance, *The Millennium Year and the Reform Process: A Contribution from the Commission on Global Governance*: 29.

18. International Campaign to Ban Landmines, "A Brief History of the ICBL: Chronology of the Ban Movement." (<www.icbl.org>, accessed May 30, 2000).

19. Richard Falk and Andrew Strauss, "On the Creation of a Global Peoples Assembly: Legitimacy and the Power of Popular Sovereignty," *Stanford Journal of International Law* 36, no. 2 (Summer 2000, forthcoming).

20. Norwegian Nobel Committee website, "The Nobel Peace Prize for 1997: International Campaign to Ban Landmines (ICBL) and Jody Williams" (<www.nobel.no/peace99_eng.html>, accessed May 31, 2000).

21. See <www.hrw.org/reports/1999/landmine/jasmine.html>, accessed May 30, 2000.

22. For a concise chronology of events leading up to and following the adoption of the Rome Statute, see the website of the Coalition for an International Criminal Court (<www.iccnow.org>, accessed June 3, 2000). See also Ken Rutherford, "The Landmine Ban and NGOs: the Role of Communications Technologies" (*Transnational Associations* 2/2000; forthcoming).

23. Falk and Strauss, "On the Creation of a Global Peoples Assembly: Legitimacy and the Power of Popular Sovereignty."

24. Ibid.

25. Coalition for an International Criminal Court website (<www.iccnow.org/html/coalition.htm>, accessed June 3, 2000).

26. William A. Dymond, "The MAI: A Sad and Melancholy Tale," in *Canada Among Nations 1999: A Big League Player?*, edited by Fen Osler Hampson, Martin Rudner, and Michael Hart (Toronto: Oxford University Press, 1999), pp. 30–31.

27. Ibid., p. 25.

28. Peter (Jay) Smith and Elizabeth Smythe, "Globalization, Citizenship and Technology: The MAI Meets the Internet," Paper presented at the annual meeting of the International Studies Association, Los Angeles, 17 March 2000, 30–31.

29. <http://mai.flora.org>, accessed June 4, 2000.

30. "After Seattle: A Global Disaster; The Non-Governmental Order," *The Economist* 353, no. 8149 (11 December 1999): 19–21.

31. United Nations, Economic and Social Council, *List of the Non-governmental Organizations in Consultative Status with the Economic and Social Council As at 31 July 1998* (<www.un.org/esa/coordination/ngo/>, accessed September 7, 1999); United Nations, Department of Public Information, *Directory of NGOs Associated with DPI* (<www.un.org/MoreInfo/ngolink/ngodir/NGODirAlph/alphabet.htm>, accessed September 7, 1999); *Yearbook of International Organizations*, 35th ed., 1998/99, Vol. 1, p. 1386; and information from Oxfam International.

32. Interview with Ernst Ligteringen, Executive Director, Oxfam International, 29 July 1999.

33. Maggie Black, *A Cause for Our Times: Oxfam, the First 50 Years* (Oxford: Oxfam and Oxford University Press, 1992).

34. Ibid., p. 172.

35. Oxfam International, *Annual Report, 1998* (Oxford: Oxfam International), p. 3.

36. Oxfam International, *Mission Statement* (<www.oxfam.org/about/mission.htm>, accessed 30 August 1999).

37. Ibid., loc. cit.

38. Oxfam International, *Programs/Kosovo* (<www.oxfam.org/programs/kosovo.htm>, accessed 30 August 1999).

39. Oxfam International, *Programs/Fair Trade* (<www.oxfam.org/programs/fair_trade.htm>, accessed 30 August 1999).

40. Oxfam International, *Annual Report, 1998*, pp. 6–7.

41. Ibid, p. 3.

42. Oxfam International, "The Timor Crisis and the OI Response" (www.oxfam.org/programs/timor.htm>, accessed October 7, 1999).

43. Oxfam International, *Annual Report, 1998*, pp. 10–11.

44. Kevin Watkins, *The Oxfam Education Report* (Oxford: Oxfam GB, 2000).

45. "Oxfam International Calls for Urgent Action to Prevent Further Bloodshed in East Timor," 3 September 1999 (<www.oxfam.org.uk>, Oxfam News Releases, accessed September 13, 1999).

46. Quoted in Black, *A Cause for Our Times*, p. 256.

47. Oxfam Great Britain, International Division, *Publications Strategy, 1996-2001* (Oxford: Oxfam GB, 1996), pp. 6–7.

48. Oxfam International, *Annual Report, 1998*, p. 3.

49. Oxfam America, "Frequently Asked Questions" (<www.oxfamamerica.org/about.html>, accessed September 3, 1999).

50. Martin Holdgate, *The Green Web: A Union for World Conservation* (London: Earthscan Publications, 1999), pp. 63–65, 203.

51. "What is IUCN?" (<www.iucn.org/info_and_news/index.html>, accessed September 21, 1999).

52. "What Is IUCN?" and other information from IUCN.

53. *A Pocket Guide to IUCN, the World Conservation Union*, 1996/1997 (Gland, Switzerland: IUCN), p. 4; and information from IUCN, November 1999.

54. United Nations, Economic and Social Council, *List of the Non-governmental Organizations in Consultative Status with the Economic and Social Council As at 31 July 1998* (<www.un.org/esa/coordination/ngo/>, accessed October 7, 1999); United Nations, Department of Public Information, *Directory of NGOs Associated with DPI* (<www.un.org/MoreInfo/ngolink/ngodir/NGODirAlph/alphabet.htm>, accessed October 7, 1999); *Yearbook of International Organizations*, 1998/99, 35th ed., Vol. 1, p. 1190; and Holdgate, *The Green Web*, pp. 253–54.

55. *Statutes of 5 October 1948, Revised on 22 October 1996 (Including Rules of Procedure of the World Conservation Congress) and Regulations, Revised on 22 October 1996* (Gland, Switzerland: IUCN, 1997).

56. *A Pocket Guide to IUCN, the World Conservation Union*, p. 4.

57. Information from IUCN, November 1999.

58. "What is IUCN?" and *A Pocket Guide to IUCN, the World Conservation Union*, pp. 4–5.

59. "What Is IUCN?"; *A Pocket Guide to IUCN, the World Conservation Union*, p. 5; and other information from IUCN.

60. "What Is IUCN?" and *A Pocket Guide to IUCN, the World Conservation Union*, p. 5.

61. *A Pocket Guide to IUCN, the World Conservation Union*, p. 4.

62. Holdgate, *The Green Web*, p. 249.

63. "What Does It Do? (IUCN in Action)" (<www.iucn.org/info_and_news/index.html>, accessed September 30, 1999).

64. Ibid; and "Integrating Gender and Social Issues Within IUCN," IUCN *Annual Report 1998*, p. 13.

65. "Themes" (<www.iucn.org/themes/themes.html>, accessed October 5, 1999).

66. Holdgate, *The Green Web*, p. 242.

67. Ibid., pp. 130–55.

68. IUCN, *World Conservation Strategy: Living Resource Conservation for Sustainable Development* (Gland, Switzerland: IUCN, 1980).

69. Holdgate, *The Green Web*, p. 152.

70. World Commission on Environment and Development, *Our Common Future* (New York: Oxford University Press, 1987).

71. *Caring for the Earth: A Strategy for Sustainable Living* (David A. Munro, project director; Gland, Switzerland: IUCN; UNEP; WWF, 1991).

72. *Caring for the Earth: A Strategy for Sustainable Living*, cited by Holdgate, *The Green Web*, p. 210.

73. Holdgate, *The Green Web*, p. 211.

74. *Global Biodiversity Strategy: Guidelines for Action to Save, Study, and Use Earth's Biotic Wealth Sustainably and Equitably* ([Washington, DC]: World Resources Institute; IUCN; UNEP, 1992).

75. James M. Sheehan, *Global Greens: Inside the International Environmental Establishment* (Washington, DC: Capital Research Center, 1998), pp. 169, 185.

76. "1998 Expenditure by Programme," IUCN *Annual Report* 1998, p. 35.

77. "Information Management Group (IMG)" (<www.iucn.org/info_and_news/index.html>; accessed September 28, 1999).

78. Holdgate, *The Green Web*.

79. *A Pocket Guide to IUCN, the World Conservation Union*, 1996/1997; IUCN, *Annual Report* (1961– ; Gland, Switzerland: IUCN); *World Conservation* (Vol. 27, No. 1, 1996– ; Gland, Switzerland: IUCN; former title: *IUCN Bulletin*, Vol. 1–26, No. 4; 1961–1995); *IUCN Membership Directory* (19??– . Gland, Switzerland: IUCN).

80. *1997 IUCN Red List of Threatened Plants*, edited by Kerry S. Walter and Harriet J. Gillett (Gland, Switzerland: IUCN, 1998); *1996 IUCN Red List of Threatened Animals*, edited by Jonathan Baillie and Brian Groombridge (Gland, Switzerland: IUCN; Washington, DC: Conservation International, 1996); *IUCN Red List Categories* (Gland, Switzerland: IUCN, 1995).

81. IUCN, *World Conservation Strategy: Living Resource Conservation for Sustainable Development* (Gland, Switzerland: IUCN, 1980); *Caring for the Earth: A Strategy for Sustainable Living* (David A. Munro, project director; Gland, Switzerland: IUCN; UNEP; WWF, 1991); *Global Biodiversity Strategy: Guidelines for Action to Save, Study, and Use Earth's Biotic Wealth Sustainably and Equitably* ([Washington, DC]: World Resources Institute; IUCN; UNEP, 1992).

82. *World Directory of Environmental Organizations: A Handbook of National and International Organizations and Programs (Governmental and Non-governmental) Concerned with Protecting the Earth's Resources*, edited by Thaddeus C. Trzyna, Elizabeth Margold, and Julia K. Osborn (Sacramento, CA; Claremont, CA: California Institute of Public Affairs; London: Earthscan, 1996).

83. *United Nations List of Protected Areas* (1st ed., 1961/1962– .; Gland, Switzerland: IUCN). Former titles: *United Nations List of National Parks and Equivalent Reserves; United Nations List of National Parks and Protected Areas*.

84. "Press Releases" (<www.iucn.org/info_and_news/index.html>, accessed September 30, 1999).

85. *IUCN Publications 1948–1998: A Catalogue of Publications Produced by IUCN—the World Conservation Union or in Collaboration with Other Organizations or Publishers*, compiled by Kevin Grose and Cécile Thiéry (3rd and 50th anniversary ed.; Gland, Switzerland: IUCN, 1998); IUCN, *The World Conservation Bookstore [Catalogue], 1948–1998* (Cambridge, UK: IUCN Publications Services Unit, 1998).

86. *IUCN Reports, 1960–1995, Including an Appendix on IUCN Periodicals*, compiled by Cécile Thiéry (1st ed.; Gland, Switzerland: IUCN, 1996).

87. "IUCN Depository Libraries" (<www.iucn.org/info_and_news/index.html>, accessed September 30, 1999).

88. *World Directory of Country Environmental Studies: An Annotated Bibliography of Natural Resources Profiles, Plans, and Strategies*, edited by Daniel B. Tunstall and Sean Gordon (Washington, DC: World Resources Institute, 1996).

89. Rony Brauman, "The Médecins Sans Frontières Experience," in *A Framework for Survival*, edited by Kevin M. Cahill ([s.l.:] Basic Books and the Council on Foreign Relations, 1991), p. 203.

90. Médecins Sans Frontières website (www.msf.org, accessed October 15, 1999).

91. Rony Brauman, op. cit., pp. 206–8.

92. Ibid., pp. 213–14.

93. Ibid., pp. 215–18.

94. Médecins Sans Frontières, *Activity Report*, July 1997/June 1998 (Brussels), back cover.

95. Médecins Sans Frontières, *Activity Report*, July 1998/June 1999 (<www.msf.org/publications/activ_rep/1999/index.htm>, accessed October 26, 1999).

96. *Populations in Danger 1995: A Médecins Sans Frontières Report*, edited by François Jean (London: Médecins Sans Frontières UK, 1995), pp. 32–46, 85–96.

97. "MSF Withdraws from Bunia and Ituri District in the DRC" (<www.msf.org/projects/africa/drc/reports/2000/02/withdrawl.htm>; accessed February 14, 2000).

98. Norwegian Nobel Committee website, "Nobel Peace Prize 1999" (<www.nobel.no/peace99_eng.html>, accessed October 15, 1999).

99. David Rieff, "The Good Doctors: Humanitarianism at Century's End," *The New Republic* 221, no. 19 (November 8, 1999): 23; James Paupst, "A Meditation on Evil," *Maclean's: Canada's Weekly Newsmagazine* 113, no. 27 (July 1, 2000): 54.

100. "The 1999 Nobel Peace Prize Speech Delivered by Dr. James Orbinski, President of the MSF International Council, in Oslo, Norway on December 10, 1999" (<www.msf.org/events/1999/nobel/reports/speech/index.htm>, accessed February 14, 2000).

101. Médecins Sans Frontières, *Activity Report*, July 1997/June 1998, pp. 82–83.

102. Information from Médecins Sans Frontières, August 1999.

103. Médecins Sans Frontières, *Activity Report* (1993– ; Brussels).

104. Brauman, "The Médecins Sans Frontières Experience," pp. 202–20.

105. "28 Years On: Milestones of a Humanitarian Movement" (<www.msf.org/msf/history.htm>, accessed November 3, 1999).

106. Roger Job, *Lettres Sans Frontières* (Bruxelles: Complexe, 1994).

107. Elliott Leyton, with photographs by Greg Locke, *Touched by Fire: Doctors Without Borders in a Third World Crisis* (Toronto: McClelland & Stewart, 1998); Leanne Olson, *A Cruel Paradise: Journals of an International Relief Worker* (Toronto: Insomniac Press, 1999); Paul B. Spiegel and Peter Salama, "War and Mortality in Kosovo, 1998–99: An Epidemiological Testimony," *The Lancet* 355, no. 9222 (24 June 2000).

108. *Populations in Danger 1995: A Médecins Sans Frontières Report*, edited by François Jean (London: Médecins Sans Frontières UK, 1995).

109. Bernard Pecoul, Pierre Chirac, Patrice Trouiller, and Jacques Pinel, "Access to Essential Drugs in Poor Countries: A Lost Battle?" *Journal of the American Medical Association* 281, no. 4 (January 27, 1999): 361–67.

110. "The 1999 Nobel Peace Prize Speech Delivered by Dr. James Orbinski" (<www.msf.org/events/1999/nobel/reports/speech/index.htm>, accessed February 14, 2000).

111. "Manuals, Guides and Handbooks" (<www.msf.org/intweb99/library/guidlist.htm>, accessed October 21, 1999).

112. "Diary of Dr. Raymond Vanholder" (<www.msf.org/projects/turkey/reports/1999/10/narrative>/, accessed October 25, 1999).

113. "A Brief History of Médecins Sans Frontières" (<www.msf.org/msf/history.htm>, accessed October 15, 1999).

114. "Webstats from a Nobel Prize" (<www.msf.org/events/1999/nobel/stats/, accessed November 2, 1999).

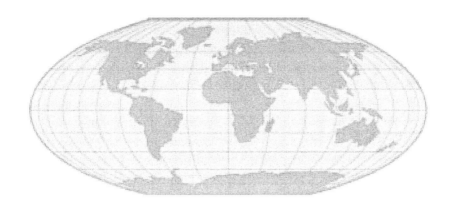

Part II

RESOURCES

CHAPTER 6
ICAO Promotes Safety and Uniformity in Aeronautical Charting Worldwide

David Lewtas

Introduction

The United Nations (UN) is central to global efforts to solve problems that challenge humanity. Cooperating in this effort are more than thirty affiliated organizations, known together as the UN system. Day in and day out, the UN and its family of organizations work to promote respect for human rights, protect the environment, fight disease, foster development and reduce poverty. UN agencies define the standards for safe and efficient transport by air and sea, help improve telecommunications and enhance consumer protection, work to ensure respect for intellectual property rights and coordinate allocation of radio frequencies. The UN leads international campaigns against drug trafficking and terrorism. Throughout the world, the UN and its agencies assist refugees and set up programs to clear landmines, help improve the quality of drinking water and expand food production, make loans to developing countries and help stabilize financial markets.

The need for geospatial information is critical to many of these activities. As well, in recent years the world has seen an unprecedented increase in natural and man-made disasters, internal conflict and cross-border disputes, and the UN has responded by making use of technological advances in cartographic automation and geographic information systems (GIS) to ensure that critical geographical information is made available at short notice and in readily digestible form to help deal with those situations at many levels.

The UN departments of Public Information, Peacekeeping Operations, Economic and Social Affairs, Political Affairs, the UN Office of Legal Affairs, the Office for the Coordinator of Humanitarian Affairs, the Food and Agriculture Organization of the United Nations (FAO), the International Civil Aviation Organization (ICAO), the International Maritime Organization (IMO), the United

Nations Centre for Human Settlements (Habitat), the United Nations Development Programme (UNDP), the United Nations Environment Programme (UNEP), the United Nations Educational, Scientific and Cultural Organization (Unesco), the Office of the United Nations High Commissioner for Refugees (UNHCR), the United Nations Children's Fund (UNICEF), the United Nations Office for Project Services (UNOPS), the World Meteorological Organization (WMO) and the World Health Organization (WHO) are just some of the UN system's agencies that are actively involved in spatial data collection, GIS development or cartographic production.

The following examples illustrate the diverse application of these efforts:

- The UN Department of Public Information undertakes a range of cartographic services related to the work of the UN Secretariat, including the preparation of small-scale, illustrative maps, large-scale stand-alone maps and GIS products and the provision of advisory geographic/cartographic services on technical and research issues.
- FAO is involved in the collection, storage, manipulation, and mapping of vast amounts of geographic data in order to improve agricultural productivity and food security, and to better the living standards of rural populations.
- ICAO, the organization that is the focus of this chapter, establishes international aeronautical charting standards as part of its work to promote safety, security and efficiency in air transport.
- IMO, in its effort to improve international shipping procedures, raise standards in marine safety, and reduce pollution by ships, works with the International Hydrographic Association (IHO), an intergovernmental organization, to develop international standards for marine navigation charts.
- UNHCR has established a GIS—essential to providing for the mass movement of refugees—to address information needs at the field (operational) level.
- WHO coordinates programs aimed at solving health problems and the attainment by all people of the highest level of health. It uses mapping and GIS in its immunization programs and in tracking and forecasting the spread of disease.

Efforts are now underway, headed by the Cartographic Section of the UN Department of Public Information, to establish a common UN geographic database so that geographic information could be more efficiently shared and coordinated among the UN and its agencies. It is envisaged that this database, utilizing advancing web technologies, will make it possible to collect and exchange spatial data from thousands of servers, national mapping agencies, and other geographic information producers.

The effects and accuracy of spatial data are very relevant to the work of the UN, its agencies, nongovernmental organizations, civil society, and industry. Cartography, whether represented by a paper chart for navigation or on the display screen of a GIS, is the art and science of displaying this spatial data so it may best be assimilated and used. The variety of requirements, users, and the global nature of the UN have created a diversity of cartographic production which is probably unique within an organization.

The International Civil Aviation Organization (ICAO)

ICAO was founded with the signing of the Convention on International Civil Aviation on 7 December 1944 to promote the safe and orderly development of international civil aviation. A specialized agency of the UN, ICAO sets international standards and regulations necessary for the safety, security, efficiency and regularity of air transport, and serves as a medium for co-operation in all fields of civil aviation among its 185 contracting states. In addition to its headquarters in Montreal, Canada, ICAO also has seven regional offices located in Bangkok, Cairo, Dakar, Lima, Mexico, Nairobi and Paris.

Improving safety is ICAO's main activity. The eighteen Annexes to the Convention on International Civil Aviation contain both technical international standards whose implementation is necessary as well as recommended practices whose implementation is desirable in the interest of safety, security, regularity and efficiency of international air navigation.[1] There is no doubt that the uniform application of these standards across the world has had the desired impact; safety in scheduled air services has improved tremendously since ICAO came into existence. In 1947, 590 passengers were killed in thirty-four fatal accidents (excluding the USSR) with 3.12 passenger fatalities per 100 million passenger-kilometres. The safety level has improved steadily since then. In 1998, the fatality rate stood at 0.035. Commercial aviation remains the safest form of transport.

The world of aviation, which by its very nature knows no geographical or political boundaries, requires aeronautical maps which are unlike those used in ground transportation. Before departure, the pilot wants to know what to expect enroute and at the destination in the way of navigation, communications and aerodrome* facilities and services. The safe and efficient flow of air traffic is facilitated by aeronautical charts produced to accepted ICAO standards. These standards are published in *Annex 4* to the *Convention on International Civil Aviation—Aeronautical Charts*.[2] Even though aeronautical charts are published by the civil aviation administrations of numerous different States and by other chart-producing organizations, the internationally understood uniformity of their specifications helps to make it possible for pilots to navigate and land safely at international aerodromes all around the world.

---

*Aerodrome is the official term used by ICAO for *airport*—ed.

Aeronautical Charts— ICAO

The ICAO series of aeronautical charts consists of seventeen types, each intended to serve a specialized purpose. They range from detailed, large-scale charts for individual aerodromes to small-scale charts for flight planning purposes. When a published aeronautical chart contains "ICAO" in its title, this indicates that the chart producer has conformed to both general *Annex 4* standards and those pertaining to a particular ICAO chart type.

Three series of charts are available for planning and visual navigation, each with a different scale. The *Aeronautical Navigation Chart—ICAO Small Scale* charts cover the largest area for a given paper size and provide a general-purpose chart series suitable for long-range flight planning. The *World Aeronautical Chart—ICAO 1:1,000,000* charts provide complete world coverage with uniform presentation of data at a constant scale and are used in the production of other charts. The *Aeronautical Chart—ICAO 1:500,000* series supplies more detail and provides a suitable medium for pilot and navigation training. This series is most suitable for use by low-speed, short- or medium-range flights performed at low and intermediate altitudes.

The vast majority of scheduled flights take place along routes equipped with radio and electronic navigation systems that make visual reference to the ground unnecessary. This type of navigation is conducted under instrument flight rules (IFR), and the flight is required to comply with the appropriate air traffic control services procedures. The *Enroute Chart—ICAO* contains the air traffic service system, radio navigation aids and other aeronautical information essential to IFR enroute navigation. It is designed for easy handling in the limited space of an aircraft flight deck, and the presentation of information is such that it can easily be read in varying conditions of natural and artificial light. Where flights cross extensive oceanic and sparsely settled areas, the *Plotting Chart—ICAO* provides a useful means of maintaining a continuous flight record of aircraft position and is often produced to complement the more complex enroute charts.

As a flight approaches its destination, more detail is required about the area around the aerodrome of intended landing. The *Area Chart—ICAO* provides pilots with information to facilitate the transition from the enroute to the final approach phase, as well as from the take-off to enroute phases of the flight. These charts are designed to enable pilots to comply with departure, arrival and holding pattern procedures and provide for a smooth transition to the information on the *Instrument Approach Chart—ICAO*.

The *Instrument Approach Chart—ICAO* provides the pilot with a graphic presentation of instrument approach and missed approach procedures to be followed should the crew be unable to carry out a landing. These charts contain both a plan and profile view of the approach with full details of associated radio navigation aids and services, and necessary aerodrome and topographical information. The format shown in Figure 6.1 illustrates the standardized layout of information for the *Instrument Approach Chart—ICAO* and highlights some

Aeronautical Charts—ICAO / 187

Figure 6.1. Format—*Instrument Approach Chart—ICAO.*

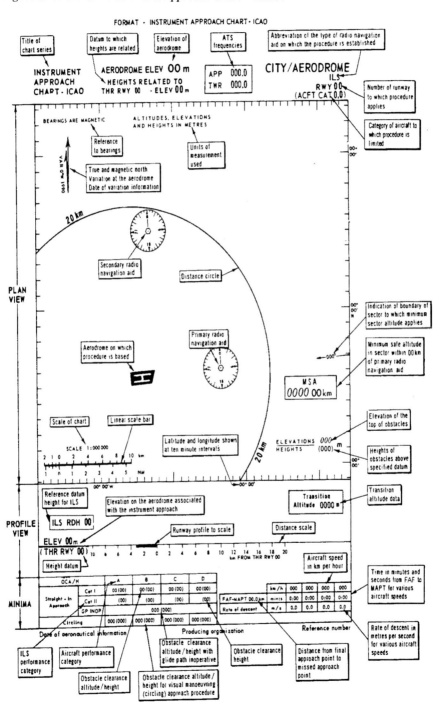

chart elements to which *Annex 4* provisions are applied. A complete sample *Instrument Approach Chart—ICAO* is shown in Figure 6.2 which illustrates the application of many *Annex 4* provisions. *Annex 4* requires that relief be shown on instrument approach charts. In this particular example, relief is shown in monochrome by the spot elevation method; however, *Annex 4* specifications are currently being reviewed to possibly include specific standards for color relief portrayal.

In the event of a visual-type approach to land, the pilot may refer to a *Visual Approach Chart—ICAO* which illustrates the basic aerodrome layout and surrounding features easily recognizable from the air. As well as providing orientation, these charts are designed to highlight potential dangers such as obstacles, high terrain, and areas of hazardous airspace.

The *Aerodrome/Heliport Chart—ICAO* provides an illustration of the aerodrome or heliport which allows the pilot to recognize significant aerodrome/heliport features necessary for landing, to rapidly clear the runway or heliport touchdown area after landing, and to follow taxiing instructions. These charts show aerodrome/heliport movement areas, visual indicator locations, taxiing guidance aids, aerodrome/heliport lighting, hangars, terminal buildings, aircraft/helicopter stands, various reference points required for the setting and checking of navigation systems and operational information such as pavement strengths and radio communication facility frequencies. At large, complex aerodromes where all the aircraft taxiing and parking information cannot be clearly shown on the *Aerodrome/Heliport Chart—ICAO*, these details are provided by the supplementary *Aerodrome Ground Movement Chart—ICAO* and the *Aircraft Parking/Docking Chart—ICAO*.

Obstacles around airports are of critical importance to aircraft operations. Information about these is given in detail on the *Aerodrome Obstacle Chart—ICAO*, Types A, B, and C. These charts are intended to assist aircraft operators in making the complex take-off mass and performance calculations required, including those covering emergency situations such as an engine failure during take-off. Aerodrome obstacle charts show the runways in plan and profile, take-off flight path areas and obstacles, and the declared distances for take-off run and accelerate-stop available at a particular runway. The detailed topographical information provided by some aerodrome obstacle charts includes coverage of areas as far as forty-five kilometres away from the aerodrome itself.

Technological Change and Safety Aspects Affecting Charting

To ensure that aeronautical charts reflect technological changes while meeting the operational requirements of modern aviation operations, ICAO is constantly monitoring and updating, as necessary, specifications for aeronautical charts. *Annex 4* is now in its ninth edition [see Endnote 2—ed.] and has been amended fifty-one times since the publication of its first edition in 1948. The following paragraphs describe some of the issues that are currently affecting aeronautical charting.

Technological Change and Safety Aspects Affecting Charting / 189

Figure 6.2. Sample *Instrument Approach Chart—ICAO*.

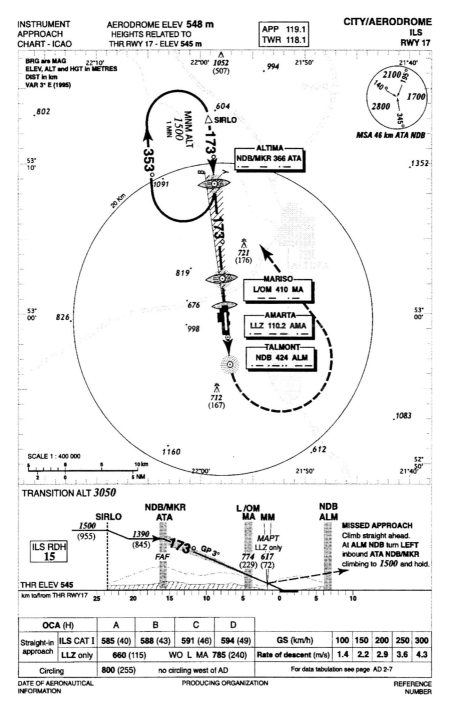

A very significant achievement by ICAO has been the development of a largely satellite-based system concept that is to meet the future communications, navigation, and surveillance/air traffic management needs of civil aviation. Satellite-based navigation extends the accuracy of airborne navigation, but this new technology also requires greater precision and compatibility of charted geographical coordinates.

There are many local geodetic reference datums* in use throughout the world providing references for the charting of particular areas. Each datum has been produced by fitting a particular mathematical earth model (ellipsoid) to the true shape of the earth (geoid) in such a way as to minimize the differences between the ellipsoid and the geoid over the area of interest. Most ellipsoids in current use were derived in the nineteenth century and were normally referenced to a local observatory. These different datums and ellipsoids produce different latitude and longitude grids and, hence, different sets of geographical coordinates.

The geographical coordinates now provided by civil aviation authorities and published on aeronautical charts are mostly referenced to different local geodetic datums while the coordinates generated by satellite navigation systems are referenced to earth-centered datums. As a consequence, the coordinates of points published on current charts will not coincide with the coordinates generated by satellite navigation systems. Differences can range from a few metres to several kilometres.

These differences are not significant to aircraft navigating by the present ground-based radio navigation aid network. However, to support the coordinate accuracy requirements of global satellite-based navigation, international acceptance of a common earth-centered geodetic datum was required. Accordingly, to realize the increased efficiencies offered by satellite-based navigation while maintaining at least the same level of safety, the earth-centered **World Geodetic System—1984 (WGS-84)** was adopted by ICAO as the common geodetic reference datum for international civil aviation.

Amendment 50 to *Annex 4* introduced new provisions concerning the promulgation, as of 1 January 1998, of **WGS-84**-related geographical coordinates on aeronautical charts. To assist States in converting their aeronautical coordinates to the **WGS-84** geodetic reference datum, an ICAO *World Geodetic System—1984 (WGS-84) Manual* (Document 9674) has been published and **WGS-84** implementation workshops have taken place throughout the world.

Electronic databases are becoming the depositories of aeronautical information promulgated by State civil aviation authorities by means of their **Aeronautical Information Publications** (AIPs) and aeronautical charts. An important

---

Datums is the plural form of the technical term *datum* used here by the author. "**Geodetic Datum** [is] an ellipsoid fixed in relation to the earth so that the polar axis, the central point and the zero meridian plane are all fixed. There are two types. (1) Local geodetic datum: the ellipsoid has been chosen and fixed to fit a region. (2) Geocentric geodetic datum: the ellipsoid has been chosen to fit the earth as a whole and its central point is based on a definition of earth's centre of mass." Canada, Department of National Defence, Directorate of Geomatics, *The Digital Geographic Information Exchange Standard*, Part 1 (Ottawa: DND, 1992).

part of the information stored in these electronic databases is transferred directly to the computers of the Flight Management System (FMS) on board aircraft, and the quality of this information may have a direct impact on the precision of air navigation. International standards and guidance material are being developed by ICAO for the quality assurance of aeronautical data, data transfer, and data protection while facilitating the global compatibility and interoperability of data formats.

"The glass cockpit" is a recently coined term describing the presentation of information on computer-like screens to flight crews. In a modern aircraft, these screens display instrumentation, the status of aircraft systems, and sometimes moving aeronautical chart displays which follow and present the aircraft's position in real time. ICAO is developing specifications and guidance material as necessary to support electronic aeronautical charts for cockpit display with particular regard to (a) the allocation of information available for display according to flight rules and phase of flight; (b) the display of color and information associated with certain colors; and (c) integration of human factors concepts in the design of the electronic chart display and its operation by the flight crew.

Many aircraft accidents have taken place in circumstances where a properly functioning aircraft has been inadvertently flown into terrain, often a mountain obscured by cloud. It is ICAO's goal to greatly reduce the occurrence of this type of accident, which is termed "controlled flight into terrain (CFIT)." As part of this initiative, the specifications for the *Instrument Approach Chart—ICAO* are being studied with the aim of increasing the pilot's awareness of terrain and preventing the misinterpretation of information contained on this type of chart. See Figure 6.2 for a sample *Instrument Approach Chart—ICAO*.

Other ICAO Products Related to Aeronautical Charting

The implementation of *Annex 4* standards is facilitated by the *Aeronautical Chart Manual*.[3] This manual provides detailed guidance (except for elementary cartographic techniques) for the design and production of all seventeen ICAO type charts. It also promotes maximum efficiency in the organization and operation of the services providing aeronautical charts and assists States in the training of personnel responsible for the production and use of aeronautical charts. Further assistance is provided to States through the ICAO regional offices, seminars, workshops, special implementation projects and ICAO-sponsored cartographic training.

The *Aeronautical Chart Catalogue* is a detailed catalog of all aeronautical charts produced by States, State-recognized agencies, and some airlines, known to be available to international civil aviation.[4] The catalog is divided into two major parts: one listing details of chart availability under the name of the producing State or agency, the other indicating the geographical coverage of specific chart series by means of index charts. With this information, chart users can make an efficient and accurate selection of the charts required for a specific flight and address chart orders to the appropriate producing or distribution agency. It should be noted that ICAO headquarters and ICAO regional offices are neither producers of nor sales agents for aeronautical charts for operational purposes.

"Aeronautical Charts" is an audio-slide presentation which provides an introduction to the contents of *Annex 4* and the *Aeronautical Chart Manual*.[5] Intended mainly for the benefit of personnel engaged in the production of aeronautical charts, it provides explanations of the purpose of each type of aeronautical chart specified in *Annex 4* and gives an outline of information to be depicted on different charts.

Annex 15[6] to the Convention on International Civil Aviation, Aeronautical Information Services (AIS), contains ICAO Standards and Recommended Practices (SARPS) governing the provision of aeronautical information, including the standards specifying those aeronautical charts which shall be a part of the Aeronautical Information Publication (AIP) published by each State. The *Aeronautical Information Services Manual* is a companion document to *Annex 15* and provides detailed guidance material aimed at facilitating the implementation of the provisions contained in the *Annex*.[7] It includes, among other material, a sample AIP illustrating those types of charts required for inclusion in an AIP.

Supporting both Annexes 4 and 15, as well as other ICAO Annexes, is the *World Geodetic System—1984 (WGS-84) Manual* mentioned earlier.[8] The purpose of this manual is to furnish guidance on the provision of geographic coordinates referenced to the WGS-84 geodetic datum in order to assist States in the uniform implementation of related ICAO technical standards and recommended practices.

The above ICAO products are prepared by the Aeronautical Information and Charts (AIS/MAP) Section which is a part of ICAO's Air Navigation Bureau. Besides the activities and duties associated with maintaining and updating these ICAO products, the section also provides a computerized chart production service for the Organization and maintains an extensive AIS technical library (Aeronautical Information Publications and aeronautical charts). In addition, ICAO issues a wide variety of aviation-related technical, economic, and legal publications as well as audiovisual aids (films, tapes, slides, posters). Most of these are available in English, French, Spanish, and Russian; some are also issued in Arabic and Chinese. A catalog of all ICAO publications and audiovisual training aids is available from the ICAO Document Sales Unit, 999 University Street, Montreal, Quebec, Canada H3C 5H7; telephone: 514-954-8022; fax: 514-954-6769; e-mail: sales_unit@icao.int. ICAO maintains a website at <www.icao.int>.

Notes and References

1. International Civil Aviation Organization, *Convention on International Civil Aviation*, signed at Chicago on 7 December 1944 and amended by the ICAO Assembly (Montreal: ICAO, 1944). Document 7300.

2. International Civil Aviation Organization, *Convention on International Civil Aviation, Annex 4—Aeronautical Charts*, 9th ed. (Montreal: ICAO, 1995).

3. International Civil Aviation Organization, *Aeronautical Chart Manual*, 2d ed. (Montreal: ICAO, 1987). Document 8697.

4. International Civil Aviation Organization, *Aeronautical Chart Catalogue*, 28th ed. (Montreal: ICAO, 1993). Document 7101.

5. International Civil Aviation Organization, "Aeronautical Charts" (Montreal: ICAO, 1990). 136 audio-slides. ICAO Order No. S690.

6. International Civil Aviation Organization, *Convention on International Civil Aviation, Annex 15—Aeronautical Information Services*, 10th ed. (Montreal: ICAO, 1997).

7. International Civil Aviation Organization, *Aeronautical Information Services Manual*, 5th ed. (Montreal: ICAO, 1995). Document 8126.

8. International Civil Aviation Organization, *World Geodetic System—1984 (WGS-84) Manual*, 1st ed. (Montreal: ICAO, 1997). Document 9674.

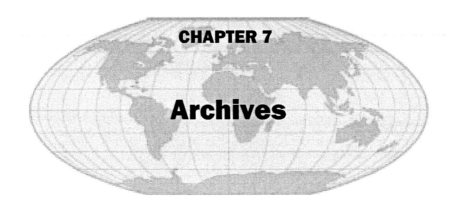

CHAPTER 7
Archives

Markku Järvinen

Introduction

Most of this book deals with printed, microform, and electronic information from international governmental organizations (IGOs). This chapter covers archives and records. Some discussion is therefore necessary to define archives and their relationship with documents and publications.

According to international terminology currently used by practising archivists, **archives** are all documents, regardless of form or medium, received or created in the course of activities by an institution, organization, or person. The *fonds* of an institution (that is, the holdings in its archives) are, as a rule, preserved as well as arranged and described in an inventory as a closed entity. Another term used in connection with archives is **records**; in general, all materials contained in archives are **records**, whatever their material support.

Another classification is **current archives** (active files), **intermediate archives** (records waiting to be appraised or waiting for their retention period to run out), and **historical archives** (records in permanent preservation.) In a restricted meaning, and especially in German and Anglo-Saxon usage, only **noncurrent records** become archives when they have been appraised as to their evidential or informational value and selected for long-term preservation in an archives repository.[1]

Formerly, the distinction was more precise between library materials (books and periodicals) and archival materials (records), and between published and unpublished information; records were (mostly) unpublished information. Today this distinction is no longer clear. The method of production of a particular type of document is irrelevant. The definition of archives also includes printed documents and even publications, especially official publications; archivists call these **printed archives**. The whole body of documentary materials or documentary heritage constitutes, in principle, the archives of an institution.[2] This is even more true of international organizations, in fact of all organizations that produce great quantities of documents by printing. In the case of Unesco, documents, resolutions, and proceedings of the General Conference are part of the archives of the Organization; it would be inconceivable to deny their archival character. At the same time, they are also official publications and become parts of library collections.

What is the relationship of archives services to libraries and documentation centers? Archive records, documents, and publications of international organizations cover the periods of existence of those organizations. Nevertheless, in practical work, requests for recent information occur more frequently in libraries and tend to predominate in documentation centers. While documentation centers and certain libraries often discard older material, archive services cannot do so. Archives comprise "documentation extended over time," and so do library collections; national libraries are sometimes termed "archival libraries" because they preserve the whole printed heritage of a nation. But the particular character of archives is that they cover all the years of existence of an organization with no special preference for recent years. In fact, archives services are somewhat cut off from new information because current and very recent records are kept by the responsible organizational units of the institution concerned. Even when archives and records services possess recent records, they cannot disclose the information therein because records may include security-classified information.

Documents and publications are, as a rule, under the bibliographic control of librarians and documentalists, and the printed documentation in its entirety is often preserved as part of library collections. Often, in international organizations, there is also an archival series of (printed) documents in the custody of the archives services. When this is not the case, the documentation kept in the library should be considered as part of the archives of the agency and should therefore be treated according to archive standards as an archival series and not only as a collection of separate individual bibliographic items.[3]

Records are "particular" because they are unique; the correspondence file of the International Institute for Intellectual Co-operation (IICI) in Paris concerning the relations with the Government of Chile and covering the years 1925–1945 exists as such only in the archives of the IICI preserved by Unesco. A counterpart file on the same subject should exist in the governmental archives in Santiago, but the two files are certainly not identical. (A subject file consists of incoming, internal, and copies of outgoing pieces.) All pieces of a correspondence file exist in very few copies (except for circular letters): the original sent to the addressee, a copy for the subject file, another for the chronological file, and perhaps some information copies to other concerned units.[4]

Documents, as contrasted with records, are "general" because they usually exist in a certain number of copies: there is a print-run according to distribution needs. A Unesco Executive Board document must be distributed to the fifty-eight members of the Board, as well as to permanent delegates of Unesco's member states, to governments and national commissions for Unesco, and

Unesco Secretariat units. The document is also available to all others interested, through free distribution. A normal Executive Board working document of a recent session is printed, in English alone, say, in eighteen hundred copies. In the Unesco Archives, there is an archival series of those documents, "archival" meaning a complete set to be kept forever, whereas other sets of the same documents serve for working purposes or for information and therefore can be discarded at some later date.

Today, recent Board documents starting from the end of 1995 are accessible also in full text in the Unesco Electronic Document Management Data Base (UNESDOC) at <http://Unesdoc.unesco.org/ulis>. The same is true for General Conference documents, the *Programme and Budget* (document C/5), and the speeches of the Director-General (documents DG); the texts of the resolutions of the Conference and the decisions of the Board since 1946 are available in the same database. If a document is stored in text mode, full-text searching is possible.

The Executive Board, the organ responsible for the execution of the Unesco program, holds open meetings and its documents are easily accessible. The working habits of secretariats are naturally different. The public is only indirectly informed of the work carried out, through public information units and news media. True, secretariats of IGOs issue and distribute (printed) documents, but their records, correspondence, internal working documents, memoranda, and notes circulate only in a few copies to be filed in the normal course of events in file stations not accessible for outsiders. When the Director-General of Unesco meets a representative of a member government to discuss collaboration, usually there is a memorandum of understanding signed by both sides. In the case of meetings between the executive head and representatives of member states where a formal document is not required, in all probability both sides take separate notes about the conversation or the exchange of views. These memoranda or notes on conversations exist perhaps only in two copies (in case of notes, possibly also in two slightly diverging versions in two different archives with no distribution or limited distribution only to those concerned).

Records are, to begin with, unpublished, closed, and inaccessible information. In general, Secretariat records in the UN system become accessible for consultation in ten, twenty, or thirty years. Records are therefore "particular" also because of restricted access. However, there exist categories of restricted (printed) documents, too, and even restricted publications. For example, Unesco field mission reports (document code FMR) are issued as restricted at least for six months, to allow the government in question in the first place to take cognizance of the contents. Another example of restricted documents are individual human rights cases submitted to the Unesco Executive Board which are treated as confidential material and discussed in private meetings. As opposed to individual cases, "questions of massive, systematic and flagrant violations" of human rights may be examined in public meetings by the Board and the Conference.[5]

Document is the general term librarians have chosen to cover all kinds of materials in libraries, and it is a term generally used by archivists as well. Pieces in a file are also documents; archivists usually call these **archive documents**, to be precise. In the context of international organizations, and in society in general,

document has also a specific, restrictive meaning referring to printed or processed documents usually identified for easy reference by a code or symbol. For example, document number 144 EX/INF.3 is a reference to the Unesco Executive Board document of the 144th session containing the report of the Director-General on the activities of the Organization since the preceding session.[6] Documents have codes [Unesco's "codes" are analogous to the UN's "document series symbols"—ed.], publications should have an ISBN number, periodicals an ISSN number. Codes serve for identification and for filing purposes; ISBN and ISSN numbers serve for identification and for book trade purposes, but not for filing.

In this chapter, **records** refer occasionally to **printed archives** with the understanding that documents and publications are part of the archival heritage of an IGO and, in fact, of every institution. Examples are drawn mostly from Unesco. There still is an important distinction between archivists and librarians: a librarian may be familiar with documents of many international organizations, having handled and used them in his or her depository collection. An archivist, on the other hand, rarely has occasion to deal with archive records of other organizations, because only a visit to the headquarters of other IGOs would bring these records within his or her reach.

Records of Intergovernmental Organizations

The history of international and intergovernmental organizations is recorded in detail in the archives and printed documentation of these organizations. How are these archives organized and what can be found in the records of the organizations?

In an ideal situation, an IGO has an archives and records management service as part of its secretariat with competent personnel working under due administrative authorization and support of the higher management echelons, having filing rules and filing plans, rules of transfer of records, and deposit of documents and publications into archival custody.[7] Normal working procedures include record retention schedules to govern the disposition of records. It is to be noted that disposition (that is, elimination) is an essential part of records management. It is possible to find a complete set of publications and printed documents, but never the totality of records created. Records are always under retention periods, say, from two to ten, twenty, or fifty years. The retention of modern records is reviewed at least twice in their lifetime. In fact, records have a life-cycle; they are created, used, filed and scheduled for temporary, short-term, long-term or permanent retention. What the researcher finds in an archives service is always a selection of records deemed, after appraisal, to be worthy of preservation for posterity.[8]

The appraisal is based on the evidential value of the records, on their value for legal, financial, and administrative information, or on their usefulness in recording the history and past activities of the organization; that is, their research value not only for the organization itself but also for independent outside researchers. It is clear that economic aspects (the cost of preservation and the need for space) have to be considered, too, when crucial decisions are taken concerning retention; the preservation of a linear metre of records and documents has a price. Are the "owners" of the organizations, that is, the member states, ready to carry the financial burden of the preservation of the archives? Experience shows that there is much more readiness, for example, to invest large sums in fancy, promising, new technology while archive services find themselves in difficult, unsatisfactory conditions.

In a broad view of the history of archives, only very partial, albeit important, archives are preserved from antiquity—thanks to the climate in the Middle East and the durable material of some of the documents. From classical antiquity (the Greek and Roman periods) nothing remains from the central archives; there are, however, a lot of inscriptions but only fragmentary records on papyrus from local archives. There are some glimpses of archives for the centuries after the collapse of the Roman Empire, but the real archival series continuing from year to year start somewhere in the eleventh or twelfth centuries A.D. in the chancelleries of the longest-standing and still existing authorities such as the Papal State and the kingdom of England.

What is the likely fate of the era of international organizations of the twentieth and twenty-first centuries? Will the records of large intergovernmental and smaller nongovernmental organizations be preserved for posterity? The history of archives, like all human history, is marked by decay and destruction. True, human history is marked also by reconstruction and rebirth; the reconstitution of an archives, however, is not possible once unique records have disappeared. Intergovernmental archives are threatened by lack of attention and unwillingness on the part of the "owners" to pay the cost of preservation and maintenance of services to the world community. Lack of space annihilates the strongest preservation motives, says a German authority.

International archives, in the long run, are a special case compared to archives and records created in nation states. In most states there are central archive repositories to receive the records of national administrations. The 1992 edition of the *International Directory of Archives* lists 173 countries that have an archival administration to preserve and provide service on records in their custody.[9] The same directory lists twenty-two archives services of international organizations. But international archives have no "competent" central repositories or special agencies to receive their past records for preservation. International organizations on the whole are obliged to preserve their archives forever. Smaller organizations such as NGOs sometimes have the opportunity to deposit their records with national archives repositories, university libraries or research institutes, but this cannot apply to large intergovernmental organizations. The League of Nations archives for 1920–1946 are well preserved by the successor body in the UN Library in Geneva, but there is no central repository for the whole UN system with its numerous specialized agencies.

However, the UN is not unaware of the problem. In the context of its fortieth anniversary, the Administrative Committee on Co-ordination decided, in 1984, to promote "the preservation of the archives of the UN and the specialized agencies, which constitute their institutional memory. Such archives are not only the primary source for present and future research on the UN..., they are also... an essential element in the day-to-day life of the organizations."[10]

There is one important exception on the regional level: the European Communities (since 1993 European Union) established in 1984 a repository for their historical archives at the European University Institute in Florence, Italy. Another deposit of documents in Florence took place in 1989, when the European Space Agency (ESA) left its historical archives in trust there. The character of the Institute as a repository for regional European archives was accentuated after the deposit in Florence, in 1992, of the archives of the Organisation for European Economic Co-operation (OEEC, the predecessor of OECD) for 1948–1961, to be made accessible for research there. (OECD is today an organization for all developed and some emerging industrial nations, but in the beginning it had solely an Atlantic/European character).[11] For international organizations in general, the question is not settled. Proposals have been made to install a central archives repository within the UN system in cities where the main headquarters are situated: New York, Geneva, Vienna, Paris, and Rome. A more concrete proposal concerning a repository in Switzerland is under study in view of the fact that many UN organizations have their headquarters in that country.[12]

Normally, researchers will locate the archives of an organization held in that same organization. In an ideal situation, described in the beginning of this chapter, there is a service to receive the visitor and answer questions. But even if there is no provision for researchers or for answering inquiries, one thing is certain: records do exist. All organizations are bound to have archives. They may not have a library or documentation center or an archives unit, but records are nonetheless created in the course of the activities of an organization or institution; records are working tools and a natural, unavoidable result of those activities.

The Secretary-General of the UN is a central figure on the international scene. His activities are described in a large number of published reports, a notable example being the very complete *Yearbook of the United Nations*.[13] But details of his actions can be traced in the voluminous records of the UN Secretariat, preserved by the UN Archives in New York. In the same way, the whole UN program, the execution of UN decisions, and the carrying out of UN missions are reflected in Secretariat records. For example, the UN sent a mission (the United Nations Emergency Force, UNEF I) to supervise the armistice between Egypt and Israel in the Sinai in 1956. UNEF I's records for 1956 to 1967, along with the records of other military or civilian missions and commissions, are accessible for consultation in the UN Archives. From 1947 to 1949 Unesco dispatched several missions to war-devastated countries, and thereafter, upon request of the governments concerned, experts and consultants to most of its member states; these missions as well as the numerous development projects in the framework of the UN technical assistance program carried out in Unesco's fields of competence are recorded in the Secretariat files located in the Unesco Archives.

Organizations, institutions—in fact all human society—work in this way; records are part of our civilization from its very early days and increasingly so after the "age of charters" (in German "Urkundenzeitalter") turned into the "age of records" ("Aktenzeitalter") in the sixteenth century. The printed documentation is the easily visible superstructure, impressive in quantity and detail, but the researcher who digs deeper below the surface will locate other layers consisting of records and archives with still more information.

It is much easier to have access to printed documentation, to documents and publications. Even if the organization itself does not have an open-access library or documentation center, books and periodicals are available in other libraries and documentation centers, because what is involved are published materials available for distribution. Letters, notes, memoranda, and other such documents are sent for action or information to other authorities and organizations, so they often exist elsewhere, too, but the archives of an organization are almost never duplicated as such anywhere else. The European Union, however, does microfilm all records transferred from Brussels to Florence, where they are consulted not in the original but on microfilm. A microfilm copy remains accessible also in Brussels; this, however, still takes place inside the same organization, the European Union. Another example concerns the records of the German Foreign Ministry archives, 1867 to 1945, microfilmed after the war by the Allied Powers because of their exceptionally high research value.[14] But these are exceptional cases. Microfilming of records in international organizations is usually confined to selected series, parts of series or individual files. Such is the case of the correspondence files of the World Health Organization (WHO) for the years 1946–1955: 2,500 microfilm jackets replace them. OECD systematically microfilms personnel files to get rid of paper. Microfilming, in general, is done for security purposes, for protection of heavily used records, for substitution to gain space or render the great volume of paper records more easily accessible, or to replace fragile files. Microfilming functions also as a publication-on-demand method.

This is the era of mass archives: increased state intervention, especially during and since World War I, led to the expansion of bureaucracy which, in turn, resulted in new methods of multiplication of documents, in increased production of records and the growth of governmental archives. International organizations are no exception: the records of the International Institute of Intellectual Co-operation in Paris (at Unesco) still take up a very reasonable 115 linear metres of shelving for 1925–1946; the League of Nations archives in Geneva already measures 4,000 linear metres. Today, Unesco archives amount to 8,000 linear metres including the registry files in intermediate storage but not counting current records in the organizational units. Archives of the UN in New York occupy more than ten linear kilometres of shelving, the Historical Archives of the European Communities take 2,000 metres, but the archives of the European Commission in Brussels already amount to 54 linear kilometres (records in intermediate and permanent preservation). Annual transfers to and deposits in Unesco Archives are about 300 linear metres.

The first important printed guide to the international archives is Unesco's three-part *Guide to the Archives of International Organizations* published in 1984–1985. The first part describes the archives of agencies in the UN system, covering thirty-four organizations and referring to at least 257 archives-creating bodies or record groups within the UN system. Part Two lists eighty archives of international organizations and papers and files of their former officials in the custody of eighteen national repositories; it includes a detailed description of the archives of Dag Hammarskjöld, the UN Secretary-General from 1953 to 1961 (deposited with the Royal Library in Stockholm, Sweden. Later, rules issued in 1984 define strictly that the Secretary-General may take away, when leaving office, only his private papers). Part Three lists sixty-four other international organizations.[15]

A new edition of the guide became accessible on the internet in May 1998 in English and French (<www.unesco.org/archives/guide/uk/sommaire2.hmtl>). It appeared in printed form one year later: *Guide to the Archives of Intergovernmental Organizations*; Unesco document CII.99/WS/2 (1999). Thirty-nine organizations, out of eighty which were invited to contribute, responded by delivering a text.[16]

How are IGO archives organized? The holdings of an archives service—the *fonds* of the agency—are first divided into archive groups or record groups which correspond to the main organs of the organization and main units of its secretariat. Groups and sub-groups are divided into series and sub-series which consist of volumes or archive boxes packed with files usually in folders. Files are created by subject, alphabetically by correspondent or name, geographically by country, or by number; and they consist of pieces, that is, individual documents. A file folder may be a few pages or hundreds of pages thick. A series comprises records or documents arranged in accordance with a filing plan or system or kept together because they:

- relate to a function or subject (for example, education of refugees);
- result from the same activity (fellowship files); or
- have a particular form (contract files).

At Unesco, archives are divided into sixteen archive groups: three of those groups are of predecessor bodies; four groups are printed archives. The most voluminous archive group is the "Records of the Secretariat" which is divided into numerous sub-groups corresponding to main Secretariat units: Sectors, Departments, Divisions, Sections, Units; there were, in 1994, some 270 series. The most comprehensive series is the **registry files**, also called **programme files** or **Secretariat subject files** on the execution of Unesco's program. The Unesco program is described in General Conference documents with the code C/5 as, for example, 27 C/5, *Programme and Budget for 1994–1995*, approved in 1993. The execution of all program actions is in one way or another reflected in the records; that is, there are files recording the action of the Secretariat in the particular issue area. This series keeps together the official correspondence of the Programme Sectors and the External Relations Sector/Bureau classified according to a filing plan adapted in 1947 from the Universal Decimal Classification (UDC) according to models applied in the Netherlands. (Unesco's fields of activity correspond rather closely to the general scheme of universal knowledge which is the basis of UDC.) However, when the File Unit of the Registry in 1997 was combined with the Archives to form the Archives, Records Management and Microform Division, a new, less laborious reference number system was put under study and should now be introduced.

Without detailing the history of the organization of files, it seems useful to refer here briefly to the central role of the registry. The League of Nations started with strict central control and preservation of files; sections had to return the official file to the registry once a transaction had been executed. Soon, however, sections started to keep parallel files, and this same phenomenon was to be repeated in other large organizations like UN Headquarters and Unesco; it was impossible, in the long run, to impose a strict discipline according to the idea of the central registry. The evolution has been toward decentralized file-keeping in file stations during the active phase of records.

In addition to registry files, there are records that are differentiated from central registry files: reports series (periodic and final reports on development projects), fellowship files, equipment purchase files for field projects. Of great importance at Unesco are: records of the Executive Office of the Director-General (CAB) and all the Services reporting directly to him such as the Inspector-General and Legal Adviser; administrative and program support services such as the Financial Comptroller, Budget Bureau, Personnel, Conferences, Publications; and, finally, records of commissions and committees concerning either the program execution or the internal administration.[17]

Here are some examples of series and coding at Unesco:

- REG/1-1632 refers to the 1,632 boxes containing the registry files for 1946–1966;

- PER/Rec.1/1-1333 is a reference to personnel files of Unesco staff members;

- NS/Mekong 1-68 relates to the project documentation recording the Mekong Delta Study (1962–1967) financed by the United Nations Development Programme (UNDP) and executed by Unesco;

- CC/CIC/1-32 denotes the documents of the MacBride Commission (International Commission for the Study of Communication Problems) (1978–1980).

This chapter largely discusses **paper records** created in central registry systems or according to filing plans by secretariat units. But sometimes such records exist only in **microform**, as some organizations have made the radical decision to destroy certain paper records, including their correspondence files, after microfilming them.[18] Researchers, thus, have access in archives services to records on paper and in microform (rolls, fiches, or jackets). A newer feature is **electronic records**. Electronic publications are commonplace; information—especially bibliographical and statistical—is available in the form of listings from databases or on diskettes and CD-ROMs, and electronic files are transferred through networks from a host computer to the client-researchers. Archivists prefer to make a distinction between document management systems and record-keeping systems. They have also introduced a new definition for electronic records; they require that an eletronic record, as part of a record-keeping system, should have a context, contents and structure, should result from a (business) transaction, and should be usable as evidence. The life-cycle of records applied to paper files, too fragmented in separate phases for electronic records, has been replaced by a "records continuum," which means that an electronic record, volatile by nature, should be under constant control of the records manager or archivist from its conception and creation to guarantee its authenticity.

Much work has been done to formulate a firm theoretical basis for the inclusion of electronic records into archives and records management concepts. According to Mrs. Gertrud Long, the long-time Chief of the Records Division of the IMF, this has been achieved, but it remains to be put into effect in organizations. Electronic mail/correspondence in the 1990s and in our new century has been growing steadily, and electronic media tend to replace paper records. But the situation is certainly not under control when paper and electronic records circulate simultaneously; this creates, according to a ICA report, "considerable chaos" in organizations. Electronic records present a formidable new challenge to archivists: how to get a hold of electronic information in volatile documents?[19]

Electronic archival records are mostly still too recent for open access. To make electronic correspondence files accessible, a new policy has to be developed. The researcher could access records in various ways: on copies of physical media, delivery through telecommunications, or online access. Physical media can be magnetic tape from mainframe systems, diskettes for PCs, or CD-ROMs for large volumes of data. It could also be printed out from databases or a computer-output microfiche. The internet will bring an electronic file to the computer screen of the researcher in the reading room or even at his or her home. Keeping archive records online requires that they have a high research potential and a very wide interest to the user community.

A major question is in which form electronic records are to be preserved permanently: on paper, microfilm, optical disk, or in another electronic medium. The need to allow the data to migrate through technological changes is also problematic. The Section of Archivists of International Organizations, in 1998, recommended that records should be preserved in the long run "on proven archival media" (paper and microfilm). The IAEA which has a thought-out policy on the matter, states specifically that optical disk is not foreseen for long-term storage for reasons such as "rapid technological change" and "resulting quick obsolescence of hard- and software." And IAEA adds that microfilm is still the cheapest medium.[20]

Finding Aids

Access to information in archive records is by means of finding aids: guides, lists, inventories, indexes, and registers. Additional special tools are the so-called "registry finding aids" created during the active phase of the records. These aids include a filing plan, a systematic listing of existing files with titles and classification numbers, different register volumes and/or indexes by name and subject formerly kept on cards and now computerized.

Archives services offer a multitude of finding aids to cover their holdings. In archives, the researcher does not encounter an information system dedicated exclusively to responding to information requests; instead, the usual way is to consult several working tools to locate references to archival documents. Technology has played an important role: finding aids are nowadays routinely edited and produced by computer. Also under development are comprehensive information systems to cover archives holdings more completely; nevertheless, to take Unesco as an example, there is nothing to match the Unesco Bibliographic Data Base (**UNESBIB**) which covers comprehensively the printed documents and publications of the Organization since 1972 and includes a great number of references for the earlier period as well. Excluded from the UNESBIB database are internal and administrative documents and certain public information documents. The "information system" (if one may use that term) of Unesco Archives, consists of its finding aids, all listed in the documents issued by the Service. Figure 7.1 shows the cover page of Unesco's *List of Documents Issued by the Archives Service, 1947–1994*; Table 7.1, page 206, is a selective list of finding aids of Unesco Archives.

References to archives, records and manuscripts are being included in public access online databases functioning as networks of research libraries and institutions. Such references are usually to record groups or series, but do not usually go beyond those. An example of an archives database in its own right is the historical archives of the European Communities in Florence, Italy, first made accessible online through the host distributor, ECHO in Luxembourg and now through the internet (EURHISTAR database, <www.arc.iue.it>). This database goes to the subject file level, and therefore shows a future trend that will likely be followed by others. Also noteworthy is the fact that the data structure is based on the new International Standard for Archival Description ISAD(G) developed in 1990–1993 and approved in 1996 by the International Council on Archives (ICA).[21] But from the point of view of an outside researcher, archives services are still far from database management systems covering archival holdings in detail and *in toto*. Databases are being created for the management of archives and the management of information found in records, but mostly for recent records which are not yet accessible and, therefore, can only be available to inside users. Therefore, the outside user must consult multiple finding aids based as far as possible on existing databases.

ILO in Geneva controls in its central filing system some 270,000 active and inactive files, out of which about 70,000 are recent records in a database system created in 1986. In addition, its historical archives hold another 70,000 files. UNICEF in New York has a database called RAMP which covers 170,000 folders in storage and office areas and can be used by staff for searches that can benefit outside clients too. At the UN Headquarters Archives, the accession database serves as a comprehensive inventory. Creation of an archival description database at the series level is underway.

Figure 7.1. Cover Page of Unesco's *List of Documents Issued by the Archives Service, 1947–1994*.

UNESCO

LIST OF DOCUMENTS

ISSUED BY THE ARCHIVES SERVICE (ARC)

1947-1994

WITH ALPHABETICAL INDEX

Liste des documents publiés par le Service des Archives (ARC)
1947-1994
avec un index alphabétique

The Archives Service has edited in the course of its activities

- **finding aids facilitating access to information in the archives**
- **circulars concerning the records management in the Secretariat**
- **documents on the history, aims and activities of the Organization**

The list is presented for practical reasons in two parts:

I. Documents indexed in the UNESBIB data base
II. Documents not indexed in the UNESBIB data base

Index - Annexes 1 - 8:

1. Bibliographies and data bases of Unesco
2-3. Unesco Archives and Unesco Secretariat
4-6. Archives in the programme of the *International Institute of Intellectual Co-operation* (IICI) and *Unesco* 1925-1994
7. Lists: Presidents and Secretaries-General of the *International Council on Archives* (ICA), Unesco Programme specialists in the field of Archives and Unesco Archivists
8. Statements on records and archives
Guides to archives of international organizations

To complete the information and for the convenience of the user some titles produced by the **Unesco Library** (DIT/LD) and the **Reports Unit** (PSD/REP of BER) have been added to the list.

Table 7.1
Finding Aids of Unesco Archives (Selective List)

Finding Aids of Unesco Archives (Selective List)

Unesco. *Conference of Allied Ministers of Education (CAME), London, 1942–1945: Index of Documents.* Paris: Unesco, 1990. 62 p. ARC.90/WS/1.

Unesco. *Conference of Allied Ministers of Education (CAME), London: List of Documents and Correspondence Files, 1942–1945, With Index.* Paris: Unesco, 1980. 16 p. PRS.80/WS/2.

Unesco. *Inventaire des Archives de l'Institut international de coopération intellectuelle (IICI), 1925–1946: dossiers, documents et publications aux Archives de l'Unesco à Paris.* Paris: Unesco, 1990. 2 vols. UIS.90/WS/1.

Unesco. *List of Documents Issued by the Archives Service, 1947–1994, With Alphabetical Index.* Paris: Unesco, 1994. 32 p. ARC.94/WS/3.

Unesco. *Publications de l'Institut international de coopération intellectuelle, 1945 = List of Publications of IICI, 1945.* Paris: Unesco, 1989. UIS.89/WS/5.

Unesco. *A Short Guide to Unesco Archives = Guide des Archives de l'Unesco.* Paris: Unesco, 1993. 2 p. ARC.93/WS/1.

Unesco. *Unesco Archives: A Short Guide.* Paris: Unesco, 1998. [Computer file: www.unesco.org/general/eng/infoserv/archives/archives.html.]

Unesco. *Unesco Archives Finding Aids: List by Archive Groups (AG) with Index = Instruments de recherche des Archives de l'Unesco.* Paris: Unesco, 1991. 42 p. ARC.91/WS/2.

Unesco. *Unesco Archives: List of Finding Aids on Microfiche: Inventories, Lists, Indexes Issued on Microfiche and/or Paper to Find References to and Trace Information from Unesco Records, Documents and Publications = Archives de l'Unesco: Liste des Instruments de recherche sur Microfiche et/ou sur papier pour trouver de références ou depister de l'information des archives, documents et publications de l'Unesco.* Paris: Unesco, 1991. 24 p. ARC.91/WS/1.

A good example of an intergovernmental organization with an advanced computerized control of records is the International Atomic Energy Agency in Vienna (IAEA). A central registry system existed from 1956 to 1979 resulting, as usual, in registry files existing parallel with departmental files. In 1979 a coordinated records management system (CRMS) was introduced with decentralized record-keeping in file stations under central control. The database related to this system, also gradually covering parts of pre-1979 files, refers to about 30,000 file titles and codes, as well as to responsible officers, and indicates the retention period. The same Section is in charge not only of records and archives but also of communications: letters, telex, fax, notes, memos, e-mail. The Section is able to retrieve not only all substantive communications but also documents and reports as they are continously indexed and microfilmed (about one million documents are online since 1986 in addition to 1979–1986 documents off-line).[22]

In general, the totality of finding aids, in different forms and formats, constitutes the "information system" of archives services. The first finding aid to be consulted is the printed guide. The most important guides to the archives of international organizations are listed in Table 7.2, pages 208–9.

In addition to guides listed in Table 7.2, short descriptions or mentions of archives of some other international organizations appear in the publications listed below:

- Co-ordinating Committee for Multilateral Export Controls (COCOM), 1949–1994. This body constituted by seventeen Western nations controlled the export of technology to countries in the Soviet orbit; its archives are deposited with the French Foreign Ministry, where they are accessible for consultation (International Conference of the Round Table on Archives (CITRA) 31, Washington, DC, 1995, pp. 198–99; in French only).

- Council for Mutual Economic Co-operation (COMECON) and Warsaw Pact archives are deposited with the Russian Government (Rudolf Pikhoya, "Documents of the COMECON and Warsaw Pact in Russian Archives," in International Conference of the Round Table on Archives (CITRA) 31, Washington, DC, 1995, pp. 200–201).

- The International Institute of Social History (IISH) in Amsterdam holds records, papers and publications of the international labor and trade union movement; for example, the first, second, and fourth Internationals, the Socialist International, the International Federation of Free Trade Unions, and the European Trade Union Confederation (Jaap Klosterman, "The International Institute of Social History," in International Conference of the Round Table on Archives (CITRA) 30, Thessaloniki, Greece, 1994, pp. 111–14; *Guide to the International Archives and Collections at the IIHS*, Amsterdam: Stichting Beheer IISG, 1989).

Table 7.2
Guides and Other References to Archives of International Organizations (Selective List)

Guides and Other References to Archives of International Organizations (Selective List)

Advisory Committee for the Co-ordination of Information Systems. *Management of Electronic Records: Issues and Guidelines*. New York: United Nations, 1990.

Bauer, George W. *International Organizations, 1918–1945: A Guide to Research and Research Materials*. Rev. ed. Wilmington, DE: Scholarly Resources, 1991.

Cook, Michael. *The Management of Information from Archives*. Aldershot: Gower, 1986. ix, 234 p.

Dollar, Charles. *Electronic Records Management and Archives of International Organizations: A RAMP Study with Guidelines*. Paris: Unesco, 1986. iv, 160 p. PGI.86/WS/12.

European Commission. Secretariat General. *Archives in the European Union: Report of the Group of Experts on the Coordination of Archives*. Luxembourg: EC, Secretariat General, 1994. xvii, 102 p.

European Commission. Secretariat General. *Guide to the Archives of the Ministries of Foreign Affairs of the Member States of the European Communities and the European Political Cooperation*. Luxembourg: Office for Official Publications of the European Communities, 1989. 78 p.

Johnston, G. A. "The Archives of International Organizations, With Special Reference to the ILO." *Journal of the Society of Archivists* 4, No. 6 (October 1972): 506–20.

Palayret, Jean Marie, and Ana Frangueira. *Guide to the Historical Archives of the European Communities*. 5th ed. Florence: European University Institute, 1998.

Thomas, Daniel H., and Lynn M. Case. *New Guide to the Diplomatic Archives of Western Europe*. Philadelphia: University of Pennsylvania Press, 1975. 441 p.

Unesco. *Access to the Archives of United Nations Agencies: A RAMP Study with Guidelines*. Prepared by Bodil Ulate Segura. Paris: Unesco, 1987. ii, 103, [v] p. PGI.86/WS/24.

(continued on p. 209.)

Unesco. *Archival Appraisal of Records of International Organizations: A RAMP Study, with Guidelines = Evaluation et tri des documents d'archives dans les organisations internationales: une étude RAMP, accompagnée de principes directeurs.* Prepared by Marilla B. Guptil. Paris: Unesco, 1985. 2, ii, 96 p. PGI.85/WS/4.

Unesco. *Development of Records Management and Archives Services Within United Nations Agencies: A RAMP Study with Guidelines.* Prepared by Marie Charlotte Stark. Paris: Unesco, 1983. iv, 215 p. PGI.83/WS/26.

Unesco. *Guide to the Archives of Intergovernmental Organizations.* Paris: Unesco,1999. 325 p. CII.99/WS/2.

Unesco. *Guide to the Archives of International Organizations, Part 1: The United Nations System.* Documentation, Libraries and Archives: Bibliographic and Reference Works, 8. Paris: Unesco, 1984. 279 .

Unesco. *Guide to the Archives of International Organizations, Part 2: Archives of International Organizations and Their Former Officials in the Custody of National and Other Archival Manuscript Repositories.* Compiled by Peter Walne. Paris: Unesco, 1985. 132 p. PGI.85/WS/18.

Unesco. *Guide to the Archives of International Organizations, Part 3: Archives of Other International Inter-governmental Organizations and Non-governmental Organizations.* Compiled by A. W. Mabbs. Paris: Unesco, 1985. 40 p. PGI.85/WS/19.

Unesco. *Selected Guidelines for the Management of Records and Archives: A RAMP Reader.* Compiled by Peter Walne. Paris: Unesco, 1990. viii, 214 p. PGI.90/WS/6.

United Nations. Library. *Guide to the Archives of the League of Nations, 1919–1946.* Rev. ed. Publications, Series E: Guides and Studies No. 2. Geneva: UN, 1978. 33 p.

United Nations. Secretariat. *Administrative Instruction: The United Nations Archives.* New York: UN, 1984. 28 December 1984. 6 p. ST/AI/326.

Welch, Thomas L. "Description of the Archives of the Organization of American States." In *International Documents for the 80s: Their Role and Use: Proceedings of the Second World Symposium on International Documentation, Brussels, 1980,* edited by Theodore D. Dimitrov and Luciana Marulli-Koenig, microfiche 2A, 100–115. Pleasantville, NY: UNIFO Publishers, 1982.

- Komintern (the Third Communist International) 1919–1943 archives are in Moscow at the Russian Centre of Conservation and Study of Records for Modern History which is one of the Federal State Archives of the Russian Federation, formerly Central Party Archives of the Institute of Marxism-Leninism of the Communist Party of the USSR (Kyrill Anderson, "The Archives of Komintern," in International Conference of the Round Table on Archives (CITRA) 30, Thessaloniki, Greece, 1994, pp. 108–10).

These guides should be available in university and research libraries and in the reading or reference rooms of national and other archives. Guides will give general orientation but not detailed references: general information, a brief administrative history, bibliography of works on the organization, and its past and present activities. The description of the archives gives a list of record groups and references to finding aids. Beyond the printed guide, other finding aids tend to be accessible in the reference room or reading room of the archives service itself. The internet is beginning to be an important source of general information on archives, too. Unesco Archives has issued a list of finding aids; some of these finding aids exist as documents on microfiche. The policy is to make finding aids available at least on microfiche and the most important ones as published documents. The *Unesco Programme and Budget* with its organizational chart is also a good source indirectly because behind all program actions there are normally records, documents or publications, often all three. The *Report of the Director-General on the Activities of the Organization* is the necessary counterpart of the Programme. Publications such as the *Register of Development Activities of the United Nations System* and the UNDP *Compendium of Approved Projects* can serve as indirect finding aids as they list by country the development projects executed by UN agencies.[23] Every entry implies or "hides" files, reports or other documentation in the archives services or elsewhere.

Records transferred into the custody of an archives service are usually accompanied by **transfer lists**, which are generally box lists, but sometimes complete lists with file titles. After appraisal and the usually necessary work of arrangement, the archives service produces, in the best case, a final **archives inventory** or descriptive inventory with an introduction to the administrative history and other details concerning the archive group or series and a description of the main subject matter and time range of records. References are mostly to file titles and not to individual documents such as letters, notes, memoranda, reports or other pieces included in the file which is usually in the physical form of a folder or under another kind of file cover.

Looking back in history, one can state that from the sixteenth century onward registries were part of the administrative life in modern European states (excluding Latin countries) and that the final stage of this development was a well-organized subject file registry based in its classical form on the principle "one subject-one file." In the course of diversification and intensification of relations between nations, several foreign ministries moved gradually, in the first years of the twentieth century, from **serial files** systems (for example, long series of chronologically filed reports from diplomatic posts abroad) to more elaborate

subject file systems.[24] International organizations inherited these systems and adapted them to their needs. The example *par excellence* is the League of Nations registry organized according to the British model.[25] Another example from Geneva is the International Labour Organisation (ILO); in 1920 it established a central registry with hierarchical alphanumeric notation. The model apparently was the British Ministry of Labour. As for the the IICI in Paris, the researcher has access, at Unesco, not only to the archives inventory of IICI (available for distribution on microfiche) with box list and detailed list of files, but also to comprehensive card-indexes. The first part gives the names of correspondents, institutions, or persons with references to all letters exchanged between the Institute and the correspondent in question complete with file numbers giving location of the letters; the second part of the index covers subjects.

This fine and elaborate system was continued by the Unesco Preparatory Commission (1945–1946). The Unesco Secretariat registry, organized in 1947 by John Pietersee from the Dutch Prime Minister's Office, included a register on cards of incoming letters and a name file series containing copies of all outgoing letters filed by correspondent. This system was very labor-intensive. In the course of a reform of the Unesco registry in 1960, the registration was discontinued (saving Unesco several posts), and thereafter the control was strictly on the file level but with special attention to the letters addressed to the Director-General. Not only was the 1947 system discontinued but the card-indexes were destroyed as well. After 1960, the already existing division of the Secretariat records into programme files—under the control of the Registry—and administrative files (files of administrative services) became clear.

Thus, access to Unesco Secretariat correspondence since 1946 is almost exclusively by subject, and as a result it is difficult to locate letters or correspondence by name. And Unesco files might very well contain correspondence with leading names in the fields of activities of the Organization. For example, Mahatma Gandhi wrote, while traveling around India by train, a letter to the Director-General in April 1947 in reply to an inquiry concerning human rights (which in his view could only be tied to duties of men and women). This letter is, in fact, a special case because it has not been possible to locate the original in the records, but happily it has been reproduced in a Unesco book. Thank God for publications![26]

Archivists have a habit of singling out what seems important to them. For example, a Unesco Executive Office file from the year 1976 which bears the title "Trésorerie BOC" (Bureau of the Financial Comptroller) contains reports of the financial situation of the Organization. (The U.S. was withholding its contribution to Unesco as a consequence of the non-inclusion, by the General Conference in 1974, of Israel in the European regional group of Unesco). The file also contains letters from the U.S. President and Secretary of State Henry Kissinger about the U.S. resuming its payments. These letters are singled out as they are something more than just routine reports. The title can never describe the contents of a voluminous file satisfactorily.

Registration at Unesco has, in fact, continued in the form of mail logging on the administrative unit level, but it serves current needs only, without being useful in research; the break with the great tradition that goes back to the sixteenth century was really detrimental to users. However, with the coming of computers and database management systems, registration has again become possible and less labor-intensive, allowing comprehensive coverage of correspondence. Since the 1970s several organizations have been running mail registration systems with databases that also incorporate telex and e-mail messages, and most have begun developing electronic records management systems. Examples include the ILO, the International Atomic Energy Agency (IAEA) in Vienna, the International Monetary Fund (IMF), and others.

Access Policy and Services

Documents and publications are accessible for consultation in libraries, documentation centers, and often also in archives services of the organizations. In addition, **publications**, in general, are deposited to a central library in the headquarters country and distributed free of charge to a network of depository libraries; they are also available through sales channels. **Documents** are distributed to those concerned or interested. In contrast to printed documentation, records of the secretariats are only working tools of the executive heads and the staff. **Records** are a byproduct of administrative processes and they are not created in order to be made accessible to outsiders. They are not publications even if in the course of events some may be published; an example is the letter signed by the U.S. Secretary of State on 28 December 1983 addressed to the Director-General of Unesco notifying the Organization of the U.S. intent of withdrawal from the Organization.[27]

Governmental archives have been inaccessible by tradition. Archives were the property of the rulers, who traditionally preferred to attend to their business with their ministers alone and not under the eyes of their subjects. Archive documents were considered as state secrets, and archives establishments preserving these precious documents were called "Secret Archives," the name still retained by the Archivio Segreto Vaticano (now open to 1922). It was the French revolution that created the public archives concept and, after further developments, records were made accessible for consultation by the citizens. This is now the rule in democracies: public inspection of governmental documents is subject to the principle of freedom of information. On the one hand, citizens have the right to see records concerning themselves; on the other hand, access to government records is part of the democratic control of the actions of the government. Archives, by their existence, contribute to the accountability of both governments and intergovernmental organizations.

Notwithstanding these principles, complete and general access does not exist; there are always limitations, applicable in particular to records concerning foreign policy, national security and defense, investigations regarding law enforcement, business secrets, and records containing information on private persons. State security and privacy of citizens are protected, and records concerning these areas become accessible only after a rather long closed period. In democracies, however, access to government records should be the general rule, and restrictions are confined to a limited list. The usual practice is to observe a general "closed" period and to provide access to more recent records within the closed period upon special authorization.

How do these principles apply to IGOs? Governments, which are the masters of IGOs, are informed directly by the executive heads of IGOs, or they receive information through IGO governing bodies, so the question of access to secretariat records usually does not arise for member states. There is, in general, no citizens' lobby pressing for access to records. Governments are far from the secretariats of IGOs, and their presence is felt less at the headquarters of IGOs than is the presence of citizens in their respective countries or the presence of news media watching their government in action or the pressure group of historians and other researchers claiming a freer access to source materials. Executive privilege (even if this term is not used) is another important feature in the life of IGOs: executive heads of the secretariats of IGOs usually have vast powers to direct their respective secretariats and to control access to information and records.[28]

Access to information in the form of printed documents and publications is an issue because librarians and documentalists are there, and they want to build up and develop collections for the benefit of their patrons such as researchers in the reading rooms. In the case of archives, there is no lobby of archivists and records are not available for collection-building anywhere except, to some degree, in microform. The only "lobby" in the archives area (unless the International Council on Archives is to be considered a pressure group) are researchers who would like to use IGO records, but this lobby is not very powerful. Recently, however, historians grouped in the Commission of History of International Relations have shown keen interest in the archives of the international organizations, and it seems that historians played a role in the opening of the archives of the European Space Agency, to name an example.[29]

In addition, not all researchers are aware of the existence of international archives. As there is already an overwhelming amount of information produced and distributed by IGOs in the international field, access to records does not, perhaps, seem as necessary. Also, there are economic constraints in all research work. Records are not part of depository collections in capital cities of the world. Most of the time, consulting archives requires a trip to the headquarters of an organization in a foreign city with considerable cost involved. Ordering microfilms tends to be a relatively costly proposition, too, so, one understands how IGO archives may be neglected in research.

IGOs have, in many cases when they have taken action promoting access to their archives, followed the example of member states. In diplomatic archives the access to documents concerning foreign policy was very restricted; the general closed period used to be fifty years, if not more. In 1966, the International Council on Archives, at its extraordinary congress in Washington, DC, adopted a recommendation for more liberal access to archives, while in the U.S. the first version of the Freedom of Information Act was enacted in the same year, regulating access by citizens to records of the federal government; it is to be noted that the twenty years' general limit was already in use in the U.S. for most public records. In 1967, the Labour government of Great Britain reduced the "closed" period to thirty years. Those two jurisdictions have been followed by several others so that the thirty-year rule now tends to be the general standard in democratic countries in matters of foreign policy and national security.

Those IGOs that have regulated access to their archival records generally apply this rule, too, as in the European Union and Unesco. The ILO has a "limited" period of only ten years, IAEA in Vienna forty years, while the UN follows the U.S. example of twenty years. All these rules allow for exceptions concerning records termed "confidential"; naturally, personnel records have a much longer closed period. At Unesco, as elsewhere, special authorization is stipulated: one may apply for permission to consult records that are not yet open. As well, there is a declassification procedure ensuring that certain records, series, or parts of series can be opened earlier than usual on the recommendation of the archivist. Safeguards are taken concerning information about living persons (in records other than personnel files, which stay closed in any case). Limitations also occur in other areas, such as in the relations between the organization and a member state or confidential information given by a government to an organization. Recent, important IGO and NGO archives being opened for consultation are, for example, the International Committee of the Red Cross in Geneva and NATO in Brussels.[30]

Access to information and documents has become an issue in the European Union in the course of its enlargement and institutional development. In 1993, citizens of the member states also became citizens of the Union, and they came to realize, sometimes to their astonishment, that the Union was issuing legislation in Brussels and Strasbourg, that passed before national laws and that might affect their private lives. The European Council, that is the Heads of State and Government of member states, had recognized in a declaration attached to the Maastricht treaty of 1992 that more transparency and openness was necessary in the functioning of the Union. There was also a move on the part of new member states joining the Union in 1995 toward more liberal access to documents following the practice in their respective countries.

In the Amsterdam Treaty of 1997 there is a paragraph stating: "Any citizen of the Union, and any natural or legal person residing . . . in a member state, shall have a right of access to European Parliament, Council and Commission documents, subject to the principles and the conditions to be defined." Principles and conditions were defined in 1993 and approved jointly by the Council of Ministers and the Commission. The general principle states: "the public will have the widest possible access to documents" held by the Commission and the Council. Exceptions are listed: the institutions will refuse access to any document where disclosure could undermine

- the protection of the public interest (public security, international relations, monetary stability, court proceedings, inspections, and investigations);
- the protection of the individual and of privacy;
- the protection of commercial and industrial secrecy;
- the protection of the Community's financial interests; and

- the protection of confidentiality as requested by the natural and/or legal persons that supplied the information or as required by the legislation of the member state that supplied the information.

Each EU institution may also refuse access in order to protect its interest in the confidentiality of its proceedings.[31]

Certain material conditions are prerequisites for a successful consultation of archives. Services that could and should be expected from an archives service in an international organization include the following:

- reading room with regular hours;

- access to a general guide and other finding aids;

- advice from a professional archivist;

- replies to information requests by letter, fax, telephone, and e-mail; replies should include lists of references and listings from databases if such databases exist;

- photocopy facilities;

- opportunity to order microfiches from complete files; and

- service of referral to resources about the organization, located elsewhere.

Even if these conditions are not fulfilled, it is possible to address a request to the organization in question. Records always exist, and there may be enough good will to give access to records even in provisional conditions on a case-by-case basis. Some organizations give privileged access to a researcher who, for example, is writing an official history of the organization.[32] A scholarly study of a subject in the areas of the organization's activity is sufficient grounds to require access to records.

Before consulting the records, one should not forget that printed documents and publications, too, are part of the archival heritage of an organization, and these materials are accessible in depository collections and sometimes in governmental archives. It is also perfectly possible to study an organization with the help of the archives of the member states; they receive documents that are distributed (but do not necessarily retain them), and they receive reports from their representatives who participate in the meetings of the deliberating bodies and in other meetings. Permanent delegations observe and follow the work of the executive heads and the secretariats. Therefore, the archives of foreign ministries and other concerned ministries are also important sources on the activities and history of IGOs.

IGOs have a public information policy addressed directly or through news media to the member states and the international audience. They should also have a policy promoting access to their archives to benefit the worldwide research community, student population, and other potential users.

Use of the Archives

The first duty of an archives and records service is to the parent organization. Records are working tools: they facilitate administrative management; they contain evidence and proof of established rights, of action taken and policies chosen; and they are part of the information resources of the organizations. Archives should include all records destined, after appraisal, for long-term preservation, and they should reflect faithfully the past and present activities of the institution. They should be the institutional memory or contribute in a basic manner to the maintenance of institutional memory in collaboration with other information services. Archives services should be able to establish facts and related source documents about the parent organization. Unesco Archives has done this, for example, by issuing documents on the history of the agency and by publishing *A Chronology of Unesco, 1945–1987*.[33]

But there are always gaps in human action. All records do not come to the archives. They may be disposed of without control, and action is sometimes taken without proper documents being created, or documents are not always put into official files. The physical medium of the documents may also be fragile; paper used for documents, especially in the 1940s, was of low quality and may not stand the test of time. New media like film and especially electronic information are volatile and are exposed to even greater risk of deterioration than paper.

In any case, what the researcher encounters in an archives service is always a selected portion of non-current records. It is impossible, but also useless, to try to keep everything. The era of "mass archives" also means massive destruction; 1975–1993 Unesco statistics show that the percentage of annual eliminations in linear metres of occupied shelving exceeds 50 percent of the volume of annual transfers (and this is probably not enough). The aim, and the duty, of the organization is to keep the significant part of records.

The first group of users is, consequently, the staff of the organization and the governing bodies. At Unesco, other users are permanent delegations of member states, governments and national commissions for Unesco, and research institutes. As for individual users, doctoral and other students and researchers in all fields of the organization's competence are the most important group; then journalists, teachers, and the public also are looking for general or precise information in archival sources, especially if other sources have not answered their questions. Archives service is a kind of last resort.

The subjects of research can be divided into two main groups. Either the organization itself is the subject or is included in the subject (for example, Unesco's role in the fight against discrimination in education; the world science information system; Brazil's collaboration with Unesco) or the subject is such that Unesco's records or documentation in general contain information on it (for example, science policy in Latin America; reconstruction in war-devastated countries; biography of Jaime Torres-Bodet, Director-General of Unesco 1948–1952).

Conclusion

As there is already too much information around, do we still need archives in today's world? What do archive records offer? An executive head of an UN agency, to give an example, has many occasions to explain in public his or her own decisions and how he or she carries out the resolutions and decisions of the governing bodies, how he or she executes with the secretariat the program of the agency, but his or her actions and the activities of the organization can only be known in full detail through archive records. Representatives of member states make a great number of public declarations at the deliberative organs of IGOs or in their respective capitals, but their intentions, policies, and real motivation can only be known in detail with the aid of governmental or IGO archive documents.

Records are mainly unpublished, restricted information, remaining confidential or even secret for a specified period. This difficulty inherent in archival information should not be exaggerated because, for example, the UN system practices open diplomacy, and through the excellent work of investigative journalists and other observers and through leaks (whether or not calculated) we know the direction that events have taken and policies that have been chosen. Excellent and well-informed works and studies have been written on the basis of what has been available publicly. Nevertheless, archive records carry weight and add considerably, sometimes in a decisive way, to our knowledge of events and persons. Archives are there to serve the quest for truth.

Notes and References

General Note

Archivists and records managers of international organizations work together in the Section of Archivists of International Organizations (SIO), founded in 1976 in the framework of the International Council on Archives (ICA), which was established in 1950. For 1992–1996 the Chair of SIO was Liisa Fagerlund, Chief, United Nations Archives, New York, and the Secretary was Robert Jurquet, NATO, Brussels; Chair since 1996 is Franz Egger, NATO, Brussels, and the Secretary is Anne-Marie Smith, NATO, Brussels (See ICA-CIA, SIO (SOI) Section *Handbook and Directory*, 5th ed., 1998; also on CD-ROM and on the internet at <www.ica.org>).

Within the UN system, Unesco is the agency that has, since 1946, had a program in the field of archives for the benefit of its member states, carried out in collaboration with ICA. This program may also benefit international organizations. In 1979, the program was renamed Records and Archives Management Programme (RAMP). To find RAMP publications, consult *Unesco List of Documents and Publications* (ULDP); the **UNESBIB** database (1972–); *List of Documents Issued by the Archives Service, 1947–1994, with Alphabetical Index* (Unesco document ARC.94/WS/3, pp. 23–29); and the latest ICA list of publications, available at <www.ica.org/cgi-bin/ica.pl?05_e>.

1. *Dictionary of Archival Terminology*, 2d, rev. ed. ICA Handbook Series, Vol. 7 (München; New Providence: K. G. Saur, 1988).

2. In an effort to standardize the disparate archival terminology in different language areas and different countries, the International Council on Archives (ICA) has introduced, on the basis of French, the term "fonds" meaning the totality of the archives of an institution; for example, the fonds of Unesco (in French: le fonds d'archives de l'Unesco). The fonds is then divided into sub-fonds and/or archive or record groups and then series consisting of volumes or boxes (items) and further into files and pieces (individual documents). An archive fonds, as a rule, is arranged and preserved as well as described in an inventory or series of inventories as an entity. Records of an archive fonds belong functionally together; they are like an organic outgrowth of the activities of the body which created the fonds. Archives are not collections of separate items like books in a library. It should be added that in libraries, serial publications and documents of IGOs are, in most cases, kept as separate collections which resemble archives.

3. *Development of Records Management and Archives Services Within United Nations Agencies: A RAMP Study with Guidelines*, prepared by Marie Charlotte Stark (Paris: Unesco, General Information Programme and UNISIST, 1983). PGI.83/WS/26. This study is a comprehensive review of the field treated in this chapter. For archives, libraries and Secretariat documentation, see pp. 20–27. In the Unesco Archives the documents are filed by document code and Unesco's own publications by the issuing sector/department/office whereas the Unesco Library files the same publications according to UDC.

4. International Institute for Intellectual Co-operation, *Relations with the Government of Chili, 1925–1945*. IICI file A I 83, microfiche 89 IICI 0013. 2 fiches.

5. Unesco, Executive Board document 104 EX/3 and decision 104EX/Dec.3.3. The argument for this treatment is that Unesco does not want to be another international juducial body, and it aims to reach solutions of human rights cases "in conditions of mutual respect, confidence and confidentiality." The UN Human Rights Commission deals with the matter more openly, as does the European Court of Human Rights established by the Council of Europe, a forty-one-nation body distinct from the European Union of fifteen States. See, by P. van Dijk and G. J. H. van Hoof, *Theory and Practice of the European Convention on Human Rights*, 3d ed. (The Hague: Kluwer Law International, 1998).

6. Unesco, Executive Board, 144th session (1993/94), Document 144 EX/INF.3. The report covers the period from November 1993 to April 1994. The orally delivered part is also recorded in the summary records of the Board, in document 144 EX/SR.1.

7. A sample of these rules for eight IGOs is reproduced in *Archivum. International Review on Archives* 41 (1996), pp. 275–330.

8. Marilla B. Guptil, *Archival Appraisal of Records of International Organizations: A RAMP Study with Guidelines* (UNESCO document PGI.85/WS/4); Luciana Duranti, "The Thinking on Appraisal of Electronic Records: its Evolution, Focuses, and Future Directions" *Janus.Archival Review* 1997.2, pp. 47–67.

9. International Council on Archives, *International Directory of Archives = Annuaire international des archives* 38 (New York; London; Paris: Saur, 1992). Series: *Archivum: International Review on Archives*, by the International Council on Archives with the financial aid of Unesco.

10.. UN/ACC decision 1984/15. The International Council on Archives revisited the problem by adopting a resolution to the same effect as ACC: International Council on Archives, CITRA 1993–1995, *Proceedings of the Thirty-first International Conference of the Round Table, Washington, DC, 1995*, p. 205.

11. *Guide to the Historical Archives of the European Communities*, 4th ed. (Florence: European University Institute, 1993).

12. "Archives and History of International Organizations: International Colloquium, Rome, 29–31 October 1998" (report not yet issued). Interventions were made, for example, concerning the archives of the following organizations: FAO (Rome), Council of Europe (Strasbourg, France), Open Society Archives (Budapest), IICI (Paris), OECE (Paris), NATO (Brussels), International Committee of the Red Cross (Geneva), Comintern (Moscow), Organization of American States (Washington DC).

13. See also *Public Papers of the Secretaries-General of the United Nations (1946–1971)*, ed. by Andrew Wellington Cordier and Wilder Foote (New York: Columbia University Press 1969–1977; 8 vols.). Records concerning this publishing enterprise with other numerous records on UN at the Columbia University Library, New York, are in the Andrew Wellington Cordier papers (see *Guide to the Archives of International Organizations*, Part II, pp. 75–121).

14. *Catalogue of Files and Microfilms of the German Foreign Ministry Archives 1867–1920* (Oxford: American Historical Association, Committee for the Study of War Documents, 1959); *Catalog of Files and Microfilms of the German Foreign Ministry Archives 1920–1945* [A joint project of the U.S. Department of State and the Hoover Institution on War, Revolution and Peace] (Stanford, California, 1962–1966; 3 vols.).

15. Unesco, *Guide to the Archives of International Organizations, Part 1: The United Nations System* (Documentation, Libraries and Archives: Bibliographic and Reference Works, 8; Paris: Unesco, 1984); *Part 2: Archives of International Organizations and Their Former Officials in the Custody of National and Other Archival Manuscript Repositories*, comp. Peter Walne (Paris: Unesco, 1985). PGI.85/WS/18; *Part 3: Archives of Other International Intergovernmental Organizations and Nongovernmental Organizations*, comp. A. W. Mabbs (Paris: Unesco, 1985). PGI.85/WS/19; "United Nations Administrative Instruction: The United Nations Archives (ST/AI/326, 28 December 1984), Annex I: Guidelines Concerning the Classification and Declassification of the Records of the Secretary-General; Annex II: Guidelines Concerning the Secretary-General's Private Papers," *Archivum* 41 (1996), pp. 288–93).

16. The new volume updates the text and introduces new organizations not covered earlier but does not make obsolete the volumes of 1984–85. Notable gaps in the new guide are, for example, FAO, the Organization of American States (OAS), and the Organization of African Unity (OAU). Notable new entries are the European Union (Florence, Brussels, Luxembourg), the International Committee of the Red Cross (Geneva) and NATO (Brussels), which all have opened their archives for research. On one hand, the internet seems to give a positive impetus for opening the archives, because some organizations, if they have not yet been able to open their archives, indicate that they are working toward that end. On the other hand, even if the internet permits daily updating of texts, some chapters are, in fact, far behind.

17. See, for example, the document concerning the Director-General's draft proposals for the Programme and Budget for 1994–1995 (27 C/5), which contains a detailed organizational chart of Unesco; and *Organization of the Unesco Secretariat Since 1946* (Paris: Unesco, 1979). PRS.79/WS/47.

18. *Guide to the Archives of International Organizations, Part 1: The United Nations System*, p. 251 (World Health Organization).

19. Electronic records are discussed, for example, in the following three studies published by the International Council on Archives, Committee on Electronic Records: *Guide for Managing Electronic Records from an Archival Point of View* (1997). Studies 8; *Electronic Records Programs. Report on the 1994/95 Survey* (1996). Studies 9; Alf Erlandsson, *Electronic Records Management. A Literature Review* (1997). Studies 10. Study 9 concerns national archives administrations; the situation in international organizations is reviewed in Tora K. Bikson, "Managing Digital Documents: Technological Challenges and Institutional Responses," International Council on Archives, CITRA XXXIII, Stockholm 1998, *Actes*, pp. 35–50). See also, Charles M. Dollar, *Electronic Records Management and Archives in International Organizations: A RAMP Study with Guidelines* (Unesco document PGI.86/WS/12) (issued in

1986, this refers only to the main-frame and mini-computer world); *Management of Electronic Records: Issues and Guidelines* (New York: UN, 1990); Advisory Committee for the Co-ordination of Information Systems, *Strategic Issues for Electronic Records Management: Towards Open Systems Interconnection* (New York: UN, 1992). A thorough review of the question with a long list of sources may also be found in Richard J. Cox, "Access in the Digital Information Age and the Archival Mission: the United States." *Journal of the Society of Archivists* 19, No.1 (1998), pp. 25–40. Says Cox: "we are living in a transition period from paper and print, to paperless and electronic information sources and records, although . . . none of us alive now are likely to see an entirely electronic information age. . . . What we know for sure is that this is a crazy time." He adds later (in the context of editing Thomas Jefferson's papers): "the Jeffersons of the 1990s might not leave any documents behind unless we solve the challenges of electronic records management."

20. Unesco, *Guide to the Archives of Intergovernmental Organizations* (1999; Unesco document CII.99/WS/2) p. 107.

21. *ISAD(G): General International Standard Archival Description* [Final ICA-approved version] (Ottawa, 1994). See also *ISAAR(CPF): International Standard Archival Authority Record for Corporate Bodies, Persons and Families* [Final ICA-approved version] (Ottawa, 1994). Also under study is the feasibility of an International Standard Archival Authority Number (ISAAN) to be used for archives-creating bodies; further still, standards for finding aids are being discussed. For a review of this question see Hugo L. Stibbe,"Standardising Description: The Experience of Using ISAD(G)." 5th European Conference on Archives: The Basics of the Profession. International Council on Archives. *Janus: Archival Review* 1998.1, pp. 132–52.

22. Unesco, *Guide to the Archives of Intergovernmental Organizations* (1999), pp. 103–14 (IAEA), 215–21 (UN), 221–31 (UNICEF).

23. Advisory Committee for the Co-ordination of Information Systems, *Register of Development Activities of the United Nations System*, 1987–1990 (New York: UN); UNDP, *Compendium of Approved Projects*, 1972– (UNDP/MIS/Series A 1972–).

24. Especially famous, historically, are Venetian ambassadors' reports. See, for example, *Relations des ambassadeurs vénitiens* (Paris: Unesco Collection of Representative Works, 1969).

25. For a description of the League of Nations registry see United Nations, Library, *Guide to the Archives of the League of Nations, 1919–1946*, rev. ed. (Geneva, 1978). An interesting brief description of the League's registry is published in "How a Registry Works: An Overview," appended to Frank Moorhouse's novel about the League, *Grand Days* (London: Picador, 1993): 545–47.

26. "I learnt from my illiterate but wise mother that all rights to be deserved and preserved came from a duty well done." "Mahatma Gandhi to the Director General of Unesco [Julian Huxley], May 25th, 1947," in *Human Rights, Comments and Interpretations: A Symposium*. Ed. by Unesco with an introduction by Jacques Maritain (London; New York: Wingate, 1949), p. 18. See also the related records: UNESCO Official correspondence files, 1 series. Comité sur les principes philosophiques des droits de l'homme REG.342.7(100):1 A 02 Parts I-II 1947–1952. (Microfiche 87 REG 0009). The work of this committee was part of the preparation, within the UN system, of the Universal Declaration of Human Rights (adopted by the UN General Assembly in Paris on 10 December 1948).

27. The letter was reproduced in the form of an official document as a circular letter addressed to the member states (CL/2897, 31 January 1984) and also as a Board document (119 EX/14).

28. Unesco Staff Regulation 1.5 requires from the staff members "utmost discretion in regard to all matters of official business" and forbids them from communicating "to any person unpublished information known to them by reason of their official position." "These obligations remain binding after separation from the Organization." Let us note in passing that the State Parties signatories of the Unesco Constitution express their belief "in the unrestricted pursuit of

objective truth" (Preamble), which can be interpreted also as supporting research involving archive records which are often necessary for getting at the whole truth.

29. "Archives of International Organizations and History of International Relations," in Commission of History of International Relations, *Newsletter*, 7–8. See also other sources in Jean Marie Palayret, "Status of Archives of Organizations in Regional Systems" (in French), International Council on Archives, CITRA 1993–1995, *Proceedings of the Thirty-First International Conference of the Round Table on Archives* (Washington, DC, 1995), pp. 189–200.

30. On access to archives, see—in addition to *Guide to the Archives of Intergovernmental Organizations* (1999, printed and Web versions)—Liisa Fagerlund, "Status of Records of the United Nations System" and Jean-Marie Palayret, "Status of Archives of Organizations in Regional Systems," both in International Council on Archives, CITRA 1993–1995, *Proceedings of the Thirty-first International Conference of the Round Table, Washington, DC, 1995*, pp. 180–200, debate pp. 202–3. Curiously, these two articles appear in the otherwise bilingual volume only in French.

31. European Commission, *Access to Commission Documents: A Citizen's Guide* (Luxembourg, 1997). The general principle and exceptions are listed in the annex containing the code of conduct concerning public access to Commission and Council documents (*Official Journal of the European Communities* 1993, L 340/41). EU's policy seems fair enough but, in fact, it rules out incoming and internal documents. Therefore access cannot be to complete files because they contain, naturally, items in both these categories. Complete files become accessible only in thirty years' time. The main interest of the member states and their citizens was, however, satisfied: the documentation leading to new legislation in the Union can now be traced. The European Ombudsman appointed by the European Parliament is empowered to investigate complaints by European citizens concerning "instances of maladministration." In 1998, about 30 percent of the complaints referred to refusals to give information. In his inquiry covering all institutions and bodies of the Union, the Ombudsman conluded that "the failure to adopt and make easily available to the public rules governing public access to documents constitute an instance of maladministration" (European Ombudsman, *Annual Report* 1996, p. 86).

32. For example, the European Organization of Nuclear Reseach (CERN) in Geneva had its history written by a four-member team, based on a wide range of sources inside and outside. See *History of CERN*, volumes I–III (Amsterdam, North Holland Publishers, 1987–1996).

33. *A Chronology of Unesco, 1945–1987: Facts and Events in Unesco's History with References to Documentary Sources in the Unesco Archives and Supplementary Information in the Annexes 1–21* (Paris: Unesco, 1987). LAD.85/WS/4 Rev.

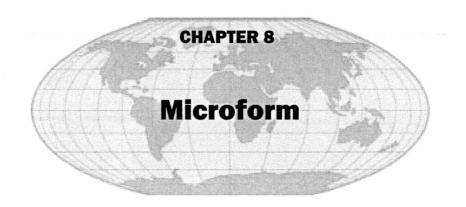

CHAPTER 8

Microform

(A) DOCUMENTATION IN MICROFORM

Robert W. Schaaf

Introduction

In this age of fast-moving technology—characterized by the development of the optical disk and the proliferation of online information systems capable of delivering full-text—documents in microform will continue to play an important role in information systems in general and those of international agencies in particular. This chapter, informed by the author's long experience at the Library of Congress (LC), will discuss the following topics: microform and the newer technologies; silver versus other types of film; secondary services making intergovernmental organization (IGO) microform available; and the author's questionnaire on IGO documentation in microform. The discussion is followed by a description of the microform programs of the United Nations and six other agencies in the UN system, the microform programs of four other international organizations, and a concluding statement.

Microform and the Newer Technologies

In recent years the Library of Congress has placed considerable emphasis on trying to secure archival quality microform for its collections of international organizations (as well as for its other collections). Although LC acquires some major IGO serials and monographs in microform, the Library's interest is mainly in securing microform for mimeographed or other near-print documentation. Its interest in microform is multifaceted. One element relates to the basic mission of the Library of Congress. It needs to acquire, organize, and service very large bodies of material that many other libraries do not have to acquire. In numerous instances, when LC is faced with questions concerning the acquisition of IGO documents, the question has to be asked: "If we do not acquire and organize this material, what other public-service institution will do so?"

Microform is particularly suitable for many of the large collections of working documents of intergovernmental organizations (as well as other government bodies) for reasons of space, preservation, ease of control, and servicing. While LC has made considerable progress in securing IGO microform, it still has a long way to go to augment the documentary collections. The Library's progress has not been entirely satisfactory. Details of the progress made or the lack of progress will become clearer during the discussion of the documentation of some of the specific organizations. At the outset, however, it would be well to point out some of the contrasting aspects of microform and the newer technologies.

Some professionals in the information field are inclined now to speak as though microform is a relic of the past.[1] Those in the computer and electronics industry are likely to discuss micrographics "as a technology fighting a rearguard action in the face of developments like high density magnetic recording and the optical disc."[2] The argument, however, is more complicated than that; it revolves partly around what kind of data are to be recorded and how often they will need to be accessed.

There are many points to take into account when comparing microform and the newer media, and it is not possible to discuss here in any detail questions about the storage and retrieval of IGO documents on laser disks. In this author's opinion, there will be a long-term need for large back-up collections of international documents in microform, and it will take longer to have viable systems that will cover the bulk of an IGO's documents on an advanced medium than some of the technical experts would lead us to believe.

There may well come a time soon when much of the new documentary output of an IGO will be in a form that can be stored on magnetic media or compact disks. This will mean both high-density storage and random access. If the text of a document is produced in machine-readable form in the first place, it can easily be made available online. Full-text transmission permits a user simply to print out the page or pages in which he is interested. Questions of public access and the costs of connect-time notwithstanding, national governmental agencies and international organizations, as well as large research libraries such as the Library of Congress, must have as complete a file of an IGO's documents as possible, even though such documentation will seldom need to be accessed. IGOs cannot expect to have such large files stored permanently on one of the newer media. It would be equally impossible, certainly in the present fiscal environment, to input the full text of large retrospective files into machine-readable form; this is another reason for having the files in microform. The full text of some newspapers and journals is already available online. Even though many research libraries have this option, permitting speedy searching as well as the printing out of urgently needed items, major libraries will still need to purchase the complete files on microfilm.

In an interesting survey of reproduction which takes up the question of microform versus the newer technologies, a British expert, Bernard J. S. Williams, favors microform over the newer media, particularly from the standpoint of preservation. Considering nonprint media, such as magnetic tape and online services (electronic printing) along with optical disks, Williams states that "the technology is far from mature [and] standards are lacking."[3] "The newer media," he declares, "pose severe problems for the conservation of knowledge." He also makes the point that "the information stored in large archives or libraries is relatively inactive (the chances of any item being accessed during a given year are slight)."[4] Thus, it seems clear that there will be room in the future for both the newer technologies and for microform, including systems that integrate microform and the newer media such as optical disks.

Although there has been considerable growth in automated systems for storage and retrieval of microfilm documents, and the term CAR (computer-assisted retrieval) is frequently seen today in the micrographic literature, such systems are not especially relevant in a discussion of IGO documentation in microform. On the other hand, computer-output microform (COM) has grown increasingly important in recent years and its use by IGOs for bibliographies and catalogs as well as statistical data is now well known. Increasingly, one finds COM substituted for statistical publications where frequent updating is necessary. This trend will doubtless continue.

Silver Versus Other Films for Libraries and Archives

The question of silver film versus other film, particularly diazo, for library and preservation purposes is still valid, although the controversy seems somewhat less important than in the past. International organizations and other publishers do not produce COM fiche on silver film. COM fiche is regularly substituted for IGO statistical publications formerly offered in a printed version. In a useful survey of microform developments, one of LC's senior officers points out that "the [U.S.] federal government has in the past and continues now to exert significant influence on microforms. It legitimatized microfiche in the U.S. in the mid-1960s and, to some extent, is legitimizing non-silver film now." He goes on to state that "it also promotes microforms by adopting them at GPO [U.S. Government Printing Office], and, by authorizing large-scale programs, it drives down the price of such items as microfiche readers.[5]

While some IGOs offer silver film at a premium price as well as diazo film for their documents, other agencies have given libraries no alternative but diazo film. Examples of the latter are the Organization for Economic Cooperation and Development,* and the European Communities [now European Union–ed].

---

*According to OECD's headquarters, the only correct spelling is Organisation for Economic Co-operation and Development, but OECD's Washington Information Center has used the form Organization for Economic Cooperation and Development, a spelling also used by the author of this chapter—ed.

LC is a depository for the European Communities, and the acquisition policy allows the Library to accept nonsilver film on deposit or gift, but for purchase, the writer and other recommending officers have to affirm that silver is not available and write a justification stating that diazo film should be acquired for the collections. Without having any technical background on the subject of silver versus nonsilver film, one may waver at times and wish the question would simply go away. Jerry Dupont, executive director of the Law Library Microform Consortium, asserts that there is no need for libraries to acquire anything other than diazo film which is the only film considered by the LLMC. "Of the available alternatives," he states, "silver film is the least suitable in a use environment."[6] In contrast, Suzanne Dodson of the University of British Columbia gives a number of reasons for preferring silver film to diazo, particularly emphasizing the fact that diazo films fade. She states that "if we accept the facts presented in the ANSI [American National Standards Institute] standard, then we must conclude that silver film in a user environment is more likely to be with us for years to come than is diazo."[7]

Secondary Services Making IGO Microform Available

Commercial firms and other organizations such as government agencies, single libraries (such as the Library of Congress), and consortia representing organizations working together have long made available microfiche copies of some IGO material. This has most often been the case for IGO periodical titles. In other instances, however, organizations have contracted for outside publishers to issue items such as their conference proceedings in microform. In still other instances, items cited in individual print or online indexes are made available in microform by the index producers. An example of a database that includes international items available for sale in microform is the ERIC (Educational Resources Information Center) database. One U.S. government agency that makes available some IGO material in microform is the National Technical Information Service. An early important example of a commercial publisher that has made certain IGO titles available in microform is University Microfilms International of Ann Arbor, Michigan. Examples of IGO conference documentation made available through commercial publishers are the International Women's Year Conference, Mexico City, 1975, and the Fifth United Nations Congress on the Prevention of Crime and Treatment of Offenders, Geneva, 1975, which were produced by UNIFO Publishers, Pleasantville, New York. As another example, Pergamon Press was given the external rights by the UN to produce a microform publication of Habitat, the United Nations Conference on Human Settlements, Vancouver, 1976.[8] In many instances, printed indexes or checklists have been produced in conjunction with the conference micropublications, but there are several problems to be noted in this connection. For example, there usually is an overlapping between some (or most) of the documentation supplied by the commercial publisher and hard copy received by the depository or standing-order library. Moreover, the quality of the commercial indexes has varied; some are mere checklists of documents with no real provision for subject access to the microform documentary collection. An example of a consortium that has produced some IGO microform publications is the Law Library Microform Consortium mentioned earlier.

A more important example of making IGO documentation available in microform is the CIS Corporation of Bethesda, Maryland, which began publishing its *Index to International Statistics (IIS)* in 1983. The great advantage of the CIS effort is that a large number of IGOs are covered in *IIS*, with detailed indexes and abstract volumes produced in hard copy. This kind of detailed indexing/abstracting makes the IGO documentation much more accessible. *IIS*, now in its fourth year, should go a long way toward making international statistical publications from IGOs more widely used and should also contribute in general to a greater awareness of the usefulness and importance of IGO documentation. A companion microfile of the documents cited in *IIS* is produced by CIS. Although there are doubtless many libraries that subscribe only to the index and abstract volumes, the CIS effort has greatly expanded the number of IGO publications available in library microform collections.

Survey of International Documentation in Microform

The author recently [in the mid-1980s—ed.] undertook to survey, by means of a questionnaire, microform programs in eighty-eight IGOs worldwide. As of June 1986, replies to the questionnaire were received from forty-seven organizations, for a response rate of fifty-three percent which is excellent for such a survey. Detailed information was received from thirty organizations; five organizations indicated possible interest for the future; and twelve other agencies said they had no microform programs and did not anticipate having any. In a number of cases where no response was received, enough information was at hand to permit some evaluation of the particular agency's microform program.

Before describing specific IGOs and their individual microform programs, it is appropriate to name the agencies to be discussed. The IGOs on which detailed information has been collected include the UN, even though no questionnaire was sent to the UN proper because details were already available. The questionnaire was sent to approximately ten of the UN's special bodies such as UNICEF. Space does not permit a description of any of these UN special bodies, although several organizations such as UNICEF and the United Nations University have substantial microform programs. Among the other organizations of the UN system discussed are Unesco, FAO, and GATT. Additional UN organizations mentioned are the International Telecommunication Union, ILO, and the IAEA. Microform programs of organizations outside the UN system worthy of discussion are those of the Organization of American States, the European Communities, the Organization for Economic Cooperation and Development, and the Andean Pact.

United Nations

The UN has had a microform program since 1947. In its earliest years the program was under the direction of the UN Archives Section and its primary purpose was preservation because the bulk of UN documents consisted of mimeographed texts on sulfide paper known to disintegrate in a relatively few years. The medium used by the Archives was 16mm roll microfilm. Documents in six official languages of the UN were filmed and the five principal organs were covered: the General Assembly, the Security Council, the Economic and Social Council, the Trusteeship Council, and the Secretariat. A printed index covering English-language documents produced from 1946 to 1961 was issued in 1963 as an "Archives Record Guide," and a supplement covering 1962–1967 was issued in 1970.[9] While the main thrust of this program was for preservation, a few libraries purchased rolls of the UN documentation on microfilm.

Beginning in 1969 the Dag Hammarskjöld Library assumed the direction of the program which was altered to permit an expanded operation emphasizing microfiche production and aiming to increase the availability of UN documentation and to achieve "economies in the storage, maintenance and distribution of materials."[10] Microfilm was still used for less frequently consulted texts, such as material in Arabic and Chinese, as well as periodicals, press releases, leaflets, and items intended for internal distribution. Sales of material were handled by the UN Sales Section. Emphasis was on microfiche production, and sales efforts were concentrated on *Official Records*, yearbooks, and other major sales publications, along with serials such as the *Treaty Series*, and works such as conference reports and major studies. Also included were the publications of the International Court of Justice at The Hague. Certain classes of mimeographed documents highlighted with a black square in the UN's new index, *UNDEX*, were also covered by the new microfiche program. In addition to moving ahead with recent material, the program also called for retrospective microfiching of major series, including early *Official Records*. The Library of Congress made its first major UN microfiche acquisition in 1975 with the purchase of a retrospective set of *Official Records* for the major UN organs. LC and other depository libraries were classed as official users entitled to a fifty percent discount.

Commercial publishers such as UNIPUB also began to utilize the expanded microform program. These publishers acquired material from the UN and were thus limited to what it produced in microform, but there were advantages for some libraries in buying from a publisher such as UNIFO which did not require prepayment and would try to customize packages according to a customer's particular interests.

One other commercial publisher, Readex, had started its own UN microform program during the UN's early years, but Readex reproduced the UN documents and *Official Records* on opaque microprint rather than on standard microfilm. Despite the disadvantages of microprint, which was more difficult to read on existing viewing machines and even more difficult to copy, the Readex program was quite comprehensive as it covered mimeographed documents as well as *Official Records* and even limited distribution (L) documents. A notable omission was Readex's exclusion of the Secretariat (ST) series of documents.

A substantial number of libraries (including the Library of Congress) subscribed to the Readex set of UN documentation. By the end of the 1970s a better reading machine was made available for viewing Readex's microprint. But in order to be able to produce hard copies (a long-standing LC concern) libraries had to use a Dennison copier which was not developed especially for Readex and was never entirely satisfactory. Dennison went out of the copying machine business in 1978.[11] Libraries that still had the machines were left with copiers that could barely reproduce hard copies from the microprint or that failed to work at all. Beginning in 1982, Readex, now owned by NewsBank, shifted over to microfiche (no longer excluding the ST series of documents), and libraries with subscriptions began to receive microfiche under their old standing orders. Today, Readex still plays a significant role in the field of UN microform, and its current UN program deserves separate coverage that is not possible here. [See Volume 1, Chapter 11 for a detailed description of the role of Readex and several other commercial firms—ed.]

Even with the advances in the UN's own microform program in the early 1970s, the Library of Congress became increasingly concerned that the UN did not offer for sale microform of mimeographed documents. In September 1974, Donald F. Wisdom, then chief of LC's Serial Division, and the author paid a visit to the UN, particularly to see the chief of the Sales Section and officers of the Dag Hammarskjöld Library. The visitors' primary aim was to emphasize the importance of making the mimeographed documents available to the public on microfiche. The UN was producing microfiche of these documents for its own internal needs, but not for sale to the public. Although the UN officials agreed there was a need to make microfiche of the mimeographed documents available for public sale, no assurance was given that the view of the visitors, likely to be shared by representatives of other major research libraries, would have any impact. The UN personnel admitted, however, that it was useful to them to be able to report that the Library of Congress was interested in having UN mimeographed documents on microfiche. This visit was followed up by a formal letter from the chief of LC's Order Division to the UN Sales Section. In a letter of 27 March 1975, however, the chief of the Sales Section, W. Scott Laing, wrote: "There are no plans presently for offering mimeographed documents or provisional summary records in microform. There are a number of technical difficulties involved and it seems unlikely that these can be resolved in the near future."

LC did not want to let matters drop, however, and continued to try and make its views heard. For example, later in 1975, Donald Wisdom and the author drafted correspondence for the Acting Librarian of Congress to send to the U.S. Ambassador to the UN in order to make sure LC's concerns were heard at that level.

In 1979, on a visit to the Dag Hammarskjöld Library and some other UN offices, the author learned from two of the UN's senior library staff during an informal talk in the Delegates' lounge that there was an "extra, unsorted set" of UN microfiche which might possibly be made available if the Library of Congress were interested. Donald Wisdom, the author's superior and Chief of the Serial and Government Publications Division, was extremely interested in this bit of intelligence. Although it took some time, negotiations were begun which eventually led to LC's purchase of this extra set of UN microfiche that included mimeographed documents, *Official Records*, and regular sales items. To estimate the number of fiche involved and to get a better picture, UN library personnel put the set in rough document-symbol order, and in 1981 LC purchased approximately 49,000 UN microfiche for a total of $25,000.

It was hoped that by now the bulk of mimeographed documents on microfiche obtained by LC through its 1981 special purchase would be included in the UN sales program. Unfortunately, much of the mimeographed documentation is still not available for purchase. For this reason, LC's acquisition of this large corpus of UN microfiche is of major importance.

After the author's 1979 UN visit, he and Donald Wisdom decided on the need to approach the UN authorities to stress again the importance of a current comprehensive UN microform program that would include the mimeographed documents. Dr. Vladimir Orlov, who had been appointed director of the Dag Hammarskjöld Library in 1979, was receptive to these concerns. While pointing out that the UN's budgetary situation would not permit the use of additional UN funds for a further expansion of the microform program and that previous contacts with potential users in the library community had not been encouraging on the matter of microform sales, he suggested, as a possible alternative, the creation of a consortium of interested libraries to purchase a guaranteed number of microfiche sets. Basically, he welcomed LC's interest and invited LC to be an initiator and catalyst in the endeavor to expand the UN microform program. It was agreed that LC and the UN would jointly develop a questionnaire to survey library interest in a comprehensive UN microform program. The drafting of the questionnaire and the covering letter was mainly in the author's hands; the questionnaire and letter were distributed on 16 January 1980, to more than five hundred libraries worldwide. It was confined to microform of English-language documents. Other libraries than those receiving the initial distribution were encouraged to participate in the survey through notices in the Library of Congress *Information Bulletin* and in the newsletter of the American Library Association's Government Documents Round Table, *Documents to the People*. More than two hundred libraries eventually responded to the questionnaire which essentially proved what LC had been saying all along—that a substantial number of libraries would be interested in having a comprehensive, continuing UN microform program. LC received copies of the individual answers and also assisted in drafting the five-page *Summary Report on UN Microforms Survey* which was distributed with a 5 June 1980 letter over Dr. Orlov's signature. The survey showed that approximately ninety libraries (sixty-two in North America) would consider joining a consortium to guarantee an assured market for UN microform. The greatest interest was in mimeographed documents, followed by *Official Records*, and finally, sales publications. The report also revealed considerable interest in regional documentation.

During a meeting at the UN in May 1980, Donald Wisdom was also asked to prepare a report and recommendations for the UN on the microform program. This six-page report, titled *Report and Recommendations on United Nations Documents in Microform Survey*, was forwarded to the UN in August 1980 with a covering letter from the Associate Librarian of Congress. In this report, Donald

Wisdom summarized the main results of the survey. He stressed the fact that the existing sales program emphasized *Official Records* and selected sales items, and that there was no subscription program for UN-produced microform. He pointed to the need for making available UN documentation in at least three groups: comprehensive sets of current documents for a calendar year; retrospective documents series; and specialized packages relating to subject or geographic interests. The logical step, he asserted, was for the UN to estimate the annual costs for current documents in microform and prorate the unit costs to libraries on the basis of the number of subscribers, say sixty or seventy. Libraries should then be circularized for letters of intent to subscribe. This would obviate the need to establish a consortium. Once a current subscription program was established, working capital for a continuing microform program for libraries could be produced through a revolving fund. The prorating of per-unit costs to libraries would amount to a share-the-cost proposal. The program could become self-sustaining over a period of time.

Priorities suggested by the additional written comments on the completed questionnaires were comprehensive coverage, archival quality, capability of reproducing hard copy readily, timeliness, and improved bibliographic control and access. Although the last was not mentioned specifically in the questionnaire, the concern was obvious from the libraries' answers. The highest priority should be given to mimeographed documents which would be made available to libraries under some kind of subscription program, with subscribers sharing costs proportionally. The UN should establish a special revolving fund to provide working capital for a current and continuing comprehensive microform program, with receipts being deposited in the fund used to carry on the activity. "The overriding goal for a UN microform program should be to provide a highly efficient mechanism for document distribution for all users that fully meets the needs for preservation, control and retrieval, and economy of space."[12]

While the UN authorities welcomed these recommendations, which were distributed by Dr. Orlov to appropriate units within the Organization, they had indicated that there would be difficulty about the idea of a revolving fund. All receipts normally go into the general funds. However, on one occasion, Donald Wisdom had asked specifically for a legal opinion from the UN whether such a fund could be established. The reply was that a revolving fund could be created with the approval of the Comptroller.

Donald Wisdom and the author came away from their 1980 meetings at the UN reasonably encouraged about improved prospects for a truly effective UN microform program but were also well aware of the obstacles. Unfortunately these obstacles have impeded progress on a more substantial UN microform program. One of the first of these, as indicated, was the resistance to a revolving fund.

As the years have gone along, LC has made progress in acquiring additional UN microfiche. For example, it purchased approximately twenty thousand additional microfiche for documents from the UN's Economic Commission for Europe (ECE), the United Nations Conference on Trade and Development (UNCTAD), and the United Nations Industrial Development Organization (UNIDO). These series included mimeographed documents and were available through the Geneva office of the UN. A major point, however, is that no subscription or standing-order program has been established. Two of LC's principal recommendations—a subscription program and a revolving fund—have never been implemented. The UN Sales Section's *Microfiche Price List* for 1980/81 stated that a "standing order service is now available," but reference to this was dropped in the next *Price List*. An inquiry on whether this was a deliberate omission did not receive a precise answer. In 1984 the Sales Section said that only the *Treaty Series* was available on standing order.

The fact that UN bodies other than the Dag Hammarskjöld Library and the Sales Section are involved in the UN microform program certainly adds to the complexity of the situation. Another factor is that the survey referred only to English-language documents, while the UN authorities have to film all languages. This greatly magnifies the problems. In the last two years, LC has made additional purchases of mimeographed series, for example, runs of *A* (General Assembly) and *E* (Economic and Social Council) documents, but when these were acquired, quite a number of items were found missing, and there have been long delays in receiving answers from UN personnel about these omissions. One of the senior Dag Hammarskjöld Library staff members involved in the program recently informed the author that she was working on an index tying the documents directly to microform numbers and that she was troubled by the number of gaps, especially when taking into account all the languages. As indicated above, one of the problems is that at least four groups are immediately involved in the UN's microform program. The Dag Hammarskjöld Library must collaborate with the UN Geneva office in deciding which office will film which document series. The Geneva office had had an outside contractor doing its part of the filming, but it has decided on an in-house operation. Apparently, however, there have been delays in getting an operational system. In addition to the Dag Hammarskjöld Library and the Geneva office, other units involved are the Sales Section in New York and the film contractor located in Ohio. In contrast, it might be noted that Readex has its own means of acquiring UN documentation (a considerable undertaking) and also handles its own marketing and sales.

It would be easy to be discouraged about the possibilities for assuring an improved UN microform program, but it is essential that interested library and information professionals make their views known to appropriate UN officials and government departments responsible for coordinating each country's position at the UN. Even though there are numerous problems—financial, technical, legal, and operational—these difficulties are certainly capable of resolution through a collaborative effort that would involve the UN (and its member governments), commercial publishers, and also the library community.

Unesco

The United Nations Educational, Scientific and Cultural Organization (Unesco) has had a large-scale microform program for some years, but from the standpoint of public availability the program cannot be described as very effective. The microfilming of documents (not publications) has taken place under the auspices of the Division of Libraries, Archives and Documentation Services.[13] The conversion of most Unesco documents into microform has been signaled since the early 1970s by the microfiche numbers given for documents cited throughout the detailed *Unesco List of Documents and Publications (ULDP)* produced since 1972. However, no workable system was established for disseminating the Unesco documentary output on microfiche. If someone contacted Unesco or the exclusive U.S. sales agent, UNIPUB, for a particular item that was out of print, that individual may or may not have been successful in obtaining the item on microfiche. But there was no systematic method for library acquisition of Unesco microform.

Overall, the distribution to depository libraries of Unesco documents, either in hard copy or microfiche, cited in *ULDP* has never been truly satisfactory. Only main documents, not working documents, are sent to depositories [the Unesco depository library network has since been scaled down drastically and is now limited to one depository per member state—ed.], but the document codes are such that experienced international documents librarians cannot always readily distinguish main documents from others in order to understand their entitlements. Because of that situation, ALA's International Documents Task Force and its parent group, the Government Documents Round Table (GODORT), adopted a resolution on the subject at the annual ALA conference in Dallas, Texas, June 1979. This resolution urged "that UNESCO, as rapidly as possible, deposit within its depository libraries a complete collection of those documents available on microfiche and indexed in the *Unesco List of Documents and Publications*. The Government Documents Round Table and its International Documents Task Force also strongly recommends the establishment of an efficient sales and distribution mechanism for both the complete microfiche collection and for individual documents which libraries and individual researchers may wish to acquire.[14] Although the resolution and covering letter were directed to the appropriate Unesco unit, and a number of librarians from major research libraries, including the Library of Congress, wrote to Unesco or discussed the matter in person with agency officials, there was never any real answer from the Organization. This unresponsiveness may have been due mainly to the absence of centralized control over documents and publications at Unesco headquarters.

In 1981 the *Unesco List of Documents and Publications* started carrying a notice to the effect that the Organization hoped to begin a microfiche sales program soon.[15] Finally, in 1982, a sales program was announced under the auspices of the Commercial Services section of the Unesco Press. From this writer's point of view, however, Unesco's notices about microform availability actually raised more questions than they answered. For example, an option for silver film was not mentioned and there were almost no specifications on the fiche. Most important of all, there was no mention of any standing-order program for acquiring either specific packages of materials or the full range of documents.

This is essentially where the situation stands today. It seems that the Unesco Press is anxious to sell microfiche because of the current budgetary crunch caused by the withdrawal from the Organization of the United States, Britain, and Singapore. Publications have now been filmed and availability of both publications and documents is announced in each issue of *ULDP* and in several separate announcements. For example, a fairly substantial six-page brochure was produced in 1984 or 1985 bearing the code LAD/UMS/01 and the title, *Books Now Available on Microfiche*. The brochure gives the ISBNs, microfiche numbers, and prices for a "non-exhaustive list of books" and also cites periodicals and their prices. As indicated earlier, however, research libraries would have little interest in purchasing publications in microform; their main concern is with the fragile and massive documentary output.

The most important advance is that full sets of the General Conference (C) and Executive Board (EX) documents are available in microform at reasonable prices, although not in silver. The price of a single fiche (98 frames, 24X reduction) is 15 French francs (FF), but for orders of more than 1,000 fiches, the unit price is 10 FF. A collection of the first through twenty-first sessions of the General Conference (2,800 fiches) is available for 18,000 FF and later sessions cost 1,200 FF per session. The 1st through the 115th sessions of the Executive Board (3,900 fiches) are available at 29,000 FF, with later sessions at 33 FF per session. It is also helpful that a *Check-List of Microfiche Numbers of General Conference Documents, 1945-1982* (LAD/83/WS/1; 12 p.) has been issued, along with a nine-page *Check-List of Executive Board Documents on Microfiche, 1946–1982* (1st–115th sessions) (no document code). Libraries can order individual books, periodicals, and these two subsets of documents, but there is no method mentioned for systematic acquisition of a full corpus of materials or any logical subsets of nonrestricted Unesco documents. The Unesco document code system, which is unnecessarily complex, is such that one cannot ask, for example, for all documents relating to communications, or culture, or the Middle East.[16] It would also be difficult to see how anyone could readily request a more specific subject package, such as all material on copyright available on microfiche.

Even though Unesco has been prudent in placing the bulk of its documentation on microform, it seems that this is a situation which cries out for some knowledgeable person's attention. Surely there are obstacles to having a satisfactory microform program, but as with the UN, these difficulties should not be such that a combination of efforts by the Organization, a commercial firm, and representatives of the library community could not work out a system permitting better access to the full panoply of information in Unesco documents.

Two final points about Unesco microform may be appropriate to mention here. In responding to the survey question: "Are current microform publications available through subscription?" Unesco's response, dated 3 March 1986, was simply "not yet." In reply to a question about microform from the director of Unesco's Washington, D.C., office* (prompted in part by the author's inquiries), the director of the Libraries, Documentation and Archives Division, M. Pobukovsky, states in the final paragraph of a letter dated 19 August 1985: "We are studying the possibility of proposing to depositary [sic] libraries the choice between printed materials and microfiche. I will keep in mind to inform you when we will take a final decision on the matter."

---

*Because of the withdrawal of the United States, Britain, and Singapore from Unesco and the resulting budget crisis, Unesco's Washington Liaison Office was closed in the spring of 1986.

Food and Agriculture Organization of the United Nations (FAO)

As with Unesco, FAO has had a comprehensive microform program for some years. However, several distinctions are exceedingly important. The first is that the FAO documents and publications cited in the Organization's regular index, *FAO Documentation*, are all listed under a systematic and simple accession-number scheme which begins with a two-digit number representing the year. According to a two-page May 1985 circular, *FAO Documentation on Microfiche*, the full collection of items cited and indexed in a year, which covers all substantive materials, amounts to about 3,500 documents, comprising about 6,600 fiches. This collection is available at a cost of $2,000 per year ($1,000 to developing countries) for silver halide microfiche (98 frames, 24X reduction). Indexes are on COM fiche (209 frames, 42X reduction).

The FAO fiches are arranged by the accession number, and the indexes provide access by author, title, subject, and geographic area. The collection is available from 1976 to date, with a retrospective coverage which started from 1978 and is eventually expected to cover all material back through 1967. In addition to offering the complete collection, the FAO library can also supply broad subject sets or collections related to specific countries. Orders for individual items on fiche are also accepted and these are supplied in diazo film. The 1985 FAO circular notes that the Organization's catalogs are also available on magnetic tape on an annual basis of U.S. $100 (U.S. $50 to developing countries) or every two months at U.S. $150 (U.S. $75 to developing countries).

While the FAO microfiche program is well designed, it has not been given any great amount of publicity. An active marketing effort would be desirable to ensure that more research libraries are aware of the access possible to FAO's rich documentation. In the same connection, however, it may be noted that although FAO's documents and publications with statistical data are indexed and abstracted in the CIS *Index to International Statistics*, the Organization was the only major IGO that did not give CIS permission to film the individual documents because FAO itself was selling the fiche. Thus, libraries that purchase the companion microfilm library to the *Index to International Statistics* are not receiving any FAO items in the *IIS* microfile.

General Agreement on Tariffs and Trade (GATT)

An almost unknown but very important IGO microform program is that of the GATT in Geneva, Switzerland. Information that GATT had a microform program was obtained in 1978 with receipt of a copy of a nine-page document, *GATT Documents on Microfiche; Revision* (INF/162/Rev.1), carrying a **restricted** symbol and dated 11 August 1976. This indicated that the Secretariat for some time had made copies of GATT documents for internal purposes. Documents issued before 1971 were copied on film and later documents on microfiche. Having learned that some delegations were interested in obtaining microfiche copies of current GATT material on a regular basis, the Secretariat document stated that it had initiated a program to supply delegations at their request. The documents, in diazo, utilized the 60-frame standard.

On a visit to GATT in 1980, the author tried to follow up on this information and obtained an updated, hand-copied list of documents available on microfiche, but the documents were still not available to libraries and were still nonsilver. In the meantime, the author had learned that an officer in the U.S. International Trade Commission was collecting GATT documents on microfiche. This made it possible to refer to this ITC staff member a number of individuals inquiring about GATT documents.

The author also had contact with two librarians interested in GATT documentation, one in the Midwest and the other in England. A meeting with the librarian from the Midwest in June 1985 at the New York conference of the American Association of Law Libraries was followed up by contacting her for more details. By chance, additional information about GATT microfiche recently came from these two librarians, the first being received in November 1985 and the second in January 1986. The librarian in the Midwest began to acquire GATT microfiche late in 1984 or in 1985. One of the documents this librarian provided late in 1985, INF/176, dated February 1978 (limited distribution) showed that the documents were still only "available to delegations," but also revealed that the fiches were now on silver-based film.

The latest and most important information, received from both librarians, was in document INF/208, *Microfiche and List & Index of GATT Documents*, dated 4 April 1984. This showed that an annual *List & Index* of GATT documents for the years 1982 and 1983 had been issued (INF/204 and INF/206) and that starting in January 1984, the Secretariat would also issue to delegations a monthly *List & Index*. The standard for microfiche, it noted, had been 60 frame (20X reduction) but henceforth would be 98 frame (24X reduction); it also stated that "documents will no longer be put on microfiche by individual series but in their chronological sequence as reflected by the new continuous numbering introduced in 1983." The price per fiche was raised from 2 to 3 Swiss francs for the 98-frame fiche. Document INF/208 states further that "the new arrangements concerning the sequence of the documents on the microfiche . . . should make filing much simpler. Document retrieval, however, will imply looking into the *List & Index* in order to identify the sequential number of the document on the basis of its symbol. Therefore, no set of new fiche will be supplied to delegations without the corresponding *List & Index*." Another consequence of the new arrangements is that for documents issued after 31 December 1983 "orders for microfiche belonging to a particular series will no longer be accepted. The loss of this facility will, however, be largely compensated by the modest price asked for a complete annual set." The current price for a year's documents is 700 Swiss francs.

A nine-page detailed list of documents accompanying INF/208 goes back to the earliest years of GATT and also includes documents of the Havana Conference on Trade and Employment, which preceded the formation of GATT. Several major GATT serial publications and monographs are also shown to have been filmed. The same listing includes a reference to a 44-fiche document in the INF series called the *List and Index of Documents Issued as from 21 Sept.*

1948–31 Dec. 1984. This list should be a most useful item for those interested in GATT documentation.

With the response to this questionnaire dated 20 February 1986, the author finally received his own copy of INF/208 along with the accompanying nine-page list of documents showing the document symbol (for particular series), the serial number, and the number of microfiche in each series.

Both librarians cited earlier referred to a restricted period of about two years before the documents are released, but the precise answer given on the questionnaire about public availability of the microforms reads: "For periods ranging between 6 months and 2 years after their date of issue, documents are available only to the governmental agencies of member states and governments or organizations with observer status."

The GATT documents, which represent a very important resource, are available to libraries and others through the Translation and Documentation Division, General Agreement on Tariffs and Trade, 54 rue de Lausanne, 1201 Geneva, Switzerland. The completed questionnaire and correspondence carry the name J. Hanus, Director, Translation and Documentation Division.

International Telecommunication Union (ITU)

The ITU set up a microfilm laboratory in 1976, and following that date the ITU Archives began filming out-of-print documents of the Union issued since its establishment in 1865. The films and microfiches currently available are only for documents and publications that are no longer in stock in accordance with the ITU's present policy. The list of currently available "Microfiches and Microfilms of ITU Documents and Publications" appears in the January 1986 issue of the Union's *Telecommunication Journal* (Vol. 53, No. 1, pp. 19–22). While the policy has been to film out-of-print material only, the text accompanying the listing of documents and publications available states that "it is proposed gradually to fill the existing gaps in these series of microfiches and microfilms." All orders are to be addressed to the Archives, General Secretariat, International Telecommunication Union, Place des Nations, CH-1211, Geneva 20, Switzerland. The price per microfiche is 8.5 Swiss francs, and the standard of 60 frames has been used. No mention is given as to whether the film is silver or diazo, but previous lists of microform received from the Union as well as the answer on the survey questionnaire indicate that the film is diazo.

International Labor Organization (ILO)

The International Labor Organization* in Geneva has not had a large-scale microform program, but has utilized the micromedium to enhance the availability

---

*Although ILO considers International Labour Organisation to be the correct spelling, its Washington, D.C. branch has used the form International Labor Organization, a spelling also used by the author of this chapter—ed.

of a number of major serials such as the *Year Book of Labour Statistics*, the *Official Bulletin*, and the *Social and Labour Bulletin* as well as the *Minutes* of successive sessions of the ILO Governing Body (1st–227th sessions, 1919–1984). The *Research Working Papers* of ILO's World Employment Programme (WEP) have also been made available on microfiche. The WEP *Research Working Papers* are preliminary research studies given a limited circulation in hard copy to specialists in order to stimulate discussion and comment. Because they are given only limited distribution, a selection of these has been microfiched. These comprise the initial collection covering 1974–1980 and supplementary packages covering 1981, 1982, and 1983. Lists of the papers included in the WEP packets for the various years have been furnished with the microfiche which are diazo and supplied in loose-leaf binders. The ILO has also published five editions of a bibliography on the World Employment Programme.[17]

In addition, ILO has used COM fiche to produce a number of bibliographic tools, including the *Register of Periodicals in the ILO Library* (1985 edition), *ILO Publications and Documents: Title List, 1965–1985*, and cumulative editions of *International Labour Documentation* for 1965–1977 and 1978–1984. *International Labour Documentation* is an abstracting bulletin produced from ILO's database, LABORDOC, which provides worldwide coverage of labor questions. LABORDOC is available online in the United States through SDC's ORBIT. More than one thousand entries per year on COM fiche are also available from ILO's Labour Information Database (LID). These details are from the April 1985 edition of a leaflet, "ILO Publications on Microfiche." This publication indicates that ILO's *International Labour Review* and *Labour Education* are available on microfilm from University Microfilms International; the *Reports* and the *Record of Proceedings* of the International Labour Conferences from 1919 onward are available on microfilm from World Microfilms Publications, London; and the *Legislative Series* is available on microfiche with a printed consolidated index from UNIFO Publishers, Sarasota, Florida.

International Atomic Energy Agency (IAEA)

No regular microform program for IAEA documentation exists, but the Agency was one of the first to develop a computerized information system, and a microfiche service for nonconventional nuclear literature is a part of the IAEA's International Nuclear Information System (INIS). INIS was designed to cover the world's nuclear literature and as indicated, does not cover IAEA's administrative and organizational documentation. INIS produces the semimonthly *INIS Atomindex* which is an announcement and abstract journal based on input from member states and international organizations. This information is also available in the form of magnetic-tape output but only to participating member governments and international agencies. Currently there are seventy-two countries and fourteen international organizations participating in the INIS system; approximately seventy-five thousand bibliographic records for nuclear literature are published yearly. At the end of 1983, the INIS bibliographic file contained more than eight hundred thousand items.

The nuclear literature reported to INIS is subdivided into two categories, conventional and nonconventional. Conventional literature is that which is commercially available through the normal book trade. The nonconventional literature consists of scientific and technical reports, patent documents, noncommercially published theses and dissertations, and standards. The INIS Clearinghouse, a unit within the INIS Section of IAEA, supplies microfiche copies on request of most of the nonconventional literature announced in *INIS Atomindex* (approximately twenty percent of the items reported to the system).

While the INIS microfiche operation is a fairly large one, with approximately 165,000 documents available on microfiche from the INIS Clearinghouse, it should be kept in mind that this service does not cover IAEA documents. Some of the nuclear literature included in the INIS system and available on microfiche comprises reports produced by other international organizations such as OECD's Nuclear Energy Agency and the European Organization for Nuclear Research (CERN). INIS is certainly an important system that has set standards for other automated information systems, but it is regrettable that IAEA has not established any microform program to cover its own documentation such as its *Annual Report, Programme and Budget*, and other documents of the General Conference or the Governing Board. Details on INIS are available in the fifty-six-page pamphlet, *INIS Today*, the latest edition of which was published in April 1984 as GEN/PUB/13 (Rev.3).

Organization of American States (OAS)

The OAS was one of the first IGOs to convert a major component of its documentation into microform and to make the material available to the public. The *Official Records (Documentos Oficiales)* series was made available initially for 1961 and subsequent years on microcards through Microcard Editions, but beginning in 1973 the OAS altered the arrangements, taking over the sale of the documentation itself and making the *Official Records* available on microfiche in yearly packages. A checklist titled *Lista General de Documentos*, prepared by the OAS's Columbus Memorial Library for the hard-copy sets, could be used for retrieving documents from the microfiche edition and was also included at the beginning of each microfiche edition.

The OAS microform operation continued through 1977, but after that date another change was made. The year 1978 was skipped over so that the documentation could be ready on a more timely basis. The 1979 fiche edition was produced with the documentation filmed in the order in which it was received and without regard to language. The *Lista General* contained a new set of microfiche numbers and these individual numbers were essential for retrieving any of the microfiched documents. This 1979 set was not entirely satisfactory, and with staff reductions and organizational changes at the OAS, it was some years before the microform sets of *Official Records* were made available again. It is thanks to the persistence of the OAS librarian, Thomas L. Welch, and the continued interest and pressure of the major research libraries that the OAS microfiche program for its *Official Records* has been saved. In 1985, the *Official Records* for 1978 as well as 1982–1984 were made available; the years 1980 and 1981 followed in 1986.[18] The fiches are now available through the OAS library, both in diazo and in silver at a small premium. The latest checklist at the time of writing is that for 1984; it was published in 1985 as volume 25 of the *Documentos Oficiales de la Organización de los Estados Americanos: Lista General de Documentos* (OEA/SER.Z/I.1; 182 p.).

The OAS has also produced catalogs of its technical reports which consist of studies and reports not included in the *Official Records* series nor offered for sale in the OAS *Catalog of Publications*. All nonrestricted items cited in the catalog are available for sale on microfiche. The initial catalog (132 p.), covering the period 1974–1976, was published in 1977 under the title, *Catálogo de Informes y Documentos Técnicos de la OEA*. Supplementary volumes have also been produced with the same title plus the word, *Suplemento*, and the year. Currently available are five supplementary volumes for 1977, 1978, 1979/80, 1981, and 1982. The two earliest supplements maintained a consecutive numbering sequence begun in the 1974–1976 edition, but starting with the 1979/80 supplement, each series begins with number 1 and indicates the year of the supplement. Examples are COOP/II/82-1 and EDU/V/82-1.[19] In addition to the offer of individual fiche, most items are also available as photocopies made from the fiche. According to the introduction to the 1982 supplement, when the print quality of the original document does not permit a clear reproduction, only the microfiche is available for sale. Standing orders are also accepted for the annual microfiche sets.

As a final item relating to the OAS, an extensive catalog received in 1985 from the OAS Secretariat for Education, Science and Culture reveals the existence of still another OAS microform program. This catalog, titled *INFOCIECC* (No. 1, 1985), is the product of a database covering regional projects of educational, scientific and technical, and cultural development. In addition to the concrete achievements resulting from these multinational cooperative projects, numerous studies, reports, and journal articles are produced; it is the documentation from the various projects that is cited and indexed in *INFOCIECC*. Included are the list by access number, the author index, meeting index, and descriptor index. For information on obtaining microfiche of the documents cited, one should address the appropriate OAS departments—Educational Affairs, Scientific and Technological Affairs, or Culture.

European Communities
[EC, now European Union]

The Library of Congress has been fortunate to be a depository for European Communities documentation since the EC initiated its depository program. Because of the number of EC institutions, the complexity of the documents, and the number of language editions, the Communities' documents and publications are just about the most complex international materials in existence. All the problems of acquisition, bibliographic control, and servicing are multiplied. Libraries and other research institutions in Washington, D.C., have been fortunate to have the Delegation of the Commission of the European Communities. The EC Information Service of the Washington, D.C., office has been outstanding, and LC is pleased this office is just a local telephone call or short subway ride away. Although the author receives inquiries quite frequently about EC documentation, the Washington, D.C., office can be depended upon for assistance on the most difficult questions and for the latest information.

In recent years the EC has concentrated its services for depository libraries and European Documentation Centres (the latter being much more common in Europe than in North America) in a separate EDC/DEP Section of the Office for Official Publications in Luxembourg. This has eased some of the problems of depository libraries.

To better illustrate the complexity of the European Communities, the survey questionnaire on microform documentation sent to the Office for Official Publications was duplicated and answered nine times by that Office. Separate answers were supplied by the Office for Official Publications for five different institutions of the EC plus replies for the three publishing services within the Commission of the European Communities as well as for the Office for Official Publications. The responses were for the European Parliament, the Council of the European Communities, the Court of Justice, the Court of Auditors, and the Economic and Social Committee, along with the response for the Office for Official Publications (a joint department under common management in which separate institutions publish through a common organ, the *Official Journal, Series L and C*). Finally, there were separate replies for the three different publishing services of the Commission in Directorates IX and XIII and the Statistical Office. The Commission is the major institution which initiates EC policy and also executes the decisions finally agreed upon by the Council.

With regard to microform documentation, it should be noted that for many years scientific and technical reports issued for the EC and described in *Euro Abstracts* were available on microfiche. These are the so-called EUR reports. A consolidated catalog of EUR documents has been issued for 1968–1979 along with a supplementary catalog for 1980–1982.[20] The *Official Journal* has also been offered for some years on microfiche as well as hard copy, but in 1983 a considerable step forward was taken when the Office for Official Publications offered depository libraries and European Documentation Centres a similar option of receiving either hard copy or fiche of Commission (COM) documents. The material in both hard copy and microfiche was to be available simultaneously. Monthly and annual indexes of the COM documents were also offered. While some of the COM documents had been publicly available in the past, for example, in the *Official Journal* or as supplements to the *Bulletin of the European Communities*, this was the first time full sets of public COM documents were offered. At the same time, subscriptions to the COM documents were offered to nondepository libraries.

Because specifications for the fiche were not given in the initial announcement, the author asked LC's acquisition staff to request further details. As indicated, the *Official Journal* had been available for some years on microfiche, but not in silver. In response to the question whether there would be an option to buy silver film at a premium, the Office for Official Publications noted that the fiche was diazo, with "no possibility to have silver halide film."[21] The letter also gave the format as 98 frames with a 25X reduction ratio and stated that the text was negative. It is a disappointment that there is no option for silver fiche, but the EC is not the only IGO that produces film in diazo only.

Since 1983 additional documentation has also been made available on microfiche. Titles include, for example, the *Reports* and *Texts Adopted* of the European Parliament and the *Opinions* of the Economic and Social Committee. Many of the EC's statistical publications are offered in either hard copy or microfiche, but some of the statistical titles are now being offered only on fiche. For example, the *Analytical Tables of Foreign Trade—SITC*, was offered in the past either in paper or on fiche, but the Library of Congress received word that beginning with 1984 the title would only be available as COM fiche. Even without the option of silver film, libraries and other institutions should be grateful that a massive corpus of EC documentation is now available in microform.

Organization for Economic Cooperation and Development (OECD)

One of the other major IGOs having a large documentary output is the Organization for Economic Cooperation and Development. OECD furnishes to libraries its publications only, not its documents. Although LC's receipt of OECD monographs and serials is very extensive, virtually all of these publications are worthy of individual cataloging and retention in hard copy in the Library of Congress. OECD for some years has also made available on microfiche the publications cited in its regular *Catalogue of Publications*. The Library of Congress has had no interest in obtaining these publications in microform for several reasons. The first, as indicated, is that the material is substantial and receives full cataloging so that it is under bibliographic control, and the second is that there are no gaps to speak of because LC is fortunate in receiving full runs of OECD material on exchange. Finally, there is no interest in OECD microfiche publications because the fiche is not silver.

The Organization has produced several bibliographic tools relating to microfiche that should be of interest. Two of these are the *Catalogue of Microfiches of English Monographs Published by OECD/OEEC, 1948–1980* and the *Catalogue of Microfiches of English and Bilingual OECD/OEEC Periodicals, 1948–1981*. A third listing of interest is *OEEC/OECD English Monographs Published for Free Distribution, 1948–1980*.

The author had no idea from the U.S. State Department or any other source that OECD was also making its documents as well as its publications available to member governments on microfiche until an officer in the library of the Canadian Department of External Affairs in Ottawa provided the information that OECD documents on microfiche were available to governments, and that the Department's library was paying to acquire these microfiches. Because these items are restricted, they cannot be made available to the public, and therefore are mostly not of concern to LC. But one can assume that it is a great boon for the

Department of External Affairs to have these documents on microfiche because the paper documents take up so much space.

Andean Pact
(Junta del Acuerdo de Cartagena)

Although a great deal of interesting information was obtained in response to the questionnaire, it is not possible to take all this information into account here. Nevertheless, it is interesting to consider a case in which it is unlikely to be known that one agency has microfilmed all its documents. Such an organization is the Andean Pact or Junta del Acuerdo de Cartagena in Lima, Peru. The organization also supplied copies of its detailed computer-assisted bibliographic tool, *JUNINDEX*, which began with Vol. 1, No. 1, in December 1984. Three issues of this title were provided, the first two numbers bearing the subtitle *Resúmenes de Documentos de la Junta del Acuerdo de Cartagena* (181 p. and 171 p.) and Vol. 2, No. 2, carrying the subtitle, *Resúmenes de Decisiones del Junta del Acuerdo*. Marina Schreiber, head of the Documentation Center of the Secretariat of the organization, stated on the questionnaire that all of the Organization's documents have been filmed, and answered "yes" to the question asking whether the documents were partially available to the public. She stated further that "if somebody pays the cost of the copy, I suppose our Organization would accept if the user is a national or international organization." This information is very interesting and certainly worth following up.

Conclusion

Though it has not been possible here to review relevant information on all the major IGOs, let alone all the smaller ones, it is clear that a substantial number of international intergovernmental organizations have converted large portions of their documentary output into microform. In some cases the microform has been produced entirely for the organization's own purposes, but in many instances substantial portions of the microform documentation have been made available to libraries, other institutions, and individuals. Nevertheless, progress in developing IGO microform collections in research libraries has been slower than most interested librarians and researchers would like.

The role microform technology will play in the future information activities of IGOs is not clear, but it might be expected that there will be a continuing need for large backup collections of IGO documents in microform for some years. These international documents should be accessible in key research libraries. Even so, the documents in large retrospective collections will not have to be accessed frequently, and automated retrieval systems are not likely to be needed. At present, the long-term storage of massive documents collections in electronic form does not appear to be feasible economically or otherwise, but it is not possible to tell what the coming years will bring and what new technologies IGOs will be able to use for information storage, retrieval, and dissemination.

The use of computers has already greatly enhanced the capacity of many IGOs to organize and service vast amounts of information, and there is no reason to think that computers will not continue to play an increasingly important part in assisting the IGOs to manage information. As stated above, there is also good reason to believe that there will continue to be a place for the microfilmed archive. Even though the organizations may be able to store and manipulate large portions of their own data through computers and other more advanced media, libraries will not necessarily be able to utilize these means for their research collections. The research library and its personnel, however, ought to be a part of the picture.

Librarians, archivists, and other information specialists should constantly monitor the latest developments and express their concerns effectively. IGO documentation as well as other government information must be accessible for researchers who do not serve in international organizations or other government bodies and who do not necessarily have all the latest technologies. As one of the major publishers of government documentation in microform has said, "Microforms will continue to be used much as they are at present—until electronic data storage and transmission technology equals or improves on microforms in quality and cost.[22]

(B) DOCUMENTATION IN MICROFORM AND ALTERNATIVE FORMATS: AN UPDATE

Michael McCaffrey-Noviss and Andrea Sevetson

Microform Technology

Since the late Robert W. Schaaf wrote his chapter for the first (1988) edition of this book, microform technology has changed very little. There are improved readers and higher-quality reproduction methods. Questions about quality and longevity of silver halide and diazo still persist although it is generally accepted that silver is preferable from an archivist's standpoint. Silver, however, is more susceptible to deterioration if not handled properly while in use. Schaaf's original chapter covered two issues concerning microform: availability and format.

When considering microforms in libraries from a public service perspective, the collection manager is often torn between catering to the needs of the average users, in particular increasing the ease with which they may gain access to material, and meeting the needs of the research community who are far more concerned with the completeness of the collection. The dilemma is offset to a certain extent by the indexing devoted to most commercially produced microform sets. For most sets, a web-based or CD-ROM index is available, often with an interface that may help even the most timid undergraduate readers overcome their fear of government documents.

When considering microforms from a collection development perspective, however, there is no such dilemma. Rare is the collection of documents shipped complete from an IGO source. If a paper document collection is to be maintained, resources must be devoted to claiming material and collating it. Once the material is considered complete, one must also preserve it and, assuming it has been printed on a paper likely to withstand the test of time, it must be bound and shelved. Commercial vendors of microforms, on the other hand, have an obligation to ship complete sets and can afford to claim material and hunt down fugitive pieces. The collections they ship to their customers take relatively little time to file and require only the cabinets to house them. The principal drawback, the often artificial order in which they arrive and the ensuing need to use vendor-specific indexes to locate material, is but a minor irritant. Congressional Information Service's *Index to International Statistics* numbering scheme and Readex's choice of shipping and providing their *United Nations Documents* collection to customers by Readex year are two examples and, in the latter case, where there have been the human resources available, Readex microfiche have been reorganized into document series symbol number order with success.

Although the costs of purchasing material from a vendor have been a source of contention in many circles, particularly where the customer is a depository for the organization and is entitled to receive material in paper, in recent years concerns over the cost of collation and binding and the demands of space have often provided a compelling argument for purchasing material in microform. This has been particularly evident in those institutions where staff positions are eliminated or filled at a snail's pace in order to free up money for electronic collections.

Another recent development in microform technology concerns the reproduction of material held in microprint. Companies such as ScreenScan in the United Kingdom have been able to adapt microform readers for the scanning and subsequent printing or saving of images. Thus, although the number of libraries in possession of a UN documents collection in microprint is dwindling, this new technology has resulted in thousands of dollars in savings for those who are unable to replace their microprint collection.

Historical Coverage

Rarely does an historical collection of IGO documents in print become available and, in the final analysis, it is not even clear if it would be desirable to acquire it this way. Those who work with early UN material or with League of Nations documents are well aware of the speed at which these collections are disintegrating. Microforms offer an effective way of acquiring a set of historical documents or a complete run of important journals such as the *Official Journal of the European Communities* in an easy-to-house and archivally sound format.

Microforms can also serve to supplement existing collections. Subscribers to the Readex *United Nations Documents and Publications* microfiche set, for instance, receive certain -/L/- (limited distribution category) documents. While this has been less frequent of late, many -/L/- documents are included in the earlier years. Users of the *League of Nations Documents and Publications, 1919–1946,* a 555-reel microfilm set, have access to a collection of League material superior to all print collections with the exception of the League collection in the Geneva Library of the UN. The GATT *List and Index of Documents Issued* microfiche is another example of a microfiche set greatly supplementing what was available through that organization's depository program.[23] Its World Trade Organization (WTO) equivalent, the web-based *Document Dissemination Facility* (DDF) will be discussed below.

Access Technology and Alternative Formats

In this area, recent advances have made the world of IGO collection management a radically different one than that envisioned when the first edition of this book appeared. When the original chapter was written, indexes were published regularly (monthly, quarterly or semiannually) and there was, in some cases, some sort of cumulative, normally annual, index. Multiyear cumulations were, to most users of IGO information, a dream. The technological advances made since then, particularly in the area of storage capacity, have made web- and CD-ROM-based multiyear databases pervasive and have changed the manner in which most IGO research is conducted. It is now much easier to search across a number of years with relatively little effort. The appearance of complete documents via the web is a more recent innovation that bodes well for those in need of IGO information.

While CD-ROM affords the library the opportunity to exert complete control over its electronic collection, that format is of questionable value in terms of its longevity. The CD-ROM is only useful when used for a replaceable product, a cumulating index such as the *UNBIS Plus* bibliographical database coproduced by the UN and Chadwyck-Healey, for instance. As a storage medium for text, however, it leaves much to be desired. Apart from the issue of archival permanence of the physical medium, one must also take care to ensure that both the hardware and software required to read and reproduce the information are kept in a good state of repair and monitored for obsolescence.

Reliance on the web, on the other hand, poses an entirely different set of problems. As its use in a reference setting is discussed throughout this book, the focus here will be on issues of collection management.

Commercial vendors and IGOs alike have begun to avail themselves of the web as a means of delivering information. In the commercial sector, CIS and Readex are industry leaders with their *Statistical Universe* and *AccessUN* products respectively. The *Statistical Universe* package will eventually include the text and datafiles of key IGO statistical publications. *AccessUN* contains the text of resolutions and the bibliographical backfile gap is being filled rapidly.

Similarly, the major IGOs are quick to mount material on the web. The WTO's *Document Dissemination Facility* is one notable recent advance.[24] Both the World Bank and the UN have made great strides in presenting material in an electronic format in recent years and continue to do so. The UN *Optical Disk System* web server (called *Official Documents Search* by the UN Sales Section), which is the official repository for parliamentary documents published by the UN, contains the full text of documents dating back to 1992 in Portable Document Format (PDF) in all official languages of the UN.[25] The trend toward making material available in electronic format will, in all likelihood, continue. The UN Administrative Committee on Co-ordination's Information Systems Coordinating Committee, in its annual report issued in 1999, stated:

> One focus (of the Organizational Committee of the ISCC) during the coming biennium will be to provide schemes for additional types of information which should be made available electronically to Member States by substantially all agencies, and for provision of relevant information to special groups (NGOs, missions, etc.).[26]

There have also been interorganizational moves toward coordinating efforts to make information available electronically and to set standards and establish gateways.

These recent developments bode well for users of IGO information and for reference librarians. There are, however, several issues which need to be kept in mind from the collection management standpoint. One is format; the other is control.

While certain formats for presenting text and image tend to predominate, there is by no means a universal standard. Adobe's PDF is the most commonly used means of delivering documents, but it is not used by all IGOs. The World Bank, for instance, on its *World Development Sources* website does not use PDF.[27] In a networked environment, a certain amount of work may need to be done by the library systems office to install plug-ins to ensure that the material made available by the World Bank is readable in the library. Similarly, the WTO provides its documents on its DDF in *WordPerfect 5.2* or *Word 97*. Apart from the problems posed by delivering editable documents to users, again, one must ensure that software is made available so that the material is readable onsite or be faced with the prospect of sending users away with unread files.

The issue of control over a collection is perhaps the most important dilemma faced by those who choose to rely on electronic products for collection development. In the final analysis, reliance on remote access is an abrogation of one's responsibility to maintain a collection. When a web-based service is chosen, it is essentially rented and the purchaser has no guarantee that it will continue to meet the needs of its users. Policies can change and commercial vendors can go bankrupt. Similarly, IGOs, no matter how noble their intent, can be affected by political decisions and budgetary constraints and cannot guarantee that whatever they make available today will be there tomorrow.

In some respects, Schaaf's words on the advisability of converting paper to microform ring even more true today than when they were originally written. The web as a means for delivering IGO information provides a useful function. It is best at getting the current and the important out to a wide audience as quickly as possible. Built-in search engines enable users to retrieve the essentials in a relatively quick and simple fashion providing almost a sense of instant gratification. In many regards, certainly for less substantial material such as UN masthead documents, paper is indeed obsolete. As a collection manager's responsibility is to ensure the integrity of a collection over time, however, microform has become the ideal medium for protecting a collection from the political and fiscal vagaries that prevent remote access from ever being completely reliable over the long term. Indeed, were the UN, for instance, to offer depositories free site-licensed access to its *Optical Disk System* in lieu of receiving masthead documents and were those libraries subsequently able to make use of the savings to purchase the material in microfiche, then they would have the best of all possible worlds. They would be able to provide quick and easy access while ensuring that the material is under their direct control and is available to users today and tomorrow.

Notes and References

1. Ellen Detlefsen, "User Costs: Information as a Social Good vs. Information as a Commodity," *Government Publications Review* 11 (September/October 1984): 390.

2. Geoffrey Charlish, "Microfilm Fights for a Future," *The Financial Times* (London), 11 September 1984, 12.

3. Bernard J. S. Williams, "Document Delivery & Reproduction Survey, October 1985," *FID News Bulletin* 35 (November 1985): 88.

4. Ibid., 87.

5. Robert C. Sullivan, "Microform Developments Related to Acquisitions," *Microform Review* 14 (summer 1985): 170.

6. Jerry Dupont, "Microform Film Stock: A Hobson's Choice; Are Librarians Getting the Worst of Both Worlds?" *Library Resources & Technical Services* 30 (January/March 1986): 81.

7. Suzanne C. Dodson, "Microfilm Types: There Really Is a Choice," *Library Resources & Technical Services* 30 (January/March 1986): 88.

8. Mary K. Fetzer, "Micropublishing Activities for United Nations and Specialized Agency Documentation: Status and Comment," *Government Publications Review* 7A, no. 5 (1980): 425.

9. United Nations, Archives Section, *Index to Microfilm of United Nations Documents in English, 1946–1961* (New York: UN, 1963) and *Index to Microfilm of United Nations Documents in English; Supplement, 1962–1967* (New York: UN, 1970).

10. Luciana Marulli-Koenig, "The Dag Hammarskjöld Library and United Nations Microforms," *Microform Review* 9 (fall 1980): 236–42.

11. Fetzer, "Micropublishing Activities," 424.

12. United States, Library of Congress, "Report and Recommendations on United Nations Documents in Microform Survey," by Donald F. Wisdom, Chief, Serial and Government Publications Division (Washington, DC, August 1980, unpublished).

13. Peter I. Hajnal, *Guide to Unesco* (Dobbs Ferry, NY: Oceana, 1983), 184.

14. Quoted in Hajnal, *Guide to Unesco*, 203–4.

15. The heading "Unesco Documents on Microfiches" first appeared in the *Unesco List of Documents and Publications*, 1981, no. 1, p. vii, with the note: "It is planned to make microfiche copies of the documents available on sale in the near future."

16. See, for example, Robert W. Schaaf's "International Organizations Documentation: Resources and Services of the Library of Congress and Other Washington Based Agencies," *Government Information Quarterly* 1, no. 1 (1984): 64.

17. International Labour Office, *Bibliography of Published Research of the World Employment Programme*, 5th ed. (Geneva: ILO, 1984). The first edition was published in 1978.

18. Letter of 17 December 1985 from the OAS Librarian, Thomas L. Welch, to the author and follow-up telephone calls.

19. See the introduction in Organization of American States, *Catálogo de Informes y Documentos Técnicos de la OEA; Suplemento, 1982* (Washington, DC, 1982).

20. European Communities, Office for Official Publications, *Catalogue of EUR Documents, 1968–1979* (Luxembourg: EC, 1983) and European Communities, Office for Official Publications, *Catalogue [of] EUR Documents, 1980–1982* (Luxembourg: EC, 1985).

21. Letter of 23 September 1983 from the Office for Official Publications of the European Communities to the Library of Congress, Exchange and Gift Division.

22. Charles Chadwyck-Healey, "The Future of Microform in an Electronic Age," *Wilson Library Bulletin* 58 (December 1983): 270.

23. General Agreement on Tariffs and Trade, *List and Index of Documents* (Geneva: GATT, 1947–1996).

24. World Trade Organization, *Document Dissemination Facility* (website); http://www.wto.org/wto/ddf/ep/index.html.

25. United Nations, *United Nations Official Documents* (New York, Optical Disk System [ODS] website); http://www.ods.un.org.

26. United Nations, Administrative Committee on Co-ordination, Information Systems Coordination Committee, *Report of the Seventh Session of the ISCC* (New York, UN, 1999). October 26, 1999, 24. ACC/1999/19.

27. World Bank, *World Development Sources: Image Bank Retrieval Page* (website); <http://www-wds.worldbank.org>.

CHAPTER 9
Electronic Information Resources of the United Nations High Commissioner for Refugees

Elisa Mason

Introduction

Refugee crises are newsworthy events. Yet despite the relatively high coverage they receive in the press, researching refugee issues can prove a challenging task. Very little has been written about refugees and other forced migrants from an information perspective. This chapter will attempt to rectify this situation by introducing one of the central players in the refugee arena, the United Nations High Commissioner for Refugees (UNHCR), and its electronic information resources.

The Organization

Background

Although refugee flows have occurred throughout history, the international community did not begin to address them formally until 1921 when the League of Nations was asked to assume responsibility for what was increasingly becoming a multilateral concern. Dr. Fridtjof Nansen of Norway was appointed the first High Commissioner for Refugees and served until his death in 1930. Although he initially focused on resolving the situation of Russian refugees in Europe, the scope of his work quickly extended to other displaced populations. An important legacy of his tenure was the Nansen Passport, a certificate that served as an identity document and allowed refugees to travel.[1]

During the 1930s and 1940s, various initiatives were mounted to alleviate the humanitarian problems of people forced from their homes (see Table 9.1). Although these endeavors responded to particular refugee situations, they shared several general characteristics: They offered assistance to the populations they served; they sought some kind of permanent settlement; and time limits were placed on their mandates, as refugee problems were considered to be temporary.

Establishment of UNHCR

In the aftermath of World War II, the United Nations was determined to assist the millions of people still displaced in Europe. As a result, the Office of the United Nations High Commissioner for Refugees was established, with an initial mandate of three years from 1 January 1951 to 31 December 1953. Like its predecessors, UNHCR was charged with resolving the refugee problem and then terminating its activities. The reality is that refugee situations continue to preoccupy the global community. Today, millions worldwide are uprooted by war and ethnic conflict. Despite this trend, UNHCR still operates on a limited mandate, although its life span was increased from three to five years at a time.[2]

The High Commissioner

UNHCR is led by a High Commissioner who is nominated by the Secretary-General and elected by the General Assembly. Since the organization's inception, eight High Commissioners have served (see Table 9.2, page 252). The present High Commissioner, Sadako Ogata of Japan, was elected in 1991. She is the first woman to head the office, and her tenure will expire in December 2000.

UNHCR's Mandate and Activities

UNHCR provides protection and assistance to some 22 million refugees and other persons of concern to the office.[3] (See Table 9.3, page 253, for categories of populations assisted.) The Statute of UNHCR outlines the agency's principal responsibilities.[4] These include, first and foremost, the provision of international protection. Refugees are people who have fled their own countries and have crossed an international frontier, often without travel documents. As such, they are in a vulnerable position from a legal perspective. UNHCR attempts to ensure the basic rights of refugees in their countries of refuge, such as the right not to be *refouled* or returned to a place where one's life is threatened. Other protection activities include:

- counseling refugees on their rights and lobbying governments on their behalf;
- promoting the granting of asylum;

Table 9.1
UNHCR's Predecessor Organizations*

Name of Organization	Life Span	Description
International Nansen Office for Refugees	1931-1938	established to settle the refugees remaining from the Nansen era over a ten-year period
High Commissioner for Refugees Coming from Germany	1933-1938	set up to secure legal status and locate employment for refugees from Germany, and later, from Austria; difference between these refugees and earlier ones is they sought refuge from persecution rather than settlement
High Commissioner for Refugees under the Protection of the League of Nations	1938-1946	created through the merging of the two previous organizations; coordinated humanitarian activities, sought resettlement, and promoted refugee conventions and other international arrangements
Intergovernmental Committee on Refugees (IGCR)	1938-1947	emerged as a result of the International Conference on Refugees (1938); tasked with helping people to escape from Germany and Austria and finding resettlement places for war refugees
United Nations Relief and Rehabilitation Administration (UNRRA)	1943-1947	created before the UN was officially established; provided relief to people displaced by the Second World War and facilitated their return home
International Refugee Organization (IRO)	1947-1952	subsumed both UNRRA's and IGCR's functions; addressed all aspects of the refugee problem: "identification, registration, and classification; care and assistance; and repatriation or resettlement and reestablishment in countries able to receive those refugees who were under the mandate of the IRO"**

* Louise Holborn, *Refugees: A Problem of Our Time. The Work of the United Nations High Commissioner for Refugees, 1951–1972*, 2 vols. (Metuchen, NJ: Scarecrow Press, 1975), 10–42. For other overviews, see Robert F. Gorman, *Historical Dictionary of Refugee and Disaster Relief Organizations* (Metuchen, NJ: Scarecrow Press, 1994) and Gil Loescher and Ann D. Loescher, *The Global Refugee Crisis: A Reference Handbook* (Santa Barbara, CA; Oxford: ABC-CLIO, 1994). For more details on a particular institution, refer to the following: Claudena M. Skran, *The International Refugee Regime and the Refugee Problem in Interwar Europe* (University of Oxford, Diss., 1989); *UNRRA: The History of the United Nations Relief and Rehabilitation Administration*, 3 vols., ed. George Woodbridge (New York: Columbia University Press, 1950); Tommie Sjöberg, *The Powers and the Persecuted: The Refugee Problem and the Intergovernmental Committee on Refugees (IGCR), 1938–1947* (Lund: Lund University Press, 1991); Louise Holborn, *The International Refugee Organization: A Specialized Agency of the United Nations, Its History and Work, 1946–1952* (London: Oxford University Press, 1956).

** Holborn, *Refugees*, 31.

Table 9.2
UN High Commissioners for Refugees*

Name	Nationality	Tenure
Mr. Gerrit J. van Heuven Goedhart	Netherlands	1950-1956
Mr. Auguste R. Lindt	Switzerland	1956-1960
Mr. Felix Schnyder	Switzerland	1960-1965
Sadruddin Aga Khan	Iran	1965-1977
Mr. Poul Hartling	Denmark	1978-1985
Mr. Jean-Pierre Hocké	Switzerland	1986-1989
Mr. Thorvald Stoltenberg	Norway	Jan.-Nov. 1990
Mrs. Sadako Ogata	Japan	1991-2000

* United Nations High Commissioner for Refugees, "Box III.1: The High Commissioners," *The State of the World's Refugees: The Challenge of Protection* (London and New York: Penguin Books, 1993). Available on the REFWORLD CD-ROM under "Reference."

- determining refugee status when a government is not able to do so;
- advising governments on the drafting of national refugee and asylum laws;
- monitoring the physical security of refugees; and
- encouraging the ratification of international refugee and statelessness conventions.[5]

The organization carries out its protection duties within the framework established by international refugee law. This framework is defined by such conventions and standards as the 1951 Convention relating to the Status of Refugees and its 1967 Protocol, the 1969 Organization for African Unity Convention Governing the Specific Aspects of Refugee Problems in Africa, and the 1984 Cartagena Declaration on Refugees. Also important are the 1954 Convention relating to the Status of Stateless Persons and the 1961 Convention on the Reduction of Statelessness, two conventions whose ratification the General Assembly has asked UNHCR to promote.

Because the refugee issue is fundamentally a human rights problem, UNHCR's work is also influenced by human rights and humanitarian law. Relevant instruments include the Geneva Conventions, the International Bill of Human Rights, and the many other human rights conventions in force such as the Convention against Torture and Other Cruel, Inhuman or Degrading Treatment or Punishment, the Convention on the Rights of the Child, and the Convention on the Elimination of Discrimination against Women.[6]

Table 9.3
Persons of Concern to UNHCR*

Population Assisted	UNHCR Definition
Refugees	"Persons outside their country of origin and recognized as refugees by governments which have signed the various United Nations or regional instruments relating to the legal status of refugees; or by UNHCR, according to the definition contained in the High Commissioner's Statute. These are known as 'mandate' refugees. This category includes persons who have been granted temporary protection on a group basis."
Asylum-Seekers	"Persons who have left their countries of origin and have applied for recognition as refugees in other countries, and whose applications are still pending decision by the appropriate government or UNHCR."
Internally Displaced Persons (IDPs)	"Like refugees, these persons may have been forced to flee their homes because their lives and/or liberty were at risk; but unlike refugees, they either could not or did not wish to cross an international border. Legally, they fall under the sovereignty of their own government, even though that government may be unable or unwilling to protect them."
Returnees	"Persons who were of concern to UNHCR when outside of their country of origin and who remain so for a limited period after their return while UNHCR assists in their reintegration and monitors their well-being."
Other Persons of Concern	"…[P]ersons living in a refugee-like situation outside their countries of origin, but who have not been formally recognized as refugees, such as victims of war in the former Yugoslavia and various groups in the Commonwealth of Independent States."

* United Nations High Commissioner for Refugees, *1999 Global Appeal* (Geneva: UNHCR, 1999). Available on the REFWORLD CD-ROM under "UNHCR." URL address: <www.unhcr.ch/fdrs/ga99/toc.htm>. UNHCR's mandate has been expanded over the years by the General Assembly to include some internally displaced persons and other people in "refugee-like situations."

The agency seeks to resolve the problems faced by refugees by implementing a "durable"—or lasting—solution to their plight. Three traditional solutions have been identified: a) local settlement (for example, asylum); b) resettlement, whereby countries like the U.S., Australia, and Canada agree to accept quotas of refugees coming from the initial country of refuge; and c) voluntary repatriation, or returning home when conditions have improved sufficiently that the safety of refugees can be guaranteed. The last solution is often controversial because it can be difficult to ascertain both the "voluntariness" of a refugee's decision to return home and the degree to which situations have become normalized.[7]

Since the 1990s, humanitarian assistance has become a more predominant focus of UNHCR's work. UNHCR, in partnership with other international governmental and nongovernmental organizations (NGOs), responds to refugee emergencies on the ground by providing aid in the form of food, shelter, sanitation, and health services. In addition to emergency relief operations, UNHCR undertakes other types of assistance programs. One example is helping refugees to become more self-sufficient in their countries of asylum or in their home countries once they have been repatriated.[8] In recognition of its work, UNHCR was twice awarded the Nobel Peace Prize, in 1954 and 1981.

Governing Bodies

UNHCR is governed by the General Assembly (GA) and the Economic and Social Council (ECOSOC). Both organs may request UNHCR to undertake specific activities. Each year, the agency submits a report to the GA through ECOSOC.[9] After examining the report, the GA adopts an "omnibus" resolution, which sets forth the policy parameters that will guide UNHCR in its work throughout the year.[10]

UNHCR also receives advice and guidance on international protection and financial matters from its Executive Committee (EXCOM). This body was established in 1958 by the General Assembly and ECOSOC.[11] Its fifty-four member states meet once a year in Geneva to review UNHCR's activities and approve the agency's assistance programs. The final report of the session is later transmitted as an addendum to UNHCR's annual report to the GA. EXCOM was preceded by the Advisory Committee on Refugees (1951–1954) and the United Nations Refugee Fund (UNREF) (1955–1958).

Two sub-committees have assisted EXCOM in its work. The Sub-Committee of the Whole on International Protection (SCIP) and the Sub-Committee on Administrative and Financial Matters (SCAF) were established in 1975 and 1980, respectively. Both were subsequently replaced in 1996 by one Standing Committee (SC). Today, the SC discusses both protection and financial issues, and can adopt decisions and conclusions accordingly. The Conclusions on International Protection are particularly important texts: "Although non-binding, the conclusions express an important international consensus on legal matters concerning refugees, and have served to fill gaps in areas of the international refugee law regime not foreseen by the 1951 Convention or 1967 Protocol relating to the Status of Refugees."[12] Relevant document symbols for reports produced by these bodies are noted in Table 9.4.

Table 9.4
UNHCR Document Symbols

Document Series	Symbol
Executive Committee (plenary sessions)	A/AC.96/#
Report of the United Nations High Commissioner for Refugees and Addendum	A/session/12 A/session/12/Add.1
Standing Committee (SC)	EC/session/SC/CRP.#
Sub-Committee of the Whole on International Protection (SCIP)	EC/SCP/# EC/year/SCP/CRP.#
Sub-Committee on Administrative and Financial Matters (SCAF)	EC/SC.2 EC/year/SC.2/CRP.#
United Nations Refugee Fund	A/AC.79/#
Advisory Committee on Refugees	A/AC.36/#

CRP=conference room paper

Staff and Budget

Today, UNHCR employs more than 5,000 staff members in both its Headquarters and its field operations in 124 countries.[13] After reaching a high of $1 billion in 1994, UNHCR's 1999 budget costs totaled $918 million. Most of its requirements are met through voluntary contributions from governments; only two percent of the budget is covered by the UN regular budget.[14]

The Information and Publication Context

UNHCR's 200-plus field offices supply the Geneva headquarters with a constant stream of reports and updates. In return, they receive guidance, policy directives, news, and information. In addition, UNHCR staff communicate regularly with government officials and donors, liaise with members of the UNHCR Executive Committee, cooperate with intergovernmental organizations (IGOs), work closely with NGOs and other implementing partners, interact with the academic community, and regularly brief the media. In all of these exchanges, information plays a key role, both internally and externally. The newly formed Division of Communication and Information (DCI) oversees most external activities. Two sections within the DCI are particularly important from an information point of view as they generate many of the materials intended for the public. These are the Centre for Documentation and Research (CDR) and the Media Relations and Public Affairs Service (formerly the Public Information Section).

CDR, formerly known as the Centre for Documentation on Refugees, was established in 1986 and was housed originally within UNHCR's legal division. It caters to the information needs not only of UNHCR staff members, but also of government officials, NGOs, intergovernmental agencies, advocates, legal practitioners, academics and students, researchers, and members of the public. Represented in its library collection is the full spectrum of refugee topics, including human rights conditions in the country of origin, international refugee issues, broader subjects of human rights and humanitarian law, national legal regimes, asylum, refugee status determination, statelessness, international cooperation, refugee camps, emergency relief, health, environment, refugee women, refugee children, voluntary repatriation, resettlement, peace efforts, and much more. In addition, it maintains a small reference collection as well as the archives for UNHCR's governing bodies, the Executive Committee and its predecessors.

The predominant focus of CDR's work has been the electronic dissemination of information in the form of the REFWORLD CD-ROM, a series of full-text databases that provide access to UNHCR and UN documents, country and legal information, bibliographic references, reference materials, and maps. A subset of REFWORLD appears on the UNHCR website. These resources are discussed in greater detail below.

Included among CDR's other publications is the *Refugee Survey Quarterly (RSQ)*, a journal which features country research, reproduces UN and UNHCR documents, updates the states parties to relevant conventions, disseminates bibliographic references, abstracts and publisher information, and highlights relevant internet resources. Each issue focuses on a particular theme. The principal Executive Committee documents from the most recent October session are published in the last issue of each year. Prior to *RSQ*, CDR compiled the monthly *Refugee Abstracts*. CDR also publishes the *International Thesaurus of Refugee Terminology*, country papers, and other specialized bibliographies.

The Media Relations Service functions as UNHCR's public affairs arm. It assumes the spokesperson duties for the office, regularly briefs the media, produces information brochures and audio-visual materials, engages in awareness-raising activities, and promotes private sector fundraising. Its principal publication is the quarterly *Refugees* magazine. The UNHCR website features a number of public information resources and publications (outlined below).

Other divisions within UNHCR are also important producers of information. For example, the Evaluation and Policy Analysis Unit is responsible for the *New Issues in Refugee Research* working paper series, the Department of International Protection issues legal guidelines, the Division of Operational Support publishes operational manuals, the Training Section produces training modules, and so forth. However, for members of the public, CDR or Media Relations will likely serve as the first point of contact for most UNHCR materials, regardless of their provenance. Likewise, the REFWORLD CD-ROM and UNHCR website provide access to a number of publications produced by other UNHCR sections besides CDR and Media Relations.

It is important to note that not all UNHCR publications are available through CDR or Media Relations. To date, UNHCR has not instituted a formal information policy. The result is less-than-perfect bibliographic control over its own publications and documents. Divisions that author manuals, reports, studies, or training modules usually publish them in-house, for consumption by UNHCR staff and partners. The value of these texts for others is not always recognized. For this reason, they are not regularly deposited with a central body like CDR, where they can at the very least be cataloged and included in the library. The newly organized DCI may help to resolve this problem.

While a significant portion of UNHCR's information is free and available to the public, the organization naturally produces a number of restricted documents. Documents are deemed confidential if they reveal personal details about an application for refugee status or if they contain information that is perceived to be politically sensitive to governments that receive refugees. Examples include internal policy memos and directives, legal opinions about individual refugee cases, refugee case files, evaluations of national refugee programs and asylum provisions, and memoranda of understanding with governments relating to repatriation arrangements. Many of these documents are distributed to field offices on an internal CD-ROM known as the Knowledge and Information Management System (KIMS). At the same time, UNHCR's Archives Section is developing an access policy for non-UNHCR personnel that, in the future, may allow a review of certain historical internal records on a selected basis.

Although UNHCR is a prolific publisher, it is also a major consumer of a variety of information sources, many of which are not necessarily refugee-specific. For anticipating refugee crises, news items about political developments and other country analyses are important. Human rights reports are useful when evaluating asylum applications. General background information on countries and maps is necessary when staff members relocate to new areas. Access to case law and international conventions is important when preparing advisory opinions on particular legal issues. Journal articles, monographs and conference papers are often consulted when drafting policy recommendations. And access to UN records is crucial for keeping abreast of related developments within the UN system.

Electronic Resources

The preceding overview should give a sense of the kind of information both produced and consumed by UNHCR. Many of the resources discussed above represent key databases in UNHCR's electronic media. What follows is an introduction to the two principal UNHCR vehicles for disseminating information: the REFWORLD CD-ROM and the UNHCR website. However, a caveat is in order: At the time of this writing, UNHCR is in the process of a significant overhaul of these two resources. Throughout 2000, greater priority will be placed on the website as the principal point of access for UNHCR's information. Therefore, many changes are slated to take place with its design, organization, and, particularly, content. The ultimate objective is to make available (for free) a greater number of the information holdings that previously were offered only on the CD-ROM. Therefore, users will be able to conduct much more of their refugee research online in the future. A new Electronic Publishing Unit has been created in order to realize these changes.

Thus, the following discussion is intended to present an overview of UNHCR's electronic resources produced to date, keeping in mind that these will evolve over the course of the year, and to acquaint readers with the wide range of information that UNHCR distributes. Whatever changes may occur with their mode of delivery, the core sources will remain the same.

REFWORLD CD-ROM

Background

The REFWORLD CD-ROM was created by CDR in recognition of the myriad information needs of both UNHCR staff and members of the public. The goal was to compile a full-text electronic library of the principal resources required for refugee work, including both UNHCR and non-UNHCR materials. The first edition was produced in January 1996 and represented the culmination of a six-year involvement in database development. The CD-ROM is issued twice each year in January and July and is available on a subscription basis (currently $250/year). It can be loaded on individual PCs or onto a network. A web version of REFWORLD also exists, but, at the time of this writing, it is not as complete as the CD-ROM. This will be described in the next section.

Sources

Each edition of REFWORLD includes six principal databases. Within each, users will find a series of secondary databases housing literally hundreds of texts. Non-UNHCR sources are identified for inclusion on the CD-ROM through a variety of mechanisms. For example, the United Nations Optical Disk System serves as the principal source for UN documents while human rights reports and legal texts are supplied through exchange agreements with information partners. CDR also relies on UNHCR's network of field offices to forward relevant materials. Although the predominant language reflected on the CD-ROM is English, most of the UNHCR materials, international instruments, and numerous country reports are also provided in French. Below is a review of the main databases and what they include. For a more detailed breakdown of the contents of the January 1999 edition, please refer to the Annex.

- **UNHCR:** In addition to general information about the organization, the UNHCR database houses current and historical policy documents. These include documents issued by and submitted to the various Executive Committee bodies as well as documents relating to both the establishment and work of the UNHCR office and the drafting of the 1951 Convention relating to the Status of Refugees. Also available are the final reports of significant UNHCR-sponsored conferences.

- **United Nations:** Given UNHCR's reporting structure, staff members are often required to consult UN documents. The United Nations database therefore includes a complete set of resolutions, along with selected reports from the Security Council, General Assembly, and Economic and Social Council. Because human rights figure prominently in the protection of refugees, a variety of documents produced by the UN's many human rights institutions are also included.

- **Country:** The Country database features human rights reports as well. The information included here is used largely in the refugee status determination process. Asylum-seekers that submit applications to either governments or UNHCR protection staff often rely on human rights reports to corroborate their stories. Likewise, decision-makers may refer to this kind of information to verify a prospective refugee's testimony. To ensure reliability, the human rights materials included in REFWORLD tend to have an international focus, represent different perspectives, and are issued by reputable sources.

- **Legal:** Because CDR was established within the Department of International Protection, it has emphasized the development of legal resources. The Legal database makes available international instruments (international and regional conventions and standards, bilateral agreements, and others), national legislation (not only refugee and asylum-related, but also citizenship and nationality laws, penal codes, constitutions, and so forth), case law from both national and international jurisdictions, legal policy directives from both UNHCR and governments, and memoranda of understanding.

- **Reference:** Most of the texts in the Reference database are UNHCR publications and therefore complement the resources in the more policy-oriented UNHCR database. Relevant sources include *The State of the World's Refugees, Refugee Survey Quarterly*, numerous legal and operational guidelines and training manuals, a directory of research organizations, and the *International Thesaurus of Refugee Terminology*.

- **Bibliographic:** The bibliographic database provides access to records for the 12,000-plus titles in CDR's literature collection as well as its 400-odd periodical subscriptions.

- **Maps:** This database includes both basic country maps and refugee-specific maps.

Platform and Structure

REFWORLD uses the FolioViews platform, which allows full-text search and retrieval and accommodates the complete spectrum of search syntax—truncation, adjacency and Boolean operators, proximity searches. At the same time, researchers can locate relevant reports by working their way through an extensive menu structure created via hypertext links. Documents tend to be organized in reverse chronological order—by date and/or document symbol—or geographically, although a few are grouped thematically. Explanatory information is provided in each database.

FolioViews can be challenging to master. Accordingly, REFWORLD provides a basic user guide as well as a more detailed training manual to help researchers get started. A number of tools are also available that point users toward relevant sources either alphabetically by the name of the source, thematically through twenty-plus "pathfinders," or geographically. Moreover, every edition includes an "update" section that reviews the existing sources, indicates which were updated, and introduces the new sources.

UNHCR Website (<www.unhcr.ch>)

Background

Most UNHCR offices have e-mail, but a majority lack full internet connectivity. For this reason, the decision was made to use the CD-ROM format for distributing REFWORLD. However, establishing an internet presence was also deemed important, particularly from a public relations point of view. CDR began posting information on a gopher as early as April 1995. With the increased prominence of the web, the organization recognized the need to take advantage of the relatively new medium. A professional design company was hired, and in October 1996, the official UNHCR website was launched. Today, the site serves the primary function of raising public awareness through the dissemination of news and information on UNHCR operations and refugees. In this respect, it differs from other organizational sites. Although it reports on UNHCR's ongoing activities, it does not present an overall picture of the organization as a whole, its structure, divisions, and functions. Rather, it focuses on UNHCR's public face and, accordingly, highlights those divisions within UNHCR which maintain a strong public component.

CDR's REFWORLD website was incorporated into the official site and given a similar look and feel. However, it continues to be maintained by CDR, while the rest of the site is maintained by Media Relations. UNHCR field offices have also expressed interest in putting up country- or region-specific websites. In order to avoid the confusion that is often created by having a multiplicity of sites on the web, all seemingly by the same organization, UNHCR decided to limit itself to sites that mirror the official one in presentation and structure but are offered in other languages. Currently, French, German, Korean, and Japanese mirrors exist.

Sources

The UNHCR website provides access to a variety of resources. For purposes of review, they are grouped below under several headings and described in greater detail. Although a search engine is included in the REFWORLD section, no mechanism is available for searching the entire site.

For general information on UNHCR and its operations, look under:

- **UNHCR and Refugees:** Broken down into "What Is UNHCR?" "UNHCR Mission Statement," "Who Is a Refugee?" "UNHCR by Numbers," and the "High Commissioner."

- **News:** Includes "Country Updates," or updates on UNHCR's current operations in certain areas, such as Kosovo, the Great Lakes region of Africa, Liberia/Sierra Leone.

- **The World:** Provides access to information on UNHCR's operations, refugee statistics, and government refugee policies on a country-by-country basis for over 100 countries; only the most recent update is provided; each profile includes links to country information located elsewhere on the site as well as to news.

- **Maps:** Operational maps depicting refugee movements, populations, camps, etc.

For refugee-related news and updates on UNHCR's activities, look under:

- **Today's News:** Headlines of breaking refugee news stories.

- **What's New:** Indicates additions to the site (last two months).

- **News:** Includes links to situation reports on the most recent refugee crisis (for example, the "Northern Caucasus Update"); "Briefing Notes" (issued twice a week); "Press Releases" (both current and archived); "Refugees Daily," a digest of news reported in public media sources such as *Agence France Presse, Reuters, The International Herald Tribune,* and others; "Refugee NewsNet," a searchable archive of the above-mentioned news sources; also provides access to the "UNHCR Newswire Section," a search service that allows users to click on the logos of Associated Press, Yahoo! News, or Excite Newstracker and automatically generate a search for >>refugees or asylum or UNHCR<< alternatively, users can enter keywords into query boxes and search those services directly for hits.

For information on the activities of specific UNHCR sections and other contact details, look under:

- **Evaluation and Policy Analysis:** Includes information on the Evaluation and Policy Analysis Unit (EPAU), which conducts assessments of UNHCR's programs and policies; this section of the site provides information on EPAU's activities, the full-text of evaluation reports since 1996, and links to related sites and handbooks.

- **Funding:** UNHCR is largely funded through voluntary contributions given by governments; this part of the site focuses on the work of the Funding and Donor Relations Section (FDRS), describes UNHCR's funding process, provides budget figures, outlines programs, lists donors, and posts appeals for funds. FDRS is responsible for the annual *Global Appeals*, UNHCR's formal requests for contributions to support its activities; the appeals give a detailed profile of UNHCR's work.

- **Statistics:** Figures for refugee populations provided by UNHCR's Food and Statistical Unit.
- **Environment:** Includes information on UNHCR's Environmental Unit and its attempts to address the environmental impact of refugee populations; the Environmental Unit also produces the maps included on the site.
- **Resettlement:** Includes information on the Resettlement Section and its work to resettle refugees to third countries either for physical protection or as a durable solution.
- **Contact:** Users can e-mail sections in UNHCR's Headquarters or locate contact information for field offices from drop-down lists.

For research and publications, look under:

- **News:** Includes a link to "New Publications."
- **Issues:** Thematic approach to accessing articles from *Refugees* magazine, as well as other UNHCR publications elsewhere on the site.
- **Publications:** Provides access to the full-text of *Refugees* magazine since 1994, as well as a selection of other publications.
- **For Teachers:** Curricula and lesson plans designed for various age groups that focus on refugees and art, history, human rights, geography and other subjects.
- **REFWORLD:** For more information on the contents of REFWORLD, see below.

For different types of graphics, look under:

- **Witness:** A multimedia documentary series coproduced with UNHCR.
- **Images:** Photographs of refugees.
- **Maps:** Operational maps depicting refugee movements, populations, camps, and so on.

Future additions:

- UNHCR will celebrate its fiftieth anniversary in December 2000. To mark this occasion, a new section will be added to the website that features "prominent refugees." Program events and additional background information on UNHCR will also be posted.

REFWORLD

Currently, the REFWORLD CD-ROM is much more comprehensive than its web counterpart (please see Annex for a comparison of contents). The web version reproduces legal texts, UNHCR policy documents, country reports, and information on related research organizations (many of which are linked to through the Weblinks section). It is also largely in English. At the same time, it tends to be more current, although less historical, than the CD-ROM. As noted above, REFWORLD on the web will change dramatically in the near future. Not only will a greater number of sources be made available, but greater integration will also occur between what once were differentiated as CDR sources versus Media Relations sources.

Conclusion

During the relatively brief period of time that this chapter was drafted, tragic events took place in Kosovo, East Timor, and Chechnya, displacing millions of people from their homes and livelihoods in the process. Yet while certain refugee crises do garner the attention and support of the global community, all too often others are left to unfold in relative obscurity. In this regard, UNHCR—as the principal refugee assistance agency—serves an important information-dissemination function. International information specialists can help to promote continuity in and commitment to the ongoing development of UNHCR's electronic resources by making use of and expressing support for the organization's information activities.

Notes and References

1. Louise Holborn, *Refugees: A Problem of Our Time. The Work of the United Nations High Commissioner for Refugees, 1951–1972*, 2 vols. (Metuchen, NJ: Scarecrow Press, 1975), 7–10.

2. United Nations, General Assembly, *Continuation of the Office of the United Nations High Commissioner for Refugees* (New York: UN, 1997). 12 December 1997; A/RES/52/104. Available on the REFWORLD CD-ROM under "UNHCR—Historical Documents—General Assembly Resolutions and Decisions Relating to UNHCR." URL: <www.un.org/ga/documents/gares52/res52104.htm>.

3. For a more complete statistical overview, see United Nations High Commissioner for Refugees, *Refugees and Others of Concern to UNHCR—1998 Statistical Overview* (Geneva: UNHCR, 1999). URL address: <www.unhcr.ch/statist/98oview/ch1.htm>.

4. United Nations, General Assembly, *Statute of the Office of the United Nations High Commissioner for Refugees* (New York: UN, 1950). 14 December 1950; G.A. Res. 428 (V), Annex. Available on the REFWORLD CD-ROM under "Legal—International Instruments—United Nations Treaties—Asylum, Refugees, and Stateless Persons." URL address: <www.unhcr.ch/refworld/refworld/legal/instrume/volrep/hcrsta_e.htm>.

5. For a review of UNHCR's protection activities, refer to either the Notes on International Protection adopted during the annual Executive Committee sessions or UNHCR's annual reports to the General Assembly. Both are available on the REFWORLD CD-ROM under "UNHCR—Executive Committee" and "UNHCR—Historical Documents," respectively. The Notes on International Protection are also available on the web at <www.unhcr.ch/refworld/refworld/unhcr/notes/menu.htm>.

6. These texts are available on the REFWORLD CD-ROM under "Legal—International Instruments." Alternatively, see either United Nations High Commissioner for Refugees, *Collection of International Instruments and Other Legal Texts Concerning Refugees and Displaced Persons*, 2 vols. (Geneva: UNHCR, 1995) or visit the REFWORLD legal information section on the web at <www.unhcr.ch/refworld/refworld/legal/instrume/refint.htm>.

7. For more information on these solutions, please refer to the following UNHCR publications: *The State of the World's Refugees: The Challenge of Protection* (London and New York: Penguin Books, 1993); *Handbook–Voluntary Repatriation: International Protection* (Geneva: UNHCR, 1996); *Resettlement Handbook* (Geneva: UNHCR, 1998). The first title is available both on the REFWORLD CD-ROM under "Reference—Publications" and on the web at <www.unhcr.ch/refworld/pub/state/sowrtoc.htm>. The latter titles are available on the CD-ROM under "Reference—Operational Guidance Materials."

8. For a review of UNHCR's assistance activities, refer to UNHCR's annual report to the General Assembly (available on the REFWORLD CD-ROM under "UNHCR—Historical Documents") or see the various updates on regional activities submitted to the Standing Committee (available under "UNHCR—Executive Committee" or on the web at <www.unhcr.ch/refworld/refworld/unhcr/excom/menu.htm>).

9. Texts are available on the REFWORLD CD-ROM under "UNHCR—Historical Documents."

10. The most recent is United Nations, General Assembly, *Office of the United Nations High Commissioner for Refugees* (New York: UN, 1999). 22 February 2000; A/RES/54/146. URL: <www.un.org/Depts/dhl/resfiles/a54r146.pdf>.

11. United Nations, General Assembly, *International Assistance to Refugees within the Mandate of the United Nations High Commissioner for Refugees* (New York: UN, 1957). 26 November 1957; G.A. Res. 1166 (XII); United Nations, Economic and Social Council, *Establishment of the Executive Committee of the Programme of the United Nations High Commissioner for Refugees* (New York: UN, 1958). 30 April 1958; E.S.C. Res. 672 (XXV). Both texts are available on the REFWORLD CD-ROM under "UNHCR—Historical Documents." For more information on EXCOM, see Elisa Mason, "Resolving Refugee Problems: An Introduction to the Executive Committee of the United Nations High Commissioner's Programme and Its Documentation," *Journal of Government Information* 27, no. 1 (2000): 1–11. All principal Executive Committee documents are available on the REFWORLD CD-ROM under "UNHCR—Executive Committee" and on the web at <www.unhcr.ch/refworld/refworld/unhcr/excom/menu.htm>.

12. *Guide to the United Nations High Commissioner for Refugees*. Available on the REFWORLD CD-ROM under "UNHCR—About UNHCR," January 1999.

13. *2000 Global Appeal* (Geneva: UNHCR, 2000). URL: <www.unhcr.ch/fdrs/ga2000.htm>.

14. The top 15 donors are Australia, Canada, Denmark, the European Commission, Finland, France, Germany, Italy, Japan, Netherlands, Norway, Sweden, Switzerland, the United Kingdom, and the United States. For more information on UNHCR's funding process, refer to the Funding and Donor Relations section of the UNHCR website at <www.unhcr.ch/fdrs/main.htm>.

Annex: Comparison of Contents on REFWORLD CD-ROM vs. REFWORLD on Web

This table provides the name of the database in which a source is located, lists the sources as they appear, briefly describes each source, and indicates the languages it is available in and the period covered on both the CD-ROM and web versions of REFWORLD.

Database: UNHCR			
Source	Contents/Description	CD-ROM Coverage	Web Coverage
About UNHCR	General information; statements made by High Commissioners	as of 1992 (for current HC's statements); 1950-1990 (past HC's statements); English	HC statements, as of 1992; English
UNHCR Executive Committee	Documents submitted to and reports of the Executive Committee; *EXCOM in Abstracts*	as of 1995 (although incomplete sets are available for 1993-1994); English and French	as of 1995; English
	Standing Committee documents	as of 1996; English and French	as of 1996; English
	Conclusions on International Protection	as of 1975; English and French	as of 1975; English
	Notes on International Protection	as of 1964; English and French	as of 1983; English
	Sub-Committee of the Whole on International Protection (SCIP) (reports and conference room papers)	1977-1995 (reports); 1995 (conference room papers); English and French	1977-1995 (reports); CRPs not available; English
	Sub-Committee on Administrative and Financial Matters (SCAF)	1995 (incomplete sets for 1992-1994); English and French	not on web version
Historical Documents	Documents submitted to Ad Hoc Committee on Statelessness and Related Problems	1950; English and French	not on web version
	A Study of Statelessness	1949; English	not on web version
	Conference of Plenipotentiaries on the Status of Refugees and Stateless Persons ("Travaux préparatoires" of 1951 Convention relating to the Status of Refugees)	1951; English and French	not on web version

	Colloquium on the Development in the Law of Refugees	1965; English and French	not on web version
	Historical General Assembly documents relating to the establishment of UNHCR and other refugee-related questions	various dates; English	not on web version
	Annual UNHCR and Executive Committee reports submitted to the General Assembly	1952-1998; English and French	not on web version
	General Assembly resolutions and decisions relating to UNHCR	as of 1949; English and French	not on web version
	Economic and Social Council resolutions and decisions relating to UNHCR	as of 1949; English and French	not on web version
Conferences	Reports from various international conferences and other meetings sponsored by UNHCR	various dates; English and French	only includes report and other documents for Regional Conference convened to address refugee problems in the Commonwealth of Independent States, 1996; English

Database: United Nations Documents

Source	Contents/Description	CD-ROM Coverage	Web Coverage
Security Council	Presidential Statements	as of 1994; English	link to Security Council site
	Resolutions	as of 1974; English	
	Reports (selected texts)	as of 1995; English	
General Assembly	Resolutions	as of 1946; English	link to General Assembly site
	Reports (selected texts)	as of 1995; English	
	Resolutions and decisions relating to UNHCR	as of 1949; English and French	not on web version
Economic and Social Council	Resolutions	as of 1946; English	link to ECOSOC site
	Reports (annual UNHCR reports)	as of 1995; English	

Annex: Comparison of Contents / 267

	Resolutions and decisions relating to UNHCR	as of 1949; English and French	not on web version
Commission on Human Rights	Reports (country and thematic)	as of 1993; English	external link to Commission on Human Rights site for documents as of 1997; includes texts of country/thematic reports for 1995 and 1996; English
	Resolutions	as of 1976; English	not on web version
Sub-Commission on Prevention of Discrimination and Protection of Minorities	Resolutions	as of 1994; English	not on web version
	Reports (selected texts)	as of 1993; English	not on web version
Committee against Torture (CAT)	Decisions, views, observations, annual reports of CAT; states parties' reports; general information; text of Convention against Torture and Other Cruel, Inhuman or Degrading Treatment or Punishment	various dates; English	not on web version
Committee on Economic, Social and Cultural Rights (ESCR)	Comments, observations of ESCR; states parties' reports; general information; text of International Covenant on Economic, Social and Cultural Rights	various dates; English	not on web version
Committee on the Elimination of Discrimination Against Women (CEDAW)	Observations, annual reports of CEDAW; states parties' reports; general information; text of the Convention on the Elimination of Discrimination Against Women	various dates; English	not on web version

Committee on the Elimination of Racial Discrimination (CERD)	Observations, decisions of CERD; states parties' reports; general information; text of International Convention on the Elimination of All Forms of Racial Discrimination	various dates; English	not on web version
Committee on the Rights of the Child (CRC)	Conclusions, observations, annual reports of CRC; states parties' reports; general information; text of Convention on the Rights of the Child	various dates; English	not on web version
Human Rights Committee (CCPR)	Comments, views, decisions, observations of CCPR; states parties' reports; general information; text of International Covenant on Civil and Political Rights	various dates; English	not on web version
Human Rights Instruments	Compilation of General Comments adopted by Human Rights Treaty Bodies; Core Documents; Annual Meeting of Chairpersons	various dates; English	not on web version

Database: Country Information

Source	Contents/Description	CD-ROM Coverage	Web Coverage
Amnesty International	Annual reports	as of 1994; English	link to Amnesty site
	Country reports	as of 1994; English and French	
	Regional reports	various dates; English and French	
	Thematic reports	various dates; English	
Federal Office for Refugees of Switzerland	Country information sheets	as of 1994; French and German	not on web version
Human Rights Watch	World reports	as of 1996; English	link to Human Rights Watch site
	Country reports	as of 1994; English	
	Thematic reports	various dates; English	

International Crisis Group	Country reports	as of 1996; English	not on web version
Lawyers Committee for Human Rights	Country reports	various dates; English	not on web version
	Thematic reports	Various dates; English	not on web version
	Critiques of U.S. Department of State Country Reports on Human Rights Practices	1994-1996; English	not on web version
Norwegian Refugee Council	Internally Displaced People: A Global Survey	1998; English	not on web version
Open Society Institute, Forced Migration Projects	Reports	as of 1995; English	not on web version
	FM Alerts (electronic bulletin)	as of 1996; English	not on web version
Research Directorate, Immigration and Refugee Board of Canada	REFQUEST (country reports)	as of 1989; English and French	not on web version
	REFINFO (responses to information requests)	as of 1989; English or French	not on web version
UNHCR Centre for Documentation and Research	Background Papers on Refugees and Asylum Seekers	as of 1994; English	as of 1994; English
UNHCR Paris	Fiches des pays (country profiles)	1996-1997; French	not on web version
U.S. Committee for Refugees	*World Refugee Survey*	1997; English	not on web version
	Issue papers	various dates; English	not on web version
U.S. Department of State	*Country Reports on Human Rights Practices*	as of 1993; English	link to State Dept. site
U.S. Immigration and Naturalization Service, Resource Information Center	Country reports	1993-1997; English	not on web version

	Responses to information requests	1998; English	not on web version
Writenet	Issue papers	as of 1993; English or French	as of 1993; English or French

Database: Legal Information

Source	Contents/Description	CD-ROM Coverage	Web Coverage
International Instruments (REFINT)	International treaties and other instruments relating to refugees, human rights, asylum and stateless persons	various dates; English and French	sub-set of CD-ROM version; organized thematically; English
	Bilateral and multilateral agreements concerning refugees	various dates; English or French	not on web version
National Legislation (REFLEG)	National laws relating to refugees, asylum, citizenship, nationality, statelessness, displaced persons; also included are constitutions, penal codes and relevant regulations	various dates; English, French or Spanish	not on web version
Case Law (REFCAS)	Decisions relating to determination of refugee status, non-refoulement, expulsion, rights of refugees and asylum seekers; mixture of abstracts/full-text jurisprudence from national courts and international bodies	various dates; English or French	searchable database that retrieves abstracts of relevant legal decisions; English or French
Refugee Policy and Practice	UNHCR guidelines and policy memoranda on protection issues	various dates; English or French	only *Handbook on Procedures and Criteria for Determining Refugee Status* (1992) available; English, French, and Spanish
Memoranda of Understanding (MOU)	Agreements between UNHCR and governments or other intergovernmental agencies relating to repatriation, cooperation and information-sharing	various dates; English or French	not on web version

Annex: Comparison of Contents / 271

Database: Reference Materials			
Source	Contents/Description	CD-ROM Coverage	Web Coverage
Publications	*The State of the World's Refugees* (UNHCR's biennial report)	1993, 1995; English	1993, 1995, 1997; English
	Refugee Survey Quarterly (CDR's quarterly journal)	1994, 1995; English	not on web version
New Issues in Refugee Research	full-text working papers that present preliminary results of refugee-related research	not on CD-ROM	various dates; English
Refugee Research Network (REFLINK)	Profiles of relevant research and academic institutions	various dates; English	various; searchable database available; English
Refugee Statistics	*Populations of Concern to UNHCR: A Statistical Overview*	as of 1994; English	as of 1995; English
Operational Guidance Materials	Manuals and guidelines designed to help UNHCR staff perform in their jobs and understand UNHCR's policies and procedures	various dates; English	not on web version
International Thesaurus of Refugee Terminology	Indexing tool	1996; English and French	not on web version
Database: Bibliographic Information			
Source	Contents/Description	CD-ROM Coverage	Web Coverage
Refugee Literature (REFLIT)	CDR's library catalogue	various dates; English, French, Spanish or German	records for three most recent years available in searchable database; English, French, Spanish or German
Refugee Periodicals (REFPERIO)	Periodical subscriptions maintained by CDR	various dates; English, French or Spanish	not on web version

Database: Maps			
Source	**Contents/Description**	**CD-ROM Coverage**	**Web Coverage**
Various Sources	Includes country maps produced by the UN Cartographic Unit and maps displaying refugee movements, camps, security situations, etc. produced by UNHCR's Environmental Unit	various dates; English	maps from UNHCR's Environmental Unit only; various dates; English
Database: Weblinks			
Source	**Contents/Description**	**CD-ROM Coverage**	**Web Coverage**
Various Sources	Searchable database of profiles of relevant Internet sites	not on CD-ROM	n/a

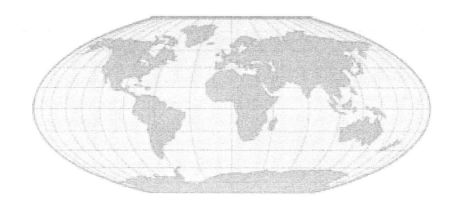

Part III

PROCESSES

CHAPTER 10

United Nations Information-Gathering for Peace and Security

A. *Walter Dorn*
Copyright © A. Walter Dorn

Introduction: The Information Cycle

The documents of the United Nations (UN), numbering over 15,000 a year,[1] are the principal means of disseminating official UN information both within the organization and to the outside world. In order to produce these documents, UN staff not only accept submissions from governments, but they must also actively gather large volumes of information covering the spectrum of human and international issues. This chapter examines this vital but little studied part of the information cycle, information-gathering, as it relates to one of the UN's most important tasks: the maintenance of international peace and security.

At the UN, information on peace and security is received from and disseminated to numerous entities, including member states, field offices, and peacekeeping missions around the world. The UN Secretariat in New York is the main focal point and clearing-house for such information. The Secretary-General (SG), as the head of the Secretariat and the chief administrative officer of the organization, is the main agent for the transmission of communications, documents, and reports to the Security Council and the General Assembly, the two organs responsible for UN policies and actions on peace and security matters. He or she is also responsible, subject to governmental oversight (mainly through the Committee on Information), for dissemination of information to the general public.

The cycle of information-gathering, analysis and dissemination—in computer jargon: input, processing, and output—is frequently repeated on a given issue, because the main bodies continually request the Secretary-General to collect new information and to report back to them. For example, in 1999, the Security Council, the body with primary responsibility for peace and security matters, asked for reports from the Secretary-General in three-quarters of its resolutions.[2] The Secretary-General may also offer his views and provide new information to the Council at his own initiative, especially in matters relating to threats to peace and the administration of UN operations.[3] Daily briefings are given by the Secretary-General or his representative to members of the Council to keep them informed of the most recent developments in UN operations.

The Secretariat also provides administrative support to the subsidiary bodies of the Security Council, which have multiplied in number, scope and responsibility since the end of the Cold War. From 1990 to 1995, the Council created five sanctions committees (for Iraq, Yugoslavia, Libya, Somalia, and Haiti), a compensation commission (Iraq), sixteen peace-keeping operations, a weapons inspection/destruction body (Iraq), and two international criminal tribunals (for the former Yugoslavia and Rwanda). To service the Yugoslavia Sanctions Committee in 1994 alone, the Secretariat had to process 45,000 communications to the committee.

The UN, not wanting to be a secretive organization, makes available to the general public most of the official documents it issues. It produces a thorough historical record of the actions of its parliamentary bodies through its *Repertoire of the Practice of the Security Council* and *Repertory of the Practice of United Nations Organs*. But many significant documents dealing with sensitive issues (for example, records of private Security Council meetings and most sanctions committee meetings) are restricted or otherwise not made available.[4] In order to gain insight into the inner workings of the UN it is often necessary to refer to the autobiographies of current or former staff members and diplomats, of which there are now an impressive number. A list of selected memoirs of staff memoirs is provided in the Appendix.

The UN also produces a large number of journals, magazines, bulletins, and brochures, most of which are not widely known, distributed, advertised, nor indexed, even by the UN. Materials in this "grey literature" can be a unique and valuable source of information, both within the UN and externally. However, for the external user, they can be hard to find. Frequently such documents do not carry UN document symbols or sales numbers. They can be obtained or even purchased upon request—providing the researcher knows what to request and to whom to make the request. This chapter should help researchers on peace and security issues to identify some of these difficult-to-find materials.

Information Sources and Methods

Figure 10.1 illustrates the information cycle at the UN and lists some possible responses to new information and events. It also lists the principal information sources and the legal authorities upon which UN information-gathering is based. The major sources of information, reviewed in detail below, are governments, the media, field missions and offices, other international agencies, nongovernmental organizations (NGOs) and individuals, and academia.

Information Sources and Methods / 277

Figure 10.1. The UN Information Cycle.

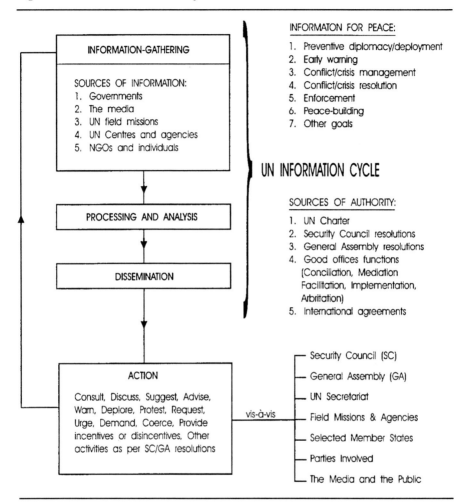

The gathering, analysis, and dissemination of information leads to action, which, in turn, leads to the need for more information. Also listed in this figure are the main information sources, the uses of information for the maintenance of international peace and security, and the potential sources of authority for information-gathering.

Governments

By far, the largest and most important sources of information for the UN are its member states. The UN, as an organization of governments, has well-codified procedures for receiving and automatically disseminating written and formal oral communications from governments. Letters intended for general distribution, with attachments if any, are customarily addressed to the Secretary-General or to the Presidents of the Security Council or the General Assembly, usually with an explicit request for circulation as documents.[5]

Official speeches made in the main deliberative bodies are a regular and important, though often redundant, information source. Mostly, they provide the current policies and views of nations, but they occasionally include breaking news or essential background to recent events. Speeches are recorded so that translations, transcriptions, and/or summaries can be provided by the Secretariat as part of the written record.

Much important information is, of course, conveyed verbally through informal discussions in the offices and corridors at the UN and at government missions. This is an essential service which the UN, as the world's largest standing diplomatic conference, provides. "Corridor diplomacy," which facilitates the informal exchange of information and views, will always be essential to the maintenance of the world's peace and security. Still, it is the public, written record that must provide the foundation and justification for UN actions. A detailed written record is essential to create the transparency necessary for the UN to work toward the "common ends" described in the Charter.

Dramatic news about important events are often heard first from governments, but communications providing written confirmation are usually not far behind. For example, Secretary-General Trygve Lie learned of the North Korean invasion of South Korea on 25 June 1950 through a midnight telephone call from a U.S. Assistant Secretary of State.[6] He immediately requested the UN Commission on Korea, which was based in Seoul, to provide a written confirmation. This came several hours later and was circulated among Council members as part of the terms of reference of the urgent Council meeting to deal with the situation.[7] Similarly, Secretary-General U Thant learned of the outbreak of the 1967 Six-Day War in a 3:00 A.M. phone call from Under-Secretary-General Ralph Bunche. Bunche had received a cable from the commander of the UN Emergency Force (UNEF), stationed in the region, containing the first information on the outbreak. At an urgent meeting of the Security Council later that day, U Thant duly reported "all the information [he] had received."[8] More recently, Secretary-General Javier Pérez de Cuéllar learned about the launch of Operation Desert Storm in a call from U.S. President George Bush only an hour before the operation began on 16 January 1991.[9] The President's televised announcement followed later in the evening. Detailed press reports immediately filled the newswires and airwaves, and the attack received front page coverage in the world's daily newspapers the next morning.

The Secretary-General has the responsibility to "immediately bring to the attention of all members of the Security Council . . . all communications from states, organs of the United Nations, or the Secretary-General" concerning any matter relevant to the mandate of the Security Council.[10] Any UN member wishing to "bring a matter to the attention of the Security Council" (i.e., place it on the agenda), must do so through a written communication, which is distributed by the Secretary-General at least forty-eight hours before the next meeting, except in urgent circumstances. Such communications usually become part of the terms of reference of the meeting.[11]

Hours after Iraq originally invaded Kuwait on 30 July 1990, the President of the Security Council received two letters asking for an immediate meeting of the Council from the representatives of Kuwait and the United States.[12] The Secretary-General was then responsible for contacting Security Council members (by fax to the missions in New York) about the meeting and providing them with copies of the letters.

After an important security issue seizes the attention of the highest levels of government, the Secretary-General often receives a rush of letters from UN ambassadors attaching statements or pronouncements by senior government officials. For instance, in the week following the Iraqi invasion of Kuwait, the Secretary-General received and disseminated, as separate documents, forty-nine letters on the invasion. Most of these communicated, in annexes, condemnations of Iraq by high-level officials (e.g., ministers of state or government), and by regional organizations (e.g., in the first four days statements were submitted for the European Community, the Gulf Cooperation Council, the League of Arab States, Organization of the Islamic Conference). This kind of response is one way of measuring the degree of importance an issue has gained for the international community.

Sometimes, important letters are hand-delivered to the Secretary-General for maximum speed, as well as for confidentiality. At the height of the Cuban Missile Crisis in October 1962, Secretary-General U Thant sent identical messages to President Kennedy and Chairman Khrushchev containing several compromise proposals to de-escalate the crisis. Soviet Ambassador Valerian Zorin, who had been denied any information from his government about Soviet nuclear arms in Cuba, criticized the Secretary-General for giving credence to the U.S. position, for seeking compromise and for not denouncing the "illegal" blockade. Shortly after he had admonished the Secretary-General, a courier from the Soviet mission arrived on the thirty-eighth floor of the UN Secretariat with an urgent message from Chairman Khrushchev. To the great embarrassment of the Ambassador, the Soviet leader thanked the Secretary-General for his important intervention in a perilous situation and accepted his proposal.[13]

Governments can request circulation of their communications to the Secretary-General as UN documents. The Secretariat provides a document symbol, translates it into the six official languages of the Security Council and the General Assembly (Arabic, Chinese, English, French, Russian and Spanish),[14] prints it, distributes it (typically within two days) and, finally, maintains proper preservation of it for future reference.

Sometimes governments use (or misuse) their right to have letters and attachments copied and circulated, in order to embarrass other governments. For example, on 20 October 1984, Nicaragua requested dissemination of a CIA manual that had been provided to Nicaraguan rebels (the *Contras*), titled "Psychological Operations in Guerilla Warfare." Despite U.S. protests, copies of the manual were duly distributed two days later.[15] Similarly, Cyprus embarrassed Turkey by requesting the circulation of an Amnesty International report titled "Turkey: Continuing Violations of Human Rights."[16]

Sometimes governments voluntarily inform the UN about their own military actions. Just after Egypt launched an attack against Israel in 1948 in coordination with other Arab countries, it informed the Secretary-General of its actions. Similarly, the United States informed the Security Council in 1964 that it had landed troops in the Dominican Republic. By providing their versions of events and their rationale to the UN first, they hope to influence the debate about UN responses.

More frequently, member states complain about the military actions of their neighbors. Iran and Iraq registered countless charges with the Secretary-General during their Gulf War (1980–88). The Secretary-General received detailed complaints during and after each campaign in the war, including long Iranian lists of incidents of Iraqi use of chemical weapons. Even after its defeat in the Second Gulf War (1991), Iraq continued to complain to the Secretary-General about violations of its airspace, in this case by U.S., British, and French aircraft.[17] Usually even the most serious complaints are conveyed in diplomatic language. The Permanent Representative of Pakistan wrote to the Secretary-General in such a style: "I have the honour to inform you that, on 22 May 1989, a Scud missile was fired by Kabul troops from within Afghanistan and fell near Bhakkar [Pakistan]."[18]

Governments circulate materials not only to defend their own actions, but also, on occasion, the actions and opinions of their nationals who are working under the Secretary-General. For instance, in 1960 the President of Ghana requested circulation of a report given to him by the Ghanaian contingent commander in the UN operation in the Congo, severely critical of the operation.[19] The Secretary-General dutifully circulated the report and soon thereafter circulated the comments of his Special Representative in the Congo, Mr. Ralph Bunche, containing a rebuttal to the criticisms (which were said to be "neither valid nor fair").[20]

At some dramatic meetings of the Security Council, the U.S. has shared one of its most prized possessions, secret intelligence. In 1962, Ambassador Adlai Stevenson displayed on two easels in the Council chamber large pictures of Soviet missile bases in Cuba taken by high-flying U-2 reconnaissance aircraft. Similarly, in 1983, Ambassador Jeane Kirkpatrick played recordings of radio conversations between the Soviet interceptor pilots and ground control at the time of the shooting down of a Korean Air Lines jet (KAL flight 007) in 1983. The U.S. did the same in 1996 when the Cuban Air Force shot down a plane belonging to the anti-Castro group, "Brothers to the Rescue." Such electronic eavesdropping is achieved through specialized and top secret satellite and airborne surveillance platforms. The decision to reveal such intelligence is usually preceded by vigorous inter-agency debates in Washington.

After the end of the Cold War, an unprecedented number of subsidiary bodies were created by the UN Security Council with new mandates for sanctions monitoring, complex peacekeeping, weapons destruction, and the prosecution of war criminals. These bodies require a great deal of specialized information and intelligence from governments. This includes declarations by governments about their own activities and intelligence reports on the behavior of other nations; for example, suspected sanctions breakers. The Sanctions Committee, set up to monitor the implementation of sanctions against Iraq (the "661 committee"),[21] has relied to a large extent on questionnaires asking governments to report on their own compliance. One month after the resolution, the Secretary-General was able to report that 106 countries had replied.[22] The committee then followed up on answers that were incomplete or unsatisfactory. Oral testimony was provided by intelligence officials, including the Director of the CIA. Similarly, the UN Special Commission, charged with finding and destroying Iraqi weapons of mass destruction, received much information from Western intelligence sources, particularly when it began its operations in 1991.

Governments provide the UN Secretariat with highly classified information only rarely and usually only on a "need to know" basis, that is, when the government thinks that specific UN officials, such as the Secretary-General, need to know. During the Cuban Missile Crisis in 1962, the Secretary-General's Military Adviser, Major-General Indar Jit Rikhye, was given Pentagon clearance to receive U-2 reconnaissance photographs of the Soviet missile sites in Cuba.[23] He visited the Pentagon to receive detailed briefings. By contrast, during the prolonged Congo crisis (1960–64), the U.S. refused to share any intelligence, although it had dozens of agents in the country. In that case, U.S. intentions were not always in harmony with those of the UN (for instance, the U.S. sought to secretly assassinate Prime Minister Patrice Lumumba[24] and it was the UN's responsibility to guard him).

Following the end of the Cold War, the U.S. has shared more intelligence with the UN than ever before. In part, this was because the UN was sponsoring important operations which the U.S. wanted to see succeed. Also, the end of the Cold War decreased the intensity of the superpower espionage game and reduced the fear that information in the hands of Soviet/Russian officials in the Secretariat would be automatically passed on to Moscow. Furthermore, the U.S. intelligence community has been looking for new reasons to justify its existence; support for certain UN operations provides one rationale. Sophisticated intelligence was shared with the operations dealing with Iraq (UNSCOM), Somalia (UNOSOM), Bosnia (UNPROFOR), and others.

In some peace-keeping operations in the Middle East, the U.S. has routinely shown, but not given, satellite photographs to UN force commanders, in order to aid the force in the performance of its monitoring and supervisory tasks. According to former force commander Major General Hannes Philipp (ret'd.) of Austria, U.S. officials once informed him of an army vehicle illegally intruding into the UN-supervised buffer zone.[25] Shortly after he had raised the matter with the side possessing the vehicle, he received word from the U.S. that everything was now satisfactory. There had been no aerial overflights over the area, so he concluded that big brother was, indeed, watching—from space!

A special computer in the Situation Centre of the Department of Peacekeeping Operations permits rapid communications to the U.S. mission and through the mission to other U.S. government departments, including the Pentagon. This access has, however, proven to be of limited utility. According to an official in the Centre, little new information is conveyed and the U.S. does not carry out research to answer specific questions from the Secretariat apart from determining if there is a U.S. study already produced which sheds light on the matter. Furthermore, there is a continuing concern by other member states about information bias and dependency. When the U.S. offered (for several million dollars) to set up an advanced system for the Situation Centre in the areas of information and communications, the proposal was declined for fear of relying too heavily on a single government and of the increased vulnerability of the communications system to U.S. interception.

Secretariat officials rely much more on publicly-available government materials than they do on secret ones. Most governments provide public information, including periodic summaries of events in their countries, through their UN missions in New York and their information services, publishing offices, as well as their embassies or consulates in foreign countries. For instance, the U.S. government and its agencies provide a wealth of public information on international issues: human rights reports from the U.S. Department of State, background reports of the Congressional Research Service of the Library of Congress, situation reports from the U.S. Agency for International Development (USAID). The Situation Centre routinely uses "open source" material from the CIA, including the CIA *World Factbook*, which is available to anyone with access to the internet.[26]

The Media

The UN relies heavily on the media for information about current international events, as do most organizations and persons, but the UN does so only in an unofficial fashion. Media articles are never referred to in UN resolutions (unlike reports of the Secretary-General which are referred to in the majority of resolutions) and are rarely used in an uncorroborated fashion in reports of the Secretary-General.

The UN requires a standard of reporting that is more objective than is normally the case for the media, or at least as it is perceived by member states. In particular, there are concerns over accuracy, emphasis, and bias in the media. Different newspapers from the same country even provide widely divergent accounts of the same events and emphasize entirely different aspects. The media of different countries can be even more divergent. Furthermore, the Western media is mostly privately owned, while the media in most developing countries is mostly controlled or supported by governments. The perception among the developing world of an "information hegemony" has even resulted in calls for a "new world information and communication order." In both the North and the South, it is clear that the media can be susceptible to considerable governmental and nongovernmental influences, as well as self-serving sensationalism, that prevent it from being used in an official way at the UN. In practice, however, the media serves to inform most persons in the UN system and thus provide the unofficial background for UN decisions. The UN relies, however, disproportionately on the Western media.

Prominent among the media providing input to the UN are the major international daily newspapers (for example, *New York Times, International Herald Tribune*) and global television networks, especially Cable News Network (CNN). In addition, "local" independent news journals called the *Diplomatic World Bulletin* and *UNDiplomatic Times*[27] are widely circulated in UN circles and provide useful news on recent UN announcements, appointments (with detailed background on the appointees), testimonies, interviews and corridor "gossip." *Secretariat News*, which sometimes provides otherwise unreported news on UN activities and personalities, is published bimonthly by the Staff Activities and Housing Unit of the UN Secretariat.

For crucial and time-sensitive decisions, information from the media is often far from sufficient. During the Six-Day War in June 1967, the situation was changing hourly. One representative of a middle-power on the Council, Canadian Ambassador George Ignatieff, complained that the two superpowers were at a distinct advantage because they had regular reports on what was happening, through satellite reconnaissance and other intelligence sources, while other representatives had to wait for the *New York Times* to find out what had happened the day before.[28] This was a tremendous handicap for those without information.

Many governments[29] and the UN Secretariat rely on in-house and external clipping services to filter and collate relevant articles from newspapers and other periodicals. The UN Secretariat's Department of Public Information (DPI, News Distribution Section) circulates to Secretariat staff the "Daily Press Clippings" of forty to fifty pages containing articles related to the UN and its work.[30] In addition to photocopied clippings, the document includes news summaries from UN Information Centres and other field offices based on press reports received there. Such summaries are included in English or French, the two working languages of the UN Secretariat.

The Department of Political Affairs (DPA) produces a similar collection, called "Daily Press Clippings from DPA," an internal document which is circulated to senior officials in DPA and other selected departments. It is typically thirty to forty pages long, with clippings from major newspapers (*Washington Times, Washington Post, Financial Times, Le Monde*, and others), wire services (Associated Press, Agence-France Presse, Itar-Tass, Reuters, and so on), and other press services (e.g., *IPS Daily Journal* [31]). The documents also include daily summaries from certain UN offices (such as *Daily Highlights* produced by Central News, and the *Daily Press Briefing* of the Office of the Spokesman for the Secretary-General) and UN agencies (for example, The World Bank's *Development News*).

Governments occasionally refer to press reports in their speeches. During the Cold War, Soviet representatives liked to cite critical Western press reports and opinion pieces to bolster their arguments, somehow thinking that if a Western paper criticized a Western government, then the criticism must be right. In one speech on the evils of the South Korean regime in 1950, a Soviet representative quoted six critical western newspapers (the *New York Times*, the *New York Post*, the London *Times*, the British *Journal of Commerce*, *The Statist*, and the Italian *24 Ore*) and told the Australian representative that he "would be well advised to read the lines" in the Australian periodical *Age*.[32]

The Secretary-General very rarely refers to specific press reports in his official statements and reports. References in a more general fashion are sometimes made, especially at times when the Secretary-General must react to a situation for which the only source of information is such press reports. For example, the Secretary-General stated in a press release in 1994 that he was "deeply concerned by press reports of an Israeli air attack" in Lebanon.[33] No mention was made if the UN peace-keeping operation in the country (UNIFIL) was able to confirm these reports.

The Foreign Broadcast Information Service (FBIS) provides English translations of current media reports from around the world, and this helps the UN monitor official government pronouncements, especially in conflict zones. Although an arm of the US government, the FBIS produces *Daily Reports* which are considered unbiased and accurate translations of items in foreign media, including whole texts or extracts from foreign radio and television, news agency transmissions, newspapers, books, and periodicals. FBIS claims that its items are processed from "the first or best available sources."

The very latest news is usually obtained not in print but rather from broadcasts (and, more recently, from the internet). Secretary-General Trygve Lie learned of the 1948 Communist coup in Czechoslovakia in a newscast on his car radio.[34] Similarly, twenty years later, U Thant learned of the Soviet invasion of Czechoslovakia through a radio newscast.[35] On an earlier occasion, U Thant, then the Burmese ambassador to the UN, first learned that he was being considered for the Secretary-Generalship in an article in the *New York Times*, published before he was approached by any delegation. In the past, it was common for diplomats and Secretariat officials to tune into the BBC World Service using a short-wave radio to obtain the latest news. Now CNN television has taken the premier position in the offices of the UN. During the Second Gulf War (1991), additional monitors were set up in corridors of the Secretariat to allow staff to follow developments during the day. Computers in the Situation Centre are now equipped to receive, record, and display current CNN programs, even while other software programs are running. In the future, it should be possible to select from an internet library of recently televised programs.

The computer information age only recently reached the UN. In 1989, the former UN information-collection agency, the Office for Research and the Collection of Information (ORCI), was still using teletype machines to print out reports from the wire services. Now, the Situation Centre uses a commercial computerized news service, "NewsEDGE," to monitor the media, particularly the wire services (such as Reuters and Agence France-Presse). Articles carrying specified keywords can be captured from a large range of publications. Computers also permit rapid searches of the World Wide Web and other parts of the internet. The very latest news, for example, can be obtained from the homepage of CNN.[36] The Situation Centre sends out daily reports on areas where there are UN operations which combine information from the media on the internet and reports from the missions themselves.

Field Operations

If it can be said that UN headquarters houses the brains of the organization, then its field operations are its own eyes and ears, and often its limbs as well. Field operations and missions are frequently established in troubled areas in an effort to contain or resolve conflicts. The vast majority of Security Council resolutions deal with conflicts in which the UN has field operations which report regularly; 94 percent of Council resolutions in 1994 were of such a nature. UN field operations are created to watch and to respond to events. They help calm hostilities, mediate settlements and then verify them (especially troop withdrawals and cease-fires), separate warring factions, and provide objective information to UN headquarters and negotiators on a continuing basis.

The smallest UN "missions" sent to an area of conflict consist of an individual, often a personal or special representative of the Secretary-General, with some administrative assistants. The mission may have a declared mandate that is different from fact-finding, such as the conduct of negotiations, but fact-finding is always a central task and the individual is expected to report back observations on conditions in the state. In some cases, fact-finding is the main task. In 1970, in order to head off a dispute between Iran and the United Kingdom, Secretary-General U Thant sent a personal representative to Bahrain to "ascertain the wishes of the people." The conclusion, that the people wanted an independent state, led to the establishment of Bahrain as a state separate from Iran in 1971. This mission was one of the forerunners of modern UN electoral activities which have, after notable successes (e.g., in Nicaragua, Namibia, and South Africa), become a recognized UN function, especially as a part of conflict resolution. It has also become common for the Secretary-General to send preliminary fact-finding missions prior to the establishment of large peacekeeping operations (for example, ONUCA in Central America and UNTAC in Cambodia).

Peacekeeping operations (PKOs), which are field operations with a military component, typically employ standard military procedures of reporting (with plenty of acronyms!). When soldiers on patrol or in an observation post (OP) or at a checkpoint (CHP) witness an unusual event, they are expected to file an incident report (INCREP) with their unit. Information is combined with other sources in a report to the PKO headquarters. From there, information is further collated before a situation report (SITREP) is prepared, usually on a daily and/or weekly basis, for transmission to New York. For serious incidents, an operational investigation may be carried out, time permitting. Less frequently, periodic summaries (PERSUMS) are sent to New York to give an operational and administrative summary of major events over the period (for instance, monthly), along with the views of senior persons in the field. PERSUMS are usually sent by the force commander (FC) to the Under-Secretary-General (USG) responsible for peacekeeping operations. Reports done outside the regular schedule, sometimes called supplementary information reports (SUPINFOREPs), may describe recent events of an important nature. In emergencies, reports are sent to the Secretary-General directly. Secretaries-General U Thant and Kurt Waldheim, for example, first learned of the outbreak of war in 1967 and 1973 from urgent messages from peacekeeping operations in the Middle East.[37]

Regular lists of personnel, nonlethal casualties, and accidents are routinely sent to New York. The death of peacekeepers, as an extremely serious matter, is reported immediately and will be handled by DPKO as well as the office of the Security Coordinator, which is responsible for the security of UN personnel worldwide. For the most serious cases, a formal Commission of Inquiry might be established by the Secretary-General, the General Assembly or the Security

Council, to investigate the circumstances leading to the deaths. For instance, the Security Council did so after some two dozen Pakistani soldiers were ambushed in Somalia in 1993. In 1961, three commissions were set up by the General Assembly to investigate the deaths in separate incidents of the Congolese Prime Minister (Patrice Lumumba), Secretary-General Dag Hammarskjöld, and the Prime Minister of Burundi. In spite of thorough investigations, however, there still remains mystery and controversy surrounding the deaths of Lumumba and Hammarskjöld.

To minimize the loss of life and to run a successful peacekeeping operation, an effective information-gathering system in the field is essential. This was one of the early lessons of the UN Operation in the Congo (ONUC, 1960–64). After the UN found itself under attack by the Katangese gendarmerie and mercenaries, and in order to suppress the secessionist efforts of Katangese leader Moise Tshombe, a Military Information Branch (MIB) was established in 1961.

The MIB used extensive means of information/intelligence gathering, more than any other UN field operation until the advent of the new generation of PKOs in the early1990s. It intercepted Katangese radio communications and, when required, proceeded to decode encrypted messages. When radio interceptions revealed Katangese plans to bomb airfields used by the UN, the UN made its final and successful push into Katanga. Aerial reconnaissance using Indian and Swedish planes facilitated estimations of the size of the Katangese Air Force and identification of ammunition stockpiles. Captured mercenaries underwent a formal interrogation procedure, using lawful and humane techniques. This did not yield as much useful information, however, as the reports of informants and asylum seekers. On one occasion, the UN was able to confiscate forty to fifty aircraft engines in an Elisabethville warehouse, after being tipped off by an informer of their whereabouts. On a daily basis, the MIB helped keep ONUC headquarters informed of developments and supplied information which was then passed on to UN headquarters. Still, the MIB constantly felt itself underequipped and understaffed, which is certainly true in comparison with most national expeditionary forces or the NATO forces sent to Bosnia (IFOR/SFOR) since 1995 or Kosovo (KFOR) in 1999. In spite of recent progress, the UN Department of Peacekeeping Operations still lacks adequate means for training for on-site investigations, for analysis of information both in the field and at headquarters, and for fulfilling urgent field requests for information and documentation. The various limitations on UN information/intelligence-gathering in peacekeeping have been explored in publications by the author of this chapter.[38]

Time-sensitive communications with UN headquarters in New York are now routinely handled by fax, though the older methods of cable and, of course, mail (via diplomatic pouch, not subject to national inspection) are also used. Fax messages are labeled with certain standard attributes. The urgency of delivery is denoted on a communication as either *routine, priority, immediate,* or *most immediate.* The security classification is also indicated: *unclassified, confidential,* or *secret.* Messages can be marked *crypto,* to denote encryption by a special device attached to the fax machine. The Situation Centre's twenty-four-hour operations room at New York headquarters has a bank of such fax machines equipped with encoders and decoders. Before the arrival of the fax machine in the late

1980s, most urgent messages were sent by cable, either coded or "in the clear." In some operations, the UN adopted a "clear" (no encryption) policy in order to build transparency, to ease potential fears of the antagonists, or to promote its impartiality in cases where only one side is capable of decryption. Finally, placing the word "only" next to the name of the addressee prevents the message from being copied or circulated widely on reception. Normally the highest security classification on communications is *secret* but the words "for SG's [Secretary-General's] eyes only" have been used at times.

To maintain the confidentiality of messages the UN has, on occasion, resorted to some unconventional means. One humorous incident happened during Secretary-General U Thant's visit to Havana during the Cuban Missile Crisis in 1962. The Secretary-General wanted to communicate important information to New York without letting the Cuban authorities know the contents of the message, recognizing that the phones were likely tapped. Having no enciphering equipment, it was decided that the Secretary-General's military adviser, Gen. Indar Jit Rikhye, should speak on the phone with his Indian colleague in New York headquarters, C. V. Narasimhan, using the Indian language Hindi. The message was successfully, if painstakingly, communicated but after Rikhye's return to New York, a senior U.S. official remarked to him that he had better improve his Hindi![39] The U.S. was listening!

Electronic mail (e-mail) communications were first used using commercial software (Higgins, or CC Mail) with limited encryption capabilities. However, a software package with a more advanced encryption capability (LotusNotes) is now being introduced, especially for sensitive areas in the UN. Some but not all field missions have e-mail connections to headquarters. Virtually all permanent UN offices have such a connection.

In response to criticisms that headquarters officials were "hard to reach after hours," even in cases of emergencies in the field, the Secretary-General established the Situation Room under the Department of Peacekeeping Operations (DPKO) in April 1993. Upgraded to the Situation Centre (SITCEN) a year and a half later, it is tasked with maintaining uninterrupted communications with all UN peacekeeping missions and to be able to communicate with all other UN missions around the globe. Another more ambitious mandate is to monitor potentially dangerous situations to UN peacekeepers and personnel. A twenty-four-hour duty room receives regular reports from the field missions, mostly by fax but increasingly by e-mail. Duty officers must know whom to contact in the Secretariat for given questions and how to contact them at any time in case of emergencies.

Peacekeeping missions provide more than half the volume of information that comes to the Situation Centre. The media provide roughly another one third, with governments and other sources providing the rest. Media reports are collected both in the field and monitored at headquarters using an online system, NewsEDGE. If the SITCEN receives an indication of important developments or potential threats from one source, then it may query specific governments and the field missions.

Over time, the SITCEN hopes to increase its analytical capacity. This includes the provision of computer databases able to respond to intelligent queries such as: "How many violations of the no-fly zone occurred in Iraq in the past year?" Ideally, an integrated database will be developed to sort, organize, prioritize, and disseminate incoming information and will be accessible to field units as well as to headquarters.

The SITCEN produces consolidated summaries for each operation. The *Daily Mission Highlights* of one or two pages for each mission, naturally, draws mainly upon the *Daily Mission Reports* but also upon media reports. A weekly *Situation Report* is also prepared.

Situation Centre staff provide daily briefings to senior UN officials. Both the SITCEN and the Department of Political Affairs prepare weekly reports for the Secretary-General. In turn, the Secretary-General submits periodic reports to the Security Council on the PKOs, typically every six months, or as specified by the Council (for example, "as soon as possible"). Such reports usually include the mission's status, current activities, recommendations and requests.

On occasion, the Security Council receives oral reports directly from the leaders of UN operations and missions in the field. This is particularly true for fact-finding missions established by the Council, as was the case, for example, for a fact-finding mission to Burundi after the 1994 Rwandan massacre.[40] Rolf Ekeus, the Chairman of the Special Commission (1991–99), which was charged with supervising the elimination of Iraq's weapons of mass destruction, also frequently appeared before the Council, since an evaluation of Iraqi compliance was considered essential in the on-going consideration of the imposed sanctions.

UN Information Centres, Field Offices, and Agencies

Unlike UN peacekeeping operations and missions, which are established on a temporary basis in a host state, the UN Information Centres (UNICs) and UNDP field offices are permanent. The primary function of these offices is not to gather information but rather to disseminate information and provide development assistance to the host state. Given their location, however, these centres and offices are well positioned to collect information for UN headquarters about activities in the state and region. At times, such information collection requires delicate diplomacy, because host countries do not want to be "spied upon." The UN has always denied that information gathering is done covertly, although it does admit to the information-gathering function of these offices. For instance, it is well known and well accepted that the UNIC in Washington keeps tabs on bills before Congress relating to UN affairs, especially those relating to UN financing.

As the concepts of early warning and preventive diplomacy became increasing fashionable after the end of the Cold War, the capacity of these field offices to play a role in such activities was recognized. In 1987, UNICs were requested by the Secretary-General's office to provide information to headquarters on potential sources of conflict. Specifically, they were asked to submit weekly reports on disputes and tensions, unusual events, displaced peoples, and disasters (natural and man-made) as well as commentaries on the UN system.

They were to base their reports primarily on official statements and media reports in the country, but first-hand observation was not discouraged.

The UN Information Centres and Information Services are located in seventy-eight countries of the world. In contrast, the United Nations Development Programme (UNDP) has field offices in more than 130 countries, including some of the poorest and most conflict-ridden areas of the world. Even though the UNDP operates at arm's length from the UN Secretariat and is not directly responsible to the UN Secretary-General, there has been a recent push to utilize its capacity as well.

Given the persistent financial crisis facing the UN, it was decided in 1992 to merge eighteen UNICs and UNDP field offices in order to present a unified image of the UN in the field, to enhance information activities in all areas, and to achieve economies through shared services. This experiment is generally viewed as successful. When new "interim offices," pending the creation of integrated offices, were created in the countries of the former Soviet Union in 1993, the offices combined the UNDP and UNIC functions into one.

Given that the information-gathering mandate is a relatively recent one, it is not surprising that personnel in the UNICs and UNDP offices receive no standardized training in observing, assessing, and reporting on conflicts. But certain offices have acquired, by necessity, specific expertise when they operate in conflict zones or are involved in peacebuilding, as for example the UNDP in its weapons collection programs in Albania. The new interim offices and similar UN field offices, e.g., the "small political offices" in conflict zones such as the Great Lakes region of Africa, were given a strong mandate for fact-finding both because of the areas in which they are located and because they are created with this objective in mind.

Several agencies within the UN system regularly provide the General Assembly and Security Council with useful information on issues relating to their specialty. Since refugees are a common occurrence during conflict, it is natural to expect that the Office of the UN High Commissioner for Refugees (UNHCR) provides information on conflict areas, in addition to the numbers, locations, and conditions of refugees. Refugees are usually first-hand witnesses of tragic events. Similarly, increasing human rights abuses are indications of current or impending conflict. The Human Rights Commission in Geneva provides the Security Council with reports from its Special Rapporteurs when so requested, as does the United Nations High Commissioner for Human Rights. These rapporteurs monitor human rights and focus on areas where the violations are most egregious, for example in the former Yugoslavia.

Within the UN system, two agencies which are mandated to carry out inspections according to arms control treaties are the International Atomic Energy Agency (IAEA) and the Organization for the Prohibition of Chemical Weapons (OPCW). In order to implement nuclear safeguards in the 1968 Non-Proliferation Treaty, the IAEA headquarters in Vienna sends out inspectors to nuclear sites in some seventy countries. The IAEA Director General makes annual reports to the General Assembly and, under special circumstances, also tables reports before the Security Council, as was the case for reports for Security Council-mandated inspections in Iraq and when North Korea was shown to be in non-compliance with its safeguards agreement. The OPCW, located in The Hague, has the most intrusive inspection rights of any permanent international organization. In a challenge inspection, it may carry out an inspection at any site on short notice (twelve hours), to locate any possible chemical weapons (or chemical precursors) present in contravention of the 1993 Chemical Weapons Treaty.

Because the governing bodies of these various agencies are composed of governments which are also members of the UN proper, it can be expected that information made available in one body will be transmitted to others through the governmental members.

NGOs and Individuals

Nongovernmental organizations (NGOs) and individuals are capable of gathering information in ways that would be out of bounds for the UN. When a state refuses the UN entry into its territory, the UN must generally desist in respect of that nation's sovereignty. Some NGOs manage to "fly under the sovereignty radar" because they have acceptable functions to perform in the state (such as humanitarian work) or because they can disguise or justify their investigative work or because they have sources within the state, such as conscientious citizens, who provide them with information. The UN, as an organization of state members, has to deal carefully and unofficially with complaints from individuals in its member states for fear of being accused by the state of violating their sovereignty. NGOs are less inhibited, in general, of investigating atrocities, of criticizing governments, and of being criticized by states. These observations are especially true of NGOs in the human rights field. Because violations of human rights are often coupled with armed conflict, human rights NGOs can be especially valuable sources of information.

A case in point is Human Rights Watch (HRW) which established an Arms Project to monitor weapons deliveries to areas where human rights violations are occurring. The Washington-based organization, using eye-witnesses, uncovered a transfer of more than eighty tons of weapons through Zaire to Rwanda in June 1994, while genocide was systematically being carried out and in violation of the UN embargo. Their findings prompted, in part, the formation of a UN International Commission of Inquiry in September 1995.[41] In presenting its report to the Security Council, the Commission acknowledged the HRW report as "a primary source of detailed information, much of which the International Commission was subsequently able to confirm for itself."[42] However, Zaire refused to cooperate with the Commission, leading to weak conclusions. HWR claimed that the UN report was incomplete and that it permitted governments who aided the Rwandan genocide, including Zaire and perhaps France, "to continue to evade accountability."[43] It is pressing for UN monitors to be stationed at airports in Zaire to prevent any further flow of armaments to Rwandan rebels.

NGOs that provide humanitarian aid can also be valuable sources of information. Because such NGOs have a presence in the field, they can obtain firsthand reports of events in troubled areas. These NGOs also have a moral right to make inquiries of their host governments on the state policies and activities that may have a bearing on their operations.

The broadening of the mandate of humanitarian NGOs would certainly help the cause of peace. It is particularly opportune now, well after the end of the Cold War, when most conflicts occur within states and have economic, social, and ethnic roots. There are many areas where such an expanded mandate is natural; for example: early warning of refugee flows is closely linked with determining threats to peace.

Furthermore, cooperation in the humanitarian field between the UN and NGOs is already well developed. The UN's Office for the Coordination of Humanitarian Affairs (OCHA) has created an excellent internet-based system, ReliefWeb, which has greatly enhanced information-sharing between NGOs, UN agencies, and governments.[44] The Inter-Agency Standing Committee (IASC), also created by OCHA to further coordinate relief efforts, meets at the executive-head level several times each year. The NGO community is represented by Inter-Action (American Council for Voluntary International Action), the International Council of Voluntary Agencies, and the Steering Committee for Humanitarian Response.[45] Inter-Action, for instance, supplies useful Situation Reports on various countries, summarizing the development and humanitarian work of NGOs in these areas.

There are fewer NGOs specializing in peace and security matters which have field experience but several are notable. International Alert seeks to identify situations of potential violent conflict and then ways of promoting prevention. It has been involved in efforts to resolve conflicts in Sri Lanka, South Africa, and the former USSR. It sent fact-finding missions to Tatarstan and northern Caucasus and has been associated with missions to Nagorno-Karabakh, Georgia, and Estonia. The Secretary-General meets occasionally with the heads of humanitarian organizations, such as International Alert and Médecins Sans Frontières, as well as human rights organizations. UN Secretary-General Pérez de Cuéllar revealed in his memoir that "before each trip abroad I was briefed confidentially by Amnesty International on individual cases of human rights abuse on which I might usefully intervene."[46]

In recent years, as the notions of preventive diplomacy and early warning became increasingly popular, some new NGOs and networks were formed, including the Preventive Diplomacy Initiative of the U.S. Institute of Peace, the Centre for Preventive Action of the Council on Foreign Relations, and the Institute for War and Peace Reporting. The latter is an "independent conflict-monitoring charity" whose bulletin, "War Report," includes reports by leading journalists and other observers of conflict.

The UN is not prohibited from receiving information from individuals and NGOs who are "in the know." The United Nations Special Commission benefited greatly from an Iraqi informer who provided information that led to the revelations of clandestine Iraqi nuclear weapons development projects and a high-level defector who revealed the continuing existence of a large clandestine biological weapons program. Similarly, the UN Operation in the Congo found that informants and asylum seekers were particularly valuable (though not trustworthy in all cases) sources of information. Planned attacks on UN forces and large weapons depots were thus identified.

The Centre for Human Rights in Geneva actively solicits information from individuals and NGOs about human rights violations. Victims, their relatives, and nongovernmental organizations are invited to send information to a twenty-four-hour fax "hot line" set up by the United Nations High Commissioner for Human Rights. The information is then used by special rapporteurs in investigations and, in the case of urgent, potentially life-saving information, by the Special Procedures branch of the Centre.

Letters from individuals and NGOs to the Security Council are not circulated unless they are annexed to a letter from a government or the Secretary-General but they are listed under thematic headings in a circulated document titled: "Communications received from private individuals and non-governmental bodies relating to matters of which the Security Council is seized."[47]

The UN sometimes draws upon the academic community for expertise in information gathering. For example, Cherif Bassiouni, a professor at DePaul University in Chicago, was appointed in 1993 chairman of the Commission of Experts established by the Security Council to investigate war crimes in the former Yugoslavia. The resulting monumental work (of some 3,000 pages)[48] was subsequently used as a basis for the work of the Prosecutor and the judges of the International Criminal Tribunal for the former Yugoslavia, who themselves were seconded from the legal systems of nation states for the duration of their work.

Commercial organizations also provide useful information. For instance, the Economist Intelligence Unit publishes *Country Reports* every three months. They include analyses of political, economic and business developments in more than 180 countries, as well as some forecasts in the short term. Similarly, Jane's Information Group publishes various reports, including *Jane's Information Review*, with detailed updates of situations around the world.

Conclusion

In this "information age," there exists a veritable ocean of information from which the UN can draw in its efforts to keep the peace in a troubled world. However, the concomitant problems of "information overload and underuse" have arisen. While organized databases and rapid computer "search engines" of systems like the internet are making retrieval faster, these new means of information-gathering add enormously to the pool of information. As a result, UN officials are often overwhelmed with data, and there is a natural tendency to overlook important sources of information.

The solution to this problem is to develop a greater analytical capability in the UN Secretariat. Currently, there are too few who analyze incoming information: perhaps two or three persons to cover each continent. To compound the problem, these analytical tasks are done in addition to many other assignments within the Departments of Peacekeeping Operations and Political Affairs. Thus, what the UN needs in order to become more effective, especially in its efforts for conflict prevention and early warning, is a greater analytical capability to turn raw information into processed information targeted to meet the current needs of the organization (some would use the term "intelligence" to describe such processed information).

Given the current financial crisis and the resulting strain on staff resources, it is difficult for the UN to consider such institution-building. But once the immediate crisis has passed, there is ample reason for the Secretary-General and member states to build the UN into a stronger instrument for rapid information-gathering and preventive action in order to achieve one of the main tasks for which it was created: the maintenance of international peace and security.

Notes and References

1. Estimates of the number of UN documents will, of course, depend on what one considers as a UN document. The current estimate is based on the restrictive definition of "parliamentary documents," almost all of which have been stored on the UN's Optical Disk System (ODS) since 1992. By March 1999, ODS had 407,300 documents in different language versions, needing 170 G-bytes of computer space [Private communication, ODS Unit, UN Secretariat, 16 Mar 1999]. ODS lists between 11,000 and 14,000 documents for each year 1992–99 and most of these documents are available in the six official languages of the UN. An estimated number of printed pages is about three-quarters of a billion based on the figure of 735,843,192 page impressions for UN headquarters in 1991 provided by Peter Hajnal in Lyonette Louis-Jacques and Jeanne Korman, *Introduction to International Organizations* (Dobbs Ferry, NY: Oceana Publications, 1996). Much UN information is now transmitted through the World Wide Web. On a typical day in 1999 (March 12), the UN transferred about four G-bytes of information from its websites in 144,000 requests for pages from 9,800 distinct client hosts [Private communication, UN Secretariat, 12 Mar 1999]. The "official Web site locator for the UN system of agencies" is found at <www.unsystem.org>.

2. Of the 65 Security Council resolutions passed in 1999, 49 resolutions (or 75 percent) specifically requested the Secretary-General to provide reports or to keep the Council informed about a matter. Similarly, five years earlier, in 1994, 70 percent of the seventy-seven Security Council resolutions made such a request.

3. The Secretary-General may make statements to the Council on any question under consideration by it (Rule 22 of the *Provisional Rules of Procedure of the Security Council* (S/96/Rev.7 or Sales No. E.83.I.4)). Furthermore, the Secretary-General may raise a new issue in the Council if it is one "which in his opinion may threaten the maintenance of international peace and security" (Article 99 of the *Charter of the United Nations*).

4. The proceedings of most of the Security Council's new subsidiary bodies are restricted and unavailable to the public. Furthermore, the UN Archives has a twenty-year rule on public viewing of UN papers. Even then, papers older than twenty years which are marked 'confidential' or messages sent by coded cable cannot be viewed without going through a laborious and lengthy declassification procedure.

5. These "letters" may come in the form of e-mails, faxes, cables, telexes, or in the traditional written form on paper delivered by hand, diplomatic courier, or regular mail.

6. Trygve Lie, *In the Cause of Peace* (New York: Macmillan, 1954), 237.

7. The document S/1495 is reproduced as a footnote in the Security Council *Official Records*, 473rd meeting, 25 June 1950.

8. Security Council *Official Records*, Twenty-Second Year (1967), 1347th meeting.

9. *UN Chronicle*, March 1991, 47.

10. Rule 6 of the *Provisional Rules of Procedure of the Security Council*.

11. See Rules 7 and 26 of the *Provisional Rules of Procedure of the Security Council*.

12. The Kuwaiti and U.S. requests in 1990 are reproduced in UN Documents S/21423 and S/21424, respectively.

13. Brian Urquhart, *A Life in Peace and War*, (New York: Harper & Row, 1987), 192–93. Khrushchev's letter can be found in the UN archives under the symbol DAG-1/5.2.2.6.1-3 #5. It is labeled "confidential" and was only declassified in 1984.

14. The six official and working languages are specified in Rule 41 of the *Provisional Rules of Procedure of the Security Council* and in Rule 51 of the *Rules of Procedure of the General Assembly*. The Secretariat itself has only two working languages (English and French).

15. Peter I. Hajnal, "A Review of 'Psychological Operations in Guerrilla Warfare'," *Government Information Quarterly* 2, no. 3 (1985): 330.

16. UN Document S/21387 of 5 July 1989.

17. "Letter dated 10 February 1996 from the Permanent Representative of Iraq to the United Nations Addressed to the Secretary-General," UN Document S/1996/97 of 12 February 1996.

18. UN Document S/20678 of 7 June 1989.

19. UN Document S/4445 of 19 August 1960.

20. Reproduced in Security Council, *Official Records* (SCOR), S/4445 of 19 August 1960, Annex II, Supplement for July, August, and September 1960, p.113.

21. Its official name is *Security Council Committee established by resolution 661 (1990) concerning the situation between Iraq and Kuwait*.

22. *UN Chronicle*, XXVII, No. 4 (December 1990) 13.

23. An album of photographs of the missile sites in Cuba remains in General Rikhye's possession.

24. United States Congress, *Alleged Assassination Plots Involving Foreign Leaders: An Interim Report of the Select Committee to Study Governmental Operations with respect to Intelligence Activities* [Church Committee], U.S. Senate, 94 Cong., 1 Sess., Report no. 94-465 (20 November 1975).

25. Major General Hannes Philipp (ret'd) of Austria was commander of the United Nations Disengagement Observer Force (UNDOF) from 1975 to 1979. Personal communication.

26. The CIA *World Factbook* can be found at <www.odci.gov/cia/publications/factbook/>.

27. The *Diplomatic World Bulletin and Delegates World Bulletin* (dedicated to serving the United Nations and the International Community) is published bi-weekly by Diplomatic World Bulletin Publications, Inc., New York. The *UNDiplomatic Times*, which incorporates and replaces the newsletter *International Documents Review*, is published monthly by Impact Communications Consultants of New York.

28. George Ignatieff, private communication to the author.

29. For example, the U.S. Information Agency's Office of Research and Media Reaction in Washington provides *Foreign Media Reaction: Daily Digest*. It includes quotes from and summaries of the media around the world.

30. DPI also compiles weekly and monthly dossiers of analytical press articles on the UN and the activities of the Secretary-General. See *Proposed Programme Budget for the Biennium 1996–1997*, Part VII, Section 25, p. 12 in the *Official Records of the General Assembly*, Fiftieth Session, Supplement No. 6; A/50/6/Rev.1.

Notes and References / 295

31. The *IPS Daily Journal*, by its own account, "provides a daily news wire service from and to more than 1,000 countries for more than 1,000 media and other clients in 12 languages."

32. Statement of Mr. Kiselev of the Byelorussian Soviet Socialistic Republic, *Official Records of the General Assembly*, Fifth Session, 293 Plenary meeting, 6 October 1950.

33. UN Press Release SG/SM/5310 of 2 June 1994.

34. Trygve Lie, *In the Cause of Peace: Seven Years with the United Nations* (New York: Macmillan, 1954), 231.

35. U Thant, *View from the United Nations* (Garden City, NY: Doubleday, 1978), 382.

36. Internet address: <www.cnn.com>.

37. Thant, p. 253 quoted in Brian Urquhart, *A Life in Peace and War* (New York: Harper & Row, 1987), 237.

38. See, for instance, A. Walter Dorn, "The Cloak and the Blue Beret: Limitations on Intelligence in UN Peacekeeping." *International Journal of Intelligence and Counter-Intelligence*, Vol. 12, No. 4 (December 1999), 414.

39. Personal communication from General Indar Jit Rikhye (ret'd).

40. UN document S/PRST/1994/47 of 25 August 1994.

41. The Security Council rarely singles out specific NGOs as providers of information in its resolutions. In resolution S/RES/1013(1995) creating the International Commission, it did not refer directly to the Human Rights Watch report. Instead, it expressed "its grave concern about allegations of the sale and supply of arms and related matériel to former Rwandan government forces in violation of the embargo. . . ." However, it did call upon "as appropriate, international humanitarian organizations, and non-governmental organizations, to collate information in their possession relating to the mandate of the Commission." The Commission subsequently had meetings with Human Rights Watch.

42. UN International Commission of Inquiry, *Second Report*, UN document S/1996/195 of 14 March 1996.

43. Human Rights Watch, *Human Rights Watch Calls for Further Investigation of Role of France and Others in Re-Arming of Former Rwandan Government Forces*, Press Release of March 22, 1996. Their original report was *Re-Arming with Impunity: International Support for the Perpetrators of the Rwandan Genocide*, Human Rights Watch (Washington, DC, 1995).

44. ReliefWeb provides Situation Reports on complex emergencies (those involving human conflict) and natural disasters. The up-to-date reports from the field come from a wide variety of organizations, including UN missions and agencies and NGOs. It is located at <www.reliefweb.int>.

45. David Biggs, "Informal, *Ad hoc* Collaboration Between the UN and NGOs in the Field of Early Warning," private manuscript, July 1995.

46. Javier Pérez de Cuéllar, *Pilgrimage for Peace: A Secretary-General's Memoir* (New York: St. Martin's Press, 1997), 6.

47. The UN document symbol is S/NC/19—/# where # is a number in a new sequence for each year 19– .

48. Letter Dated 24 May 1994 from the Secretary-General to the President of the Security Council, Addendum, Annexes to the *Final Report of the Commission of Experts Established Pursuant to the Security Council Resolution 780 (1992)*, Volume I - Annexes I to V, 31 May 1995; UN Doc. S/1994/674/Add.2.

Appendix: Memoirs of UN Officials and Peacekeepers

The memoirs of UN staff and peacekeepers provide some of the best insights into the inner workings of the UN, as demonstrated by the use of such writings in this chapter. A bibliography is provided here.

UN Secretariat Staff (Including Secretaries-General)

Boutros-Ghali, Boutros. *Unvanquished: A U.S.–U.N. Saga.* New York: Random House, 1999.

Lie, Trygve. *In the Cause of Peace: Seven Years with the United Nations.* New York: Macmillan, 1954.

Narasimhan, C.V. *The United Nations: An Inside View.* New Delhi: UNITAR, 1988.

———. *The United Nations at 50: Recollections.* Delhi, India: Konark Publishers PVT, 1996.

Pérez de Cuéllar, Javier. *Pilgrimage for Peace: A Secretary-General's Memoir.* New York: St. Martin's Press, 1997.

Picco, Giandomenico. *Man Without a Gun : One Diplomat's Secret Struggle to Free the Hostages, Fight Terrorism, and End a War.* New York: Times Books, 1999.

Tavares de Sá, Hernane. *The Play Within the Play: An Inside Story of the UN.* New York: Knopf, 1966.

U Thant. *View from the United Nations.* Garden City, NY: Doubleday, 1978.

Urquhart, Brian. *A Life in Peace and War.* New York: Harper and Row, 1987.

Waldheim, Kurt. *In the Eye of the Storm.* London: Weidenfeld and Nicolson, 1985.

Peacekeepers and Individuals on Secondment

Bull, Odd. *War and Peace in the Middle East: The Experiences and Views of a U.N. Observer.* London: L. Cooper, 1976.

Burns, E. L. M. *Between Arab and Israeli.* Toronto: Clarke, Irwin, 1962.

Dayal, Rajeshwar. *Mission for Hammarskjöld*. Princeton: Princeton University Press, 1976.

Erskine, E. A. *Mission with UNIFIL: An African Soldier's Reflections*. New York: St. Martin's Press, 1992.

Harbottle, Michael. *The Blue Berets*. London: Leo Cooper, 1975.

———. *The Impartial Soldier*. London: Oxford University Press, 1970.

Rikhye, Indar Jit. *Military Adviser to the Secretary-General: United Nations Peacekeeping and the Congo Crisis*. London: St. Martin's Press, 1993.

———. *The Sinai Blunder*. New Delhi: Oxford & IBH Publishing Co., 1978.

Siilasvuo, Ensio. *In the Service of Peace in the Middle East, 1967–1979*. New York: St. Martin's Press, 1992.

Von Horn, Carl. *Soldiering for Peace*. New York: David Mackay, 1966.

CHAPTER 11

Trends in Reference Service for United Nations System Materials

Mary Fetzer

The caption to an Associated Press article published near the end of 1999 read, "Click if you want to fight world hunger."[1] Ten years earlier, few reasonably literate readers would have immediately understood the term "click" that, by the year 2000, had become commonplace terminology. Who would have expected back then that the United Nations Development Programme would sponsor Netaid, a series of live concerts designed to form a perpetual stream of music and information and featuring popular performers such as Sting, David Bowie, and Puff Daddy, to be simulcast live on the organization's website as a means of inspiring a new generation of philanthropists to contribute to flagging development aid? Just as many other activities in our lives have been transformed dramatically at the dawn of the new millennium as a result of the internet, so too have the information-seeking patterns of users of materials that emanate from the international intergovernmental organizations (IGOs) that form the basis of this book. Consider, for instance, the following:

- Since 1996, the United Nations (UN) official website (<www.un. org/>) has enabled thousands to access resolutions, selected documents, and related materials from the comfort of their homes or offices, saving many the often arduous trek into a library's mysterious collections of print and microfiche UN resources. More on this later.

- The serious researcher, needing to gauge the necessity of a costly sabbatical trip to Switzerland to examine the holdings of the UN's Geneva Library at the Palais des Nations, could suddenly in 1999 conduct a remote search of the institution's web-based catalog (<www.unog.ch/>) as well as obtain a detailed description of its League of Nations Archives.

- The doctoral candidate in the information sciences, in the last year of the twentieth century, could now partake of discussions on digital libraries held by the Information Systems Co-ordination Committee (ISCC) of the United Nations System of Organizations via a webcast that was made available live for public viewing on September 16, 1999 (<www.unsystem.org/iscc/>) directly from UN Headquarters in New York.

Such examples, indicative not only of the change but also of the speed of change, have confronted librarians and researchers alike in the past ten years. This chapter will explore some of the changes affecting users of IGO resources and look at some emerging trends in that context. Unfortunately, the rapidity of change precludes a gradual absorption, integration, and analysis of every important activity currently underway within the information area of IGOs. The change is dramatic rather than evolutionary. Therefore, this chapter provides but a snapshot of the fast-changing reference scene at the turn of the century.

Accessibility of Information: A Time to Reassess

In the late 1990s, several of the institutions of the UN system that were in their infancy fifty years earlier drew strength through their issuance of anniversary commemoratives or through scholarly analyses of their activities. The UN issued *The UN at 50: Statements by World Leaders*[2] and *The Future of the United Nations System: Potential for the Twenty-First Century*;[3] scholars delved into the recesses of IGOs and brought forth new works such as *The International Court of Justice, 1946–1996*[4] and *The World Health Organization*.[5] Compilations appeared which focused light on various international programs; examples include *Organized Crime: A Compilation of U.N. Documents 1975–1998*[6] and *Encyclopedia of Human Rights Issues Since 1945*.[7] Valuable additions to the secondary literature appeared, including *The Procedure of the UN Security Council*[8] and *Key Resolutions of the United Nations General Assembly 1946–1996*.[9] A spate of works, focused specifically on reform of the UN, emerged such as *Renewing the United Nations System*[10] and *UN21: Accelerating Managerial Reform for Results*.[11] A bibliography on UN reform covering 1945–1996 appears at <www.un.org/Depts/dhl/reform.htm>. A new journal, *Global Governance*,[12] from the Academic Council of the United Nations System, a relatively new organization formed as an international association of scholars, teachers, practitioners, and others active in the work and study of international organizations, also focused attention on IGOs.

Efforts to provide the novice with a starting point for exploring the publishing framework of the complex organizational structures of IGOs continued through conferences of librarians and other scholars. Traditional guides to the massive documentation of IGOs continued in print manifestation through publication of works such as *Introduction to International Organizations*,[13] representing the proceedings of a four-day American Association of Law Librarians Institute on International Organizations at Harvard University; and volume one of the present work, *International Information*,[14] took its place on library shelves. To meet the challenges of the rapid pace of change, however, some books are now being updated between editions via publishers' websites or individual author or institution home pages. Robert V. Williams's *The Information Systems of International Intergovernmental Organizations: A Reference Guide*[15] is updated at his academic department's home page <www.libsci.sc.edu/Bob/IGOs.htm>.

More specialized guides have begun to appear full-text online. An example is Jeanne Rehberg's thirteen-page *WTO/GATT Research* guide, which appeared on the Law Library Resource Exchange's Webzine <www.llrx.com> October 15, 1999. In addition to the more traditional venues for staying abreast of changes in IGO information activities, the curious can also follow the "What's On Line in International Law" column distributed through the online *ASIL* (American Society of International Law) *Newsletter* at <www.asil.org/newsletter/>.

Publishers continue to produce new editions of standard directories to help identify IGOs. After all, where better to search for the answer to a thorny reference question than with the IGO that originated the information? Also, directories offer an excellent tool for ascertaining e-mail and web addresses. And, while experience tempts the sophisticated to guess at appropriate URLs (Uniform Resource Locators), an assumption that the correct address for the World Meteorological Organization should be <www.wmo.org> may yield either a laugh or frustration when the World Missionary Organization, Inc. site appears. *The Europa Directory of International Organizations*[16] became a new entry in the directory category, and the Union of International Associations began to provide freely available web links (<www.uia.org/webints/websys80.htm>) for organizations listed in its *Yearbook of International Organizations.*[17]

A number of other general IGO-oriented web locator services quickly became established guides or jumping-off points for quick access to organization websites. The UN System Locator (<www.unsystem.org/>), which provides both an alphabetical and a classified arrangement for websites, serves as the official locator for the UN system of organizations. Its "Frequently Requested Information" link offers seamless access to conference schedules, library and documentation services, and press releases. A searchable online service called "unions: The United Nations International Organizations Network Search" (<www.3.itu.int/unions/>) allows the user to enter a search and locate information across a variety of UN agencies. The UN's Drug Control Programme also maintains a useful directory at <www.undcp.org/unlinks.html>.

Various other institutions and professional organizations have developed metasites to assist the stranded traveler. An example of an excellent academic site is the University of Michigan Document Center's International Agencies and Information on the Web (<www.lib.umich.edu/libhome/Documents.center/intl.html>) which includes links for international and foreign governments, to various IGO simulations, to statistics, and to treaties. The International Documents Task Force of the American Library Association's Government Documents Round Table (GODORT) has an evolving web presence linked from GODORT's home page (<www.library.berkeley.edu/GODORT/>) and currently housed at

<www.ucsd.edu/idtf/links.html>. It serves as a clearinghouse and provides the beginnings of an IGO document librarians' tool kit.

The UN: Moving Forward

From the standpoint of the information service provider, developments within the UN proper have contributed, in some respects, to a most welcome, more open, and information-accessible organization. From publication of the brochure *Dear United Nations . . . : How to Order UN Publications, Where to Find "Freebees," What Is on the Internet*[18] (UN, 1997, DPI/1887) to major transformational websites, the UN's information dissemination activities have been on the move in a positive and fast-paced manner. The organization's masterpiece is the official UN website at <www.un.org/>. Its home page provides the public entree to a wealth of information. While certain considerations regarding its use will be noted later, the amount of information it opens up to the world is a significant achievement. Consider this:

- Until recently, locating current UN press releases presented a major challenge to scholars with limited access to its New York distribution desk. Staying abreast of these press releases, valuable for accessing information not yet available in official form is now as simple as the click of the mouse (<www.un.org/News/>).

- Until the Earth Summit and the Cairo International Conference on Population and Development, when conference proceedings first began to appear through a gopher site, most interested outsiders might have expected to wait for years to obtain some edited or micropublished version of the conference proceedings. Conference documentation is now frequently available through the <www.un.org/> site.

- Reading lead articles in the *United Nations Chronicle* required either a personal subscription or a trip to the library. Selected articles are now on the web at <www.un.org/Pubs/chronicle/>.

For many, however, the most outstanding contribution is the easy access to the full text of many of the documents which appear on the UN's website. Suddenly, librarians at smaller public and academic institutions who were unable to collect UN materials can flush out essential documents online if they can fine-tune their understanding of the UN and its specialized agencies. Although the official site offers no guarantee of archiving documents, and "what you see is what you get," it offers an immense amount of documentation that will frequently fulfill current needs. While the press releases, conference proceedings, and articles from the *Chronicle* were noted above, some of the most important offerings of the official website include:

- Resolutions and Decisions for the three main organs are available retrospectively as follows:

    General Assembly, 1981+
    <www.un.org/ga/documents/gadocs.htm>

    Security Council, 1974+
    <www.un.org/Docs/sc.htm>

    Economic and Social Council, 1982+
    <www.un.org/esa/coordination/ecosoc/archives.htm>

  Fortunately, the UN appears to have a commitment to maintain these time series on their website.

- A very few, recent series symbol or so-called "masthead" documents are available full-text. Since there is a moving wall for what is retained on the site, users are well advised to note carefully the document symbol in the event that they need to refer to the document subsequently in a print, fiche, or other online alternative.

- Selective social and economic data from the UN and its specialized agencies.

- Links to official databases such as the subscription-based *United Nations Treaty Series*, *Monthly Bulletin of Statistics*, and *WISTAT*, as well as to free databases such as *REFWORLD* (<www.unhcr.ch/refworld/welcome.htm>).

- Links to the Dag Hammarskjöld Library's home page.

The Dag Hammarskjöld Library: Leading the Way

Noticeable differences in the availability of information from the Dag Hammarskjöld Library (DHL) have been in evidence in recent years and are of growing utility to the information community as well as to the public. Cracks in the elusive nature of IGO materials are sometimes found first in an organization's library, since it is often from that vantage point that broader needs are perceived. A momentous advance came with the DHL's introduction of its own home page on July 4, 1996: <www.un.org/Depts/dhl>. Some observations on it are warranted:

- UN Info Quest (UN-I-QUE; <www.un.org/Depts/dhl/unique.html>) is a reference librarian's and cataloger's dream. Many libraries holding substantial collections of UN sales publications checked in and maintained their collections in past years according to the sales number assigned by the Sales Section. Increasingly, libraries have begun to fully catalog and reclassify their collections, often making their holdings available remotely through web-based public access catalogs. To accomplish this, however, staff needed to pull together the individual years or editions of recurrent titles sometimes dispersed within the sales number. UN-I-QUE provides a publishing history of recurrent serial titles by giving each year/edition's corresponding symbol or sales number, thereby allowing technical service staff to locate volumes with a minimum of effort.

- For years, professors struggled to find a source to explain succinctly the use of the UN's prolific documentation to their students. Relatively few guides existed in the early years of the UN, and, in fact, this author was drawn into documenting UN research methodology by a graduate professor exasperated by the lack of available tools. With the DHL's website, it has produced its own official *UN Documentation: A Research Guide* (<www.un.org/Depts/dhl/resguide/index.html>) from which others may draw knowledge or adapt guides to their own library collections. The DHL's *Research Guide* explains in simple fashion the document symbols used by the UN, the various indexes available, types of documents, and strategies for locating resolutions, decisions, and speeches in the main organs along with relevant links.

- Simply locating an up-to-date list of UN depositories proved elusive for all but the most experienced UN documents librarians for years. Learning that a *List of Depository Libraries* existed often eluded one's physical, if not bibliographic, grasp. The home page now advises visitors not only of the UN's own depositories, but also of those of their specialized agencies through its DEPOLIB data base at <www.un.org/Depts/dhl/dls.htm>.

- In a remarkable move, the UN Publications Board cleared the first addition in roughly twenty years of several new depositories in the U.S. between 1997 and 1999. Added were three private institutions: St. John's University, Long Island, New York; Seton Hall University, South Orange, New Jersey; the University of Pittsburgh, Pittsburgh, Pennsylvania; and one public library, the Farmingdale Public Library in Farmingdale, New Mexico. Some institutions have, however, dropped or are considering dropping depository status as factors such as cost and staffing are weighed against alternative modes of delivering service.

- The recently debuted United Nations System Pathfinder helps one identify major publications of the organizations of the UN, its history, work, and structure (<www.un.org/Depts/dhl/pathfind/frame/start.htm>).

- More than one hundred general maps from the UN's Cartographic Section are now accessible in PDF (portable document format) and linked under "Maps."

Indexes and Catalogs of United Nations Materials

Changes in major tools that provide access to UN documentation have occurred since the topics were originally presented in this author's Chapter 14 of Volume 1 of *International Information*. The major changes can be summed up by the following:

- *UNDOC*, the DHL's main print index since 1979, ceased publication in September 1996. With January 1998, the Dag Hammarskjöld Library began issuance of a print *United Nations Documents Index* (ST/LIB/SER.N/1; Vol. 1, No.1 covered January–March 1998) with author, title, and subject indexes. The intervening period of October 1996–December 1997 was covered by a 1,152-page *United Nations Documents Checklist* (UN, E.99.I.10).

- Chadwyck-Healey continued production of its *UNBIS Plus on CD-ROM* through cooperative arrangements with the UN.

- The Readex Corporation continues to produce the *Index to United Nations Documents and Publications* on CD-ROM to accompany its fiche collection of the documentation of the UN; backfiles to 1945 are available. Through its affiliation with Newsbank, it has also produced a popular web-based index called *AccessUN* which is available retrospectively to 1961. It contains full-text resolutions, and provides numerous web links to UN documents. The 1945–1960 backfiles are being added in five-year segments.

- The UN has made available for purchase its own *ODS: Official Documents Search* (<www.ods.un.org>; formerly, *ODS: Optical Disk System*) which provides access to more than 300,000 pre-, in- and post-session meeting documents from 1992 forward. It includes *Official Records* and parliamentary documents for the period, plus resolutions of the main and subsidiary organs from 1946 onward. Sales publications are excluded.

- Crucial *Indexes to Proceedings* continue to be published in print for the General Assembly, Security Council, and Economic and Social Council, while a similar *Index* for the Trusteeship Council ceased when that organ became inactive.

Changes in the production of catalogs of the UN and its specialized agencies have been a topic of debate within agencies attempting to cut costs and among librarians seeking to preserve traditional print access while at the same time enjoying the currency and convenience of web-based catalogs. Following a hiatus of a couple of years, the UN issued its own print *United Nations Publications Catalogue 2000* late in 1999. The UN's catalog is also available online at <www.un.org/Pubs/catalog.htm/> in PDF. Catalogs of many of the specialized agencies are linked through the Frequently Requested Information site of the UN

System Locator at <www.unsystem.org/>. A catalog of the UN's *Official Records* is anticipated in the year 2000.

In the United States, Bernan remains the primary distributor for publications of a number of IGOs, and their site at <www.bernan.com/PublisherIndex.asp/> is useful for locating products available for purchase from that firm. Databuero, also a specialist in international official publications, has instituted a weekly e-mail newsletter available by subscription for organizations such as the World Trade Organization, International Monetary Fund, World Bank, European Union, Council of Europe, and UN.[19] IGO publishers have continued to partner with commercial publishers in order to achieve lower costs and increased revenues. Examples include the International Labour Organisation which makes its LABORDOC on CD-ROM database available through Nordic AB in Sweden; the United Nations Development Programme's flagship *Human Development Report* is published by Oxford University Press.

Bundling and Blurring: Collection and Service Implications

The same practices and challenges that librarians have encountered in recent years with collecting and servicing U.S. federal government information have also arrived on the international organizations' bibliographic scene. These practices include bundling of information and the blurring of content with service.

Bundling, considered here to be the aggregation of individual titles, or pieces of titles, from a variety of sources, into a composite that then results in a separate database under a new title has been occurring. American librarians have become increasingly familiar with the trend through government products such as the U.S. Department of Commerce's *National Trade Data Bank*. Within the UN one now finds products such as *REFWORLD* (E.GV.99.0.99); *WISTAT: Women's Indicators and Statistics Database*, Version 3 (E.95.XVII.6); and *TRAFIX* (*Trade Facilitation Information Exchange*; E.GV.98.0.7) which illustrate the bundling concept. Typically these are produced in a CD-ROM format and bring together, for a specialized audience, resources important to research within a discrete area. Included may be texts of documents available in other but dispersed venues, speeches not readily available elsewhere, legal instruments affecting the topic, statistical information gathered from various entities, and bibliographic information leading to further exploration of the subject. Portions of what the organization makes available on the priced CD-ROM products may be made available gratis on the IGO's website, as is the case with both *REFWORLD* and *WISTAT*. Commercial products such as the *International Statistical Yearbook* (Reinberg, Germany: DSI Data Services and Information GMBH, 10th ed., 1999) and the *CNTS: Cross-National Time-Series* (Binghamton, New York: Computer Solutions Unlimited) further complicate choices of available data and formats.

For the reference librarian, specialized researcher, or student, these bundled products offer convenience and time-saving research. They can, however, present challenges in the bibliographic arena. The CD-ROM may be cataloged under its own unique title. However, much like the major microform sets that became popular several decades ago, providing awareness of the actual contents of the CD-ROM (or web-based counterpart) can be problematic, particularly when the producer fails to maintain a consistent corpus of source material in the database. Providing proper "analytics" for the product can become the cataloger's nightmare and the collection development specialist's nemesis because it may be tempting to drop individual titles from a library's collection once it is known that a given title is incorporated into the bundled product.

The notion of blurring is in an evolutionary stage within the IGO environment; used here, it represents the melding of content with service and opens new frontiers for librarians. As stated by Lippincott and Cheverie, "In the future world of government information, the links between content and services will become more tightly coupled and more complex."[20] While individuals are less likely to interact directly with an IGO than they are to transact business with agencies of their national government, occasions do arise. At the most general level, individuals may wish to purchase greeting cards from UNICEF (an online function not yet activated, though one can make donations to UNICEF online); obtain current requirements for vaccinations; or acquire health advice for overseas travel destinations. At the opposite end, companies and other organizations constantly require data produced by IGOs; need to understand standards and protocols for the conduct of business with a given organization; and need to transact business with them. Increasingly, such transactions may be accomplished directly through internet services. As less of the librarian's time is required to serve as direct intermediary with the organization, the opportunity arises, however, to serve in other capacities. Librarians may find their expertise in accessing databases and developing strategies for use, in moving data into spreadsheets and web applications, in locating additional sources of information, and in advising on citation format just as significant as the functions of helping users pinpoint information in traditional print formats were earlier. In so doing, however, they may find the need to make "house calls," to move beyond the physical walls of the library itself to assist users via e-mail, in dormitory rooms and faculty offices, and over the phone with remote users of these resources. At the same time, institutions will still require a seasoned corps of librarian specialists able to understand and to mine the full extent of IGO documentation.

Statistics in Electronic Formats: Enhancing the Options

With statistics now readily available in electronic formats—whether as a CD-ROM or online—we have moved from an era of dead data to one in which the end user is often able to massage it, move it into spreadsheets, and manipulate the figures in myriad ways using statistical software packages. Specialized agencies of the UN create a tremendous amount of data, some of which is, however, difficult to use. The International Monetary Fund's important *International Financial Statistics* print series, available also as the *IFS CD-ROM*, is one example of a computer file that challenges the infrequent user but that can now be exported into Microsoft Access and moved into an easier-to-negotiate web interface using Cold Fusion software.

Traditional indexes to the statistical output of the UN, its specialized agencies, and other IGOs continue via the *Index to International Statistics*. The title is now being delivered under the web-based *Statistical Universe* umbrella by Congressional Information Service, Inc., as well. At the same time, direct online access to a wide spectrum of IGO statistics is becoming more commonplace as agencies refine their websites and decide what data they wish to make freely available on the web versus what portions will be withheld for purchase only. An early entry in the online field was the UN's own *Monthly Bulletin of Statistics*, available in its original incarnation in a print version but offered online free of charge to its print subscribers. Selections from other IGO data compilations can often be located online, although an IGO's complete database is generally available for a fee. The UN's own home page links users to a wide range of subject-matter aggregations of social indicators at <www.un.org/Depts/unsd/social/main.htm>. Much of the data is gathered from the *WISTAT* data discussed previously in this chapter.

In addition, substantial amounts of data may be located online from the specialized agencies of the UN system. The World Health Organization's WHOSIS (WHO Statistical Information System; <www.who.int/whosis/>) provides detailed data on AIDS/HIV and basic health indicators. The International Labour Organisation has a well-developed ILOSTAT site (<www.ilo.org/public/english/120stat/index.htm>) with excellent statistics on child labor and selected articles from the organization's *Bulletin of Labour Statistics*. Their "Database" link offers free searches of their statistical resources for requestors of small volumes of data.

While the Unesco Statistics website (<http://unescostat.unesco.org/>) is in the developmental stages, the Food and Agriculture Organization (FAO) has a richly developed site at <http://apps.fao.org> which provides a wide range of options for combining data in areas such as forest and fishery products, fertilizers and pesticides. The UNICEF site (<www.unicef.org/statis/indexr.htm>) provides a considerable amount of data from its popular *Progress of Nations* and *State of the World's Children* reports.

An important advance in linking the growing number of IGO statistical websites was introduced in 1999 when the UN Statistical Office brought up its Global Statistics index at <www.un.org/Depts/unsd/global.htm>.

FAQs, AAL Services and Listservs: Their Influence on the Reference Process

Researchers and librarians have increasingly resorted to new methods for posing reference queries. These methods include the FAQ, or Frequently Asked Questions; AAL, or Ask-a-Librarian services; and listservs, all of which offer alternatives to the traditional telephone call or reference desk encounter. These services sometimes lighten the burden at busy reference desks but, at the same time, shift responsibility to other venues.

The FAQ has become the websites' version of a larger library's information desk or "Rolodex." For example, the International Civil Aviation Organization's home page (<www.icao.int>) offers a FAQ service which readily provides the user answers to questions such as job vacancies, medical facilities at international airports, and visual requirements for commercial pilots.

FAQs have the potential to answer the same question over and over again, as well as simultaneously, for thousands of "callers" without draining costly staff resources. This capability has undeniable potential for answering queries in times of emergencies or natural disasters. It can also cut down on ennui for information dispatchers, allowing them to spend valuable time on more challenging or unique questions. FAQs assume, however, awareness of both the organization and its website; the ISCC may soon need to employ a web spider or robot to fetch and index this scattered information.

In a similar vein, some institutions have established Ask-a-Librarian services. The services are of particular value to the institution's remote faculty and doctoral students, to students attempting to complete assignments from satellite locations, and to researchers from afar who need to conduct preliminary investigations regarding a library's special collections before traveling to campus. Such services are often supported by a team of librarians or specialists and allow catalog records and other pertinent information to be cut and pasted into the requestor's e-mail. The team approach generally allows referral of questions to other specialists within the institution. Unlike the FAQ, however, response is not instantaneous, but is contingent upon normal turn-around time needed to research and respond to questions of a more extensive nature.

Popular among librarians and researchers within subject areas are the numerous listservs that have been established in recent years. While REF-L serves a more general audience, the international documents librarian community has developed several such discussion groups with considerable utilitarian value. The listserv most closely aligned with the ability to respond to information requests requiring the use of IGO documentation is probably INTL-DOC. This moderated listserv carries a very manageable volume of discussion on issues germane to the IGO community. While it carries information items such as job postings, needs and offers, notices of events, and so on, it can be a particularly useful venue for the resolution of difficult reference queries. Occasional questions requiring expert knowledge of IGO documentation, whether recent or historical, are posted to the list and often receive the generous attention of librarians with either the requisite expertise or with rich collections which lend themselves to an answer. Increasingly, responses have come from staff within the IGOs themselves. This is especially beneficial, because the answers lend a sense of "officialese" to them. While immediacy of response to questions posted on listservs is not guaranteed, replies within this collegial network are often swift and are of benefit to other readers on the list as well. Replies to questions on a listserv can often prevent others from duplicating research regarding a similar question or problem.

Other listservs with relevance to the reference process and to IGO-oriented questions include prolific discussion groups such as INT-LAW and GOVDOC-L, though the latter has a decidedly U.S. federal bent. Both listservs can be accessed in the traditional one-message-at-a-time mode or, for the more casual observer, in digest mode. More recently developed discussion lists include the Academic Council of the United Nations System's ACUNS-IO; and DOCWORLD-L, sponsored by the International Documents Task Force of ALA's GODORT. The latter is an unmoderated list geared to persons interested in sharing government information worldwide and covers subjects such as freedom of access to government information, trends in government publishing, and issues of broad general concern. Instructions for joining the various listservs mentioned are included in the Notes.[21] An excellent list of nearly 200 international law-related lists, including the subscription address and a brief description of each is maintained by Lyonette Louis-Jacques at <www.lib.uchicago.edu/~llou/law/lists/international.html>.

Changing Patterns in Model UN Research: Chat Rooms and Remote Access

Noticeable differences in patterns of use among on-site users of Model-UN resources are being observed. To the uninitiated, Model UN students serve as mock delegates, representing the interests and politics of various member states of the UN through a series of conferences hosted by academic institutions. More than 300 conferences are listed on the Model UN Calendar of Conferences at the United Nations Association of the United States of America (UNA-USA) site at <www.unausa.org>; and a UNA-USA Model UN Summit and Leadership Conference is held annually in the summer. Model UN activity centers most heavily around peak periods of activity on the spring and fall calendars of many academic institutions and occurs at both the college and high school levels. Students at the college level often serve, in fact, as mentors for those participating in high school simulations. The documentation needs of this enthusiastic corps of users have often placed heavy demands on sometimes ill-trained staff and scarce resources of institutions.

Lately, institutions with substantial UN resources, particularly the oft-sought *Official Records* series and masthead documents, have been experiencing a diminution in the number of on-site users if comments on listservs, discussions among colleagues, and dialogue at conferences are accurate. Other indicators of use are the lower rate of refiles of masthead documents on microfiche, decreased queues for workstations offering CD-ROM indexes or web access to UN index products; and less frequent reshelving of print volumes at several institutions. Ready availability of selected UN documents on the UN's own website, discussed earlier, likely contributes to this change. It may also contribute, however, to a "make do" attitude among participants eager to complete delegated assignments. Perceptions that "everything is on the Net" sometimes lead students to sidestep the more scholarly and traditional routes to uncovering pertinent citations, routes such as searching the more comprehensive indexes; for example, *Access UN* or its counterpart *Index to United Nations Documents and Publications* on CD-ROM, *UNBIS*, the UN's *ODS: Official Documents Search*, the *Index to Proceedings*, or the recently restructured *United Nations Documents Index*, with the result that numerous important materials on the topic under scrutiny may be missed.

Model UN students are, understandably, turning to a variety of Model UN websites which they can discover by surfing the internet, employing a growing number of search engines, or by relying on related sites such as that of the UNA-USA or by following Model UN links from <www.undcp.org/unlinks.html> or from the University of Michigan site at <www.lib.umich.edu/libhome/Documents. center/intl.html>. The United Nations Scholars' Workstation at Yale University (<www.library.yale.edu/un/>) was an early entry allowing users to access research materials of value to the Model UN student as well. Institutions with access to Nexis can subscribe to a separate UN package; full-text documents are available in their INTLAW Library with coverage going back to January 1980.

Through its development of the CyberSchoolBus the UN acknowledges the importance of its documentation to high school and college Model UN groups. With versions in English, French, and Spanish, CyberSchoolBus, at <www.un.org/Pubs/CyberSchoolBus/> offers project materials, links to Model UN conferences and organizations, an online newsletter and more. For students who need to contact "their" country's UN mission to ascertain its current stance on a particular topic, easy access to addresses and phone numbers of member state missions to the UN in both New York and Geneva is now available at the click of the mouse through MUNDA's Country at a Glance link. MUNDA (Model UN Discussion Area) is a chatroom, hosted by CyberSchoolBus, where interested parties can discuss research topics, ask for, and receive information. MUNDA requires a simple registration process. The UN's CyberSchoolBus was called "a tough cyberact to follow" as well as a "teacher's bonanza" in the July 9, 1998 issue of *DummiesDaily* (<www.dummiesdaily.com>).

The UNA-USA has also expanded its website to include a chat room, Model United Nations E-News, in which anyone in the Model UN program can notify the organization to ask that his or her information be sent out over this moderated MUN E-News circuit. Membership requires sending an empty message to mun-e-news-subscribe@makelist.com. A searchable archive is maintained. Another listserv created for Model UN students is available at LISTSERV@INDYCMS.IUPUI.EDU.

With so many new options available to them, it is no wonder that on-site use of UN materials is being reserved for the more diligent student and the traditional scholar. Unfortunately, however, Model UN research through remote access may tend to rely on that portion of the documentation currently available on the UN website rather than the more complete documentation available onsite at libraries or through subscriber access to the UN's *ODS: Official Documents Search* system.

Independent Learning

Not only are the information-seeking patterns of IGO librarians and researchers evolving; so also are modes of learning and teaching about IGOs and their documentation. Few schools in either the United States or Canada regularly teach an entire course on international documents; exceptions include the University of South Carolina and the State University of New York at Albany in the U.S. and the University of Toronto in Canada. The Readex division of NewsBank, Inc., through its annual seminars begun in 1986, has introduced a substantial number of U.S. and Canadian librarians to documentation in the field; so have a variety of professional associations. Within the International Federation of Library Associations (IFLA), its Official Publications Section has developed and sponsored workshops for librarians in other countries. In the U.S., the American Library Association's GODORT, especially through its International Documents Task Force, has sponsored numerous programs to educate librarians in this genre and has expanded the horizons of many, novice and experienced librarians alike.

New forums are appearing, however, which promise a more direct form of education for the end user interested in IGO material. John V. Williams, who teaches the international documents course at the University of South Carolina and has written the previously mentioned *Information Systems of International Intergovernmental Organizations,* published his book through conventional means but maintains periodic updates to web sources cited in the book in the online environment at <www.libsci.sc.edu/Bob/IGOs.htm>, thereby making this information more widely available. A website for the course International Organizations: Their Documents and Publications, taught by Peter Hajnal and Michael McCaffrey-Noviss can be found at <www.fis.utoronto.ca/courses/LIS/2137>. Other new developments include e-college (<www.ecollege.com>) and e-books. Examples of their potential influence on the dissemination of IGO information and documentation follow. Already available through e-College are courses in political science and librarianship so that one may expect courses in international organizations and international governmental organizations to emerge online as well.

In spring 1999, for instance, e-College.com joined forces with the G8 Research Group based at the University of Toronto (<www.g7.utoronto.ca>) to present the 1999 G8 Summit Online (<www.g8online.org>) which, according to the project director, represented an "unprecedented interactive dialogue with the world's top leaders at the G8 Summit."[22] Registration was free; access allowed professors, students, media, and other interested parties direct access to "quality analysis of Summit history and current proceedings provided by top scholars from the G8 Research Group." While UN conference proceedings have previously been made available online by the UN itself beginning with Agenda 21, such an interactive approach may set a new precedent for direct involvement.

In another development, the American Society for International Law reports that Professor Enrique Carrasco and his students at the University of Iowa College of Law recently produced an e-book on International Finance and

Development (<www.uiowa.edu/ifdebook/#E-Book>). This e-book is "an interactive web site that helps lay people understand what 'development' means, how law affects the development process, and how international finance and international financial institutions operate in the era of globalization."[23] Furthermore, e-journals already exist that have integrated multimedia—datasets, interactive graphs, spreadsheets and tables, sound—with their e-articles.[24]

Preserving the IGO Legacy: A Final Note

It is well known that websites generally have no archives or retention policies. In fact, the viability for preserving information via web technology is uncertain at this writing. And, in what might be a premature move, some agencies, the FAO, for instance, have suspended their programs for making documentation available on microfiche. Concern arises then over who will take responsibility for the preservation of international information in the future and what format that archiving will take. Digitization projects are well underway at various institutions, but coordination of efforts needs to be addressed and accessibility issues resolved. Not all institutions currently digitizing IGO information are prone to share the efforts of their projects, but make the material available solely on a proprietary basis via passwords.

One recent announcement involving Cornell University's New York State School of Industrial and Labor Relations indicates their plan to make freely available web mirror sites for the International Labour Organisation and the International Court of Justice for researchers and the public. The announcement was most welcome and may be indicative of the larger role other institutions will be forced to play if we are to preserve the documentation that our users require and retain the thread of our increasingly global society. Cornell developed the mirror sites with several goals in mind, perhaps the most important of which is "to permit the yearly capture and retention of the information found at these sites on CDs or other electronic storage media, thereby providing long-term access and archiving necessary for researchers and decision-makers. In addition, to serve as a secure backup location for these international organizations."[25]

Significant strides have been made in recent years to reclaim bibliographic control over UN system documentation, control that was lost in the early 1960s when the chief bibliographic tool, the *United Nations Documents Index*, ceased to cover selected documents and publications of the specialized agencies.[26] With the opening up of the internet, and through the efforts of the ISCC, through advances such as the UN System Locator and Global Statistics metasites, we have begun to close the circle in achieving fuller access. Of increasing importance will be the development of a clearinghouse to track scattered preservation efforts and to link to archival sites wherever they may reside.

Conclusion

Noted international organizations scholar Richard Falk, referring to the macro-trends of our times, wrote, "in these circumstances only a stubborn fool would have any confidence about anticipating what the future holds in store for us."[27] That said, one can but meekly project continuing and rapid change in the delivery of information as it relates to IGOs and to our global society and acknowledge that corresponding adjustments in the kinds of reference service we provide will present endless challenges for the foreseeable future.

Notes and References

1. "Click If You Want to Fight World Hunger," *Star Ledger* [Newark, NJ] (2 October 1999): 2.

2. *The UN at 50: Statements by World Leaders: New York, 22–24 October 1995* (New York: United Nations, 1996).

3. Chadwick F. Alger, *The Future of the United Nations System: Potential for the Twenty-First Century* (New York: United Nations University Press, 1998). E.98.II.A.4.

4. Arthur Eyffinger, ed., *The International Court of Justice, 1946-1996* (The Hague; Boston: Kluwer Law International, 1996).

5. Yves Beigbeder, *The World Health Organization* (The Hague; Boston: M. Nijhoff, 1998).

6. M. Cherif Bassiouni and Eduardo Vetere, eds., *Organized Crime: A Compilation of U.N. Documents 1975–1998* (Ardsley, NY: Transnational Publishers, Inc., 1998).

7. Winston E. Langley, *Encyclopedia of Human Rights Issues Since 1945* (Westport, CT: Greenwood Press, 1999).

8. Sydney Dawson Bailey, *The Procedure of the UN Security Council*; 3d ed. (Oxford; New York: Clarendon Press, 1998).

9. Dietrich Rauchning, Katja Wiesbrock, and Martin Lailach, eds., *Key Resolutions of the United Nations General Assembly 1946–1996* (New York: Cambridge University Press, 1997).

10. Erskine Childers and Brian Urquhart, *Renewing the United Nations System* (Uppsala, Sweden: The Dag Hammarskjöld Foundation, 1994). Development dialogue 1994:1.

11. *UN21: Accelerating Managerial Reform for Results* (New York: United Nations, 1997). E.97.I.10.

12. *Global Governance: A Review of Multilateralism and International Organizations*, vol.1, no.1-, winter 1995- (Boulder, CO: Lynne Reinner).

13. Lyonette Louis-Jacques and Jeanne S. Korman, eds. *Introduction to International Organizations*. Sponsored by the American Association of Law Libraries at the Harvard University Law Library (Dobbs Ferry, NY: Oceana Press, 1996).

14. Peter I. Hajnal, ed., *International Information: Documents, Publications, and Electronic Information of International Government Organizations*, 2d ed. (Englewood, CO: Libraries Unlimited, 1997).

15. Robert V. Williams, *The Information Systems of International Intergovernmental Organizations: A Reference Guide* (Stamford, CT; London: Ablex, 1998).

16. *The Europa Directory of International Organizations* 1st ed.- , 1999- (London: Europa Publications).

17. *Yearbook of International Organizations*, Union of International Associations, 1st ed.- , 1948- (Brussels: G.K. Saur).

18. *Dear United Nations...: How to Order UN Publications, Where to Find "Freebees," What Is on the Internet* (New York: UN, Department of Public Information, 1997). DPI/1887.

19. To subscribe to the free newsletter, send an e-mail to: subscribe@databeuro.com. In the subject line type "Subscribe."

20. J. K. Lippincott and J. F. Cheverie, "The 'Blur' of Federal Information and Services: Implications for University Libraries," *Journal of Government Information* 26, No.1 (1999): 25–31.

21. Instructions for subscribing to listservs:

    ACUNS-IO   LISTSERV@LISTS.YALE.EDU
    Discussion of issues related to international organization studies and the UN System

    DOCWORLD-L   LISTSERV@LISTSERV.INDIANA.EDU
    Document interests worldwide

    GOVDOC-L   LISTSERV@LISTS.PSU.EDU
    Government Document Librarians

    INTL-DOC   LISTSERV@LISTSERV.ACNS.NWU.EDU
    International Document Librarians

    INT-LAW   MAJORDOMO@LISTHOST.CIESIN.ORG
    International and Foreign Legal Resources

    MODEL UN   LISTSERV@INDYCMS.IUPUI.EDU
    Students involved in Model UN simulations

In general, to subscribe to a listserv, submit your request as: subscribe [listname] Your Name; send to the address of the software that runs the list. For example, to subscribe to INTL-DOC, send e-mail to LISTSERV@LISTSERV.ACNS.NWU.EDU. Do not fill in the "Subject" line, but in the body of the message type "subscribe INTL-DOC Your Name." If the e-mail goes to a MAJORDOMO address, omit your name; just type, "subscribe list name."

22. Paul Nielson, "1999 G8 Summit Online: Open Registration." 26 May 1999. <http://INTL-DOC@listserv.acns.nwu.edu>.

23. "What's New On Line in International Law," *ASIL Newsletter*. January–February 1999: 1. <www.asil.org/newsletter/>.

24. Gerry Mckiernan, "WE NEED SUBJECT LINE OF THIS EMAIL." 28 October 1999. Personal email to Mary Fetzer.

25. Stuart Basefsky, "Cornell Mirrors ILO & ICJ—Two International Web Mirror Sites." 21 October 1999. <OVDOC-L@lists.psu.edu>.

26. More detailed information on the publication history of the *United Nations Documents Index* and its successor titles appears in volume one of *International Information*, 2d ed., at pages 32 and 435–38, and 446–47.

27. Richard Falk, *Predatory Globalization: A Critique* (London: Blackwell/Polity Press, 1999). See Acknowledgement page.

CHAPTER 12

Citation Forms

Diane L. Garner

Introduction

Citations are a major access route to international governmental organization (IGO) documentation. Complete and accurate citations are a critical element of the research process, but knowing how to cite government information sources has always been problematical. Citations often lack sufficient information to make retrieval straightforward, because the documentation does not always lend itself to the citation styles prescribed in most manuals. In recent years the proliferation of electronic information resources has added further to the confusion over the way to cite a source. Standards are beginning to emerge, but will remain tentative until the media are more stable.

Citations have several purposes: to give credit to one's sources or to provide authoritative support for one's opinions, to name but two. Writer and reader would probably agree that the primary purpose is to lead the reader to the source cited. A good citation has two characteristics: it contains the necessary data, and it is easy to understand. What data are necessary depends on the way libraries and data banks, through indexes, catalogs and searching software, have described a source; this varies with the sources being cited. Thus, a journal article, a book, a parliamentary speech, a numeric data file on diskette, and a message from the internet are all cited differently from one another. The second criterion, ease of comprehension, is rather subjective, but consistency is its hallmark. Consistency means that a reader can expect to find the same data in the same order throughout the text, and that certain conventions, such as highlighting a title with underlining or italic print, are always observed.

Citation style is largely governed by the wishes and needs of publishers (in the case of published material) or institutions (in the case of unpublished items such as term papers and theses). A consistent style is usually achieved through the use of style manuals written or sanctioned by the press, the association, or the institution. In the United States commercial and academic publishers and institutions most generally accept the style of the University of Chicago Press. In the legal profession the style of the "Harvard Bluebook" is the universal standard. In the social sciences many follow the style of the American Psychological Association, and in the humanities, the style of the Modern Language Association.[1] These style manuals prescribe content and form for a wide variety of publications, but they do not adequately represent government documents, and citation forms for electronic media are only now being developed.

Print Formats

Over the years, certain conventions in print publishing have become established. Among these is placing bibliographic information (title, author, publisher, place and date of publication or copyright) on the title page and on the verso of the title page. Libraries, publishers, and booksellers use this information to catalog printed books. On this basis certain standard ways of citing works have developed. These may vary slightly in form or punctuation, but they are all basically alike in content.

For a book:

(Bibliography) Author. *Title.* Place: Publisher, Date of publication.

(Note) Author. *Title.* (Place: Publisher, Date), page cited.

For a journal article:

(Bibliography) Author. "Title of Article." *Journal Title* Volume (Date of issue): pages

(Note) Author, "Title of Article," *Journal Title* Volume (Date of issue): page cited

IGO printed documents and publications do not always fit these models, and even when they do, the models do not provide enough data to identify certain kinds of documentation. IGO information sources as a separate class of material requiring special rules are represented only to a very limited extent in the traditional style manuals. While it is true that rules that apply to other kinds of books and periodicals can sometimes be applied to IGO documents and publications, often these rules do not cover all the facts of publication. General style manuals do not take into account, for example, the difficulties of corporate-author (jurisdictional, governmental or organizational) entries, the central importance of document-numbering systems, or the complexities of publishing styles.

Electronic Formats

IGO information in electronic format offers the further challenge of providing fixed data for often elusive and technologically complex media. Just what information is needed to retrieve precisely the same text of a multinational treaty that was found on the UN gopher via the internet? How much information does one need to provide about the technical demands of the format? The International Organization for Standardization (ISO) published a draft international standard for bibliographic citations that includes electronic documents in 1995. Only a few manuals have been published so far that deal with these issues. In general, the styles for electronic media include some of the same elements as for print media, but they also include information about the medium, the pathway to retrieval of the source, and for volatile online media, the date the source was accessed.

For a book:

(Bibliography) Author. *Title.* Place: Publisher, Date of publication. Medium and notes about the medium. Source/Pathway/[Date of Access].

(Note) Author. *Title.* (Place: Publisher, Date), page cited. Medium and notes about the medium. Source/Pathway/[Date of Access].

For a journal article:

(Bibliography) Author. "Title of Article." *Journal Title* Volume (Date of issue): pages. Medium and notes about the medium. Source/Pathway/[Date of Access].

(Note) Author, "Title of Article," *Journal Title* Volume (Date of issue): page cited. Medium and notes about the medium. Source/Pathway/[Date of Access].

Online electronic media have also introduced other types of sources into scholarly discourse—e-mail, discussion lists, newsgroups, audio, video, and graphic files, to name a few.

Standards

Two bodies, the International Organization for Standardization (ISO) and the American National Standards Institute (ANSI), have set basic rules for citations. ISO Standard 690-1975 and ANSI Standard Z39.29-1977 agree on the basic elements necessary for a bibliographic citation. The ANSI standard is much more thorough in its consideration of all the elements and all the possibilities of a citation; it requires eighty pages of text as compared with ISO's eight pages. Neither considers documents as a separate class of citation. The rules that apply to books, conference proceedings, reports, articles, or the like, of any provenance apply also to the products of government organizations.

ISO Standard 690-1975

The first part of this standard lists the ways in which a bibliographic reference might be used: in a heading, a bibliography, a footnote or endnote, partially in a text and partially in a note, and wholly in a text. It distinguishes three kinds of works referred to: a book, a serial, and a contribution to a book or serial. The rest of the standard describes in some detail recommendations for the essential elements of a citation, that is, author, title, and imprint. The following parts are of special significance for IGO documentation:

> Recommendation 5.2, for corporate authors, follows *Anglo-American Cataloguing Rules II* (*AACR 2*), that is, when an organization is clearly responsible for a work, it is considered the author.[2] When a subordinate part of a larger group is named, the large group comes first (for example, United Nations. General Assembly). When a body, although subordinate or allied to another body, has its own functions and independent identity, its own name is used alone. The example given is "World Health Organization," not "United Nations World Health Organization."

> Recommendations 6.1 and 6.2 allow for the shortening of a long title and the translation of a title, if necessary.

> Recommendations 7.1.2 and 7.1.3, for publisher, allow the use of a publisher and a sponsoring body, or a publisher and a distributor. The frequency of copublication between IGOs; between IGOs and commercial presses; and the difficulty of locating sources of IGO documentation make this an especially important element for IGO citations. The publisher statement is not a required element for all citations, but it ought to be required for most document citations.

> Recommendation 7.6.3 allows for the "elucidation of a title that is ambiguous." Given the characterless titles of much official documentation (for example, *Report*...), this can be a useful option.

It should be stressed that these are recommended standards. ISO Standard 690-1975 is not a citation manual, but rather a set of principles that forms the basis of a manual. Although examples are given to illustrate the recommendations, they are not adequate to meet the practical needs of a writer.

ISO Standard 690-2

This standard is an extension of the standard for bibliographic references, with specific provisions for the elements to be included in electronic documents. It prescribes an order for the elements of a bibliographic reference and rules for how the information from the source documents is to be presented. An important part of this standard is that the identifying data come from the source itself and that it refer to the copy that was used, so as to distinguish it from other possible sources and copies. For this reason, the place, time, and pathway by which a source is accessed are important citation elements. ISO 690-2 covers citations to both the whole and the parts of electronic monographs, databases, computer programs, serials, bulletin boards, discussion lists, and other message systems, such as electronic mail. It is intended that the standard will be revised as new formats come into use.

ANSI Standard for Bibliographic References Z39.29-1977

The purpose of this ANSI standard is to provide a bibliographic format with enough information to identify a work. It aims at a consistent format, but one that can be varied to suit different needs. Although this sounds paradoxical, it is not. There is wide latitude about what to include that varies from publication to publication.

The ANSI standard defines all the data elements that could be used in a citation and divides them into groups that correspond to the bibliographic groups of Anglo-American cataloging rules. The groups are:

AUTHORSHIP//TITLE STATEMENT//EDITION//IMPRINT//

PHYSICAL DESCRIPTION//SERIES STATEMENT//NOTES

Not all of the groups apply to every kind of publication. A typical citation to a book, for instance, will only include authorship, title statement, and imprint. For general purposes the ANSI standard recommends that either the authorship group or the title statement group be used first in a citation, followed by the other groups in the order given above; for example:

International Labour Office. *Collective Bargaining.* 2d ed. Geneva: ILO, 1986.

or

Collective Bargaining. International Labour Office. 2d ed. Geneva: ILO, 1986.

There may be several elements within each group. A corporate author may have several levels that are named in hierarchical order; for example, United Nations. General Assembly. Special Political Committee. The title statement may include a title proper, a subtitle, a report number, a medium designation for media other than paper, and so on. The order of the elements within a group is illustrated by examples.

An introduction explaining the scope and purpose of the standard is followed by an exhaustive glossary of terms and bibliographic elements. The glossary is not merely a convenience but a prescriptive standard, defining such concepts as "author." The glossary is followed by a summary of the possible elements in each group and a statement of principles and guidelines giving the rationale for the standards. This section includes statements on the source of the information, the content, the sequence of elements within a citation, the use of punctuation, typography, abbreviations, and other details.

A matrix of elements for different kinds of print and nonprint material indicates which elements within each group are essential, recommended, or optional for each type of publication. There is also a lengthy appendix with examples to show the order of elements. IGO documents are not treated as a separate category in the matrix or in the examples. In fact, many IGO materials, and especially publications, fit under the types considered—journals, monographs, conference proceedings, reports, legal materials, maps, audiovisual materials, and data files. A Unesco document is described in the examples for conference proceedings, and a NATO document is used for an example of a technical report. For some classes of IGO documentation, such as official records and meeting records, the matrix and the examples are lacking. It is difficult to decide where the rules might put such data elements. It is not that the standard is incompatible with these kinds of documents; the elements needed to identify them are already included in the basic groups. It is more a matter of adding the various kinds of IGO documentation to the matrix, indicating essential, recommended, and optional elements, and of giving examples.

Manuals

(see Appendix for full citations)

The citation style of the University of Chicago Press is the best known. It is illustrated in *The Chicago Manual of Style* (popularly known as *The Chicago Manual*) and in Kate Turabian's *Manual for Writers of Term Papers, Theses, and Dissertations*. The importance of the Chicago style cannot be overemphasized. It is required by more publishers, journals, and schools than any other, at least in the United States; it can, however, be very difficult to use for IGO citations. The latest editions of both manuals acknowledge the complexity of document citations to a far greater degree than earlier editions. The *Manual for Writers*, for instance, advises that "it is better to err on the side of giving too much rather than too little information. . ." and the library card catalog is a good model for deciding what data are necessary. A typical citation has the issuing body in hierarchical order, followed by the title; other citations depend on the material being cited. The problem for IGO documents is that there are too few examples. The latest edition of Turabian's *Manual for Writers* covers only League of Nations and UN documents and gives only one IGO citation in eight different styles in its section on public documents. *The Chicago Manual* gives thirteen. Additional examples can be found in other sections, such as those on treaties, but nowhere is the complexity of IGO documentation given its due. A writer might have many questions that are simply not covered by these few examples. The Chicago style does provide for a variety of document numbers; both series symbols and sales numbers are shown in examples.

Another serious problem in the Chicago style for many IGO documents is the lack of imprint data. In none of the examples in Turabian is the place of publication given. This is not crucial for documents produced at the headquarters of the organization, nor is it important for the examples given. Almost everyone knows that UN headquarters is in New York. But it leads one to believe that imprint is not important (it is not included in *any* of the examples), and this could result in incomplete citations. The locations of regional offices, to give one case, are not as well known. Furthermore, to an experienced librarian the presence of a regional office in a citation is a signal that the search will probably require more esoteric indexes, will be more difficult, and may not succeed.

The Library of Congress (LC) Reference Department's *Bibliographic Procedures and Style* (an internal document) devotes six pages to corporate authors and twelve pages to documents, two of which give examples for international documents. The LC style provides for the name of the issuing organization (in hierarchical form), the title, a statement of responsibility (for personal authors, speakers, and so on), the place and date, the number of pages, series name and number, and a note section with a variety of possible data, including series symbol, sales, and LC classification number. As the LC manual was written for LC staff, that is, librarians familiar with cataloging rules, it is difficult for a layperson without cataloging knowledge to interpret. It is necessary to move from section to section to find out where specific rules apply. One problem, for example, is deciding when to use a corporate author and when a personal author.

Three citation styles of professional groups enjoy wide use in the United States, and some refer to documents: the MLA (Modern Language Association) style, the APA (American Psychological Association) style, and the legal citation style of the Harvard Bluebook. The MLA and the APA manuals cover documents, but they give little or no space to IGO documents. The Harvard Bluebook deals more extensively with IGO documents, but is limited in other ways.

The MLA style manual advises one to give the issuing agency as author unless the personal author's name is known, in which case it uses the author's name instead of the issuing agency (or in addition to it) placed after the title. This is followed by the title, and the imprint as it appears on the title page. The MLA manual advises that full publishing information be included since not all UN documents are issued from a central office. It does not, however, recommend other essential data, such as series symbol, or include any examples other than two UN documents.

The APA style is used by many in the social sciences. It calls for author, date, title, and imprint. It does not include any IGO examples, but there are several for U.S. documents which could be easily applied to some IGO documents. Again, the problem is lack of examples and of consideration of documents that do not fit the pattern. The APA does, however, have examples for electronic media. Using the APA and MLA styles requires so many interpretations on the part of a writer that neither is recommended for document citations, unless one's publisher or institution requires it.

Of the professional citation manuals, the Harvard Bluebook is most relevant to international documents. It has twenty-six pages on treaties, court cases, arbitration, official records, document series, parliamentary publications, official journals, and yearbooks. It is especially good for the United Nations, the European Union, the Council of Europe, and the League of Nations. For obvious reasons it focuses on legal publications. The legal citation style is wonderfully consistent and simple. It typically consists of an abbreviated issuing agency, a year or volume number, a title or an abbreviated series title, and a page number, with a series symbol, sales number, or other identifying number. With a legal citation the knowledgeable user can go straight to the source. The limitations of the style stem from its simplicity. If the user is not familiar with the abbreviations, as is usually the case with novices or infrequent users, recourse to a list of standard abbreviations is a necessary intermediate step before retrieval of the source. The latest edition (1996) has added numerous examples of monographic publications from IGOs. One useful bit of advice is to explain the source's availability in a parenthetical note if it is particularly difficult to find; for example, "(photocopy on file with author)."[3]

The Dag Hammarskjöld Library of the United Nations published its *Bibliographical Style Manual* in 1963 to establish uniformity in the compilation of UN bibliographies. In 1963 international standards for citations did not yet exist, so this manual follows *ALA Cataloging Rules for Author and Title Entries* (1949) and the Library of Congress *Rules for Descriptive Cataloging* (1949, 1952). It is very thorough in its treatment of United Nations and League of Nations documents, and is still used for some purposes in the compilation of UN bibliographies.

Since the 1963 manual was issued, ISO and ANSI standards have been accepted and new Anglo-American cataloging rules (*AACR 2*) have come into effect. Bibliographic standards and new cataloging rules were spurred on and molded to a great extent by the increasing use of computers for bibliographic control. It is not surprising, then, that the manuals currently in use by the UN are governed by the formats and standards needed for machine-readable copy.

The United Nations Editorial Manual is the UN's comprehensive set of rules for editorial practice. It prescribes policies on everything from language to the use of punctuation. "Footnotes and Other References" (Article E3) gives detailed rules on how to cite—in text, footnotes, and reference lists produced by the UN—all kinds of material including books, articles, reports, UN and other IGO documents. In treating citation style for bibliographies, the *Editorial Manual* distinguishes between bibliographies prepared by the Dag Hammarskjöld Library and those prepared by other entities of the UN (and by extension, bibliographies prepared by a writer using the UN style). Staff at the Dag Hammarskjöld Library must follow the style of the *Reference Manual for Bibliographic Description* and the *Cataloguing Manual* (both of which are based on a machine-readable format for bibliographic description). For other units of the UN and other organizations, the *Editorial Manual* advises that the 1963 *Bibliographical Style Manual* continue to be used.

The *Reference Manual for Bibliographic Description* and the *Cataloguing Manual* are in-house guides for input of bibliographic data into UNBIS, the UN's computerized database (*U*nited *N*ations *B*ibliographic *I*nformation *S*ystem). Neither manual was distributed to the general public, although some libraries received copies. They are mentioned here because the citation style, being derived from the same format as the library's online catalog, achieves the ideal mesh of library practice and citation style. It must be stressed, however, that these are not style manuals for writers but cataloging manuals for librarians.

The *Editorial Manual* also distinguishes between bibliographies that contain only UN publications and "mixed" bibliographies containing both UN and non-UN material. In UN-only bibliographies, less information might be required and such bibliographies are likely to be organized by series symbol rather than by author or issuing agency.

Marie Rothman's *Citation Rules and Forms for United Nations Documents and Publications* was written to bridge the gap between the specialized UN citation style ("primarily a tool for librarians and bibliographers") and the more widely accepted Chicago style. She applies the principles of the Chicago style to UN documents and publications. Rothman tries to cover all of the circumstances in which UN documents might be cited. She gives long and short forms for first and second references, forms for official records, mimeographed documents, and documents of subsidiary organs. For citations to UN publications it is the most complete guide in general use.

The *Complete Guide to Citing Government Information Resources* attempts to create a consistent format for all kinds of government documents—international, national (both U.S. and foreign), and local. It pays heed to both the ANSI standards and the format of the Chicago style, but does not completely follow either. Unlike the Rothman manual, *The Complete Guide* gives neither alternate forms for shortened, abbreviated or long references, nor examples for both bibliography and footnote forms as does Turabian. It does give examples to cover every variation of bibliographic data for international documents known to the authors. This expanded and revised edition of the earlier *The Complete Guide to Citing Government Documents* (CIS, 1984) has extensive chapters, with examples, for foreign government publications and for electronic formats.

The citation of electronic formats presents issues that many are wrestling with. As technology presents new formats, it is not always clear what data elements should be included in a citation. The standard advice—when in doubt, leave nothing out—applies especially with electronic media. Tangible electronic media, such as CD-ROMs, DVDs, or diskettes, are like printed materials in that their content and form are more or less fixed. Online media, like the World Wide Web, where the content can change from minute to minute, offer more challenges. It might be claimed that the ANSI and ISO standards cover all formats. However, the standards, by themselves, are not sufficient to guide the average user to a useful citation.

A few manuals have been published as of this writing that attempt to address these problems. *The Complete Guide to Citing Government Information Resources* (1993) gives the most examples for government information. *Electronic Styles* (1996) and *The Columbia Guide to Online Style* (1998) are more comprehensive for the whole range of electronic formats, especially online, but are less specifically geared to government information resources. Neither creates its own citation style; instead they fit the necessary citation elements for electronic resources into existing styles.

Electronic Styles is based on the APA citation style, with the date shown early in the citation, after the author. It has a good sample of international government information sources and the forms are adaptable enough to accommodate a variety of other sources. It is a general manual with the strengths (uniformity) and limitations (lack of expertise in documents) of all general manuals. The citations tend to be briefer and simpler than those of *The Complete Guide*. The examples include all media, but most are online rather than CD-ROM, diskettes, and other tangible media so that it is primarily useful for online sources. The most salient feature of the citation is the path used to retrieve the information.

Cheney, in *The Complete Guide,* also stresses the path to retrieval, but counsels much fuller information. Based on her experience as both a government documents librarian and a cataloger, Cheney's citations tend to be long and complex. She uses, for example, extensive notes to describe the system requirements for a particular product.

The Columbia Guide to Online Style is the most recent printed guide. Published by Columbia University Press, it has an added advantage of updates on its website, <http://www.columbia.edu/cu/cup/cgos>. *The Columbia Guide* gives formats for both APA (scientific) and MLA (humanities) styles. It does not single out government information as such. Instead it provides citation forms and examples for the media available as of 1998—the World Wide Web, e-mail, discussion lists, newsgroups, gopher, File Transfer Protocol (FTP), Telnet, synchronous communication sites, online references sources, online databases, and electronic publications. It can be expected that as new media are developed, the online updates to *The Columbia Guide* will provide for them. It might be considered on a par with *The Chicago Manual* as a basic citation guide for electronic resources.

The specialized document citation manuals—Rothman, Garner and Smith, and UN—show an expertise in IGO documentation that sets them apart from the more general manuals. Not surprisingly, they all tend to require more data elements than all-purpose manuals. They give so many examples that it is difficult to describe precisely the content of a typical citation. The sample citations that follow the discussion of citation elements will give an idea of what each style requires.

Bibliography Formatting Software

Computer programmers have written software programs that will automatically format citation elements into a predetermined style. Several software packages for DOS and Macintosh computers include all the major styles—Chicago, APA, MLA, and Turabian—as well as user-defined styles. Up to 1994 these were reviewed in an annual column in *Database*.[4] Most library catalogs and many other bibliographic databases for IGO information are now in electronic formats, and the citation elements in these databases can be downloaded and imported directly into formatting software. Researchers could certainly save time and aggravation by investing in one of these programs. Given the vagaries of IGO documentation, there would still be instances requiring further intervention, but with a carefully thought out user-determined base style, most difficulties could be avoided.

The Citation

It is advisable to investigate which style of citation is to be used before starting any research work. It will save time later if, before compiling sources and taking notes, one has a clear idea of what style (and therefore, what manual) is required and what bibliographic data are used in that style. Citation style is usually determined by one's publisher or institution. Sometimes it is left up to the individual researcher, with a requirement only that it be consistent. In that case the style might depend on the kinds of works that are likely to be included. If a mixed bibliography of books, journals, and documents were anticipated, one should choose a general manual like *The Chicago Manual*, plus a compatible documents manual such as Garner and Smith, or Rothman. If electronic media are included, one would probably wish to consult *The Columbia Guide* as well. If a bibliography is composed entirely of older UN documents, the 1963 UN manual might be used.

Sources of Information

The first question confronting a writer is where to look for the correct and pertinent bibliographic data. This question is easily answered if one has used a standard source for locating the document and has recorded the search process, for example, by downloading the record from the library's online public access catalog. It is also fairly easy with some documents in hand. Many IGO publications are laid out like standard books or journals. One can find an easily discernible title, author, publisher, place and date of publication on the title page. In addition, many have Cataloging-in-Publication (CIP) data or its equivalent, usually facing the title page, on the verso of the title page, or on the last page of the book (an example is given in Figure 12.4). CIP data can help in indicating the correct bibliographic information; for example, the proper title, the corporate author's name, or data which it would be useful to include in a note (sales number, document number, and so on). It is easy to write a useful citation for such material (see the citations with Figure 12.4 for examples of "easy" citations). More difficult citations involve materials, particularly documents, which do not conform to standard commercial publishing styles (see Figure 12.1, and its citations). Figure 12.4 has an author, a title, a place, publisher and date, all in the usual places, but Figure 12.1 has two possible authors (is it the General Assembly or the Secretary-General?); three possible titles; no place; questionable publisher (is it the United Nations General Assembly?); and several numbers which it might be important to cite.

Styles of presenting bibliographic data vary widely. The UN, for one, has a standard masthead for its mimeographed documents, now often called "masthead documents" (see Figure 12.1). Other organizations have standard styles that may be applied to some classes of documents, but not to others. Some documents, especially those not meant for circulation ("gray literature"), have scarcely any bibliographic data at all.

For a document lacking a title page or a masthead on which to base a citation, one may be forced to rely on other sources. The first and most obvious recourse would be to the index, bibliography, catalog, or other finding aid that led to the work in the first place. If such finding aids are not available, it may be necessary to take information from a preface, a letter of transmittal, or the text itself (see Figure 12.6). Information about the facts of publication may be buried in small print on the back pages. It is preferable to take information from unorthodox sources rather than omit it because it does not appear in the prescribed place.

Authorship

The question of authorship probably causes more confusion and uncertainty than any other aspect of IGO publications and documents, not just for researchers but also for catalogers and indexers. It is an issue not sufficiently considered by any of the standards committees, in *AACR 2*, ANSI, or ISO. *AACR 2* ignores the problem of corporate authorship by entering a work under its title if it has no personal author, except in a few well-defined cases. ANSI and ISO, and most manuals, use either personal or corporate authors, but do not give any guidance about which is preferred when both are given in the work being cited. This writer recommends that the problem be circumvented, not by leaving anything out, as *AACR 2* does, but by placing the IGO as the main author in the "authorship" slot and putting personal authors' names after the title.

Title

The title is taken exactly as it is given on the title page of the document; all standards and manuals recommend this. In some cases, there is no traditional title page. Instead there may be a title only on an outside cover or a simple heading on the first page (e.g., in UN masthead documents), both of which may serve as the authoritative source of title. Electronic formats can be especially tricky. Usually "hard copy" (e.g., CD-ROMs, diskettes, video disks) materials have titles affixed to them or on their accompanying holders or documentation. Online sources with address fields, such as electronic bulletin boards or electronic mail, usually have a subject line that may be considered a title if there is no title proper. In both print and electronic media there may be no title at all. In such cases most standards and manuals allow for a descriptive title to be made up and placed in brackets or for the citation to say simply "Untitled."

In sales publications it is usually not difficult to determine the title. They follow modern standard commercial practices of typography and layout. Moreover, many have CIP or other cataloging information (see Figure 12.4). The title in many documents may not be obvious, and the length and complexity of a title may be daunting. Figure 12.1 is a good example and will be discussed in detail.

When it is difficult to determine the correct title, one may have to use all the possibilities that present themselves on a title page, or better yet, consult another source. There may be CIP to indicate what the publishers consider to be the title. The catalog or index source that brought the writer to the document may be a legitimate source. Most manuals allow for lengthy titles to be shortened by using ellipses (...). The initial three or four words of a title should not be eliminated, however, because they are vital in any index or catalog that lists documents by title.

The *United Nations Editorial Manual* distinguishes three kinds of titles in UN documents (all of which may be used simultaneously): general, secondary, and descriptive (see Figure 12.1). Any or all of these may have titles or subtitles. The general title is the first title given, in capital letters. It may appear as part of the corner notation under the masthead when it corresponds to the title of an agenda item.

The secondary title (*not* a subtitle) is given second, in both uppercase and lowercase letters, and underlined. It relates to a more specific subject within the general title. In fact, it is often the more distinctive title and is used as the title of UNDOC in preference to the general title.

The third or descriptive title tells what kind of document is represented; for example, letter, report, note, and the author or originating body. For indexing purposes, this is probably the least descriptive access point and, unless it is the only title given, can often be eliminated in a citation.

No nonspecialist writer could be expected to know all the details of UN editorial practice. Citing a "correct" title is at best an educated guess. Because of this, for UN documents and for many other IGO documents, a number may be the single most informative data element.

Most IGOs assign identifying numbers to at least some of their documents. The best known of these numbering systems is the UN document series symbol, but Unesco, the Food and Agriculture Organization of the United Nations (FAO), the International Atomic Energy Agency (IAEA), and the Organization of American States (OAS) use similar numbers. The European Union catalog number and the Organisation for Economic Co-operation and Development (OECD) stock number, although they look rather different, are based on roughly the same principles of issuing agency and document serial number. These numbers are useful in a citation because they are often indexed in the finding tools for

IGO documents and because many libraries use the number as a basis for shelf location.

Other numbers may be found in addition to or instead of document numbers, namely the International Standard Book Number (ISBN), the International Standard Serial Number (ISSN), the Library of Congress card number, and stock or sales numbers. Only two of the works discussed, Garner and Smith, and the ANSI standard, provide for the citation of ISBN, ISSN, and LC card numbers, usually in an optional note. These universally used numbers can be searched on some automated systems. Stock or sales numbers are, on the other hand, unique in form and content to the IGO that uses them. With the exception of UN sales numbers, most of these numbers cannot be searched in book indexes, card catalogs, or automated systems. Nevertheless, sales or stock numbers are useful and recommended in the absence of other identifying numbers.

Edition

Edition is a standard data element in book citations for anything beyond the first edition. It does not often appear as a separate statement in print documents, even though many are issued in draft and final editions, with one or more revisions, and as official or unofficial documents. Often the title or the document number will indicate edition, making a separate statement redundant. This is probably why most of the manuals do not even consider the edition as a separate element for print-format documents. It is another compelling reason for including complete document numbers.

The question of edition or version in electronic resources is problematical. What is an edition? The potential exists for electronic media, especially online, to be altered easily and often. How does one convey the exact source of the exact text one used so that a future researcher can retrieve it? Barring the possibility that exactly the same text cannot be retrieved in the future, one aims at giving the reader the optimum chance.[5] The time that a source was retrieved may be important. Many electronic resources are "nested" in layers of directories; in those instances the pathway by which the item was found becomes an essential element of the citation. A different pathway might produce a different version.

Imprint

The standard imprint consists of place, publisher, and date of publication. There is a great deal of variation in what is considered necessary. Turabian and *The Chicago Manual* use only the date of registration or of publication. While this practice is sufficient for most UN documents issued from headquarters in New York, it is not recommended to adopt it as a general practice.

Omitting the publisher's name is accepted if the publisher has already been identified as the issuing agency. Omitting the place of publication is trickier. Its omission causes no great harm when the work cited comes from the headquarters city of a well-known IGO. When it comes from an IGO which has more than one seat (e.g., the European Union in Luxembourg and Brussels) or a regional office of an IGO (e.g., Unesco Regional Office for Education in Africa in Dakar, Senegal), knowing all the facts of publication can make a difference in one's ability to locate the work. International organizations and their agencies are scattered all over the world. None has a completely centralized and well-controlled system of documentation. Documents from the UN's New York headquarters or Geneva may require one source for locating; documents from a regional office in Turkey may require another. Turabian advises writers to use "common sense" when deciding what to include in a citation. Better advice might be: "When in doubt, leave nothing out."

Series Statement

All the manuals allow for the series name and number for monographs in series (except for the Harvard Bluebook which does not cover citations for monographs). In most cases the series information comes after the imprint data, and is usually placed between parentheses. While the series statement may not be absolutely necessary, it does make it easier to locate a work. A large percentage of IGO monographs is released in series. Most libraries provide access by series name; some libraries, to cut cataloging costs, provide access *only* by series name. Knowing the series may also allow clearer identification of ambiguous or similar titles. Some IGO monographs are part of more than one series.

Although no manual prohibits naming both series, only Turabian, Chicago, LC, UN 1963, and Garner and Smith specify that both series should be mentioned.

Notes

"Notes" is a catchall element where useful information, which does not fit anywhere else, is given. Some notes may be necessary; others, while not strictly necessary, may be very helpful in identifying and locating a work. Notes may include facts about the availability and distribution of an item (especially when these differ from data in the imprint); ISBN/ISSN (Garner and Smith also include sales or stock numbers); language of the work, and so on. In citing electronic media notes take on a great importance that will be discussed below.

Knowledge of IGO documents is helpful in deciding what information to include in a note. For example, in deciding whether to give information about alternate distribution it helps to know how hard it is to obtain a given document. A UN masthead document of the *limited* distribution category may not be easily available in paper copy, but it may be widely distributed in the Readex microform version. If one has this information, it is a useful note. The guiding principle should be to give the reader as many avenues of access as are consistent with a reasonable length and complexity of the citation.

All the UN citation manuals (1963 manual, UN *Editorial Manual,* and Rothman) require supplying information about documents of limited or restricted distribution. This may be shown by an L or an R in the series symbol. If it

330 / 12—Citation Forms

is not so indicated, it should be explicit in a note, because it obviously affects the availability of documents.

Citing Nontraditional Media

More and more IGOs are increasing the use of nonbook media to disseminate information. These include microfiche, microfilm, 35mm film, audiocassettes, magnetic tapes, floppy disks, CD-ROMs, and so on. It is important to cite the medium if it is not paper, because the medium may have an effect on locating the materials. Libraries may house it in a different way. Special indexes and catalogs may be needed to locate it. Special equipment will probably be needed to use it.

Photographic reproductions of works on paper should be cited the same way as the paper edition, with the addition of information about the microform edition, such as the producer's accession number. This is not required by the ANSI standard, but it is useful to the reader. The basic bibliographic information should be taken from the frame reproducing the title page and not from the header; information on headers is often abbreviated or otherwise changed. Other nontraditional media, (e.g., sound recordings, computer programs, magnetic tapes) may require that one consult accompanying material to get the bibliographic data—covers, containers, user guides, or documentation.

The ANSI standard uses author, title, imprint, and physical description for most nonbook formats. It puts the medium designation after the title and data about the medium (size, reduction ratio, recording speed, and so forth) in the physical description, after the imprint data. Of the manuals previously described only *The Complete Guide* and *Electronic Styles* give examples of IGO citations to nonprint media. *The Complete Guide* follows ANSI standards:

> International Bank for Reconstruction and Development. *Place in the City* (film). Washington, 1976. (16 mm, 15 min, col.). Available from UN Centre for Human Settlements (HABITAT). Nairobi, Kenya.

Electronic Styles follows the APA style:

> United Nations. General Assembly, 49th Session. (1995) *Resolution 215: Assistance in mine clearance* [Online]. Available: <gopher://undp.org: 70/11/undocs/gad/RES/49/9576321E> [1995, August 11].[6]

Another manual, *A Style Manual for Citing Microform and Nonprint Media* by Eugene B. Fleischer, provides extensive coverage of nonprint media (except for computer-related products) and the situations one might encounter in trying to cite them. This is probably the only manual, except for Garner and Smith, where one can find citation styles for games and kits.

Much has changed since the first edition of *International Information* was published in 1988. What were nontraditional media then—microfiche, microfilm, audiocassettes, audiodisks, film—now seem like old technology. New technologies in electronic publishing have transformed and continue to change the way information is disseminated and accessed. Standards of production, the electronic equivalent of title pages and imprint data are still in flux, and so, too, are standards of bibliographic access. Technology that we take for granted with print media plays a larger role in determining how and whether an electronic information product can be used. And technologies themselves are developing and changing rapidly. A computer file may no longer be accessible if the software and hardware needed to run it are no longer available. The volatility of electronic media is another factor. Is the online text that was called up on Monday still there on Friday? All these issues are beyond the scope of this chapter, but their disposition will have a bearing on the citation styles of the future.

Translation and Romanization

Some manuals require that works be cited in the language used; some allow translation of certain data elements, such as corporate author, place, and publisher. APA requires translation of titles into English as well as the original language. There are a few exceptions to the rule of using the original language. In bilingual or multilingual works no manual requires one to cite all languages used; one may choose the language of the bibliography (English for English speakers, Spanish for Spanish speakers, and so on). The other exception is a language in a nonroman script that may be romanized, using ISO or ANSI standards. The UN citation style is an exception; guided by diplomatic and political necessities, it uses the language of the original, whatever the script. For most writers who do not have access to fonts for several scripts, romanization is perfectly acceptable.

Sample Citations

The citations in this section are based upon this writer's interpretation of the rules in the manuals described earlier. They are all in bibliography (as opposed to footnote) form, and are long or first references rather than abbreviated subsequent references. Some of the figures do not have sample citations from every manual discussed because not enough information could be found in some manuals to be sure of the correct citation form. The citations represent only a very small number of the possible citations for IGO documents and publications in the manuals. The following examples illustrate typical document citations. They are meant to show the similarities and differences of the citation styles. For more thorough explanations and examples, the reader is urged to consult the manuals themselves.

Figure 12.1   UN Masthead Document
Figure 12.2   UN Official Record
Figure 12.3   UN Sales Publication
Figure 12.4   IGO Item Copublished with Another Press

332 / 12—Citation Forms

Figure 12.5   Multiple Authors
Figure 12.6   Annual Report without Imprint. Necessary to Consult Text for Imprint Data
Figure 12.7   Journal Article
Figure 12.8   Microformat, Multiple Series
Figure 12.9   IGO Material Online Source: Website
Figure 12.10 IGO Material in Tangible Electronic Medium

Figure 12.1. UN Masthead Document.

UNITED NATIONS

General Assembly

```
                                        Distr.
                                        GENERAL

                                        A/49/202
                                        1 July 1994
                                        ENGLISH
                                        ORIGINAL:   ENGLISH/RUSSIAN
```

```
Forty-ninth session
Item 64 (g) of the preliminary list*
```

GENERAL AND COMPLETE DISARMAMENT: REGIONAL DISARMAMENT

Report of the Secretary-General

CONTENTS

		Page
I.	INTRODUCTION	2
II.	REPLIES RECEIVED FROM GOVERNMENTS	2
	Austria	2
	Bulgaria	5
	Ukraine	6

*   A/49/50/Rev.1.

94-26528 (E)   110794   130794   *14/07/94*   /...

Turabian, Chicago
United Nations. General Assembly, 49th Session, 1 July 1994. *General and Complete Disarmament: Regional Disarmament* (A/49/202).

Harvard Bluebook
United Nations, General Assembly, General and Complete Disarmament: Regional Disarmament; Report of the Secretary General, U.N. Doc. A/49/202 (1994)

LC
United Nations. General Assembly. General and complete disarmament: Regional disarmament; report of the Secretary General: [New York]. 1994. 7 p. A/49/202.

MLA
United Nations. General Assembly. *General and Complete Disarmament: Regional Disarmament.* New York: United Nations, 1994. (A/49/202).

UN 1963 Manual; *UN Editorial Manual* (mixed bibliography of UN and other materials)
United Nations. General Assembly. General and complete disarmament: Regional disarmament. Report of the Secretary-General. 1 July 1994. 7 p. (A/49/202).

UN Editorial Manual (bibliography of UN materials only)
A/49/202
General and complete disarmament: Regional disarmament: report of the Secretary-General. New York: UN, 1 July 1994. 7 p.

Rothman
United Nations. General Assembly. "General and Complete Disarmament: Regional Disarmament." Report of the Secretary-General. A/49/202, 1 July 1994.

Garner and Smith
U.N. General Assembly, 49th Session. *General and Complete Disarmament: Regional Disarmament; Report of the Secretary-General.* (A/49/202). 1 July 1994. (Mimeo).

Figure 12.2. UN Official Record.

A/48/44

Report of the Committee against Torture

General Assembly
Official Records · Forty-eighth Session
Supplement No. 44 (A/48/44)

United Nations · New York, 1993

Chicago
United Nations. General Assembly. *Report of the Committee Against Torture*, Suppl. 44 (A/48/44). 1993.

Turabian
United Nations. General Assembly, 48th Session. 24 June 1993. *Report of the Committee Against Torture* (A/48/44).

Harvard Bluebook
48 U.N. GAOR Supp. (No. 44), UN Doc. A/48/44 (1993).

UN 1963, *UN Editorial Manual* (mixed bibliography)
United Nations. General Assembly. Report of the Committee Against Torture. 1993. 89 p. (A/48/44: GA Official records, 48th sess. Supplement no. 44).

Rothman
United Nations. General Assembly. "Report of the Committee Against Torture 24 June 1993." (General Assembly, *Official records*, Forty-eighth Session, Supplement no. 44. A/48/44).

Garner and Smith
U. N. General Assembly, 48th Session. *Report of the Committee Against Torture.* Supp. No. 44 (A/48/44). Official Record. New York, 1993.

Figure 12.3. UN Sales Publication.

ST/TCD/SER.E/15

United Nations
Department of
Technical
Co-operation for
Development

Government Financial Management in Least Developed Countries

United Nations   New York, 1991

Recto

ST/TCD/SER.E/15

UNITED NATIONS PUBLICATION

Sales No. E.91.II.H.1

ISBN 92-1-123115-9

Copyright © United Nations 1991
All rights reserved
Manufactured in the United States of America

Verso

Turabian, Chicago
United Nations. Department of Technical Co-operation for Development. *Government Financial Management in Least Developed Countries.* 1991. (ST/TCD/SER.E/15).

LC
United Nations. Department of Technical Co-operation for Development. Government financial management in least developed countries. New York, 1991. 234 p.
United Nations [Document] ST/TCD/SER.E/15
"United Nations publications. Sales no. E.91.II.H.1"

Harvard Bluebook
U. N. Dep't of Technical Co-operation for Development, Government Financial Management in Least Developed Countries. [pages cited], U. N. Doc. ST/TCD/SER.E/15, U.N. Sales No. E.91.II.H.1 (1991).

MLA
United Nations. Department of Technical Co-operation for Development. *Government Financial Management in Least Developed Countries.* New York: United Nations, 1991.

APA
United Nations. Department of Technical Co-operation for Development. (1991). *Government Financial Management in Least Developed Countries.* New York, United Nations.

UN 1963 (mixed bibliography)
United Nations. Department of Technical Co-operation for Development. Government financial management in least developed countries. 1991. 234 p. (ST/TCD/SER.E/15).

UN Editorial Manual (UN bibliography)
Government financial management in least developed countries. New York, UN, 1991. 234 p. (ST/TCD/SER.E/15 - Sales no. E.91.II.H.1).

Rothman
United Nations. Department of Technical Co-operation for Development. *Government Financial Management in Least Developed Countries.* ST/TCD/SER.E/15. New York, United Nations, 1991. (E.91.II.H.1)

Garner and Smith
U. N. Department of Technical Co-operation for Development. *Government Financial Management in Least Developed Countries* ST/TCD/SER.E/15). New York, 1991.

Figure 12.4. IGO Item Copublished with Another Press.

National Security Concepts of States

NEW ZEALAND

Kennedy Graham

UNIDIR
United Nations Institute for Disarmament Research

Taylor & Francis
New York · Philadelphia · Washington DC · London

Recto

Copyright © 1989 United Nations Institute for Disarmament Research

All rights reserved. No part of this publication may be reproduced, stored in a retrieval system, or transmitted, in any form or by any means, electronic, electrostatic, magnetic tape, mechanical, photocopying, recording or otherwise, without the prior permission of the copyright owner.

First published 1989
Printed in the United States of America

Library of Congress Cataloging in Publication Data

Graham, Kennedy
    National security concepts of states : New Zealand / Kennedy Graham.
        p.   cm.-- (UNIDIR series)
  ISBN 0-8448-1614-0
    1. New Zealand--National security. I. Title. II. Series.
UA874.3.G72 1989
355'.033093--dc20   89-4458
                                                                CIP

Verso

Turabian, Chicago
Graham, Kennedy. *National Security Concepts of States: New Zealand.* New York: Taylor and Francis, 1989.

LC
Graham, Kennedy. National security concepts of states: New Zealand. New York: Taylor and Francis, 1989. 180 p.

MLA
Graham, Kennedy. *National Security Concepts of States: New Zealand.* United Nations Institute for Disarmament Research series. New York: Taylor and Francis, 1989.

APA
Graham, Kennedy. (1989). *National Security Concepts of States: New Zealand.* United Nations Institute for Disarmament Research. New York, Taylor and Francis.

UN 1963, *UN Editorial Manual*
Graham, Kennedy. National security concepts of states: New Zealand. New York, Taylor and Francis, 1989. 180 p.

Garner and Smith
United Nations Institute for Disarmament Research. *National Security Concepts of States: New Zealand* by Kennedy Graham. New York: Taylor and Francis, 1989.

Figure 12.5. Multiple Authors.

**ADJUSTMENT AND EQUITY
IN DEVELOPING COUNTRIES**

GENERAL EDITOR
Christian Morrisson

ADJUSTMENT AND EQUITY IN INDONESIA

By
Erik Thorbecke

with

Roger Downey, Steven Keuning, Byung Kim,
David Roland-Holst, David Berrian

and

The Center for World Food Studies

DEVELOPMENT CENTRE
OF THE ORGANISATION FOR ECONOMIC CO-OPERATION AND DEVELOPMENT

Turabian, Chicago
Thorbecke, Erik; Downey, Roger; Keuning, Steven; Kim, Byung, Roland-Holst, David; and Berrian, David. *Adjustment and Equity in Indonesia.* OECD Adjustment and Equity in Developing Countries Series. Paris: Organisation for Economic Cooperation and Development, 1992.

LC
Thorbecke, Erik and others. Adjustment and equity in Indonesia. Paris: Organisation for Economic Cooperation an d Development, 1992. 264 p. (OECD Adjustment and Equity in Developing Countries Series).

MLA
Thorbecke, Erik et al. *Adjustment and equity in Indonesia.* OECD Adjustment and Equity in Developing Countries Series. Paris: Organisation for Economic Cooperation and Development, 1992.

APA
Thorbecke, E.; Downey, R.; Keuning, S.; Kim, B., Roland-Holst, D.; & Berrian, D. (1992). *Adjustment and Equity in Indonesia.* (OECD Adjustment and Equity in Developing Countries Series). Paris: Organisation for Economic Cooperation and Development.

UN 1963
Organisation for Economic Cooperation and Development. Adjustment and equity in Indonesia by Thorbecke, Erik and others. Paris, 1992. 264 p. (OECD Adjustment and Equity in Developing Countries Series).

UN Editorial Manual
Adjustment and equity in Indonesia. Paris, Organisation for Economic Cooperation and Development, 1992. 264 p. (OECD Adjustment and Equity in Developing Countries Series).

Garner and Smith
Organisation for Economic Cooperation and Development. *Adjustment and equity in Indonesia* by Thorbecke, Erik et al. Paris, 1992. (OECD Adjustment and Equity in Developing Countries Series)

Figure 12.6. Annual Report without Imprint. Necessary to Consult Text for Imprint Data.

UNEP PROFILE

Title Page

Introduction

accomplished and, more importantly, what it has encouraged others to attempt. A gigantic task looms ahead. All of us who work for UNEP will be grateful for your help in these efforts.

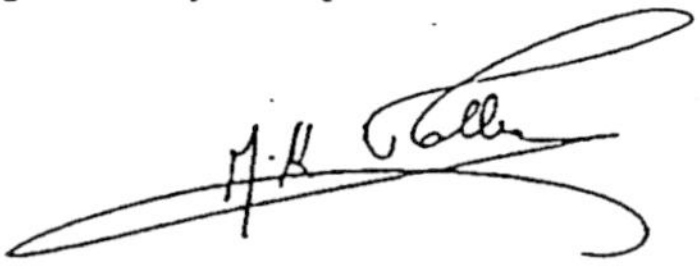

MOSTAFA KAMAL TOLBA
Executive Director
United Nations Environment Programme
Nairobi, July 1990

Turabian, Chicago, MLA, Garner and Smith
United Nations Environment Programme. *UNEP Profile.* Nairobi, 1990.

APA
United Nations Environment Programme. (1990). *UNEP Profile.* Nairobi.

LC, UN 1963, *UN Editorial Manual*
United Nations Environment Programme. UNEP profile. Nairobi, 1990. 48 p.

Figure 12.7. Journal Article.

First Call for Children

"The essential needs of children should be given priority in bad times as well as good" — *Plan of Action, World Summit for Children*

A UNICEF Quarterly/1992/No. 1   January-March 1992

NEW PRIORITY TAKES SHAPE FOR COMING EARTH SUMMIT

Placing children on the environment agenda

By Yin Yin Nwe

In less than six months, the United Nations Conference on Environment and Development (UNCED), also called the Earth Summit, will take place in Rio de Janeiro. Commitments will be made at Rio and a process will be initiated to "find a common basis for action to protect the future of planet Earth, and to secure for all its inhabitants a more sustainable and more equitable future", according to an UNCED booklet.

In that process, the first call should be for children. Many of the most publicized environmental issues, such as global warming, depletion of the ozone layer and destruction of tropical rain forests, however, don't appear, at first glance, to have much to do with children. I was told by an UNCED official that the link is that children are the most vulnerable to environmental degradation —a much-repeated phrase, but one which nonetheless bears repeating. The right to protection and care, already affirmed by the Convention on the Rights of the Child, should also be seen as protection from environmental degradation, which affects every aspect of children's well-being. This concept needs to be included in the statement of principles that will be made in Rio, to be called the Earth Charter or the Rio Declaration.

Vulnerability, however, is certainly not the only aspect of the link between children and the environment, nor should children be seen merely as passive victims. For it is they who in the next century will be responsible for looking after the earth. It is, therefore, only fair that their concerns be addressed in any action the international community takes now to deal with environmental degradation.

Getting down to basics

One of the greatest challenges of the UNCED meeting will be to reconcile the perspectives of the industrialized North and the underdeveloped South, whose differences are clear.

About four fifths of the world's people live in developing countries, with children making up almost half the population in many cases. Nearly one fourth of humanity lives in absolute poverty in the South, unable to fulfil their most basic needs for food, shelter and clothing. Hunger, malnutrition, dirty water and preventable diseases kill 40,000 children every day. For the majority of people in the South, meeting survival needs is an overriding priority and their view of the environment is a very basic one.

In contrast, the affluent in the North (and in the South) no longer worry about fulfilling basic survival needs. For them the environment has lost its immediacy, so they see it in terms of saving the rain forests, stemming ozone depletion, acid rain and greenhouse gases, and buying 'environmentally friendly' consumer goods. Forests are seen as carbon sinks and population issues only as a strain on the earth's resources.

Ironically, many of the passionate
continued on page 8

CONTINENT'S STRENGTHS TO BE A FOCUS

Donor conference on African Child set for year-end

By Patricia Lone

Concerned about the continuing crisis in Africa, and the widening gap between the continent's many reform efforts and the external resources required for their success, UNICEF will be supporting a range of actions and strategies to alleviate the crisis and narrow the resource gap.

The most prominent will be support for a donors' conference on the African Child called for by the Organization of African Unity (OAU) and scheduled for the end of the year. It promises to provide an opportunity for Africa to show the progress it has made in child survival and development efforts as well as its plans to meet Summit goals, as a way of eliciting increased donor support.

Buttressing this approach is a substantial and productive resolve Africa has shown in tackling its problems, in the wave of democratization that is sweeping the continent and in the growing consensus that only human-centred development can spur and support the changes needed in Africa.

The past decade has offered Africa bitter but useful insights into the value of strategies designed to help it cope. For years, many African countries struggled to implement structural economic changes in order to qualify for continued loans from international funding agencies, eliminating jobs and subsidies on staples, reducing salaries and opening their economies to competition from imports. By the end of the decade, however, it was evident that structural adjustment programmes offered an important but only a partial remedy to

After a rooming-in policy, enabling mothers to breastfeed their infants on demand, was introduced in one hospital in the Philippines, the incidence of neonatal deaths due to infection dropped by 95 per cent.

Baby-friendly hospital

Turabian, Chicago
Nwe, Yin Yin. "Placing children on the environment agenda." *First Call for Children,* January-March 1992, pp. 1, 8.

LC
Nwe, Yin Yin. "Placing children on the environment agenda." First call for children, January-March 1992: 1, 8.

MLA
Nwe, Yin Yin. "Placing children on the environment agenda." *First Call for Children,* January-March 1992: pp. 1+.

APA
Nwe, Yin Yin. (1992, January-March). Placing children on the environment agenda. *First Call for Children*, 1, 8.

UN 1963, *UN Editorial Manual*
Nwe, Yin Yin. "Placing children on the environment agenda." *First call for children* (New York) January-March 1992: 1.

Garner and Smith
Nwe, Yin Yin. "Placing children on the environment agenda." *First Call for Children: A UNICEF Quarterly.* (January-March 1992) pp. 1, 8.

Figure 12.8. Microformat, Multiple Series.

```
                          FAO  yearbook
                               annuaire
                               anuario
FAO Forestry Series       ...........................
No. 26
FAO Statistics Series
No. 110                   Forest
Collection FAO:
Forêts N° 26              products
Collection FAO:
Statistiques N° 110       ...........................
Colección FAO:
Montes N° 26
Colección FAO:            Produits
Estadística N° 110
                          forestiers

                          ...........................

                          Productos
                          forestales

                          ...........................
                          1980-1991

FOOD
AND AGRICULTURE                    1991
ORGANIZATION
OF THE
UNITED NATIONS
Rome, 1993
ORGANISATION
DES NATIONS UNIES
POUR
L'ALIMENTATION
ET L'AGRICULTURE
Rome, 1993
ORGANIZACION
DE LAS
NACIONES UNIDAS
PARA
LA AGRICULTURA
Y LA ALIMENTACION
Roma, 1993
```

Garner and Smith
Food and Agriculture Organization of the United Nations. *FAO Forest Products Yearbook, 1991,* Rome, 1993. (FAO Forestry Series No. 26; FAO Statistics Series No. 110). (1993 IIS microfiche 3410-S1).

Fleischer
Food and Agriculture Organization of the United Nations. *FAO Forest Products Yearbook, 1991.* Rome: FAO, 1993. Located in IIS Microfiche Library, Bethesda, Md.: Congressional Information Service, 1993, 4 fiche, 3410-S1.

Figure 12.9. IGO Material Online Source: Website.

Tuesday, September 21, 1999   9923160e.htm   Page: 1

UNITED NATIONS

Distr.
GENERAL

S/1999/862
9 August 1999

ORIGINAL: ENGLISH

QUESTION OF EAST TIMOR

Report of the Secretary-General

1. The Security Council, by its resolution 1246 (1999) of 11 June 1999, established the United Nations Mission in East Timor (UNAMET) to organize and conduct a popular consultation. In accordance with that resolution, the United Nations is authorized to operate in East Timor throughout the consultation process, which ends by the announcement of its results. However, in accordance with the Agreement between the Republic of Indonesia and the Portuguese Republic on the question of East Timor signed on 5 May 1999 (hereinafter referred to as "the 5 May Agreement") (A/53/951-S/1999/513, annex I), the United Nations will be required to play a substantive role in East Timor in the post-ballot period.

Post-ballot scenarios 2. The 5 May Agreements provide for the United Nations to play a significant role in the implementation of either possible result of the consultation. Should the East Timorese vote to accept autonomy, the constitutional framework for a special autonomy (ibid., appendix) gives the Secretary-General of the United Nations the responsibility and the authority to monitor and verify the implementation of autonomy for East Timor and to establish such offices as are deemed necessary to do so in the Special Autonomous Region of East Timor (SARET). Additionally, the autonomy framework requires the Secretary-General to appoint a broadly representative Transitional Council, which would remain in place until the election of the Regional Council of People's Representatives of the SARET, which the Secretary-General is called upon to monitor and verify. 3. Should the consultation result in a rejection of autonomy, the 5 May Agreement provides that Indonesia, Portugal and the Secretary-General shall reach agreement on arrangements for the peaceful and orderly transfer of authority in East Timor to the United Nations. The Secretary-General shall then, subject to the appropriate legislative mandate, initiate the procedure enabling East Timor to begin a process of transition towards independence.

Interim phase 4. There will be an interim phase between the conclusion of the popular consultation and the start of the implementation of its result, during which the parties will undertake the necessary steps, legal and otherwise, for implementation to begin. Under article 7 of the 5 May Agreement, the Governments of Indonesia and Portugal requested the Secretary-General to maintain an adequate United Nations presence in East Timor during this period, regardless whether autonomy is accepted or rejected in the popular consultation. The purpose of the present report is to convey to the Security Council my views concerning this presence.

5. During this interim phase, the situation in East Timor will be rather delicate as the Territory prepares for the implementation of the result of the popular consultation, whichever it may be. Thus the United Nations efforts must be redoubled following the ballot to build confidence and support stability in the Territory and reassure all groups, in particular those who were in the minority in the ballot, that they have a role to play in the future political life of East Timor. In order to do this, the United Nations should be closely involved in the work of East Timorese bodies. The establishment of an interim representative council, and subsequently an elected representative council, foreseen in the special autonomy proposal, would also be highly desirable if autonomy is rejected. It would be highly desirable if this body could be established before or immediately following the ballot. The United Nations will also liaise with and advise the Indonesian authorities and maintain close contact with pro-integration and pro-independence groups. Again, these tasks would be the same under either ballot outcome. A further important task for the United Nations during the interim phase will be to prepare to adjust its role for the implementation of either option.

Restructuring of UNAMET

6. In order to accomplish these tasks, I wish to propose to the Council that UNAMET continue through the post-ballot period until the implementation phase of the result, and that its tasks and structure be adjusted in the manner described in the paragraphs below. One aim of these adjustments would be to ensure a United Nations presence in all 13 regencies (districts) of East Timor.

Electoral component

7. As the United Nations Volunteers serving as district electoral officers will have completed their task of conducting the ballot process, the majority of them will be withdrawn, although a portion, those with requisite skills and background to fulfil other tasks outlined herein, may be retained in order that the Mission may continue to draw upon their expertise and experience in East Timor. The electoral component itself would be temporarily reduced to a unit that would plan and prepare for the monitoring of the election of the Regional Council which is foreseen in the autonomy plan or for elections that will take place if autonomy is rejected. The unit will also assist in developing an appropriate legal framework, institutions and technical capacity for elections in either scenario.

Civilian police component

8. The police component would be increased to 410 to enable it to operate in all 13 regencies (districts). It would continue to advise the Indonesian police. It would be augmented by a small team to prepare for the recruitment and training of a new East Timorese police force, a requirement in both scenarios. The training personnel would eventually number about 50, bringing the overall strength of the police component to close to 460.

Military component

http://www.un.org/peace/etimor/9923160e.htm

APA, *Electronic Styles*
United Nations. Secretary General. *The question of East Timor*, report of the Secretary General (9 August 1999) [On-line]. Available : http://www.un.org/peace/etimor /9923160e.html [1999, September 21]

Garner and Smith
United Nations. Secretary General. "The question of East Timor," 9 August 1999 (S/1999/862). Text on United Nations Web site, Document No. 9923160e.html. Referenced: 9/21/99, 11:10 a.m. EDT. Internet address: http://www.un.org/peace/etimor/9923160e.html

Walker and Taylor, *The Columbia Guide*
Humanities Style
United Nations. Secretary General. " The question of East Timor," 9 August 1999. http://www.un.org/peace/etimor/9923160E.html (21 Sept. 1999)

Scientific Style
United Nations. Secretary General. (9 August 1999). " The question of East Timor." http://www.un.org/peace/etimor/9923160E.html (21 Sept. 1999)

Figure 12.10. IGO Material in Tangible Electronic Medium.

ST/ESA/STAT/SER.K/10

Department of Economic and Social Development
Statistical Division
Social Statistics and Indicators   Series K No. 10

Wistat
Women's Indicators
and Statistics Spreadsheet Database
for Microcomputers (Version 2)

Users Guide and Reference Manual

United Nations
New York, 1992

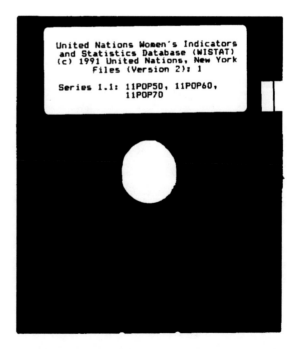

Garner and Smith

United Nations. Statistical Office. *United Nations Women's Indicators and Statistics Microcomputer Database: WISTAT* (Serial no. 001-2.0-01093) (Floppy disk). Version 2. New York, 1991. (Contains 84 data files and 9 reference files in Lotus spreadsheet format, file size ranges from 20 KB to 150KB; 7 disks; accompanied by: *User's Guide*, 183 pp.; UN/ST/ESA/WISTAT/ver.2).

Electronic Styles

United Nations. Statistical Office. (1991) *United Nations Women's Indicators and Statistics Microcomputer Database: WISTAT* (Version 2), [diskette]. Available: UN, New York: UN/ST/ESA/WISTAT/ver.2).

The examples of availability statements used in *Electronic Styles* do not fit the resource being cited here. The author has freely interpreted the manual's frequent admonition to give information sufficient for retrieval.

Appendix— Manuals Consulted

American National Standards Institute, *American National Standard for Bibliographic References*. New York: ANSI, 1977. ANSI Z39.29-1977.

Fleischer, Eugene B. *A Style Manual for Citing Microform and Nonprint Media*, 1st ed. Chicago: American Library Association, 1978.

Garner, Diane, Diane Smith, Debora Cheney, and Helen Sheehy. *The Complete Guide to Citing Government Information Resources*. Rev. ed. Bethesda, MD: Congressional Information Service, 1993.

Gibaldi, Joseph. *MLA Handbook for Writers of Research Papers, Theses and Dissertations*. 5th ed. New York: Modern Language Association, 1999, 143–45, 178–202.

"International Materials," *The Bluebook: A Uniform System of Citation*, 16th ed. Cambridge, MA: Harvard Law Review Association, 1996, 138–63.

ISO 690-1975: Documentation, Bibliographical References, Essential and Supplementary Elements," in *Information Transfer, Handbook on International Standards Governing Information Transfer: Texts of ISO Standards*, 1st ed., ISO Standards Handbook 1. Geneva: International Organization for Standardization, 1977, 29–36.

ISO 690-2: *Information and Documentation, Bibliographic Reference, Part 2, Electronic Documents or parts thereof.* 1st ed., Geneva: International Organization for Standardization, 1997.

Li, Xia, and Nancy B. Crane. *Electronic Styles: A Handbook for Citing Electronic Information*. 2d edition. Medford, NJ: Information Today, 1996.

"Public Documents," *The Chicago Manual of Style*, 14th ed. Chicago: University of Chicago Press, 1993, 602–28.

Publication Manual of the American Psychological Association, 4th ed. Washington, DC: American Psychological Association, 1994, 168–234.

Rothman, Marie H. *Citation Rules and Forms for United Nations Documents and Publications*. Brooklyn, NY: Long Island University Press, 1971.

Turabian, Kate L. " Documents of International Bodies," *A Manual for Writers of Term Papers, Theses, and Dissertations*, 6th ed., rev. by John Grossman and Alice Bennett. Chicago: University of Chicago Press, 1996, 237–38.

United Nations, Dag Hammarskjöld Library, *Bibliographical Style Manual* New York: UN, 1963. ST/LIB/SER.B/18.

United Nations, Dag Hammarskjöld Library, *UNBIS Reference Manual Bibliographic Description.* New York: UN, 1985.

United Nations, Department of Conference Services, "Article E3: Footnotes and Other References," *United Nations Editorial Manual.* New York: UN, 1983, 212–90. ST/DCS/2.

United States, Library of Congress, Reference Department, "Documents," in *Bibliographic Procedures and Style*, by Blanche Prichard McCrum and Helen Dudenbostel Jones. Washington, DC: Government Printing Office, 1954, 67–80.

Walker, Janice R., and Todd Taylor. *The Columbia Guide to Online Style.* New York: Columbia University Press, 1998.

Notes and References

1. "Public Documents," *The Chicago Manual of Style*, 14th ed. Chicago: University of Chicago Press, 1993, 602–28; Joseph Gibaldi, *MLA Handbook for Writers of Research Papers, Theses and Dissertations.* 5th ed. New York: Modern Language Association, 1999, 143–45 and 178–202; *Publication Manual of the American Psychological Association*, 4th ed. Washington, DC: American Psychological Association, 1994, 168–234; "International Materials," *The Bluebook: A Uniform System of Citation*, 16th ed. Cambridge, MA: Harvard Law Review Association, 1996, 138–63.

2. *Anglo-American Cataloging Rules.* 2d ed. Chicago: American Library Association, 1978, 288–91.

3. *Bluebook*, 161.

4. The latest review column appeared as Sue Stigleman, "Bibliography formatting software: an updated buying guide," *Database* 17 (February 1994): 53–65. There was also a later article, Sue Stigleman, "Bibliography programs do Windows," *Database* 19 (April/May 1996): 57–66.

5. The issues of archiving electronic resources and the reliability of texts are too complex to be discussed here. Suffice it to say that the responsibilities for ensuring that electronic texts are archived in usable formats for the future and for maintaining an authoritative text are yet to be settled.

6. This citation is taken from *Electronic Styles*, 74.

7. This citation is taken from Garner and Smith, 162.

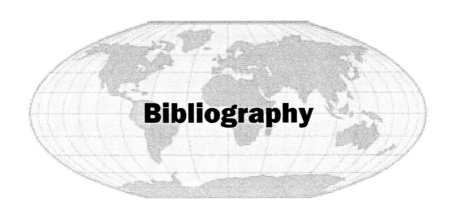

Bibliography

*Compiled by Peter I. Hajnal
and Gillian R. Clinton*

Advisory Committee for the Co-ordination of Information Systems. *Management of Electronic Records: Issues and Guidelines*. New York: United Nations, 1990.

Advisory Committee for the Co-ordination of Information Systems. *Register of Development Activities of the United Nations System*. 1988– . New York: United Nations.

Advisory Committee for the Co-ordination of Information Systems. *Strategic Issues for Electronic Records Management: Towards Open Systems Interconnection*. New York: United Nations, 1992.

"After Seattle: A Global Disaster" *The Economist* 353, no. 8149; 11 December 1999: 19–20.

Agence de la Francophonie. *Echoweb du CIFTI*. <http://cifdi.francophonie.org/Echow/> (June 25, 2000).

Agence de la Francophonie. *Liaison Francophone*. <www.francophonie.org/liaison/> (June 25, 2000).

Agence universitaire de la Francophonie. *Cahiers Sécheresse*. 1990– . <www.aupelf-uref.org/revues/sech/sommfm.htm> (June 25, 2000).

Ager, Dennis. *Francophonie in the 1990s: Problems and Opportunities*. Clevedon, UK: Multilingual Matters, 1996.

Alger, Chadwick F. *The Future of the United Nations System: Potential for the Twenty-First Century.* New York: United Nations University Press, 1998. E.98.II.A.4.

Alger, Chadwick F. "The United Nations System and Civil Society." Paper presented at the International Studies Association Convention, Washington, DC, February 1999.

American Historical Association. Committee for the Study of War Documents. *Catalogue of Files and Microfilms of the German Foreign Ministry Archives 1867–1920.* Oxford, 1959.

American Historical Association. Committee for the Study of War Documents. *Catalog of Files and Microfilms of the German Foreign Ministry Archives 1920–1945.* A joint project of the U.S. Department of State and the Hoover Institution on War, Revolution, and Peace. Stanford, CA, 1962–1966. 3 vols.

Anglo-American Cataloging Rules. 2d ed. Chicago: American Library Association, 1978.

"Archives of International Organizations and History of International Relations." In Commission of History of International Relations. *Newsletter.* 7–8.

Archivum: International Review on Archives. Vol. XLI. München and New Providence, 1996.

Assemblée internationale des parlementaires de langue française. *Parlements et Francophonie.* 1985– . Paris: AIPLF. Continues *Revue des parlementaires de langue française.*

Assemblée parlementaire de la Francophonie. *La Lettre de l'Assemblée parlementaire de la Francophonie.* 1996– . <www.francophonie.org/aiplf/> (June 25, 2000).

Assemblée parlementaire de la Francophonie. *Parlons Doc.* <www.francophonie.org/aiplf/parlons.html> (June 25, 2000).

Association des Universités Partiellement ou Entièrement de Langue Française. *Universités.* 1980– . Montréal: AUPELF. Formed by the merger of: *Bulletin de nouvelles brèves*; *Études françaises dans le monde*, and *Nouvelles universitaires africaines.*

Bailey, Sydney Dawson. *The Procedure of the UN Security Council.* 3d ed. Oxford; New York: Clarendon Press, 1998.

Barrat, Jacques. *Géopolitique de la Francophonie*. Paris: Presses Universitaires de France, 1997.

Basefsky, Stuart. "Cornell Mirrors ILO & ICJ—Two International Web Mirror Sites." 21 October 1999. <GOVDOC–L@lists.psu.edu>.

Bassiouni, M. Cherif, and Eduardo Vetere, eds. *Organized Crime: A Compilation of U.N. Documents 1975–1998.* Ardsley, NY: Transnational Publishers, Inc., 1998.

Bauer, George W. *International Organizations, 1918–1945: A Guide to Research and Research Materials*. Rev. ed. Wilmington, DE: Scholarly Resources, 1991.

Beigbeder, Yves. *The World Health Organization*. The Hague, Boston: M. Nijhoff, 1998.

Biggs, David. *Informal, Ad Hoc Collaboration Between the UN and the NGOs in the Field of Early Warning*. July, 1995. Unpublished.

Black, Maggie. *A Cause for Our Times: Oxfam, the First 50 Years*. Oxford: Oxfam and Oxford University Press, 1992.

The Bluebook: A Uniform System of Citation. 16th ed. Cambridge, MA: Harvard Law Review Association, 1996.

Boli, John, and George M. Thomas, eds. *Constructing World Culture: International Nongovernmental Organizations Since 1875.* Stanford: Stanford University Press, 1999.

Bostock, William F. *Francophonie: Organisation, Coordination, Evaluation*. Melbourne, Australia: River Seine, 1986.

Boutros–Ghali, Boutros. *Unvanquished: A U.S.–U.N. Saga*. New York: Random House, 1999.

Brauman, Rony. "The Médecins Sans Frontières Experience." In *A Framework for Survival*, edited by Kevin M. Cahill. [s.l.:] Basic Books and the Council on Foreign Relations, 1991: 202–20.

Brooke, James. "A Meeting of Francophones, with Insults in Plain English." *New York Times* (4 September 1999): A6 [National].

Bull, Odd. *War and Peace in the Middle East: The Experiences and Views of a U.N. Observer*. London: L. Cooper, 1976.

Burns, E. L. M. *Between Arab and Israeli*. Toronto: Clarke, Irwin, 1962.

Caiola, Marcello. *A Manual for Country Economists*. Washington, DC: IMF, 1995.

Canada. Department of External Affairs. *Overview: Canada and la Francophonie*. Ottawa: DEA, 1998.

Canada. Directorate of Geomatics. Department of National Defence. *The Digital Geographic Information Exchange Standard (DIGEST), Part 1, General Description*. Ottawa: DND, 1992.

Caring for the Earth: A Strategy for Sustainable Living. David A. Munro, project director. Gland, Switzerland: IUCN; UNEP; WWF, 1991.

Chadwyck-Healey, Charles. "The Future of Microform in an Electronic Age." *Wilson Library Bulletin* 58 (December 1983): 270–73.

Charlesworth, Bernard. "The Need for Modernization in Production, Editing and Distribution of IGO Documentation." In *Sources, Organization, Utilization of International Documentation; Proceedings of the International Symposium on the Documentation of the United Nations and Other Intergovernmental Organizations, Geneva, 1972*, 263–67. The Hague: International Federation for Documentation, 1974. FID Publication no. 506.

Charlish, Geoffrey. "Microfilm Fights for a Future." *The Financial Times* (London) (11 September 1984): 12.

Cherns, J. J. *Official Publishing: An Overview; An International Survey and Review of the Role, Organisation and Principles of Official Publishing*. Oxford: Pergamon, 1979.

The Chicago Manual of Style. 14th ed. Chicago: University of Chicago Press, 1993.

Childers, Erskine with Brian Urquhart. *Renewing the United Nations System*. Uppsala, Sweden: Dag Hammarskjöld Foundation, 1994. Development Dialogue 1994:1.

"Click If You Want to Fight World Hunger." *Star Ledger*. [Newark, NJ] (2 October 1999): 2.

CNN.com. <www.cnn.com> (June 3, 2000).

Commission on Global Governance. *The Millennium Year and the Reform Process: A Contribution from the Commission on Global Governance*. London: Commission on Global Governance, 1999.

Commission on Global Governance. *Our Global Neighbourhood: The Report of the Commission on Global Governance.* Oxford; New York: Oxford University Press, 1995.

Congressional Information Service. *Index to International Statistics.* 1983– . Washington, DC: CIS. Also available on computer file.

Congressional Information Service. *Statistical Universe.* 1997– . Bethesda, MD: CIS. Computer file.

Cook, Michael. *The Management of Information from Archives.* Aldershot: Gower, 1986.

Cordier, Andrew Wellington, and Wilder Foote, eds. *Public Papers of the Secretaries-General of the United Nations.* 8 vols. New York: Columbia University Press, 1969–1977.

Cox, Richard J. "Access in the Digital Information Age and the Archival Mission: The United States." *Journal of the Society of Archivists* 19, no. 1 (1998): 25–40.

Daley, Suzanne. "More and More, Europeans Find Fault with the U.S." *New York Times* (9 April 2000): A1, A8 [National].

Dayal, Rajeshwar. *Mission for Hammarskjöld: The Congo Crisis.* Princeton, NJ: Princeton University Press, 1976.

Dear United Nations . . . : How to Order UN Publications, Where to Find "Freebees," What Is on the Internet. New York: UN, Department of Public Information, 1997. DPI/1887.

Defining and Certifying Electronic Publication in Science: A Proposal to the International Association of STM Publishers. Frankfurt: AAAS/ACSU Press, 1999.

Detlefsen, Ellen. "User Costs: Information as a Social Good vs. Information as a Commodity." *Government Publications Review* 11 (September/October 1984): 385–94.

Development in Practice. Vol. 1– , 1991– . Oxford: Carfax Publishing on behalf of Oxfam GB.

Dictionary of Archival Terminology. 2d rev. ed. Munich and New Providence: K. G. Saur, 1988. ICA Handbook Series, Vol. 7.

Dijk, P. van, and G. J. H. van Hoof. *Theory and Practice of the European Convention on Human Rights.* 3d ed. The Hague; Boston: Kluwer Law International, 1998.

Dimitrov, Theodore D. *Documents of International Organisations: A Bibliographic Handbook.* London and Chicago: International University Publications/American Library Association, 1973.

Diplomatic World Bulletin and Delegates World Bulletin. 1975– . New York: Diplomatic World Bulletin Publications. Continues *Diplomatic World Bulletin.* 1970–1974; *Delegates World Bulletin* 1970–1974.

Dodson, Suzanne C. "Microfilm Types: There Really Is a Choice." *Library Resources & Technical Services* 30 (January/March 1986): 84–90.

Dollar, Charles M. *Electronic Records Management and Archives in International Organizations: A RAMP Study with Guidelines.* Paris: Unesco, 1986. PGI.86/WS/12.

Driscoll, David D. *What Is the International Monetary Fund?* Washington, DC: IMF, 1998.

Dupont, Jerry. "Microform Film Stock: A Hobson's Choice; Are Librarians Getting the Worst of Both Worlds?" *Library Resources & Technical Services* 30 (January/March 1986): 79–83.

Duranti, Luciana. "The Thinking of Appraisal of Electronic Records: Its Evolution, Focuses, and Future Directions." *Janus: Archival Review* 2 (1997): 47–67.

Dymond, William A. "The MAI: A Sad and Melancholy Tale." In *Canada Among Nations 1999: A Big League Player?* Edited by Fen Osler Hampson, Martin Rudner, and Michael Hart, 25–53. Toronto: Oxford University Press, 1999.

Eade, Deborah, and Suzanne Williams. *The Oxfam Handbook of Development and Relief.* Oxford: Oxfam, 1995. 3 vols.

Erlandsson, Alf. *Electronic Records Management: A Literature Review.* Ottawa: The Committee of Electronic Records, 1996. On CD-ROM.

Erskine, E.A. *Mission with UNIFIL: An African Soldier's Reflections.* New York: St. Martin's Press, 1992.

The Europa Directory of International Organizations 1st ed– , 1999– . London: Europa Publications.

European Commission. *Access to Commission Documents: A Citizen's Guide.* Luxembourg: Office for Official Publications of the European Communities, 1997.

European Commission. Secretariat General. *Archives in the European Union: Report of the Group of Experts on the Coordination of Archives.* Luxembourg: EC, Secretariat General, 1994.

European Commission. Secretariat General. *Guide to the Archives of the Ministries of Foreign Affairs of the Member States of the European Communities and the European Political Cooperation.* Luxembourg: Office for Official Publications of the European Communities, 1989.

European Communities. Office for Official Publications. *Catalogue of EUR Documents, 1968–1979.* Luxembourg: EC, 1983.

European Communities. Office for Official Publications. *Catalogue [of] EUR Documents, 1980–1982.* Luxembourg: EC, 1985.

European Communities. Office for Official Publications. *Official Journal of the European Communities.* 1952– . Luxembourg: EC. Continues *Journal officiel de la Communauté européenne du charbon et de l'acier* (1952–1958); and *Journal officiel des Communautés européennes* (1958–1972). Four parts: *Legislation-L Series*; *Communications-C Series*; *Annex-Debates*; and *Supplement-S Series.* The *L* and *C* Series and *Annex* are available on microfiche.

European Ombudsman. *Annual Report.* 1995– . Luxembourg: Office for Official Publications of the European Communities.

Eyffinger, Arthur, ed. *The International Court of Justice, 1946–1996.* The Hague and Boston: Kluwer Law International, 1996.

Falk, Richard. *Predatory Globalization: A Critique.* London: Blackwell/Polity Press, 1999.

Falk, Richard, and Andrew Strauss. "On the Creation of a Global Peoples Assembly: Legitimacy and the Power of Popular Sovereignty." *Stanford Journal of International Law* 36, no. 2 (Summer 2000, forthcoming).

Fetzer, Mary K. "Micropublishing Activities for United Nations and Specialized Agency Documentation: Status and Comment." *Government Publications Review* 7A, no. 5 (1980): 423–28.

Fleischer, Eugene B. *A Style Manual for Citing Microform and Nonprint Media.* Chicago: American Library Association, 1978.

Fletcher, J. "International Comparative Statistics Produced by International Organizations." In *International Documents for the 80's: Their Role and Use*. Edited by Theodore D. Dimitrov and Luciana Marulli-Koenig, 32–47. Pleasantville, NY: UNIFO Publishers, 1982.

France. Haut Conseil de la Francophonie. *État de la francophonie dans le monde*. 1987– . Paris: Documentation Française. Continues *Rapport sur l'état de la francophonie dans le monde*.

Freeman, Alan. "The English Patience of France." *The Globe and Mail* (1 April 2000): A13.

Furstenberg, R. "Distribution and Acquisition of UN Documents." In *International Documents for the 80's: Their Role and Use*. Edited by Theodore D. Dimitrov and Luciana Marulli-Koenig, 63–68. Pleasantville, NY: UNIFO Publishers, 1982.

Garner, Diane L. *The Complete Guide to Citing Government Information Resources: A Manual for Writers & Librarians*. Rev. ed. by Diane L. Garner, Diane H. Smith, et al. Bethesda, MD: Congressional Information Service, c1993.

General Agreement on Tariffs and Trade. "Agreement on Government Procurement." *Basic Instruments and Selected Documents*. Supplement 26. 33–55. Geneva: GATT, 1980.

General Agreement on Tariffs and Trade. "Agreement on Implementation of Article VI of the General Agreement on Tariffs and Trade." *Basic Instruments and Selected Documents*. Supplement 26. 171–88. Geneva: GATT, 1980.

General Agreement on Tariffs and Trade. "Agreement on Implementation of Article VII of the General Agreement on Tariffs and Trade." *Basic Instruments and Selected Documents*. Supplement 26. 116–50. Geneva: GATT, 1980.

General Agreement on Tariffs and Trade. "Agreement on Import Licensing Procedures." *Basic Instruments and Selected Documents*. Supplement 26. 154–61. Geneva: GATT, 1980.

General Agreement on Tariffs and Trade. "Agreement on Interpretation and Application of Articles VI, XVI and XXIII of the General Agreement on Tariffs and Trade." *Basic Instruments and Selected Documents*. Supplement 26. 56–83. Geneva: GATT, 1980.

General Agreement on Tariffs and Trade. "Agreement on the Organization for Trade Cooperation." *Basic Instruments and Selected Documents*. Volume I (revised). 75–84. Geneva: GATT, 1955.

General Agreement on Tariffs and Trade. "Agreement on Trade in Civil Aircraft." *Basic Instruments and Selected Documents*. Supplement 26. 162–70. Geneva: GATT, 1980.

General Agreement on Tariffs and Trade. "Agreements on Technical Barriers to Trade." *Basic Instruments and Selected Documents*. Supplement 26. 8–32. Geneva: GATT, 1980.

General Agreement on Tariffs and Trade. *Analytical Index: Guide to GATT Law and Practice*. 6th ed. Geneva: GATT, 1994. ST/LEG/2.

General Agreement on Tariffs and Trade. *The Annecy Protocol of Terms of Accession*. Geneva: GATT, 1949.

General Agreement on Tariffs and Trade. *Basic Instruments and Selected Documents*. Vols. 1–4, 1952; 1st–supplement, 1953–1995. Geneva: Contracting Parties to the General Agreement on Tariffs and Trade.

General Agreement on Tariffs and Trade. "Central African Economic and Customs Union." *Summary Record of the Ninth Meeting*. Geneva: GATT, 1968: 176. SR.25/9.

General Agreement on Tariffs and Trade. "Consultative Group of Eighteen." *Basic Instruments and Selected Documents*. Supplement 22. 15–16. Geneva: GATT, 1976. L/4204.

General Agreement on Tariffs and Trade. "Consultative Group of Eighteen." *Basic Instruments and Selected Documents*. Supplement 26. 284–90. Geneva: GATT, 1980. L/4869.

General Agreement on Tariffs and Trade. "Dispute Settlement Procedures." *Basic Instruments and Selected Documents*. Supplement 31. 9–10. Geneva: GATT, 1985. L/5752.

General Agreement on Tariffs and Trade. *Final Act Embodying the Results of the Uruguay Round of Multilateral Trade Negotiations*. Geneva: GATT, 1994.

General Agreement on Tariffs and Trade. "Functioning of the GATT System." *Basic Instruments and Selected Documents*. Supplement 36. 403–6. Geneva: GATT, 1990. L/6490.

General Agreement on Tariffs and Trade. *GATT Activities in . . . 1970–1996*. Geneva: GATT.

362 / Bibliography

General Agreement on Tariffs and Trade. *GATT WTO News: From GATT to the World Trade Organization.* 1994– . Geneva: Information and Media Relations Division of the General Agreement on Tariffs and Trade. Continues *News of the Uruguay Round of Multilateral Trade Negotiations.*

General Agreement on Tariffs and Trade. *General Agreement on Tariffs and Trade, with Annexes and Schedules of Tariff Concessions.* Geneva: GATT, 1947. 4 vols.

General Agreement on Tariffs and Trade. *Geneva 1979 Protocol.* Geneva: GATT, 1979. 4 vols.

General Agreement on Tariffs and Trade. "Improvements to the GATT Dispute Settlement Rules and Procedures." *Basic Instruments and Selected Documents.* Supplement 36. 61–67. Geneva: GATT, 1990. L/6489.

General Agreement on Tariffs and Trade. *International Trade: Trends and Statistics.* 2 vols. 1994–1995. Continued by WTO *Annual Report.* (Continued *International Trade: Statistics.* 1991/92–1993. Continued *International Trade.* 1952–1990/91.) Geneva: GATT.

General Agreement on Tariffs and Trade. "Intersessional Procedures." *Basic Instruments and Selected Documents.* Supplement 3. 9–15. Geneva: GATT, 1955.

General Agreement on Tariffs and Trade. *List and Index of Documents.* Geneva: GATT, 1947–1996. Also available in microform.

General Agreement on Tariffs and Trade. "Mandate of Consultative Group of Eighteen." *Basic Instruments and Selected Documents.* Supplement 26. 289–90. Geneva: GATT, 1980. L/4869.

General Agreement on Tariffs and Trade. "Ministerial Declaration: Dispute Settlement Procedures." *Basic Instruments and Selected Documents.* Supplement 29. 13–16. Geneva: GATT, 1983.

General Agreement on Tariffs and Trade. "Organizational and Functional Questions." *Basic Instruments and Selected Documents.* Supplement 3. 231–52. Geneva: GATT, 1955. L/327.

General Agreement on Tariffs and Trade. "Procedures Under Article XXII on Questions Affecting the Interests of a Number of Contracting Parties." *Basic Instruments and Selected Documents.* Supplement 7. 24. Geneva: GATT, 1958.

General Agreement on Tariffs and Trade. "Procedures Under Article XXIII." *Basic Instruments and Selected Documents.* Supplement 14. 18–20. Geneva: GATT, 1980.

General Agreement on Tariffs and Trade. "Protocol to the Agreement on Implementation of Article VII of the General Agreement on Tariffs and Trade." *Basic Instruments and Selected Documents.* Supplement 26. 151–53. Geneva: GATT, 1980.

General Agreement on Tariffs and Trade. *Protocol to the General Agreement on Tariffs and Trade Embodying the Results of the 1960–61 Tariff Conference.* Geneva: GATT, 1962.

General Agreement on Tariffs and Trade. *The Results of the Uruguay Round of Multilateral Trade Negotiations: The Legal Texts.* Geneva: GATT, 1994.

General Agreement on Tariffs and Trade. "Rules of Procedures for Sessions of the Contracting Powers." *Basic Instruments and Selected Documents.* Supplement 9. 7–9. Geneva: GATT, 1961.

General Agreement on Tariffs and Trade. *Status of Legal Instruments.* 1971– . Geneva: GATT. ST/LEG/1.

General Agreement on Tariffs and Trade. *The Torquay Protocol and the Torquay Schedule of Tariff Concessions.* Geneva: GATT, 1951.

General Agreement on Tariffs and Trade. "Trade Policy Review Mechanism (TPRM)." *Basic Instruments and Selected Documents.* Supplement 36. 403–6. Geneva: GATT, 1990. L/6490.

General Agreement on Tariffs and Trade. "Understanding Regarding Notification, Consultation, Dispute Settlement and Surveillance." *Basic Instruments and Selected Documents.* Supplement 26. 210–18. Geneva: GATT, 1980. L/4907.

Gibaldi, Joseph. *MLA Handbook for Writers of Research Papers, Theses and Dissertation*s. 5th ed. New York: Modern Language Association, 1999.

Global Biodiversity Strategy: Guidelines for Action to Save, Study, and Use Earth's Biotic Wealth Sustainably and Equitably. [Washington, DC]: World Resources Institute; IUCN; UNEP, 1992.

Global Governance: A Review of Multilateralism and International Organizations. Vol. 1– , no. 1, Winter 1995– . Boulder, CO: Lynn Rienner Publishers.

Gorman, Robert F. *Historical Dictionary of Refugee and Disaster Relief Organizations.* Metuchen, NJ: Scarecrow Press, 1994.

Guide to the Historical Archives of the European Communities. 4th ed. Florence: European University Institute, 1993.

Guptil, Marilla B. *Archival Appraisal of Records of International Organizations: A RAMP Study, with Guidelines = Evaluation et tri des documents d'archives dans les organisations internationales: une étude RAMP, accompagnée de principes directeurs.* Paris: Unesco, 1985. PGI.85/WS/4.

Haden, J. W. "Some Previous Attempts at Organizing International Documentation." In *Sources, Organization, Utilization of International Documentation; Proceedings of the International Symposium on the Documentation of the United Nations and Other Intergovernmental Organizations, Geneva, 1972,* 271–74. The Hague: International Federation for Documentation, 1974. FID Publication no. 506.

Hajnal, Peter I. *Guide to Unesco.* London, Rome and New York: Oceana, 1983.

Hajnal, Peter I. *Guide to United Nations Organization, Documentation and Publishing for Students, Researchers, Librarians.* Dobbs Ferry, NY: Oceana, 1978.

Hajnal, Peter I., ed. *International Information: Documents, Publications, and Electronic Information of International Government Organizations.* 2d ed. Englewood, CO: Libraries Unlimited, 1997.

Hajnal, Peter I. "A Review of 'Psychological Operations in Guerrilla Warfare.' " *Government Information Quarterly* 2, no. 3 (1985): 330–32.

Hamilton, Janice. *Canada in Action: The Commonwealth, La Francophonie.* Rupert J. Taylor, ed. Waterloo, ON: R/L Publishing Consultants, 1994.

Harbottle, Michael. *The Blue Berets.* London: Leo Cooper, 1975.

Harbottle, Michael. *The Impartial Soldier.* London: Oxford University Press, 1970.

Harden, Blaine. "United Nations Sees Violation of a Diamond Ban by Angola Rebels." *New York Times* (11 March 2000): A1, A4 [National].

Harper, Richard H. R. *Inside the IMF: An Ethnography of Documents, Technology and Organisational Action.* London: Academic Press, 1998.

Harvey, Claire. "Une université populaire: L'université virtuelle francophone manque déjà de fonds." *Le Devoir* (28 August 1999): E10.

Hébert, Michel. "Air France scandalise Louise Beaudoin." *Le Devoir* (29 March 2000): A2.

Hermann, Armin, Lanfranco Belloni, and John Krige. *History of CERN*. 3 vols. Amsterdam; New York: North–Holland Physics Publishers, 1987–1996.

Hinds, Thomas S. "The United Nations as a Publisher." *Government Publications Review* 12 (July/August 1985): 297–303.

Holborn, Louise. *The International Refugee Organization: A Specialized Agency of the United Nations, Its History and Work, 1946–1952*. London: Oxford University Press, 1956.

Holborn, Louise. *Refugees: A Problem of Our Time. The Work of the United Nations High Commissioner for Refugees, 1951–1972*, 2 vols. Metuchen, NJ: Scarecrow Press, 1975.

Holdgate, Martin. *The Green Web: A Union for World Conservation*. London: IUCN; Earthscan Publications, 1999.

Hudec, Robert. *Enforcing International Trade Law: The Evolution of the GATT Legal System*. Salem, NH: Butterworths, 1993.

Human Rights Watch. *Human Rights Watch Calls for Further Investigation of Role of France and Others in Re-Arming of Former Rwandan Government Forces*. Press Release of 22 March 1996. Original report by the Human Rights Watch is *Re-Arming with Impunity: International Support for the Perpetrators of the Rwandan Genocide*. Washington, DC: Human Rights Watch, 1995.

Ignatieff, George. (Former Canadian Ambassador to the United Nations.) Personal communication to A. Walter Dorn.

Index to International Statistics. Vol. 1– , 1983– . Washington, DC: Congressional Information Service.

International Bank for Reconstruction and Development. *Report on the Cost-Effectiveness Review*. Washington, DC: IBRD, 1997.

International Civil Aviation Organization. *Aeronautical Chart Catalogue*. 28th ed. Montreal: ICAO, 1993. Doc. 7101.

International Civil Aviation Organization. *Aeronautical Chart Manual*. 2d ed. Montreal: ICAO, 1987. Doc. 8697.

International Civil Aviation Organization. *Aeronautical Charts*. Montreal: ICAO, 1990. 136 audio–slides. ICAO Order no. S690.

International Civil Aviation Organization. *Aeronautical Information Services Manual*. 5th ed. Montreal: ICAO, 1995. Doc. 8126.

International Civil Aviation Organization. *Convention on International Civil Aviation*, signed at Chicago on 7 December 1944 and amended by the ICAO Assembly. Montreal: ICAO, 1944. Doc. 7300.

International Civil Aviation Organization. *Convention on International Civil Aviation, Annex 4—Aeronautical Charts*. 9th ed. Montreal: ICAO, 1995.

International Civil Aviation Organization. *Convention on International Civil Aviation, Annex 15—Aeronautical Information Services*. 10th ed. Montreal: ICAO, 1997.

International Civil Aviation Organization. *World Geodetic System—1984 (WGS–84)*. Montreal: ICAO, 1997. Doc. 9674.

International Colloquium. *Archives and History of International Organizations*. Rome: 1998. Unpublished.

International Congress on Universal Availability of Publications, Paris, 1982. *Main Working Document*. Paris: Unesco, 22 March 1982. PGI–82/UAP/2; PGI–82/CONF.401/COL.2.

International Council on Archives. *International Directory of Archives = Annuaire international des archives* 38 (1992). New York, London and Paris: Saur. Series: *Archivum: International Review on Archives*, by the International Council on Archives with the financial aid of Unesco.

International Council on Archives. *ISAAR(CPF): International Standard Archival Authority Record for Corporate Bodies, Persons and Families*. Ottawa: ICA, 1994.

International Council on Archives. *ISAD(G): General International Standard Archival Description*. Ottawa: ICA, 1994.

International Council on Archives. "Managing Digital Documents: Technological Challenges and Institutional Responses." By Tora K. Bikson. *Actes*. Stockholm (1998): 35–50.

International Council on Archives. "Status of Archives of Organizations in Regional Systems." By Jean Marie Palayret. In *Proceedings of the Thirty First International Conference of the Round Table on Archives*. Washington, DC: ICA, 1995: 189–200.

International Council on Archives. "Status of Records of the United Nations System." By Liisa Fagerlund. In *Proceedings of the Thirty First International Conference of the Round Table on Archives*. Washington, DC: ICA, 1995: 180–88.

International Council on Archives. Committee on Electronic Records. *Electronic Records Programs, Report on the 1994/95 Survey*. Studies 9. Paris: ICA, 1996.

International Council on Archives. Committee on Electronic Records. *Guide for Managing Electronic Records from an Archival Point of View*. Studies 8. Paris: ICA, 1997.

International Council on Archives. Section of Archivists of International Organizations. *Handbook and Directory*. 5th ed. 1998. Also available at <www.ica.org>.

The International Criminal Court Monitor. Issue 1, July/August 1996– . New York: NGO Coalition for an International Criminal Court.

International Institute for Intellectual Co–operation. *Relations with the Government of Chili, 1925–1945*. IICI file A I 83, microfiche 89 IICI 0013. 2 fiches.

International Labour Office. *Bibliography of Published Research of the World Employment Programme*. 5th ed. Geneva: ILO, 1984.

International Monetary Fund. *Annual Report of the Executive Board*. 1946/47– . Washington, DC: IMF.

International Monetary Fund. *Articles of Agreement of the International Monetary Fund*. Washington, DC: IMF, 1993.

International Monetary Fund. *Balance of Payments Manual*. 5th ed. Washington, DC: IMF, 1993.

International Monetary Fund. *Direction of Trade Statistics Quarterly*. 1994– . Washington, DC: IMF.

International Monetary Fund. *Direction of Trade Statistics Yearbook*. 1981– . Washington, DC: IMF.

International Monetary Fund. *Finance and Development*. 1968– . Washington, DC: IMF. Continues *Fund and Bank Review*. 1964–1968. Also available at <www.imf.org/external/pubs/ft/fandd/fda.htm> (June 25, 2000).

International Monetary Fund. *IMF Glossary*. English, French, Arabic. Washington, DC: IMF, 1996.

International Monetary Fund. *IMF Glossary*. English, French, Russian. Washington, DC: IMF, 1998.

International Monetary Fund. *IMF Glossary*. 5th ed. English, French, Spanish. Washington, DC: IMF, 1997.

International Monetary Fund. *IMF Survey* 1– , 1972. Washington, DC: IMF.

International Monetary Fund. *International Financial Statistics*. Vol. 1– , 1948– . Washington, DC: IMF. Also available on CD-ROM, 1991?– .

International Monetary Fund. *The International Monetary Fund, 1972–1978: Cooperation on Trial*. By Margaret Garritsen de Vries. Washington, DC: IMF, 1985. 3 vols.

International Monetary Fund. *Selected Decisions and Selected Documents of the International Monetary Fund*. 1962– . Washington, DC: IMF.

International Monetary Fund. *Summary Proceedings of the Annual Meeting of the Board of Governors*. 1946– . Washington, DC: IMF. From the Fiftieth Meeting report also available at <www.imf.org/external/pubs/ft/summary/sum50.htm> (June 27, 2000).

International Monetary Fund. *World Economic Outlook: A Survey by the Staff of the International Monetary Fund*. 1980– . Washington, DC: IMF. World Economic and Financial Surveys.

International Monetary Fund. Balance of Payments Division. *Balance of Payments Statistics Yearbook*. 1981– . Washington, DC: IMF.

International Monetary Fund. Government Finance Statistics Division. *Government Finance Statistics Yearbook*. 1977– . Washington, DC: IMF.

IUCN Membership Directory. 19??– . Gland, Switzerland: IUCN.

IUCN Publications 1948–1998: A Catalogue of Publications Produced by IUCN—the World Conservation Union or in Collaboration with Other Organizations or Publishers. 3rd and 50th anniversary ed. Compiled by Kevin Grose and Cécile Thiéry. Gland, Switzerland: IUCN, 1998.

IUCN Reports, 1960–1995, Including an Appendix on IUCN Periodicals. 1st ed. Compiled by Cécile Thiéry. Gland, Switzerland: IUCN, 1996.

IUCN. *Annual Report*. 1961– . Gland, Switzerland: IUCN. Earlier titles: *IUCN Yearbook: Annual Report of the International Union for Conservation of Nature and Natural Resources*; *Annual Report by the Director General*.

IUCN. *A Pocket Guide to IUCN, the World Conservation Union, 1996/1997*. Gland, Switzerland: IUCN, 1997.

IUCN. *Statutes of 5 October 1948, Revised on 22 October 1996 (Including Rules of Procedure of the World Conservation Congress) and Regulations, Revised on 22 October 1996*. Gland, Switzerland: IUCN, 1997.

IUCN. *The World Conservation Bookstore [Catalogue], 1948–1998*. Cambridge, UK: IUCN Publications Services Unit, 1998.

IUCN. Species Survival Commission. *IUCN Red List Categories*. Gland, Switzerland: IUCN, 1995.

IUCN. Species Survival Commission. *1996 IUCN Red List of Threatened Animals*. Edited by Jonathan Baillie and Brian Groombridge. Gland, Switzerland: IUCN; Washington, DC: Conservation International, 1996.

IUCN. Species Survival Commission. *1997 IUCN Red List of Threatened Plants*. Edited by Kerry S. Walter and Harriet J. Gillett. Gland, Switzerland: IUCN, 1998.

Jackson, John. *World Trade and the Law of GATT*. New York: Bobbs-Merrill, 1969.

Jeffries, John. *A Guide to the Official Publications of the European Communities*. 2d ed. London: Mansell, 1981.

Job, Roger. *Lettres Sans Frontières*. Bruxelles: Complexe, 1994.

Johnston, G. A. "The Archives of International Organizations, With Special Reference to the ILO." *Journal of the Society of Archivists* 4, no. 6 (October 1972): 506–20.

Joint Inspection Unit. *Publications Policy and Practice in the United Nations System*. Geneva: JIU, 1984. JIU/REP/84/5. Printed in United Nations, General Assembly, 39th sess., *Questions Relating to Information*. New York: UN, 1984. 14 May 1984. A/39/239.

Joint Inspection Unit. *Report on United Nations Documentation and on the Organisation of the Proceedings of the General Assembly and Its Main Bodies*. Geneva: JIU, 1971. JIU/REP/71/4. Printed in United Nations, General Assembly, 26th sess., *Pattern of Conferences*. New York: UN, 1971. 2 June 1971. A/8319.

Kono, Masamichi. *Opening Markets in Financial Services and the Role of the GATS*. Geneva: World Trade Organization, 1997.

LaFleur, Claude. "Brancher le Sud et joindre le Nord sur Internet: Art, culture, éducation ou législation lancés sur une inforoute francophone." *Le Devoir* (28 August 1999): E11.

Langley, Winston E. *Encyclopedia of Human Rights Issues Since 1945.* Westport, CT: Greenwood Press, 1999.

Le Devoir. 1910– . Montréal: Le Devoir, Inc.

Le Scouarnec, François–Pierre. *La Francophonie.* Montréal: Boréal, 1997.

League of Nations Documents and Publications, 1919–1946. New Haven, CT: Research Publications, 1971–1972. Microfilm set.

Leyton, Elliott, with photographs by Greg Locke. *Touched by Fire: Doctors Without Borders in a Third World Crisis.* Toronto: McClelland & Stewart, 1998.

Li, Xia, and Nancy B. Crane. *Electronic Styles: A Handbook for Citing Electronic Information.* 2d ed. Medford, NJ: Information Today, 1996.

Lie, Trygve. *In the Cause of Peace: Seven Years with the United Nations.* New York: Macmillan, 1954.

Lippincott, J. K., and J. F. Cheverie. "The 'Blur' of Federal Information and Services: Implications for University Libraries." *Journal of Government Information* 26, no.1 (1999): 25–31.

Loescher, Gil, and Ann D. Loescher. *The Global Refugee Crisis: A Reference Handbook.* Santa Barbara, CA and Oxford: ABC-CLIO, 1994.

Louis–Jacques, Lyonette, and Jeanne S. Korman, eds. *Introduction to International Organizations.* Sponsored by the American Association of Law Libraries at the Harvard University Law Library. Dobbs Ferry, NY: Oceana Publications, 1995.

"Mahatma Gandhi to the Director General of Unesco [Julian Huxley], May 25th, 1947" In *Human Rights, Comments and Interpretations: A Symposium.* Edited by Unesco with an introduction by Jacques Maritain, 18. London and New York: Wingate, [1949].

Mamère, Noël, and Olivier Warin. *Non Merci, Oncle Sam!* Paris: Ramsay, 1999.

Marulli-Koenig, Luciana. "The Dag Hammarskjöld Library and United Nations Microforms." *Microform Review* 9 (Fall 1980): 236–42.

Marulli-Koenig, Luciana. "Documentation of the United Nations System: Bibliographic Control and Coordination." In *International Documents for the 80's: Their Role and Use.* Edited by Theodore D. Dimitrov and Luciana Marulli-Koenig, 420–38. Pleasantville, NY: UNIFO Publishers, 1982.

Mason, Elisa. "Resolving Refugee Problems: An Introduction to the Executive Committee of the United Nations High Commissioner's Programme and Its Documentation." *Journal of Government Information* 27, no. 1 (January/February 2000): 1–11.

Mckiernan, Gerry. "E-journals with Integrated Multimedia." 28 October 1999. Personal communication to Mary Fetzer.

Médecins Sans Frontières. *Clinical Guidelines: Diagnostic and Treatment Manual*. 3rd ed. 1993.

Médecins Sans Frontières. *Essential Drugs: Practical Guidelines*. 1st ed. 1993.

Médecins Sans Frontières. *International Activity Report*. 1993– . Brussels.

Médecins Sans Frontières. *Living in a Minefield: An MSF Report on the Mine Problem in Afghanistan*. 1997.

Médecins Sans Frontières. *Minor Surgical Procedures in Remote Areas*. 1st ed. 1989.

Médecins Sans Frontières. *Nutrition Guidelines*. 1st ed. 1995.

Médecins Sans Frontières. *Obstétrique en situation d'isolement*. 1st ed. 1992.

Médecins Sans Frontières. *Populations in Danger 1995: A Médecins Sans Frontières Report*. Edited by François Jean. London: Médecins Sans Frontières UK, 1995.

Médecins Sans Frontières. *Public Health Engineering in Emergency Situations*. 1st ed. 1994.

Millennium Forum, New York, 22–26 May 2000. *We the Peoples: Millennium Forum Declaration and Agenda for Action*. New York, 26 May 2000.

Moorhouse, Frank. *Grand Days*. London: Picador, 1993.

Narasimhan, C. V. *The United Nations: An Inside View*. New Delhi: UNITAR, 1988.

Narasimhan, C. V. *The United Nations at 50: Recollections*. Delhi: Konark Publishers, 1996.

Nielson, Paul. "1999 G8 Summit Online: Open Registration." 26 May 1999. <INTL-DOC@listserv.acns.nwu.edu>.

"The Non-Governmental Order." *The Economist* 353, no. 8149; 11 December 1999: 20–21.

Office for Official Publications of the European Communities. 23 September 1983. Letter to the Library of Congress, Exchange and Gift Division.

Olson, Leanne. *A Cruel Paradise: Journals of an International Relief Worker.* Toronto: Insomniac Press, 1999.

Onishi, Norimitsu. "African Dictator Faces Trial Where He Once Took Refuge." *New York Times* (1 March 2000): A1, A3 [National].

Onishi, Norimitsu. "With Africa Watching, Senegal Casts Votes That Count." *New York Times* (27 February 2000): A3 [National].

Organization of American States. *Catálogo de Informes y Documentos Técnicos de la OEA; Suplemento.* Washington, DC: OAS, 1982.

Oxfam Great Britain. International Division. *Publications Strategy, 1996–2001.* Oxford: Oxfam GB, 1996.

Oxfam International. *Annual Report.* 1997– . Oxford.

Oxfam International. *Mission Statement.* <www.oxfam.org/about/mission.htm> (accessed 30 August 1999).

Oxfam International. *Programs/Fair Trade.* <www.oxfam.org/programs/fair_trade.htm> (accessed 30 August 1999).

Oxfam International. *Programs/Kosovo.* <www.oxfam.org/programs/kosovo.htm> (accessed 30 August 1999).

Palyret, Jean Marie and Ana Franqueira. *Guide to the Historical Archives of the European Communities.* 5th ed. Florence: European University Institute, 1998.

Paupst, James. "A Meditation on Evil." *Maclean's: Canada's Weekly Newsmagazine* 113, no. 27 (July 1, 2000): 54–56.

Pecoul, Bernard, Pierre Chirac, Patrice Trouiller, and Jacques Pinel. "Access to Essential Drugs in Poor Countries: A Lost Battle?" *Journal of the American Medical Association* 281, no. 4 (January 27, 1999): 361–67.

Pérez de Cuéllar, Javier. *Pilgrimage for Peace: A Secretary–General's Memoir.* New York: St. Martin's Press, 1997.

Philipp, Major General Hannes, (ret'd). Commander, United Nations Disengagement Observer Force (UNDOF), 1975–1979. Personal communication to A. Walter Dorn.

Picco, Giandomenico. *Man Without a Gun: One Diplomat's Secret Struggle to Free the Hostages, Fight Terrorism, and End a War.* New York: Times Books, 1999.

Publication Manual of the American Psychological Association. 4th ed. Washington, DC: American Psychological Association, 1994.

Rauchning, Dietrich, Katja Wiesbrock, and Martin Lailach, eds. *Key Resolutions of the United Nations General Assembly 1946–1996.* New York: Cambridge University Press, 1997.

Readex. *AccessUN.* 1997– . Chester, VT: NewsBank. Available on CD-ROM or internet.

Reclus, Onésime. *France, Algérie, et colonies.* Paris: Hachette, 1880.

Refugee Health: An Approach to Emergency Situations. Basingstoke, Hampshire, England: Macmillan, 1997.

Refugee Survey Quarterly. Vol. 13, no. 1– , 1994– . Oxford: Oxford University Press. Formerly *Refugee Abstracts*, OUP assumed publishing responsibilities with vol. 15, 1996.

Refugees. Vol. 1– (1982–). Geneva: UN High Commissioner for Refugees.

Rieff, David. "The Good Doctors: Humanitarianism at Century's End." *The New Republic* 221, no. 19 (November 8, 1999): 23.

Rikhye, General Indar Jit, (ret'd). Military Adviser to the Secretary-General, United Nations. Personal communication to A. Walter Dorn.

Rikhye, Indar Jit. *Military Adviser to the Secretary-General: United Nations Peace-keeping and the Congo Crisis.* London: St. Martin's Press, 1993.

Rikhye, Indar Jit. *The Sinai Blunder.* New Delhi: Oxford & IBH Publishing Co., 1978.

Rioux, Christian. "Une nouvelle agence au service de 160 millions de personnes: Le Sud ne fera plus les frais de la politique de "dumping" du Nord." *Le Devoir* (28 August 1999): E9.

Rioux, Christian. "Québec fait reculer Air France." *Le Devoir* (7 April 2000): A1, A10.

Rothman, Marie H. *Citation Rules and Forms for United Nations Documents and Publications*. Brooklyn, NY: Long Island University Press, 1971.

Schaaf, Robert W. "International Organizations Documentation: Resources and Services of the Library of Congress and Other Washington Based Agencies." *Government Information Quarterly* 1, no. 1 (1984): 59–73.

Séguin, Rhéal. "France not French Enough, PQ Says." *The Globe and Mail* (29 March 2000): A1, A9.

Sheehan, James M. *Global Greens: Inside the International Environmental Establishment*. Studies in Organization Trends, no. 12. [Washington, DC:] Capital Research Center, 1998.

Siilasvuo, Ensio. *In the Service of Peace in the Middle East, 1967–1979*. New York: St. Martin's Press, 1992.

Sjöberg, Tommie. *The Powers and the Persecuted: The Refugee Problem and the Intergovernmental Committee on Refugees (IGCR), 1938–1947*. Lund, Sweden: Lund University Press, 1991.

Skran, Claudena M. *The International Refugee Regime and the Refugee Problem in Interwar Europe*. Ph.D. diss., University of Oxford, 1989.

Smith, Peter (Jay), and Elizabeth Smythe. "Globalization, Citizenship and Technology: The MAI Meets the Internet." Paper presented at the annual meeting of the International Studies Association, Los Angeles, 17 March 2000.

Smith, Russell. "A Quiz Show about Grammar Would Be Inconceivable on English-language Television. But *Des Mots et des Maux* Reflects a Passion We Lack." *The Globe and Mail* (1 April 2000): R7.

Spiegel, Paul B., and Peter Salama, "War and Mortality in Kosovo, 1998-99: An Epidemiological Testimony," *The Lancet* 355, no. 9222 (24 June 2000).

Stibbe, Hugo. "Standardising Description: the Experience of Using ISAD(G)." *Janus: Archival Review* 1 (1998): 132–152.

Stigleman, Sue. "Bibliography Formatting Software: An Updated Buying Guide." *Database*. 17 (February 1994): 53–65.

Stigleman, Sue. "Bibliography Programs Do Windows." *Database*. 19 (April/May 1996): 57–66.

Sullivan, Robert C. "Microform Developments Related to Acquisitions." *Microform Review* 14 (Summer 1985): 164–70.

Tavares de Sá, Hernane. *The Play Within the Play: An Inside Story of the UN.* New York: Knopf, 1966.

Thant, U. *View from the United Nations.* Garden City, NY: Doubleday, 1978.

Thomas, Daniel H., and Lynn M. Case, eds. *New Guide to the Diplomatic Archives of Western Europe.* Philadelphia: University of Pennsylvania Press, 1975.

Transnational Social Movements and Global Politics: Solidarity Beyond the State. Edited by Jackie Smith, Charles Chatfield, and Ron Pagnucco. Syracuse Studies on Peace and Conflict Resolution. Syracuse, NY: Syracuse University Press, 1997.

Turabian, Kate L. *A Manual for Writers of Term Papers, Theses, and Dissertations.* 6th ed. Rev. by John Grossman and Alice Bennett. Chicago: University of Chicago Press, 1996.

UN21: Accelerating Managerial Reform for Results. New York: UN, 1997. E.97.I.10.

The UN at 50: Statements by World Leaders: New York, 22–24 October 1995. New York: United Nations, 1996.

UNBIS Plus on CD–ROM. Quarterly. 1979– . Cambridge: Chadwyck–Healey in cooperation with the United Nations, 1995–.

UNDiplomatic Times. 1999– . Teaneck, NJ; Impact Communications Consultants. Continues *International Documents Review.* 1990– .

Unesco. *Access to the Archives of United Nations Agencies: A RAMP Study with Guidelines.* Prepared by Bodil Ulate Segura. Paris: Unesco, 1987. PGI.86/WS/24.

Unesco. *A Chronology of Unesco, 1945–1987: Facts and Events in Unesco's History with References to Documentary Sources in the Unesco Archives and Supplementary Information in the Annexes 1–21.* Paris: Unesco, 1987. LAD.85/WS/4 Rev.

Unesco. *Conference of Allied Ministers of Education (CAME), London, 1942–1945: Index of Documents.* Paris: Unesco, 1990. ARC.90/WS/1.

Unesco. *Conference of Allied Ministers of Education (CAME), London: List of Documents and Correspondence Files, 1942–1945, With Index.* Paris: Unesco, 1980. PRS.80/WS/2.

Unesco. *Development of Records Management and Archives Services Within United Nations Agencies: A RAMP Study with Guidelines.* Prepared by Marie Charlotte Stark. Paris: Unesco, 1983. PGI.83/WS/26.

Unesco. *Guide to the Archives of Intergovernmental Organizations.* Paris: Unesco, 1999. CII.99/WS/2. Also available at <www.unesco.org/archives/guide/uk/sommaire2/html>.

Unesco. *Guide to the Archives of International Organizations, Part 1: The United Nations System.* Documentation, Libraries and Archives: Bibliographic and Reference Works, 8. Paris: Unesco, 1984. PGI.85/WS/18; PGI.85/WS/19. *Part 2: Archives of International Organizations and Their Former Officials in the Custody of National and Other Archival Manuscript Repositories.* Compiled by Peter Walne. Paris: Unesco, 1985. PGI.85/WS/18. *Part 3: Archives of Other International Intergovernmental Organizations and Non-governmental Organizations.* Compiled by A. W. Mabbs. Paris: Unesco, 1985. PGI.85/WS/19.

Unesco. *Inventaire des Archives de l'Institut international de coopération intellectuelle (IICI), 1925–1946: dossiers, documents et publications aux Archives de l'Unesco à Paris.* 2 vols. Paris: Unesco, 1990. UIS.90/WS/1.

Unesco. *List of Documents Issued by the Archives Service, 1947–1994, With Alphabetical Index.* Paris: Unesco, 1994. ARC.94/WS/3.

Unesco. *Organization of Unesco Secretariat since 1946.* Paris: Unesco, 1979. PRS.79/WS/47.

Unesco. *Publications de l'Institut international de coopération intellectuelle, 1945 = List of Publications of IICI, 1945.* Paris: Unesco, 1989. UIS.89/WS/5.

Unesco. *Relations des ambassadeurs vénitiens.* Paris: Unesco Collection of Representative Works, 1969.

Unesco. *A Short Guide to Unesco Archives = Guide des Archives de l'Unesco.* Paris: Unesco, 1993. ARC.93/WS/1.

Unesco. *Unesco Archives Finding Aids: List by Archive Groups (AG) with Index = Instruments de recherche des Archives de l'Unesco.* Paris: Unesco, 1991. ARC.91/WS/2.

Unesco. *Unesco Archives: A Short Guide.* 1998. <www.unesco.org/general/eng/infoserv/archives/archives.html> (8 May 2000).

Unesco. *Unesco Archives: List of Finding Aids on Microfiche: Inventories, Lists, Indexes Issued on Microfiche and/or Paper to Find References to and Trace Information From Unesco Records, Documents and Publications = Archives de l'Unesco: Liste des Instruments de recherche sur Microfiche et/ou sur papier pour trouver de références ou depister de l'information des archives, documents et publications de l'Unesco*. Paris: Unesco, 1991. ARC.91/WS/1.

Unesco. Computerized Documentation System. *Unesco List of Documents and Publications*. 1972– . Paris: Unesco.

Unesco. Executive Board. *Study of the Procedures Which Should be Followed in the Examination of Cases and Questions Which Might Be Submitted to Unesco Concerning the Exercises of Human Rights in the Spheres of Its Competence, in Order to Make Its Action More Effective: Report of the Working Party of the Executive Board Set Up in Pursuance of 120 EX/Dec. 5.6.2* Mar. 1978. 104th Session, 1978.

Unesco. General Information Programme and UNISIST. *Availability and Use of Official Publications in Libraries*, prepared by J. J. Cherns. Paris: Unesco, 1983. PGI–83/WS/30.

United Nations. *United Nations Documents and Publications*. 1982– . New Canaan, CT: Readex Microprint Corp. Continues *Documents and Official Publications in Microprint*.

United Nations. *United Nations Treaty Series*. 1947– . New York: UN.

United Nations. Administrative Committee on Co–ordination. Information Systems Co-ordination Committee. *Report of the Seventh Session of the ISCC*. New York: UN, 1999. ACC/1999/19.

United Nations. Archives Section. *Index to Microfilm of United Nations Documents in English, 1946–1961*. New York: UN, 1963. Archives Special Guide, no. 14.

United Nations. Archives Section. *Index to Microfilm of United Nations Documents in English: Supplement, 1962–1967*. New York: UN, 1970. Archives Special Guide, no. 14, Supplement no. 1.

United Nations Conference on Trade and Employment. *Final Act and Related Documents*. Havana: UN, 1948. ICITO/1/14 1948; E/Conf.2/78

United Nations. Dag Hammarskjöld Library. *Bibliographical Style Manual*. Bibliographical Series, no. 8. New York: UN, 1963. ST/LIB/SER.B/18; S/N 63.I.5.

United Nations. Dag Hammarskjöld Library. *Guide to the Archives of the League of Nations, 1919–1946*. Rev. ed. Geneva: UN, 1978. Publications, Series E: Guides and Studies, no. 2.

United Nations. Dag Hammarskjöld Library. *Reference Manual for Bibliographic Description*. New York: UN, 1985.

United Nations. Department of Conference Services. *United Nations Editorial Manual: A Compendium of Rules and Directives on United Nations Editorial Style, Publication Policies, Procedures, and Practice*. New York: UN, 1983.

United Nations. Department of Public Information. *Charter of the United Nations and Statute of the International Court of Justice*. New York: UN, 1989. DPI/511.

United Nations. Department of Public Information. *Secretary–General, Addressing Participants at Millennium Forum, Calls For Intensified 'NGO Revolution'*. Press Release SG/SM/7411; GA/9710. New York: UN, 22 May 2000.

United Nations. Department of Public Information. *Secretary-General Says 'Global People-power' Best Thing for United Nations in Long Time, Needing Response in Partnership with Civil Society*. Press Release SG/SM/7249/Rev.1. New York: UN, 7 December 1999.

United Nations. Department of Public Information. *UN Chronicle*. 1965– . New York: UN.

United Nations Development Programme. *Compendium of Approved Projects*. 1972– . New York: UNDP. UNDP/MIS/Series A 1972– .

United Nations. Economic and Social Council. *Establishment of the Executive Committee of the Programme of the United Nations High Commissioner for Refugees*. New York: UN, 1958. 30 April 1958. E/RES/672 (XXV).

United Nations. General Assembly. *Continuation of the Office of the United Nations High Commissioner for Refugees*. New York: UN, 1997. 12 December 1997. A/RES/52/104.

United Nations. General Assembly. *International Assistance to Refugees Within the Mandate of the United Nations High Commissioner for Refugees*. New York: UN, 1957. 26 November 1957. A/RES/1166 (XII).

United Nations. General Assembly. *Office of the United Nations High Commissioner for Refugees.* New York: UN, 1999. 12 February 1999. A/RES/53/125.

United Nations. General Assembly. *Publications Policy and Practice in the United Nations System; Comments of the Administrative Committee on Co-ordination.* New York: UN, 2 October 1984. A/39/239/Add.2.

United Nations. General Assembly. *Publications Policy and Practice in the United Nations System; Comments of the Secretary-General.* New York: UN, 7 August 1984. A/39/239/Add.1/.

United Nations. General Assembly. *Publications Policy and Practice in the United Nations System; Comments of the Secretary-General; Corrigendum.* New York: UN, 10 October 1984. A/39/239/Add.1/Corr.1.

United Nations. General Assembly. *Statute of the Office of the United Nations High Commissioner for Refugees.* New York: UN, 1950. 14 December 1950. A/RES/428 (V), Annex.

United Nations. General Assembly. *Universal Declaration of Human Rights.* New York: UN, 1949. Sales no.: 1949.I.3.

United Nations. General Assembly. Executive Committee of the High Commissioner's Programme. *Overview of UNHCR Activities: 1997–1999.* Geneva: UN, 1998. 17 August 1998, A/AC.96/900.

United Nations List of Protected Areas. 1st– ed., 1961/1962– . Gland, Switzerland: IUCN. Earlier titles: *United Nations List of National Parks and Equivalent Reserves*; *United Nations List of National Parks and Protected Areas.*

United Nations. Office for the Coordination of Humanitarian Affairs. *ReliefWeb.* <www.reliefweb.int> (3 June 2000).

United Nations. Office of the United Nations High Commissioner for Refugees. *Collection of International Instruments and Other Legal Texts Concerning Refugees and Displaced Persons*, 2 vols. Geneva: UNHCR, 1995.

United Nations. Office of the United Nations High Commissioner for Refugees. *Handbook – Voluntary Repatriation: International Protection.* Geneva: UNHCR, 1996.

United Nations. Office of the United Nations High Commissioner for Refugees. *International Thesaurus of Refugee Terminology*, 2nd ed. New York and Geneva: UN, 1996.

United Nations. Office of the United Nations High Commissioner for Refugees. *1999 Global Appeal.* Geneva: UNHCR, 1999.

United Nations. Office of the United Nations High Commissioner for Refugees. *Refugees and Others of Concern to UNHCR—1998 Statistical Overview.* Geneva: UNHCR, 1999.

United Nations. Office of the United Nations High Commissioner for Refugees. *Resettlement Handbook.* Geneva: UNHCR, 1998.

United Nations. Office of the United Nations High Commissioner for Refugees. *The State of the World's Refugees: The Challenge of Protection.* London and New York: Penguin Books, 1993.

United Nations. Office of the United Nations High Commissioner for Refugees. *The State of the World's Refugees: In Search of Solutions.* Oxford: Oxford University Press, 1995.

United Nations. Office of the United Nations High Commissioner for Refugees. *The State of the World's Refugees: A Humanitarian Agenda.* Oxford: Oxford University Press, 1997.

United Nations. Secretariat. 12 March 1999. Communication to Walter Dorn.

United Nations. Secretariat. *Administrative Instruction: The United Nations Archives.* New York: UN, 1984. 28 December 1984. ST/AI/326.

United Nations. Secretariat. ODS Unit. 16 March 1999. Communication to Walter Dorn.

United Nations. Secretary–General. *Letter Dated 2 July 1990 from the Permanent Representative of Cyprus to the United Nations Addressed to the Secretary-General.* New York: UN, 1990. S/21387; A/44/962.

United Nations. Secretary-General. *Letter Dated 7 June 1989 from the Permanent Representative of Pakistan to the United Nations Addressed to the Secretary-General.* New York: UN, 1989. S/20378; A/44/307.

United Nations. Security Council. *Exchange of Messages Between the Secretary-General and the President of Ghana.* New York: UN, 1960. S/4445.

United Nations. Security Council. *Letter Dated 2 August 1990 from the Permanent Representative of Kuwait to the United Nations Addressed to the President of the Security Council.* New York: UN, 1990. S/21423.

United Nations. Security Council. *Letter Dated 2 August 1990 from the Permanent Representative of the United States of America to the United Nations Addressed to the President of the Security Council.* New York: UN, 1990. S/21424.

United Nations. Security Council. "Letter Dated 24 May 1994 from the Secretary-General to the President of the Security Council." Addendum, Annexes to the *Final Report of the Commission of Experts Established Pursuant to the Security Council Resolution 780 (1992)*, Volume I – Annexes I to V. New York: UN, 1995. 31 May 1995. S/1994/674/Add.2 (Vol. I).

United Nations. Security Council. *Letter Dated 10 February 1996 from the Permanent Representative of Iraq to the United Nations Addressed to the Secretary-General.* New York: UN, 1996. 12 February 1996. S/1996/97.

United Nations. Security Council. *Letter Dated 13 March 1996 from the Secretary-General Addressed to the President of the Security Council.* New York: UN, 1996. S/1996/195.

United Nations. Security Council. *Resolution 1013 on Establishment of the International Commission of Inquiry for the Investigation of Arms Flows to the Former Rwandan Government Forces in the Great Lakes Region.* New York: UN, 1995. S/RES/1013.

United Nations. Security Council. Presidential Statement. *Statement on the Item Entitled 'The Situation in Burundi.'* New York: UN, 1994. S/PRST/1994/47.

United Nations. Security Council. *Provisional Rules of the Procedure of the Security Council.* New York: UN, 1983. S/96/Rev.7; S/N E.83.I.4.

United Nations. Statistical Office. *System of National Accounts, 1993.* Brussels/Luxembourg: European Communities, Statistical Office; New York: UN; Paris: Organisation for Economic Co-operation and Development; Washington, DC: International Monetary Fund, 1993.

United Nations. United Nations Official Documents. *UN Optical Disk System (ODS).* <www.ods.un.org/> (16 May 2000).

United Nations System. *Official Web Site Locator for the United Nations System of Organizations.* 9 March 2000, <www.unsystem.org> (12 March 2000).

United States. Central Intelligence Agency. *The World Factbook.* 1981– . Washington, DC: CIA. Also available online at <www.odci.gov/cia/publications/factbook/>.

United States. Congress. *Alleged Assassination Plots Involving Foreign Leaders: An Interim Report of the Select Committee to Study Governmental Operations with Respect to Intelligence Activities* [Church Committee], U.S. Senate, 94th Congress, 1st Session, Report no. 94-465 (20 November 1975). Washington, DC, 1975.

United States. Department of State. *Proposals for Expansion of World Trade and Employment.* Washington, DC: U.S. Department of State, 1945. Commercial Policy Series no. 79; Department of State Publication no. 2411.

United States. Department of State. *United States Suggested Charter.* Washington, DC: U.S. Department of State, 1946. Commercial Policy Series no. 92; Department of State Publication no. 2598.

United States. Library of Congress. Descriptive Cataloging Division. *Rules for Descriptive Cataloging in the Library of Congress; Motion Pictures and Filmstrips.* Prelim. ed. Washington, DC: LC, 1952.

United States. Library of Congress. "Report and Recommendations on United Nations Documents in Microform Survey." By Donald F. Wisdom, Chief, Serial and Government Publications Division. Washington, DC, August 1980. Unpublished.

Université des réseaux d'expression française. *Cahiers Agricultures.* 1992– . Montrouge, France: John Libbey Eurotext.

Université des réseaux d'expression française. *Cahiers Santé.* 1991– . Montrouge, France: John Libbey Eurotext.

Urquhart, Brian. *A Life in Peace and War.* New York: Harper and Row, 1987.

Vallée, Pierre. "Déclaration de Monaco: Un espace francophone élargi." *Le Devoir* (28 August 1999): E3.

Vallée, Pierre. "Le Forum francophone des affaires est l'acteur privilégié de la Francophonie économique." *Le Devoir* (28 August 1999): E10.

Venne, Michel. "Anne-Marie contre les dictateurs." *Le Devoir* (7 September 1999): A1, A8.

Venne, Michel. "L'après-Moncton: Une série de réalisations à portée limitée." *Le Devoir* (11 March 2000): E3.

Venne, Michel. "Boutros Boutros-Ghali: Francophonie, médiateur pour la paix et la démocratie." *Le Devoir* (28 August 1999): E3.

Venne, Michel. "Les droits de la personne, invité surprise de la Francophonie." *Le Devoir* (3 September 1999): A1, A10.

Venne, Michel. "L'Ontario dans la Francophonie? Pourquoi pas!" *Le Devoir* (28 August 1999): E6.

Venne, Michel. "Les parlementaires font la leçon aux chefs d'État: L'APF a exclu des ses rangs quatre pays coupables de violations." *Le Devoir* (1 September 1999): A5.

Venne, Michel. "Le ton se durcit face aux dictateurs." *Le Devoir* (4 September 1999): A1, A12.

Von Horn, Carl. *Soldiering for Peace*. New York: David Mackay Co., 1966.

Waldheim, Kurt. *In the Eye of the Storm*. London: Weidenfeld and Nicolson, 1985.

Walker, Janice R., and Todd Taylor. *The Columbia Guide to Online Style.* New York: Columbia University Press, c1998.

Walne, Peter, comp. *Selected Guidelines for the Management of Records and Archives: A RAMP Reader*. Paris: Unesco, 1990. PGI.90/WS/6.

Watkins, Kevin. *The Oxfam Poverty Report*. Oxford: Oxfam, 1995.

Weiss, Thomas G., and Leon Gordenker. *NGOs, the UN, and Global Governance.* Boulder, CO: Lynne Rienner Publishers, 1996.

Welch, Thomas L. "Description of the Archives of the Organization of American States." In *International Documents for the 80s: Their Role and Use: Proceedings of the Second World Symposium on International Documentation, Brussels, 1980*. Edited by Theodore D. Dimitrov and Luciana Marulli–Koenig, microfiche 2A, 100–115. Pleasantville, NY: UNIFO Publishers, 1982.

Welch, Thomas L. Organization of American States. 17 December 1985. Personal communications to Robert W. Schaaf.

"What's New On Line in International Law." *ASIL Newsletter*. January–February 1999: 1. <www.asil.org/newsletter/>.

Williams, Bernard J. S. "Document Delivery & Reproduction Survey, October 1985." *FID News Bulletin* 35 (November 1985): 87–89.

Williams, Robert V. *The Information Systems of International Intergovernmental Organizations*. Stamford, CT and London: Ablex, 1998.

Williams, Suzanne; Janet Seed; and Adelina Mwau. *The Oxfam Gender Training Manual.* Oxford: Oxfam, 1995.

Woodbridge, George, ed. *UNRRA: The History of the United Nations Relief and Rehabilitation Administration,* 3 vols. New York: Columbia University Press, 1950.

World Bank. *The World Bank Group Publications Catalog 2000.* Washington, DC: World Bank. <www.worldbank.org/html/extpb/search.htm> (8 June 2000).

World Bank. *The World Bank Policy on Disclosure of Information.* Washington, DC: World Bank, 1994.

World Bank. *World Bank Publications Style Guide.* Washington, DC: World Bank, 1997.

World Bank. *World Development Report.* 1978– . New York: Oxford University Press for the World Bank.

World Bank. *World Development Report 1998/99: Knowledge for Development.* New York: Oxford University Press for the World Bank, 1999.

World Bank. *World Development Sources.* <www.wds.worldbank.org/> (15 May 2000).

World Commission on Environment and Development. *Our Common Future.* New York: Oxford University Press, 1987.

World Conservation. Vol. 27, no. 1; 1996– . Gland, Switzerland: IUCN. Former title: *IUCN Bulletin* (New Series). no. 1– Vol. 26, no. 4; 1961–1995.

World Directory of Country Environmental Studies: An Annotated Bibliography of Natural Resources Profiles, Plans, and Strategies. Edited by Daniel B. Tunstall and Sean Gordon. Washington, DC: World Resources Institute, 1996.

World Directory of Environmental Organizations: A Handbook of National and International Organizations and Programs (Governmental and Nongovernmental) Concerned with Protecting the Earth's Resources. Edited by Thaddeus C. Trzyna, Elizabeth Margold, and Julia K. Osborn. Sacramento, CA; Claremont, CA: California Institute of Public Affairs; London: Earthscan, 1996.

World in Crisis: The Politics of Survival at the End of the 20th Century. Edited by Médecins Sans Frontières; MSF project coordinator: Julia Groenewold; associate editor: Eve Porter. London; New York: Routledge, 1996.

World Trade Organization. *Document Dissemination Facility.* <www.wto.org/wto/ddf/ep/index.html> (15 May 2000).

World Trade Organization. *Electronic Commerce and the Role of the WTO.* Special Study no. 2. Geneva: WTO, c1998.

World Trade Organization. Information and Media Relations Division. *Trading into the Future: WTO, the World Trade Organization.* 2d ed. Geneva: WTO, 1998.

World Trade Organization. *Regionalism and the World Trading System.* Geneva: WTO, 1995.

World Trade Organization. Secretary-General to the Advisory Committee on Administration and Budgetary Questions. *Internal and External Printing Practice at the Organization: Note by the Secretary-General.* Geneva: WTO, 1999.

World Trade Organization. *Trade and the Environment.* Special Study no. 4. Geneva: WTO, 1999.

World Trade Organization. *Trade and Environment Bulletin.* 1997– . Geneva: Information and Media Relations Division, WTO. Continues *Trade and the Environment.*

World Trade Organization. *Trilingual Glossary.* Geneva: WTO, 1998.

World Trade Organization. *World Trade Organization Dispute Settlement Decisions: Bernan's Annotated Reporter.* 1998– . Lanham, MD: Bernan Press.

World Trade Organization. *WTO Focus.* January 1995– . Geneva: Information and Media Relations Division, WTO. Continues *GATT Focus* (1981–95).

World Trade Organization. *WTO Status of Legal Instruments.* 1997– . Geneva: WTO Publications. ST/LEG/1.

Yearbook of International Organizations. 1st ed., 1948– . Brussels: Union of International Associations/G.K. Saur.

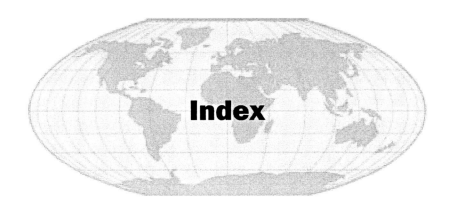

Index

AAL (Ask-a-Librarian) services, 307, 308
Abbreviations and acronyms, xxv–xxxiv
Academic Council of the United Nations System, 299
Access to the Archives of the United Nations Agencies: A RAMP Study with Guidelines, 208table
AccessUN, 245, 304, 309
Acronyms, xxv–xxxiv
Activities of GATT series, 101
Administrative Instruction: The United Nations Archives, 209table
Advisory Committee for the Co-ordination of Information Systems, 208table
Aerodrome Ground Movement Chart—ICAO, 188
Aerodrome/Heliport Chart—ICAO, 188
Aerodrome Obstacle Chart—ICAO, 188
Aeronautical Chart—ICAO 1:500,000, 186
Aeronautical Chart Catalogue, 191–92
Aeronautical Chart Manual, 191
"Aeronautical Charts," 192
Aeronautical Information Publications (AIPs), 190–91
Aeronautical Information Services Manual, 192
Aeronautical Navigation Chart—ICAO Small Scale, 186
Age, 283
Agence France-Presse, 284
Agreement Establishing the World Trade Organization, 73, 75
Agreement on Government Procurement (WTO), 85
Agreement on Trade in Civil Aircraft (WTO), 85
Agreement on Trade Related Aspects of Intellectual Property (TRIPs Agreement) (WTO), 85, 86
Aircraft Parking/Docking Chart—ICAO, 188
ALA Cataloging Rules for Author and Title Entries, 322
Alger, Chadwick F., 141
American Library Association (ALA), Government Documents Round Table, 229
Analytical Tables of Foreign Trade—SITC (EC), 241
Andean Pact (Junta del Acuerdo de Cartagena), 242
  microform program, 242
Anderson, Kyrill, 210
Annual Report (WTO), 84, 91, 96
Annual Report on Exchange Arrangements and Exchange Restrictions, 57, 58
ANSI (American National Standards Institute), 317, 322
APA (American Psychological Association) citation style, 316, 321–22, 324, 325
Archival Appraisal of Records of International Organizations: A RAMP Study, with Guidelines = Evaluation et tri des documents d'archives dans les organisations internationales: une etude RAMP, accompagnee de principes directeurs, 209table
Archives, 194–221
  access policy and services, 212–15
  definitions, 194–97, 210
  Doctors Without Borders, 174
  finding aids, 203–12
  intergovernmental organizations (IGOs), 197–203

Archives (*continued*)
  microfilm type considerations, 224–25
  Oxfam International (OI), 155
  Unesco involvement, 217
  United Nations and United Nations High Commissioner for Refugees, 256, 257
  use of, 216
Archives in the European Union: Report of the Group of Experts on the Coordination of Archives, 208table
"Archives of International Organizations, With Special Reference to the ILO, The," 208table
"Archives of Komintern,The," 210
"Archives Record Guide," 227
Area Chart—ICAO, 186
ASIL (American Society of International Law) *Newsletter*, 300
Availability and Use of Official Publications in Libraries, 9–10, 19, 21
Aviation. *See* International Civil Aviation Organization (ICAO)

Balance of Payments Manual (IMF), 54
Balance of Payments Statistics Yearbook (IMF), 55
Banque de Terminologie, 134
Bauer, George W., 208table
Bernan (company), 17, 305
Bibliographic Procedures and Style (LC), 321, 329
Bibliographic Style Manual (UN–Dag Hammarskjöld Library), 322, 323, 329
BISD. See *Basic Instruments and Selected Documents [BISD]* under General Agreement on Tariffs and Trade (GATT)
Black, Maggie, 150
Bourse d'affaires, 132
Brundtland Commission, 160
Bulletin of Labour Statistics, 307
Bulletin of the European Communities, 240

Cahiers Agricultures, 130
Cahiers Santé, 130
Cahiers Secheresse, 130
Caiola, Marcello, 53
Caring for the Earth: A Strategy for Sustainable Living, 160–61, 162
Carrasco, Enrique, 311–12
Case, Lynn M., 208table

Cataloging Manual, 322–23
Catálogo de Informes y Documentos Técnicos de la OEA, 239
Catálogo de Informes y Documentos Técnicos de la OEA Supplemento, 239
Catalogue of Microfiches of English and Bilingual OECD/OEEC Periodicals, 1948–1981, 241
Catalogue of Microfiches of English Monographs Published by OECD/OEEC, 1948–1980, 241
Cause for Our Times, A: Oxfam, the First 50 Years, 150
Chadwyck-Healey (company), 245, 304
Charlesworth, Bernard, 9
Chat rooms, 310
Check-List of Executive Board Documents on Microfiche, 1946–1982, 233
Check-List of Microfiche Numbers of General Conference Documents, 1945–1982, 233
Cheney, Debora, 324
Cherns, J. J., 6, 23, 25, 27, 28
Chicago Manual of Style, The, 320, 321, 324, 325, 328, 329
"Choksi Report" (World Bank), 33
Chronology of Unesco, 1945–1987, A, 216
CIA, 282
Citation forms, 315–51
  elements of, 325–31
    authorship, 326
    edition, 328
    imprint, 328–29
    nontraditional media, 330–31
    notes, 329–30
    series statement, 329
    sources of information, 325–26
    title, 326–28
    translation and romanization, 331
  introduction to, 315–16
    electronic formats, 317
    print formats, 316
  manuals, 320–24
    bibliographic information for, 350–51
  sample citations, 331–49
    annual report without imprint, 342fig, 342
    IGO item copublished with another press, 338fig, 339
    IGO material in tangible electronic medium, 348fig, 349
    IGO material online source, website, 346fig, 347
    journal article, 343fig, 344

microformat, multiple series, 345fig, 345
multiple authors, 340fig, 341
UN masthead document, 332fig, 333
UN Official Record, 334fig, 335
UN sales publication, 336fig, 337
software, bibliography formatting, 325
standards, 317–20
   ANSI Standard for bibliographic references, 319–20
   bibliographic reference, electronic document-ISO Standard 690-2, 319
   bibliographic reference-ISO Standard 690-1975, 318
Citation Rules and Forms for United Nations Documents and Publications, 323, 324, 329
"Click if you want to fight world hunger," 298
Clinical Guidelines: Diagnostic and Treatment Manual, 173
CNN (Cable News Network), 282, 284
CNTS: Cross-National Time-Series, 305
Cocoa Producers' Alliance, 8
Columbia Guide to Online Style, The, 324, 325
Comments of the Administrative Committee on Co-ordination (UN), 11, 18
Comments of the Secretary-General (UN), 11
Commission on Global Governance, 141, 142
"Communications received from private individuals and nongovernmental bodies relating to matters of which the Security Council is seized," 292
Complete Guide to Citing Government Documents, The, 323
Complete Guide to Citing Government Information Sources, The, 323, 324, 330
Conference of Allied Ministers of Education (CAME), London, 1942–1945: Index of Documents (Unesco), 206table
Conference of Allied Ministers of Education (CAME), London: List of Documents and Correspondence Files, 1942–1945, With Index (Unesco), 206table
Congressional Information Service (CIS), 226, 234, 244, 245
   statistical output, 307
Congressional Research Service, 282
Convention on International Civil Aviation, Annex 4—Aeronautical Charts, 185, 186, 192

Convention on International Civil Aviation, Annex 15—Aeronautical Information Services, 192
Cook, Michael, 208table
Cost Effectiveness Review (CER) (World Bank), 24, 26, 29–30, 33–34
Council of Europe, 305
Country Statistical Appendices (IMF), 52
Cruel Paradise, A: Journals of an International Relief Worker, 172

Dag Hammarskjöld Library (DHL). *See under* United Nations
Database, 325
Databuero, 305
Dear United Nations...: How to Order UN Publications, Where to Find "Freebees," What Is on the Internet, 301
Declaration on the Contribution of the World Trade Organization to Achieving Greater Coherence in Global Economic Policy-making, 90
Defining and Certifying Electronic Publication in Science: A Proposal to the International Association of STM Publishers, 27
"Description of the Archives of the Organization of American States," 209table
Development in Practice, 154
Development News (World Bank), 72
Development of Records Management and Archives Services Within United Nations Agencies: A RAMP Study With Guidelines (Unesco), 209table
Dimitrov, Theodore, 5
Diplomatic World Bulletin, 282
Direction of Trade Statistics (IMF), 55
Disclosure of Information Policy (World Bank), 25
Dissemination activities, 301–2
"Distribution and Acquisition of UN Documents," 11
Doctors Without Borders. (Médecins Sans Frontierès [MSF]), 165–74
   activities, 169–71
   Activity Report, 169, 171
   autonomous sections, 166–68
   financing, 171
   information and publishing, 171–74
   library and archival resources, 174
   mandate, governance, and structure, 168
   origins, history, and presence, 165–68
   website, 166

"Documentation of the United Nations System: Bibliographic Control and Coordination," 4
Documentos Oficiales de la Organización de los Estados Americanos: Lista General de Documentos, 239
Documents of International Organizations: A Bibliographic Handbook, 4, 5
"Documents of the COMECON and Warsaw Pact in Russian Archives," 207
Documents to the People, 229
Dollar, Charles, 208table
Driscoll, David D., 44

Eade, Deborah, 154
Echoweb, 129
Economic Issues (IMF), 58
Economic Reviews (IMF), 58
Économies francophones, 132
The Economist, 1457
Education Now: Break the Cycle of Poverty, 154
Electronic Commerce and the Role of the WTO, 91
Electronic Records Management and Archives of International Organizations: A RAMP Study with Guidelines, 208table
Electronic Styles, 324, 330
Encyclopedia of Human Rights Issues Since 1945, 299
Enroute Chart—ICAO, 186
Essential Drugs: Practical Guidelines, 173
État de la Francophonie dans le monde, 125
Euro Abstracts, 240
Europa Directory of International Organizations, The, 300
European Commission, Secretariat General, 208table
European Communities (EC), 4, 8, 10, 17. *See also* European Union (EU)
  archives, 199
    microfilm type, 224–25
    microform program, 239–41
European Union (EU), 4. *See also* European Communities (EC)
  archives, 199
    access to, 214–15
    microfilm type, 224–25
  e-mail newsletter, 305
  microform program, 239–41
  Official Journal Series C, 240–41
  Official Journal Series L, 240–41
  Reports, 241
  Texts Adopted, 241

FAO Documentation, 234
FAO Documentation on Microfiche, 234
FAQ (Frequently Asked Questions), 307–8
Final Act Embodying the Results of the Uruguay Round of Multilateral Trade Negotiations (GATT), 93
Finance and Development (IMF), 57
Financial Times, 283
Fleischer, Eugene B., 330
Fletcher, J., 15
Food and Agriculture Organization (FAO), 11, 16
  electronic information, 307
  geographic data, 184
  microform program, 234
Foreign Broadcast Information Service (FBIS) *Daily Reports*, 284
Framework for Survival, A, 172
Frangueira, Ana, 208table
Furstenberg, R., 11
Future of the United Nations System, The: Potential for the Twenty-First Century, 299

Garner, Diane, 324, 329
GATT: Status of Legal Instruments, 94
GATT Activities in... (annual report), 91
GATT and Uruguay Round Documents September 1986–December 1996, 98
GATT Bibliography, 96
GATT Depository Libraries, 101
GATT Depository Libraries, List of Publications Deposited in Each Library, 101
GATT Documents on Microfiche; Revision, 234
GATT Focus, 91
GATT Studies in International Trade series, 101
GATT WTO News: From GATT to the World Trade Organization, 91
General Agreement on Tariffs and Trade (GATT), 75–80
  Analytical Index, 93
  Analytical Index: Guide to GATT Law and Practice, 93
  Annecy Protocol of Terms of Accession, 93
  Annual Report of the Director General, 91
  Basic Instruments and Selected Documents [BISD], 92, 101

Basic Instruments and Selected Documents [BISD]. Supplements, 92
decision-making, 77
documentation, internal (GATT 1947, Tokyo Round, Uruguay Round), 97–98, 97tables, 98table
   derestriction, 104
functions, 78–80
   dispute settlement, 78–80
   trade barrier reduction, 78
governance, 76–77
Legal Texts, 94
List and Index of Documents Issued, 99, 245
List and Index of Documents Issued from 21 Sept. 1948–31 Dec. 1984, 235–36
List and Index of Uruguay Round Documents Issued Between 1986–1994, 99
List of Documents Issues, 99
membership, 75
Microfiche and List & Index of GATT Documents, 235
microform program, 234-36
origin, 73–74
panel reports, 95
Plurilateral Agreements, 94
publications program, 99
   availability and dissemination, 101–3
      depository libraries, 101
      distribution, Internet, 103
      distribution, microfilm, 102
      distribution, print, 102
      restrictions on distribution, 101–2
      sales, 101
   bibliographic control
      documentation, 99, 100table
      Uruguay Round, 99
   series and areas, 91-96
      analytical indexes, 93
      annual reports, 91
      Basic Instruments and Selected Documents (BISD), 92
      current awareness, 91–92
      website, 92
   reference material, 96
Schedules of Specific Commitments for Trade in Services, 94
Schedules on Services and Goods, 94
Secretariat, 77–78
statistics, 95–96
Trade Policy Reviews, 95
trade rounds and associated legal texts, 93–94
Uruguay Round, 94
General Agreement on Tariffs and Trade, with Annexes and Schedules of Tariff Concession, 93
General Agreement on Trade in Services (GATS) (WTO), 85
Geneva 1979 Protocol (GATT), 93
Global Biodiversity Strategy: Guidelines for Action to Save, Study, and Use Earth's Biotic Wealth Sustainably and Equitably, 161, 162
Global Governance, 299
Global Refugee Crisis, The: A Reference Handbook, 251
Gordenker, Leon, 141
Gorman, Robert F., 251
Government Finance Statistics (GFS) (IMF), 54
Government Finance Statistics (GFS) Manual (IMF), 54
Government Finance Statistics Yearbook, 55
Government Publications Review, 11–13
Green Web, The: A Union for World Conservation, 160, 162
Group of 8 (G8), 110
Guide to the Archives of Intergovernmental Organizations, 201, 209table
Guide to the Archives of International Organizations, Part 1: The United Nations System, 201, 209table
Guide to the Archives of International Organizations, Part 2: Archives of International Organizations and Their Former Officials in the Custody of National and Other Archival Manuscript Repositories, 209table
Guide to the Archives of International Organizations, Part 3: Archives of Other International Inter-governmental Organizations and Non-governmental Organizations, 209table
Guide to the Archives of the League of Nations, 1919–1946, 209table
Guide to the Archives of the Ministries of Foreign Affairs of the Member States of the European Communities and the European Political Cooperation, 208table
Guide to the Historical Archives of the European Communities, 208table
Guide to the International Archives and Collections at the IIHS, 207

Guide to the Official Publications of the European Communities, A, 2d ed., 17
Guide to United Nations Organization, Documentation and Publishing for Students, Researchers, Librarians, 5, 20
Guinness Book of Records, 7
Guptil, Marilla B., 209table

Haden, J. W., 20
Hajnal, Peter, 5, 20, 311
Harper, Richard H. R., 45
Harvard Bluebook, 316, 321, 322
Havana Charters, 74–75
Havana Conference, 73–74, 75
Her Majesty's Stationary Office (HMSO), 17
Hinds, Thomas S., 8, 11
Historical Dictionary of Refugee and Disaster Relief Organizations, 251
Holborn, Louise, 251
Holdgate, Martin, 160
Human Rights Watch (HRW), 290
Hyman Development Report, 305

IAEA (International Atomic Energy Agency), 237–38
  Annual Report, 238
  Programme and Budget, 238
ILO Publications and Documents: Title List, 1965–1985, 237
"ILO Publications on Microfiche," 237
Improvements to the GATT Dispute Settlement Rules and Procedures, 78
Independent learning, 311–12
Index to International Statistics [IIS], 99, 226, 234, 244, 307
Index to United Nations Documents and Publications, 304, 309–10
INFOCIECC, 239
Information Systems of International Intergovernmental Organizations, The: A Reference Guide, 300, 311
INIS Atomindex, 237
INIS Today, 238
Inside the IMF: An Ethnography of Documents, Technology and Organizational Action, 45
Institute for War and Peace Reporting, 291
Instrument Approach Chart—ICAO, 186, 187fig, 188, 189fig, 191
Integrated Database (GATT), 96
interalia (WTO), 84

International Atomic Energy Agency (IAEA), microform program, 237–38
International Bank for Reconstruction and Development, 24, 29
International Bibliography, Information, Documentation (GATT and WTO), 99
International Bovine Meat Agreement (WTO), 85
International Capital Markets Report (IMF), 57
International Civil Aviation Organization (ICAO), 3–4, 183–92
  aeronautical charts, 186, 188, 191–92, 187fig, 189fig
  technological change and safety, 188, 190–91
"International Comparative Statistics Produced by International Organizations," 15
International Congress on Universal Availability of Publications (1982), 5, 19, 20, 21, 22
International Council on Archives (ICA). Section of Archivists of International Organizations (SIO). *Handbook and Directory*, 217
International Court of Justice, 1946–1996, The, 299
International Criminal Court Monitor, The, 145
International Dairy Agreement (WTO), 85
International Directory of Archives, 198
International Documents for the 80's: Their Role and Use, 20
International Financial Statistics (IFS), 53, 55, 305
International governmental organizations (IGOs), 3–43
  activity frameworks, 6–10
  archives, 197–203
    access to, 213–14
  case study (*see* World Bank)
  defined, 3
  external aspects, 18–22
  organization of, 10–14
  "publications"/"documents" distinctions, 4–6
  size of, 14–18
  suggestions, 22–23
  websites, 142
International Herald Tribune, 282

International Information: Documents, Publications, and Electronic Information of International Government Organizations, 300, 304, 330
International Labour Documentation, 237
International Labour Organization (ILO), 5, 11, 16, 236–37
   archives, microform, 236–37
   electronic information, 305, 307
   microform program, 236–37
   Minutes, 237
   Official Bulletin, 237
   Record of Proceedings, 237
   Reports, 237
   website, ILOSTAT, 307
   World Employment Programme (WEP), Research Working Papers, 237
International Labour Review, 237
International Monetary Fund (IMF), 44–71, 72
   Annual Report, 59, 62
   Annual Report of the Executive Directors, 62
   Annual Report on Exchange Arrangements and Exchange Restrictions, 57, 58
   archives, 65–66
   Articles of Agreement, 47, 57, 59, 61, 63
   Articles of Agreement, 1946–As Amended, 47, 53
   Board of Governors, 62
   By-Laws Rules and Regulations. Part II. Rules and Regulations of the International Monetary Fund, Section C, Minutes, 60
   By-Laws Rules and Regulations. Part II. Rules and Regulations of the International Monetary Fund, Section N Staff Regulations. [Rule] N5, 55
   data and research compilation, 53–55
   Departmental Memorandum (DM) series, 55, 61
   documentation, research, 55–58
   documents and publications, 47–58, 59–62
      translation of, 58–59
   economic developments, recent, 52–53
   electronic information,
      IMF website, 49, 57, 61, 64
      Joint BIS-IMF-OECD-World Bank Statistics on External Debt, 55
      JOLIS Library Catalog, 64
   Executive Board, 59–62
      Annual Report of the Executive Directors (IMF), 62
      BUFF Eds, 61
      BUFFs, 61
      Executive Board Administrative Matters (EBAMSs), 61
      Executive Board Administrative Papers (EBAPs), 61
      Executive Board Document (EBD) series, 60, 61
      Executive Board Specials (EBS) series, 60–61
      meeting, minutes of, 59–60
      Recent Economic Developments (REDs), 61
      Research Department
         Departmental Memorandum (DM) series, 55
      Staff Memoranda (SM) series, 61
      Surveillance (SUR) series, 61
   financial assistance missions, 50–52
   locating publications and documents, 64
      website, 64
   history, 45–47
   IMF Glossary, 58
   IMF Occasional Papers, 58
   IMF Pamphlet Series, 58
   IMF Policy Discussion Papers, 58
   IMF Public Information Notices, 58
   IMF Staff Papers, 57
   IMF Survey, 58
   IMF Working Papers, 55, 58
   International Monetary and Financial Committee, 62–64
   International Monetary Fund Publications Catalog, 58
   and ITO, creation of, 73
   mission travel, reporting, and review, 47–50
   operations and their documentation, 47
   Papers on International Financial Statistics (PIFs), 55
   Policy Discussion Papers, 56
   Policy Framework Papers (PFPs), 50
   poverty reduction and growth, 52
   Poverty Reduction Strategy Paper (PRSP), 52
   Public Information Notices (PINs), 50, 58
   Recent Economic Developments (REDs), 52–53, 61
   Research Working Papers, 56

394 / Index

International Monetary Fund (IMF) (*continued*)
   Statistics Department, 53, 54–55
      Dissemination Standards Bulletin Board (DSBB), 55
      General Data Dissemination System (GDDS), 55
      Special Data Dissemination Standards (SDDS), 55
      Summary Proceedings of the Annual Meeting of the Board of Governors, 63–64
      Supporting Studies for the World Economic Outlook, 57
   translation of publications, 58–59
   WEO Database, 56
   Working Papers, 58
   World Economic and Financial Surveys, 57, 58
International Monetary Fund Publications Catalog, 58
International Nuclear Information System (INIS), 237
International Organizations, 1918–1945: A Guide to Research and Research Materials, 208table
International Refugee Organization, The: A Specialized Agency of the United Nations, Its History and Work, 1946–1952, 251
International Refugee Regime and the Refugee Problem in Interwar Europe, The, 251
International Statistics Yearbook, 305
International Symposium (1972), 5
International Telecommunication Union (ITU), microform program, 236
International Thesaurus of Refugee Terminology, 256, 259
International Trade (GATT), 91, 101
International Trade (WTO), 95
International Trade Organization (ITO), 72
   charter, 73
   structure, proposed, 74–75
International Trade Statistics (WTO), 84, 95
International Trade: Trends and Statistics (WTO), 95
International Union for the Conservation of Nature and Natural Resources (IUCN). *See* World Conservation Union
International Union for the Protection of Nature (IUPN). *See* World Conservation Union

Introduction to International Organizations, 299
Inventaire des Archives de l'Institut international de coopération intellectuelle (IICI), 1925–1946: dossiers, documents, et publications aux Archives de l'Unesco a Paris, 206table
IPS Daily Journal, 283
ISCC, 312
ISO (International Organization for Standardization), 317, 318–19, 322
IUCN Bulletin. *See World Conservation*, 162
IUCN Publications 1948–1998: A Catalogue of Publications Produced by IUCN—the World Conservation Union or in Collaboration with Other Organizations or Publishers, 163
IUCN Publications Available from Regional and Country Offices, 163
IUCN Red List Categories, 162
IUCN Reports, 1960–1995, Including an Appendix on IUCN Periodicals, 163
IUCN. *See* World Conservation Union

Jeffries, John, 17
Johnson, G. A., 208table
Journal of Commerce, 283
Journal of the American Medical Association, 172
JUNINDEX: Resúmenes de Documentos de la Junta del Acuerdo de Cartagen, 242
JUNINDEX: Resúmenes Decisiones del Junta del Acuerdo, 242

Key Resolutions of the United Nations General Assembly 1946–1996, 299

La Francophonie. *See* Organisation internationale de la Francophonie (OIF)
La Lettre d'Alexandrie, 131
La Lettre de L'Assemblee Parlementaire de la Francophonie, 131–32
LABORDOC database, 305
Labour Education, 237
Lancet, The, 172
Landmine Monitor Report 1999: Toward a Mine-Free World, 144
L'année francophone internationale, 124
Le Devoir, 125
Le Journal de l'Agence Intergouvernemental de la Francophonie, 129

Le Monde, 283
League of Nations, 5
League of Nations Documents and Publications, 1919–1946, 245
Legal Instruments Embodying the Results of the Uruguay Round, 94
Lettre de la Francophonie, 129
Lettres Sans Frontières, 172
Leyton, Elliott, 172
Liaison, 132
Liaison Francophone, 129
Library of Congress
  Information Bulletin, 229
  Reference Department, 321, 329
  Rules for Descriptive Cataloging, 322
Listservs, 307, 308–9
Living in a Minefield: An MSF Report on the Mine Problem in Afghanistan, 172
Locke, Greg, 172
Loescher, Ann D., 251
Loescher, Gil, 251
London *Times*, 283

Mabbs, A. W., 209table
Macleans's: Canada's Weekly Newsmagazine, 171
Main Working Document (International Congress on Universal Availability of Publications, Paris, 1982), 19, 20, 21
Management of Electronic Records: Issues and Guidelines, 208table
Management of Information from Archives, The, 208table
Manual for Country Economists, A, 53
Manual for Writers of Term Papers, Theses, and Dissertations, 320–21, 325, 328, 329
Marulli-Koenig, Luciana, 4
McCaffrey-Noviss, Michael, 311
Médecins Sans Frontierès (MSF). *See* Doctors Without Borders (Médecins Sans Frontierès [MSF])
"Médecins Sans Frontierès Experience, The," 172
Microfiche Collection for Governments, 102
Microfiche Collection for Libraries, 102
"Microfiches and Microfilms of ITU Documents and Publications," 236
Microform, 222–48
  access technology and alternative formats, 245–47
  collection development, 244
  historical coverage, 244–45

secondary services providing, 225–26
silver versus other film, 224–25
survey of programs, 226–42
  Andean Pact, 242
  European Communities (EC), 239–41
  Food and Agriculture Organization (FAO), 234
  General Agreement on Tariffs and Trade (GATT), 234–36
  International Atomic Energy Agency (IAEA), 237–38
  International Labor Organization (ILO), 236–37
  International Telecommunications Union (ITU), 236
  Organization for Economic Cooperation and Development (OECD), 241–42
  Organization of American States (OAS), 238–39
  Unesco, 231–33
  United Nations, 227–31
versus newer technologies, 222–25
Minor Surgical Procedures in Remote Areas, 173
MLA (Modern Language Association) citation style, 316, 321, 322, 324, 325
Model UN
  research patterns, 309–10
  websites, 310
Monthly Bulletin of Statistics (UN), 302, 307
Mwau, Adelina, 154

National Trade Data Bank, 305
"Need for Modernization in Production, Editing and Distribution of IGO Documentation, The," 9
New Guide to the Diplomatic Archives of Western Europe, 208table
New Issues in Refugee Research, 256
New Republic, The, 171
New York Post, 283
New York Times, 282, 283, 284
"NewsEDGE," 284
NGOs, the UN, and Global Governance, 141
1996 IUCN Red List of Threatened Animals, 162
1997 IUCN Red List of Threatened Plants, 162
1999 Global Appeal, 253
Non merci, Oncle Sam!, 135

Nongovernmental organizations (NGOs) and
civil society, 138–79
  case studies, 148–74
    Doctors Without Borders, 165–74
      Activity Report, 169, 171
    OXFAM International, 36, 148–56
      Annual Report, 150, 153, 154, 155
    World Conservation Union, 156–65
  civil society, influence by, 142–47
    "Battle of Seattle"—WTO meeting, 146–47
    International Criminal Court, 144–45
    landmines, 142–44
    Multilateral Agreement on Investment (MAI), 145–46
  definitions, 139–40
  Internet information sources, 147–48
  UN system and other IGOs, relations with, 140–42
Nordic AB, 305
Nutrition Guidelines, 173

Obstétrique en situation d'isolement, 173
OECD *Catalogue of Publications*, 241
OEEC/OECD English Monographs Published for Free Distribution, 1948–1980, 241
Official Journal of the European Communities, 244
Official Publishing: An Overview; An International Survey and Review of the Role, Organization and Principles of Official Publishing, 6
Olson, Leanne, 172
Open Markets in Financial Services and the Role of GATS, 91
Organisation internationale de la Francophonie (OIF), 108–37
  history, 112, 114–18
  information about, 124–25
    electronic, 124
    print, 124–25
  member countries, 109table
  modernization through summits, 118–24
  relationships between/among units in, 113fig
  structure and documentation of components, 126–33
    Agence Intergouvernemental de la Francophonie (AIF), 128–29
    Agence Universitaire de la Francophonie (AUF), 129–30
    Assemblée Parlementaire de la Francophonie (APF), 131–32
    Association Internationale des Maires Francophones (AIMF), 131
    Conférence Ministérielle de la Francophonie (CMF), 127
    Conseil Permanent de la Francophonie (CPF), 128
    Forum Francophone des Affaires (FFA), 132
    Organisations Internationales Non Gouvernementales (OING), 132–33
    other sectoral conferences, 127
    Secretariat and Secretary General, 126
    summits, 126
    TV5, 130
    Universite Senghor in Alexandria, 130–31
Organization for Economic Cooperation and Development (OECD), 110, 241–42
  archival microfilm, 224–25
  documents and publications
    as publisher, 10, 13, 17
  microform program, 241–42
Organization of American States (OAS), microform program, 238–39
  Catalog of Publications, 239
  Lista General de Documentos, 238
  Official Records (Documentos Oficiales), 238–39
Organized Crime: A Compilation of U.N. Documents 1975–1998, 299
Our Common Future, 160
Our Global Neighbourhood, 141, 142
Oxfam Education Report, The, 154
Oxfam Gender Training Manual, The, 154
Oxfam Handbook of Development and Relief, The, 154
Oxfam International (OI), 36, 148–56
  activities, 152
  affiliate locations and websites, 148–49
  Annual Report, 150, 153, 154, 155
  financing, 153
  information and publishing, 153–55@sub =
  library and archival resources, 155
  mandate, governance, and structure, 150–51
Oxfam Poverty Report, The, 154
Oxford University Press, 305

Palayret, Jean Marie, 208table
Parlements et Francophonie, 131
Patrimoine francophone, 131

Paupst, James, 171
Plotting Chart—ICAO, 186
Pocket Guide to IUCN, the World Conservation Union, A, 162
Populations in Danger, 172
Powers and the Persecuted, The: The Refugee Problem and the Intergovernmental Committee on Refugees (IGCR) 1938–1947, 251
Procedure of the UN Security Council, The, 299
Procedures for the Circulation and Destriction of WTO Documents, 102
Progress of Nations (UNICEF), 307
"Proposals Concerning an International Trade Organization," 73
"Proposals for Consideration by an International Conference on World Trade and Employment," 73
Protocol Embodying the Results of the 1960–61 Tariff Conference (GATT), 93
"Psychological Operations in Guerilla Warfare," 279
Public Health Engineering in Emergency Situations, 173
Publications Policy and Practice in the United Nations System, 11–13
Publications Policy and Practice in the United Nations System; Comments of the Administrative Committee on Co-ordination, 11–13
Publications Policy and Practice in the United Nations System; Comments of the Secretary-General, 11–13
Publications Policy and Practice in the United Nations System; Comments of the Secretary-General; Corrigendum, 11–13
Publications Update (World Bank), 32

Rapport du Secrétaire général de la Francophonie: de Hanoi à Moncton, 126
Readex Corporation, 245, 304, 311
Refugee Abstracts, 256
Refugee Health: An Approach to Emergency Situations, 172
Refugee Survey Quarterly (RSQ), 256, 259
Refugees. *See* United Nations High Commissioner for Refugees
Refugees: A Problem of Our Time. The Work of the United Nations High Commissioner for Refugees, 1951–1972, 251

Refugees magazine, 256
Regionalization and the World Trading System (WTO), 91
Register of Development Activities of the United Nations System, 210
Register of Periodicals in the ILO Library, 237
Registry of Print Publications (World Bank), 25, 26
Rehber, Jeanne, 300
Remote access, 309–10
Renewing the United Nations System, 299
Repertoire of the Practice of the Security Council, 276
Repertory of the Practice of United Nations Organs, 276
Report and Recommendations on United Nations Documents in Microform Survey, 229
Report on the Cost-Effectiveness Review, 24, 29
Report on United Nations Documentation and on the Organization of the Proceedings of the General Assembly and Its Main Bodies, 10
Results of the Uruguay Round of Multilateral Trade Negotiations, The: The Legal Text, 94
Reuters, 284
Review of Developments in International Trade and the Trading System (GATT), 91
Review of Developments in International Trade and the Trading System (WTO), 95
Rothman, Marie, 323, 324, 329
Rules for Descriptive Cataloging (LC), 322

Safeguards agreement (WTO), 86
Salama, Peter, 172
Schaff, Robert W., 243, 246
Second World Symposium on International Documentation (1980), 5
Secretariat News, 283
Seed, Janet, 154
Selected Decisions and Selected Documents of the International Monetary Fund, 61, 63
"Shell" Guides, 7
Short Guide to Unesco Archives = Guide des Archives de l'Unesco, A, 206table
Shreiber, Marina, 242
Sjöberg, Tommie, 251

Skran, Claudena M., 251
Smith, Diane, 324, 329
Social and Labour Bulletin, 237
"Some Previous Attempts at Organizing International Documentation," 20
Spiegel, Paul B., 172
Stark, Marie Charlotte, 209table
State of the World (UNICEF), 307
State of the World's Refugees, The, 259
State of the World's Refugees, The: The Challenge of Protection, 252
Statist, The, 283
Statistical Universe website, 99, 245, 307
Statistics in electronic format, 306–7
Study Abroad (Unesco), 15
Style Manual for Citing Microform and Nonprint Media, A, 330
"Suggested Charter for an International Trade Organization of the United Nations," 74
Summary Report on UN Microforms Survey, 229
Supporting Studies for the World Economic Outlook, 57
System of National Accounts (IMF), 54

Tariff Schedules for Trade in Goods, 94
Telecommunications Journal, 236
Thomas, Daniel H., 208table
Tokyo Round Antidumping Code (GATT), 80, 86
Torquay Protocol (GATT), 93
Touched by Fire: Doctors Without Borders in a Third World Crisis, 172
Trade Policy Review series (GATT), 101
Trading into the Future: Introduction to the World Trade Organization, 96
TRAFIX (Trade Facilitation and Information Exchange), 305
"Tresorerie BOC" (Unesco Bureau of the Financial Comptroller), 211
Trilingual Glossary (WTO), 96
Turabian, Kate, 320, 325, 328, 329
"Turkey: Continuing Violations of Human Rights," 279
24 Ore, 283

The UN at 50: Statements by World Leaders, 299
UN Documentation: A Research Guide, 303
UNDiplomatic Times, 282

UN21: Accelerating Managerial Reform for Results, 299
UNBIS, 20, 310
UNBIS Plus, 245, 304
UNBIS Reference Manual for Bibliographic Description, 322–23
Understanding on Rules and Procedures Governing the Settlement of Disputes (WTO), 85
Understanding Regarding Notification, Consultation, Dispute Settlement and Surveillance (GATT), 78
UNDEX, 227
Unesco
   archives, 104-221, 217
      Unesco Bibliographic Data Base (UNESBIB), 204
      finding aids, selected list, 206table
   Books Now Available on Microfiche, 233
   documents and publications, 11, 14, 15–16, 17, 21
   electronic information, 307
   Executive Board
      Documents, 195–96, 233
   General Conference (C) documents, 233
   General Information Programme and UNISIST, 9–10, 21
   List of Documents Issued by the Archives Service, 1947–1994, 204, 205fig
   List of Documents Issued by the Archives Service, 1947–1994, with Alphabetical Index, 206table, 217
   microform program, 231–33
   Programme and Budget, 196, 210
   Programme and Budget for 1994–1995, 201
   Publications de l'Institut international de cooperation intellectuelle, 1945 = List of Publications of IICI, 1945, 206table
   Report of the Director-General on the Activities of the Organization, The, 210
   Secretariat, records, 196
   Selected Guidelines for the Management of Records and Archives: A RAMP Reader, 209table
   subject range, 8
Unesco Archives: A Short Guide, 206table
Unesco Archives Finding Aids: List of Archive Groups (AG) with Index = Instruments de recherche des Archives de l'Unesco, 206table

Unesco Archives: List of Finding Aids on Microfiche: Inventories, Lists, Indexes Issued on Microfiche and/or Paper to Find References To And Trace Information from Unesco Records, Documents and Publications = Archives de l'Unesco: Liste des Instruments des Instruments de recherche sur Microfiche et/ou sur papier pour trouver de references ou depister de l'information des archives, documents et publicatiaons de l'Unesco, 206table
Unesco Courier, The, 15, 17
Unesco List of Documents and Publications (ULDP), 217, 232
UNESCO Statistics Website, 307
UNICEF, electronic information, 307
UNIPUB, 17
UNISIST, 21
United Nations, 4, 8, 245. *See also* United Nations System
  citation styles, 322–23, 329
  Corrigendum (UN), 11
  Dag Hammarskjöld Library, 302-3, 322, 329
  website, 302
  Daily Highlights, 283
  Daily Press Briefings, 283
  Department of Political Affairs
    "Daily Press Clippings from DPA" (UN), 283
  Department of Public Affairs (DPA), 283
  Economic and Social Council
    Indexes to Proceedings, 304
  Economist Intelligence Unit
    Country Reports, 292
  electronic information, 305, 307
    e-mail communications, 287
    UNBIS, 20, 310
    UNBIS Plus, 245, 304
    website, 298
  General Assembly, 304
  General Assembly, 39th Session
    Publications Policy and Practice in the United Nations System; Comments of the Administrative Committee on Co-ordination, 11
    Publications Policy and Practice in the United Nations System; Comments of the Secretary-General, 11
    Publications Policy and Practice in the United Nations System; Comments of the Secretary-General; Corrigendum, 11
  Indexes to Proceedings series, 304
  information-gathering, 275–97
    information cycle, 276, 277fig
    sources and methods, 276–92
      field operations, 284–88
      governments, 277–82
      information centers, field offices and agencies, 288–90
      media, 282–84
      nongovernmental organizations (NGOs) and individuals, 290–92
  Library, 209table
  List of Depository Libraries, 303
  memoirs of officials and peacekeepers, 296–97
  Microfiche Price List, 231
  microform program, 227–31
  optical disk system
    ODS: Official Documents Search, 246, 304, 310
    ODS: Optical Disk System, 246–47, 304
  as publishers, 17
  Secretariat
    Administrative Instruction: The United Nations Archives, 209table
    Department of Public Information, "Daily Press Clippings," 283
  Security Council
    Indexes to Proceedings, 304
  spatial data collection (*see* International Civil Aviation Organization)
  Statistical Office
    Global Statistics index (UN), 307
  Trusteeship Council, 304
    Index, 304
"United Nations as a Publisher, The," 8, 11
United Nations Chronicle, 301
United Nations Development Programme (UNDP)
  collaboration with external publishers, 305
  Compendium of Approved Projects, 210
  Human Development Report, 305
United Nations Documents and Publications, 244–45
United Nations Documents Checklist, 304
United Nations Documents Index, 99, 304, 310, 312
United Nations Editorial Manual, The, 322, 323, 327, 329, 331
United Nations Educational, Scientific and Cultural Organization. *See* Unesco

United Nations High Commissioner for Refugees, 249–71
  background and predecessor organizations, 249–50, 251table
  Centre for Documentation and Research (CDR), 255, 256
  electronic resources, 256, 257–58
  establishment of, 250–55
    document symbols, 255table
    governing bodies, 254
    High Commissioner, 250, 252table
    mandate and activities, 250, 252–54, 253table
    staff and budget, 255
  information and publications, 255–57
  REFWORLD CD-ROM, 258–60
    background, 258
    content comparison with REFWORLD website, 265–71table
    platform and structure, 259–60
    source databases, 258–59
  website, 260–63
    background, 260
    content comparison with REFWORLD CD-ROM, 265–71table
    REFWORLD, 263
    sources, 260–62
United Nations List of Protected Areas, 163
United Nations Official Records, 227, 228–29, 230, 304, 305, 309
United Nations Publications Catalogue 2000, 304
United Nations Situation Centre (SitCen)
  Daily Mission Highlights, 288
  Daily Mission Reports, 288
  Situation Report, 288
United Nations system, 4, 9, 10, 11. *See also* United Nations
  bundling and blurring, melding content with service, 305-6
  dissemination activities, 301–2
  Economic and Social Council (ECOSOC), 73
  electronic information, 307
    chat rooms and remote access, 309–10
    home page, 302
    statistics, 306–7
  geospatial information need, 183
  independent learning, 311–12
  indexes and catalogs, 304–5
  Joint Inspection Unit
    Publications Policy and Practice in the United Nations System, 11

Report on United Nations Documentation and on the Organization of the Proceedings of the General Assembly and Its Main Bodies, 10
  melding content and service, 305–6
  Model-UN research, 309–10
  preservation of information, 312
  reference service, 298–302, 307-9
    information dissemination moving forward, 301-2
    new methods of reference query, 307–9
    UN website, 298
    United Nations System Pathfinder website, 303
    website locator services, IGO-related, 300-301
  spatial data collection (*see* International Civil Aviation Organization)
"United Nations System and Civil Society, The," 141
United Nations Treaty Series, 94, 227, 231, 302
United States
  Department of Commerce
    National Trade Data Bank, 305
  Department of State, 73
Universal Bibliographic Control (UBC), 5
Universités, 130
University Availability of Publications (UAP), 22
UNRRA: The History of the United Nations Relief and Rehabilitation Administration, 251

Visual Approach Chart—ICAO, 188

Walne, Peter, 209table
"War Report," 291
Washington Post, 283
Washington Times, 283
Watkins, Kevin, 154
We the Peoples: Millennium Forum Declaration and Agenda for Action, 142
Weiss, Thomas, 141
Welch, Thomas L., 209table
WEO Database, 56
What Is the International Monetary Fund?, 44
"What's On Line in International Law," 300
Who Is Killing France? The American Strategy, 135
WHOSIS (WHO Statistical Information System), 307

Williams, John V., 311
Williams, Robert V., 300
Williams, Suzanne, 154
Wisdom, Donald, 229–30
WISTAT (Women's Indicators and Statistics Database), 302, 305, 307
Woodbridge, George, 251
World Aeronautical Chart—ICAO 1:1,000,000, 186
World Bank, 3, 23–43, 72
  governance and development—Office of the Publisher, 28–33
    background, 28–29
    cost effectiveness review, 29–30
    current organization and mission, 30, 32–33, 31fig, 32fig
    policies, 33–34
  and ITO, creation of, 73
  policies—Office of the Publisher, 33–40
    copublishing and licensing, 38–39
    cost-sharing, 35
    free dissemination of publications, 38
    pricing, 35–37
    pricing, internal, 37
    results of, numeric, 40table
    revenue sharing, 34
  publications described, 25–28
    documents, 25–27
    electronic, 27–28, 245–46, 305
    governance and development of, 28–33
    Registry of Print Publications, 26
  special initiative, African Publishing Institute, 40–41
World Bank Publications Style Guide, The, 14, 28
World Conservation, 162
World Conservation Bookstore, 1948–1998, The, 163
World Conservation Strategy: Living Resource Conservation for Sustainable Development, 160, 162
World Conservation Union, 156–65
  activities and themes, 158–61
  financing, 161
  information and publishing, 161–64
  library and archival resources, 164
  mandate, governance, and structure, 157–58
Statutes and Regulations, 157
World Development Report 1998/99: Knowledge for Development, 24, 39
World Development Sources website, 246
World Directory of Country Environmental Studies, 164

World Directory of Environmental Organizations: A Handbook of National and International Organizations and Programs, 162
World Economic and Financial Surveys, 57, 58
World Economic Outlook (WEO) Report (IMF), 53, 56, 57, 59
World Factbook (CIA), 282
World Geodetic System—1984 (WGS-84) Manual, 190, 192
World Health Organization, The, 299
World Health Organization (WHO), 8, 11, 16, 17
  electronic information, 307
World in Crisis: The Politics of Survival at the End of the 20th Century, 172
World Intellectual Property Organization (WIPO), 16
World Is Not Merchandise, The, 135
World Symposium on International Documentation, 1980, 20
World Trade and the Environment (WTO), 91
World Trade Organization (WTO), 80–80
  decision-making, 83
  documentation, 96–97, 98, 98table
  functions, 84–90
    cooperation with IMF and World Bank, 90
    dispute settlement, 87, 88fig
    negotiation forum, 86
    policy monitoring, 89–90
    trade barrier reduction, 84–86
  governance, 80–83
    general council, 82
    ministerial conference, 81
    structure, 81fig
    subsidiary bodies, 82–83
  historical overview, 73
  as information provider, 103
    copublishing, 104
    derestriction, 104
    website, 103
List & Index of Documents Issued, 99
  membership, 80
  panel reports, 95
  publication availability and dissemination, 101–3
    depository library, 101
    distribution, Internet, 103
    distribution, microform, 102
    distribution, print, 102
    Document Dissemination Facility, 245
    restrictions, 101–2
    sales program, 101

World Trade Organization (WTO) (*continued*)
   publication series and areas
      analytical index, 93
      annual reports, 91
      Basic Instruments and Selected Documents (BISD), 92
      current awareness, 91–92
      website, 92
   reference material, 96
   Secretariat, 84
   statistics, 95–96
   Trade and the Environment press release series (PRESS/TE), 92
   Trade Policy Reviews, 95
   trade rounds and associated legal texts, 93–94
      certified legal instruments, 94
   WTO Agreement, 73, 75, 82, 83, 84, 85, 89, 90

WTO Basic Instruments and Selected Documents series, 92
World Trade Organization Dispute Settlement Decisions: Bernan's Annotated Reporter, 95
World Trade Organization Guide to Documentation (GATT and WTO), 96–97
World Trade Organization: Status of Legal Instruments, 94
WTO Focus, 84, 92
WTO Press Release series, 92
WTO/GATT Research guide, 300

Year Book of Labour Statistics, 237
Yearbook of International Organizations, 138, 139, 300
Yearbook of the United Nations, 14, 15, 199